Eleventh Edition

TECHNIQUES OF FINANCIAL ANALYSIS

A Guide to Value Creation

ERICH A. HELFERT, D.B.A.

McGraw-Hill Irwin

Boston   Burr Ridge, IL   Dubuque, IA   Madison, WI   New York
San Francisco   St. Louis   Bangkok   Bogotá   Caracas   Kuala Lumpur
Lisbon   London   Madrid   Mexico City   Milan   Montreal   New Delhi
Santiago   Seoul   Singapore   Sydney   Taipei   Toronto

Mcgraw-Hill Higher Education

A Division of The **McGraw-Hill** Companies

TECHNIQUES OF FINANCIAL ANALYSIS: A GUIDE TO VALUE CREATION
Published by McGraw-Hill/Irwin, a business unit of The McGraw-Hill Companies, Inc., 1221
Avenue of the Americas, New York, NY, 10020. Copyright © 2003, 2000, 1997, 1994, 1991,
1987, 1982, 1977, 1972, 1967, 1963 by The McGraw-Hill Companies, Inc. All rights reserved.
No part of this publication may be reproduced or distributed in any form or by any means, or
stored in a database or retrieval system, without the prior written consent of The McGraw-Hill
Companies, Inc., including, but not limited to, in any network or other electronic storage or
transmission, or broadcast for distance learning.
Some ancillaries, including electronic and print components, may not be available to customers
outside the United States.

This book is printed on acid-free paper.

domestic   2 3 4 5 6 7 8 9 0 DOC/DOC 0 9 8 7 6 5 4 3
internationionl   1 2 3 4 5 6 7 8 9 0 DOC/DOC 0 9 8 7 6 5 4 3 2

ISBN   0-07-248729-1

Executive editor: *Stephen M. Patterson*
Sponsoring editor: *Michele Janicek*
Editorial coordinator: *Barbara Hari*
Executive marketing manager: *Rhonda Seelinger*
Producer, Media technology: *Melissa Kansa*
Project manager: *Laura Griffin*
Production supervisor: *Debra R. Sylvester*
Senior designer: *Pam Verros*
Senior digital content specialist: *Brian Nacik*
Cover design: *JoAnne Schopler*
Cover images: *© Wei Yan/Masterfile and © Digital Vision*
Typeface: *10/12 Times Roman*
Compositor: *GAC Indianapolis*
Printer: *R. R. Donnelley & Sons Company*

Library of Congress Cataloging-in-Publication Data
Helfert, Erich A.
    Techniques of financial analysis: a guide to value creation / Erich A. Helfert.--11th ed.
    p. cm. -- (The McGraw-Hill/Irwin series in finance, insurance, and real estate)
    Includes index
    ISBN 0-07-248729-1 -- ISBN 0-07-119547-5 (International ed.)
    1. Corporations--Finance. 2. Cash flow. 3. Financial statements. 4. Ratio analysis. I.
Title. II. Series.
HG4026 .H44 2003
658.15'1--dc21

                                                                    2002025458

INTERNATIONAL EDITION ISBN 0-07-119547-5
Copyright © 2003. Exclusive rights by The McGraw-Hill Companies, Inc. for manufacture and
export. This book cannot be re-exported from the country to which it is sold by McGraw-Hill.
The International Edition is not available in North America.

www.mhhe.com

THE MCGRAW-HILL/IRWIN SERIES IN FINANCE, INSURANCE, AND REAL ESTATE

Stephen A. Ross
Franco Modigliani Professor of Finance and Economics
Sloan School of Management
Massachusetts Institute of Technology
Consulting Editor

FINANCIAL MANAGEMENT

Benninga and Sarig
Corporate Finance: A Valuation Approach

Block and Hirt
Foundations of Financial Management
Tenth Edition

Brealey and Myers
Principles of Corporate Finance
Seventh Edition

Brealey, Myers, and Marcus
Fundamentals of Corporate Finance
Third Edition

Brooks
FinGame Online 3.0

Bruner
Case Studies in Finance: Managing for Corporate Value Creation
Fourth Edition

Chew
The New Corporate Finance: Where Theory Meets Practice
Third Edition

DeMello
Cases in Finance

Grinblatt and Titman
Financial Markets and Corporate Strategy
Second Edition

Helfert
Techniques of Financial Analysis: A Guide to Value Creation
Eleventh Edition

Higgins
Analysis for Financial Management
Seventh Edition

Kester, Fruhan, Piper, and Ruback
Case Problems in Finance
Eleventh Edition

Nunnally and Plath
Cases in Finance
Second Edition

Ross, Westerfield, and Jaffe
Corporate Finance
Sixth Edition

Ross, Westerfield, and Jordan
Essentials of Corporate Finance
Third Edition

Ross, Westerfield, and Jordan
Fundamentals of Corporate Finance
Sixth Edition

Smith
The Modern Theory of Corporate Finance
Second Edition

White
Financial Analysis with an Electronic Calculator
Fourth Edition

INVESTMENTS

Bodie, Kane, and Marcus
Essentials of Investments
Fourth Edition

Bodie, Kane, and Marcus
Investments
Fifth Edition

Cohen, Zinbarg, and Zeikel
Investment Analysis and Portfolio Management
Fifth Edition

Corrado and Jordan
Fundamentals of Investments: Valuation and Management
Second Edition

Farrell
Portfolio Management: Theory and Applications
Second Edition

Hirt and Block
Fundamentals of Investment Management
Seventh Edition

FINANCIAL INSTITUTIONS AND MARKETS

Cornett and Saunders
Fundamentals of Financial Institutions Management

Rose
Commercial Bank Management
Sixth Edition

(continued)

Rose
Money and Capital Markets: Financial Institutions and Instruments in a Global Marketplace
Eighth Edition

Santomero and Babbel
Financial Markets, Instruments, and Institutions
Second Edition

Saunders and Cornett
Financial Institutions Management: A Risk Management Approach
Fourth Edition

Saunders and Cornett
Financial Markets and Institutions: A Modern Perspective

INTERNATIONAL FINANCE

Beim and Calomiris
Emerging Financial Markets

Eun and Resnick
International Financial Management
Second Edition

Levich
International Financial Markets: Prices and Policies
Second Edition

REAL ESTATE

Brueggeman and Fisher
Real Estate Finance and Investments
Eleventh Edition

Corgel, Ling, and Smith
Real Estate Perspectives: An Introduction to Real Estate
Fourth Edition

FINANCIAL PLANNING AND INSURANCE

Allen, Melone, Rosenbloom, and Mahoney
Pension Planning: Pension, Profit-Sharing, and Other Deferred Compensation Plans
Ninth Edition

Crawford
Life and Health Insurance Law
Eighth Edition (LOMA)

Harrington and Niehaus
Risk Management and Insurance

Hirsch
Casualty Claim Practice
Sixth Edition

Kapoor, Dlabay, and Hughes
Personal Finance
Sixth Edition

Skipper
International Risk and Insurance: An Environmental-Managerial Approach

Williams, Smith, and Young
Risk Management and Insurance
Eighth Edition

ABOUT THE AUTHOR

Erich A. Helfert is an internationally recognized management consultant, author, and speaker in corporate finance, strategic planning, and executive education in financial/economic decision making and shareholder value creation. He gained his professional experience from a combination of distinguished business and academic careers. Dr. Helfert was vice president, corporate planning, at Crown Zellerbach Corporation, a major integrated paper and forest products company. Prior to his 20-year corporate career, he served on the faculty of the Harvard Graduate School of Business for eight years, teaching finance and managerial economics in the MBA program, and consulting in management development and strategy with major companies.

A native of the Sudetenland, a former region of Austria, he received his BS from the University of Nevada and earned both an MBA (with high distinction) and a DBA (as a Ford Foundation Fellow) at the Harvard Business School. Dr. Helfert writes and lectures extensively in his field, and his books and articles have been published in the United States and abroad. His first literary work, *Valley of the Shadow,* a factual historical novel about his experiences in the ethnic cleansing of the Sudetenland by Czechoslovakia after the end of World War II, was published recently. Dr. Helfert's website is www.heleassoc.net.

Dr. Helfert is also cofounder, chairman and CEO of Modernsoft, Inc., San Mateo, California, developers of *Financial Genome*, an advanced knowledge-based financial analysis and business planning software. A special educational version of this program is available with the 11th edition of *Techniques of Financial Analysis.*

PREFACE

With more than half a million copies in nine languages over the past 39 years, this best-selling guide to financial analysis has consistently provided the student of business, financial analyst, and business executive with a concise, practical, usable, and up-to-date overview of key financial/economic analysis tools. Its unique presentation format was always carefully designed to help the reader understand the linkage between management decisions and their impact on the financial performance and economic value of a business. Every technique and measure is described and demonstrated in the context of the key underlying financial and economic concepts, but without delving into theoretical abstraction. The book helps the reader interpret financial reports, develop basic financial projections, evaluate business investment decisions, assess the implications of financing choices, derive the value of a business or a security, and understand the role of analysis in achieving the goal of shareholder value creation.

A Unique Systems Approach to Financial Management

The book's unique foundation is the concept that any business is essentially an integrated system of cash flows driven by management decisions, an intuitive approach that clearly differentiates the book from other texts. All analytical tools and related financial/economic concepts are discussed within this systems perspective, which reflects the three basic types of decisions made continuously by the management of any ongoing business: *investment, operating*, and *financing*. The materials are also related to the viewpoints of the major parties interested in the analysis and performance of a business: managers, owners, and creditors.

The book begins with a detailed exploration of the business system and its relationships to financial/economic analysis and financial statements. This overview sets the stage for all ensuing chapters, which explain the various techniques and concepts in a logical progression. Closure is provided by returning to the business system in the final chapters on valuation and on managing for shareholder value, further illustrating the integrated nature of sound financial/economic analysis. The systems approach is also reflected in the accompanying *Interactive Templates* and the special educational version of the professional business analysis and planning software, *Financial Genome*, which are available for download with this book.

Throughout the book's structure and coverage, however, practicality always remains paramount. Any issues and concepts beyond essential aspects are left to the more specialized textbooks and articles identified in the references.

The Audience

Ever since the first edition appeared in 1963, *Techniques of Financial Analysis* has consistently maintained a unique appeal both for business students (graduate and undergraduate) and practitioners, because of its clarity and commonsense presentation. Straddling the educational and professional markets, the book requires little background in finance and accounting and provides an accessible, self-contained overview of the essential financial/economic management concepts and tools. Countless students have found the book to be an understandable and useful guide for their studies and have kept the book for ready reference in their careers. Large numbers of business professionals—whether financial practitioners or nonfinancial managers—recognized the practicality and applicability of the book's approach to their analytical needs and decision making.

Originally an outgrowth of the compact technical briefing notes used in the MBA program at the Harvard Business School, which supplement practical case study discussion with essential background, the book has been regularly updated and modified approximately every four years. This eleventh edition reflects not only the latest practice in the use of the various financial techniques, but also the experience gained over 10 editions from the widespread use the book has enjoyed in university finance courses, both graduate and undergraduate, and from hundreds of executive development seminars and in-company programs in the United States, Canada, Latin America, and overseas, including those conducted by the author at numerous Fortune 100 client companies. Repeatedly translated into nine foreign languages over the years, the book has transcended the confines of American business practice on which it is built, because the way in which the analytical methods are described makes them almost universally applicable.

What's New in This Edition

The entire eleventh edition of *Techniques of Financial Analysis* has been refined and updated while preserving the logical, integrated flow of the materials. The coverage begins, as before, with an overview of the business system and the key financial analysis tools, leading all the way to the development of business valuation and the more recent and expanded materials on managing for shareholder value. Among the new concepts added is a discussion in Chapter 1 of the attributes of the modern "economic manager" as related to the effective use of financial/economic analysis, and a review of the characteristics of a value-creating company in Chapter 11. The sobering lessons from the recent dot-com boom and bust have also been recognized where appropriate. The financial statements and annual report background of 3M Corporation have been incorporated as examples in the first three chapters, and also integrated into the analytical support structure. In addition, the various graphics supporting the text—tested for their effectiveness in numerous executive development programs over the past 15 years—have again been updated and refined for this edition. Many of them are represented in live format within the set of *Interactive Templates* described on the next page. Where appropriate, specific references to spreadsheet analysis have been made and examples are presented in this readily accessible format to ease the mechanical aspects of analysis.

As before, Chapters 1 through 5 of the book form an integrated set, built around the conceptual overview of the business system, its decisional context, and its relationship to financial statements and analytical tools as presented in Chapter 1. The coverage of analytical methods begins in Chapter 2 with funds flow analysis, moves on to financial performance analysis, covers financial projections, and culminates in a discussion of the financial dynamics useful in modeling financial conditions and growth capabilities. Chapters 6 through 10 deal with more specialized topics such as business investment analysis, the cost of capital, financing choices, and valuation of securities and businesses, and the final chapter returns to the systems context in an expanded discussion of the conceptual and analytical aspects of managing for shareholder value.

The process of revising the eleventh edition has not, however, affected the book's primary focus on the doable and practical—it effectively provides a form of "executive briefing"—and on building the reader's basic ability to grasp financial relationships and issues. As before, the book presupposes only that the user has some familiarity with basic accounting concepts.

The eleventh edition features two major new enhancements in the form of unique analytical support software packages:

The first support software is a set of *Interactive Templates* provided without charge to aid the reader's insights and understanding. These Excel-based live displays were specifically designed by Modernsoft, Inc., to accompany *Techniques of Financial Analysis,* as indicated below. There are 11 templates included in the *Interactive Templates* workbook:

The Business System: An Overview

Ratios as a System: Key Ratios and Their Elements

Cash Budget Example: Projections and Key Drivers

Break-Even Model: Key Variables

Sustainable Growth Model and Related Statements

Policies Impacting Growth: Comparative Cases

Integrated Growth Model: Projecting Financial Results

Present Value Model: Cash Flows and Key Measures

Impact of Financing Choices on EPS

Business Valuation Model: Cash Flows and Firm Value

Comparing Economic Measures: An Illustration.

The templates activate many of the key diagrams and exhibits of the book, beginning with the core display of the business system in Chapter 1, p. 8. The displays enhance the reader's learning experience by graphically illustrating the impact of changes in assumptions and conditions; they are also integrated into the suggested end-of-chapter exercises where appropriate. Many of the templates

INTERACTIVE TEMPLATES

Example: The Business System: An Overview

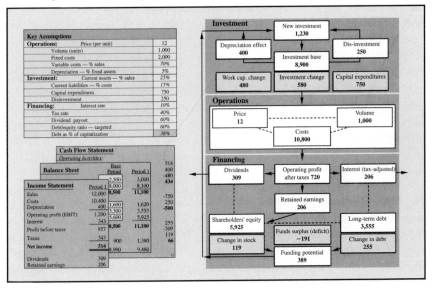

Each template is laid out in a similar fashion: Key assumptions are contained in a special table, whereas the impact of changing assumptions is shown in graphic form and/or in a summary financial statement mode.

are appropriate tools for general business use, such as sustainable growth analysis, high-level planning projections, present value project analysis, and business valuation. The *Interactive Templates* can be downloaded from the book's website: www.mhhe.com/helfert11e.

The second support software is a special time-limited educational version of the advanced, knowledge-based financial analysis and business planning application, *Financial Genome*, an Excel add-in also created by Modernsoft, Inc. This professional software tool enables the user to freely develop sets of financial statements, the whole range of key financial measures, and fully integrated financial projections and plans, as well as carry out ad hoc financial analyses. The program's patented knowledge-based technology allows the user to readily perform these tasks from spreadsheet data or databases with assured internal consistency, without having to worry about spreadsheet cell locations or formulas. Knowledge of financial terms, relationships, and statement structures is built into the software, and the user can access and display this knowledge at will to enhance understanding of the definitions and linkages. *Financial Genome* is described in detail in Appendix I (p. 471). It contains special databases supporting the financial information relevant to key examples used in the book, and it is also integrated into the end-of-chapter problems where appropriate. The special educational version can be downloaded without charge from the book's website www.mhhe.com/helfert11e by using the unique code provided with this copy of the book. After expiration of the six-month period of free use, *Financial Genome* can be upgraded to the then current commercial version and registered for permanent use at a discount from the list price by visiting Modernsoft Inc.'s website at www.modernsoft.com and again using the unique code provided with this copy of the book.

Acknowledgments

I would again like to express my appreciation to my former colleagues at the Harvard Business School for the opportunity to develop the original concept of the book. My thanks also go to my business associates and to my colleagues at universities and in executive development programs here and abroad, too numerous to mention individually, for their continued extensive use of the book and for the many expressions of interest and constructive suggestions that have supported the book's evolution.

My special thanks go to my colleagues at Modernsoft, Inc., Edgar P. Canty, Dr. William J. Clancey, and John W. Wu for their enthusiasm and expertise in adapting the major concepts of the book and its approach in our development of the *Financial Genome* software and the *Interactive Templates*. Their insights and suggestions have been most valuable during the recent revisions of this book, and their unwavering dedication to creating this unique professional financial analysis and planning software advance has been exemplary.

I would also like to express my sincere appreciation to the McGraw-Hill/ Irwin publishing team who made this eleventh edition a reality. Michele Janicek, sponsoring editor, Barbara Hari, editorial coordinator, Rhonda Seelinger, executive marketing manager, Laura Griffin, project manager, and Gretlyn Cline, copy editor, have been enthusiastic and tireless in their efforts to continue the long tradition of excellence that has characterized the publication and marketing processes of the many editions of *Techniques of Financial Analysis*. Their expertise and dedication are key contributions to making the book successful.

I am grateful to John Draut, Benedictine University, and Sudhir Singh, Frostburg State University, for their thoughtful and constructive inputs during the revision of the book.

Finally, I continue to be most gratified by the positive responses from so many individual users, past and current, who have found the book helpful in their studies and an ongoing supportive resource in their professions.

Erich A. Helfert

CONTENTS

Chapter 3

Assessment of Business Performance   107

Chapter 6

Cash Flows and the Time Value of Money   245

Chapter 7

Analysis of Investment Decisions   279

Chapter 8

Cost of Capital and Business Decisions 325

Chapter 11

Managing for Shareholder Value   431

INTRODUCTION

When a student of business, an analyst, or an executive is dealing with a financial issue, or wishes to understand the financial implications and economic trade-offs involved in decisions about business investment, operations, and financing, a wide variety of analytical techniques—and sometimes rules of thumb—is available to generate quantitative answers. Selecting the appropriate tools from these choices is clearly an important part of the analytical task. Yet experience has shown again and again that just as important as the choice of the tools themselves, is the need to first develop a proper perspective by carefully framing the problem or issue. Therefore, this book not only presents the key financial tools generally used, but also explains the broader context of how and where they're applied to obtain meaningful answers. To this end, Chapter 1 provides an integrated conceptual backdrop both for the financial/economic dimensions of systematic business management and for understanding the nature of financial statements, data, and processes underlying financial analysis techniques. All analytical concepts and tools are viewed in the context of creating shareholder value—a fundamental principle that is revisited in detail in the final chapter on managing for shareholder value.

Although the tools and techniques covered in this book are discussed and demonstrated in detail, the user must not be tempted to view them as ends in themselves. It's simply not enough to master the techniques alone! Financial/economic analysis is both an analytical and a judgmental process which helps answer questions that have been carefully framed in a managerial context. The process is at its best when the analyst's efforts are focused primarily on structuring the issue and its context, and only secondarily on data manipulation. We can't stress enough that the basic purpose of financial analysis is to help those responsible for results make sound business decisions within a cash flow framework using relevant inputs!

Apart from providing specific numerical answers, "solutions" to financial problems and issues depend significantly on the points of view of the various parties involved, on the relative importance of the issue, and on the nature and reliability of the information available. In each situation, the objective of the analysis must be clearly understood before pencil is put to paper or computer keys are touched—otherwise the process becomes wasteful "number crunching," even if the numerical task itself is eased by analytical software.

Management has been defined as "the art of asking significant questions." The same applies to financial analysis, which must be targeted toward finding meaningful answers to these significant questions—whether or not the results are fully quantifiable. In fact, the qualitative judgments involved in finding answers to financial/economic issues can often count just as heavily as the quantitative, and no analytical task is complete until these aspects have been carefully spelled out and weighed.

The degree of precision and refinement to which any financial analysis is carried also depends on the specific situation. Given the uncertain nature of many of the estimates used in calculations, it's often preferable to develop ranges of potential outcomes rather than precise answers. At the same time, a lot of effort can be wasted in further refining answers that clearly suggest the choice of particular alternatives—there's no need to belabor the obvious! Moreover, common sense dictates that most of the analytical effort should be directed at areas where the likely payoff from additional analysis is largest—to match the amount of energy expended with the significance of the results.

The following points are a suggested checklist for review and consideration in "framing" the issue before any financial analysis task is begun. This list should be helpful to the person actually doing the work as well as to the manager who may have assigned the question or project to an associate:

1. What is the exact nature and scope of the issue to be analyzed? Is the issue and its relative importance within the overall business context truly understood, and have its attributes been clearly spelled out, including all the relevant alternatives that should be considered?

2. Which specific variables, relationships, and trends are likely to be helpful in analyzing the issue? What is the order of their importance, and in what sequence should they be addressed?

3. Are there possible ways to obtain a quick "ballpark" estimate of the likely result to help decide (a) what the critical data and steps might be, and (b) how much effort should be spent on refining these?

4. How precise an answer is necessary in relation to the importance of the issue itself? Would additional refinement truly be worth the effort?

5. How reliable are the available data, and how is this uncertainty likely to affect the range of results? What confirmation might be possible, and at what degree and cost of effort?

6. Are the input data to be used expressed in cash flow terms—essential for economic analysis—or are they to be applied within an accounting framework to test only the financial reporting implications of a decision?

7. What limitations are inherent in the tools to be applied, and how will these likely affect the range of results obtained? Are the tools chosen truly appropriate to solving the issue?

8. How important are qualitative judgments in the context of the issue, and what is the ranking of their significance? Which analytical steps might in fact be made unnecessary by such considerations?

Only after having thought through these questions should specific analytical work on any issue proceed. The amount of care and effort expended on taking this critical first step to properly frame the issue at the beginning of the task will pay off in much more focused and meaningful work and results. In effect, we're talking about using a rational approach to problem solving in financial/economic analysis. In the end, this is what effective support of decision making involving a company's investments, operations, and financing is all about, because shareholder value creation is the logical result of sound business decisions carefully analyzed and successfully implemented.

Eleventh Edition

TECHNIQUES OF FINANCIAL ANALYSIS

A Guide to Value Creation

To Anne

CHAPTER 1

A SYSTEMS CONTEXT FOR FINANCIAL MANAGEMENT

$\mathbf{A}$ny business, large or small, is a system of financial relationships and cash flows which are activated by management decisions. This concept gained initial importance in the 1990s, when creation of shareholder value emerged as a critical performance challenge and became one of the primary goals of modern management. More recently it has been reinforced by the events of the first two years of the new century, when the speculative bubble of the dot-com phenomenon was deflated by sobering reality, and the basic criteria of business success were slowly rediscovered. This "return to the basics" reinstated the time-honored concept that creating shareholder value depends on bringing about a positive pattern of cash flows in excess of investor expectations. A business that is successfully managed in all parts as an integrated system will generate such cash flows over time and well into the future—thereby becoming a value-creating company.

Given that the basic purpose and value of business activity depend on long-term cash flow generation, it's necessary for us to understand more specifically how the dynamics of the integrated business system work. Moreover, we must directly relate the various analytical concepts and tools we'll discuss in this book to the business system. Financial/economic tools should assist decision makers at all levels in specific ways to support cash flow generation and shareholder value creation. Finally, we must provide an appropriate context for the use of commonly available financial information with which such analytical activity is supported.

In this chapter we'll set the stage by presenting three conceptual overviews for the context and meaning of financial/economic analysis and the key economic trade-offs involved in it. The purpose is to provide the reader with a realistic structure that goes beyond mere coverage of technical tools and methods:

- A graphic representation of the generalized, integrated business system, showing the relationships and dynamics of the three basic management

1

decision areas that are common to all organizations which have an economic purpose:

Investment decisions

Operating decisions

Financing decisions

- A broad perspective of the nature, meaning, and limits of the major published financial statements, which are the primary source of financial data, and their relationship to the business system:

Balance sheets

Income (operating) statements

Cash flow statements

Statements of changes in shareholders' (owners') equity

- A generalized overview of the key analytical processes used in interpreting the performance and value of the business system, grouped by three major viewpoints:

Financial accounting

Investor analysis

Managerial economics

In our discussions we'll differentiate between purely financial analysis on one hand, and economic analysis and trade-offs on the other. The first is largely based on financial statements and accounting data, whereas the second focuses on cash flows and their impact. We make this important distinction because the tasks of analyzing, judging, and guiding a firm's activities are far broader and more complex than the mere manipulation of reported financial data. Ultimately, the performance and value of any business must be judged in economic terms; that is, expressed both in cash flows achieved and future cash flows expected.

Yet we must remind ourselves that much of the available data and many of the analytical techniques generally used are based on financial accounting and its special conventions, which by their nature don't necessarily reflect current and future economic performance and value. Therefore, the manager or analyst must at all times carefully interpret and even translate the available data to properly match the context and purpose of the analysis. It's both the manager's and the analyst's duty to make sure that the process selected and the results obtained in any analysis clearly fit the desired objectives, whether they express a financial viewpoint or an economic insight when judging performance, expectations, or valuation.

A Dynamic Perspective of Business

Decision Context

Successful operation, performance, and long-term viability of any business depend on a continuous sequence of sound decisions made individually or collectively by the management team. Every one of these decisions ultimately causes, for better or worse, an economic impact on the business. In essence, the process of managing any enterprise requires making an ongoing series of economic choices; each time trading off costs and benefits. These choices in turn activate specific, identifiable shifts in the physical and financial resources supporting the business. Ultimately these shifts cause movements of cash, which is the final economic result.

For Example

Hiring an employee means incurring a future series of salary or wage payments in exchange for useful services. Selling merchandise on credit releases goods from inventory to the customer and creates a documented obligation by the customer to remit payment within 30 or 60 days. Investing in a new physical facility causes, among other effects, a potentially complex set of future financial obligations to be fulfilled. Developing a new software application involves a significant period of repeated cash commitments for salaries, technical support, and testing before marketing efforts result in a revenue stream. Successful negotiation with a lender of a line of credit brings an inflow of cash into the business, to be repaid in future periods.

Some decisions are major, such as investing in a new manufacturing plant, raising large amounts of debt, or adding a new line of products or services. Most other decisions are part of the day-to-day processes through which every functional area of a business is managed. Common to all, however, is the basic concept that decisions are economic trade-offs; that is, before a decision is made the decision maker must weigh the cash benefits expected against the cash costs incurred.

In normal day-to-day decisions, these underlying trade-offs can be quite apparent and identifiable. In complex situations, however, managers must carefully evaluate whether the net pattern of resources committed directly or indirectly by the decision is likely to be profitably recovered over time through the changes in revenues and expenses caused by this commitment. Managers also must identify the relevant information needed to support this analysis. The collective effect of the ongoing series of trade-off analyses and decisions ultimately impacts both the performance and value of the business. Results are then judged periodically, either by means of financial statements or with the help of special economic analyses.

Fundamentally, managers make decisions on behalf of the owners of the business while addressing the interests of the various stakeholders involved, that is, employees, suppliers, creditors, and the community. In this process, managers are responsible for effectively deploying available internal and external resources in ways that create an economic gain for the owners—a gain reflected over time in the combination of dividends and share price appreciation received by the owner/shareholders. This concept, called *total shareholder return (TSR),* is one of the key criteria for measuring the success of the company relative to its peers and the market as a whole, as we'll discuss in Chapters 3 and 11.

Despite the great variety of issues faced every day by managers of different businesses, and within the hierarchy of business activities, most management

The Three Basic Business Decisions

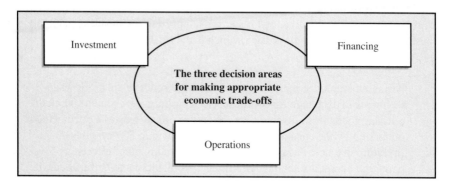

tasks are so similar in principle that we can effectively group all business decisions into three basic areas:

- The investment of resources.
- The operation of the business using these resources.
- The proper mix of financing that funds these resources.

Figure 1–1 reflects the continuous interrelationship of these three areas.

Today's business world has infinite variety. Enterprises of all sizes engage in activities such as trade, manufacturing, finance, and myriad services, using a variety of business models, and legal and organizational structures. They frequently involve international operations, far-flung investments, and growing Internet support. Common to all businesses, however, is the following definition of the basic economic purpose of sound management:

> Strategic deployment of selected resources in order to create, over time, economic value sufficient to recover all of the resources employed while earning an acceptable economic return on these resources under conditions that match the owners' expectations of risk.

Over time, therefore, successful resource deployments should result in a net improvement in the economic position of the owners of the business. Only when such an improvement is achieved has additional shareholder value been created, as we'll discuss later. The primary effect of value creation normally will be a higher valuation of the business. If the company's stock is traded publicly, its value is judged by the securities markets. If the company is privately held, its value will be reflected in the price offered by potential buyers of the business. If no value increment is achieved over time, or if there is a declining trend, the firm's economic viability might be in question.

Therefore, creating shareholder value ultimately depends on properly managing the three basic decision areas common to all organizations:

F I G U R E   1–2

The Process of Value Creation

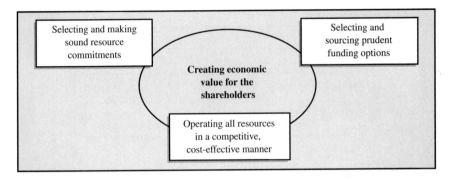

- Selecting, implementing, and monitoring all *investments* on the basis of sound, sustainable strategies, economic analysis, and effective management.
- Guiding the *operations* of the business profitably through proper trade-off decisions and cost-effective use of all resources employed.
- Prudently *financing* the business by consciously trading off the rewards expected against the risks encountered in balancing internal and external financing in the capital structure.

Making successful economic trade-offs in all of these decisions is fundamental to driving the value creation process. These trade-offs must also be explicitly chosen and managed in a consistent way to achieve long-run success, instead of focusing on occasional short-term improvements that cannot be sustained or might detract from longer-term results. Figure 1–2 depicts the definition and purpose of the three interrelated decision areas.

The basic task—and the fundamental challenge—of financial/economic analysis lies in constructing and sharing a reasonably consistent and meaningful set of data and relationships that will support the decision-making process for the purpose of value creation. If this is done well, the chosen frameworks and tools should enable the analyst and the manager to judge the economic trade-offs involved in investment choices, financing options, and operational effectiveness, and help define and judge the company's economic performance, future expectations, and value.

Figure 1–3 illustrates, in the form of background layers, the analytical framework and tools, data sources, and the general backdrop of competitive and economic conditions to the three decision areas. This picture presents an integrated set of concepts for the ideal interplay of management decisions and the interpretation of results.

FIGURE 1-3

The Broad Context of Financial/Economic Analysis

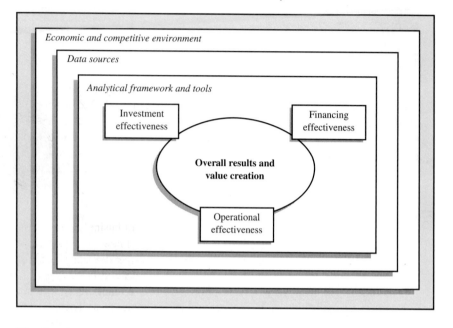

The Business System

As we've established, the daily decisions made by managers impact the resources under their control in one way or another in a dynamic interrelationship. Decisions cause resource movements in various forms that ultimately change the cash flow pattern of the business as a whole. The process might involve some intermediate steps before cash movements occur, as we'll discuss in Chapter 2, but increases or decreases in cash will invariably follow any decision made. In a successful business, the balancing of cash uses and sources over time generates positive cash flow patterns that lead to the desired buildup of economic value and long-term viability. In fact, creation of shareholder value and cash flow patterns—achieved and expected—are inseparable concepts.

As we take up the analytical concepts and tools in the book, we'll relate them, as appropriate, to the simple principle of "cash in" versus "cash out," which is the key to any economic analysis that focuses on creating shareholder value. The principle applies whether one is judging a new facilities investment, evaluating the performance prospects of a product line, or weighing the pros and cons of a research project or new service offering. In Chapter 2, we'll discuss the formal ways of tracking and analyzing overall resource flow patterns and their cash impact. In Chapters 6, 7, 10, and 11 we'll show how the specific cash flows associated with an investment project or a business as a whole can be developed, analyzed, and valued.

Let's now turn to a practical, simplified view of how a typical business operates. With the help of an intuitive systems diagram we'll demonstrate the basic cash flow patterns, the key relationships, and the key decisions involved in an integrated fashion. Then we'll show how the major financial/economic analysis measures and key business strategies relate to this business system. Every one of the measures and concepts will, of course, be discussed in greater depth in the appropriate chapters of this book, but this overview provides a structure for keeping the individual elements in proper perspective.

Figure 1–4 presents the basic flowchart of the business system, which contains all major elements necessary to understand the broad cash flow patterns of any business. The arrangement of boxes, lines, and arrows is designed to show that we're dealing with a system in which all parts are interrelated with each other—and which therefore has to be managed as a whole. The solid lines with arrows represent cash flows, whereas the dashed lines symbolize trade-off relationships. The system is organized into three segments that match the three major decision areas we've already defined: investment, operations, and financing.

- The top segment represents the three components of business investment: the *investment base* already in place, the addition of *new investments,* and any *disinvestment* (divestment) of resources no longer deemed effective or strategically necessary. In addition, it shows the *depreciation effect* caused by accounting write-offs of portions of depreciable assets against the investment base and against profits. This box, which effectively enhances the funding potential shown in the bottom segment, represents available cash that was masked when the accounting-based operating profit after taxes was calculated, as we'll discuss in Chapter 2.

- The center segment represents the operational interplay of three basic elements: *price, volume,* and *costs* of products and/or services. It also recognizes that usually costs are partly fixed and partly variable relative to volume changes, as we'll discuss in Chapter 5. The ultimate result of the complex set of continuously occurring trade-offs in the operations area is the periodic operating profit or loss, after applicable income taxes. Operating profit is shown as part of the bottom segment in the diagram, because profit represents one of the key elements of financing the business.

- The bottom segment represents, in two parts, the basic financing choices open to a business:

  1. The normal disposition of the *operating profit after taxes* (or loss after taxes) that has been achieved for a period:

     This is a three-way split among *dividends* paid to owners, *interest* paid to lenders (adjusted for taxes because of its tax deductibility), and *earnings* retained for reinvestment in the business. As the arrows indicate, the cash used for paying dividends and interest leaves the system.

FIGURE 1–4

The Business System: An Overview*

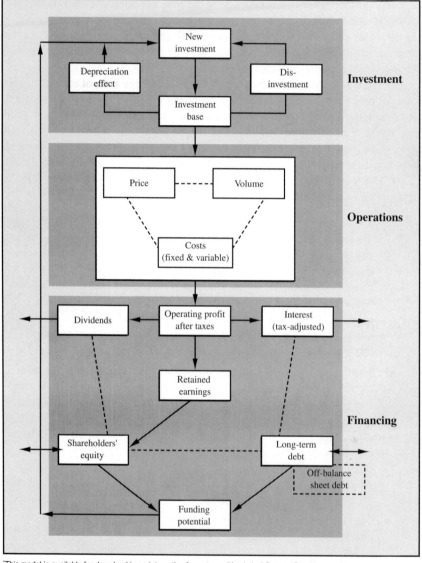

'This model is available for download in an interactive format; see "Analytical Support," p. 41.

2. The available choices for using long-term capital sources:

This reflects *shareholders' equity* (ownership), augmented by retained earnings, and *long-term debt* held by outsiders. Trade-offs and decisions that affect the levels of shareholders' equity, retained profits, or long-term capital sources impact the company's *funding potential,* which, as the arrow moving from the left to the top indicates, affects the amount of new investment that can be added to the investment base. As was already mentioned, the depreciation effect shown in the top segment enhances the funding potential, because it reflects cash that was masked in the accounting profit calculation.

Alternatively, some of the enhanced funding potential can be used to reduce long-term debt, or to repurchase outstanding ownership shares in the market. These actions will, of course, change the capital structure proportions and, as the arrows indicate, cause cash to leave the system—just as issuing new shares or additional debt will bring cash into the system.

Now we'll examine each part of the business system in further detail to highlight the three types of decisions and the various interrelationships among them. We'll also introduce the key measures and strategic considerations applicable to each area.

Investment Decisions

Investment is the basic driving force of any business activity. It's the source of growth, it supports management's explicit competitive strategies, and it is normally based on careful plans (capital budgets) for committing existing or new funds to three main areas:

- Working capital (cash balances, receivables due from customers, and inventories, less trade credit from suppliers and other normal current obligations).

- Physical assets (land, buildings, machinery and equipment, office furnishings, computer systems, laboratory equipment, etc.).

- Major spending programs (research and development, product or service development, promotional programs, etc.) and acquisitions.

Note that investment is broadly defined here in terms of resource commitments to be recovered over time, not by the more narrow accounting classification which would, for example, categorize most spending programs as ongoing expenses, despite their longer-range impact. Figure 1–5 shows the investment portion of the systems diagram, accompanied by major yardsticks and key strategies that can be identified in this area.

During the periodic planning process, when capital budgets are formulated, management normally chooses from a variety of options those new investments that are expected to exceed or at least meet targeted economic returns. The level of these returns generally is related to shareholder expectations via the cost of capital calculation, as described in Chapter 8. Making sound investment choices and implementing them successfully—so that the actual results in fact exceed the cost of capital

FIGURE 1–5

The Business System: Investment Segment

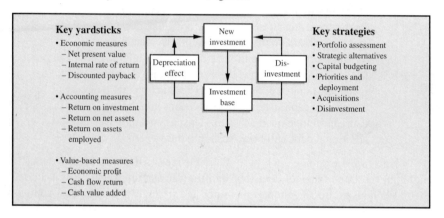

standard—is a key management responsibility that leads to value creation. New investment is the key driver of growth strategies that cause enhanced shareholder value, but only if carefully established investment standards are met or exceeded.

At the same time, successful companies periodically make critical assessments of how their existing investment base (portfolio) is deployed, to see if the actual performance and outlook for the individual products, services, and business segments warrant continued commitment within the context of the company's strategic posture. If careful analysis demonstrates below-standard economic results and expectations about a particular market or activity, then the opposite of investment, *disinvestment,* becomes a compelling option. As we'll see, such poorly performing activities destroy shareholder value. Disposing of the assets involved or selling the operating unit as a going concern will allow the funds received to be redeployed more advantageously elsewhere, such as making new investments, reducing debt, or repurchasing outstanding shares. Also, the sale of any equipment being replaced by newer facilities will provide funds for such purposes. Shareholder value creation thus depends on a combination of ongoing successful performance of existing investments, and the addition of successful new investments—a continued reassessment of the company's total portfolio of activities.

The yardsticks helpful in selecting *new investments* and *disinvestments* are generally economic criteria. They are based on cash flows, measuring the trade-off between investment funds committed now and the expected stream of future operational cash flow benefits and residual values. The cash flow tools listed here—net present value, internal rate of return, and discounted payback—are discussed in detail in Chapter 6. In contrast, common yardsticks that measure the effectiveness of the existing investment base generally are based on accounting data and relationships, as we'll describe in Chapter 3. These measures—return on investment, return on assets, and return on assets employed—relate balance sheet and income statement data as basic ratios. We'll show that there's a real disconnect between the economic

FIGURE 1–6

The Business System: Operations Segment

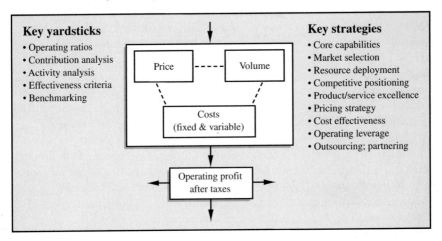

measures commonly used for new investments, and the accounting-based measures for existing investments. The gap in comparability must be bridged in order to achieve a consistent approach to shareholder value creation. In fact, this bridging process has been underway since the 90s with the significant shift of corporate America toward *value-based management* in which measures such as economic profit, cash flow return on investment, and cash value added have become widely used in judging the performance and value of existing operations. As we'll discuss in Chapter 11, these measures are cash flow oriented and thus are comparable to the economic yardsticks used for new investment, which are described in Chapter 6.

Operating Decisions

Here key strategies and decisions should focus on effective utilization of the funds invested to ensure that their implementation and continued operation meet the criteria and expectations on which the commitment was originally based. The basic set of trade-offs in operations, as was already mentioned, lies in the price, volume, and cost relationship, but surrounding this simple concept is an extensive array of complex choices and decisions. Figure 1–6 shows the operational segment of the business system in its broader context.

To begin with, the company must identify its core capabilities and match them to appropriate market segments. This is followed not only by effective deployment of human and physical resources, but also by careful positioning of products and services relative to its competition. The company must seek to differentiate its offerings in the market for competitive advantage, and strive for excellence in serving real customer needs. This requires making appropriate trade-offs in pricing strategy, while striving for cost effectiveness, and taking advantage of operating leverage as well as the potential for outsourcing and part-nering to enhance operational effectiveness and service.

Apart from the broader strategic context, we're talking here about making practical use of such advantages as cost-effective facilities, superior skills and sys-tems in delivery and customer service, highly effective information systems linked with customer networks, and unique technology or research capabilities. All along, management must anticipate and deal with the impact of changing prices and competitors' actions on sales volume and on the profitability of indi-vidual products or services. At the same time, all operations of the business, whether carried on inside the company or outsourced with others must be made cost effective, and also maintained as such to achieve competitive success.

Sound operating results also depend on a realistic understanding of the busi-ness processes employed, the economic costs and benefits of each part of the orga-nization, and the relative contribution of products and services to overall results. This requires the use of appropriate information systems, data collection, and re-porting. Part of the insights is the effect on the company's profitability of the level and proportion of fixed (period) costs committed to the operations versus the amount and nature of variable (direct) costs incurred in manufacturing, service, or trading operations. These concepts will be discussed in detail in Chapter 5.

Sound operational planning is an essential support process. Goals and in-centives are established to reinforce the need for making economic decisions. Budgeting and analysis processes are designed to give relevant feedback, and pro-vide action signals for corrective measures should targets not be met. Enterprise modeling and activity-based accounting represent modern information structures made possible by ever more powerful computer systems and networks. We'll dis-cuss basic budgeting and projection of operating activity in Chapter 4, and take up the subject of financial modeling in Chapter 5.

The key yardsticks in the operations segment include a variety of operating ratios that measure the effectiveness with which revenues and costs are managed. Among these are financial expressions such as operating profit percentages and various ratios of cost elements to sales revenue. There are overall expressions such as sales and assets per employee, and a host of operating statistics such as output per hour, yield percentages in production, or indicators of customer satis-faction with services rendered. Operating ratios vary greatly by type of business, because they have to be tailored to the specific variables that drive performance. In fact, operating ratios are ideally derived from those variables that represent key drivers for the business, whether they be physical conditions, human skills and at-titudes, resource utilization, or technology application. From an economic stand-point, the relative profit and cash flow contribution margins of different products and services are important measures for tracking current performance and as an input to strategic decisions about the portfolio of products and services.

The distinction between accounting ratios and economic analysis is again important in the operations segment, because the answers provided by each can vary significantly. This problem has led to the wide use of a relatively recent methodology that directly addresses the need for economic answers, namely, *activity-based analysis*, which was mentioned earlier. This process is essentially a step-by-step identification of the physical activities involved in a specific function of the company, or the activities required to support a particular product line, followed by a careful economic analysis of the costs and benefits incurred in each step and in total. Because it amounts to an economic assessment, activity-based analysis has become an important technique for supporting the current emphasis on corporate reengineering and value-based management. In addition, benchmarking activities against best practices in the specific industry or in general business usage represent yet another popular way of refining the measures and standards to be applied. We'll discuss a variety of key financial and economic operational criteria in Chapters 3, 4, and 5.

Financing Decisions

Here we must deal with the various choices available to management for funding the investments and operations of the business over the long term. Note that the financing section begins with profit after taxes, which normally is a major source of funding for a company. Two key areas of strategy and trade-off decisions are identified:

- The disposition of profits.
- Shaping the company's capital structure.

Normally this set of trade-offs and decisions is made at the highest levels of management and endorsed by the board of directors of a corporation because the choices are crucial to the firm's long-term viability. Figure 1–7 displays the relationships, yardsticks, and strategies in the financing segment. The first area, the disposition of profits, amounts to a basic three-way split of after-tax profit among:

- Owners.
- Lenders.
- Reinvestment in the business.

Every one of these choices is affected by current or past management policies, trade-offs, and decisions. For example, payment of dividends to owners is made at the discretion of the board of directors. Here, the critical trade-off choice is the relative amount of dividends to be paid out to shareholders as part of their overall return versus the alternative of retaining these funds to invest in the company's growth, with the goal of creating additional value which will be reflected in greater share price appreciation for the shareholders.

Payment of interest to lenders is a matter of contractual obligation. The level of tax-adjusted interest payments incurred (the cost to the company is the net amount after applying the corporate tax rate) relative to operating profit, however, is a direct function of management policies and actions regarding the use of debt, symbolized by the dashed line. The higher the proportion of debt in the capital structure, the greater the demand will be for profit dollars to be used as interest

FIGURE 1–7

The Business System: Financing Segment

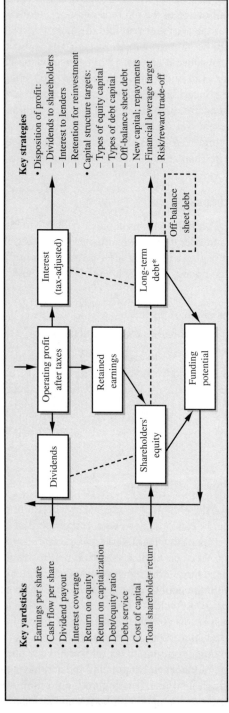

Key yardsticks
- Earnings per share
- Cash flow per share
- Dividend payout
- Interest coverage
- Return on equity
- Return on capitalization
- Debt/equity ratio
- Debt service
- Cost of capital
- Total shareholder return

Key strategies
- Disposition of profit:
  - Dividends to shareholders
  - Interest to lenders
  - Retention for reinvestment
- Capital structure targets:
  - Types of equity capital
  - Types of debt capital
  - Off-balance sheet debt
  - New capital; repayments
  - Financial leverage target
  - Risk/reward trade-off

Operating profit after taxes

Interest (tax-adjusted)

Dividends

Retained earnings

Shareholders' equity

Long-term debt*

Off-balance sheet debt

Funding potential

*Assumes a continuous rollover of debt (refinancing), that is, there is no reduction in existing debt levels from repayments, as new funds are raised to cover these—unless a policy change in debt proportions is specified. No specific provision is made here for use of off-balance sheet debt, such as operating leases.

expense, and the greater the firm's risk exposure will be; that is, its potential inability to meet interest obligations and/or repayment during a business downturn.

Retained earnings represent the residual profit after taxes for the period, a net amount which remains in the company after payment of interest and dividends. This normally forms a significant part of the funding potential for additional investment and growth as shown on the bottom of the chart. We recall that the depreciation effect was added to this funding potential and reflected in the investment section in order to correct for the amount of cash masked by the depreciation deduction made in calculating operating profit after taxes, as will be discussed in Chapter 2. Additional funding potential can be found in new funds provided by investors and lenders, depending on the company's policies governing the use of such long-term sources.

Key measures in the area of earnings disposition are earnings and cash flow (after-tax profit plus the depreciation effect), calculated on a per share basis, which are viewed as broad indicators of the company's ability to compensate both lenders and owners. In addition, specific ratios are used that measure the proportion of dividends paid out, the degree to which earnings cover the current interest on debt, and how well total debt service requirements are covered. These measures are discussed in Chapter 3.

The second area, the planning of capital structure targets, involves selecting and balancing the relative proportions of funding obtained over time from ownership sources and long-term debt obligations. The chosen combination, after taking into account business risk and debt service requirements, is intended to support an acceptable level of overall profitability while matching the degree of risk exposure deemed appropriate by management and the board of directors. A key consideration in choosing funding methods is the impact of financial leverage(see Chapter 5). It can be defined as the prudent use of funds obtained from fixed-cost debt obligations for financing opportunities that promise potential earnings higher than the interest cost on the borrowed funds—the difference benefiting the owners of the company.

Again, this process requires a series of economic trade-offs, which include weighing the rewards obtained versus the risks involved in the different alternatives open to management. As we'll discuss in Chapter 9, numerous types of equity, ranging from straight common equity to convertible shares and preferred stocks, can be used for new ownership funding. On the other hand, existing ownership funds also can be returned through repurchase of the company's shares in the open market, using some of the current funding potential. The latter choice has become an important aspect of capital structure management, because repurchasing stock with corporate cash flow reduces the number of shares outstanding, making each remaining share proportionally more valuable. At the same time, no dividends need be paid on the purchased shares, which can be used at a later time for purposes such as acquisitions. The trade-off is between adding value through new investment and adding share value through a reduced number of shares.

The choices among debt instruments are even more varied, as we'll discuss in Chapter 9. These include operating leases and similar long-term obligations, which are called *off-balance sheet debt* because they are not listed on the balance sheet and only impact the income statement as annual expenses. Major measures in the area of capital structure strategy include ratios that measure the return on equity and the return on capitalization (equity and long-term debt combined), various debt service coverage ratios (Chapter 3), ratios for relative levels of debt and equity (Chapter 5), measures of the cost of various forms of capital as well as the combined cost of capital for the company as a whole (Chapters 8 and 9), and, finally, shareholder value creation concepts, such as total shareholder return, economic value added, and so forth (Chapters 10 and 11). As we'll see, one of the fundamental principles of running a successful business system is that the returns from the investments supported by the capital structure must exceed the combined cost of the equity and debt capital employed, in order to create shareholder value and a satisfactory total shareholder return. Returns just matching the cost of capital will leave value unchanged, whereas returns below the cost of capital will destroy value. As we'll discuss in Chapter 11, the analyst again must distinguish carefully between accounting-based and cash flow–based measures in this area.

The footnote to Figure 1–7 refers to an assumption about continuous rollover of debt. This is necessary because the business system as described here is a simple growth model with stable capital structure policies, also called target proportions. Normally, as the amount of shareholders' equity grows with incremental retained earnings, management will likely wish to match this increase, in the proper proportion, with an incremental amount of new debt—unless management decides that a change in debt policy is appropriate for a variety of reasons. In that case, specific assumptions will have to be made about the pattern of repayments planned, which, of course, will change the relative proportions of debt and equity outstanding, and also change the cash flow patterns in the model.

Interrelationship of Strategy and Value Creation

It should be obvious by now that our concept of the basic business system (Figure 1–4) forces us to recognize and deal with the many dynamic interrelationships of key management strategies, policies, and decisions, and the major cash flows they cause. In effect, the system amounts to a basic financial growth model which illustrates the interplay of key variables in support of the ultimate goal—value creation through positive cash flows in excess of the cost of capital over time. Achieving consistency in the choices and decisions regarding these variables is critical to managing a firm's long-term success and shareholder expectations, because only a well-tuned business system will perform in a superior fashion.

For Example

It would be ineffective for a company to set aggressive growth strategies for its operations, while at the same time restricting itself to a set of rigid and conservative financial policies—especially when operating margins are narrow and funding needs sizable. Similarly, paying out a high proportion of current operating profit in the form of dividends, or repurchasing significant amounts of the company's shares, while at the same time maintaining a restrictive debt policy, would clash with an objective to hold market share in a rapidly expanding business that requires substantial funding. Under such circumstances, adequate funds for new investment simply wouldn't be available, unless new equity was raised in the market. The company's strategic position could be at risk, and the stock market would adversely assess future cash flow expectations, thereby lowering the valuation of the company.

The basis for successful management, therefore, is to develop and maintain a consistent set of business strategies, investment objectives, operating goals, and financial policies that reinforce each other rather than conflict. They must be chosen through conscious and careful analysis of the various economic trade-offs involved, both individually and in combination. Proper measures and incentives must be employed, all reinforcing a long-term pattern of performance that will establish and reinforce positive shareholder expectations about current and future cash flows from successful existing investments and sound new investments—or from divestments of underperforming parts of the company. As we'll demonstrate in later chapters, understanding the dynamics of business strategies and financial policies is essential, whether they involve operational cash flow management, key drivers of financial performance, investment and divestment analysis, or capital structure planning. Our simplified systems diagram has provided a way to recognize the main interrelationships within a broad context of management decisions and cash flows.

The Economic Manager

A few words should be said at this point about the role of managers in successfully building and operating the business system. We consider it to be the role of *economic manager.* This appellation certainly doesn't imply requirement of a degree in economics, or a stint in an economic consulting firm. Instead, we define the economic manager as a person operating from a mind-set of deliberate economic trade-offs, applied to every decision made. This mind-set always leads to the question: What are the ultimate cash flow benefits to be derived from this action, and what are the cash flow commitments involved—is this trade-off appropriate, given the risks involved? There is a degree of basic common sense about this point of view, because whether knowingly, instinctively, or even subconsciously, just about all individuals make such trade-offs in their daily lives. We all have a sense of weighing value received for value given in our purchases or investments, or in reverse, of value given for value received when we sell assets, or provide our own services. It's only the degree of understanding, quantification, and analytical discipline applied in practice that distinguishes the economic manager from the average individual, and we'll discuss the key attributes in a little more detail.

Understanding Business Economics

The economic manager has a very clear understanding of the business economics of the company and its parts, and especially of the segment he or she manages. This understanding begins with the dimensions and implications of the business model used, including customer needs and attributes, the supply chain, competitive positioning, and the company's operational design and effectiveness, all within the larger societal setting. It extends to insights about the specific contributions and requirements of the various stakeholders, both inside and outside the business system, and the obligations the organization owes them.

With such solid background knowledge the economic manager is in a position to identify and prioritize key value drivers that are essential to the long-term success of the business. A value driver can be as basic as a sustainable cost and/or quality advantage because of a patented process, a protected resource, or a unique set of operational skills. It can be as intangible as the technical expertise of a product development team or a group of service providers, or it can be an attribute of the business model that is hard for others to emulate. Positioning on the preference spectrum of the customers, such as brand recognition, or enjoying the advantage from an installed base of products or services can be value drivers. The point is, most businesses can identify one or more of these drivers, and if properly addressed, managed, and measured the drivers can lead to a tangible advantage or at least acceptable results. In the end every value driver is a lever for improved cash flow performance, and the economic manager will be very familiar not only with the nature of the value drivers impacted by decisions, but also by the trade-offs to be made in using the drivers well. Thus the economic manager views the business not only as a complete system, but also as a finely tuned assembly of interrelated parts. The economic manager knows where the priority areas of attention are and how to enhance them, and understands the business model and its parts sufficiently to have a positive impact through carefully analyzed and executed decisions.

Parallel to this understanding is the economic manager's comfort with the decision-making process itself. The mind-set is oriented toward clearly defining the issue at hand, establishing the appropriate alternatives, identifying which information and data are relevant for the purpose, and judging the analytical results from a long-term viewpoint of value creation. The economic manager is sufficiently familiar with information sources within the company, and works in close collaboration with financial and other staff persons to make sure that relevant data are at hand for sound analysis and judgments. There's sufficient understanding of such data to know what to ask for, to judge whether data or analyses provided by others are truly relevant, and to hold one's own in discussions with specialized personnel whose job it is to delve into the details of analytical data, constructs, and tools. We're talking about a level of practical insight that stops well short of the intricate specialization implicit in accounting, economic analysis, and planning expertise, but which is pronounced enough to insist on and achieve justifiable approaches and answers. The economic manager thus actively and successfully merges practical line experience with effective use of available staff capabilities.

Appropriate Economic Tools

Specifically, the economic manager knows the major tools for economic analysis described in this book well enough to be comfortable with their application and the interpretation of the results achieved. This is part of a deliberate effort to take responsibility for the process, and to draw in assistance from specialized staffs as needed. It's a natural aspect of managerial leadership to be cognizant of the need to apply the best techniques whenever necessary, and to base the choice on the cost benefit trade-off involved in such an effort.

Once appropriate analytical tools for preparing the groundwork for a decision have been identified, the economic manager acts in the role of decision maker—one who guides the process, probes for the appropriate information, and challenges the preliminary results and insights presented by staff, until a level of comfort is reached with the output of the analysis. Practicality is paramount at all times, as is realism stemming from the collective experience of the players involved. In line with this principle, for example, we'll discuss in Chapters 6 and 7 the technical aspects of the investment analysis tools presented there and frame their meaning and use in the larger context of the decision process involved. Economic tools must be an extension of management practice, not an exercise in number crunching.

The economic manager embracing such an approach will be in a better position to interpret and argue the case for a significant initiative with the ultimate decision makers, whether senior executives or even the board of directors. The manager's involvement in the framing of the issue, the choice of tools, and guidance of analytical effort leads to greater effectiveness not only in the manager's ability to handle decisions large and small, but also, by virtue of the manager's leadership, in the organization's ability to operate the business by appropriate economic criteria and by making the necessary trade-offs. This is, of course, a key prerequisite for creating shareholder value.

The Nature of Financial Statements

To apply the insights gained from the conceptual overview of the business system and how it should be managed, we must now look for available information that will:

- Allow the manager or analyst to track the financial condition and operating results of the business.
- Assist in understanding the cash flow patterns in more specific terms.

In the process of financial/economic analysis, a variety of formal or informal data are normally reviewed and tested for their relevance to the specific purpose of the analysis. The most common form in which basic financial information is available publicly, unless a company is privately held, is the set of financial statements issued under the guidelines of the Financial Accounting Standards Board (FASB) of the public accounting profession and governed by the U.S. Securities and Exchange Commission (SEC). Such a set of statements, prepared according to generally accepted accounting principles (GAAP), usually contains balance sheets as of given dates, income statements for given periods, and cash flow statements for the same periods. A special statement highlighting changes in owners' equity on the balance sheet is commonly provided as well.

Because financial statements are the source for a good portion of analytical efforts, we must first understand their nature, coverage, and limitations before we can use the data and observations derived from these statements for our analytical judgments. Financial statements reflect the cumulative effects of all of management's past decisions. However, they involve considerable ambiguity. Financial statements are governed by rules that attempt to consistently and fairly account for every business transaction using the following conservative principles:

- Transactions are recorded at values prevailing at the time.

- Adjustments to recorded values are made only if values decline.

- Revenues and costs are recognized when committed to, not when cash actually changes hands.

- Periodic matching of revenues and costs is achieved via accruals, deferrals, and accounting allocations.

- Allowances for negative contingencies are required in the form of estimates that reduce both profits and recorded value, usually affecting shareholders' equity or special set-asides.

These rules leave reported financial accounting results open to considerable interpretation, especially if the analyst seeks to understand a company's economic performance and to establish the basis for shareholder value results. It's common practice among professional analysts to adjust the data reflected on financial statements for known accounting transactions which do not affect cash flows, and to make assumptions about the economic values underlying recorded asset values. We'll discuss the most important of these adjustments in Chapters 3 and 11.

The Balance Sheet

The balance sheet, prepared as of *a specific date*, records the categories and amounts of assets employed by the business (i.e., the resources committed) and the offsetting liabilities incurred to lenders and owners (i.e., the funds obtained). Also called the *statement of financial condition* or *statement of financial position*, it must always balance. By definition, the recorded value of the total assets invested in the business at any point in time must be matched precisely by the recorded liabilities and owners' equity supporting these assets. Liabilities are specific obligations that represent claims against the assets of the business, ranking ahead of the owners in repayment priority. In contrast, the recorded shareholders' equity in effect represents a residual claim of the owners on the remaining assets after all liabilities have been subtracted.

The major categories of assets, or resources committed, are:

- Current assets (items that turn over in the normal course of business within a relatively short period of time, such as cash, marketable securities, accounts receivable, and inventories).

- Fixed assets (such as land, mineral resources, buildings, equipment, machinery, and vehicles), all of which are used over a longer time frame.

- Other assets, such as deposits, patents, and various intangibles, including goodwill that arose from an acquisition.

Major sources of the funds obtained are:

- Current liabilities, which are obligations to vendors, tax authorities, employees, and lenders due within one year or less.

- Long-term liabilities, which are a variety of debt instruments repayable beyond one year, such as bonds, loans, and mortgages, as well as a number of calculated set–asides recognizing potential future claims.

- Owners' (shareholders') equity, which represents the recorded net amount of funds contributed by various classes of owners of the business as well as the accumulated earnings retained in the business after payment of dividends.

Balance sheets are *static* in that, like snapshots, they reflect conditions on the date of their preparation. They're also cumulative because they represent the effects of all decisions and transactions that have taken place since the inception of the business and have been accounted for up to the date of preparation.

As we indicated earlier, financial accounting rules require that all transactions be recorded at costs and values as incurred at the time, and retroactive adjustments to recorded values are made only under very limited circumstances. As a consequence, balance sheets (being cumulative) display assets and liabilities acquired or incurred at different times. Because the current economic value of assets can change, particularly in the case of longer-lived items (such as buildings and machinery) or basic resources (such as land and minerals), the costs stated on the balance sheet are not likely to reflect true economic values. Moreover, changes in the value of the currency in which the transactions are recorded can, over time, distort the balance sheet.

Ultimately, the recorded book value of owners' equity is affected by all of these value differentials. There generally is quite a divergence between this residual accounting value and the current economic value of the business as reflected in share prices or in valuations for acquisition. In fact, the shares of successful companies are usually traded at price levels far above their recorded book value (see Chapter 11).

Finally, a number of relatively recent accounting rules require the estimation and recording of contingent liabilities arising from a variety of future obligations, such as pension and health care costs, further introducing a series of value judgments. These are frequently shown as "other liabilities," listed just ahead of

FIGURE 1–8

The Balance Sheet in Decisional Context

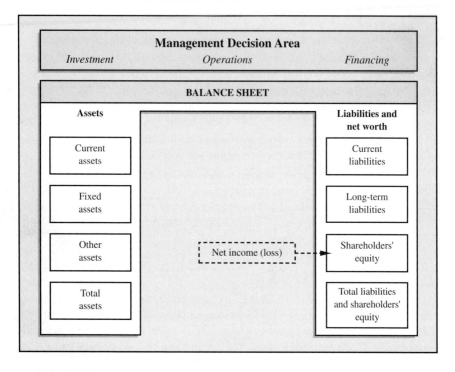

shareholders' equity, and, in effect, amount to a reclassification from being part of the owners' residual claims to a special form of long-term liability.

The accounting profession's FASB is expending a great deal of effort to resolve these and other issues affecting the meaning of the balance sheet, but only with partial success. Accounting standards continue to evolve, and a manager or analyst must be aware of the underlying issues and processes when reviewing and analyzing this statement. We'll discuss the most important of these more specifically as we examine analytical techniques in later chapters.

In our decisional context of investment, operations, and financing, the balance sheet is a cumulative listing of the impact of past investment and financing decisions, and of the net operational results from using these resources. It's a historical record of all transactions that affected the current business over time. The net effect of operations in the form of periodic profit or loss is reflected in the changing shareholders' equity account. Figure 1–8 is a simple conceptual picture of the balance sheet as it relates to the three areas of management decisions.

Only the major categories normally found on the balance sheet are listed in Figure 1–8, which is an oversimplification. In actual practice, the analyst encounters a large variety of detailed asset, liability, and net worth accounts because balance sheets reflect the unique nature of a given company and the business sector to which it belongs. But the actual accounts always can be grouped into the basic categories listed.

To provide an example of the balance sheet for a major corporation, Figure 1–9 shows the consolidated balance sheets for December 31, 2000, and December 31, 1999, of Minnesota Mining and Manufacturing Company (3M), as published in its 2000 annual report, but presented here without accompanying notes. (These are reproduced at the end of Chapter 2, Addendum 2–1). 3M is a global technology and manufacturing company headquartered in St. Paul, Minnesota. It is focused on building brands in 21 strategic areas worldwide, some of these going back 75 years, like the original Scotch® brand. Founded 100 years ago, 3M is organized into six business segments: Industrial products, transportation, graphics and safety products, health care products, consumer and office products, electro and communication products, and specialty materials. Producing and marketing several tens of thousands of products with 2000 sales of $16.7 billion dollars, the company employs about 75,000 people, and is ranked 118th in sales in the Fortune 500 listing for 2001. More descriptive details can be found in the company's notes to financial statements at the end of Chapter 2, beginning with page 90. We'll use 3M's published financial statements as examples in Chapters 2 and 3 and demonstrate the use of analytical techniques on the company's data.

The Income Statement

The income statement reflects the effect of management's operating decisions on business performance and the resulting accounting profit or loss for the owners of the business *over a specified period of time.* The profit or loss calculated in the statement increases or decreases owners' equity on the balance sheet. Thus, the income statement is a necessary adjunct to the balance sheet in explaining this major component of change in owners' equity, and it provides a variety of performance assessment information. The income statement, also referred to as the *operating statement, earnings statement,* or *profit and loss statement,* displays the revenues recognized for a specific period, and the costs and expenses charged against these revenues, including write-offs (e.g., depreciation and amortization of various assets) and taxes. Revenues and costs involve elements such as:

- Sales for cash or credit.
- Purchases of goods for resale or manufacture, or cost of services provided.
- General and administrative expenses.
- Sales and marketing expenses.
- Research and development costs.

FIGURE 1-9

MINNESOTA MINING AND MANUFACTURING COMPANY AND SUBSIDIARIES
Consolidated Balance Sheets
December 31, 1999 and 2000 ($ millions)

	2000	1999
Assets		
Current assets:		
Cash and cash equivalents	$ 302	$ 387
Accounts receivable—net	2,891	2,778
Inventories	2,312	2,030
Deferred income taxes	143	88
Other current assets	731	783
Total current assets	6,379	6,066
Investments	310	487
Property, plant, and equipment at cost	14,170	13,652
Less: Accumulated depreciation	8,347	7,876
Total property, plant and equipment—net	5,823	5,776
Intangible assets—net	852	573
Other assets	1,158	1,030
Total assets	$14,522	$13,896
Liabilities and Shareholders' Equity		
Current liabilities:		
Short-term debt	$ 1,220	$ 1,094
Accounts payable	1,081	1,008
Accrued compensation	382	361
Income taxes	462	464
Other current liabilities	963	856
Current portion of long-term debt	646	36
Total current liabilities	4,754	3,819
Long-term debt	971	1,480
Other liabilities:		
Nonfunded pension and postretirement benefits	754	761
Minority interest in subsidiaries	346	371
Deferred income taxes	362	332
Other	804	844
Total other liabilities	2,266	2,308
Shareholders' equity:		
Common stock, par value $.01 per share in 2000	5	236
Capital in excess of par value	291	60
Retained earnings	11,517	10,741
Treasury stock	(4,065)	(3,833)
Unearned compensation	(303)	(327)
Accumulated other comprehensive income (loss)	(914)	(588)
Shareholders' equity—net	6,531	6,289
Total liabilities and shareholders' equity	$14,522	$13,896

Source: Adapted from 2000 3M annual report.

The income statement represents the best effort of the firm's accountants to match the relevant items of revenue with the relevant items of cost and expense for the period, a process which involves accrual accounting and extensive use of allocation of prior and future revenues and costs.

Among the judgmental areas involving costs are:

- Recognizing the incidence of revenues received in advance or delayed in time.

- Depreciation of assets being used over more periods than the current reporting period.

- Cost of goods purchased or manufactured in previous periods.

- Proper allocation of general expenses to a specific period.

We'll take up the more critical of these elements and choices as we apply the analysis techniques in later chapters.

When viewed in our decisional context, the income statement in the center column of Figure 1–10 expands the details of the transactions and allocations that make up one of the key performance elements, profit or loss.

F I G U R E   1–10

The Income Statement in Decisional Context

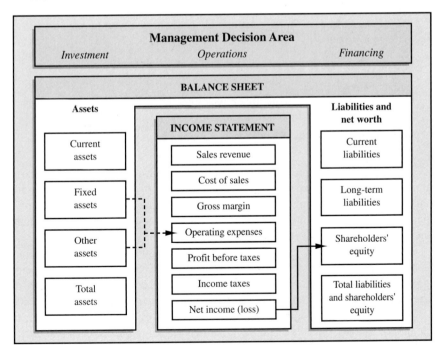

Again, we are providing an actual example of an income statement in Figure 1–11, 3M's consolidated income statements for the years ending December 31, 2000, and December 31, 1999.

The Cash Flow Statement

Because we are interested in the combined effects of investment, operating, and financing decisions, analyzing both the income statement for the period and the balance sheets at the beginning and the end of the period together provides more basic insights than either statement alone. Management decisions not only affect the profit for the period, but also cause accompanying changes in most assets and liabilities, particularly in the accounts making up working capital, such as cash, receivables, inventories, and current payables. The statement that captures both the current operating results and the accompanying changes in the balance sheet is the *cash flow statement, statement of cash flows,* or *funds flow statement.* It gives us a dynamic picture of the ultimate changes in cash resulting from the combined decisions made during a given period.

The statement is prepared by comparing beginning and ending balance sheets and using key items of the income statement for the period, all interpreted in terms of uses and sources of cash:

- Cash generated by profitable operations or drained by unprofitable results.
- Cash impact of changes in working capital requirements.
- Commitments of cash to invest in assets or to repay liabilities.
- Raising of cash through additional borrowing or by reducing asset investments.
- Cash impact of issuance of new shares or repurchase of shares.
- Cash impact of dividends paid.
- Adjustments for accounting allocations, write-offs, and other noncash elements in the income statement and the balance sheets.
- Net impact of the period's cash movements on the company's cash balance.

The cash flow statement thus offers a ready overview of the combined cash impact of all management decisions during the period. The user can judge both the magnitude and the relationships of these cash movements, such as the company's ability to fund investment needs from operational results, the magnitude and appropriateness of financing changes, and disproportional movements in working capital needs. Observing the cash flow patterns can stimulate questions about the effectiveness of management strategies as well as the quality of operational decisions. The amount of detail can vary widely, depending on the nature of the business and the different types of movements emphasized.

In the past, basic formats for these statements differed widely as well. In more recent times, the FASB and SEC required that all published cash flow statements follow a common format, listing uses and sources by the familiar three

FIGURE 1–11

MINNESOTA MINING AND MANUFACTURING COMPANY AND SUBSIDIARIES
Consolidated Statements of Income
For the Years December 31, 1999 and 2000 ($ millions)

	2000	1999
Net sales:		
Domestic sales	$ 7,858	$ 7,559
International sales	8,866	8,189
Total net sales	16,724	15,748
Cost of sales	8,787	8,126
Gross profit	7,937	7,622
Operating expenses:		
Selling, general and administrative	3,963	3,712
Research, development, and related expenses	1,101	1,056
Other expense (income)	(185)	(102)
Total operating expenses	4,879	4,666
Operating income	3,058	2,956
Other income and expense:		
Interest expense	111	109
Interest and other income	(27)	(33)
Total other income and expense	84	76
Income before income taxes, minority interest, extraordinary loss, and cumulative effect of accounting change	2,974	2,880
Provision for income taxes	1,025	1,032
Minority interest	92	85
Income before cumulative effect of accounting change	1,857	1,763
Cumulative effect of accounting change	(75)	—
Net income	$ 1,782	$ 1,763
Per share of common stock:		
Weighted average common shares outstanding (millions):		
Basic	395.7	402.0
Diluted	399.9	406.5
Earnings per share—basic:		
Income before cumulative effect of accounting change	$ 4.69	$ 4.39
Cumulative effect of accounting change	(0.19)	—
Basic net earnings per share	$ 4.50	$ 4.39
Earnings per share—diluted:		
Income before cumulative effect of accounting change	$ 4.64	$ 4.34
Cumulative effect of accounting change	(0.19)	—
Diluted net earnings per share	$ 4.45	$ 4.34
Dividends per share	2.32	2.24
Book value per share (year-end)	16.49	15.77

Continues

F I G U R E   1–11

Continued

	2000	1999
Other data ($ millions):		
Depreciation of property, plant, and equipment	$ 915	$ 822
Amortization of software	45	39
Amortization of patents, acquisition intangibles, and goodwill	65	39
Capital expenditures (property, plant, and equipment)	1,115	1,050
Dispositions (sales of property, plant, and equipment)	104	108
Acquisitions of businesses	472	374
Dispositions (sales of businesses)	1	249
Dividends paid	918	901

Source: Adapted from 2000 3M annual report.

F I G U R E   1–12

The Cash Flow Statement in Decisional Context

Management Decision Area		
Investment	*Operations*	*Financing*

CASH FLOW STATEMENT		
Investments	**Operations**	**Financing**
Investments (increases) in all types of assets are uses of cash; disinvestments (reductions) in all types of assets are sources of cash.	Profitable operations are a source of cash; losses drain cash from the system. Accounting write-offs or write-downs do not affect cash; their profit impact must be adjusted for.	Trade credit and new financing (increases in liabilities and shareholders' equity are sources of cash; repayments of liabilities, dividends, and share repurchases are uses of cash).

decision areas: investments, operations, and financing. This rule recognized the usefulness of this arrangement in understanding the dynamics of the business system, as described earlier. Figure 1–12 shows how the cash flow statement fits into our management decision context.

One aspect of the cash flow statement that requires some explanation is the treatment of accounting write-offs. From a cash flow standpoint, write-offs such as depreciation and amortization merely represent bookkeeping entries that have *no* effect on cash. The reason is simply that the assets being amortized by these entries represent cash that was committed in *past* periods. Consequently, the write-off categories, insofar as they reduced net profit, must be added back as a positive cash flow, thus restoring the cash generated by operations to the original level before the write-off was made. The reader will recall that we recognized the cash flow implications of the depreciation effect in the earlier discussion of the business system. Handling of this adjustment will be illustrated more specifically in Chapter 3.

The cash flow statement has the same inherent limitations as the balance sheet and the income statement, because it's derived from the accounting data contained in these statements. However, because it focuses on the *changes* incurred during the period, the limitations due to historical valuation are usually not significant. However, we must remember that by displaying the net change from the beginning to the end of the chosen period in each asset, liability, and ownership account reported, the statement might "bury" major individual transactions that occurred during the period and perhaps offset each other. Normally, however, material transactions of this kind (such as major investments, acquisitions, or divestitures) are noted specifically in the company's cash flow statement. The statement therefore affords the user the most detailed picture of the impact of major events of the period.

3M's consolidated cash flow statement for the years ended December 31, 2000, and December 31, 1999, shows in Figure 1–13 how the various elements are listed in practice. A number of adjustments based on information only internally available have been made by 3M to show more clearly the nature of cash movements during the periods covered, as we'll discuss in Chapter 2.

The Statement of Changes in Shareholders' (Owners') Equity

The fourth financial statement commonly provided by a business is an analysis of the main changes, during a specific period, in the shareholders' capital accounts, or net worth. We know from the earlier discussion that one of these changes is the net income or loss for the period, as displayed in the income statement. But other management decisions could have affected shareholders' equity.

For example, most corporations, including 3M, pay dividends on a quarterly basis. Such dividends are normally paid in cash, reducing both the cash balance and retained earnings, the latter being part of shareholders' equity. Another decision might be to provide additional capital through sale of new shares of common stock, or conversely, the repurchase of shares in the open market using excess cash balances—some of which may be resold to employees under stock purchase or option plans. A third area might involve write-offs or adjustments of asset values connected with disposition of assets or with business combinations. A fourth area concerns other comprehensive income (loss) categories, including the complex adjustments related to the exchange of foreign currencies by companies doing business internationally, adjustments to pension funds, and unrealized gains and losses on securities held.

The net change in owners' equity can thus be selectively split into its major components to highlight the impact of these decisions. Figure 1–14 provides a conceptual view of this special analytical statement. Its limitations largely depend on how much the issuing company chooses to disclose beyond what's legally required.

FIGURE 1-13

MINNESOTA MINING AND MANUFACTURING COMPANY AND SUBSIDIARIES
Consolidated Statements of Cash Flows
For the Years December 31, 1999 and 2000 ($ millions)

	2000	1999
Cash Flows from Operating Activities:		
Net income	$1,782	$1,763
Adjustments to reconcile net income to net cash provided by operating activities:		
Depreciation and amortization	1,025	900
Asset impairment and restructuring	48	(31)
Deferred income tax provision	89	95
Implant litigation—net	49	93
Changes in assets and liabilities:		
Accounts receivable	(171)	(186)
Inventories	(261)	96
Other current assets	(172)	(256)
Other assets—net of amortization	(145)	119
Income taxes payable	27	196
Accounts payable and other current liabilities	119	89
Other liabilities	(92)	173
Other—net	28	30
Net cash provided by operating activities	2,326	3,081
Cash Flows from Investing Activities:		
Purchases of property, plant, and equipment	(1,115)	(1,050)
Proceeds from sales of property, plant, and equipment	104	108
Acquisitions of businesses	(472)	(374)
Proceeds from sale of businesses	1	249
Purchases of investments	(12)	(56)
Proceeds from sale of investments	121	9
Net cash used in investing activities	(1,373)	(1,114)
Cash Flows from Financing Activities:		
Change in short-term debt—net	(236)	(164)
Repayment of long-term debt	(23)	(179)
Proceeds from marketable securities and long-term debt	495	2
Purchases of treasury stock	(814)	(825)
Reissuances of treasury stock	425	347
Dividends paid to shareholders	(918)	(901)
Distributions to minority interests	(60)	(51)
Net cash used in financing activities	(1,131)	(1,771)
Effect of exchange rate changes on cash	93	(20)
Net increase (decrease) in cash and equivalents	(85)	176
Cash and cash equivalents at beginning of year	387	211
Cash and cash equivalents at end of year	$ 302	$ 387
Supplemental Cash Flow Information:		
Interest payments	$ 104	$ 114
Income tax payments	852	653

Source: Adapted from 2000 3M annual report.

The Statement of Changes in Shareholders' Equity in Decisional Context

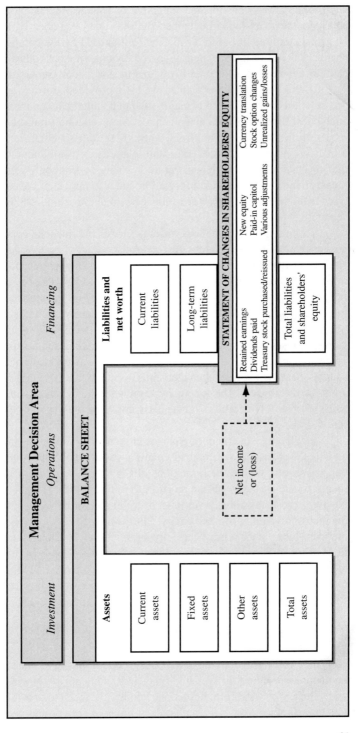

Again 3M's consolidated statement of changes in shareholders' (owners') equity for the years ended December 31, 2000, and December 31, 1999, is given as an actual example in Figure 1–15. The format used by the company displays the changes in each of the key areas involved, by type of stock, other capital, retained earnings, currency translation effects, and treasury stock (repurchased shares).

In this portion of the chapter, we have provided an overview of the nature and relationships of the four major financial statements as the background for analysis of the results of management decisions and their impact on funds movements. Within our decisional framework, these four statements can be combined to help us visualize their coverage and relationship as an integrated whole. Note that the generalized overview in Figure 1–16 displays not only what the four statements cover in terms of key information, but also how they are related, being derived from the same basic information. The dotted lines indicate the impact of any accounting write-offs.

To summarize, the balance sheet describes the financial condition of a business at a point in time. It shows the cumulative effect of previous decisions and includes the profits or losses for preceding periods. The income statement matches revenues and expenses for a specific period, including write-offs and allocations. It provides more detail about the elements making up the after-tax net profit and loss that was recorded in arriving at the owners' equity on the balance sheet.

In contrast to the two previous statements, the cash flow statement is a dynamic representation in that it highlights the net changes in assets, liabilities, and ownership accounts over a specific period. It reflects the pattern of cash uses and sources that resulted from management's decisions concerning investments, operations, and financing. The statement corrects for the fact that write-offs and amortization of assets acquired in the past are bookkeeping entries and not cash movements.

Finally, the statement of changes in owners' equity gives more details concerning the change in ownership accounts as recorded on the beginning and ending balance sheets. Within the limitations of GAAP rules and the accountants' judgments, financial statements are an effort to reflect, with reasonable consistency, all business transactions that, over time, result in a net improvement or worsening of the recorded value of owners' equity. But as we'll discuss in the ensuing chapters, the manager or analyst must carefully interpret their meaning, due to the implications of recorded values and their conservative bias. This requires using standard techniques as well as explicit judgments and adjustments in evaluating the financial, and more important, the economic performance of the business under review.

The Context of Financial Analysis

Now that we've explored the broad background of business system dynamics and the nature of commonly available financial statements that describe performance and values from a specific, limited viewpoint, it's useful to provide one more context that allows us to put the materials of the book into proper perspective. It will

FIGURE 1-15

MINNESOTA MINING AND MANUFACTURING COMPANY AND SUBSIDIARIES
Consolidated Statements of Changes in Shareholder Equity and Comprehensive Income
For the Years December 31, 1998, 1999 and 2000 ($ millions except per share amounts)

	Total	Common Stock and Capital in Excess of Par	Retained Earnings	Treasury Stock	Unearned Compensation ESOP	Accumulated Other Comprehensive Income (Loss)
Balance at December 31, 1998	$5,936	$ 296	$ 9,980	$(3,482)	$ (350)	$(508)
Net income	1,763		1,763			
Cumulative translation adjustment—net	(176)					(176)
Minimum pension liability adjustment—net of tax of $36 million	(30)					(30)
Debt and equity securities, unrealized gain—net of tax of $77 million	126					126
Total comprehensive income	1,683					
Dividends paid ($2.24 per share)	(901)		(901)			
Amortization of unearned compensation	23				23	
Reacquired stock (9.0 million shares)	(825)			(825)		
Issuances for stock option and benefit plans (5.7 million shares)	373		(101)	474		
Balance at December 31, 1999	$6,289	$ 296	$10,741	$(3,833)	$ (327)	$(588)
Net income	1,782		1,782			
Cumulative translation adjustment—net	(191)					(191)
Minimum pension liability adjustment—net of tax of $37 million	(28)					(28)
Debt and equity securities, unrealized loss—net of tax of $65 million	(107)					(107)
Total comprehensive income	1,456					
Dividends paid ($2.32 per share)	(918)		(918)			
Amortization of unearned compensation	24				24	
Reacquired stock (9.1 million shares)	(814)			(814)		
Issuances for stock option and benefit plans (6.3 million shares)	483		(88)	571		
Issuances for acquisitions (129 thousand shares)	11			11		
Balance at December 31, 2000	$6,531	$ 296	$11,517	$(4,065)	$(303)	$(914)

Source: Adapted from 2000 3M annual report.

FIGURE 1–16

Generalized Overview of the Key Financial Statements

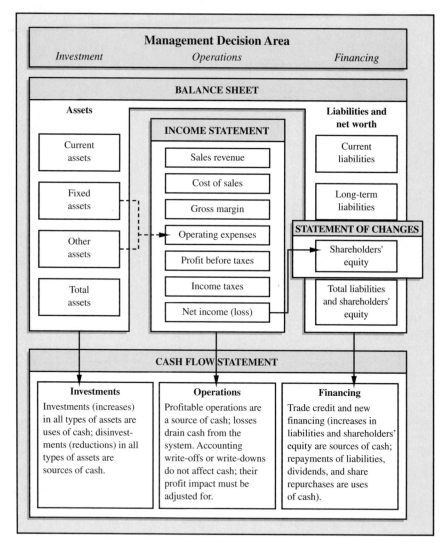

reinforce a number of the references we have made earlier to the judgmental aspects involved in financial analysis, and to the distinction between financial and economic analysis.

Managers or analysts performing various kinds of financial/economic analysis normally do so with a specific purpose in mind. During the process of analysis, financial statements, special analyses, databases, and other information sources are

FIGURE 1–17

The Different Objectives of Financial/Economic Analysis Processes

Analytical Viewpoint		
Financial Accounting	**Investor Analysis**	**Managerial Accounting**
Profit Determination	**Financial Information**	**Activity Economics**
• Revenue recognition	• Adjustment processing	• Task analysis
• Expense recognition	• Trend analysis	• Economic allocation
• Cost allocation	• Profit projection	• Contribution analysis
• Profit definition	• Cash flow projection	• Trade-off determination
Value Determination	**Comparative Data**	**Resource Effectiveness**
• Historical costs	• Industry analysis	• Investment base
• Conservatism	• Competitor analysis	• Capital investments
• Equity as residual value	• Economic conditions	• Capital divestments
• Contingency recognition	• Adjustment areas	• Human resources
Tax Determination	**Market Analysis**	**Shareholder Value Creation**
• Legal data requirements	• Share price patterns	• Cash flow patterns
• Income/expense timing	• Market trends	• Cost of capital
• Tax management issues	• Value drivers	• Investor expectations
• Statement adjustments	• Market models	• Ongoing business value

used to derive reasonable judgments about past, current, and prospective conditions of a business and the effectiveness of its management.

We must recognize that not only does the person performing the analysis and interpretation have a purpose and viewpoint, but so do the preparers and providers of the various types of data and information on which the analysis is based. For example, during our discussion of financial statements, we referred to the accounting rules and principles governing the compilation of these documents, and to the need to allow for the specific biases introduced by them. This isn't to say that financial statements are right or wrong in an absolute sense, but rather that the information might have to be adjusted in some cases, or discarded in others, in order to suit the purpose of the analysis.

Figure 1–17's descriptive overview presents the key objectives of three major financial/economic processes as a context for understanding the differences in data generation and analytical orientation involved in each:

- Financial accounting.
- Investor analysis.
- Managerial economics.

The table identifies these three as processes whose objectives differ, although they frequently have to draw on each other for information and data. We must consider the orientation and focus of these processes when information is shared between them, or exchanged for use by any one of them. Our ultimate aim is to analyze and judge business problems, company performance, and shareholder value in *economic* terms, which requires careful adjustment of data and analyses that often were prepared with different objectives in mind.

When we speak of basic financial analysis in this book, we put more emphasis on the objectives of the left column (financial accounting) and to some extent on the middle column (investor analysis). When we refer to economic analysis, however, the focus is on the right column (managerial economics) and also on a number of the areas in the center column. Despite the obvious differences among the three areas, the majority of the available data are originated on the left, by financial accounting, whereas some are obtained from the right, from analytical efforts or internal databases on which managerial economics depends. In addition, databases covering the stock market and economic activity come into play in the center column.

Financial accounting has three major objectives, as governed by professional standards and SEC regulations:

- Profit determination
- Value determination
- Tax determination

Profit determination focuses on recognizing when revenue is earned during a period, and how to determine the matching costs and expenses. A clear distinction must be drawn between the recording of a revenue or expense transaction, and the actual receipt or disbursement of cash, which might lag by days or months. Similarly, costs incurred in the past are allocated to current or future periods with the objective of determining a profit figure that matches only "recognized" revenue and expense elements. A similar allocation process might apply to anticipated future costs that are apportioned to current periods. These allocations have significant implications for cash flow analysis, as we'll see in Chapter 4.

Value determination rests firmly on the principle of historical costs, a conservative concept that uses only actual transaction evidence as the value criterion. When economic values of assets acquired in the past change, adjustments to values are generally made only if they decline. This is commonly done for accounts receivable that have become uncollectible, or inventories where market value has declined below cost. A recent FASB rule also requires periodic downward adjustments of goodwill as warranted. Increases are recognized (realized) only when assets are sold, not while they're being held. The residual value of the business, that is, its recorded shareholders' equity (book value), therefore might over time bear only limited resemblance to the equity's market value (economic value). In addition, the growing emphasis on recording contingencies of all kinds in the liability section of the balance sheet introduces a negative bias in value, because only potential liabilities are established, not potential gains. Examples are long-term pension and benefit obligations, and potential liabilities arising from all types of operational, legal, and contractual issues. Generally such contingent liabilities are set-asides of shareholders' equity, further diminishing the recorded book value of equity.

Meanwhile, appreciation of assets like land, buildings, natural resources, technologies, and patents is left unrecognized until they're disposed of. As the wave of corporate takeovers in the past 15 years demonstrated, careful analysis of the target companies' balance sheets often uncovered massive amounts of unrecorded potential gains, which could be turned into cash from the eventual breakup of the acquired companies, and used in part to pay for the acquisition.

Tax determination is governed by the legal requirements of the current income tax code, which often requires modified principles of income and expense recognition, including disallowance of certain costs and expenses—in effect amounting to a different set of books. Tax rules tend to speed up the timing of revenue recognition compared with financial accounting rules, and at the same time, delay expense recognition. These rules are clearly designed to enhance current tax receipts for the government. Differences between financial accounting for reporting purposes and for tax accounting give rise to tax management issues (legally minimizing taxes) in companies and industries where the amounts involved could be significant enough to affect actual decisions on investments, operations, and financing.

From the standpoint of financial analysis, the important question is what effect tax accounting has on the financial statements used for analysis. As we'll see, the amount of taxes actually paid versus the amount shown on the income statement can differ materially, and adjustments made on the balance sheet to compensate for this situation might involve significant funds movements. From an analytical standpoint, we'll show the importance of recognizing the tax implications of various types of decisions in Chapters 6 through 11.

Investor analysis in this context has three objectives:

- Interpretation of financial information.
- Use of comparative data.
- Analysis of financial markets.

Interpretation of financial information essentially amounts to analyzing financial statements and other financial data about a company in order to assess and project its performance and value. The key judgments focus on the adjustment process through which reported accounting data are modified or converted into information that permits economic and cash flow assessments to be made. Only rarely can financial data, as generally provided, be used in their exact form to derive analytical judgments. Applying the various ratios and relationships discussed in Chapter 3, for example, often leads to significant questions and actual adjustments during the analysis.

Trend analysis uses various series of adjusted past data to look for and analyze significant changes in magnitudes and ratio relationships over time, and it becomes one of the bases of profit projection. Finally, the ultimate adjustment leads to understanding the pattern of net cash flows generated by the business, and the projection of these cash flows as an indicator of expected economic performance and value.

Comparative data are an essential part of financial analysis, because they help put judgments about a particular company or business in perspective. By implication, all judgments made about performance and value are relative to the standards and perceptions of the analyst; comparable data assist in confirming these judgments. Industry analysis involves the selection of relevant groupings of companies and compiling appropriate data and ratios (generally available in on-line databases) against which to measure the attributes of the company being studied. The important issue here again is the need to interpret and adjust the financial data so that they match the data used for the original company.

Competitor analysis applies the same process to individual companies or divisions of those companies that compete directly with the business. Economic conditions and the competitive dynamics of the markets served are brought into the analysis as a backdrop for explaining past variations, and as a guide to projecting future performance and value.

Market analysis involves the study and projection of the pattern of share prices of the company and its competitors relative to trends in the stock market, in relation to general economic and political conditions, and with reference to industry and company-specific forces. It is here that financial analysis becomes a bridge between published financial statements and stock market trends that reflect the economic value of a company. The analyst focuses on the value drivers behind the market value of the shares, which are basic economic variables like cash flow generated and the relative cost effectiveness of the business, along with judgments about the expected impact of known strategies in the competitive setting. Market models range from simple relationships of key variables and share price to complex computer simulations, in an effort to determine the current and potential shareholder value created by the expected cash flows of the business. The discussion in Chapter 11 provides some of the key aspects involved in these approaches.

Managerial economics encompasses three basic objectives:

- Determining activity economics.
- Determining resource effectiveness.
- Creating shareholder value.

All three areas deal with economic insights managers can use to make decisions that will enhance shareholder value. In that sense, the orientation of managerial economics is closely allied to the basic purpose of economic analysis as we define it here. In fact, the third objective directly supports the ultimate question: Is the business creating value for its owners? In later chapters, we'll address the most important aspects of these areas.

Activity economics is a summary term for various types of processes and analyses that define and establish economically relevant data to describe and judge the relative attractiveness of any operational aspect of a business and its subdivisions. Among these, task analysis amounts to determining the true economic cost of a task, whether it be a functional area like purchasing, or legal services, or a line area like selling. This is done by identifying and measuring the series of steps required to provide a service, or the phases of a manufacturing process, and to establish the resources used directly or indirectly in each case. This kind of analytical process, referred to previously as activity-based accounting, goes far beyond normal cost accounting principles. These principles often fall short of a proper economic allocation of jointly used resources or often they can't recognize all aspects of a task or an activity.

Contribution analysis refers to measuring the difference between revenues created and the economic costs involved in a given line of business or a particular product or service. Such information on economic contribution helps management plan which combination of activities will create the most economic value over time. The choices always require economic trade-offs based on economic data, not accounting information. By using activity-based accounting information, management can make both operational and strategic choices in monitoring and adjusting its portfolio of products and services.

Resource effectiveness addresses the important question of how well, from an economic standpoint, the resources employed by a business are currently being utilized or will be utilized in the future. The process includes measuring the returns from the existing investment base, gauging the economic justification of new capital investments or capital divestments, and measuring the returns from human resources. These questions will be discussed in more detail in Chapters 2, 6, and 7, where again we'll highlight the need to develop an economic basis for these judgments.

Shareholder value creation, management's ultimate goal, is measured by means of a combination of past and projected cash flow patterns, the cost of capital of the particular company, and the overall return expectations of investors for this type of business. In essence, shareholder value creation becomes a tangible expression of the risk/reward trade-off the investor has to judge when investing in the equity of a company. Management has to assess at all times whether cash flow expectations from the strategies, policies, and decisions employed are likely to serve the investors' interest by creating additional shareholder value. The approach will be discussed in detail in Chapters 7, 10, and 11.

Key Issues

The following is a recap of the key issues raised directly or indirectly in this chapter. They are enumerated here to help the reader keep the materials discussed within the perspective of financial theory and business practice.

1. Managing a business successfully requires an understanding of the systematic relationships among the key elements in the areas of investment, operations, and financing, and the impact of decisions on these relationships. Total systems thinking is a critical requirement both in setting strategies and in their execution.

2. Cash flow is the ultimate driver of business performance and value, but its use in internal and external analysis generally requires considerable care in selecting data, constructing proper analytical frameworks, and interpreting the results.

3. Expectations by shareholders about future cash flows are the basis for deriving shareholder value. The value of a business relative to its peers and the stock market as a whole will change with these expectations. This requires a future orientation in analyzing business performance.

4. Creating shareholder value is a key responsibility of business management, the success of which depends on consistent use of sound economic trade-offs in all decisions made by the management team. This requires an understanding of the economics and drivers of the business, the cash flow implications of decisions, the risks involved, and an organizational climate and incentives that will foster such consistency in strategies and policies, and in making and implementing management decisions.

5. Although published financial statements are the most widely available source for financial analysis, the limitations inherent in their preparation (based on generally accepted accounting principles and leeway available to management) require a basic understanding on the part of the user of how analytical results in the areas of performance and valuation can be distorted and what adjustments might be necessary.

6. The context of any analytical effort is critical to successfully addressing the issue or problem to be resolved by the analysis. Much of the thought process underlying an analysis should be directed to ensuring consistency between the objectives and the data sources and processes employed.

Summary

First, we provided a conceptual overview of the business system to show the dynamic interrelationship of cash flows activated by management decisions. Three basic decision areas were recognized—investment, operations, and financing—that underlie all business activity. The cash impact of decisions in any or all of these areas on the system was shown. The systems view also demonstrated how decisions in each area were affected by key strategies and policies, and how consistency was essential in optimizing the system to achieve the ultimate goal—enhanced shareholder value. The overview also provided a first look at major areas of financial and economic analysis, and how these were related to management strategies and decisions. We characterized the key role of managers operating the system as an economic role, necessary to ensure ultimate value creation from sound, economically reasoned analysis and decisions.

Second, we gave an overview of the major financial statements commonly prepared by companies, and their relationships both to each other and to the three decisional areas defined earlier. We also indicated how the origin, rationale, and limitations of financial statements affect the potential for analyzing performance and value, and how important the cash flow statement is as a useful dynamic view of the changing cash flow patterns in the system.

Third, we established the context within which most financial analysis takes place, and provided an overview of the various objectives of analysis and data preparation. This was done to highlight the need for building a bridge between accounting-oriented data and the ultimate objective of financial/economic analysis, that is, judging business performance and shareholder value creation in economic terms. Adjustment areas were suggested as prerequisites for developing useful information, and the analyst's judgmental role was emphasized.

The chapter served as a contextual preview of the various analytical concepts explored in the remainder of the book. Its intent was to reinforce the point that financial/economic analysis is not a freestanding activity or an end in itself, but rather an effort to understand and judge the characteristics and economic performance of a highly interrelated system of financial relationships.

Analytical Support

To enhance the reader's insights into the dynamics of a company's cash flows, a set of Excel-based templates (*Interactive Templates*) is downloadable at no charge from the Web at www.mhhe.com/helfert11e. The first of these templates, "The Business System—An Overview" activates the business system model in Figure 1–4 on page 8. The template allows you to vary a given set of key assumptions about the investments, operations, and financing conditions of a sample company, and to observe the numerical changes resulting from these modifications on a graphic representation of the business system. The template also contains a set of abbreviated financial statements linked to the systems diagram, instantly displaying the results of any changes made. Moreover, the major positive and negative cash flow movements are highlighted on an active bar graph. The live template helps you explore and understand in depth the linkages within the business system and its accompanying financial statements, and to simulate and test the impact of any one, or a combination of, modifications in key financial policies, investment commitments, and price/volume/ cost conditions.

Financial Genome, the advanced financial analysis software application described in Appendix I, is built around the business system context of this chapter. It is a fully integrated analytical and planning model for both the professional user and the business student. Financial Genome contains a transparent information structure and financial dictionary that provides instant display of the meaning of all terms and relationships that are built into its knowledge base and provides the platform for working Problem 2 on pages 43 and 44.

Financial Genome is downloadable from the Web, using the unique code provided with this book. (See details in "Downloads" at the end of Appendix 1, p. 479.)

Selected References

Copeland, Tom; Tim Koller; and Jack Murrin. *Valuation: Measuring and Managing the Value of Companies.* New York: Wiley, 1990.

Johnson, H. Thomas, and Robert S. Kaplan. *Relevance Lost: The Rise and Fall of Management Accounting.* Boston: Harvard Business School Press, 1987.

Johnson, Roy E. *Shareholder Value—A Business Experience.* Boston: Butterworth-Heinemann, 2001.

Kaplan, Robert S., and David P. Norton. *The Balanced Scorecard.* Boston: Harvard Business School Press, 1996.

Knight, James A. *Value Based Management: Developing a Systematic Approach to Creating Shareholder Value.* Burr Ridge, IL: Irwin/McGraw-Hill, 1998.

Martin, John D., and J. William Petty, *Value Based Management.* New York: The Financial Management Association Survey and Synthesis Series, 2000.

McTaggart, James M.; Peter W. Kontes; and Michael C. Mankins. *The Value Imperative: Managing for Superior Shareholder Returns.* New York: Free Press, 1994.

Porter, Michael E. *Competitive Advantage: Creating and Sustaining Superior Performance.* New York: Free Press, 1985. (A classic.)

Rappaport, Alfred. *Creating Shareholder Value.* New York: Free Press, 1997.

Stewart, B. Bennett. *The Quest for Value.* New York: HarperBusiness, 1991.

Self-Study Exercises, Problems, and Discussion Questions

Exercises and Problems

The exercises for this introductory chapter are designed mainly to reinforce the systems view of a business. They are based on the use of the Interactive Template and the Financial Genome application as means for exploring the structure of the business system and its interrelationships. Note that the all-inclusive overview of Chapter 1 touches on many of the subjects covered in later chapters of the book, and it will therefore be useful to periodically revisit the business systems template as the detailed concepts and techniques are taken up. The templates for some of the later chapters again include the business systems model. The Financial Genome software, of course, provides a full integration of all aspects covered.

1. Using the first interactive template, "The Business System—An Overview," examine the flow diagram, the key assumptions field, and the abbreviated financial statements to become familiar with the structure of the template (for help turn to the illustrative template in the "Read Me" tab). Note the additional boxes (light blue color) on the systems diagram. They have been added to highlight the incremental changes that take place as assumptions are varied. Because the system is designed to be self-balancing, the "Funds surplus/deficit" box above the funding potential reflects the impact of separate assumptions, such as the level of capital expenditures, which may exceed or fall short of the funding potential created. The system is also partially driven by ratios, such as the debt/equity ratio and dividend payout, which requires keeping track

of the incremental changes in dollar amounts. Examine all the red explanation symbols to understand the contents of boxes and statements.

a. Successively vary operational assumptions (such as price, volume, variable costs, and depreciation) and watch their impact on the diagram, the statements, and the bar chart. Note that the changes trigger movements throughout the system. Check your understanding.

b. Successively vary investment assumptions (such as capital expenditures, disinvestments, and current assets and liabilities) and watch their impact on the diagram, the statements, and the bar chart. Explain the apparent effect on the funding potential. Check your understanding.

c. Successively vary financing assumptions (such as debt/equity ratio, dividends, interest and tax rates) and watch their impact on the diagram, especially on the financing portion and funding potential. Note the changes in the balance sheet and cash flow statements, and the bar chart. Check your understanding.

d. Successively vary the five assumptions in the base period of the balance sheet, and watch their impact on the diagram, the cash flow statement, and the bar chart. Check your understanding.

e. Develop a full set of desired assumptions and enter them in the key assumptions field. Observe the results and examine the conditions in the financing areas, especially the funds deficit. Modify assumptions to try to bring the funds deficit to zero.

f. What insights have you gained? Discuss your findings.

2. Use Financial Genome to explore the structure and interconnection of financial statements by selecting one of the sample projects in the software's project file and successively displaying the historical balance sheets, income statements, and cash flow statements. Moving between the statements, and selecting individual terms click on the (?) button for each term to obtain its definition and its relationships to other terms. Also browse the dictionary and similarly display the meaning of terms and relationships.

a. Find the "Funds deficit" term in the liabilities section of the balance sheet and obtain its definition. In the last column of the project's series of balance sheets, override the dollar amounts of any of the input terms (not calculated terms), checking the impact on the funds deficit in each case (restore the overrides to the original database value by highlighting and pressing "return"). What similarities are there to the business system model?

b. Override the dollar amounts of selected input terms (not calculated terms) in the final column of the income statement series and check the impact on both the balance sheet's funds deficit and the cash flow statement. Note that at the bottom of both statements there will be an "out of balance" condition matching the override (restore the overrides to the original database value by highlighting and pressing "return").

    c.   What advantages are there to having such an integrated financial system for planning purposes? How helpful can the fund deficit line be when forecasting expected conditions?

Discussion Questions

1. Why is the business systems model designed as an integrated flow diagram? Does it have to be, or could it be open-ended? What constraints are introduced by keeping it integrated?
2. Is working capital different from capital expenditures? What are the underlying drivers for working capital versus capital expenditures?
3. What are the constraints in the operational area of the business system, where only price, volume, and fixed and variable costs are shown? What additional elements would be useful?
4. Why is the depreciation effect shown as an addition to the funding potential for new investment?
5. Where do depreciation charges enter the calculation of after-tax profit? Are they the same as the depreciation effect?
6. How does a change in debt/equity proportions impact the funding potential? Why is this so? What are the key drivers of such a change?
7. How does a disinvestment affect the investment base? How does it affect the funding potential?
8. Relate the various measures and strategic aspects as discussed in this chapter to the results of your systems modification.
9. Why is the cash flow statement the most meaningful part of the normal set of financial statements?
10. Are there other contexts and viewpoints of financial/economic analysis beyond the three discussed (financial accounting, investor analysis, and managerial economics) in the chapter?

CHAPTER 2

MANAGING OPERATING FUNDS

We now turn to the key issues surrounding the flow of funds through a business, that is, how to properly manage, on an ongoing basis, cash inflows and funding needs for day-to-day operations. Managers must understand the specific cash movements within the business system, which are caused by their daily decisions on investment, operations, financing, and the many external circumstances affecting the business. These decisions and events, in one form or another, affect the company's ability to pay its bills, obtain credit from suppliers and lenders, extend credit to its customers, and maintain a level of operations that matches the demand for the company's products or services, supported by appropriate investments. In the end, the combined effect of these decisions is the creation of shareholder value—but, as we've stated before, only if the net cash flows achieved by the business exceed the stock market's expectations over time.

It should be obvious by now that every decision has a monetary impact on the ongoing pattern of uses and sources of cash. Management's job is to maintain at all times an appropriate balance between cash inflows and outflows, and to plan for the cash impact of any changes in operations—whether caused by management's decisions or by outside influences—that might affect these flows. Properly managing operating cash flows is, therefore, fundamental to successful business performance.

The principle is quite simple: Obtain the most performance over time with the least commitment of resources. In practice, however, leads and lags in receipts and payments, unexpected deviations from planned conditions, delays in receiving cash from funding sources, and myriad other factors can make cash flow management a complex challenge. New businesses often find that balancing operating funds needs and sources is a continuous struggle for survival. Yet even well-established companies need to devote considerable management time and effort to balance the ongoing funding of their operations as they strive for optimal economic results.

In addition to managing working capital, balancing operating funds flows requires dealing with the changing cash flow patterns of periodic profits and losses, and with the ultimate cash impact of current decisions on both new investment and new financing choices.

As we'll demonstrate, managing operating funds requires a thorough understanding of the combined systems effect of investment, operating, and financing decisions. This includes recognizing the impact on fund uses and sources caused by various basic operating conditions, such as seasonal peaks and valleys, cyclical variations, rapid growth, or gradual decline. In every circumstance the resulting cash flow patterns will behave in very different ways, and will put stresses on the financial system at different points and in different time frames.

For Example

Managing working capital soundly is a major operating cash flow challenge. The key components of working capital, accounts receivable, inventories, and accounts payable often represent significant funds commitments and sources for a business. In fact, the basic level of working capital (commonly defined as the difference between current assets and current liabilities) with which a business operates represents a long-term investment supported by long-term capital sources. Each component, however, must be carefully managed to match the changing requirements of operations—with the objective of minimizing the resources committed at any point in time while meeting all operational needs, such as ensuring smooth production and customer service goals.

Management should plan for fluctuations in working capital as a result of changing conditions, rather than be surprised by soaring inventories or overextended supplier credit. As in all business decisions, economic trade-offs apply here: Is the cost of carrying extra inventory outweighed by better service to customers? Is the cost of granting higher discounts for early payment offset by the potential reduction in receivables? What is the real cost of not meeting the credit terms extended by the company's vendors?

Current assets	Current liabilities
Working capital	Long-term debt
Fixed assets (net)	Share-holders' equity
Other assets	

In Chapter 3, we'll examine a variety of performance measures drawn from financial statements, which we know to be periodic summaries of financial condition and operating results. As we'll see, these summaries often mask peaks and valleys of funds movements—for example, a seasonal buildup causing critical near-term financing needs—because these points might lie within the period spanned by the statements. Obviously, managing a business is an ongoing day-to-day process, which must deal with peaks and valleys of cash flows as they occur.

In this chapter, we'll describe how operating funds cycle through a business, what the implications of these movements are, and how to identify the critical financial variables that must be weighed in making daily operating decisions. We'll demonstrate how significantly different types of operations impact a company's cash flow pattern, and also highlight key accounting issues, such as inventory costing and methods of depreciation. Then we'll return to the interpretation of cash flow statements, using our sample of 3M's 2000 and 1999 financial data, and demonstrate how to use cash flow statements in a meaningful way. Finally, we'll discuss the key levers available to managers with which to minimize funds needs, moderate the impact of fluctuations, and generally optimize the management of operating funds as part of shareholder value creation.

Funds Flow Cycles

Businesses vary widely in orientation, size, structure, and products or services, but they all experience operating funds cycles that eventually affect cash needs and availability. To illustrate the simplest of circumstances, let's observe one day's activities of a concession vendor who sells warm snacks from his stand at the ball park, strictly on a cash basis. To carry on his business, he invested some of his own money in the portable setup stand one year ago, equipment which will be serviceable for a number of seasons ahead.

In the morning our vendor needs to provide an inventory of food well before game time. As the day progresses, he will slowly convert this supply into cash. Let's first assume that he has used his own money to purchase the fresh snacks from his supplier. He obviously hopes not only to recoup these funds, but also to pocket a profit by the end of the day. The ball park management will charge him a commission fee that allows him to operate his stand and to plug the food warmer into the electricity supply. This commission is due in cash when the game is over.

Our vendor's decision to commit his own cash to inventory can be visualized in Figure 2–1, which traces the funds movements in a simple diagram. Note that the layout reflects the three decision areas we discussed in Chapter 1. The heavy arrows and shaded boxes indicate the flow of current cash necessary to purchase the fresh snacks. The owner provides the cash, which increases his stake in the business (owner's equity), and the cash becomes the funding source. The original equipment investment was also financed by funds from the owner, but the cash impact of this action occurred well in the past and does not affect the cash flow pattern of his current operations. The diagram simply notes the existing equipment as a freestanding unshaded box under the investment area, implicitly balanced by owner's equity.

As an alternative, if our vendor was short of cash that day, he could arrange for short-term credit from the supplier, promising to pay for the food the next morning, perhaps signing an IOU. The day's expected cash receipts would then be used as a source for repayment. This assumption modifies the diagram, as shown in Figure 2–2. Here, the creditor's funds effectively supplant the owner's funds, if only for a single day.

F I G U R E 2–1

Ball Park Vendor: Initial Cash Investment to Start the Day

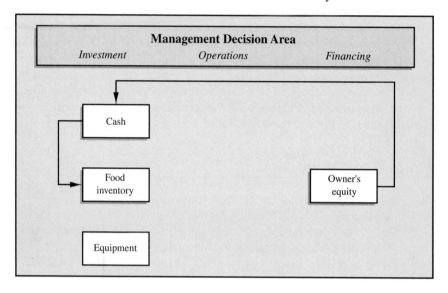

F I G U R E 2–2

Ball Park Vendor: Initial Use of Credit to Start the Day

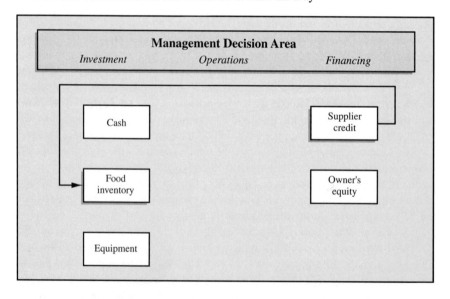

FIGURE 2–3

Ball Park Vendor: Profitable Operations During the Day

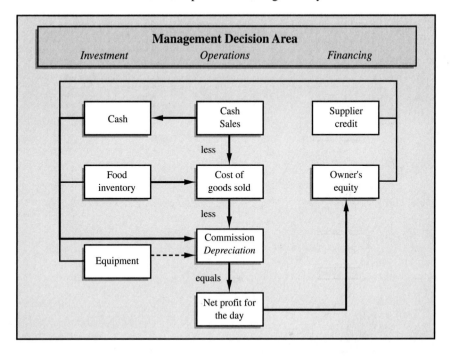

In any event, our vendor's funds cycle is very short. The morning's initial investment in inventory, funded either with his own cash or with credit from his supplier, is followed by numerous individual cash sales during the day. These receipts build up his cash balance as a source for the following day's operations.

To illustrate the cash implications we've represented the effect of the day's operations—assuming the vendor financed the inventory himself—in Figure 2–3. Cash on hand is built up by sales receipts, food inventory is drawn down during the day, and the difference between sales revenue and the cost of the snacks sold leads to profit earned—but not until two other elements are subtracted. First, there is the cash commission, which must be paid to the ball park after the end of the game. This will reduce the cash balance obtained through the day's receipts. Second, some amount of depreciation of the equipment must be recognized as an expense. This periodic charge does not represent a cash outlay, it is simply a notation that a fraction of the cost of the equipment must be counted as an expense because of the wear and tear of a day's use. The cash balance will be unaffected, but both the net profit for the day, and the original cost of the equipment must be reduced by this write-off. In the end, the net profit earned increases ownership equity, reflecting the value created during the day. We have again highlighted the affected

FIGURE 2–4

Ball Park Vendor: Repayment of Credit After Profitable Day

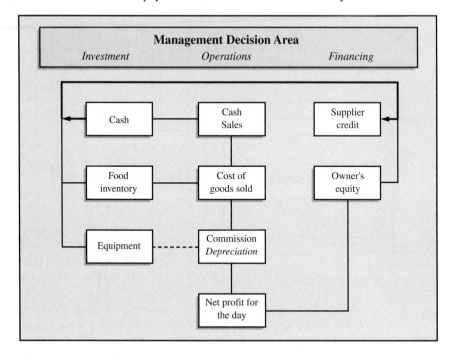

boxes by shading them, indicating cash movements by heavy lines with arrows. The depreciation charge is italicized and represented by a dotted arrow, because it does not involve a cash movement.

The following morning, our vendor can use the accumulated cash to replenish his inventory and start the cycle all over again. Any profit he has earned above the cost of the food sold and the cash commission paid will, of course, be his to keep, or to invest in more inventory for the next day. At some point he will have to pay income tax on his earnings, of course, but we are ignoring this fact because we are only illustrating one day's activities.

Figure 2–4 shows the alternative funds movement that would arise had our vendor used supplier credit for the first day. He can now use cash provided by the profitable operations to repay the supplier. He would find, however, that the amount of cash left after repayment of the initial supplier credit—the difference between his sales receipts on the one hand, and the cost of the food plus the cash commission paid to the ball park on the other—would likely purchase only a portion of the next day's inventory. To continue operating on the second day he would have to decide whether to

- Ask for renewed credit from his supplier.

- Provide the additional cash needed from any resources of his own that aren't yet committed to the business, in effect increasing his owner's equity.

Note that even in these simplest of circumstances cash flow is the critical element in managing a business. Funds cycles of larger and more structured businesses differ from this basic situation only in complexity, not in concept. Even for the most diverse international conglomerate, the ultimate form of settlement of any transaction is cash. However, such a company's operational funds cycle usually involves a variety of partially offsetting credit extensions, advances and prepayments, changes in inventories, supplier credit, transformations of assets, and so forth that precede the cash collections or payments.

In essence, funds cycles arise because of a series of lags (or leads) in the timing of business transactions. Our ball park vendor has a lag of only a few hours between acquiring the inventory and converting it into cash through many small transactions. In contrast, a large manufacturer might have a lag of months between the time a product is made in the factory and the ultimate collection of the selling price from customers who purchased on trade credit. A service company might have a lag of weeks between the time salaried or contract professionals are paid for their work and the ultimate collection of service fees. In contrast, a magazine publisher often has a reverse lag (lead), as subscriptions are solicited and collected ahead of the period served. Similarly, some Web-based business models, like Dell Computer's, provide products built to order after receipt of credit card payment. Such situations, of course, can significantly reduce the need for working capital.

Management must plan for and find the financing for company funds which are tied up because of timing lags. This is important because such funds will remain committed for the foreseeable future, unless there are significant changes in the company's operations. As with any type of investment, management should attempt to minimize this resource commitment while maintaining operational effectiveness. Ways to reduce the funding required include methods such as "just-in-time" delivery of materials or parts in manufacturing, or purchasing merchandise on consignment in retailing.

To illustrate the nature of the concept further, we'll explore the following three processes:

- The funds cycle of a simplified manufacturing operation.
- The funds cycle for selling the manufactured products.
- The funds cycle for a service organization.

We've separated the cycles for purposes of illustration and discussion, even though the first two are always intertwined in any ongoing business that both produces and sells products. The sales cycle alone, of course, applies to any retail, wholesale, or trading operation that purchases goods for resale, whereas the service cycle amounts to a modification of the sales cycle.

The Funds Cycle for Manufacturing

To keep the illustration simple, let's assume that the Widget Manufacturing Company has just begun operations and is going to produce widgets for eventual sale. Figure 2–5 shows the company's funds flow cycle in the form of an overview, using minimal detail. We've again arranged the diagram to reflect the three management decision areas.

As is readily apparent, the company was initially financed through a combination of shareholders' equity, long-term debt, and three kinds of short-term debt:

- Accounts payable due vendors of materials and supplies.
- Some short-term loans from banks.
- Other current liabilities, such as accrued wages and taxes.

The initial investments involve fixed assets (such as plant facilities), other assets (such as patents and licenses), and three kinds of current assets:

- Cash.
- Raw materials inventory.
- Finished goods inventory.

F I G U R E   2–5 ────────────────────────────────

Funds Flow Cycle for Manufacturing

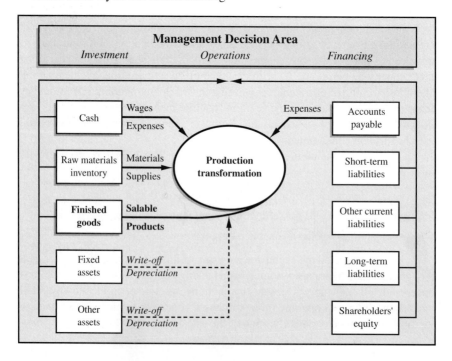

Of course, the last of these won't appear until the plant actually starts producing widgets. We can assume that long-term debt and owners' equity are the logical sources of funds for investing in plant and equipment, because they match the long-term funding commitment involved. In contrast, the short-term loans most likely provided the ready cash needed to start operations. Materials and supplies were bought with short-term trade credit extended by the company's vendors.

As production begins, a basic transformation process takes place. Some of the available cash is used to pay weekly wages and various ongoing expenses. Materials and supplies are withdrawn from inventory and are used in manufacturing widgets. Inventories are replenished with additional credit. Some operating inputs, like power and fuel oil, are obtained on credit, and are temporarily financed through accounts payable.

Use of the plant and equipment is reflected in the form of a depreciation charge, which becomes part of the cost of the transformation process. Any patents and licenses are similarly amortized and charged to the production cost. As widgets are finished on the factory floor, they're moved into the warehouse and their cost is added to the growing finished goods inventory account.

In the absence of any widget sales, the production process continuously transforms cash, raw materials, expense accruals, and trade credit into a growing buildup of finished goods inventory. A fraction of the original cost of the building, machinery, and other depreciable assets used has now become part of the cost of finished goods via the depreciation charge—even though no cash is actually moved by this allocation process. This accounting write-off merely affects the company's books by transferring a portion of the recorded cost of the assets into the cost of the inventory. Remember, the only time cash actually changed hands was when the assets were originally acquired.

What are the funds implications of this transformation? The operational funds flows, which occurred after the business was established, to this point had affected only working capital components. The major sources of funding for the production process largely came from drawing down cash and raw materials, which were among the initial funds committed. An additional source was found in increased trade credit and in expenses accrued but not yet paid.

The major use of these funds was in the buildup of finished goods inventory. Unless the company can eventually turn finished goods into cash through successful sales to its customers, the continued inventory buildup will eventually drain both the cash reserves and the stores of raw material. These will have to be replenished by new infusions of credit or shareholders' equity, or both. Adding to the cash drain is the obligation to begin repayment—on normal terms such as 30 or 45 days from the invoice date—of accounts payable for trade credit incurred.

From a funds flow standpoint, several timing lags are significant in our example:

- A supply of raw materials sufficient for several days of operation has to be kept on hand to ensure uninterrupted manufacturing, assuming that just-in-time delivery arrangements are not possible.

- The physical lag in the number of days required to produce a widget causes a buildup of an inventory of work in process, that is, widgets in various stages of completion.

- A sufficient number of widgets must be produced and kept at all times in finished goods inventory to support an ongoing sales and service effort.

The combined funds commitment caused by these lags has to be financed on a *continuous* basis through resources provided by owners and creditors, as long as the pattern of lags remains unchanged.

Offsetting this funding requirement, but only in part, is the length of time over which credit is extended by the company's suppliers. This is a favorable lag because purchases of raw material and supplies, as well as certain other expenses, will be financed by vendors as accounts payable for 30 or 45 days, or for whatever length of time is common usage in the industry. New credit will continue to be extended as repayments are made of the accounts coming due.

Another significant favorable lag is the temporary funding provided by the employees of the company whose wages are paid periodically. In effect, employees are extending credit to their employer for a week, two weeks, or even a month, depending on the company's payroll pattern. Such funding is recognized among current liabilities as accrued wages. Other expense accruals, such as income taxes currently owed, will provide temporary funds as well.

As we observed before, however, the buildup of finished goods in the warehouse cannot go on indefinitely, and at some point, revenues from the sale of the widgets become essential to replenishing cash in order to meet the company's obligations as accounts become due. To complete the picture, we must examine the funds implications of the selling process.

The Funds Cycle for Sales

The funds flows caused by selling the widgets can be examined within our decisional framework, as shown in Figure 2–6. The operations segment in the center of the diagram now includes the main elements of an income statement:

- Sales revenue.
- Cost of goods sold.
- Selling expenses.
- General and administrative expenses.
- Net income.

The selling cycle is based on a major timing lag, which arises from the extension of credit to the company's customers. If the widgets were sold for cash, collection would, of course, be instantaneous. If the company provides normal trade credit, however, the collection of accounts receivable will be delayed by the terms extended to customers, such as 30 or 45 days, depending on prevailing practice in the business sector.

Funds Flow Cycle for Sales

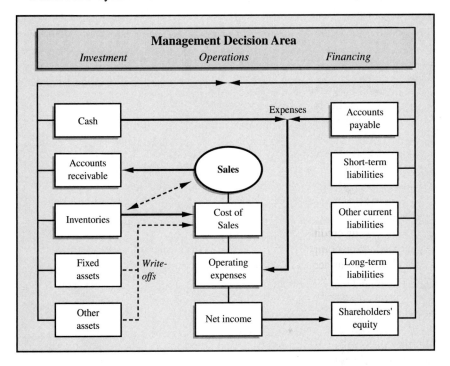

This sales lag, like the lags incurred during the production cycle, has to be financed *continuously*, because for any given volume of sales, the equivalent of 30, 40, or 50 days' worth of sales will always be outstanding. As accounts becoming due are collected, new credit will be extended to customers on current sales—as was the case with the vendors supplying materials and other items to the company itself.

Cost of goods sold represents the value of the widgets withdrawn from finished goods inventory, each of which contains a share of the labor, raw material, and overhead. Other costs expended in its manufacture include apportioned depreciation for the use of the facilities and a share of the amortization of any patents or licenses involved.

Selling expenses, which consist of the salaries of the sales force, the marketing support staff, and advertising and promotional costs, will be paid partly in cash and partly with funds obtained from creditors. General and administrative expenses will be paid in a similar fashion. Once all these costs and expenses have been subtracted from sales revenue, the resulting net income (or loss), after allowing for state and federal income taxes, causes an increase (or decrease) in shareholders' equity.

What are the funds flow implications of this picture? First of all, assuming that the company is maintaining a level volume of sales and manufacturing operations, management must plan for a continuous long-term commitment of funds to support the necessary amount of working capital. This means that sufficient funds must be provided to carry inventories of raw materials and work in process in support of production. In addition, funds are needed to maintain a proper level of finished goods to support smooth sales and deliveries, and to allow for sufficient accounts receivable balances outstanding to permit normal credit extension to customers. Also, a minimum cash balance must be maintained for punctual payment of currently due obligations.

Beyond these working capital requirements, additional funds are likely to be needed for any investment outlays on fixed and other assets that support growing operations. Finally, arrangements have to be made for payment of declared dividends, any scheduled repayment of debt, or for refinancing long-term obligations.

The sources of this financing will be derived only in relatively small part from outstanding accounts payable, which can usually support a portion of raw materials, supplies, and ongoing operating expenses in line with the normal number of days' credit extended by the suppliers. The difference between the amount of funds continually tied up in inventories and receivables, and the funds provided by current accounts payable, must come from sources that are relatively permanent, such as long-term debt and owners' equity—the latter augmented by after-tax profits or diminished by net losses.

The dynamics of the system are such that once desired conditions and relationships have been reached, the requirement for operating funds will be constant as long as the business operates on a sustained level. As we shall see in the section on the variability of funds flows, however, the level of funding requirements will change significantly when operational conditions themselves change.

The Funds Cycle for Services

The funds flows characterizing a service organization are similar to the sales cycle we just discussed. Service businesses for the most part do not produce any physical goods, but instead make available a wide range of activities to their customers. These include providing information and advisory services, electronic communication, equipment servicing, physical or electronic delivery, retailing or wholesaling functions, transportation services, temporary staffing, data processing, and so on. Services, whether based on contractual arrangements, trade credit, or cash remittances, will produce periodic cash inflows to the provider, with normal lags in collection matching the service pattern. Whereas certain service businesses require extensive physical infrastructure resources, such as stores and warehouse facilities, delivery fleets, diagnostic and repair equipment, or data processing networks, the funds flow cycle tends to be centered more on working capital elements and their leads and lags. Infrastructure resources are frequently obtained through leasing arrangements, which effectively transform their funding into periodic cash payments. Human re-sources are a significant portion of the funds flow mix, again representing near-term cash requirements.

Thus the funds flow implications are largely the interplay of payment for current expenses, current infrastructure support, and collection of services billed. Inventories have a significant role in manufacturing but are minor ele-ments in many service businesses. There they are limited to supplies or parts used in carrying out service activities—except in the case of retailing and wholesaling operations, where they are a critical part of the funds picture. The funds flow cycle pattern of Figure 2–6 applies to service businesses with minor modifications, the main differences being the relative importance of working capital elements and the relative impact of infrastructure elements represented by fixed assets. As in the case of the sales cycle, basic working capital needs will require permanent funding, and the interplay of sales, cost of services (or goods) sold, and attendant support expenses will result in operational cash in-flows. Increased infrastructure needs will have to be funded over time through leasing or ownership. Major marketing or new service initiatives also will re-quire funding from the normal mix of profit, the depreciation effect, and long-term sources. Under stable conditions, operational cash flow patterns for service businesses will level out, given an integrated set of operational and financial policies. But stable conditions are the exception rather than the rule, and we now turn to the funds flow implications of changing conditions.

Variability of Funds Flows

Unless there are significant changes in a company's internal conditions or in its markets, the level of ongoing financing needed to support operations will mainly depend on effective inventory management, sound management of cus-tomer credit, and prudent use of supplier credit, as well as reliable relations with other lenders, such as banks. Also, cost-effective and profitable operations will generate cash that can be used as part of the funding pattern. The com-pany's continuous funding needs will, of course, be increased if collections from customers worsen, credit terms extended by suppliers or lenders tighten, or profits decline.

Rarely does a company enjoy the steady-state conditions that made financ-ing so predictable in our simple illustrations. In reality, several internal and exter-nal factors can affect any business. Major internal forces include management's ability to seize growth opportunities, its effectiveness in managing all activities, or its inability to stem a decline in the company's volume of operations. Major ex-ternal forces include the competitive interplay in the industry, as well as seasonal variations and cyclical movements in the economy, which go beyond the impact of specific actions taken by the company's competitors. Each of these conditions has its own particular cash flow implications, and we'll illustrate the most impor-tant of these now.

Growth/Decline Variations

Growth

A pattern of steady growth in a business brings with it the need to fund the underlying expansion of all financial requirements. Successful growth can't be achieved without providing for appropriate increases in working capital, long-term investments, and other expenditures. These growing funds commitments will be permanently tied up as long as growth continues or as long as operations remain at a given level. Normal profits earned from successful operations usually supply only a portion of these funding needs.

Consider the following rules of thumb:

- If the business sells on 30-day credit, the value of each incremental layer of sales will be added to accounts receivable for 30 days and must be funded continually, because as prior sales are collected, new and larger current sales are added.

- Similarly, if the business turns over its inventory nine times per year, the value of the incremental cost of the goods sold will have to be added to inventories in the form of 40 days' worth of inventory (360 ÷ 9), which must also be funded continually.

- Offsetting this additional use of funds, but only in part, will be the incremental growth in accounts payable and other minor accruals. The credit from the company's vendors will amount to an equivalent value of the additional purchases for, say, 30 days, if that is the usual credit pattern.

For Example

Let's take the simple example of a wholesaling company that sells on terms of 45 days, buys on terms of 40 days, and turns over its inventory every 30 days (12 times per year). Cost of goods sold is 72 percent of sales, and profit after taxes 6 percent. As the company grows, funding needs for every *incremental* $100 in annual sales will be:

- Accounts receivable increase by $12.50 [($100 × 45)/360].
- Inventories of goods purchased increase by $6.00 [($72 × 30)/360].
- Accounts payable to vendors increase by $8.00 [($72 × 40)/360].

The net effect is a funding requirement of $10.50 in additional working capital ($12.50 + $6.00 − $8.00), assuming no other changes take place in the company's business system. At the normal level of after-tax profits of 6 percent, the company could provide only $6.00 of the funding needed— that is, if no other uses of these profits existed, such as paying dividends to shareholders, or expanding the warehouse and associated equipment to support the growth trend. Thus, a minimum of $4.50 would have to be continuously financed for every $100 in additional sales generated.

Because the required investment in accounts receivable and inventories is normally much more than twice the credit obtained from current payables and accruals, it should be clear that successful growth requires extensive funding of additional working capital. Add to this the funds required for any expansion of physical facilities or for contractual arrangements to support the growth in sales.

The pattern of sales, operating assets (working capital plus fixed and other assets supporting operations), and profits of the typical growing company will look something like the graph shown in Figure 2–7, where growth requires additional working capital every single year as receivables and inventories expand. This growth is only partially offset by increasing accounts payable. Periodically, new investments must be made in expanded facilities, as is indicated by the jump in the operating assets in 2003 and again in 2006. The asset column continues to grow as long as volume growth persists, and constant funding of this increase will be necessary through a combination of profit and other sources.

The dotted funding line indicates the total need for funds required to finance growing operating assets, reduced by total after-tax profits in every year. It is assumed that an amount equal to annual depreciation is spent every year on maintaining the facilities. No dividend payments have been allowed for in this line, and as a result the actual funding need is understated. Note that growing profits in the later years are able to gradually reduce the total funding requirements.

When dividend payments are provided for, however—in this case rising gradually from $20 in 1999 to $40 in 2006—what was essentially a level funding need becomes a steadily growing requirement for permanent funding, as shown in

FIGURE 2–7

Typical Growth Pattern

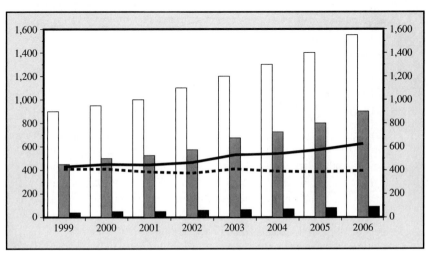

the solid line. By now it should be clear that successful growth typically requires an ongoing and growing funding commitment, which must be financed over the long term through the use of additional owners' equity and long-term debt. Frequently, reinvestment of profits alone is not a sufficient source, because in a high-growth business, the contribution from the profit margin might be far outweighed by the cumulative funding demands (as Chapter 4 details).

Decline

In the opposite case, when a business declines in volume and is deliberately managed to achieve such shrinkage efficiently—a difficult assumption not always realized—the company will in fact turn into a strong generator of cash. Here the reverse of the growth situation prevails. As sales decline, management must carefully seek to reduce operations, working capital, and other operating assets to match the decline in volume, thus releasing the funds that had been tied up over time.

This idealized situation is demonstrated in Figure 2–8. Note the dramatic decline in the basic funding needs, which turned into positive funds generation during the last two years. When dividend payments of as much as 50 percent of after-tax profits are assumed in every year, the funding requirements decline more slowly, but still represent only a fraction of the level at the beginning of the period.

Basically, the ability of the business system to release cash depends on the careful removal of all layers of activity that no longer need to be supported. A proportional shrinkage of receivables and inventories, partially offset by declining payables, becomes the major potential cash source, apart from the disposal of

FIGURE 2–8

Managed Decline Pattern

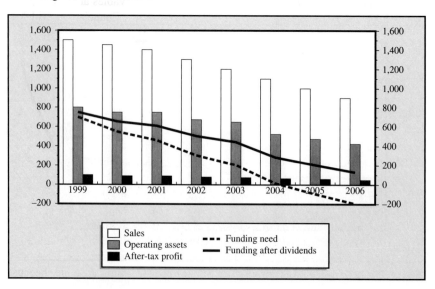

other assets no longer needed. If the decline pattern becomes precipitous or cannot be managed properly, however, the specter of inventory markdowns, operating inefficiencies, and emergency actions will seriously impede the release of funds. Under these conditions, real difficulties can arise and the expected cash flows might not materialize.

Seasonal Variations

A fairly large number of industries experience distinct seasonal operating patterns (specific months or weeks of high sales, followed by a dramatic decline in demand). These ups and downs repeat themselves quite predictably. Examples are most common in retailing operations, many of which are geared to special holiday periods or specific customer segments with seasonal style or gift requirements. Producers of seasonal items, like snowmobiles or bathing suits, will experience high fluctuations in demand, unless they can sell into global markets that have offsetting climates, or diversify their offerings. Similar patterns impact businesses such as canneries that process specific crops or other seasonal foods, or service firms that prepare income tax returns.

Common to all seasonal businesses is a funds cycle with large short-term swings during the period of a year or less. The financial implications of such a pattern are quite obvious. During the low point of demand, ongoing operations have to be supported with cash from internal or external sources, unless the business can be shut down, as some seasonal resorts are. In many seasonal manufacturing businesses, inventories are gradually built up, either through production or through purchases from suppliers.

As was the case in our earlier example, funding for this buildup must come from credit, loans, and owners' equity. Once the selling activity begins, growing amounts of receivables due from customers buying on normal credit terms have to be funded by the company. It is not until the first receivables are actually collected that cash starts flowing back into the business. The financial lags are usually such that collection of the receivables from peak sales will occur well after the peak of funding requirements has occurred.

Figure 2–9 demonstrates a typical seasonal pattern on a month-by-month basis which reflects the dramatic rise and fall in funding needs over the year, before any dividends are even considered. In this case, management must make several critical decisions. Among them are the size of the buildup of inventories needed to support anticipated demand, the level of operating and other expenditures to be made during the different phases of the operating cycle, and the nature of the funding to finance the bulge in requirements. Contingencies—such as lower-than-expected demand or prices, or both, delays in collections from customers, or the time involved in arranging for short-term financing with banks and other lenders—must be allowed for. Otherwise, the business could find itself strapped because its own financial obligations must be met well before collections are made.

We'll discuss applying turnover relationships and the aging of receivables as a means of judging the effectiveness of asset use by management in Chapter 3. Under highly seasonal conditions such relationships become unstable, because

FIGURE 2–9

Typical Seasonal Pattern

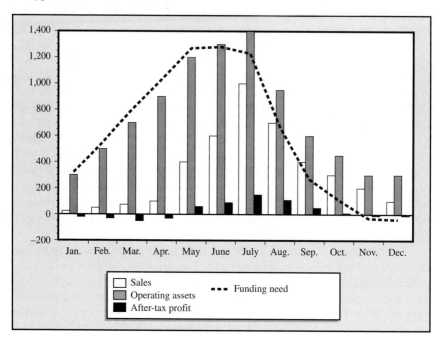

lags and surges in the accounts within the period spanned by financial statements make most ratio comparisons difficult.

As we'll see in Chapter 4, a more direct evaluation of a seasonal business is possible. Rather than comparing quarterly or year-end financial statements, a month-to-month (or week-to-week) analysis of funds movements and a careful assessment of changes in the funds cycle of the company from peak to peak, or trough to trough can be done.

Cyclical Variations

A variant of the seasonal picture is the cyclical pattern of funds movements. It mainly reflects external economic changes that impact the company over a period of several years. Economic variations and specific industry cycles are generally long term and not as regular and predictable as seasonal variations. Economic swings that affect a business or industry tend to bring many more variables into play, such as changes in raw materials, prices and availability, competitive conditions in the market, and capital investment needs. Nevertheless, the cash flow principles we observed in dealing with the seasonal pattern apply here as well.

Funds lags during a cyclical upturn or downturn tend to be magnified by a mostly unavoidable lag in decision making. As conditions begin to change, it can be very difficult for management to gauge, from daily experience, whether the economy or the market is undergoing a long-term shift and what the specific timing is likely to be.

Thus a cyclical downturn results in significant challenges: First, management must recognize, with reasonable confidence, that a turning point has indeed arrived. Next, management must prevent inventories from rising by curtailing purchases and production. This is usually followed by reducing staffing levels, and by cutting ongoing costs wherever possible. Careful management of credit, both extended and used, becomes critical as well. Meeting these challenges is easier said than done, because data on current economic trends available at any one time tend to lag significantly behind actual conditions, while economic forecasts often fall short of predicting both the timing and the degree of economic change.

For Example

> A gradual downturn in housing construction will leave many producers and wholesalers of building materials with inventories in excess of declining demand. As the sales slump accelerates, and prices of lumber, plywood, and other commodities fall, management faces a funding crisis. Continuing normal production will transform raw material into products that cannot be sold; thus, production must be curtailed. Lower volume and prices also decrease the eventual cash flow generated from current sales, while the stream of collections from past higher sales begins to run out.

Figure 2–10 demonstrates a typical cyclical pattern, where sales volume and prices swing with economic conditions, but, because of the factors just mentioned,

FIGURE 2–10

Typical Cyclical Pattern

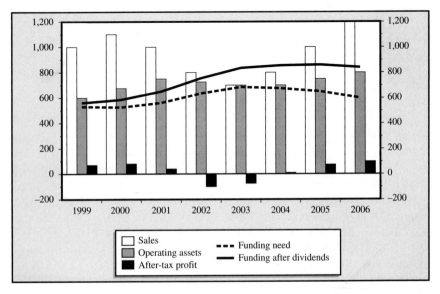

operating asset levels and their accompanying funding needs lag behind the volume changes. Note that the steady increase in funding required during the decline phase is brought about by a combination of rising investment (mostly a buildup of working capital) and plummeting profits. If dividends are maintained at the level of $30, and if we assume that these are paid every year, the funding line rises to a new high, indicating that the company isn't able to make up for the funds drain of the cyclical decline.

In the cyclical upswing, lags in decision making can cause inventory and production levels to be insufficient as sales volume begins to surge. To compensate, extra shifts or outside purchases might be used, even though the costs incurred with these alternatives are typically higher than normal and will depress profitability. Growing sales will also raise the amount of receivables credit extended to customers.

Thus, a cyclical boom will likely require the infusion of additional funds to provide the increased working capital needed and to finance increased physical operations. The latter might involve additional investment in plant and facilities. Overall, it can be said that a cyclical upswing will usually require an increase in medium- to long-term financing to support added levels of working capital and other financial requirements. A downswing, however, will first result in rising inventories—until management can adjust its operations—and then will begin to release cash, which can be used to repay credit obligations. The latter condition, however, will hold true only if both working capital and production levels are carefully managed downward.

In summary, variability in funds flows is caused by management actions, by external conditions, or by both. We know that a business operating in a steady state must maintain a permanent stock of working capital, as well as properties, facilities, equipment, and other assets. As a general rule of thumb, the amount of funds tied up in current assets far exceeds trade credit sources and normal short-term borrowings. Therefore, when significant variability in the level of operations is introduced, major shifts in the company's financial condition might be caused by changes in working capital alone. Funding for other needs, such as investments in facilities or infrastructure and major spending programs, must be superimposed on this pattern. In Chapter 4, we'll discuss these issues in the context of the techniques of forecasting funds requirements.

Generalized Funds Flow Relationships

At this point, it's useful once again to examine the overall relationships of funds movements in a generalized framework, as shown in Figure 2–11. The diagram is applicable to any type of business, large or small. We have added flow lines, which show the potential funds movements and linkages between the main accounts of the balance sheet and the income statement. A summary, in terms of our familiar management decision context, of the sources and uses of the ultimate cash flows is given at the bottom of the diagram.

This representation will be a useful reference when we discuss the interpretation of cash flow statements in the next section, as we follow the convention of the three decisional areas, and the general rules governing cash inflows and outflows.

FIGURE 2–11

Generalized Funds Flow Model

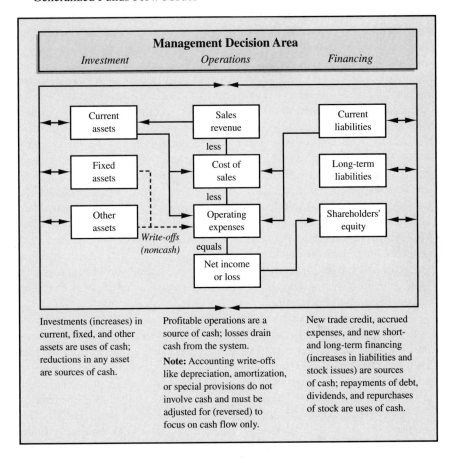

Interpreting Funds Flow Data

We're now ready to examine in more detail the use and implications of a company's funds flow information, as normally represented in its cash flow statements. As we discussed in Chapter 1, companies that are publicly held and publish regular financial statements are required by the SEC to provide a statement of cash flows along with balance sheets and income statements. Where such statements aren't readily available, however, or in situations where the analyst wishes to project future funds movements, it's relatively straightforward to develop meaningful cash flow statements from standard balance sheets and income statements. With the help of the cash flow statement, we can develop many insights about the actual funds changes that took place, and also obtain clues for further analysis of the nature and quality of management decisions in operations, investments, and financing.

In this section, we'll illustrate how to quickly draw up a basic cash flow statement from available balance sheets and income statements, and discuss the major principles involved in transforming this accounting information into the funds flow pattern in which we are interested. For this purpose, we'll again use the 2000 and 1999 3M financial statements originally shown in Chapter 1 as Figures 1–9, 1–11, and 1-13.

We'll work back from these to develop a derived cash flow statement, which we can then compare to the more detailed one published by 3M. Not having access to the detailed records of the company, we'll find that our own version of the cash flow statement will only approximate some of the specific funds movements shown in 3M's own statement, and some items will differ. This is because a variety of transactional background elements required for precision are not directly represented on the published statements, although the statement notes in the annual report go a long way toward providing additional insights. These are reproduced at the end of this chapter as Addendum 2-1, starting on page 90.

We'll begin with a look at the changes in key balance sheet items between the two dates, and sort these into a listing of funds sources and uses as a convenient way of identifying positive and negative cash flows. This format is called a *sources and uses statement*, mainly distinguished from the formal cash flow statement by the arrangement of the information, which in the latter case follows our three familiar decisional areas. It is the key to preparing cash flow statements in all situations. Then we'll turn to the income statement to obtain additional details necessary to expand our insights in the operational area of funds movements. We'll also briefly refer to the statement of changes in shareholders' equity for insights into retained earnings, and into the relatively new area of *comprehensive income (losses)*, which separates some of the elements previously recorded under retained earnings. Our objective is not accounting refinement, but simply an understanding of the principles involved in transforming key balance sheet changes into cash flow patterns.

3M's consolidated balance sheets are reproduced as Figure 2–12, which also shows changes in the accounts between the two balance sheet dates. To develop a cash flow statement, these changes must be classified as either funds uses or sources. We've done this in Figure 2–13, where the various increases and decreases in assets and liabilities are assigned to the appropriate categories, following the rules we displayed earlier in Figure 2–11. However, some of the balance sheet categories are too broad for our purpose. As a result, several of the underlying funds flows cannot be specifically delineated:

- Net profit (or loss) from operations is not recognized as such, but is part of the net change in retained earnings.

- Cash dividends are also immersed in the net change in retained earnings.

- Depreciation and amortization write-offs are buried in the changes in accumulated depreciation and amortization, respectively.

- New investments in facilities, as well as acquisitions, disposals, and divestments, are netted out in the changes in the property, plant, and equipment account. Acquisitions and sales of businesses often affect other balance sheet accounts as well.

FIGURE 2–12

MINNESOTA MINING AND MANUFACTURING COMPANY AND SUBSIDIARIES
Consolidated Balance Sheets
December 31, 1999 and 2000 ($ millions)

	2000	1999	Change
Assets			
Current assets:			
Cash and cash equivalents	$ 302	$ 387	$ (85)
Accounts receivable—net	2,891	2,778	113
Inventories	2,312	2,030	282
Deferred income taxes	143	88	55
Other current assets	731	783	(52)
Total current assets	6,379	6,066	313
Investments	310	487	(177)
Property, plant, and equipment at cost	14,170	13,652	518
Less: Accumulated depreciation	8,347	7,876	471
Total property, plant, and equipment—net	5,823	5,776	47
Intangible assets—net	852	573	315
Other assets	1,158	1,030	128
Total assets	$14,522	$13,896	$ 626
Liabilities and Shareholders' Equity			
Current liabilities:			
Short-term debt	$ 1,220	$ 1,094	$ 126
Accounts payable	1,081	1,008	73
Accrued compensation	382	361	21
Income taxes payable	462	464	(2)
Other current liabilities	963	856	107
Current portion of long-term debt	646	36	610
Total current liabilities	4,754	3,819	935
Long-term debt	971	1,480	(509)
Other liabilities:			
Nonfunded pension and postretirement benefits	754	761	(7)
Minority interest in subsidiaries	346	371	(25)
Deferred income taxes	362	332	30
Other	804	844	(40)
Total other liabilities	2,266	2,308	(42)
Shareholders' equity:			
Common stock, par value $.01 per share in 2000	5	236	(231)
Capital in excess of par value	291	60	231
Retained earnings	11,517	10,741	776
Treasury stock	(4,065)	(3,833)	(232)
Unearned compensation	(303)	(327)	24
Accumulated other comprehensive income (loss)	(914)	(588)	(326)
Shareholders' equity—net	6,531	6,289	242
Total liabilities and shareholders' equity	$14,522	$13,896	$ 626

Source: Adapted from 2000 3M annual report.

FIGURE 2–13

MINNESOTA MINING AND MANUFACTURING COMPANY AND SUBSIDIARIES
Statement of Balance Sheet Changes
For the Year Ended December 31, 2000
($ millions)

Sources:	
Decrease in cash and cash equivalents	$ 85
Decrease in other current assets	52
Decrease in investments	177
Increase in accumulated depreciation	471
Increase in short-term debt	126
Increase in accounts payable	73
Increase in accrued compensation	21
Increase in other current liabilities	107
Increase in current portion of long-term debt	610
Increase in capital in excess of par value	231
Increase in retained earnings	776
Increase in unearned compensation	24
Total sources	$2,753
Uses:	
Increase in accounts receivable	$ 113
Increase in inventories	282
Increase in deferred income taxes (net)	25
Increase in property, plant, and equipment	518
Increase in intangible assets	315
Increase in other assets	128
Decrease in income taxes payable	2
Decrease in long-term debt	509
Decrease in nonfunded pension and postretirement benefits	7
Decrease in minority interest in subsidiaries	25
Decrease in other liabilities	40
Decrease in common stock par value	231
Increase in treasury stock	232
Increase in accumulated other comprehensive loss	326
Total uses	$2,753

- Special items, such as write-offs and adjustments incurred with acquisitions, restructuring activities, employee stock options, and currency translation, can affect several balance sheet accounts, including retained earnings and accumulated other comprehensive income.

3M's income statement, reproduced in Figure 2–14, provides us with information on net income for the period, but we have to rely on additional information

FIGURE 2–14 ───

MINNESOTA MINING AND MANUFACTURING COMPANY AND SUBSIDIARIES
Consolidated Statements of Income
For the Years December 31, 1999 and 2000 ($ millions)

	2000	1999
Net sales:		
Domestic sales	$ 7,858	$ 7,559
International sales	8,866	8,189
Total net sales	16,724	15,748
Cost of sales	8,787	8,126
Gross profit	7,937	7,622
Operating expenses:		
Selling, general and administrative	3,963	3,712
Research, development, and related expenses	1,101	1,056
Other expense (income)	(185)	(102)
Total operating expenses	4,879	4,666
Operating income	3,058	2,956
Other income and expense:		
Interest expense	111	109
Interest and other income	(27)	(33)
Total other income and expense	84	76
Income before income taxes, minority interest, extraordinary loss, and cumulative effect of accounting change	2,974	2,880
Provision for income taxes	1,025	1,032
Minority interest	92	85
Income before cumulative effect of accounting change	1,857	1,763
Cumulative effect of accounting change	(75)	—
Net income	$ 1,782	$ 1,763
Per share of common stock:		
Weighted average common shares outstanding (millions):		
Basic	395.7	402.0
Diluted	399.9	406.5
Earnings per share—basic:		
Income before cumulative effect of accounting change	$ 4.69	$ 4.39
Cumulative effect of accounting change	(0.19)	—
Basic net earnings per share	$ 4.50	$ 4.39
Earnings per share—diluted:		
Income before cumulative effect of accounting change	$ 4.64	$ 4.34
Cumulative effect of accounting change	(0.19)	—
Diluted net earnings per share	$ 4.45	$ 4.34
Dividends per share	2.32	2.24
Book value per share (year-end)	16.49	15.77

Continues

FIGURE 2-14

Continued

Other data ($ millions):	2000	1999
Depreciation of property, plant, and equipment	$ 915	$ 822
Amortization of software	45	39
Amortization of patents, acquisition intangibles, and goodwill	65	39
Capital expenditures (property, plant, and equipment)	1,115	1,050
Dispositions (sales of property, plant, and equipment)	104	108
Acquisitions of businesses	472	374
Dispositions (sales of businesses)	1	249
Dividends paid	918	901

Source: Adapted from 2000 3M annual report.

about depreciation, amortization, dividends paid, and the amount of new investments, acquisitions, disposals, and divestments usually stated separately. These items are commonly contained in the notes to financial statements mentioned earlier and we've provided such key information in summarized form at the bottom of the income statement. Also, 3M's statement of changes in shareholders' equity, reproduced in Figure 2–15, displays more details on the various movements in the shareholders' equity section of the balance sheet.

The simple sources and uses statement in Figure 2–13, which was derived solely from the two balance sheets in Figure 2–12 provides an indication of the broad financial consequences of another year of 3M's growth in both sales volume and earnings, some financing changes, and the impact of acquiring the remainder of two business investments in 2000.

The key net funds sources were:

- A net increase in retained earnings of $776 million, in which profits and dividends paid are the key components.

- An increase of $471 million in accumulated depreciation, reflecting the net effect of new depreciation charges and reductions from assets and businesses disposed of. The period's depreciation expense, which we expect to be a major source, is so far hidden in the overall change shown on the balance sheet.

- An increase of $610 million in the current portion of long-term debt, an increase in short-term debt of $126 million, and growth in other current liabilities of $107 million.

- An increase of $231 million of capital in excess of par value, resulting from a change in the par value of common stock from $.50 per share to $.01 per share. This accounting change is precisely offset by the decrease of $231 million in the recorded common stock par value shown below as a use. Therefore there is no cash effect, because positives and negatives cancel each other and can they be left out of the analysis.

FIGURE 2-15

MINNESOTA MINING AND MANUFACTURING COMPANY AND SUBSIDIARIES
Consolidated Statements of Changes in Shareholder Equity and Comprehensive Income
For the Years December 31, 1998, 1999 and 2000 ($ millions except per share amounts)

	Total	Common Stock and Capital in Excess of Par	Retained Earnings	Treasury Stock	Unearned Compensation ESOP	Accumulated Other Comprehensive Income (Loss)
Balance at December 31, 1998	$ 5,936	$ 296	$ 9,980	$(3,482)	$ (350)	$ (508)
Net income	1,763		1,763			
Cumulative translation adjustment—net	(176)					(176)
Minimum pension liability adjustment—net of tax of $36 million	(30)					(30)
Debt and equity securities, unrealized gain—net of tax of $77 million	126					126
Total comprehensive income	1,683					
Dividends paid ($2.24 per share)	(901)		(901)			
Amortization of unearned compensation	23				23	
Reacquired stock (9.0 million shares)	(825)			(825)		
Issuances for stock option and benefit plans (5.7 million shares)	373		(101)	474		
Balance at December 31, 1999	$ 6,289	$ 296	$10,741	$(3,833)	$ (327)	$ (588)
Net income	1,782		1,782			
Cumulative translation adjustment—net	(191)					(191)
Minimum pension liability adjustment—net of tax of $37 million	(28)					(28)
Debt and equity securities, unrealized loss—net of tax of $65 million	(107)					(107)
Total comprehensive income	1,456					
Dividends paid ($2.32 per share)	(918)		(918)			
Amortization of unearned compensation	24				24	
Reacquired stock (9.1 million shares)	(814)			(814)		
Issuances for stock option and benefit plans (6.3 million shares)	483		(88)	571		
Issuances for acquisitions (129 thousand shares)	11			11		
Balance at December 31, 2000	$ 6,531	$ 296	$11,517	$(4,065)	$ (303)	$ (914)

Source: Adapted from 2000 3M annual report.

- A net decrease of $177 million in investments held by the company.
- A reduction in cash and cash equivalents of $85 million.
- The remaining sources, representing working capital items, include an increase in accounts payable of $73 million, a decrease in other current assets of $52 million, an increase in unearned compensation, and an increase in accrued compensation of $21 million.

The major net funds uses during 2000 were:

- A net increase of $518 million in property, plant, and equipment, reflecting new capital spending as well as asset disposals, and the impact of the acquisitions made.
- A net decrease in long-term debt of $509 million, representing a variety of financing changes during the year.
- Working capital requirements caused by an increase in inventories of $282 million, an increase in accounts receivable of $113 million, and a minor $2 million decrease in income taxes payable.
- An increase of $326 million in accumulated other comprehensive loss, which according to the last column in 3M's statement of changes in shareholders' equity (Figure 2–15 on p. 71) represents currency translation losses of $191 million, unrealized losses on debt and equity securities of $107 million, and a pension liability adjustment of $28 million.
- A net increase of $315 million in intangible assets, largely due to acquisition activity.
- A net increase of $232 million in treasury stock, because of share repurchases in the open market in excess of treasury shares reissued for stock options and acquisitions.
- An increase in other assets of $128 million, which are a collection of special receivables, benefit adjustments, and other items.
- A minor use is the net increase in deferred income tax assets of $25 million. Note that 3M shows deferred income tax items both under current assets (an increase of $55 million) and under other liabilities (an increase of $30 million) on its balance sheet. This is a common practice that reflects the several different conditions under which deferred taxes can arise. They are caused by timing differences in tax treatment and in accounting methods for calculating the tax impact of write-offs and various other accounting transactions. For simplicity we've netted out the changes in the two items here.
- Other minor uses are a decrease in other liabilities of $40 million, a decrease in minority interest of $25 million, and a $7 million decrease in nonfunded benefits.

Although we do, at this point, have a broad picture of 3M's sources and uses of funds, we should make a few modifications to our statement using what information is readily available to us:

1. The net change in retained earnings of $776 million can be separated into its key elements, profit from operations and cash dividends paid. We know from 3M's income statement that there was net income (earnings) for 2000 of $1,782 million. This result must have been added to retained earnings. The income statement further contains information that cash dividends paid were $918 million, which must have been subtracted from retained earnings. The net result of these two amounts is $864 million, a difference of $88 million from the change shown on the balance sheet in Figure 2–12. When we examine the statement of changes in shareholders' equity in Figure 2–15, we find in the retained earnings column that this $88 million represents the negative earnings impact of 6.3 million shares of reissued treasury stock for stock options and benefit plans.

2. The increase of $326 million in accumulated other comprehensive loss can be separated into its key components by examining the last column in the statement of changes in shareholders' equity, which lists currency translation losses of $191 million, unrealized losses on debt and equity securities of $107 million, and a pension liability adjustment of $28 million.

3. The amount of depreciation and amortization charged against income during the period should be shown as a positive funds movement in order to reverse the impact of these noncash charges. Normally the largest is depreciation of plant and equipment, followed by amortization of patents, goodwill, software, and other intangibles. In some cases, depletion of mineral deposits and standing timber is charged. We remember that such write-offs reflect the apportionment of past expenditures and do not involve current cash flows, serving to mask the total cash generation implicit in net income. Therefore, they must be added back to income to arrive at cash flow. This proper practice, however, results in a common misconception—to view depreciation and amortization as actual sources of cash. Remember that depreciation and amortization as such do not create any cash—they are only accounting entries that reduce reported income and thus understate the actual cash flow obtained. They do, of course, directly affect the provision for income taxes, but this positive funds impact has already been recognized in the income tax charge which was deducted before arriving at net income. In 3M's case, depreciation as shown at the bottom of the income statement was $915 million, and amortization was $110 million. These amounts should be listed as sources because their addition in effect restores net income to its pre–write-off level.

4. Capital expenditures for new investment are often provided as a line item in published statements and in a company's annual report. If we did not

have direct information about new investments, acquisitions, disposals, and divestments made during the period, we would have to approximate the amount of funds used by arguing that the net change of the property, plant, and equipment account was affected by two main elements:

- The amount of depreciation charged during the year.
- All the other transactions combined.

Because we know from Figure 2–12 that the net increase in 3M's property, plant, and equipment was $47 million (increase in gross property of $518 million less increase in allowances for depreciation of $471 million), we can derive the net effect of all the other movements by adding back the amount of depreciation of $915 million to this net increase. This results in a net change in property, plant, and equipment of $962 million. However, as shown below the income statement in Figure 2–14, 3M's actual new capital expenditures were $1,115 million. When we subtract the stated dispositions of $104 million the net addition amounts to $1,011 million. Thus there must have been some additional changes to property, plant, and equipment, to explain the $49 million difference between $1,011 million and the $962 million we calculated. This is likely due to the acquisitions made, where the company took full ownership of two partially owned businesses. From the notes to the financial statements we learn that $179 million of property, plant, and equipment was acquired, but we do not have any information on the offsetting reductions that must have occurred in the plant, property, and equipment account to explain the $49 million difference.

5. We can use the same approach to approximate the net change in intangible investments by adding back the amortization charge of $110 million to the net balance sheet change of $315 million, for a total of $425 million. Again, these intangibles are largely due to the acquisitions the company made, as we learn from the notes to financial statements, which indicate that purchased intangible assets amounted to $326 million. As before, we do not have enough information to explain the difference between $326 million and the $425 million we calculated.

6. Finally, we can turn to the statement of changes in shareholders' equity in Figure 2–15 to determine the components of the $232 million change in treasury stock. We find that $814 million of treasury stock was reacquired, and $582 million was reissued for stock options, benefits, and acquisitions. Separately, we have already learned that retained earnings was affected by $88 million in connection with reissuances of treasury stock to employees.

Now we can assemble a modified sources and uses statement as shown in Figure 2–16, using the basic information displayed earlier in Figure 2–13. For every item we have indicated the source of the data, reflecting our discussion of the adjustments. The statement was enhanced by these adjustments in net income;

FIGURE 2–16

MINNESOTA MINING AND MANUFACTURING COMPANY AND SUBSIDIARIES
Derived Cash Sources and Uses Statement
For the Year Ended December 31, 2000
($ millions)

	Sources	Uses	Data Source
Cash from Operations:			
Net income	$1,782*		Income statement
Depreciation (noncash item)	915		Income statement note
Amortization (noncash item)	110		Income statement note
Change in deferred income taxes (net of $55 asset & $30 liability)		$ 25	Balance sheet changes
Change in current assets other than cash ($113 receivables, $282 inventories, $52 other)		343	Balance sheet changes
Change in current liabilities ($73 payables, $21 accruals, $107 other, less $2 income taxes payable)	199		Balance sheet changes
Total operational cash flows	3,006	368	
Net cash from operations	$2,638		
Cash for Investment:			
Capital investments (adjusted for depreciation of $915)		962	Balance sheet/derived
Intangible assets (adjusted for amortization of $110)		425	Balance sheet/derived
Decrease in investments	177		Balance sheet change
Increase in other assets		128	Balance sheet change
Total investment cash flows	177	1,515	
Net cash for investment		$1,338	
Cash for Financing:			
Increase in short-term debt	126		Balance sheet change
Increase in long-term debt (net of $610 change in current portion)	101		Balance sheet changes
Decrease in nonfunded pension and postretirement benefits		7	Balance sheet change
Decrease in other liabilities		40	Balance sheet change
Decrease in minority interest		25	Balance sheet change
Treasury stock acquired		814	Stmt. of chges in s/h equ.
Treasury stock issued (net after retained earnings impact of $88)	494		Stmt. of chges in s/h equ.
Dividends paid		918	Income statement note
Currency translation losses		191	Stmt. of chges in s/h equ.
Unrealized losses on investments		107	Stmt. of chges in s/h equ.
Pension liability adjustment after tax		28	Stmt. of chges in s/h equ.
Increase in unearned compensation	24		Balance sheet change
Total financing cash flows	745	2,130	
Net cash for financing		$1,385	
Change in Cash:	$ 85		Balance sheet change
Total net sources and uses	$2,723	$2,723	

*Not adjusted for the cumulative effect of accounting change of $(75); cash impact not clear.

property, plant, and equipment; and shareholders' equity, but will mainly be lacking in terms of understanding the specific impact of 3M's acquisitions in 2000 and a number of internal accounting transactions We've rearranged the derived 3M data in our three familiar areas of management decisions: operations, investment, and financing, as well as by sources and uses to highlight the specific impact of each element. This provides a preliminary picture of the effect of 3M management decisions in 2000.

We observe that operating decisions resulted in a net funds source of $2,638 million, which represents the 2000 net income of $1,782 million, depreciation of $915 million, amortization of $110 million, and net change in deferred taxes of $25 million. The final two items represent changes in various working capital elements, with net changes in current liabilities providing a source of $199 million, and net changes in current assets (other than cash; see bottom of statement for change in cash) amounting to a use of $343 million.

Funds for financing decisions, a net amount of $1,385 million, are characterized by net increases in 3M's debt, with short-term debt raised by $126 million and long-term debt growing by a net of $101 million. Dividends paid were the largest item at $918 million, followed by net repurchases of treasury stock of $814 million, of which $494 million was reissued for options, benefit plans, and acquisitions. Currency translation losses affected cash negatively by $191 million, whereas unrealized investment losses were $107 million, and offsetting pension and benefit adjustments were $7 million and $28 million, respectively. The last three items may not be strictly cash flow items, but in the absence of additional information we have included them here. Finally, there were minor funding needs for other liabilities, minority interest, and benefits.

In the end, all three areas netted out to the decrease in cash during the year of $85 million, which we observed earlier as the first change on the balance sheet.

When we compare 3M's actual cash flow statement, reproduced in Figure 2–17, to our derived statement in Figure 2–16, we find that, apart from differences in presentation, many of the figures we have developed are only directionally representative. The various items on which the statements disagree—and several of them are significant—require more detailed inside knowledge. In the operations section, we find that 3M lists such noncash items as asset impairments and restructuring and net litigation, which were not available from the notes. The net change in deferred taxes differs because of acquisition activity, as do the individual working capital items. Thus we have in effect understated the operating cash flows by $312 million, because we had to rely on the published information alone. In the investment section, our derived categories are reasonably close in total, but the specific details about purchases, acquisitions, sale of businesses, and proceeds from investments differ because the internal accounting information was not available to us. Finally, the financing section, although again directionally indicative in total, reflects the detailed movements in the various forms of debt, treasury stock, minority interest, and exchange rate effects about which we only had partial information available to us. Note also that the elements of comprehensive loss were redistributed to various categories. In the end, exact agreement was possible

FIGURE 2–17

MINNESOTA MINING AND MANUFACTURING COMPANY AND SUBSIDIARIES
Consolidated Statements of Cash Flows
For the Years December 31, 1999 and 2000 ($ millions)

	2000	1999
Cash Flows from Operating Activities:		
Net income	$1,782	$1,763
Adjustments to reconcile net income to net cash provided by operating activities:		
Depreciation and amortization	1,025	900
Asset impairment and restructuring	48	(31)
Deferred income tax provision	89	95
Implant litigation—net	49	93
Changes in assets and liabilities:		
Accounts receivable	(171)	(186)
Inventories	(261)	96
Other current assets	(172)	(256)
Other assets—net of amortization	(145)	119
Income taxes payable	27	196
Accounts payable and other current liabilities	119	89
Other liabilities	(92)	173
Other—net	28	30
Net cash provided by operating activities	2,326	3,081
Cash Flows from Investing Activities:		
Purchases of property, plant, and equipment	(1,115)	(1,050)
Proceeds from sales of property, plant, and equipment	104	108
Acquisitions of businesses	(472)	(374)
Proceeds from sales of businesses	1	249
Purchase of investments	(12)	(56)
Proceeds from sale of investments	121	9
Net cash used in investing activities	(1,373)	(1,114)
Cash Flows from Financing Activities:		
Change in short-term debt—net	(236)	(164)
Repayment of long-term debt	(23)	(179)
Proceeds from marketable securities and long-term debt	495	2
Purchases of treasury stock	(814)	(825)
Reissuances of treasury stock	425	347
Dividends paid to shareholders	(918)	(901)
Distributions to minority interests	(60)	(51)
Net cash used in financing activities	(1,131)	(1,771)
Effect of exchange rate changes on cash	93	(20)
Net increase (decrease) in cash and equivalents	(85)	176
Cash and cash equivalents at beginning of year	387	211
Cash and cash equivalents at end of year	$ 302	$ 387
Supplemental Cash Flow Information:		
Interest payments	$ 104	$ 114
Income tax payments	852	653

Source: Adapted from 2000 3M annual report.

only on net income, depreciation and amortization, dividends to shareholders, and the change in the cash balance. This is common with large companies.

Nevertheless, the exercise was useful to understand the broad cash movements caused by management decisions at 3M. Note that the company's operational cash flow by far exceeded its internal investment and acquisition requirements, allowing management to continue paying cash dividends at more than 50 percent of net income, and to repurchase an almost equal amount of its own stock. Only relatively minor changes in debt financing took place, even though cash flow from operations decreased by almost three-quarters of a million dollars from the prior year. In working capital, inventories increased significantly during the period, largely a result of slowing business conditions. In short it can be said that strong net income and cash flow have characterized 3M's conditions over many years.

To summarize, in this section we constructed a cash flow statement that goes beyond simply listing the changes readily observed in a comparison of beginning and ending balance sheet accounts. Note, however, that developing the changes in a company's balance sheets is the first, critical step in constructing the cash flow statement for any business, large or small. We were then able to make a number of refinements by examining the income statement, and the statement of changes in shareholders' equity, as well as related supporting notes publicly available. The purpose of the refinements was to highlight in more detail significant results stemming from management decisions about investments, operations, and financing. But the analysis is by nature limited to public information, and lack of accounting details forces the analyst to stop short of achieving the information on published cash flow statements. At any rate, if a company's cash flow statement is not made available as a matter of course, the analyst can usually approximate the main elements of the statement, and obtain at least directional insights. In a less complex business the results will be quite close, of course. In the case of a major international company like 3M an insider can prepare a much more precise statement by going far beyond the basic adjustment process we've demonstrated.

Funds Management and Shareholder Value

It will be useful to reflect once more on the nature of funds movements in the context of shareholder value creation. We've demonstrated the complex interrelationship of funds movements, driven by management decisions, external forces, and the intrinsic nature of a company's business. We've further shown how to determine and illustrate the impact of funds movements on cash flows.

The overriding principle for successful management of operating funds is constant attention to the economical use of the resources these funds represent. The best-managed companies tailor their information systems and management incentives to minimize funds use relative to the level of each activity. If the foundation of shareholder value creation is to earn returns on the resources employed at levels above shareholder expectations, taking a "scarcity" approach to resource deployment should be natural for managers at all levels. Such thinking must not be limited to funding new capital outlays alone, as we'll discuss in Chapters 7 and 8, but must reach into all aspects of the business, including working capital management, employment practices, funding of research, product and service development, marketing and promotional programs, and so on. We'll now briefly discuss some of the key elements involved in managing operational funds.

Cash Management

As we've stated before, all management decisions and the funds movements caused by them eventually materialize in the form of a cash impact. But we also must realize that a company's cash balance at any one time represents a resource commitment, even though its movements are more frequent and extensive than those of other investments. The principle that applies to this resource is the same as with any other resource:

> Minimize its size relative to the needs it supports, and obtain the greatest possible return by investing cash balances in ways that reflect its unique characteristics.

Therefore, the economics of sound cash management requires that any time there is a lag in cash receipts it should be minimized, and disbursements should be made no sooner than required by commercial and legal terms. Ways to achieve time compression range from the use of lockboxes, to which remittances from customers are mailed for speedier processing, to the growing use of electronic funds transfers, which allows immediate collection of amounts due without the delays of paperwork. Effective banking relationships are a great asset in this process, and companies with widespread locations will attempt to concentrate cash management into regional processing arrangements.

Minimization of cash balances can be achieved by transferring any excess cash into marketable securities of short maturities, including U.S. treasury bills, commercial paper issued by corporations, and certificates of deposit issued by banks. Although returns from these temporary investments will not approach the returns from a company's normal business activities, the trade-off between leaving cash idle versus earning a modest return until the cash can be used for longer-term investments, dividends, or repurchase of shares, will be positive and therefore in the shareholders' interest.

Working Capital Management

Investments in customer credit in the form of accounts receivable, and in inventories of goods or materials, are long-term resource commitments as part of the stock of working capital, as we discussed earlier. Minimization of these investments relative to the level and pattern of a company's operations is a crucial element in the total management of operating funds. The key to successful management of customer credit and inventories is a clear understanding of the economic trade-offs involved.

Credit terms are a function of the competitive environment as well as of a careful assessment of the nature and creditworthiness of customers. For example, the issue might be whether extended credit terms, and the resulting rise in receivables outstanding, are compensated for by the contribution from any incremental sales gained. Similarly, extending normal credit to marginal customers has to be judged in terms of the risk of late payment or default versus the contribution from the sales gained. Techniques in the customer credit area include constant updating of credit performance, aging of accounts receivable into time categories, and developing sound criteria for credit extension.

Inventory management in successful companies has evolved into a rigorous process of asset minimization. Information technology has permitted a general reduction in inventory levels, whether in manufacturing, wholesaling, or retailing. In an effort to push inventories as low as possible, techniques such as just-in-time deliveries by suppliers to their customers' manufacturing or trading locations, and carefully scheduled restocking triggered by instantaneous purchase data from major wholesalers and retailers, have become widespread. In effect, these techniques have created a very close relationship between major suppliers and major customers, often with electronic linkages of inventories, order processing, and production scheduling. Such ties allow for timely coordination of schedules and minimization of inventories on both sides.

Normal trade credit from suppliers in the form of accounts payable helps offset receivables and inventories. Here the appropriate principle is to make use of the credit terms extended, but to watch for potential favorable trade-offs such as discounts for early payment. Accounts payable is one form of financing working capital, and therefore, maximum use of trade terms is appropriate. If discounts offered for early payment are attractive—for example, 2 percent for payment in 10 days rather than 30 days amounts to a sizable interest rate of 36 percent per year (2 percent gained for a 20-day speed up in remittance)—there is an obvious advantage in using less-expensive bank credit in order to remit to the vendor in 10 days. Deliberately exceeding the normal credit terms might make the interest trade-off more favorable, but there is the risk of affecting the company's credit standing if delays beyond the terms granted become habitual. Sound management of supplier credit, as was true with customer credit, relies on current up-to-date information on accounts and aging of payables to ensure proper payment.

As we discussed earlier, funding of working capital must be considered a long-term commitment, unless the business is characterized by significant seasonal or cyclical fluctuations. Given that even tightly managed receivables and inventories require long-term financial support, successful management of operational funding requires the use of a combination of reinvested earnings and long-term debt, augmented as needed by temporary short-term funding.

Investment Management

Funding of operations also involves periodic investments in facilities, programs, and other long-term resource commitments beyond working capital needs. As we'll discuss in Chapters 6 and 7, the principles of sound investment management are no different in terms of shareholder value creation—the minimization of funds needs relative to the expected benefits is paramount. The main complications arise because of the longer time frame and greater degree of uncertainty surrounding the expectations about the cash flows to be generated. The techniques of analysis are somewhat more involved, but still are based on the basic notion of cash flow trade-offs. The funding for such commitments will naturally tend to have a longer time horizon as well.

Key Issues

The following is a recap of the key issues raised directly or indirectly in this chapter. They are enumerated here to help the reader keep the materials discussed within the perspective of financial theory and business practice.

1. Operational funding needs and sources are woven into the larger systems context of managing the company for shareholder value, and must also be viewed from both short-term and a long-term perspective. It's not appropriate to attempt to separate specific operational funding issues from this larger context.

2. Operational funding is affected by both internal and external conditions and causes, which must be understood in terms of the business environment, economic conditions, and specific company processes and policies. Identifying the key drivers of operational funds patterns and tracing their impact over appropriate periods of time is a valuable effort for minimizing unexpected shortfalls or ineffective use of resources.

3. Operational funding requirements and the trade-offs surrounding them are special applications of the broader economic principles that govern all resource commitments and sources. The main difference lies in the timing of the flow patterns, which are generally more short-term oriented, but still belong within the larger framework of resource management.

4. Several key questions arise as funds movements are analyzed. Most relate to the types of funds commitments (uses) made compared to the sources of funds available. Are enough long-term funds provided to fund ongoing growth in working capital and fixed asset expansion given a strategic context? Are most sources of funds temporary loans and credit extensions? Is the business counting on profits to fund peak needs that might exceed such expectations?

5. As modern management embraces greater degrees of cash flow thinking, the interpretation and use of cash flow statements increases,

as does the amount of detail presented in them. Analysis of published sets of financial statements materially benefits from these displays of cash flow patterns, and familiarity with the development and limitations of the statements is a necessary skill for the financial analyst and manager.

6. Funds flow patterns represent the essential nature of business decisions, and are the key ingredient in shareholder value creation. The challenge to the analyst and manager is to understand the difference between economic cash flows and noncash accounting transactions, and to interpret the pattern of funds movements accordingly. Judging the performance and value of a business largely depends on such discriminating insights by the economic managers of modern business.

Summary

In this chapter, we've demonstrated the funds flow cycle involved in any business, large or small, and its implications for management. We began with a highly simplified illustration of basic funds movements, and then discussed operating funds cycles from the standpoints of manufacturing, sales, and service. We observed the nature and behavior of working capital, highlighted the impact of different types of variability in operations, and demonstrated the effect of funds lags on the nature and duration of financing required to support a business. Major insights gained included the need to consider the permanence of basic working capital requirements, the financial drain encountered even with successful growth, and the potential funds release from a decline in volume.

We then turned to a demonstration of how public financial statement information can be used to develop a meaningful cash flow statement, which summarizes the major trends in the cash flow picture of a business. It became clear that much of the insight to be gained about the cash impact of a company's decision pattern could be expressed by analyzing balance sheet changes and supplementary information from the income statement and the statement of changes in shareholders' equity. At the same time, the need for underlying specific detail not normally published was apparent, in order to further refine the cash flow information. Fortunately, publicly held companies are required to publish detailed cash flow statements arranged in a standard format, allowing direct access to the major cash effects of significant management decisions.

In essence, funds flow analysis is a broad-brush dynamic view of the management of the business. It relates changes in major conditions to their key financial implications by making apparent the cash implications of major transactions during the period. The techniques are relatively simple, requiring only basic accounting knowledge to provide this extra dimension in assessing balance sheets and income statements. The transformation into cash flow thinking achieved by funds flow analysis matches the dynamics of the business systems concept we discussed in

Chapter 1. It is also a precursor to the topics covered in later chapters, where cash flow patterns and expectations are a significant aspect of financial analysis techniques and practices.

Analytical Support

Financial Genome, the advanced financial analysis software application described in Appendix I, is a fully integrated analytical and planning model for both the professional user and the business student. It is designed to develop fully integrated financial statements, including the cash flow statement, from historical data inputs as well as for projections of financial performance. The software contains a five-year database (1996 to 2000) for 3M Corporation, matching the company's financial statements reproduced in this chapter. It also contains databases and project files with which to work Problems 3, 4, 5, and 6 on pages 86 through 89.

Financial Genome is downloadable from the Web, using the unique code provided with this book. (See details in "Downloads" at the end of Appendix I, p. 479.)

Selected References

Anthony, Robert N. *Essentials of Accounting.* 5th ed. Reading, MA: Addison-Wesley, 1993. (A classic.)

Brealey, Richard, and Stewart Myers. *Principles of Corporate Finance.* 5th ed. Burr Ridge, IL: Irwin/McGraw-Hill, 1996.

Ross, Stephen; Randolph Westerfield; and Bradford Jordan. *Fundamentals of Corporate Finance.* 5th ed. Burr Ridge, IL: Irwin/McGraw-Hill, 2000.

Weston, J. Fred, and Thomas E. Copeland. *Managerial Finance.* 10th ed. Hinsdale, IL: Dryden Press, 1992.

Self-Study Exercises, Problems, and Discussion Questions

Exercises and Problems (Selected Solutions Provided in Appendix VI)

1. Work the following exercises:
   a. The following data about the ABC Company's operations and conditions for the year 2003 are available from a variety of sources:

Depreciation	$ 21,000
Net loss	14,100
Common dividends paid	12,000
Amortization of goodwill, patents	15,000
Inventory write-down	24,000
Loss from sale of equipment	4,000
Capital investments	57,500
Balance of retained earnings 12/31/02	167,300

Which of the preceding items affect retained earnings during 2003, and what's the balance of retained earnings as of 12/31/03? Which of these items are cash sources, and which are cash uses? Can depreciation be considered a cash flow item even though the operating results are negative? What would be different if the $4,000 loss from the sale of equipment had been a gain instead? Discuss.

b. The following items, among others, appear on the cash flow statement of DEF Company for the year 2003:

Capital investments	$1,250,500
Operating profit after taxes	917,500
Depreciation charges	1,613,000

The only other information readily available is:

Gross property, plant and equipment, 12/31/02	$8,431,500
Gross property, plant and equipment, 12/31/03	8,430,000
Accumulated depreciation, 12/31/03	3,874,000

From this information determine the change in *net* property, plant and equipment during the year. What assumptions do you need to make? Discuss.

c. The XYZ Company experienced the transactions and changes listed below, among many others, during 2003. These affected its balance sheet as follows:

- Fixed assets originally recorded at $110,000 and carrying accumulated depreciation of $81,000 were sold for $45,000 (the capital gain was reflected in net income).
- Accumulated depreciation for the company as a whole decreased by $5,000 during 2003.
- Total depreciation charges for the year were $78,500.
- Gross property, plant and equipment showed a balance of $823,700 on 12/31/02 and $947,300 on 12/31/03.

From this information, determine the amount of new investment in property, plant and equipment that should be shown in the cash flow statement. What was the amount of change in *net* property, plant and equipment during 2003? Which other items shown above or derived from these should be shown on the cash flow statement? What assumptions do you need to make? Discuss.

2. Develop a statement of cash flow sources and uses from the balance sheets and income statements of the CBA Company for the year 2003. Make appropriate assumptions and comment on the results.

CBA COMPANY
Income Statements for 2002 and 2003

	2002	2003
Net sales	$1,133,400	$1,147,700
Cost of goods sold*	740,500	813,300
Gross margin	392,900	334,400
Expenses:		
Selling expense	172,500	227,000
General and administrative	65,500	71,800
Other expenses	22,200	25,000
Interest on debt	9,700	14,300
Total expenses	269,900	338,100
Profit (loss) before taxes	123,000	(3,700)
Income taxes	56,600	(1,700)
Net income (loss)†	$ 66,400	$ (2,000)

*Includes depreciation of $31,500 for 2002 and $32,200 for 2003.
†Dividends paid were $30,000 for 2002 and $15,000 for 2003.

CBA COMPANY
Balance Sheets
December 31, 2002 and 2003

	2002	2003
Assets:		
Current assets		
Cash	$ 39,700	$ 27,500
Marketable securities	1,000	11,000
Accounts receivable (net)	81,500	72,700
Inventories	181,300	242,000
Total current assets	303,500	353,200
Fixed assets:		
Land	112,000	112,000
Plant and equipment (net)	445,200	464,800
Total fixed assets	557,200	576,800
Other assets	13,300	21,500
Total assets	$874,000	$951,500
Liabilities and shareholders' equity		
Current liabilities:		
Accounts payable	$ 71,200	$ 83,000
Notes payable	50,000	140,000
Accrued expenses	33,400	36,300
Total current liabilities	154,600	259,300
Long-term debt:		
Mortgage payable	106,000	90,800
Shareholders'equity:		
Common stock	225,000	230,000
Retained earnings	388,400	371,400
Total shareholders' equity	613,400	601,400
Total liabilities and shareholders' equity	$874,000	$951,500

3. Develop a standard cash flow statement for the year 2003 from the balance sheets, income statements, and retained earnings statements of the FED Company as shown below. Additional data about company actions are as follows:

   a. Sold fully depreciated machinery for 4,000.

   b. Issued $20,000 of common stock ($1.00 par) to reduce the outstanding note payable.

   c. Issued $4,000 of preferred stock to outsiders.

Make appropriate assumptions and comment on the results. If you net out the various changes in working capital items into a single figure, will significant information be obscured? Discuss.

Financial Genome contains the historical data for this problem in a separate database. You can create the cash flow statement from this information, and also test your figures by varying your assumptions. Discuss your findings.

FED COMPANY
Balance Sheets, December 31, 2002 and 2003
($ thousands)

	2002	2003	Change
Assets:			
Current assets			
Cash	$ 12	$–0–	– $12
Marketable securities	18	–0–	– 18
Accounts receivable–net	68	73	+ 5
Notes receivable	30	50	+ 20
Inventories	131	138	+ 7
Total current assets	259	261	+ 2
Property, plant, and equipment	268	283	+ 15
Less: Accumulated depreciation	157	160	+ 3
Net plant and equipment	111	123	+ 12
Total fixed assets	136	148	+ 12
Other assets:			
Prepaid expenses	12	14	+ 2
Patents, organization expense	30	27	– 3
Total other assets	42	41	– 1
Total assets	$437	$450	+ $13
Liabilities and net worth			
Current liabilities:			
Bank overdraft	$–0–	$4	+ $ 4
Accounts payable	73	97	+ 24
Notes payable	100	70	– 30
Accrued expenses	13	22	+ 9
Total current liabilities	186	193	+ 7
Long-term liabilities:			
Secured notes payable	40	20	– 20
Other liabilities:			
Deferred income taxes	25	27	+ 2

Continues

FED COMPANY
Continued

	2002	2003	Change
Shareholders'equity:			
Preferred stock	35	39	+ 4
Capital surplus	90	109	+ 19
Retained earnings	51	51	–0–
Common stock	10	11	+ 1
Total net worth	186	210	+ 24
Total liabilities and shareholders' equity	$437	$450	+$13

FED COMPANY
Income Statement for 2002 and 2003
($ thousands)

	2002	2003
Sales	$1,115	$1,237
Cost of goods sold:		
Material	312	345
Labor	274	341
Depreciation	24	26
Overhead	158	210
Cost of goods sold	768	922
Gross profit	347	315
Expenses:		
Selling and administrative expense	268	297
Patent, other amortization	3	3
Interest on debt	9	7
Total expenses	280	307
Profit before taxes	67	8
Income taxes	32	5
Net income	$ 35	$ 3

FED COMPANY
Statement of Retained Earnings for 2003
($ thousands)

Balance 12–31–02		$51
Additions:		
Net income from 2003 operations	$3	
Gain from sale of fixed assets	4	7
		58
Deductions:		
Preferred dividends	2	
Common dividends	5	7
Balance 12-31-03		$51

4. The ZYX Company, a vegetable packaging plant, operates on a highly
    seasonal basis, which affects its financial results during various parts of
    its fiscal year and forces a financial planning effort in tune with these
    fluctuating requirements. From the company's nine quarterly balance
    sheets (covering two fiscal years at ZYX Company's history), and

using a spreadsheet approach, develop a cash flow analysis that appropriately reflects the funds needs and sources as balanced by company management.

Additional data about company operations are available as follows:

a. Purchases of machinery, $48,000 in April 2003, and $50,000 in April 2004.

b. Depreciation charged at $6,000 per quarter through April 2003, and at $8,000 per quarter through July 2004.

c. Dividends paid at $15,000 per quarter through October 2003, and at $18,000 per quarter through July 2004.

Comment on the various alternative ways in which this analysis can be developed, and state your reasons for your choices. What are your key findings?

Financial Genome contains the historical data for this problem in a separate database. You can create the quarterly cash flow statements from this information, and also test your figures by varying your assumptions. Discuss your findings.

ZYX COMPANY
Balance Sheets by Fiscal Quarters
July 31, 2002, to July 31, 2004
($ thousands)

	2002		2003				2004		
	7–31	10–31	1–31	4–30	7–31	10–31	1–31	4–30	7–31
Assets									
Cash	$ 21	$ 30	$ 74	$ 91	$ 7	$ 28	$ 90	$103	$ 16
Accounts receivable	114	247	319	128	141	293	388	151	103
Inventories	231	417	315	131	271	467	351	98	310
Net plant and equipment	239	233	227	269	262	255	248	291	283
Other assets	15	16	16	15	15	14	18	18	17
Total assets	$620	$943	$951	$634	$696	$1,057	$1,095	$661	$729
Liabilities and net worth									
Accounts payable	$ 68	$297	$121	$103	$ 79	$ 314	$ 188	$ 97	$ 84
Notes payable	35	126	294	—	63	178	342	—	80
Mortgage payable	80	80	75	75	70	70	65	65	60
Preferred stock	100	100	100	100	100	100	100	100	100
Common stock	100	100	100	100	125	125	125	125	125
Retained earnings	237	240	261	256	259	270	275	274	280
Total liabilities and net worth	$620	$943	$951	$634	$696	$1,057	$1,095	$661	$729

5. 3M Corporation's five-year database contained in Financial Genome can be used to create cash flow statements for each of these years. Examine these statements and compare them to the statement for 2000 discussed in the chapter. You can vary the results by overriding selected

input items (not calculated terms) on the income statements and balance sheets and trace the impact to the cash flow statements (restore original database values by highlighting and pressing the return key). Observe the linkage between the various statements and how temporarily altering historical values causes statements to show an "out of balance" condition.

6. Using Financial Genome follow the process of entering data as described in the "help" system and create integrated sets of financial statements for companies of your choice. Note the feature which requires you to make certain enough appropriate data are entered to ensure that historical balance sheets and income statements show no "out of balance" condition.

Discussion Questions

1. Differentiate between cash flow and funds movements. What is "cash flow from operations"?
2. In what ways does a cash flow statement correspond to the income statement for a period? In what ways does it differ? Can the two be readily reconciled?
3. In what ways are the concepts of debit and credit related to cash uses and sources? Drawing up a simple balance sheet, derive the key principles of this relationship.
4. Does a sizable profit for the period necessarily mean an increase in a company's cash account? If not, why not?
5. Does a company whose operations are shrinking always throw off cash? If not, why not?
6. Why is depreciation a "source of cash" when it is clear that a mere bookkeeping entry is involved?
7. If a company incurred an operating loss for the period, is depreciation still treated as a "cash inflow"?
8. What is the tax impact of depreciation? Are there any cash movements involved?
9. Why is it necessary in cash flow analysis to "reverse" such transactions as amortization of goodwill and the write-down of an asset?
10. What is the cash impact when accelerated depreciation is used for tax reporting while using straight-line depreciation for book purposes?
11. What criteria determine the selection of the proper time period for cash flow analysis? Can you derive any rules?
12. What are the major ways in which inflation distorts the cash flow picture? Should adjustments be made?

MINNESOTA MINING AND MANUFACTURING COMPANY AND SUBSIDIARIES

Notes to Consolidated Financial Statements

Note 1 Significant Accounting Policies

Consolidation—All significant subsidiaries are consolidated. All significant intercompany transactions are eliminated. As used herein, the term "3M" or "company" refers to Minnesota Mining and Manufacturing Company and subsidiaries unless the context indicates otherwise.

Foreign Currency Translation—Local currencies generally are considered the functional currencies outside the United States, except in countries treated as highly inflationary. Assets and liabilities for operations in local-currency environments are translated at year-end exchange rates.

Income and expense items are translated at average rates of exchange prevailing during the year. Cumulative translation adjustments are recorded as a component of accumulated other comprehensive income in stockholders' equity.

For operations in countries treated as highly inflationary, certain financial statement amounts are translated at historical exchange rates, with all other assets and liabilities translated at year-end exchange rates. These translation adjustments are reflected in income and are not material.

Reclassifications—Certain prior-period amounts have been reclassified to conform with the current-year presentation. Research, development and related expenses have been reclassified from cost of sales and are now presented separately. Pursuant to FASB Emerging Issues Task Force Issue No. 00-10, Accounting for Shipping and Handling Fees and Costs, the company has also reclassified freight billed to customers from selling, general and administrative expenses to net sales, and has reclassified related freight costs from selling, general and administrative expenses to cost of sales.

Use of estimates—The preparation of financial statements in conformity with generally accepted accounting principles requires management to make estimates and assumptions that affect the reported amounts of assets and liabilities and the disclosure of contingent assets and liabilities at the date of the financial statements, and the reported amounts of revenues and expenses during the reporting period. Actual results could differ from these estimates.

Cash and cash equivalents—Cash and cash equivalents consist of cash and temporary investments with maturities of three months or less when purchased.

Investments—Investments primarily include debt securities held by captive insurance operations, the cash surrender value of life insurance policies, and real estate and venture capital investments. Unrealized gains and losses relating to investments classified as available-for-sale are recorded as a component of accumulated other comprehensive income in stockholders' equity.

Inventories—Inventories are stated at lower of cost or market, with cost generally determined on a first-in, first-out basis.

Property, Plant and Equipment—Depreciation of property, plant and equipment generally is computed using the straight-line method based on estimated useful lives of the assets. Estimated useful lives range from 5 to 40 years for buildings and improvements and 3 to 20 years for machinery and equipment. Fully depreciated assets are retained in property and accumulated depreciation accounts until removed from service. Upon disposal, assets and related accumulated depreciation are removed from the accounts and the net amount, less proceeds from disposal, is charged or credited to operations.

Other assets—Other assets include product and other insurance receivables, goodwill, patents, other intangible assets, deferred income taxes and other noncurrent assets. Goodwill is amortized on a straight-line basis over the periods benefited, ranging from 5 to 40 years. Other intangible assets are amortized on a straight-line basis over their estimated economic lives.

Impairment of long-lived assets—Long-lived assets, including identifiable intangibles and goodwill, are reviewed for impairment whenever events or changes in circumstances indicate that the carrying amount of an asset may not be recoverable. An impairment loss would be recognized when the carrying amount of an asset exceeds the estimated undiscounted future cash flows expected to result from the use of the asset and its eventual disposition. The amount of the impairment loss to be recorded is calculated by the excess of the asset's carrying value over its fair value. Fair value is determined using a discounted cash flow analysis.

Revenue recognition—Revenue is recognized when the risks and rewards of ownership have substantively transferred to customers regardless of whether legal title has transferred. This condition is normally met when the product has been delivered or upon performance of services. The company sells a wide range of products to a diversified base of customers around the world and, therefore, believes there is no material concentration of credit risk. Prior to 2000, the company recognized revenue upon shipment of goods to customers and upon performance of services (refer to "Accounting Change" that follows).

Advertising and merchandising—These costs are charged to operations in the year incurred.

Internal-use software—The company capitalizes direct costs of materials and services used in the development of internal-use software. Amounts capitalized are amortized on a straight-line basis over a period of 3 to 5 years and are reported as a component of machinery and equipment within property, plant and equipment.

Environmental—Environmental expenditures relating to existing conditions caused by past operations that do not contribute to current or future revenues are expensed. Liabilities for remediation costs are recorded on an undiscounted basis when they are probable and reasonably estimable, generally no later than the completion of feasibility studies or the company's commitment to a plan to action.

Derivatives and hedging activities—The company uses interest rate swaps, currency swaps, and forward and option contracts to manage risks generally associated with foreign exchange rate, interest rate and commodity market volatility. All hedging instruments are designated and effective as hedges, in accordance with U.S. generally accepted accounting principles. Instruments that do not qualify for hedge accounting are marked to market with changes recognized in current earnings. The company does not hold or issue derivative financial instruments for trading purposes and is not a party to leveraged derivatives.

Realized and unrealized gains and losses for qualifying hedge instruments are deferred until offsetting gains and losses on the underlying transactions are recognized in earnings. These gains and losses generally are recognized either as interest expense over the borrowing period for interest rate and currency swaps, as an adjustment to cost of sales for inventory-related hedge transactions, or as a component of accumulated other comprehensive income in stockholders' equity for hedges of net investments in international companies. If the underlying hedged transaction ceases to exist, all changes in fair value of the related derivatives that have not been settled are recognized in earnings. Cash flows attributable to these financial instruments are included with the cash flows of the associated hedged items.

Accounting for stock-based compensation—The company uses the intrinsic value method for the Management Stock Ownership Program (MSOP). The General Employees' Stock Purchase Plan is considered noncompensatory.

Comprehensive income—Total comprehensive income and the components of accumulated other comprehensive income are presented in the Consolidated Statement of Changes in Stockholders' Equity and Comprehensive Income.

Accumulated other comprehensive income is composed of foreign currency translation effects, including hedges of net investments in international companies, minimum pension liability adjustments, and unrealized gains and losses on available-for-sale debt and equity securities.

Earnings per share—The difference in the weighted average shares outstanding for calculating basic and diluted earnings per share is attributable to the assumed exercise of MSOP stock options, if dilutive.

Net accounting pronouncements—In June 1998, the Financial Accounting Standards Board issued Statement of Financial Accounting Standards (SFAS) No. 133, "Accounting for Derivative Instruments and Hedging Activities." SFAS No. 133, as amended, was adopted by the company on January 1, 2001. Based on the company's analysis of its current derivative positions, this standard will not materially affect its financial position or results of operations.

Note 2   Accounting Change

During the fourth quarter of 2000, the company changed its revenue recognition policy. Essentially, the new policies recognize that the risks and rewards of ownership in many transactions do not substantively transfer to customers until the product has been delivered, regardless of whether legal title has transferred. In addition to this change in accounting that affects a substantial portion of its product sales, the company has revised aspects of its accounting for services provided in several of its smaller businesses. These new policies are consistent with the guidance contained in SEC Staff Accounting Bulletin No. 101. The effect of these changes in revenue recognition policies, as of January 1, 2000, is reported as the cumulative effect of an accounting change in the fourth quarter of 2000. This change did not have a significant effect on previously reported 2000 quarters or on prior years.

Note 3   Restructuring Charge

To reduce costs and improve productivity, the company initiated a restructuring program in the second half of 1998 to streamline corporate structure, consolidate manufacturing operations and exit certain product lines. Related to this, the company recorded a restructuring charge of $493 million ($313 million after tax). A portion of this restructuring charge ($39 million) has been classified as a component of cost of sales. In 1999, the company recorded a change in estimate that reduced the restructuring charge by $28 million. The restructuring charge does not include the write-down of goodwill or other intangible assets. As of December 31, 1999, this restructuring program was substantially complete.

Of the total restructuring charge, $275 million related to employee termination benefits for personnel reductions in each business segment and geographic area of the company and in all major functions. Under the plan, the company terminated 1,225 employees in the second half of 1998 and 3,288 employees in 1999, of whom about one-third were in the United States and two-thirds were abroad. Because certain employees can defer receipt of termination benefits, cash payments lag job eliminations. After subtracting payments of $268 million made through December 31, 2000, the company had a remaining liability of $7 million related to employee termination benefits at year-end. This amount is classified in current liabilities (payroll) on the Consolidated Balance Sheet.

The company has consolidated or downsized manufacturing operations, including actions in seven locations in the United States, nine in Europe, four in the Asia Pacific area and two in Latin America. As part of the restructuring plan, the company has discontinued product lines that had combined annual sales of less than $100 million and marginal operating income.

Restructuring Information

(Millions)	Employee Termination Benefits	Write-down of Property, Plant and Equipment	Inventory	Other	Total
1998 restructuring charge					
Third quarter	$102	$161	$29	$40	$332
Fourth quarter	169	—	10	—	179
Fourth quarter change in estimate	—	(18)	—	—	(18)
Total-year 1998	$271	$143	$39	$40	$493
1999 change in estimate	4	(31)	—	(1)	(28)
Total restructuring charge	$275	$112	$39	$39	$465

Restructuring Liability

(Millions)	Employee Termination Benefits	Other	Total
September 30, 1998 liability	$ 102	$ 40	$ 142
Fourth-quarter 1998 employee termination benefits charge	169	—	169
Fourth-quarter 1998 cash payments	(39)	(8)	(47)
December 31, 1998 liability	$ 232	$ 32	$ 264
1999 cash payments	(205)	(23)	(228)
1999 change in estimate	4	(1)	3
December 31, 1999 liability	$ 31	$ 8	$ 39
2000 cash payments	(24)	(4)	(28)
December 31, 2000 liability	$ 7	$ 4	$ 11

The restructuring charge included $112 million, net of salvage value, for the write-down of assets included in property, plant and equipment. These assets primarily included specialized 3M manufacturing machinery and equipment. Estimated salvage values are based on estimates of proceeds upon sale of certain affected assets.

The restructuring charge also included $78 million for losses on inventory write-downs and other exit costs. The company has taken an inventory write-down of $39 million, which has been classified as a component of cost of sales, for certain product lines that were discontinued primarily in 1998. Other exit costs included $39 million in incremental costs and contractual obligations for items such as leasehold termination payments and other facility exit costs incurred as a direct result of the plan. After subtracting $35 million in payments made through December 31, 2000, the company had a remaining balance of $4 million in other current liabilities for these exit costs at December 31, 2000.

Note 4   Acquisitions and Divestitures

Year 2000 acquisitions—During 2000, 3M acquired 91 percent of Quante AG (a telecommunications supplier), 100 percent of the multi-layer integrated circuit packaging line of W. L. Gore and Associates, and seven smaller businesses for a total purchase price of $472 million in cash (net of cash acquired) plus 128,994 shares of 3M common stock. The stock had a fair market value of $11 million at the acquisition date and was previously held as 3M treasury stock. All of these transactions were accounted for using the purchase method of accounting. The preliminary

estimated fair values of assets acquired and liabilities assumed relating to these acquisitions are summarized in the Note 4 Acquisitions and Divestitures table.

(Millions)	Asset (Liability)
Accounts receivable	$ 86
Inventories	112
Other working capital—net	(80)
Property, plant and equipment	179
Purchased intangible assets	326
Other assets	30
Interest bearing debt	(123)
Long-term liabilities	(47)
Net assets acquired	$ 483

The 2000 purchased intangible assets, including goodwill, are being amortized on a straight-line basis over the periods benefited, ranging from 3 to 20 years. In-process research and development charges associated with these acquisitions were not significant. Pro forma information related to these acquisitions is not included because the impact of these acquisitions on the company's results of operations is not considered to be significant.

Year 1999 acquisition—On December 28, 1999, 3M finalized the acquisition of the outstanding 46 percent minority interest in Dyneon LLC from Celanese AG for approximately $340 million in cash, primarily financed by debt. The purchase method of accounting was used for this acquisition. The purchase price exceeded the fair value of the minority interest net assets by approximately $267 million, of which approximately $242 million represents goodwill and other intangible assets that will be amortized over 20 years or less. Dyneon's assets, liabilities, revenues and expenses were already fully consolidated in 3M's financial statements, with the 46 percent minority interest eliminated on the minority interest line to reflect 3M's net position. If this acquisition had occurred at the beginning of 1999, the effect on results of operations would not have been material.

Year 1999 divestitures—On June 30, 1999, the company closed on the sale of Eastern Heights Bank, a subsidiary banking operation, and on the sale of the assets of its cardiovascular systems business. These divestitures generated cash proceeds of $203 million and, net of an investment valuation adjustment, resulted in a pre-tax gain of $104 million ($55 million after tax) in the second quarter of 1999. 3M also recorded a pre-tax gain of $43 million ($26 million after tax) related to divestitures, mainly in the Health Care segment, in the third quarter of 1999. These pre-tax gains are recorded in the other expense (income) line within operating income.

Note 5 Supplemental Statement of Income Information

(Millions)	2000	1999	1998
Research, development and related expenses	$1,101	$1,056	$1,028
Advertising and merchandising costs	544	484	448

Research and development expenses, covering basic scientific research and the application of scientific advances to the development of new and improved products and their uses, totaled $727 million, $688 million and $648 million in 2000, 1999 and 1998, respectively. Related expenses primarily include technical support provided by the laboratories for existing products.

Note 6 Supplemental Balance Sheet Information

(Millions)	2000	1999
Accounts receivable		
Accounts receivable	$ 2,975	$2,860
Less allowances	84	82
Accounts receivable—net	$ 2,891	$2,778
Inventories		
Finished goods	$ 1,231	$1,103
Work in process	663	544
Raw materials	418	383
Total inventories	$ 2,312	$2,030
Other current assets		
Product and other insurance receivables	$267	$ 291
Deferred income taxes	152	172
Other	455	408
Total other current assets	$ 874	$ 871
Investments		
Available-for-sale (fair value)	72	254
Other (cost, which approximates fair value)	238	233
Total investments	$ 310	$ 487
Property, plant and equipment - at cost		
Land	$ 249	$ 265
Buildings and leasehold improvements	3,477	3,429
Machinery and equipment	9,958	9,356
Construction in progress	486	602
	14,170	13,652
Less accumulated depreciation	8,347	7,876
Property, plant and equipment—net	$ 5,823	$5,776
Other assets		
Intangible assets—net	$ 852	$ 537
Product and other insurance receivables	541	634
Prepaid pension benefits	412	265
Deferred income taxes	143	88
Other	62	43
Total other assets	$ 2,010	$1,567
Other current liabilities		
Product and other claims	$ 107	$141
Nonfunded pension and postretirement benefits	93	72

(Millions)	2000	1999
Other	763	643
Total other current liabilities	$ 963	$ 856
Other liabilities		
Nonfunded pension and postretirement benefits	$ 754	$ 761
Product and other claims	339	397
Minority interest in subsidiaries	346	371
Deferred income taxes	362	332
Other	465	447
Total other liabilities	$2,266	$2,308

Note 7 Supplemental Stockholders' Equity and Comprehensive Income Information

Common stock ($.01 par value per share; $.50 par value at December 31, 1999 and 1998) of 1.5 billion shares is authorized (1 billion shares at December 31, 1999), with 472,016,528 shares issued in 2000, 1999 and 1998. Common stock and capital in excess of par includes $231 million transferred from common stock to capital in excess of par value during 2000 in connection with the change in par value of the company's common stock to $.01 per share. Preferred stock, without par value, of 10 million shares is authorized but unissued.

The following table shows the ending balances of the components of accumulated other comprehensive income (loss).

Accumulated Other Comprehensive Income (Loss)

(Millions)	2000	1999	1998
Cumulative translation—net	$(885)	$(694)	$(518)
Minimum pension liability adjustments—net	(58)	(30)	—
Debt and equity securities, unrealized gain—net	29	136	10
Total accumulated other comprehensive income (loss)	$(914)	$(588)	$(508)

Reclassification adjustments in 2000 for realized gains included in net income totaled $62 million ($101 million before tax). These gains related to the sale of appreciated equity securities. Reclassification adjustments in 1999 for realized gains included in net income totaled $25 million ($41 million before tax). These gains related to appreciated equity securities donated to the 3M Foundation in December 1999. In 2000, 1999 and 1998, other reclassification adjustments were not material. Income tax effects for cumulative translation are not material since no tax provision has been made for the translation of foreign currency financial statements into U.S. dollars.

Note 8   Supplemental Cash Flow Information

Supplemental Cash Flow Information

(Millions)	2000	1999	1998
Income tax payments	$852	$553	$467
Interest payments	104	114	130
Depreciation	915	822	798
Amortization of software	45	39	28
Amortization of patents, other identifiable acquisition intangibles, and goodwill	65	39	40

As required by a third-quarter 2000 Emerging Issues Task Force consensus, stock option tax benefits have been classified as a component of cash flows from operating activities. Prior-period Consolidated Statement of Cash Flows amounts have been restated to conform with this presentation.

Individual amounts on the Consolidated Statement of Cash Flows exclude the effects of acquisitions, divestitures and exchange rate impacts, which are presented separately. The net impact of cumulative effect of accounting changes is recorded in "Other–net" within operating activities.

In 1999, 3M exchanged assets used in the business, but not held for sale, with a fair market value of $61 million plus cash of $12 million, for similar assets having a fair market value of $73 million. No gain was recognized on this nonmonetary exchange of productive assets. Also in 1999, 3M donated to the 3M Foundation appreciated equity securities with a market value of $66 million, resulting in $8 million of pre-tax expense, which represented the company's cost of securities.

In 1998, the 3M Employee Stock Ownership Plant (ESOP) refinanced its existing debt by issuing new debt of $385 million. Because the company has guaranteed repayment of the ESOP debt, the debt and related unearned compensation are recorded on the Consolidated Balance Sheet. The repayment of principal and proceeds of long-term debt relating to the ESOP have been excluded from the financing activities of the company in the Consolidated Statement of Cash Flows because the funds involved were received and disbursed by the ESOP trust.

Note 9   Debt

Short-Term Debt

(Millions)	Effective Interest Rate*	2000	1999
Commercial paper	6.49%	$ 655	$ 786
Long-term debt —current portion	5.94%	646	36
6.325% dealer remarketable securities	5.67%	352	—
Other borrowings	7.79%	213	308
Total short-term debt		$1,866	$1,130

Long-Term Debt

(Millions)	Effective Interest Rate*	Maturity Date	2000	1999
ESOP debt guarantee	5.62%	2002–2009	$303	$ 333
U.S. dollar 6.375% note	6.38%	2028	330	330
Japanese yen 1% eurobond	1.00%	2003	139	—
Sumitomo 3M Limited 0.795% note	0.80%	2003	87	98
Other borrowings	6.11%	2002–2037	112	719
Total long-term debt			$971	$1,480

*Reflects the effects of interest rate and currency swaps at December 31, 2000.

At December 31, 2000, debt with fixed interest rates includes the ESOP, U.S. dollar 6.375 percent note, Japanese yen eurobond, Sumitomo 3M Limited note and a portion of other borrowings. The ESOP debt is serviced by dividends on stock held by the ESOP and by company contributions. These contributions are reported as an employee benefit expense in the Consolidated Statement of Income. At December 31, 2000, debt not denominated in U.S. dollars includes the Japanese yen eurobond, the Sumitomo 3M Limited note and most of other borrowings. Other borrowings include debt held by 3M's international companies, and floating rate notes and industrial bond issues in the United States. Other borrowings in long-term debt significantly decreased in 2000 as a result of certain debt securities becoming due in 2001, with the corresponding increase reflected in the current portion of long-term debt.

Maturities of long-term debt for the next five years are: 2001, $646 million; 2002, $33 million; 2003, $261 million; 2004, $36 million; and 2005, $38 million.

The company estimates that the fair value of short-term debt approximates the carrying amount of this debt. The fair value of long-term debt, based on third-party quotes, is estimated at $950 million. Debt covenants do not restrict the payment of dividends. At year-end 2000, the company had available short-term lines of credit totaling about $694 million.

Note 10   Other Financial Instruments

Interest rate and currency swaps—The company uses interest rate and currency swaps to manage interest rate risk related to borrowings. The notional amounts shown in the table below serve solely as a basis for the calculation of payment streams to be exchanged. These notional amounts are not a measure of the company's exposure through its use of derivatives. These instruments generally mature in relationship to their underlying debt and have maturities extending to 2001. Unrealized gains and losses and exposure to changes in market conditions were not material at December 31, 2000 and 1999, for interest rate swaps. Currency swaps at December 31, 2000, had unrealized gains of $29 million and unrealized losses of $47 million. Currency swaps at December 31, 1999, had unrealized gains of $13 million and unrealized losses of $61 million. In both years, unrealized gains and losses relating to underlying debt instruments largely offset these unrealized amounts.

Notional Amounts

(Millions)	2000	1999
Interest rate swaps	$615	$550
Currency swaps	365	465

Foreign exchange forward and option contracts— The company has entered into foreign exchange forward and option contracts, the majority of which have maturities of less than one year. The face amounts represent contracted U.S. dollar equivalents of forward and option contracts denominated in foreign currencies. The amounts at risk are not material because the company has the ability to generate offsetting foreign currency cash flows. Unrealized gains and losses at December 31, 2000 and 1999, were not material. In 2000, realized gains totaled $132 million and realized losses totaled $45 million, with most of this net impact offset by underlying hedged items.

Face Amounts

(Millions)	2000	1999
Forward contracts	$442	$997
Options purchased	113	140

The company engages in hedging activities to reduce exchange rate risks arising from cross-border cash flows denominated in foreign curren-cies. The company operates on a global basis, generating more than half its revenues internationally and engaging in substantial product and financial transfers among geographic areas. Major forward contracts at December 31, 2000, were denominated in European euros and Japanese yen.

Credit risk—The company is exposed to credit loss in the event of nonperformance by counterparties in interest rate swaps, currency swaps, and option and foreign exchange contracts. However, the company's risk is limited to the fair value of the instruments. The company actively monitors its exposure to credit risk through the use of credit approvals and credit limits, and by selecting major international banks and financial institutions as counterparties. The company does not anticipate nonperformance by any of these counterparties.

Note 11   Income Taxes

At December 31, 2000, about $2.6 billion of re-tained earnings attributable to international com-panies were considered to be indefinitely invested. No provision has been made for taxes that might be payable if these earnings were re-mitted to the United States. It is not practical to determine the amount of incremental taxes that might arise were these earnings to be remitted.

Income before Income Taxes, Minority Interest, Extraordinary Loss and Cumulative Effect of Accounting Change

(Millions)	2000	1999	1998
United States	$1,580	$2,020	$1,326
International	1,394	860	626
Total	$2,974	$2,880	$1,952

Provision for Income Taxes

(Millions)	2000	1999	1998
Currently payable			
Federal	$ 385	$ 494	$186
State	64	72	52
International	487	371	308
Deferred			
Federal	92	100	149
State	7	9	13
International	(10)	(14)	(23)
Total	$1,025	$1,032	$685

In 2000, the company recorded a cumula-tive effect of accounting change, reducing earn-ings by $75 million net of tax. The provision for income taxes excludes a $42 million tax benefit related to this cumulative effect.

In 1998, the company refinanced debt re-lated to its Employee Stock Ownership Plan. The provision for income taxes excludes a $21 mil-lion tax benefit (classified as part of the extraor-dinary loss) related to this refinancing.

Components of Deferred Tax Assets and Liabilities

(Millions)	2000	1999
Accruals currently not deductible		
Employee benefit costs	$278	$288
Product and other claims	170	205
Product and other insurance receivables	(308)	(353)
Accelerated depreciation	(436)	(423)
Other	221	206
Net deferred tax asset (liability)	$(75)	$(77)

Reconciliation of Effective Income Tax Rate

(Millions)	2000	1999	1998
Statutory U.S. tax rate	35.0%	35.0%	35.0%
State income taxes—net	1.6	1.8	2.4
International income taxes—net	(.8)	.2	.8
All other—net	(1.3)	(1.2)	(3.1)
Effective worldwide tax rate	34.5%	35.8%	35.1%

Note 12   Business Segments

Net sales in prior periods have been reclassified to conform with the current-year presentation. In the first quarter of 2000, business segment operating income for 1999 was restated for minor amounts to be consistent with year 2000 management reporting practices. Certain costs previously included in Corporate and Unallocated were allocated to the individual business segments. 3M's businesses are organized, managed and internally reported as six operating segments based on differences in products, technologies and services. These segments are Industrial; Transportation, Graphics and Safety; Health Care; Consumer and Office; Electro and Communications; and Specialty Material. These segments have worldwide responsibility for virtually all of the company's product lines. 3M is not dependent on any single product or market.

Transactions among reportable segments are recorded at cost. 3M is an integrated enterprise characterized by substantial intersegment cooperation, cost allocations and inventory transfers.

Therefore, management does not represent that these segments, if operated independently, would report the operating income and other financial information shown. The allocations resulting from the shared utilization of assets are not necessarily indicative of the underlying activity for segment assets, depreciation and amortization, and capital expenditures.

Operating income in 2000 includes a non-recurring net loss of $23 million. Non-recurring costs include $168 million in the Specialty Material segment related to the company's phaseout of perfluorooctanyl-based chemistry products. This $168 million includes $56 million of accelerated depreciation (included in the Specialty Material segment depreciation and amortization), $48 million of impairment losses, and severance and other costs. Other non-recurring costs include a $20 million write-down of corporate and unallocated assets, and $20 million of other non-recurring expenses ($13 million related to acquisitions in the Electro and Communications segment). Non-recurring operating income gains in 2000 of $135 million were largely related to corporate and unallocated asset dispositions, principally the sale of available-for-sale equity securities. Operating income in 2000 also included a $50 million gain from the termination of a product distribution agreement in the Health Care segment.

Operating income in 1999 includes a non-recurring net gain of $100 million. This relates to divestitures of certain health care businesses and Eastern Heights Bank, litigation expense, an investment valuation adjustment, and a change in estimate that reduced the 1998 restructuring charge. Of this $100 million gain, $62 million was recorded in Health Care and $38 million in Corporate and Unallocated. Operating income in 1998 includes a restructuring charge of $493 million in Corporate and Unallocated.

Business Segments	Major Products
Industrial	Tapes, coated and nonwoven abrasives, and specialty adhesives
Transportation, graphics, and safety	Reflective sheeting, commercial graphics systems, respirators, automotive components, safety and security products, and optimal films
Health care	Medical and surgical supplies, skin health products, infection prevention, pharmaceuticals, drug delivery systems, dental and orthodontic products, health information systems, microbiology products, and closures for disposable diapers
Consumer and office	Sponges, scour pads, high-performance cloths, consumer and office tapes, repositioning notes, carpet and fabric protectors, energy control products, home improvement products, floor matting, commercial cleaning products, and visual systems
Electro and communications	Packaging and interconnection devices, insulating and splicing solutions for the electronics, telecommunications and electrical industries
Specialty material	Specialty materials for automotive, electronics, telecommunications, textile and other industries, and roofing granules

Business Segment Information

(Millions)		Net Sales	Operating Income	Assets[†]	Depreciation and Amortization	Capital Expenditures
Industrial	2000	$ 3,525	$ 641	$ 2,392	$ 213	$ 214
	1999	3,409	612	2,357	220	202
	1998	3,372	561	2,394	199	281
Transportation, graphics	2000	3,518	783	2,741	186	239
and safety	1999	3,234	675	2,673	140	199
	1998	3,025	532	2,652	170	336
Health care	2000	3,135	675	2,025	188	189
	1999	3,138	680	2,076	203	189
	1998	3,102	571	2,168	161	225
Consumer and office	2000	2,848	434	1,711	101	134
	1999	2,705	401	1,589	118	123
	1998	2,624	398	1,614	136	182
Electro and communications	2000	2,467	404	1,961	158	208
	1999	2,017	402	1,359	130	194
	1998	1,743	263	1,177	111	225
Specialty material	2000	1,197	57	1,230	144	131
	1999	1,194	185	1,323	79	143
	1998	1,133	194	1,112	66	188
Corporate and unallocated[*]	2000	34	64	2,462	35	—
	1999	51	1	2,519	10	—
	1998	95	(480)	3,036	23	16
Total Company	2000	$16,724	$3,058	$14,522	$1,025	$1,115
	1999	15,748	2,956	13,896	900	1,050
	1998	15,094	2,039	14,153	866	1,453

[*]Corporate and Unallocated operating income principally includes corporate investment gains and losses, certain derivative gains and losses, insurance-related gains and losses, banking operating results (divested June 30, 1999), certain litigation expenses, restructuring charges and other miscellaneous items. Because this category includes a variety of miscellaneous items, it is subject to fluctuation on a quarterly and annual basis.

[†]Segment assets primarily include accounts receivable; inventory; property, plant and equipment–net; and other miscellaneous assets. Assets included in Corporate and Unallocated principally are cash and cash equivalents; insurance receivables; deferred income taxes; certain investments and other assets; and certain unallocated property, plant and equipment.

Note 13   Geographic Areas

Information in the table below is presented on the basis the company uses to manage its businesses. Export sales and certain income and expense items are reported within the geographic area where the final sales to customers are made. Prior-year amounts have been retroactively restated to conform to the current-year presentation.

In 1999, operating income for eliminations and other includes a $100 million non-recurring net benefit related to gains on divestitures, litigation expense, an investment valuation adjustment, and a change in estimate that reduced the 1998 restructuring charge. In 1998, operating income for eliminations and other includes a $493 million restructuring charge.

Geographic Area Information

(Millions)		United States	Europe and Middle East	Asia Pacific	Latin America, Africa and Canada	Eliminations and Other	Total Company
Net sales to customers	2000	$7,858	$3,946	$3,329	$1,564	$ 27	$16,724
	1999	7,559	3,808	2,887	1,467	27	15,748
	1998	7,297	3,863	2,375	1,539	20	15,094
Operating income	2000	$1,160	$ 589	$ 961	$ 376	$(28)	$ 3,058
	1999	1,198	574	768	348	68	2,956
	1998	1,185	515	512	339	(512)	2,039
Property, plant and	2000	$3,699	$1,046	$ 711	$ 367	$ —	$ 5,823
equipment—net	1999	3,647	1,017	757	355	—	5,776
	1998	3,504	1,116	718	376	—	5,714

Note 14   Retirement and Postretirement Benefit Plans

3M has various company-sponsored retirement plans covering substantially all U.S. employees and many employees outside the United States. Pension benefits are based principally on an employee's years of service and compensation near retirement. In addition to providing pension benefits, the company provides certain postretirement health care and life insurance benefits for substantially all of its U.S. employees who reach retirement age while employed by the company. Most international employees and retirees are covered by government health care programs. The cost of company-provided health care plans for these international employees is not material.

The company's pension funding policy is to deposit with independent trustees amounts at least equal to accrued liabilities, to the extent allowed by law. Trust funds and deposits with insurance companies are maintained to provide pension benefits to plan participants and their beneficiaries. In addition, the company has set aside funds for its U.S. postretirement plan with an independent trustee and makes periodic contributions to the plan.

The company's U.S. non-qualified pension plan had an unfunded accumulated benefit obligation of $187 million at December 31, 2000, and $171 million at December 31, 1999. There are no plan assets in the non-qualified plan due to its nature.

Certain international pension plans were underfunded as of year-end 2000 and 1999. The accumulated benefit obligations of these plans were $499 million in 2000 and $467 million in 1999. The assets of these plans were $300 million in 2000 and $353 million in 1999. The net underfunded amounts are included in current and other liabilities on the Consolidated Balance Sheet.

Benefit Plan Information

(Millions)	Qualified and Non-qualified Pension Benefits				Postretirement Benefits	
	United States		International			
	2000	1999	2000	1999	2000	1999
Reconciliation of benefit obligation						
Beginning balance	$5,597	$6,201	$2,234	$2,153	$1,016	$1,030
Service cost	125	150	83	88	39	42
Interest cost	416	387	98	98	82	69
Participant contributions	—	—	6	7	11	9
Foreign exchange rate changes	—	—	(199)	(34)	—	1
Plan amendments	1	8	—	3	—	—
Actuarial (gain) loss	117	(823)	199	(21)	109	(56)
Benefit payments	(351)	(326)	(53)	(60)	(91)	(79)
Ending balance	$5,905	$5,597	$2,368	$2,234	$1,166	$1,016
Reconciliation of plan assets at fair value						
Beginning balance	$6,813	$6,233	$2,155	$2,028	$ 537	$ 523
Actual return on plan assets	384	807	5	173	4	19
Company contributions	90	86	60	51	139	64
Participant contributions	—	—	6	7	11	9
Foreign exchange rate changes	—	—	(157)	(45)	—	—
Benefit payments	(333)	(313)	(58)	(59)	(90)	(78)
Ending balance	$6,954	$6,813	$2,011	$2,155	$ 601	$ 537
Funded status of plans -						
Plan assets at fair value less benefit obligation	$1,049	$1,216	$ (357)	$ (79)	$ (565)	$ (480)
Unrecognized transition (asset) obligation	—	—	16	21	—	—
Unrecognized prior service cost	129	142	25	36	(26)	12
Unrecognized (gain) loss	(1,012)	(1,325)	311	13	160	(37)
Net amount recognized	$ 166	$ 33	$ (5)	$ (9)	$ (431)	$ (505)
Amounts recognized in the Consolidated Balance Sheet consist of:						
Prepaid assets	$ 319	$ 184	$ 80	$ 74	$ —	$ —
Accrued liabilities	(187)	(171)	(229)	(157)	(431)	(505)
Intangible assets	5	6	8	1	—	—
Accumulated other comprehensive income—pre-tax	29	14	136	73	—	—
Net amount recognized	$ 166	$ 33	$ (5)	$ (9)	$ (431)	$ (505)

Benefit Plan Information

(Millions)	Qualified and Non-qualified Pension Benefits						Postretirement Benefits		
	United States			International					
	2000	1999	1998	2000	1999	1998	2000	1999	1998
Components of net periodic benefit cost									
Service cost	$ 125	$ 150	$ 130	$ 83	$ 88	$ 80	$ 39	$ 42	$ 36
Interest cost	416	387	377	98	98	95	82	69	62
Expected return on assets	(565)	(501)	(440)	(117)	(108)	(103)	(47)	(34)	(32)
Amortization of transition (asset) obligation	—	(37)	(37)	2	2	(1)	—	—	—
Amortization of prior service cost or benefit	13	45	38	8	8	8	(11)	(11)	(11)
Recognized net actuarial (gain) loss	(14)	14	—	7	2	3	3	—	—
Net periodic benefit cost	$ (25)	$ 58	$ 68	$ 81	$ 90	$ 82	$ 66	$ 66	$ 55
Weighted average assumptions									
Discount rate	7.50%	7.50%	6.50%	5.40%	5.67%	5.58%	7.50%	7.50%	6.50%
Expected return on assets	9.00%	9.00%	9.00%	7.14%	6.69%	6.72%	8.19%	8.19%	6.25%
Compensation rate increase	4.65%	4.65%	4.65%	4.28%	4.12%	4.02%	4.65%	4.65%	4.65%

The company expects its health care cost trend rate for postretirement benefits to slow from 5.8 percent in 2001 to 5.0 percent in 2004, after which the rate is expected to stabilize. A one percentage point change in the assumed health care cost trend rates would have the effects shown in the following table:

Health Care Cost

(Millions)	One Percentage Point Increase	One Percentage Point Decrease
Effect on current year's benefit expense	$16	$(13)
Effect on benefit obligation	119	(103)

Note 15   Leases

Rental expense under operating leases was $119 million in 2000, $113 million in 1999 and $125 million in 1998. The table below shows minimum payments under operating leases with non-cancelable terms in excess of one year, as of December 31, 2000.

(Millions)	2001	2002	2003	2004	2005	After 2005	Total
Minimum lease payments	$ 83	$ 67	$ 50	$ 29	$ 20	$ 83	$332

Note 16   Employee Savings and Stock Ownership Plans

The company sponsors employee savings plans under Section 401(k) of the Internal Revenue Code. These plans are offered to substantially all regular U.S. employees. Employee contributions of up to 6 percent of compensation are matched at rates ranging from 20 to 35 percent, with additional company contributions depending upon company performance.

The company maintains an Employee Stock Ownership Plan (ESOP). This plan was established in 1989 as a cost-effective way of funding the majority of the company's contributions under 401(k) employee savings plans. Total ESOP shares are considered to be shares outstanding for earnings per share calculations.

In 1998, the ESOP refinanced its existing debt by issuing new debt of $385 million at an interest rate of 5.62 percent. This refinancing extended the life of the original ESOP from 2004 to 2009. The company incurred a one-time charge of $59 million ($38 million net of tax), or 9 cents per diluted share, which is reported as an extraordinary loss from early extinguishment of debt.

Dividends on shares held by the ESOP are paid to the ESOP trust and, together with company contributions, are used by the ESOP to repay principal and interest on the outstanding notes. Over the life of the notes, shares are released for allocation to participants based on the ratio of the current year's debt service to the remaining debt service prior to the current payment.

The ESOP has been the primary funding source for the company's employee savings plans. Expenses related to the ESOP include total debt service on the notes, less dividends. The company contributes treasury shares, accounted for at fair value, to employee savings plans to cover obligations not funded by the ESOP. These amounts are reported as an employee benefit expense.

Unearned compensation, shown as a reduction of stockholders' equity, is reduced symmetrically as the ESOP makes principal payments on the debt.

Employee Savings and Stock Ownership Plans

(Millions)	2000	1999	1998
Dividends on shares held by the ESOP	$31	$31	$31
Company contributions to the ESOP	15	7	44
Interest incurred on ESOP notes	19	21	29
Expenses related to ESOP debt service	12	14	37
Expenses related to treasury shares	35	50	2

ESOP Debt Shares

	2000	1999	1998
Allocated	6,898,666	6,596,898	6,586,192
Committed to be released	194,187	280,615	85,153
Unreleased	6,116,961	6,709,549	7,457,885
Total ESOP debt shares	13,209,814	13,587,062	14,129,230

Note 17   General Employees' Stock Purchase Plan

In May 1997, shareholders approved 15 million shares for issuance under the company's General Employees' Stock Purchase Plan (GESPP). Substantially all employees are eligible to participate in the plan. Participants are granted options at 85 percent of market value at the date of grant. There are no GESPP shares under option at the beginning or end of each year because options are granted on the first business day and exercised on the last business day of the same month.

Note 18   Management Stock Ownership Program

In May 1997, shareholders approved 35 million shares for issuance under the Management Stock Ownership Program (MSOP). Management stock options are granted at market value at the date of grant. These options generally are exercisable one year after the date of grant and expire 10 years from the date of grant. In May 2000, at the time of the grant, there were 11,073 participants in the plan.

General Employees' Stock Purchase Plan

	2000 Shares	2000 Exercise Price*	1999 Shares	1999 Exercise Price*	1998 Shares	1998 Exercise Price*
Options granted	1,206,262	$77.40	1,210,189	$72.25	1,271,120	$69.91
Options exercised	(1,206,262)	77.40	(1,210,189)	$72.25	(1,271,120)	$69.91
Shares available for grant— December 31.	10,563,726		11,769,988		12,980,177	

*Weighted average

Management Stock Ownership Program

	2000 Shares	2000 Exercise Price*	1999 Shares	1999 Exercise Price*	1998 Shares	1998 Exercise Price*
Under option—January 1	30,702,415	$74,67	29,330,549	$67.72	26,831,852	$59.75
Granted	6,612,707	89.20	5,697,333	94.32	5,872,537	92.78
Exercised	(4,684,779)	62.19	(4,201,886)	52.50	(3,300,215)	47.76
Canceled	(283,087)	86.77	(123,581)	93.35	(73,625)	93.35
December 31	32,347,256	$79.34	30,702,415	$74.67	29,330,549	$67.72
Options exercisable— December 31	26,159,345	$77.02	25,213,683	$70.27	24,031,395	$62.09
Shares available for grant— December 31	11,738,624		18,088,285		23,780,604	

*Weighted average

Options Outstanding and Exercisable at December 31, 2000

	Options Outstanding			Options Exercisable	
Range of Exercise Prices	Shares	Remaining Contractual Life (months)*	Exercise Price*	Shares	Exercise Price*
$42.50–54.52	4,542,274	34	$47.96	4,542,274	$47.96
54.57–82.91	6,855,135	60	62.02	6,855,135	62.02
86.70–119.60	20,949,847	101	91.86	14,761,936	93.01

*Weighted average

Note 19   Stock-Based Compensation

No compensation cost has been recognized for the General Employees' Stock Purchase Plan (GESPP) or the Management Stock Ownership Program (MSOP). Pro forma amounts based on the options' estimated fair value, net of tax, at the grant dates for awards under the GESPP and MSOP are presented below.

Pro Forma Net Income and Earnings per Share

(Millions)	2000	1999	1998
Net income			
As reported	$1,782	$1,763	$1,175
Pro forma	1,668	1,652	1,072
Earnings per share—basic			
As reported	$ 4.50	$ 4.39	$ 2.91
Pro forma	4.22	4.11	2.66
Earnings per share—diluted			
As reported	$ 4.45	$ 4.34	$ 2.88
Pro forma	4.17	4.06	2.63

The weighted average fair value per option granted during 2000, 1999 and 1998 was $13.65, $12.75 and $12.34, respectively, for the GESPP, and $22.45, $22.86 and $20.41, respectively, for the incentive MSOP grants. The weighted average fair value was calculated by using the fair value of each option on the date of grant. The fair value of GESPP options was based on the 15 percent purchase discount. For MSOP options, the fair value was calculated utilizing the Black-Scholes option-pricing model and the weighted average assumptions that follow.

MSOP Assumptions

	2000	1999	1998
Risk-free interest rate	6.7%	5.4%	5.7%
Dividend growth rate	4.3%	5.0%	5.8%
Volatility	22.3%	22.3%	17.6%
Expected life (months)	68	66	69

The MSOP options, if exercised, would have the following dilutive effect on shares outstanding for 2000, 1999 and 1998, respectively: 4.2 million, 4.5 million and 4.7 million shares. Certain MSOP options outstanding for years 2000, 1999 and 1998 (11.5, 8.7 and 10.8 million

shares, respectively) were not included in the computation of diluted earnings per share because they would not have a dilutive effect.

Note 20   Quarterly Data (Unaudited)

(Millions, Except per Share Amounts)	First	Second	Third	Fourth	Year
Net sales*					
2000	$4,075	$4,243	$4,270	$4,136	$16,724
1999	3,795	3,885	4,021	4,047	15,748
Cost of sales*					
2000	$2,091	$2,181	$2,295	$2,220	$8,787
1999	1,991	2,010	2,072	2,053	8,126
Income before cumulative effect of accounting change*					
2000	$487	$470	$499	$401	$1,857
1999	384	476	459	444	1,763
Net income*					
2000	$487	$470	$499	$326	$1,782
1999	384	476	459	444	1,763
Basic earnings per share—income before cumulative effect*					
2000	$1.22	$1.19	$1.26	$1.02	$4.69
1999	.95	1.18	1.14	1.11	4.39
Basic earnings per share—net income*					
2000	$1.22	$1.19	$1.26	$0.83	$4.50
1999	.95	1.18	1.14	1.11	4.39
Diluted earnings per share—income before cumulative effect*					
2000	$1.21	$1.18	$1.25	$1.00	$4.64
1999	.95	1.17	1.13	1.10	4.34
Diluted earnings per share—net income*					
2000	$1.21	$1.18	$1.25	$0.82	$4.45
1999	.95	1.17	1.13	1.10	4.34
Stock price comparisons (NYSE composite transactions)					
2000 high	$103.81	$98.31	$97.44	$122.94	$122.94
2000 low	78.19	80.44	80.40	83.94	78.19
1999 high	81.38	96.38	100.00	103.38	103.38
1999 low	69.31	70.06	85.00	87.44	69.31

*Net sales in prior periods have been reclassified to conform to the current-period presentation. Fourth-quarter and third quarter 2000 operating income include non-recurring costs of $90 million and $118 million, respectively, included in cost of sales, and non-recurring gains of $16 million and $119 million, respectively, primarily relating to the sale of equity securities. Non-recurring costs in both quarters primarily relate to the company's phaseout of perfluorooctanyl-based chemistry products. Fourth-quarter 2000 non-recurring items include an operating loss of $74 million ($46 million after tax) and a cumulative effect of accounting change that reduced earnings by $75 million net of tax, or a total of 30 cents per diluted share on a combined basis. First quarter 2000 includes a gain from termination of a product distribution agreement of $50 million ($31 million after tax), or 8 cents per diluted share. Third quarter 1999 includes gains on divestitures of $43 million, litigation expense of $73 million and a change in estimate that reduced the 1998 restructuring charge by $26 million. These items resulted in a net loss of $4 million ($3 million after tax), or 1 cent per diluted share. Second quarter 1999 includes gains on divestitures, net of an investment valuation adjustment, of $104 million ($55 million after tax), or 14 cents per diluted share.

Note 21   Legal Proceedings

General—The company and certain of its subsidiaries are named as defendants in a number of actions, governmental proceedings and claims, including environmental proceedings and products liability claims involving products now or formerly manufactured and sold by the company. In some actions, the claimants seek damages as well as other relief, which, if granted, would require substantial expenditures. The company has recorded certain liabilities, which represent reasonable estimates of its probable liabilities for these matters. The company also has recorded receivables for the probable amount of insurance recoverable with respect to these matters.

Some of these matters raise difficult and complex factual and legal issues, and are subject to many uncertainties, including, but not limited to, the facts and circumstances of each particular action, the jurisdiction and forum in which each action is proceeding and differences in applicable law. Accordingly, the company is not always able to estimate the amount of its possible future liabilities with respect to such matters.

While the company currently believes that the ultimate outcome of these proceedings and claims, individually and in the aggregate, will not have a material adverse effect on the consolidated financial position, results of operations, or cash flows of the company, there can be no absolute certainty that the company may not ultimately incur charges, whether for governmental proceedings and claims, products liability claims, or other actions, in excess of presently recorded liabilities.

While the company currently believes that a material adverse impact on its consolidated financial position, results of operations, or cash flows from any such future charges is remote, due to the inherent uncertainty of litigation, there exists the remote possibility that a future adverse ruling could result in future charges that could have a material adverse impact on the company. The current estimate of the potential impact on the company's financial position for the above legal proceedings could change in the future.

Breast implant litigation—The company and certain other companies have been named as defendants in a number of claims and lawsuits alleging damages for personal injuries of various types resulting from breast implants formerly manufactured by the company or a related company. The company entered the business of manufacturing breast implants in 1977 by purchasing McGhan Medical Corporation. In 1984, the company sold the business to a corporation that also was named McGhan Medical Corporation.

As of December 31, 2000, the company is currently named as a defendant, often with multiple co-defendants, in 1,223 lawsuits and 29 claims in various courts, all seeking damages for personal injuries from allegedly defective breast implants. These lawsuits and claims purport to represent 3,715 individual claimants.

3M has confirmed that 70 of the 3,715 claimants have opted out of the Revised Settlement Program (discussed below) and have 3M implants. Approximately 93 percent of the claimants in these confirmed cases have alleged an unspecified amount of damages above the jurisdictional limit of the courts in which the cases were filed. The company has one claimant who filed a lawsuit in New York state court alleging damages of $20 million.

The company believes that most of the remaining 3,645 claimants will be dismissed either because the claimants did not have 3M implants or the claimants accepted benefits under the Revised Settlement Program. Approximately 88 percent of these claimants have filed lawsuits that either do not allege a specific amount of damages or allege an unspecified amount of damages above the jurisdictional limit of the court. The rest of these claimants allege damages aggregating approximately $300 million in their lawsuits. Approximately 412 claimants have filed lawsuits in New York state courts alleging damages in excess of $20 million each. 3M expects that virtually all of these New York cases will be dismissed without payment for the reasons stated above. The company continues to work to clarify the status of these lawsuits and claims.

Based on 3M's experience in resolving thousands of these lawsuits, 3M believes that the amount of damages alleged in complaints is not a reliable or meaningful measure of the potential liability that 3M may incur in the breast implant litigation. Investors should place no reliance on the amount of damages alleged in breast implant lawsuits against 3M.

On December 22, 1995, the United States District Court for the Northern District of Alabama approved a revised class action settlement program for resolution of claims seeking damages for personal injuries from allegedly defective breast implants (the "Revised Settlement Program"). The Court ordered that, beginning after November 30, 1995, members of the plaintiff class may choose to participate in the Revised Settlement Program or opt out, which would then allow them to proceed with separate products liability actions.

The company believes that approximately 90 percent of the registrants, including those claimants who filed current claims, have elected to participate in the Revised Settlement Program. It is still unknown as to what disease criteria all claimants have satisfied, and what options they have chosen. As a result, the total amount and timing of the company's prospective payments under the Revised Settlement Program cannot be determined with precision at this time. As of December 31, 2000, the company had paid $296 million into the court-administered fund as a reserve against costs of claims payable by the company under the Revised Settlement Program (including a $5 million administrative assessment). Additional payments will be made as necessary. Payments to date have been consistent with the company's estimates of the total liability for claims under the Revised Settlement Program.

Under the Revised Settlement Program, additional opt outs are expected to be minimal since the opt-out deadline has passed for virtually all U.S. class members. The company's remaining obligations under the Revised Settlement Program are limited since (i) most payments to current claimants have already been made, (ii) no additional current claims may be filed without court approval, and (iii) late registrants are limited by the terms of the Revised Settlement Program.

The company's current best estimate of the amount to cover the cost and expense of the Revised Settlement Program and the cost and expense of resolving opt-out claims and recovering insurance proceeds (from inception of the litigation through December 31, 2000) is $1.2 billion. After subtracting cumulative payments of $1.168 billion as of December 31, 2000, for defense and other costs and settlements with litigants and claimants,

the company had remaining liabilities for the breast implant litigation of $32 million.

The company's insurers initiated a declaratory judgment action in Ramsey County Minnesota against the company seeking adjudication of certain coverage and allocation issues. The jury trial phase of this action finished on February 24, 2000. The jury returned a verdict favorable to the company by rejecting all of the insurers' remaining defenses to coverage for breast implant liabilities and costs. The court has considered additional remedies requested by the company and the insurers including eliminating, limiting or extending allocation among the insurers providing occurrence-based coverage (before 1986), pre- and post-judgment interest, attorneys' fees and further equitable relief.

The court's rulings in post-verdict motions are considered to be generally favorable to the company. The court awarded the company prejudgment interest on amounts owing by insurers including reasonable attorney fees. However, the court has yet to determine the amount of attorneys' fees recoverable by the company. The court has indicated a formula to be used for this calculation that would result in the company being reimbursed for less than all of its fees. Exact amounts cannot yet be determined. The company expects entry of judgment to occur during the first half of 2001.

As of December 31, 2000, the company had receivables for insurance recoveries of $519 million, representing settled but yet to be received amounts as well as amounts contested by the insurance carriers. During 2000, the company received payments from its occurrence carriers. Various factors could affect the timing and amount of proceeds to be received under the company's various insurance policies, including (i) the timing of payments made in settlement of claims; (ii) the outcome of occurrence insurance litigation in the courts of Minnesota (as discussed above) and Texas; (iii) potential arbitration with claims-made insurers' (iv) delays in payment by insurers' and (v) the extent to which insurers may become insolvent in the future. There can be no absolute assurance that the company will collect all amounts recorded as being probable of recovery from its insurers.

While the company currently believes that the ultimate outcome of these proceedings and claims, individually and in the aggregate, will not have a material adverse effect on the consolidated financial position, results of operations, or cash flows of the company, there can be no absolute certainty that the company may not ultimately incur charges for breast implant claims in excess of presently recorded liabilities.

While the company currently believes that a material adverse impact on its consolidated financial position, results of operations, or cash flows from any such future charges is remote, due to the inherent uncertainty of litigation, there exists the remote possibility that a future adverse ruling could result in future charges that could have a material adverse impact on the company. The current estimate of the potential impact on the company's financial position for breast implant litigation could change in the future.

CHAPTER 3

ASSESSMENT OF BUSINESS PERFORMANCE

When we wish to assess the performance of a business, we're looking for ways to measure the financial and economic consequences of past management decisions that shaped investments, operations, and financing over time. The important questions to be answered are whether all resources were used effectively, whether the profitability of the business met or even exceeded expectations, and whether financing choices were made prudently. Shareholder value creation ultimately requires positive results in all these areas—which will bring about favorable cash flow patterns exceeding the company's cost of capital.

As we'll see, there is a wide range of choices among many individual ratios and measures, some purely financial and some economic. No one ratio or measure can be considered predominant. In this chapter, we'll demonstrate primarily the analysis of business performance based on published financial statements. These represent the most common data source available for the purpose, even though they are not designed to reflect economic results and conditions. We'll also discuss the more important measures that help assess economic performance aspects. Our focus will be on key relationships and indicators that allow the analyst to assess past performance and also to project assumed future results (as discussed in Chapter 4). We'll point out their meaning as well as the limitations inherent in them. In the final chapters we'll discuss the larger context of valuing a company or its parts in economic terms, a process that is based on an intense assessment of performance drivers and strategic positioning, and that requires developing expected cash flow results for which past performance is only a starting point.

Ratio Analysis and Performance

Because there are so many tools for doing performance assessment, we must remember that different techniques address measurement in very specific and often narrowly defined ways. One may be tempted to "run all the numbers," particularly given the speed and ease of computer spreadsheets. Yet normally, only a few selected relationships will yield information the analyst or manager really needs for useful insights and decision support. By definition, a ratio can relate any magnitude to any other—the choices are limited only by the imagination. To be useful, both the meaning and the limitations of the ratio chosen have to be understood. Before beginning any task, therefore, the analyst must define the following elements:

- The viewpoint taken.
- The objectives of the analysis.
- The potential standards of comparison.

Any particular ratio or measure is useful only in relation to the applicable viewpoint and the specific objectives of the analysis. When there is such a match, the measure can become a standard for comparison. Moreover, ratios are not absolute criteria: They serve best when used in selected combinations to point out changes in financial conditions or operating performance over several periods and as compared to similar businesses. Ratios help illustrate the trends and patterns of such changes, which, in turn, might indicate to the analyst the risks and opportunities for the business under review.

A further caution: Performance assessment via financial statement analysis is based on past data and conditions from which it might be difficult to extrapolate future expectations. Yet, any decisions to be made as a result of such a performance assessment can affect only the future—the past is gone, or sunk, as an economist would call it.

No attempt to assess business performance can provide firm answers. Any insights gained will be relative, because business and operating conditions vary so much from company to company and industry to industry. Comparisons and standards based on past performance are especially difficult to interpret in large, multibusiness companies and conglomerates, where specific information by individual lines of business is normally limited. Accounting adjustments of various types present further complications. To deal with all these aspects in detail is far beyond the scope of this book, although we'll point out the key items. The reader should strive to become aware of these issues and always be cautious in using financial data for analysis and interpretation.

To provide a coherent structure for the many ratios and measures involved, the discussion will be built around three major viewpoints of financial performance analysis. Although there are many different individuals and groups interested in the success or failure of a given business, the most important are:

- Managers.
- Owners (investors).
- Lenders and creditors.

Closest to the business on a day-to-day basis, but also responsible for its long-range performance, is the management of the organization, whether its members are professional managers or owner/managers. Managers are responsible and accountable for operating efficiency, the effective deployment of capital, useful human effort, appropriate use of other resources, and current and long-term results—all within the context of sound business strategies.

Next are the various owners of the business, who are especially interested in the current and long-term returns on their equity investment. They usually expect growing earnings, cash flows, and dividends, which in combination will bring about growth in the economic value of their "stake." They are affected by the way a company's earnings are used and distributed, and by the relative value of their shares within the general movement of the security markets.

Finally, there are the providers of "other people's money," lenders and creditors who extend funds to the business for various lengths of time. They are mainly concerned about the company's liquidity and cash flows that affect its ability to make the interest payments due them and eventually to repay the principal. They'll also be concerned about the degree of financial leverage employed, and the availability of specific residual asset values that will give them a margin of protection against their risk.

Other groups such as employees, government, and society have, of course, specific objectives of their own—the business's ability to pay wages, the stability of employment, the reliability of tax payments, and the financial wherewithal to meet various social and environmental obligations. Financial performance indicators are useful to these groups in combination with a variety of other data.

The principal financial performance areas of interest to management, owners, and lenders are shown in Figure 3–1, along with the most common ratios and measures relevant to these areas. We'll follow the sequence shown in the figure and discuss each subgrouping within the three broad viewpoints. Later, we'll relate the key measures to each other in a systems context.

Management's Point of View

Management has a dual interest in the analysis of financial performance:

- To assess the efficiency and profitability of operations.
- To judge how effectively the resources of the business are being used.

Judging a company's operations is largely done with an analysis of the income statement, whereas resource effectiveness is usually measured by reviewing both the balance sheet and the income statement. In order to make economic

FIGURE 3–1

Performance Measures by Area and Viewpoint

Management	Owners	Lenders and Creditors
Operational Analysis	**Investment Return**	**Liquidity**
Gross margin	Return on total net worth	Current ratio
Profit margin	Return on common equity	Acid test
EBIT; EBITDA; NOPAT	Earnings per share	Quick sale value
Operating expense analysis	Cash flow per share	
Contribution analysis	Share price appreciation	
Operating leverage	Total shareholder return	
Comparative analysis		
Resource Management	**Disposition of Earnings**	**Financial Leverage**
Asset turnover	Dividends per share	Debt to assets
Working capital management	Dividend yield	Debt to capitalization
• Inventory turnover	Payout/retention of earnings	Debt to equity
• Accounts receivable patterns	Dividend coverage	
• Accounts payable patterns	Dividends to assets	
Human resource effectiveness		
Profitability	**Market Performance**	**Debt Service**
Return on assets (after taxes)	Price/earnings ratio	Interest coverage
Return before interest and taxes	Cash flow multiples	Burden coverage
Return on current value basis	Market to book value	Fixed charges coverage
EVA and economic profit	Relative price movements	Cash flow analysis
Cash flow return on investment	Value drivers	
Free cash flow	Value of the firm	

judgments, however, it's often necessary to modify the available financial data to reflect current economic values and conditions.

For purposes of illustration, we'll again use information from the sample statements of 3M for 2000 and 1999, which were reproduced in Chapters 1 and 2. They are shown here in Figures 3–2, 3–3, and 3–4. We'll use this information for the remainder of this chapter. For added convenience, we've also expressed the various items on the income statement as a percent of sales, a common way of highlighting the relative magnitude of the various categories in relation to the base of sales.

The reader will recall that Addendum 2–1 at the end of Chapter 2 (p. 90) contains 3M's "Notes to Consolidated Financial Statements," as published in the company's 2000 annual report. We already made use of some of the detail provided during our preparation of the cash flow statement in Chapter 2. The notes represent useful explanatory background for the company's key accounting policies,

FIGURE 3-2

MINNESOTA MINING AND MANUFACTURING COMPANY AND SUBSIDIARIES
Consolidated Balance Sheets
December 31, 1999 and 2000 ($ millions)

	2000	1999
Assets		
Current assets:		
Cash and cash equivalents	$ 302	$ 387
Accounts receivable—net	2,891	2,778
Inventories	2,312	2,030
Deferred income taxes	143	88
Other current assets	731	783
Total current assets	6,379	6,066
Investments	310	487
Property, plant, and equipment at cost	14,170	13,652
Less: Accumulated depreciation	8,347	7,876
Total property, plant and equipment—net	5,823	5,776
Intangible assets—net	852	537
Other assets	1,158	1,030
Total assets	$14,522	$13,896
Liabilities and Shareholders' Equity		
Current liabilities:		
Short-term debt	$ 1,220	$ 1,094
Accounts payable	1,081	1,008
Accrued compensation	382	361
Income taxes	462	464
Other current liabilities	963	856
Current portion of long-term debt	646	36
Total current liabilities	4,754	3,819
Long-term debt	971	1,480
Other liabilities:		
Nonfunded pension and postretirement benefits	754	761
Minority interest in subsidiaries	346	371
Deferred income taxes	362	332
Other	804	844
Total other liabilities	2,266	2,308
Shareholders' equity:		
Common stock, par value $.01 per share in 2000	5	236
Capital in excess of par value	291	60
Retained earnings	11,517	10,741
Treasury stock	(4,065)	(3,833)
Unearned compensation	(303)	(327)
Accumulated other comprehensive income (loss)	(914)	(588)
Shareholders' equity—net	6,531	6,289
Total liabilities and shareholders' equity	$14,522	$13,896

Source: Adapted from 2000 3M annual report.

FIGURE 3–3

MINNESOTA MINING AND MANUFACTURING COMPANY AND SUBSIDIARIES
Consolidated Statements of Income
For the Years December 31, 1999 and 2000 ($ millions)

	2000	Percent of Sales	1999	Percent of Sales
Net sales:				
Domestic sales	$ 7,858	47.0%	$ 7,559	48.0%
International sales	8,866	53.0%	8,189	52.0%
Total net sales	16,724	100.0%	15,748	100.0%
Cost of sales	8,787	52.5%	8,126	51.6%
Gross profit	7,937	47.5%	7,622	48.4%
Operating expenses:				
Selling, general and administrative	3,963	23.7%	3,712	23.6%
Research, development, and related expenses	1,101	6.6%	1,056	6.7%
Other expense (income)	(185)	−1.1%	(102)	−0.6%
Total operating expenses	4,879	29.2%	4,666	29.6%
Operating income	3,058	18.3%	2,956	18.8%
Other income and expense:				
Interest expense	111	0.7%	109	0.7%
Interest and other income	(27)	−0.2%	(33)	−0.2%
Total other income and expense	84	0.5%	76	0.5%
Income before income taxes, minority interest, extraordinary loss, and cumulative effect of accounting change	2,974	17.8%	2,880	18.3%
Provision for income taxes	1,025	6.1%	1,032	6.6%
Minority interest	92	0.6%	85	0.5%
Income before cumulative effect of accounting change	1,857	11.1%	1,763	11.2%
Cumulative effect of accounting change	(75)	−0.4%	—	—
Net income	$ 1,782	10.7%	$ 1,763	11.2%
Per share of common stock:				
Weighted average common shares outstanding (millions):				
Basic	395.7		402.0	
Diluted	399.9		406.5	
Earnings per share—basic:				
Income before cumulative effect of accounting change	$ 4.69		$ 4.39	
Cumulative effect of accounting change	(0.19)		—	
Basic net earnings per share	$ 4.50		$ 4.39	
Earnings per share—diluted:				
Income before cumulative effect of accounting change	$ 4.64		$ 4.34	
Cumulative effect of accounting change	(0.19)		—	
Diluted net earnings per share	$ 4.45		$ 4.34	
Dividends per share	2.32		2.24	
Book value per share (year-end)	16.49		15.77	
Other data ($ millions):				
Depreciation of property, plant, and equipment	$ 915		$822	
Amortization of software	45		39	
Amortization of patents, acquisition intangibles, and goodwill	65		39	
Capital expenditures (property, plant, and equipment)	1,115		1,050	
Dispositions (sales of property, plant, and equipment)	104		108	
Acquisitions of businesses	472		374	
Dispositions (sales of businesses)	1		249	
Dividends paid	918		901	

Source: Adapted from 2000 3M annual report.

FIGURE 3-4

MINNESOTA MINING AND MANUFACTURING COMPANY AND SUBSIDIARIES

Consolidated Statements of Changes in Shareholder Equity and Comprehensive Income
For the Years December 31, 1999 and 2000 ($ millions except per share amounts)

	Total	Common Stock and Capital in Excess of Par	Retained Earnings	Treasury Stock	Unearned Compensation ESOP	Accumulated Other Comprehensive Income (Loss)
Balance at December 31, 1998	$5,936	$ 296	$ 9,980	$(3,482)	$ (350)	$(508)
Net income	1,763		1,763			
Cumulative translation adjustment—net	(176)					(176)
Minimum pension liability adjustment—net of tax of $36 million	(30)					(30)
Debt and equity securities, unrealized gain—net of tax of $7 million	126					126
Total comprehensive income	1,683					
Dividends paid ($2.24 per share)	(901)		(901)			
Amortization of unearned compensation	23				23	
Reacquired stock (9.0 million shares)	(825)			(825)		
Issuances for stock option and benefit plans (5.7 million shares)	373		(101)	474		
Balance at December 31, 1999	$6,289	$ 296	$10,741	$(3,833)	$ (327)	$(588)
Net income	1,782		1,782			
Cumulative translation adjustment—net	(191)					(191)
Minimum pension liability adjustment—net of tax of $37 million	(28)					(28)
Debt and equity securities, unrealized loss—net of tax of $65 million	(107)					(107)
Total comprehensive income	1,456					
Dividends paid ($2.32 per share)	(918)		(918)			
Amortization of unearned compensation	24				24	
Reacquired stock (9.1 million shares)	(814)			(814)		
Issuances for stock option and benefit plans (6.3 million shares)	483		(88)	571		
Issuances for acquisitions (129 thousand shares)	11			11		
Balance at December 31, 2000	$6,531	$ 296	$11,517	$(4,065)	$ (303)	$(914)

Source: Adapted from 2000 3M annual report.

restructuring, acquisitions and divestitures, supplemental financial statement data, debt and financial instruments, income tax conditions, business segments, geographic areas, retirement and postretirement benefit plans, leases, employee savings, stock ownership, and stock purchase plans, stock-based compensation, quarterly data, and legal proceedings. Because many of these items can affect the development of the ratios in this chapter, the notes will help in understanding some of the choices an analyst must make in using financial statement information, and we'll use them selectively for illustration.

Operational Analysis

An initial assessment of the operational effectiveness for the business as a whole or any of its subdivisions is generally performed through a "common numbers" or percentage analysis of the income statement. Individual costs and expense items are normally related to sales, that is, gross sales revenues adjusted for any returns and allowances. The common base of sales permits a ready comparison of the key costs and expenses from period to period, over longer stretches of time, and against competitor and industry databases.

Expense to sales ratios are used both to judge the relative magnitude of selected key elements and to determine any trends toward improving or declining performance. However, we must always keep in mind the type of industry involved and its particular characteristics, as well as the individual trends and special conditions of the company being studied. For example, the gross margin of a jewelry store with slow turnover of merchandise and high markups will be far greater (75 percent is not uncommon) than that of a supermarket, which depends on low margins and high volume for its success (gross margins of 10 to 15 percent are typical). In fact, comparing a particular company's ratios to those of similar companies in its industry over a number of time periods will usually provide the best clues as to whether the company's performance is improving or declining.

Many published annual overviews of company and industry performance use ranking approaches, such as the annual Fortune 500 listings. Individual companies usually develop their own comparisons with the performance of comparable units within the organization or with relevant competitors on the outside. It's also often useful to graphically depict a series of performance data over time, a process now easily achieved with the ubiquitous availability of computer spreadsheets and online financial databases and services.

Gross Margin and Cost of Goods Sold Analysis

Two of the most common ratios in operational analysis are the calculation of cost of goods sold (cost of sales) and the gross margin as a percentage of sales. These ratios indicate the magnitude of the cost of goods purchased or manufactured, or the cost of services provided, in relation to sales, and the gross margin (gross profit) left over for operating expenses and profit.

The ratios calculated from our 3M sample statements appear as follows:

$$\text{Cost of goods sold ratio } \frac{\$8,787}{\$16,724} = 52.5\% \quad (1999: 51.6\%)$$

$$\text{Gross margin } \frac{\$7,937}{\$16,724} = 47.5\% \quad (1999: 48.4\%)$$

The cost of goods sold (52.5 percent) resulting in the gross margin (47.5 percent) reflect the margin of "raw profit" from operations. Remember that gross margin represents the relationship of prices, volume, and costs. A change in gross margin can result from a combination of changes in:

- The selling price of the product.
- The level of manufacturing costs for the product.
- Any variations in the product mix of the business.

In a trading or service organization, gross margin can be affected by a combination of changes in:

- The price charged for the products or services provided.
- The price paid for merchandise purchased on the outside.
- The cost of services from internal or external sources.
- Any variation in the product/service mix of the business.

The volume of operations also can have a significant effect if, for example, a manufacturing company has high fixed costs (see Chapter 5 for a discussion of operating leverage), or a small trading company has less buying power and economies of scale than a large competitor.

In the case of 3M, the cost of goods sold and the gross margin shown in the annual report represented a consolidation of the company's six major business segments and of its domestic and worldwide operations. In other words, the income statement combined the results of 3M's industrial segment, the transportation, graphics and safety segment, the health care segment, the consumer and office segment, the electro and communications segment, and the specialty material segment. We observe an overall gross margin decline of nine tenths of a percentage point from the prior year, which was largely caused by the slowing of the U.S. economy and uncertain economic conditions overseas. For a more detailed insight, we should calculate the specific gross margins for the individual business segments, if this information were publicly available.

3M did provide a selective breakdown, by major product line, of sales, operating profit, identifiable assets, depreciation and amortization, and capital expenditures, in its notes to financial statements, which allow the analyst to make some overall comparisons (see Note 12 in Addendum 2–1, p. 97, "Business Segments"). These data would have to be supplemented by additional internal information, however, to be able to perform a detailed ratio analysis—something that is routinely done within the company, of course.

There are particular complications in the analysis of manufacturing companies. The nature of manufacturing cost accounting systems governs the specific costing of products for inventory and for current sale. Significant differences can exist in the apparent cost performance of companies when using standard full-cost systems (all costs, fixed and variable, are allocated to each unit of production on the basis of an estimate of normal cost levels) as compared to using direct costing (fixed manufacturing costs are not allocated to individual products but charged as a block against operations). The charges against a particular period of operations can be affected to some degree by the choice of accounting methods. Increasingly, however, companies are turning to various forms of activity-based accounting for internal purposes, which provides a more precise basis for judging the real economic costs and contributions of products and services. Inflation, which affects the prices of both cost inputs and goods or services sold, or currency fluctuations, in the case of international businesses, further distort the picture. We'll take up some of these issues later.

Any major change in a company's cost of goods sold or gross margin over a relevant period of time would call for further analysis to identify the cause. The length of the time period chosen for such trend analysis depends on the nature of the business. For example, as we demonstrated in Chapter 2, many businesses have normal seasonal fluctuations, whereas others are affected by longer-term business cycles. Thus, this ratio serves as a signal rather than an absolute measure, as is the case with most of the measures discussed.

Profit Margin

The relationship of reported net profit after taxes (net income) to sales indicates management's ability to operate the business profitably. Success in this case means not only recovering the cost of the merchandise or services, the expenses of operating the business (including depreciation), and the cost of borrowed funds, but also leaving a margin of reasonable compensation to the owners for putting their capital at risk. The ratio of net profit (income) to sales (total revenue) essentially expresses the overall cost/price effectiveness of the operation. As we'll demonstrate later, however, a more significant ratio for this purpose is the relationship of profit to the amount of capital employed in generating it.

At this point, we should note that earnings can be affected significantly by mandated changes in accounting methods issued from time to time by FASB. There might be sizable adjustments, as occurred in the early 90s, when future employee medical benefits had to be recognized as a liability with an offsetting charge to earnings. For purposes of ratio analysis and for period-to-period comparisons, extraordinary adjustments should be excluded, along with any other extraordinary gains or losses a company might encounter in a particular period. In most cases, significant items of this kind are highlighted in the company's financial statements, allowing the analyst to choose whether to include them in the analysis. In the case of 3M, we find that net income in 2000 was lowered by an accounting change of $75 million. In Note 2 on page 92 the company explains that this represented a change in revenue recognition in line with SEC guidance, and that past periods were not materially affected. Under these conditions we saw no reason to exclude the item from our ratio analysis.

The calculation of the net profit (net earnings) ratio is simple, as the figures from our 3M example show:

$$\text{Profit margin} = \frac{\$1,782}{\$16,724} = 10.7\% \quad (1999: 11.2\%)$$

Note the decline of one-half of a percentage point from 1999, which the company largely ascribed to economic conditions.

A variation of this ratio uses net profit *before* interest and taxes. This figure represents the operating profit before any compensation is paid to debt holders. It's also the profit before the calculation of federal and state income taxes, which are often based on modified sets of deductible expenses and accounting write-offs. The ratio provides a purer view of operating effectiveness, undistorted by financing patterns and tax calculations. Referred to as earnings before interest and taxes (EBIT), this pretax, pre-interest income ratio for 3M appears as follows:

$$\text{EBIT margin} = \frac{\$1,782 + \$1,025 + \$84}{\$16,724} = \frac{\$2,891}{\$16,724} = 17.3\% \quad (1999: 18.2\%)$$

In developing this corporate total we have left intact the subtraction for minority interest ($92 million), and the effect of the accounting change discussed earlier ($75 million), by starting with net income and simply adding back income taxes and interest. Alternatively, one could consider operating income ($3,058 million) as equivalent to EBIT. The choice depends on the specific view desired: adjusted bottom-line net income or a purely operational analysis.

In line with the latter view, 3M reported sales and pretax operating income for each of its six major businesses, in Note 12 on page 97, from which we can calculate their respective operational EBIT figures. The industrial business (largest with 21 percent of 3M's sales) achieved EBIT of 18.2 percent (18.1 percent for 1999); transportation, graphics, and safety (also 21 percent of 3M's sales) had EBIT of 22.2 percent (20.9 percent for 1999); health care (19 percent of 3M's sales) had EBIT of 21.5 percent (21.7 percent for 1999); consumer and office (17 percent of 3M's sales) had EBIT of 15.2 percent (14.8 percent for 1999); electro and communications (15 percent of 3M's sales) had EBIT of 16.4 percent (19.9 percent in 1999); and specialty material (7 percent of 3M's sales) had EBIT of only 4.7 percent (sharply down from 15.5 percent in 1999).

Note 13 on page 98 provides a geographic breakdown of sales, operating income, and assets, on which a similar analysis can be performed. For example, the Asia Pacific region (20 percent of sales) had the highest EBIT of 28.9 percent when compared with the U.S. region (47 percent of sales), which had EBIT of 14.7 percent. Europe with 24 percent of sales had a similar EBIT of 14.9 percent, but the rest of the world with 9 percent of sales achieved the second highest EBIT of 24.0 percent. Such comparisons provide additional useful insights for performance analysis, which are more specific than dealing with overall results alone.

A ratio frequently used by security analysts is a modified EBIT, adjusted for depreciation and amortization. This is an attempt to show earnings unaffected by both taxes and the allocation of past expenditures in the form of depreciation and amortization. Called EBITDA, this income measure affects the ratio as follows, when we use the EBIT figure we just developed:

$$\text{EBITDA margin} = \frac{\$2{,}891 + \$915 + \$110}{\$16{,}724} = 23.4\% \quad (1999{:}\ 23.9\%)$$

A sound argument can be made, however, that income taxes should be considered an ongoing expense of being in business. The EBIT formula can therefore be modified by using profit *before* interest but *after* taxes (EBIAT), which requires an adjustment for the tax impact of the interest cost. Again, the intent is to focus on operational results by leaving out any compensation to the various holders of capital. For convenience in removing the tax effect of interest, we usually assume that the interest paid during the period was fully tax deductible. Thus, we simply add back to the net income figure, which has been reduced by both interest and taxes, the after-tax cost of interest. We obtain the latter by multiplying the stated pretax interest by a factor of "1 minus the tax rate," employing either the effective (average) tax rate paid on earnings (approximately 35.0 percent in 3M's case) or, ideally, the marginal (highest-bracket) corporate tax rate for the firm in question.

Using 3M's figures, we begin with net income and add back the tax effect of interest. The modified result appears as follows:

$$\text{EBIAT margin} = \frac{\$1{,}782 + (1 - 0.35)\,\$84}{\$16{,}724} = 11.0\% \quad (1999{:}\ 11.5\%)$$

The choice of tax rates depends on the complexity of the company's taxation pattern. 3M operates worldwide, and therefore is subject to a variety of taxes, which are combined in the provision for income taxes on the income statement. It's most straightforward to rely on this effective overall rate (provision for income taxes divided by income before taxes), which for 3M approximated the marginal U.S. corporate tax rate prevailing in 2000. Chapter 8 contains a specific discussion of the cost of debt and the nature of the necessary tax adjustments to be made to interest cost.

The EBIAT concept can be further refined in the form of NOPAT, the net operating profit after taxes, which excludes interest expense and income as well as any nonoperating income and expense items. The NOPAT measure has gained in importance with the shift toward shareholder value measures, which we'll discuss in more detail in Chapter 11. As an expression of the after-tax earnings power of the operations of the business, NOPAT becomes an input to such measures as economic value added. In 3M's case, the calculation from its published income statement is similar to the EBIAT approach we just demonstrated. In order to emphasize operations, we'll start with income before taxes ($2,974 million), subtract the provision for income taxes, and add back the tax-adjusted interest:

$$\text{NOPAT margin} = \frac{\$2,974 - \$1,025 + (1 - 0.35)\,\$84}{\$16,724} = 11.9\% \text{ (1999: 12.0\%)}$$

This approach leaves out minority interest and the accounting change, which could be viewed as the only nonoperating elements in 3M's statements. This is a choice for the analyst to decide. As a general rule, when there are unusual or nonrecurring income and expense elements not directly related to ongoing operations, the analyst should adjust the ratios by excluding these items when measuring operating effectiveness. The adjustment should be done on the same basis as we demonstrated for interest—that is, the tax effect of revenue or expense items must be calculated and recognized if after-tax comparisons are desired.

Operating Expense Analysis

Various expense categories are routinely related to sales. These comparisons include such items as administrative expenses, selling and promotional expenses, and many others typical of particular businesses and industries.

The general formula used to calculate this expense ratio is:

$$\text{Expense ratio} = \frac{\text{Various expense items}}{\text{Sales}} = \text{Percent}$$

There are relatively few expense categories shown in 3M's abbreviated income statement, but the ratio to sales was calculated for each item shown in the income statement (Figure 3–3). In practice, a much finer breakdown would be desirable, something that is internally available as a matter of course. Most trade associations collect extensive financial data—many of them company confidential—from their members and compile published summary statistics on expense ratios, as well as on most of the other ratios discussed in this chapter. These publications help provide broad standards of comparison and can serve as a basis for trend analysis. As in any statistical references, however, care must be taken to select reasonably comparable groupings of companies and businesses to obtain meaningful insights.

In such statistics, businesses should be carefully categorized within an industry by size and other characteristics to reduce the degree of error introduced by large-scale averaging. Moreover, companies with complex product or service offerings, or companies with many international operations, might be hard to categorize. 3M serves as an example of this type of company. Yet even without specific comparative data available, a skilled analyst will scan the revenue and expense categories on an income statement as a matter of course over a number of time periods to see if any of them seem out of line or are trending adversely within the particular company's experience.

Contribution Analysis

This type of analysis has been used mainly for internal management, although it is increasingly applied in broader financial analysis. It involves relating sales to the contribution margin of individual product groups or of the total business. Such calculations require a very selective analysis or estimate of the fixed and variable costs and expenses of the business, and take into account the effect of *operating leverage* (see Chapter 5). Usually only directly variable costs are subtracted from sales to show the contribution of operations toward fixed costs and profits for the period.

The contribution margin is calculated as follows:

$$\text{Contribution margin} = \frac{\text{Sales} - \text{Direct costs (variable costs)}}{\text{Sales}} = \text{Percent}$$

Significant differences can exist in the contribution margins of different industries, because of varying needs for capital investment and the resultant cost-volume conditions. Even within a particular company, various lines of products or services might contribute quite differently to fixed costs and profits. Note that the measure is sensitive to three key drivers—volume, price and direct costs—which are traded off in the process of managing the operations of the business. Understanding changes in contribution therefore depends on understanding the changes in the drivers underlying this result, as we pointed out in our discussion of the business system in Chapter 1.

Contribution margins as derived from financial statements are useful as a broad, if limited, tool in judging the risk characteristics of a business. The measure suggests the amount of leeway management enjoys in pricing its products and services, and the scope of its ability to control costs and expenses under different economic conditions. Analysis of operating leverage and pricing strategies as related to volume becomes important in this context. Chapter 5 contains a more extensive discussion of these points.

As mentioned before, a great deal of effort has been expended in recent years on so-called activity-based accounting analysis. This approach can be used for an assessment of the relative economic contribution of various parts of a company, thereby going beyond the limitations of existing cost accounting systems. During this process, all phases of an activity are first carefully defined in terms of physical relationships and process steps. Then a specific financial/economic allocation is made of all resources and cost elements, direct or indirect, internal or external, which support the activity, product line, operation, or line of business. The result serves as the basis for periodic strategic assessment of the current and prospective relative economic contribution of the area under study. The insights gained often differ from a straight accounting analysis, because the activity-based process is much more precise in defining and allocating relative effort, cost, and support capital required. The techniques involved go beyond the scope of this book; for more information see the references at the end of the chapter.

Resource Management

Here we are interested in judging the effectiveness with which management has employed the assets entrusted to it by the owners of the business. When examining a balance sheet, an analyst can draw company-specific conclusions about the size, nature, and value of the assets listed, look at relative proportions, and judge whether the company has a viable asset base. Clues such as high accumulated depreciation relative to recorded property, plant, and equipment may suggest that aging facilities are in need of upgrading. Similarly, a significant jump in cash balances might suggest lagging new investments and an accumulation of excess funds. Surges in working capital items like inventories and receivables might signal problems with inventory management or customer credit policies. As pointed out in Chapter 2, the cash flow statement provides useful insights into the variations in resource commitments that are derived from balance sheet changes.

In a more overall sense, a few ratios are used to judge broad trends in resource utilization. Such ratios essentially involve turnover relationships and express, in various forms, the relative amount of capital used to support the volume of business transacted.

Asset Turnover

The most commonly used ratios relate sales to gross assets, or sales to net assets. The measure indicates the size of the recorded asset commitment required to support a particular level of sales or, conversely, the sales dollars generated by each dollar of assets.

Although simple to calculate, overall asset turnover is a crude measure at best, because the balance sheets of most well-established companies list a whole variety of assets recorded at widely differing cost levels of past periods. These stated values often have little relation to current economic values, and the distortions grow with time, with any significant change in the level of inflation, or with the appreciation of assets such as real estate. Such discrepancies in values can attract corporate raiders intent on realizing true economic values through the breakup and selective disposal of the company, as we'll discuss in Chapter 11.

Another distortion is caused by a company's mix of product or service lines. Most manufacturing activities tend to be asset-intensive, whereas others, like services or wholesaling, need a relatively low asset base to support the volume of revenues generated. Again, wherever possible, a breakdown of total financial data into major product or service lines should be attempted when a company has widely different businesses.

Basically, the turnover ratio serves as one of several clues that, in combination, can indicate favorable or unfavorable performance. If total assets are used for the purpose of averaging the beginning and ending amounts for the year, the calculation for 3M's turnover ratios appears as follows:

Sales to assets:

$$\frac{\text{Sales}}{\text{Average total assets}} = \frac{\$16,724}{0.5\,(\$14,522 + \$13,896)} = 1.18 \text{ times (1999: 1.07 times)}$$

or

Assets to sales:

reciprocal= .85 for every $ of Sales we need b $85 assets

$$\frac{\text{Average total assets}}{\text{Sales}} = \frac{\$14,209}{\$16,724} = 85.0\ \% \ (1999:\ 89.1\%)$$

If net assets (total assets less current liabilities, representing the capitalization of the business) are used, the calculations are either:
Sales to net assets:

$$\frac{\text{Sales}}{\text{Average net assets}} = \frac{\$16,724}{\$0.5\,(\$9,768 + \$10,077)} = 1.68 \text{ times (1999: 1.59 times)}$$

or

Net assets to sales:

$$\frac{\text{Average net assets}}{\text{Sales}} = \frac{\$9,922}{\$16,724} = 59.3\ \% \ (1999:\ 63.0\%)$$

The difference between the two sets of calculations lies in the choice of the asset figure, that is, whether to use total assets or net assets. Using net assets eliminates current liabilities from the ratio. Here the assumption is that current liabilities, which are mostly operational in nature (accounts payable, current taxes due, current repayments of short-term debt, and accrued wages and other obligations), are available to the business as a matter of course. Therefore, the amount of assets employed in the business is effectively reduced by these ongoing operational credit relationships. This concept is especially important for trading firms, where the size of accounts payable owed suppliers is quite significant in the total balance sheet.

Again 3M provided the necessary information in Note 12, page 97, to allow calculation of the turnover of identifiable assets in its six major businesses. The respective results and changes varied: In the industrial segment turnover was 1.47 times (1.45 in 1999), in the transportation segment 1.28 times (1.21 in 1999), in the health care segment 1.55 times (1.51 in 1999), in the consumer and office segment 1.66 times (1.7 in 1999), in the electro and communications segment 1.26 times (1.48 in 1999), and in the specialty material segment 0.97 times (0.90 in 1999).

Working Capital Management

Among the assets of a company, the key working capital accounts, inventories and accounts receivable, are usually given special attention. The ratios used to analyze them attempt to express the relative effectiveness with which inventories and receivables are managed. They aid the analyst in detecting signs of deterioration in value, or excessive accumulation of inventories and receivables. The amounts as stated on the balance sheet are generally related to the single best indicator of activity levels, such as sales or cost of sales (cost of goods sold), on the assumption that a reasonably close relationship exists between the asset and the indicator.

Inventory levels cannot be judged precisely, short of an actual count, verification, and appraisal of current value. Because an outside analyst can rarely do this, the next best step is to relate the recorded inventory value to sales or to cost of goods sold, to see whether there is a shift in this relationship over time. Normally, *average* inventories are used to make this calculation (the average of beginning and ending inventories). At times, it might be desirable to use only ending inventories, especially in the case of rapidly growing firms where inventories are being built up to support steeply rising sales.

Furthermore, it's necessary to closely observe the method of inventory costing employed by the company—such as last-in, first-out (LIFO), first-in, first-out (FIFO), average costing—and any changes made during the time span covered by the analysis, because these can significantly affect the amounts recorded on the balance sheet. (We'll discuss inventory costing and other key accounting issues later.)

Although the simple relationship of sales and inventories will often suffice as a broad measure of performance, it's usually more precise to relate inventories to the cost of sales. Only then will both elements of the ratio be stated on a comparable cost basis. Using sales causes a distortion, because recorded sales include a profit markup that is not included in the stated cost of the inventories on the balance sheet.

The difference in the two methods of calculating the size of inventory relative to sales or cost of sales is reflected in the equations below:

Inventory to sales:

$$\frac{\text{Average inventory}}{\text{Sales}} = \frac{0.5\,(\$2,312 + \$2,030)}{\$16,724} = 13.0\% \ (1999:\ 13.5\%)$$

or
Inventory to cost of sales:

$$\text{Average inventory} = \frac{\$2,172}{\$8,787} = 24.7\% \ (1999:\ 26.1\%)$$

In the sample calculations, we've used total 3M sales and total cost of goods and services. The fact that 3M has six major businesses and numerous product lines within each again suggests that a more refined analysis is desirable. Given the different nature of these businesses, it would be useful to develop separate ratios for each, if detailed inventory information were available to the outsider.

When dealing with any manufacturing company, we also must be particularly aware of the problem of accounting measurements—so often encountered when using other analytical methods—because the stated value of inventories can be seriously affected by the specific cost accounting system employed.

In assessing the effectiveness of a company's inventory management, it's more common to use the number of times inventory has turned over during the period of analysis, again using average amounts.

The 3M inventory turnover figures appear as follows:

Inventory turnover (sales basis):

$$\frac{Sales}{Average\ inventory} = \frac{\$16,724}{\$2,172} = 7.7\ times\ (1999:\ 7.4\ times)$$

or
Inventory turnover (cost of sales basis):

$$\frac{Cost\ of\ sales}{Average\ inventory} = \frac{\$8,787}{\$2,172} = 4.0\ times\ (1999:\ 3.8\ times)$$

These calculations reflect the frequency with which the inventory was turned over during the operating period. In 3M's case, turnover improved somewhat because of a combination of inventory management and some changes in the mix of products. Generally speaking, the higher the turnover number the better, because low inventories often suggest a minimal risk of nonsalable goods and indicate efficient use of capital. Electronic linkages and just-in-time deliveries have materially improved turnover in recent years.

However, inventory turnover figures that are well above prevailing industry practice might signal the potential for inventory shortages, resultant poor customer service, and thus the risk of suffering a competitive disadvantage. The final judgment about what a desirable turnover goal should be depends on the specific circumstances and the business model employed, industry practices, and a much finer breakdown of inventory data into separate businesses and product lines.

The analysis of *accounts receivable* again is based on sales. Here, the question is whether accounts receivable that are outstanding at the end of the period closely approximate the amount of credit sales we would expect to remain uncollected under prevailing credit terms. For example, a business selling under terms of net/30 would normally expect an accounts receivable balance approximating the recorded sales of the prior month. If 40 or 50 days' sales were reflected on its balance sheet, this could mean that some customers had difficulty paying or were abusing their credit privileges, or that some sales had to be made on extended terms.

An exact analysis of accounts receivable can only be made by examining the *aging* of the individual accounts recorded on the company's books. Aging involves classifying accounts receivable into brackets of days outstanding, 10 days, 20 days, 30 days, 40 days, and so on, and relating this pattern to the credit terms applicable in the business. Because this type of analysis requires access to detailed inside information about individual customer accounts, financial analysts assessing the business from the outside must be satisfied with the relatively crude overall approach of restating accounts receivable outstanding in terms of the number of days' sales they represent.

This is done in the following two steps, using 3M's figures:

1.   Sales per day:

$$\frac{Sales}{Days\ of\ the\ year} = \frac{\$16,724}{360} = \$46.4/day\ (1999:\ \$43.7/day)$$

and

2.   Days outstanding:

$$\frac{\text{Accounts receivable}}{\text{Sales per day}} = \frac{\$2,891}{\$46.4} = 62.3 \text{ days (1999: 64.5 days)}$$

3M is showing an improvement in the turnover of its total receivables from the prior year. A complication arises when a company's sales are normally made to different types of customers under varying terms, or when sales are made partly for cash and partly on account. If at all possible, cash and credit sales should be separated. If no detailed information is available on this aspect and on the terms of sale used, the rough average calculated above must suffice to provide a broad indication of trends.

A similar process can be used to judge a company's performance regarding the management of *accounts payable*. The analysis is a little more complicated, because accounts payable should be related specifically to the purchases made during the operating period. Normally purchasing information is not readily available to the outside analyst, except in the case of trading companies, where the amount of purchases can be readily deduced by adding the change from beginning to ending inventories to the cost of goods sold for the period. In a manufacturing company, purchases of goods and services are buried in the cost-of-goods-sold account and in the various inventories at the end of the operating period. We can make a crude approximation in such cases by relating accounts payable to the average daily use of raw materials, if this expense element can be identified from the available information.

In most cases, we can follow the approach used for analyzing accounts receivable, if it's possible to approximate the average daily purchases for the period. The number of days of accounts payable is then directly related to the normal credit terms under which the company makes purchases, and serious deviations from that norm can be spotted.

Optimal management of accounts payable involves remitting payment within the stated terms, but no sooner—yet taking discounts whenever offered for early payment, such as 2 percent if paid in 10 days versus remitting the full amount due in 30 days. Credit rating agencies can be a source of information to the analyst because they will express an opinion on the timeliness with which a company is meeting its credit obligations, including accounts payable.

The ultimate issue in interpreting working capital conditions is the flow of cash through the business, as we discussed in detail in Chapter 2. Over time, all working capital elements are converted into cash, and the analyst must assess the nature and quality of the company's cash conversion cycle. Excessive lags in receivables and payables, and a steady buildup in inventories, for example, can significantly affect the normal cash conversion patterns and lead to distortions in the company's financial system performance.

Human resource effectiveness has been gaining increased attention in recent years. Ratios used in measuring this complex area often go beyond purely financial relationships, and are based on carefully developed statistics on output data, such as various productivity indicators, call volume for sales personnel, deliveries completed, and so forth. They also extend to managing human resources, such as costs of employment, training, and development, and the complex issue of compensation and benefits administration. Examples of broad measures, per employee, are units of output, dollars of investment, costs of hiring and training, benefits costs, and so on. In 3M's case, the company published overall employee totals of 75,026 at the end of 2000 (70,549 in 1999); from this we can calculate sales per average employee at $222,910 ($223,220 in 1999); operating income per employee at $40,759 ($41,900 in 1999); and year-end assets per employee at $193,560 ($196,969 in 1999).

Profitability

Here the issue is the effectiveness with which management has employed both the total assets and the net assets as recorded on the balance sheet. This is judged by relating net profit, defined in a variety of ways, to the resources utilized in generating the profit, for the company as a whole or for any of its parts. The relationship is used quite commonly, although the nature and timing of the stated values on the balance sheet and the accounting aspects of recorded profit will again tend to distort the results. As we'll see later, the approach can be refined to reflect the cash flow concepts underlying shareholder value creation.

Return on Assets (ROA or RONA)

The easiest form of profitability analysis is to relate reported net profit (net income) to the total assets on the balance sheet. Net assets (total assets less current liabilities) might also be used, with the argument (already mentioned earlier) that current operating liabilities are available essentially without cost to support a portion of the current assets. Net assets are also called the *capitalization* of the company, or *invested capital*, representing the portion of the total assets supported by equity and long-term debt. Whether total or net assets are employed, it's also appropriate to use *average* assets for the period, instead of ending balances. Using average assets allows for changes due to growth, decline, or other significant influences on the business.

The calculations for both forms of return on assets for 3M, in this case using ending balances, appear as follows:

Return on total assets:

$$\frac{\text{Net profit}}{\text{Assets}} = \frac{\$1,782}{\$14,522} = 12.3\% \ (1999: 12.7\%)$$

or

Return on net assets:

$$\frac{\text{Net profit}}{\text{Net assets (capitalization)}} = \frac{\$1,782}{\$14,522 - \$4,754} = 18.2\% \ (1999: 17.5\%)$$

Although either ratio is a broad indicator of overall profitability, the results can be seriously distorted by nonrecurring gains and losses during the period, changes in the company's capital structure (the relative proportions of interest-bearing long-term debt and owners' equity), significant restructuring and acquisitions, and changes in the federal income tax regulations applicable for the period analyzed. It's usually desirable to make further adjustments if some of these conditions prevail.

Return on Assets before Interest and Taxes

As we stated before, net profit (net income, or net earnings) is the final operating result after interest and income taxes. It's therefore directly affected by the proportion of debt contained in the capital structure, because of the resultant interest charges that were deducted from profit before taxes. A more meaningful result can be obtained when we eliminate both interest and taxes from the profit figure and use EBIT (earnings before interest and taxes), which was demonstrated earlier. Moreover, it will again be useful to eliminate any significant unusual or nonrecurring income and expense items. The revised return ratio expresses the gross earnings power of the capital employed in the business, independent of the pattern of financing that provided the capital, and independent of changes in the tax laws.

The calculation of return on assets before interest and taxes, based on average assets, is as follows for 3M:

Return on average total assets before interest and taxes:

$$\frac{\text{Net profit before interest and taxes(EBIT)}}{\text{Average assets}} = \frac{\$2,891}{\$14,209} = 20.3\% \ (1999: 20.5\%)$$

or

Return on average net assets before interest and taxes:

$$\frac{\text{Net profit before interest and taxes (EBIT)}}{\text{Average net assets (capitalization)}} = \frac{\$2,891}{\$9,922} = 29.1\% \ (1999: 28.9\%)$$

If we accept the argument that income taxes are a normal part of doing business, this result can be modified by using net profit before interest but after taxes. We can again employ the simple adjustment shown earlier to add back to net profit the after-tax cost of interest and the after-tax effect of any nonrecurring income and expense items.

When there is reason to believe that income taxes paid were modified for any reason and the effective tax rate does not reflect normal conditions, the marginal income tax rate should be used to calculate the net effect of interest and other items added back by determining the earnings before interest, after taxes (EBIAT), which were developed earlier.

The calculations for 3M are as follows:

Return on average total assets before interest, after taxes:

$$\frac{\text{Net profit after taxes, before interest}}{\text{Average assets}} = \frac{\$1,837}{\$14,209} = 12.9\% \ (1999: 12.9\%)$$

or

Return on average net assets before interest, after taxes:

$$\frac{\text{Net profit after taxes, before interest}}{\text{Average net assets (capitalization)}} = \frac{\$1,837}{\$9,922} = 18.5\% \ (1999: 18.3\%)$$

Note that the results of the last two sets of more refined calculations show relatively little change in 3M's overall effectiveness of asset utilization, whereas the first calculation, which was based on net profit alone, yielded slightly contradictory results. A key reason is the use of ending balances in the first calculation, which is affected by a temporary shift in current liabilities because of the scheduled repayment of long-term debt in 2000. This is an example of the need to carefully examine whether the basis of calculations is truly meaningful under the circumstances. Again, it would also be useful to break down these results into major product lines, but in most cases there's not enough information to make all the adjustments from published data.

Another refinement used at times is the relationship of profit, defined in the various ways we have described, to the net assets of the business restated on a *current value* basis. This requires a series of very specific assumptions about the true economic value of various assets or business segments of a company, and it is employed particularly by analysts developing a case for the takeover of a company that might be underperforming on this basis. The Financial Accounting Standards Board (FASB) is engaged in developing new rules that are designed to take some changes in value into account, which are already being applied to certain financial investments held by banks and other financial institutions.

A relatively recent measure of profitability that is finding wide use is the concept of *economic profit,* or *economic value added* (EVA). It is based on the premise that to create shareholder value, the profits earned on the resources employed must exceed the cost of the capital that supports these resources. In its simplest form, economic profit is derived by subtracting from after-tax operating profits a capital charge that represents this cost of capital. To arrive at the capital charge, it's necessary first to define the asset base involved, which usually is net assets (with some adjustments to arrive at net operating assets), and second, to derive the weighted cost of capital of the company's capital structure (discussed in detail in Chapter 8). Then the asset base is multiplied by the cost of capital percentage, and the result is subtracted from after-tax operating profits. If the net amount is positive, value has been created; if it's negative, value has been destroyed. We'll explore this concept in more detail in Chapter 11.

As we'll discuss in Chapters 6 and 7, profitability also depends on the economic analysis and successful implementation of new investment projects. Here it's critical to define and develop the relevant cash flow changes brought about by the investment decision, and to judge the results through an economic appraisal process based on discounted cash flow techniques. In recent years, this methodology has been expanded to measure the *cash flow return on investment* on both existing and new investments, in effect treating the company as a whole or its major parts as if they were a series of investment projects. This calls for a number of specialized techniques, and we will return to this subject when we discuss valuation concepts in Chapters 10 and 11.

The concept of *free cash flow* also will be discussed in Chapter 11. It's the basis for cash flow valuation techniques that help establish the value of a company or its parts. In its simplest form, free cash flow is the net amount of (1) reported profit, adjusted for depreciation, depletion, and other noncash accounting elements; less (2) net new investment in facilities and net acquisitions; and plus or minus (3) changes in working capital. Free cash flow comes closest to a cash-in, cash-out concept of performance, and is used in valuing current and prospective cash flow as the driver of a company's value.

In summary, the various ratios available for judging a business from management's point of view deal with the effectiveness of operations, the effectiveness of capital deployment, and the profitability achieved on the assets deployed. These measures are all affected to some degree by uncertainties involving accounting and valuation methods, but together they can provide reasonable clues to a firm's performance, and suggest areas for further analysis.

Owners' Point of View

We now turn to the second of the three viewpoints relevant in analyzing performance, that of the owners of a business. These are the investors to whom management is responsible and accountable. It should be quite clear that the management of a business must be fully cognizant of, and responsive to, the owners' viewpoint and their expectations in the timing, execution, and appraisal of the results of operations. This is the basis for shareholder value creation, as we've said before. Similarly, as we'll learn, management must be alert to the lender's viewpoint and criteria.

The key interest of the owners of a business—the shareholders in the case of a corporation—is investment return. In this context, we are talking about the returns achieved, through the efforts of management, on the funds invested by the owners. The owners are also interested in the disposition of earnings that belong to them; that is, how much is reinvested in the business compared to how much is paid out to them as dividends, or, in some cases, through repurchase of outstanding shares. Finally, they are concerned about the effect of business results achieved—and future expectations about results—on the market value of their investment, especially in the case of publicly traded stock. The key concepts related to this last aspect are discussed in detail in Chapters 9 and 10; therefore we'll make only brief reference to them here.

Investment Return

The relationship of profits earned to the shareholders' stated investment in a company is watched closely by the financial community. Analysts track several key measures that express the company's performance in relation to the owners' stake. Two of these, return on shareholders' equity and return on common equity, address the profitability of the total ownership investment, whereas the third, earnings per share, measures the proportional participation of each unit of investment in corporate earnings for the period.

Return on Equity (Shareholders' equity)

The most common ratio used for measuring the return on the owners' investment is the relationship of net profit to equity, or total shareholders' equity. In performing this calculation, we don't have to make any adjustment for interest, because the net profit available for shareholders already has been properly reduced by interest charges, if any, paid to creditors and lenders. However, we do have to consider the impact of nonrecurring and unusual events, such as restructuring and major accounting changes and adjustments.

Net profit for purposes of this calculation is the residual result of operations and belongs totally to the holders of common and preferred equity shares. Within the shareholder group, only those holding common shares have a claim on the residual profit after obligatory preferred dividends have been paid.

The ratio is calculated for 3M's shareholders' equity as follows:

Return on equity:

$$\frac{\text{Net profit}}{\text{Shareholders' equity}} = \frac{\$1,782}{\$6,531} = 27.3 \text{ \% (1999: 28.0\%)}$$

Here we have used 3M's ending shareholders' equity. It's quite common, however, to use the average equity for this calculation, on the assumption that profitable operations build up equity during the year, and that therefore the annual profit should be related to the midpoint of this buildup. Moreover, as Figure 3–4 indicates, significant changes in shareholder's equity were brought about in 2000 and 1999 by stock repurchases, reissuances of treasury shares, currency effects and other adjustments.

The revised ratio for 3M is calculated as follows:

Return on average equity:

$$\frac{\text{Net profit}}{\text{Average shareholders' equity}} = \frac{\$1,782}{\$0.5\,(\$6,531\,+\,6,289)} = 27.8\% \text{ (1999: 28.8\%)}$$

There is an issue that involves so-called other liabilities, which are generally shown after interest-bearing long-term debt on the liability side of the balance sheet. Among these are significant amounts that represent the results of changes in accounting rules designed to establish estimated liabilities—and corresponding reductions in equity—for such obligations as postretirement benefits, previously paid as incurred ($754 million and $761 million in the case of 3M). Such liabilities are non-interest-bearing estimates, and in effect, represent permanent setasides of portions of the shareholder's investment.

Some analysts argue that such liabilities should be treated as equity, whereas others argue that they represent a form of long-term debt. Because there is no consensus on the analytical treatment, significant benefits obligations, deferred income taxes, and other liabilities are often not included in any of the ratio calculations. However, because their combined accumulation on the liability side of the balance sheet might be quite large, material differences can result depending on how they are considered in the calculations. Again, the analyst has to use judgment about the context in which the analysis is performed and decide accordingly.

Return on Common (Shareholders') Equity (ROE)

A somewhat more refined version of the calculation of return on the shareholders' equity is necessary if there are several types of stock outstanding, such as preferred stock in different forms. The goal is to develop a return based on earnings accruing to the holders of common shares only. The net profit figure is first reduced by dividends paid to the holders of any preferred shares and by other obligatory payments, such as distributions to minority interests. The total equity is likewise reduced by the stated amount of any preferred equity and minority elements, to arrive at the residual common equity figure. 3M in has only common stock outstanding, and therefore we'll show only the formula for the calculation, because the results will be the same as developed earlier:

Return on common equity:

$$\frac{\text{Net profit to common equity}}{\text{Average common equity}} = \text{Percent}$$

Return on common equity is a widely published statistic. Rankings of companies and industry sectors are compiled by major business magazines and rating agencies. The ratio is closely watched by stock market analysts and, in turn, by management and the board of directors. Because the ratio focuses only on the ownership portion of the capital structure, however, the ROEs of companies with widely different proportions of long-term debt in their capital structure are not directly comparable. As we observed before, successful use of leverage will boost the owners' return and make it higher than that of an otherwise identical company that uses no debt. Moreover, the accuracy of recorded balance sheet values and earnings calculations is an issue in this ratio as well, and adjustments might be necessary if the analyst is aware of major inconsistencies. Such inconsistencies could include assets with sizable economic values, such as well-known brands, proprietary technologies, and unique processes that are not reflected on the balance sheet and thereby leave owners' equity understated.

Finally, there is the basic issue of using book value versus market value. Because recorded common equity is the residual value of all accounting transactions and adjustments, the value shown on the balance sheet is generally quite different from the market value of the shares representing it. In publicly traded companies with successful operations and outlook, the market value of common shares will be much higher than the book value of these shares, often two to three times or even more. In the case of 3M, the book value per share was $16.49 at the end of 2000, whereas the market price at that point was $120.50 per share ($15.77 and $97.86, respectively, in 1999). When return on common equity is calculated on a market value basis, the result will therefore be proportionally lower. Consequently, despite the widespread use of return on equity on a book value basis, the measure is certainly not a reflection of the economic return to the shareholder. We'll discuss these issues in more detail when we return to valuation and value-based management in Chapter 11.

Earnings per Share

The analysis of earnings from the owners' point of view usually centers on earnings per share in the case of a corporation. This ratio simply involves dividing the net profit to common equity by the average number of shares of common stock outstanding:

Earnings per share:

$$\frac{\text{Net profit to common equity}}{\text{Average number of shares outstanding}} = \text{Dollars per share}$$

Earnings per share is a measure to which both management and shareholders pay a great deal of attention. It is widely used in the valuation of common stock, and often is the basis for setting specific corporate objectives and goals as part of strategic planning. Earnings per share are announced regularly on both an annual and a quarterly basis and are a matter of record for any company whose shares are publicly traded.

A recent requirement by the Financial Accounting Standards Board and the Securities and Exchange Commission calls for the calculation of earnings per share on two bases: The first is the so-called *basic* earnings per share, which uses average shares actually outstanding during the period. The second basis recognizes all shares to be potentially issued and counts these in additional to the actual shares outstanding. Such potential shares include those resulting from the exercise of stock options, conversion of preferred and debt securities that are convertible into common shares under various provisions, as well as exercise of rights and warrants. In 3M's 2000 annual report, basic earnings per share were reported as $4.50 for 2000, and $4.39 for 1999 (see Figure 3–3).

The second result is referred to as *diluted* earnings per share, and reflects the reduced earnings per share that would result from any overhang of such potential shares—putting the investment community on notice that such a dilutive effect is possible. In 3M's case, there is no significant potential dilution, and diluted earnings per share within five cents of basic earnings in both years ($4.45 and $4.34, respectively), as can be seen in Figure 3–3.

Even though the earnings per share figure is one of the most readily available statistics reported by publicly held corporations, there are some complications in its calculation. Apart from possible unusual elements in the quarterly and annual net profit pattern, the number of shares outstanding varies during the year in many companies, either because of newly issued shares (new stock offerings, stock dividends paid, options exercised, and so on), or because outstanding existing shares are repurchased (acquired as treasury stock). Therefore, the *average* number of shares outstanding during the year is commonly used in this calculation. Moreover, any significant change in the number of shares outstanding (such as would be caused by a stock split) requires retroactive adjustments in past data to ensure comparability.

A great deal of interest among analysts is focused on past earnings per share, both quarterly and annual. Future projections are frequently made on the basis of past earnings levels. Fluctuations and trends in actual performance are compared to the projections and watched closely for indications of strength or weakness. Again, great caution is advised in interpreting these data. Allowances must be made for unusual elements both in the earnings figure and in the number of common shares outstanding.

It is important to emphasize here that the rise of shareholder value concepts during the past decade has been causing a reassessment of the importance of earnings per share which, as a pure accounting measure, does not adequately reflect cash flow performance and expectations that drive shareholder value creation. Chapters 9, 10, and 11 contain more background on the uses and limitations of this measure. The importance of earnings per share for performance analysis and valuation is waning, and the concept is increasingly supplanted by cash flow–based measures, which will be discussed in more detail in Chapter 11.

Cash Flow per Share

Representing a calculation to approximate the cash flow per share from operating results this figure is frequently used as a very rough indicator of the company's ability to pay cash dividends. It's developed from the net profit figure to which accounting write-offs such as depreciation, amortization, and depletion have been added back. We recall from our earlier discussion of the cash flow statement that such write-offs do not represent cash movements. Adding back these accounting entries restates the net profit in a form that partially reflects the cash generated by operations, but leaves out many other significant funds movements, such as changes in working capital, investments in new assets, and so on.

The calculation parallels the earnings per share ratio:

Cash flow per share:

$$\frac{\text{Net profit to common equity plus write–offs}}{\text{Average number of shares outstanding}} = \text{Dollars per share}$$

In the case of 3M, we know that depreciation and amortization amounted to $915 million and $110 million, respectively, for a total of $1,025 million. The average number of shares outstanding was given in the annual report as 395.7 million for purposes of calculating basic earnings per share. Write-offs thus amounted to $2.59 per share, which when added to basic earnings per share of $4.50, results in a cash flow per share from continuing operations of $7.09 in 2000, and $6.63 in 1999.

Because the use of all funds movements in a business is largely at the discretion of management, this limited cash flow per share concept is at best only a crude indication of the ability to pay dividends, which in 3M's case were $2.32

and $2.24 per share in 2000 and 1999. A more extensive analysis of overall cash flows is required to judge the total pattern of sources and uses, including dividend payments, as demonstrated in Chapter 2.

Share Price Appreciation

Apart from current earnings generated for the shareholders, some of which will be received as dividends, investors expect an appreciation in the value of their common shares in the stock market over time. The main driver for this appreciation is the creation of additional economic value by management, that is, the generation of more positive cash flows than outlays in the long run through the combined effect of sound investment, operating, and financing decisions. We'll discuss shareholder value creation more fully in Chapter 11, but suffice it to say that the analyst will look for movement in the share prices that at least matches and hopefully outperforms the trend in the stock market as a whole. Similarly, the performance trend of particular business segments in a large company will be related to the share price trends of relevant composites of comparable companies.

Total Shareholder Return (TSR)

The return achieved by investors holding shares in a company is a combination of share price appreciation (or decline) and cash dividends received over appropriate time periods selected for analysis. Because usually only part of the earnings belonging to shareholders is paid out in the form of dividends, the relevant positive inflow to the shareholder is the stream of dividends received, not the announced earnings per share. The full economic benefit received by the shareholder is the sum of this stream of dividends plus any change in the price of the stock. The calculation simply involves taking the market price of stock at the beginning of the period, summing the quarterly dividends for the period, determining the change in price at the end of the period, and calculating the annualized return this pattern represents on the initial market price (the present value techniques of Chapter 6 are helpful in this calculation).

The results of this process are published annually in the spring by *Fortune* magazine for publicly held companies in the Fortune 500 listings. The previous year's TSR and the annual rate of TSR for the prior 10-year period is provided for companies in each major segment. 3M was listed as the largest in revenues among 13 companies in the scientific, photo, and control equipment segment, along with Eastman Kodak and Applied Materials. The breadth of 3M's product line certainly extends beyond this classification, but this is the closest fit Fortune could achieve. 3M's TSR for 2000 was 26 percent (41 percent for 1999), whereas the more meaningful long-term return from 1990 to 2000 was 15 percent (13 percent for 1989 to 1999). Comparable figures for the median of the segment were 36 percent for 2000 (27 percent for 1999), and 21 percent for the decade (13 percent for 1989 to 1999).

The TSR concept is critical to assessing the relative performance of a company within the market as a whole, compared with its peers, and within broad industry groupings. We'll again discuss TSR in relation to shareholder value analysis in Chapter 11.

Disposition of Earnings

The periodic split of earnings (net profit) into dividends paid and earnings retained for reinvestment is watched closely by shareholders and the financial community, because of the trade-off between cash leaving the financial system and the retained residual, which builds up the owners' equity and is a source of funds for management's use. The trade-off amounts to giving value directly to the shareholders as part of TSR, versus reinvesting the funds for future value creation. This is not an either/or proposition, however, because dividend policy is hardly ever changed abruptly. Instead, the board of directors usually considers whether dividends should be increased incrementally as earnings grow, focusing on the stability of the dividend record which shareholders can expect from the company. Only in dire circumstances will the dividend be reduced or omitted.

Cash dividends are the most common form of payment, although stock dividends are also frequently used. In the latter case, no cash is involved. Instead, additional shares are issued to the holder in proportion to the shares owned. If a regular cash dividend is paid as well, stock dividends will, in the end, result in fractionally higher cash dividends to the holder.

Dividends per Share

Dividends are generally declared on a per share basis every quarter by a corporation's board of directors, the elected representatives of the shareholders. Therefore no calculation is necessary. Dividend policy is the prerogative of the board, which has legal authority to set payments at any level it deems appropriate. Because the market value of common stock is partially influenced by both dividends paid and dividends anticipated, the board generally deals with this periodic decision carefully. Dividends are declared each quarter and paid subsequently on a specified date, which can lead to slight differences between the dividends declared and those actually paid in a given year, if dividend levels change from period to period. 3M Inc. paid common dividends of $2.32 per share in 2000 and $2.24 in 1999.

Dividend Yield

Annual dividends paid per share can be related to current or average share prices to derive the dividend yield:

Dividend yield:

$$\frac{\text{Annual dividend per share}}{\text{Average market price per share}} = \text{Percent}$$

This is a measure of the return on the owners' investment from cash dividends alone. In the case of 3M, the 12-month range of closing stock prices from January 2000 to December 2000 was $120.5 to $83.00, with an average of approximately $101.75. The dividend yield at $2.32 per share thus amounts to 2.3 percent on the average price. This ratio falls short as a basis for comparison with other companies, however, because dividend policies differ widely. As we stated earlier, the more important measure is TSR, a combination of dividends and market appreciation (or decline) of the stock.

Payout/Retention

A ratio commonly used in connection with dividend policy is the so-called payout ratio, which represents the proportion of earnings paid out to the shareholders in the form of cash during any given year:

Payout ratio:

$$\frac{\text{Cash dividend per share}}{\text{Earnings per share}} = \frac{\$2.32}{\$4.50} = 51.6\% \ (51.0\% \text{ in } 1999)$$

Because most boards of directors tend to favor paying a fairly stable dividend per share, adjusted only gradually, the payout ratio of a company might fluctuate widely in the short run in response to swings in earnings performance. Over a period of several years, however, the payout ratio can often be used to indicate the attitude of the board toward reinvesting funds in the business versus paying out earnings to the shareholders.

There are no firm standards for this ratio, but the relationship is significant in characterizing the style of the corporation. High-growth companies tend to pay out relatively low proportions of earnings because they prefer to reinvest earnings to support profitable growth. Stable or moderate-growth companies tend to pay out larger proportions. Some companies pay no cash dividends at all, or provide stock dividends only. Many more factors must, of course, be considered in making judgments in this area. The reader is directed to the references at the end of this chapter for further insight into both concepts and practices.

Dividend Coverage

Owners are also interested in the degree to which their dividends are covered by earnings and cash flow. Furthermore, they are concerned about the degree to which the proportion of debt in the capital structure and its associated interest and repayment requirements will affect management's ability to achieve reasonably stable and growing earnings, and to pay dividends commensurate with the owners' expectations. A variety of coverage ratios can be calculated, but they hardly differ from the ones we'll take up in the discussion of the lender's point of view.

Dividends to Assets

Finally, it is sometimes useful to relate the annual dividends paid by a company to the total assets or net assets involved in generating them. The rationale is similar to the dividend yield discussed earlier, except that in this case, it's not the market value of the shares but the book value of the assets they represent, which is used as the denominator. It can be argued that market valuation is a more current indicator for the yield relationship than the historical basis of the asset values as recorded on the balance sheet. Nevertheless, dividends to assets is at times found as part of an analytical set of performance data.

Market Indicators

We'll briefly mention two ratios commonly used as indicators of stock market values: the price/earnings ratio and the market to book ratio. The subject of market valuation will be covered in more detail in Chapters 10 and 11.

Price/Earnings Ratio

The simple relationship between current or expected earnings per share and the current market price of the stock is often quoted by both management and owners. The ratio also is called the earnings multiple, and it is used as a broad indicator of how the stock market is judging the company's earnings performance and prospects. The calculation is quite straightforward, and relates current market prices of common shares to the most recent available earnings per share on an annual basis:

Earnings multiple (price/earnings ratio):

$$\frac{\text{Market price per share}}{\text{Earnings per share}} = \text{Factor}$$

The result is a simple factor. If diluted earnings differ significantly from basic earnings per share, the calculation can be done on both bases. The earnings multiple is used quite commonly as a rough rule of thumb in valuing companies for purposes of acquisition to arrive at a first approximation of value.

Earnings multiples vary widely by industry and by company, and are, in effect, a simple overall approximation of the market's current judgment of industry and company risk versus past and prospective earnings performance. They are tracked by various investor services and related to total market averages, as well as to average price earnings multiples for selected industry groups, to assess the relative performance of a particular company. Earnings multiples will tend to be higher in emerging industries, such as high technology companies or Internet-based firms, than in more established industries, such as public utilities or basic manufacturing. The reason for this divergence lies in the collective expectations of the market about the ability of an industry to achieve superior growth, technological breakthroughs with above-average earnings, cash flow potential, and other ways of achieving shareholder returns well above average through sustainable differentiation. The same is true for individual companies in their respective industry classifications—standouts like innovative Wal-Mart within the mature retailing field come to mind.

The reverse of the earnings per share formula is the so-called earnings yield, which relates earnings per share to the market price. Although it is sometimes used to express the current yield the owner enjoys, the measure can be misleading, because earnings are not normally paid out in full as dividends. Thus, the earnings yield cannot be compared to, for example, the yield on a bond where interest payments are contractual cash remittances. As we already know, the real economic return to the shareholder is a combination of the dividends received and the appreciation (decline) of the stock.

Cash Flow Multiples

A variant of relating current earnings performance to current market value is the use of cash flow per share, as discussed earlier, where we learned that 3M's cash flow per share in 2000 was $7.28 ($6.63 in 1999). Usually the definition of cash flow for this purpose is after-tax profit plus depreciation and amortization, divided by the average number of shares outstanding. We know from the discussion in Chapter 2 that this represents only a limited view of the actual cash generation of the business, but the measure is widely used and quoted as a rule of thumb that relates this definition of operating cash flow to share values.

Market to Book Ratio

This indicator relates current market value on a per share basis to the stated book value of owners' equity on the balance sheet, also on a per share basis. 3M's December 31, 2000, book value per share was $16.49, whereas the average market value for 2000 at $101.75 was more than six times this figure. The market to book ratio leaves much to be desired as a measure of performance for many of the reasons mentioned in earlier discussions of other ratios. It's not an economic measure of performance, because it relates market values to stated historical accounting values, which are further affected by equity set-asides and similar accounting effects. In addition, while in a given company the relationship between stated balance sheet values and market values might be favorable, the ratio doesn't truly help the analyst judge what the comparable expectations for other firms should be. Thus, the measure is only a beginning step in the appraisal of long-term performance and outlook.

Relative Price Movements

Although the typical investor is interested in the absolute change in the value of the shares held, the insights from the relative performance of the stock to the market as a whole and to appropriate averages for specific industries can be useful in assessing the trend of a particular company. As we'll discuss in Chapter 11, targeting for shareholder value creation is often based on relative price performance as one of the measures used. Price movements can be expressed in absolute dollar terms, or in several of the ratios mentioned above. In view of the growing importance of cash flow thinking, fueled by the acquisition and leveraged buyout boom of the past decade, services like Value Line provide trends in cash flow multiples as an additional indicator of relative price movements, as do the various online services that give access to published company statistics.

Value Drivers

An approach that has gained increased recognition in recent years is the identification of key elements that stand out as significant in the creation of shareholder value of a specific company. From the owners' standpoint, key value drivers might be the growth potential of key products or services of the company, key technology capabilities that provide a competitive advantage, superior cost-effectiveness in its processes, or differentiated strategic positioning. All of these affect the market's expectations about the future success and cash flow generation potential of the company. Clearly, these and many more narrowly defined value drivers, which may be specific operational ratios, have to be developed and managed by the organization, and are part of an integrated value-based management process, as we'll discuss in Chapter 11.

Value of the Firm

This is a common concept which recognizes that the two main components of a company's capital structure, equity and debt, are valued separately in the marketplace. At any time, the market value of the firm is the sum of the market values of its shares and its debt:

$$VF = VS + VD$$

where VS is the market price per share times the number of shares outstanding, and VD is the market value of the various classes of long-term debt the company has outstanding. The formula can, of course, be restated to show that the value of the company's shares is a function of the total value of the firm less the value of its debt:

$$VS = VF - VD$$

We'll return to a more detailed discussion of valuation principles and shareholder value creation in Chapters 10 and 11.

In summary, the ratios pertinent to the *owners' view* of a company's performance are measures of the return owners have earned on their stake and the cash rewards they have received in the form of dividends, as well as their expectations about future returns. These results depend on the earning power of the company and on management policies and decisions regarding the use of financial leverage and reinvestment, and the exploitation of the company's value drivers. Ultimately, all management actions affect the economic value of the owners' capital commitment, as reflected in stock market prices. This will be discussed in more detail in Chapter 11.

Lenders' Point of View

Although the main orientation of management and owners is toward the business as a going concern, the lender—of necessity—has to be of two minds. Lenders are interested in funding the needs of a successful business that will perform as expected. At the same time, they must consider the possible negative consequences of default and liquidation. Sharing none of the rewards of success other than receiving regular payments of interest and principal, the lender must carefully assess the risk involved in recovering the original funds extended—particularly if they have been provided for a long period of time. Part of this assessment must be the ultimate value of the lender's claim in case of serious difficulty.

The claims of a general creditor rank behind federal tax obligations, accrued wages, and the claims of secured creditors, who lend against a specific asset, such as a building or equipment. Thus caution often dictates that lenders look for a margin of safety in the assets held by the company, a cushion against default.

Several ratios are used to assess this protection by testing the liquidity of the business. Another set of ratios tests the relative debt exposure, or leverage of the business, in order to weigh the position of lenders versus owners. Finally, there are so-called coverage ratios relating to the company's ability to provide debt service from funds generated by ongoing operations.

Liquidity

One way to test the degree of protection afforded lenders focuses on the short-term credit extended to a business for funding its operations. It involves the liquid assets of a business, that is, those current assets that can readily be converted into cash, on the assumption that they form a cushion against default.

Current Ratio

The ratio most commonly used to appraise the debt exposure represented on the balance sheet is the current ratio. This relationship of current assets to current liabilities is an attempt to show the safety of current debt holders' claims in case of default. The calculation is shown using 3M's relevant totals from Figure 3–2:

Current ratio:

$$\frac{\text{Current assets}}{\text{Current liabilities}} = \frac{\$6{,}379}{\$4{,}754} = 1.34{:}1 \ (1999{:} 1.59{:}1)$$

Presumably, the larger this ratio, the better the position of the debt holders. From the lender's point of view, a higher ratio would certainly appear to provide a cushion against drastic losses of value in case of business failure. A large excess of current assets over current liabilities seems to help protect claims, should inventories have to be liquidated at a forced sale and should accounts receivable involve sizable collection problems.

Seen from another angle, however, an excessively high current ratio might signal slack management practices. It could indicate idle cash balances, high inventory levels that have become unnecessary when compared to current needs, and poor credit management that results in overextended accounts receivable. At the same time, the business might not be making full use of its short-term borrowing power.

A very common rule of thumb suggests that a current ratio of 2:1 is about right for most businesses, because this proportion appears to permit a shrinkage of up to 50 percent in the value of current assets, while still providing enough cushion to cover all current liabilities. The problem with this concept is that the current ratio measures an essentially static condition and assesses a business as if it were on the brink of liquidation. The ratio does not reflect the dynamics of a going concern, which should be the top priority of management. A lender or creditor looking for future business with a successful client should bear this in mind, and will likely turn to the type of cash flow analysis described in Chapters 2 and 4 to judge the viability of the business as a client. In 3M's case, the rise in the short-term portion of financing of over $600 million related to the imminent repayment of some long-term debt during 2000 caused a temporary decline in the ratio, with no implication about any liquidity issues.

Acid Test

An even more stringent test, although again on a static basis, is the acid test or quick ratio, which is calculated using only a portion of current assets—cash, marketable securities (cash equivalents), and accounts receivable—which are then related to current liabilities as follows:

Acid test:

$$\frac{\text{Cash + cash equivalents + receivables}}{\text{Current liabilities}} = \frac{\$302 + \$2,891}{\$4,754} = 0.67{:}1$$

$$(1999{:}\ 0.83{:}1)$$

The key concept here is to test the collectibility of current liabilities in the case of a real crisis, on the assumption that inventories would have no value at all. As drastic tests of the ability to pay in the face of disaster, both the current ratio and acid test are helpful.

From an operational standpoint, however, it is better to analyze a business in terms of the expected total future cash flow pattern, which projects inflows and outflows over the period for which credit is extended. The proportion of current assets to current liabilities normally covers only a small part of this picture.

Quick Sale Value

Another stringent test that can be applied to the business as a whole is to determine, through a series of assumptions, what cash value the various assets of the company would bring in a hurried sale, and relating this total to the liabilities of the business. Again, this is a liquidation point of view that does not allow for recognizing the ongoing cash flow patterns achieved and expected.

Financial Leverage

As we'll discuss in greater detail in Chapters 6 and 10, successful use of debt enhances earnings for the owners of the business, because the returns earned on these funds—over and above the interest paid—belong to the owners, and thus will increase the return on owners' equity. From the lender's viewpoint, however, when earnings do not exceed or even fall short of the interest cost, fixed interest and principal commitments must still be met. The owners must fulfill these claims, which might severely affect the value of owners' equity. The positive and negative effects of leverage increase with the proportion of debt in a business. With higher leverage, the risk exposure of the providers of debt grows, as does the risk exposure of the owners.

From the lender's point of view, a variety of ratios that deal with total debt, or long-term debt only, in relation to various parts of the balance sheet, are more inclusive measures of risk than leverage alone. These ratios measure the risk exposure of the lenders in relation to the available asset values against which all claims are held.

Debt to Assets

The first and broadest test is the proportion of total debt, both current and long-term, to total assets, which is calculated as follows:

Debt to assets:

$$\frac{\text{Total debt}}{\text{Total assets}} = \frac{\$4,754 + \$971 + \$2,266}{\$14,522} = \frac{\$7,991}{\$14,522} = 55.0\% \ (1999: 54.7\%)$$

Note that we've included the whole category of other liabilities ($2,266 million), which contains pension and postretirement benefits obligations that could be considered a set-aside of shareholders' equity, given that such benefits are paid as a matter of course from ongoing operations, and deferred income taxes, which are differences arising from tax accounting that are continuously adjusted and cannot be considered debt in the full sense of the term. Some analysts choose to leave these elements out when calculating the ratio.

Debt to assets is used to describe the proportion of "other people's money" to the total claims against the assets of the business. The higher the ratio, the greater the risk for the lender. This is not necessarily a true test of the ability of the business to cover its debts, however. As we've already observed, the asset amounts recorded on the balance sheet are generally not indicative of current economic values, or even liquidation values. Nor does the ratio give any clues as to likely earnings and cash flow fluctuations that might affect current interest and principal payments.

Debt to Capitalization

A more refined version of the debt proportion analysis involves the ratio of long-term debt to capitalization (total invested capital). The latter is again defined as the sum of the long-term claims against the business, both debt and owners' equity, but doesn't include short-term (current) liabilities. This total also corresponds to net assets, unless some adjustments were made, such as ignoring deferred taxes.

The calculation appears as follows, when the current portion of long-term debt and other liabilities are included in the debt total:

Debt to capitalization:

$$\frac{\text{Long–term debt}}{\text{Capitalization (net assets)}} = \frac{\$971 + \$646 + \$2,266}{\$14,522 - \$4,764} = 39.8\% \ (1999: 37.9\%)$$

The ratio is one of the elements that rating companies such as Moody's take into account when classifying the relative safety of debt. Another definition of debt is sometimes used, which includes (1) short-term debt (other than trade credit), (2) the current portion of long-term debt, and (3) all long-term debt in the form of contractual obligations. In this case, long-term liabilities like set-asides representing potential employee benefit claims and deferred taxes are not counted as part of the capitalization of the company, which is (1) the sum of debt as defined above, plus (2) minority interests, and (3) shareholders' equity (equity). In 3M's case, the debt total thus becomes $2,837 ($1,220 + $646 + $971), and the capitalization becomes $9,714 ($2,837 + $346 + $6,531), resulting in a ratio of 29.2 percent for 2000 and 28.2 percent for 1999. As is apparent, the greater the uncounted portions of the capital structure, the less this version of the debt ratio represents the full balance of the various elements of the capital base of a company.

A great deal of emphasis is placed on the ratio of debt to capitalization, carefully defined for any particular company, because many lending agreements of both publicly held and private corporations contain covenants regulating maximum debt exposure expressed in terms of debt to capitalization proportions. There remains an issue of how to classify different liabilities, and how to deal with accounting changes, because most companies, including 3M, experienced establishment of long-term liabilities for future employee benefits. As we'll see later, however, there is growing emphasis on a more relevant aspect of debt exposure, namely, the ability to service the debt from ongoing funds flows, a much more dynamic view of lender relationships.

Debt to Equity

A third version of the analysis of debt proportions involves the ratio of total debt, frequently defined as the sum of current liabilities and all types of long-term debt, to total owners' equity, or shareholders' equity. The debt to equity ratio is an attempt to show, in another format, the relative proportions of all lender's claims to ownership claims, and it is used as a measure of debt exposure. The measure is expressed as either a percentage or as a proportion, and in the example shown below, we are using the 3M total debt figure developed earlier when we discussed debt to assets:

Debt to equity:

$$\frac{\text{Total debt}}{\text{Shareholders' equity}} = \frac{\$7,991}{\$6,531} = 122\% \ (1999: 121\%)$$

In preparing this ratio, as in some earlier instances, the question of deferred income taxes and other estimated long-term liabilities is often sidestepped by leaving these potential long-term claims out of the debt and capitalization figures altogether. We have included all of these elements here. One specific refinement of this formula uses only long-term debt, including the current portion due during the year, as related to shareholders' equity, ignoring long-term obligations and deferred taxes.

Debt to equity (alternate):

$$\frac{\text{Long--term debt}}{\text{Shareholders' equity}} = \frac{\$971 + \$646}{\$6,531} = 24.8\% \ (1999: 24.1\%)$$

The various formats of these relationships suggest the great care with which the ground rules must be defined for any particular analysis, and for testing compliance with the covenants governing specific lending agreements. They only hint at the risk/reward trade-off implicit in the use of debt, which we'll discuss in more detail in Chapters 9 and 11.

Debt Service

Regardless of the specific choice from among the several ratios just discussed, the analysis of debt proportions is by nature a static view, and does not take into account the operating dynamics and economic values of the business. The analysis is totally derived from the balance sheet, which in itself is a static snapshot of the financial condition of the business at a single point in time.

Nonetheless, the relative ease with which these ratios are calculated probably accounts for their popularity. Such ratios are useful as indicators of trends when they are applied over a period of time. However, they still don't get at the heart of an analysis of creditworthiness, which involves a company's ability to pay both interest and principal on schedule as contractually agreed upon, that is, to service its debt over time.

Interest Coverage

One very frequently encountered ratio reflecting a company's debt service uses the relationship of net profit (earnings) before interest and taxes (EBIT) to the amount of the interest payments for the period. This ratio is developed with the expectation that annual operating earnings can be considered the basic source of funds for debt service, and that any significant change in this relationship might signal difficulties. Major earnings fluctuations are one type of risk considered.

No hard and fast standards for the ratio itself exist; rather, the prospective debt holders often require covenants in the loan agreement spelling out the number of times the business is expected to cover its debt service obligations. The ratio is simple to calculate, and we can employ the EBIT figure developed for 3M earlier in the management section:

Interest coverage:

$$\frac{\text{Net profit before interest and taxes (EBIT)}}{\text{Interest expense}} = \frac{\$2,891}{\$111} = 26.0 \text{ times}$$

$$(1999: 26.4 \text{ times})$$

The specifics are based on judgment, often involving a detailed analysis of a company's past, current, and prospective conditions.

Burden Coverage

A somewhat more refined analysis of debt coverage relates the net profit of the business, before interest and taxes, to the sum of current interest and principal repayments, in an attempt to indicate the company's ability to service the burden of its debt in all aspects. A problem arises with this particular analysis, because interest payments are tax deductible, whereas principal repayments are not. Thus, we must be on guard to think about these figures on a comparable basis.

The first format expresses the coverage in pretax profit terms, utilizing the EBIT figure we developed earlier in the chapter on page 117. For comparability, the principal repayments are then converted into an equivalent pretax amount, because they have to be paid with after-tax dollars. This adjustment is done by dividing the principal repayment by the factor "1 minus the effective tax rate." The resulting calculation for 3M appears as follows, using the $36 million in principal repayments on long-term debt due at the end of 1999 and paid during 2000, as shown on the 1999 balance sheet in Figure 3–2 as the current portion of long-term debt. Note that a significantly higher amount ($646 million) was scheduled for future repayment during 2001, which will adversely affect the result of a similar calculation at the end of that year. Note also that 3M's published interest expense is not segregated into the respective amounts paid on long-term versus short-term debt, which causes us to apply the total interest amount to the calculation of long-term debt coverage, thus adversely affecting the result.

Burden coverage:

$$\frac{\text{Net profit before interest and taxes (EBIT)}}{\text{Interest expense} + \dfrac{\text{Principal repayments}}{(1 - \text{Tax rate})}} = \frac{\$2,891}{\$111 + \dfrac{\$39}{0.65}} = \frac{\$2,891}{\$171} =$$

16.9 times

An alternate approach expresses the burden coverage in after-tax cash flow terms. It uses operating cash flow (net profit after taxes plus write-offs), to which after-tax interest has been added back. This amount is then compared to the sum of after-tax interest and principal repayment. We can develop operating cash flow by beginning with income before taxes of $2,974 million, in Figure 3-3, subtract the provision for taxes of $1,025 million, and add back depreciation of $915 million and amortization of $110 million. The result is $2,974 million, which happens to be identical to income before taxes—because by chance the provision for taxes, and the sum of depreciation and amortization in 2000 turned out to be the same amounts. The result of the alternative calculation is much more favorable, of course, because it is based on after-tax cash flow, a higher figure than net profit because of the add-back of non-cash items:

Burden coverage:

$$\frac{\text{Operating cash flow} + \text{Interest expense}\left(1 - \text{Tax rate}\right)}{\text{Interest expense}\left(1 - \text{Tax rate}\right) + \text{Principal repayments}} = \frac{\$2{,}974 + \$72}{\$72 + \$39} =$$

$$\frac{\$3{,}046}{\$111} = 27.4 \text{ times}$$

Again, more exact coverage calculations would require access to internal information, and judgment has to be used in interpreting these results.

Fixed Charges Coverage

A more inclusive concept is the combination of interest and rental expenses into a fixed charges amount, which is then compared to pretax earnings to which these fixed charges are added back. Such a calculation depends on the availability of detailed information on leasing and rental charges, and can be appropriately performed by internal analysts. 3M did not publish rental and leasing expense information in its 2000 annual report.

Cash Flow Analysis

Determining a company's ability to meet its debt obligations is most meaningful when a review of past profit and cash flow patterns is made over a long enough period of time to indicate the major operational and cyclical fluctuations that are normal for the company and its industry. This might involve financial statements covering several years or several seasonal swings, as appropriate, in an attempt to identify characteristic high and low points in earnings and funds needs. The pattern of past conditions must then be projected into the future to see what margin of safety remains to cover interest, principal repayments, and other fixed payments, such as major lease obligations. These techniques will be discussed in Chapter 4.

If a business is subject to sizable fluctuations in after-tax cash flow, lenders might be reluctant to extend credit when the debt service cannot be covered several times at the low point in the operational pattern. In contrast, a very stable business would encounter less-stringent coverage demands. The type of dynamic analysis involved is a form of financial modeling that can be greatly enhanced both in scope and in the number of possible alternative conditions explored by using spreadsheets or full-fledged corporate planning models.

Ratios as a System

The ratios discussed in this chapter have many elements in common, because they are derived from key components of the same financial statements. In fact, they're often interrelated and can be viewed as a system. The analyst can turn a series of ratios into a dynamic display highlighting the elements that are the most important levers used by management to affect operating performance.

In internal analysis, many companies employ a variety of systems of ratios and standards that segregate into their components the impact of decisions affecting operating performance, overall returns, and shareholder expectations. DuPont was one of the first to do so early in the last century. The company published a chart showing the effects and interrelationships of decisions in these areas, which focused on the linkages to return on equity as the key result and represented a first "model" of its business. The DuPont system was built on accounting relationships only, because cash flow concepts and measures were not in vogue at that time. Companies that engage in value-based management, as we'll discuss in Chapter 11, develop relationships in their planning models and operational systems that focus on value drivers and shareholder value creation, using a mix of cash flow measures and appropriate physical and accounting ratios.

For purposes of illustrating the basic principles here we'll demonstrate the relationships between major accounting ratios discussed earlier, using two key parameters segregated into their elements: *return on assets*, which is of major importance for judging management performance, and *return on equity*, which serves as the key measure from the owners' viewpoint. We'll leave aside the refinements applicable to each to concentrate on the linkages. As we'll show, it's possible to model the performance of a given company by expanding and relating these ratios. Needless to say, careful attention must be paid to the exact definition of the elements entering into the ratios for a particular company to achieve internal consistency. Also, it's important to ensure that the ratios are interpreted in ways that foster economic trade-offs and decisions in support of shareholder value creation.

Elements of Return on Assets

We established earlier that the basic formula for return on assets (ROA) was a simple ratio, into which different versions of the elements can be inserted:

$$\text{Return on assets} = \frac{\text{Net profit}}{\text{Assets}}$$

We also know that net profit was related both to asset turnover and to sales. Thus, it is possible to restate the formula as follows:

$$\text{Return on assets} = \frac{\text{Net profit}}{\text{Sales}} \times \frac{\text{Sales}}{\text{Assets}}$$

Note that the element of sales cancels out in the second formula, resulting in the original expression. But we can expand the relationship even further by substituting several more basic elements for the terms in the equation:

$$\text{ROA} = \frac{(\text{Gross margin} - \text{Expenses})(1 - \text{Tax rate})}{\text{Price} \times \text{Volume}} \times$$

$$\frac{\text{Price} \times \text{Volume}}{\text{Fixed assets} + \text{Current assets} + \text{Other assets}}$$

The relationships expressed here serve as a simple model of the key drivers on which management can focus to improve return on assets. For example, improvement in gross margin is important, as is control of expenses. Price/volume relationships are canceled out, but we know they are essential factors in arriving at a satisfactory gross margin, as is the management of gross margin via pricing and cost of goods sold. (We could have substituted "price times volume less cost of goods sold" for the term "gross margin" in the first part of the equation.)

All along we've said that asset management is very important. This simple model shows that the return on assets will rise if fewer assets are employed and if all the measures of effective management of working capital are applied. Minimizing taxes within the legal options available to management also will improve the return.

Elements of Return on Equity

A similar approach can be taken with the basic formula for return on owners' equity (ROE), which relates profit and the amounts of recorded equity:

$$\text{Return on equity} = \frac{\text{Net profit}}{\text{Equity}}$$

If we use some of the basic profit and turnover relationships to expand the expression, the following formula emerges:

$$\text{Return on equity} = \frac{\text{Net profit}}{\text{Assets}} \times \frac{\text{Assets}}{\text{Equity}}$$

Note that, in effect, the formula states that return on equity (ROE) consists of two elements:

- The net profit achieved on the asset base.
- The degree of leverage or debt capital used in the business.

"Assets to equity" is a way of describing the leverage proportion. We can expand the formula even more to include the key components of return on assets:

$$\text{ROE} = \frac{\text{Net profit}}{\text{Sales}} \times \frac{\text{Sales}}{\text{Assets}} \times \frac{\text{Assets}}{\text{Assets} - \text{Liabilities}}$$

Once again we can look for the key drivers management should use to raise the return on owners' equity. It's not a surprise that improving profitability of sales (operations) comes first, combined with effective use of the assets that generate sales. An added factor is the boosting effect from successful use of debt in the capital structure. The greater the liabilities, the greater the improvement in return on equity—assuming, of course, that the business is profitable to begin with and at a minimum continues to earn more on its investments than the cost of debt. As we know, of course, value creation depends on overall returns above the cost of capital, which is not expressed in this particular formula.

Using other people's money can be quite helpful—until the risk of default on debt service in a down cycle becomes significant. The analyst can use this simple framework to test the impact on the return on equity from one or more changed conditions, and to test how sensitive the result is to the magnitude of any change introduced.

A more inclusive format of the relationship of key ratios to each other and to the three major decision areas is displayed in Figure 3–5. We've added the major drivers behind the ratios on the left, as an indication of the levers management can use in managing the company. Note that in this diagram, we've included the cost of interest on debt as part of the "net contribution from leverage" in the financing area, while properly defining operating earnings as excluding the cost of interest.

This representation can be viewed as a simple model of a business in an accounting ratio format, and it is available as an interactive template for testing the results of various assumptions (see "Analytical Support" on p. 163). It can be useful in tracing through the ultimate effects from changes in any of the basic drivers that are brought about by management decisions. For example, note that an increased level of inventories will reduce working capital turnover, which lowers the return on investment, and in the end, the return on equity. Or take an increase in debt (leverage), where the funds obtained are successfully invested with a rate of return higher than the interest cost—this will make a positive contribution to the return on equity. The latter example also illustrates that different degrees of leverage employed by companies being compared can affect the comparability of the return on equity measure.

A word of caution is in order, however. The neat precision implied in this arrangement must not blind us to the fact that while accounting ratios are commonly used indicators, the ultimate driver of TSR and shareholder value is the pattern of cash flows achieved and, more important, expected by the stock market. This represents an economic viewpoint that transcends the shortcomings of accounting statements and relationships, and expresses market valuation as a cash flow mechanism—a concept confirmed by many empirical studies. The roots of the system on the left of the diagram are the basic conditions which drive success or failure as expressed in these accounting ratios. These drivers are common to accounting and cash flow reasoning. The difference is in the way the results are expressed. As we'll discuss in Chapter 11, value creation depends on effective management of all the basic drivers, but the ultimate result must be viewed in cash flow terms.

Does this mean that we cannot really use the various tools and relationships we've discussed in this chapter? Not at all. The challenge to analysts and managers is to constantly be aware of the cash flow implications of their decisions in addition to any accounting-based analysis. Accounting ratios and data at times will conflict with economic choices, especially in the near term, and some of them will not be useful for a particular decision. Over the long run, measures such as return on equity and return on net assets will tend to converge with cash flow results. The rule to observe at all times is that true economic

FIGURE   3–5

A Systems View of Key Ratios and Their Elements[*]

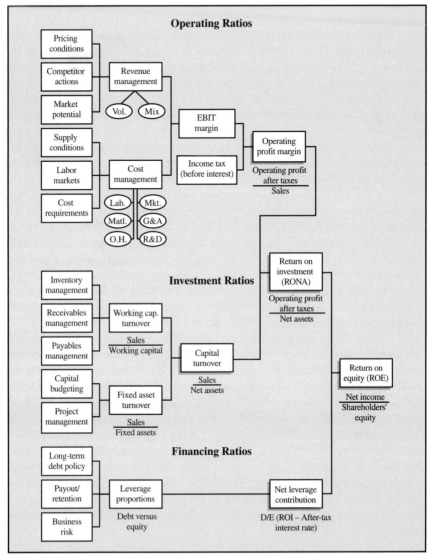

'This model is available for download in an interactive format; see "Analytical Support," p. 163.

trade-offs must be based on cash flows, and if decisions are consistently ana-lyzed and executed in this manner, positive accounting results will follow in due course.

We'll return to the subject of business modeling again in Chapters 4 and 5, and highlight economic cash flow trade-offs in Chapters 6 through 11.

Integration of Financial Performance Analysis

We've discussed the great variety of financial ratios and measures available to anyone wishing to analyze the performance of a company and its various units, or of an individual business. We've also grouped the measures by points of view and shown their many interrelationships as well as the key management drivers that impact them. At this point, it'll be helpful to provide a few practical guidelines for structuring the process of using the measures. We'll briefly address the following key points:

- Carefully defining the issue being analyzed and the viewpoint to be taken.
- Identifying a combination of primary and secondary measures and tools.
- Identifying key value drivers that affect performance.
- Finding comparative indicators and supplementary information.
- Trending performance data over time, both historical and prospective.
- Using past performance as a clue to future expectations.
- Recognizing systems issues and obstacles to optimal performance.

First, there is nothing more important in any kind of financial/economic analysis than a clear *definition of the issue* to be addressed, and the *viewpoint to be taken*. For example, when a banker ponders whether to extend a short-term loan to a business for working capital needs, the key issue is the company's ability to repay within a relatively short time period. Immediately, the analysis focuses on past and prospective cash flow patterns, supplemented by measures on working capital management and profitability. When a security analyst wishes to assess the quality of a company's management, the focus will be on past and prospective strategic direction, competitive position, and investment effectiveness. Measures of profitability benchmarked against comparative industry data will be important, as will be indicators of shareholder return and value creation. The point is that every type of analysis—complex or simple—should be preceded by a careful issue definition and choice of viewpoint that will naturally lead to a focused selection of measures to be applied.

Second, it should be obvious that most financial/economic analysis has to use a *combination of primary and secondary measures* to be effective. Rarely will a situation require only a single measure or indicator, because all ratios are limited to some extent both by the nature of the data and by the relationships underlying them. Looking only at the return on equity as a measure of profitability, for example, falls far short of the insights gained when it is combined with key measures of operating earnings, asset turnover, and contribution from leverage, as we saw earlier. It's good practice to decide which key indicators best fit the specific issue, and which subsidiary ratios or other measures can provide additional insight or verification. The analytical results should then be expressed in these terms.

Third, sound analytical practice includes *identifying the key value drivers* underlying the performance of any business. Whether production oriented, such as the yield in producing electronic chips, or service based, such as call volume by sales personnel, performance ratios and measures are usually directly affected by variations in these key drivers. Although one can find many kinds of value drivers—internal or external—varying greatly between types of business, there are generally just a few in each situation that really make a difference. The effective analyst makes it a practice to understand what these drivers are, how they affect the broader financial/economic measures used, and how trends in the drivers themselves impact both past and prospective performance. It's good practice to test the sensitivity of key measures chosen to various value driver conditions, and to include critical value drivers as part of the combination of measures chosen to address the performance issue under review.

Fourth, the results of performance analysis are much more meaningful when placed in the *context of comparative data* about the industry, key competitors, or intracompany comparisons of organizational units. It's here that both the level of performance and key trends can be judged in relative terms. Although it's often hard to find truly comparable data, particularly for multidivisional businesses, the notion of benchmarking business results whenever possible has grown in the past decade as U.S. management has begun to focus on improving competitive effectiveness. The references at the end of this chapter and in Appendix III contain published sources of industry data and ratios, which companies often supplement with special efforts to develop even more specific data through detailed benchmarking activities, that is, by sharing experiences with noncompeting companies. Depending on the importance of the issue being analyzed, the industry/competitive context for viewing performance results can be critical.

Fifth, it's an axiom of good analysis that *trends in financial/economic performance* be judged in a time frame befitting the nature of the business and its industry, including the aspects of cyclicality, seasonality, growth, and decline discussed in Chapter 2. This calls for developing data series that cover at least several years, in order to judge the trends affecting various aspects of the company's performance. Sound analysis uses the perspective gained from positive or adverse trends in the primary and secondary performance indicators, and carefully weighs their relative importance to the issue being addressed. Remember also that performance analysis is not just an exercise in historical assessment—rather, it's the basis from which future expectations are developed. Trend analysis becomes especially important in this context, because the analyst often needs to project future conditions and must decide whether the trends observed are likely to continue, or change, because of foreseeable events.

Sixth, viewing past performance as a *clue to potential future expectations* is a common practice in financial/economic analysis. We've already touched on this aspect in our discussion of trend analysis. A word of caution is necessary, however. Although it's proper to identify past trends in both value drivers and the broader ratios and measures, and to extrapolate them into the future, this is only a first step. As we'll see in Chapter 4 and later chapters, historical conditions are merely an indication that might not be relevant for the company's prospective results. Past performance trends have to be carefully tested against expectations about future conditions, both internal to the company and external in the broader context of business, competitive, and economic conditions. It might very well be true that recent actions taken by management, or discernible changes in the environment, require a different set of assumptions about the future.

Finally, performance analysis in the broadest sense has to be viewed in the *context of the business system,* as described in Chapter 1. When the issue selected is an overall assessment of a company or a major business unit, it's good practice to test the results and trends of the various measures not only in the form of absolute and relative performance against proper benchmarks, but also in relation to each other. As we pointed out in Chapter 1, sound economic/financial performance requires optimizing the systems results over time. This simply means that policies and strategies in the areas of investment, operations, and financing should reinforce each other. The skilled analyst will put performance analysis into this broader context, and view the historical results as well as the projected expectations as indicators of systems balance. Are growth policies matched by appropriate financing plans? Are operating results in cash flow terms sufficient to support dividend policies and investment plans? Do the results reflect sound trade-offs over time? Many of these points will be discussed in more detail in later chapters.

To provide a degree of historical perspective and some trends of significant financial and other statistics, we have reproduced as Figure 3–6 the 10-year financial summary published by 3M in its 2000 annual report. It contains key operating results, financial ratios, and selected background information on a comparable 10-year basis, adjusted for all accounting changes, restructurings, and acquisition and divestiture activity. Some of the data are taken directly from the financial statements we analyzed both in Chapter 2 and in this chapter, whereas other data represent data calculated by 3M as well as information on employees and shares outstanding. The reader is invited to examine this information to gain a wider perspective on 3M's growth and performance during the last decade of the 20th century. As we also pointed out, a full assessment would require much additional analysis along the lines discussed in this and the previous chapter.

Some Special Issues

The impact of accounting practices and decisions on the management of funds was briefly mentioned in Chapter 2, where accounting write-offs and deferred taxes were identified as aspects to be considered. At this point, it'll be useful to refine our understanding of these issues a little further because possible alternative treatments of these matters at times significantly affect the assessment of operations as well as understanding the patterns of cash flows. Addendum 2–1 at the end of Chapter 2 contains the notes to 3M's financial statements as an illustration of the many accounting and tax considerations underlying the reported financial data of any large U.S. corporation. Appendix V contains some

MINNESOTA MINING AND MANUFACTURING COMPANY AND SUBSIDIARIES
Consolidated 10-Year Financial Summary

Financial Summary
(Dollars in millions, except per share amounts)

	2000	1999	1998	1997	1996	1995	1994	1993	1992	1991
Operating Results										
Net sales	$16,724	$15,748	$15,094	$15,133	$14,295	$13,516	$12,199	$11,099	$10,862	$10,324
Operating income	3,058	2,956	2,039	2,675	2,491	2,221	2,095	1,796	1,811	1,683
Income from continuing operations	1,857	1,763	1,213	2,121	1,516	1,306	1,207	1,133	1,116	984
Per share—basic	4.69	4.39	3.01	5.14	3.63	3.11	2.85	2.61	2.55	2.24
Per share—diluted	4.64	4.34	2.97	5.06	3.59	3.09	2.84	2.59	2.54	2.23
Net income	1,782	1,763	1,175	2,121	1,526	976	1,322	1,263	1,233	1,154
Per share—basic	4.50	4.39	2.91	5.14	3.65	2.32	3.13	2.91	2.81	2.63
Per share—diluted	4.45	4.34	2.88	5.06	3.62	2.31	3.11	2.89	2.80	2.62
Economic profit	959	907	307	720	629	502	530	429	404	270
Financial Ratios										
Percent of sales										
Cost of sales	52.5%	51.6%	53.2%	52.0%	52.0%	52.6%	51.2%	51.9%	51.5%	52.1%
Selling, general and administrative expenses	23.7	23.6	23.5	23.7	24.0	23.9	24.8	24.7	25.2	24.7
Research, development, and related expenses	6.6	6.7	6.8	6.6	6.6	6.5	6.8	7.2	7.4	6.9
Operating income	18.3	18.8	13.5	17.7	17.4	16.4	17.2	16.2	16.7	16.3
Income from continuing operations	11.1	11.2	8.0	14.0	10.6	9.7	9.9	10.2	10.3	9.5
Return on invested capital	19.2	19.1	13.0	18.0	17.3	16.3	17.4	16.0	16.8	16.1

Continues

Continued	2000	1999	1998	1997	1996	1995	1994	1993	1992	1991
Total debt to total capital	30	29	34	30	24	23	22	19	18	19
Current ratio	1.3	1.6	1.5	1.5	1.8	1.8	1.8	1.8	1.8	1.7
Additional Information										
Cash dividends paid	$ 918	$ 901	$ 887	$ 876	$ 803	$ 790	$ 744	$ 721	$ 701	$ 685
Per share	2.32	2.24	2.20	2.12	1.92	1.88	1.76	1.66	1.60	1.56
Stock price at year-end	120.50	97.88	71.13	82.06	83.00	66.38	53.38	54.38	50.31	47.63
Book value per share	16.49	15.77	14.77	14.64	15.08	16.44	16.04	15.16	15.06	14.36
Working capital	1,625	2,247	1,997	2,185	2,880	2,847	2,516	2,348	2,246	1,899
Capital expenditures	1,115	1,050	1,453	1,406	1,109	1,088	972	898	968	1,065
Depreciation	915	822	798	800	825	795	793	768	754	710
Research, development, and related expenses	1,101	1,056	1,028	1,002	947	883	828	794	800	713
Number of employees at year-end*	75,026	70,549	73,564	75,639	74,289	85,313	85,296	85,940	86,793	88,370
Average shares outstanding—basic (in millions)	395.7	402.0	403.3	412.7	418.2	419.8	423.0	434.3	438.2	439.1
Average shares outstanding—diluted (in millions)	399.9	406.5	408.0	418.7	422.1	422.5	425.3	436.8	440.2	441.0

2000 results include a nonrecurring net loss of $23 million ($15 million after tax), or 4 cents per diluted share, and a cumulative effect of accounting change related to revenue recognition that reduced earnings by $75 million net of tax, or 19 cents per diluted share.

1999 results include nonrecurring items of $100 million ($52 million after tax), or 13 cents per diluted share. Nonrecurring items consist of a $73 million charge related to litigation; gains on divestitures of $147 million (net of an investment valuation adjustment); and a $26 million gain related to a change in estimate of the restructuring liability.

1998 results include a restructuring charge of $493 million ($313 million after tax), or 77 cents per diluted share, and an extraordinary loss on early extinguishment of debt of $38 million (net of tax), or 9 cents per diluted share.

1997 results include a gain of $803 million ($495 million after tax), or $1.18 per diluted share, on the sale of National Advertising Company.

*Includes both continuing and discontinued operations; decrease in 1996 primarily reflects Imation Corp. spin-off.

Source: Adapted from 2000 3M annual report.

of the more specialized issues of interpreting performance statements in an *international setting*, especially the problem of judging the profitability of parts of a multibusiness company operating in different countries.

We'll limit ourselves to a review of the key choices available to management in the areas of *inventory costing* and *depreciation methods* to help the reader form individual judgments when faced with interpreting financial statements and cash flows. We'll also briefly mention the effects of *inflation*, although no satisfactory methods of dealing with that issue have been established so far.

Inventory Costing

One accounting challenge present at all times is the proper allocation of a portion of the costs that are accumulated in the inventory account to the actual goods being sold. We can visualize *layers of cost* built up over time in the inventory account, which correspond to the physical movement of raw materials, work in process, and finished goods into storage. The accountant wants to *match revenues and expenses* in keeping track of the inventory account, yet from a physical standpoint, it is just as possible to ship the oldest unit on hand as it is to ship the most recent arrival. The warehouse supervisor can even pick the goods at random.

If unit costs never changed, matching costs to revenues would not be a problem, because the accountant would simply track the number of units shipped and multiply them by the unchanged unit cost, regardless of the actual physical choices made by the warehouse supervisor. In real life, however, several problems arise. A manufacturing company might experience fluctuations that affect the recorded unit cost of the products inventoried. This effectively results in different layers of cost in the finished goods inventory account. Further, the prices of raw materials and other inputs might be positively or negatively influenced by supply and demand. The materials inventory account will therefore reflect different layers of cost. A merchandising company will similarly encounter variations in the cost of inventory items, as supplier prices change. Most cost accounting systems allow for variances to the extent they are predictable, but larger swings do affect costs that are charged to periodic income statements.

Finally, there is the impact of general inflation, or, more rarely, deflation. The impact of inflation on inventories generally is a steady rise in the cost of the more recent additions, resulting in successive layers of escalating costs.

The accountant is therefore faced with a real problem in the effort to match costs and revenues. If unit costs are growing significantly from period to period, deciding which costs to charge against the revenues for a period can have significant effects on the financial statements. If the more "logical" method of removing the oldest units first is used, the oldest, and presumably lowest, unit costs will be charged against current revenues. Depending on how quickly the inventory turns over, such costs might lag current conditions by months and even longer. Therefore, under rising price levels, first-in, first-out (FIFO) inventory costing causes the profit on the income statement to be higher than it would be if current unit costs had been charged. At the same time, the balance sheet will reflect inventory values that are reasonably current, because the oldest, lowest cost units are being removed.

If the opposite method is employed, that is, last-in, first-out (LIFO) costing, the income statement will be charged with current costs and thus reflect lower but more realistic profits. The balance sheet, however, will show inventory values that in time, might be highly *understated,* because only the oldest and lowest layers of cost remain.

We could argue that the choice of methods does not really matter, because one of the two financial statements will be distorted in *either* case. The question then simply becomes whether more realistic balance sheet values or more realistic reported profits are preferred. There is a significant *cash flow* aspect involved, however. The choice of methods affects the amount of income taxes paid for the period. The higher earnings under FIFO are taxed as income from operations, even though they contain a profit made from old inventories. Therefore, one criterion in making the choice is the difference in tax payments, which *does* affect the company's funds. LIFO is preferable from this standpoint, even though with continued inflation, inventory values stated on the balance sheet will become more and more obsolete. Yet surprisingly, FIFO has remained a very common form of inventory costing, despite the fact that it can lead to a funds drain from higher tax payments. Apparently, the higher reported profit under FIFO costing is attractive enough to many managers to outweigh the actual tax disadvantage—a trade-off between reporting and economics.

In contrast to other permissible choices of accounting methods for tax purposes, current federal tax laws do not allow the use of one inventory costing method for tax calculation and another for bookkeeping and reporting. Thus, the ideal combination of LIFO for tax purposes and FIFO for reporting earnings is not possible. In fact, many firms employ an averaging method for inventory costing, or a combination of methods.

Trading firms, retailers, and companies experiencing significant fluctuations in the current values of inventories often adjust inventory values, usually at year-end, using the conservative method of restating inventories at cost or market value, whichever is lower, and writing off the difference against current profits. Such periodic adjustments tend to reduce stated values, not raise them, and allow the company to reflect the negative effects of changed conditions so as not to overstate inventory values. Under inflationary conditions, this practice does not, of course, assist in resolving the inventory costing issues we have just discussed.

Depreciation Methods

Depreciation is based on the accountant's objective to reflect as a charge against current operations some appropriate fraction of the cost of assets employed in producing revenues. Because physical assets other than land deteriorate with use and eventually wear out, the accounting challenge is to establish an appropriate period of time over which portions of the cost of the asset are charged against revenues. Moreover, the accountant has to decide on the pattern of the depreciation write-off, that is, level, declining, or variable depreciation. Another issue involves estimating any salvage value that might be realized at the end of an asset's useful life. Only the difference between asset cost and such salvage value is normally depreciated.

A similar rationale is applied to intangible assets such as patents and licenses, which are amortized and charged against operations over an appropriate period of years, and to specialized assets such as mineral deposits and timber, on which depletion allowances are calculated.

In the case of physical assets, the depreciation write-off is shown as a charge in the income statement, and is accumulated on the balance sheet as an offset to the fixed assets involved, in an account called accumulated depreciation or reserve for depreciation. Thus, over time, the original asset value stated on the balance sheet is reduced because periodic charges are made against operations. For performance assessment, the significance of depreciation write-offs is in the appropriateness of the charges in light of the nature of the assets and industry conditions, and thus, depreciation's impact on profits and balance sheet values. The significance for purposes of cash flow management is the tax impact of depreciation. Under normal circumstances, depreciation is a tax-deductible expense, even though it is only an accounting allocation of past expenditures. The highest depreciation write-off legally possible will normally be taken by management to minimize the cash outlay for taxes, unless operating profits are insufficient during the taxable period (including tax adjustments like operating-loss carryback and carryforward, which permit using losses to reduce the taxes of profitable periods) to take full advantage of the deductions.

The choice of depreciation methods is made easier by the provision in the current tax laws allowing the use of one method for bookkeeping and reporting purposes and another for income tax calculation. Recall that this was not possible for inventory valuation. Thus a company can enjoy the best aspects of both depreciation concepts: slower depreciation for reporting higher profits, and faster depreciation for paying lower taxes.

The difference between the taxes actually paid versus what would be due had the book profit been taxed, is accumulated on the balance sheet as a liability called deferred taxes, which we encountered earlier in our discussion. This liability will keep growing if a company continually adds to its depreciable assets, and consistently uses faster write-offs for tax purposes. If the company stops growing or changes its depreciation policies, actual tax payments in future periods will increase and the differences will begin to reduce the deferred taxes account. There is no current consensus on how to treat this often significant amount in the calculation of performance assessment measures.

What are the most common choices for depreciation write-offs? Historically, accounting practice has favored *straight-line depreciation*. This is determined by dividing the cost of the asset (less the estimated salvage value) by its expected life. For example, an asset costing $10,000, with a salvage value of $400 and a six-year life, would be depreciated at the annual rate of $1,600 (one-sixth, or 162/3 percent of $9,600). A variant of this method is *unit depreciation*, in which the allocation is based on the total number of units estimated to be produced over the life of the asset and the annual depreciation is based on the number of units produced in that year.

Because many types of assets, such as automobiles, lose more of their value in early years, and because allowing faster write-offs provides an incentive to reduce current income taxes, several methods of *accelerated depreciation* were developed over time. The two most common methods are described here.

Double-declining balance depreciation is calculated by using twice the annual rate of straight-line depreciation (33⅓ percent for a 6-year life), multiplying the full original cost of the asset for the first year with this factor, and the declining balance for each successive year. In other words, in our example, one-third of the remaining balance would be depreciated in each year (see Figure 3–7). The last year's depreciation is the remaining balance, and any salvage value is recognized by reducing the amount charged in the *final* year.

Sum-of-years digits depreciation is calculated by adding the digits for all the years of the asset's life (1 + 2 + 3, and so on). The total is the denominator in a fraction (for a 6-year life, this sum would be 21: 1 + 2 + 3 + 4 + 5 + 6). The numerators represent each year of useful life, in reverse order. (In our example, the fractions are 6/21, 5/21, 4/21, 3/21, 2/21, and 1/21.) In a given year, the depreciation write-off is the asset's original cost (less salvage value) multiplied by the fraction for that year.

The different patterns of depreciation resulting from the use of the various methods for accounting purposes are shown in Figure 3–7, using our simple example for illustrating the differences in the annual amounts.

The depreciation methods permitted under prevailing IRS codes have changed frequently, especially during the 1980s. Under the 1986 revision of the tax code, the IRS lengthened the lives over which various classes of depreciable assets could be written off. Six asset classes were established for personal property, with lives of 3, 5, 7, 10, 15, and 20 years. For real property (e.g., buildings), two classes of 27.5 and 31.5 years were defined, which must be depreciated straight-line. All classes have in common the assumption that new assets are in

---

FIGURE   3–7

Comparative Annual Depreciation Patterns
($10,000 Asset with Six-Year Life and $400 Salvage Value)

	Straight-Line Method	Double-Declining Balance Method*	150 Percent Declining Balance Method†	Sum-of-Years Digits Method
Year 1	$1,600	$3,333	$2,500	$2,743
Year 2	1,600	2,222	1,875	2,286
Year 3	1,600	1,482	1,407	1,829
Year 4	1,600	988	1,406	1,371
Year 5	1,600	658	1,406	914
Year 6	1,600	917	1,006	457
Total:	$9,600	$9,600	$9,600	$9,600

*Year 6 is shown net of salvage value of $400.

†Switch to straight-line in year 4; required for 15- and 20-year IRS asset classes.

F I G U R E 3–8

Tax Depreciation Percentages by ACRS Asset Class

Year(s)	3–Year	5-Year	7-Year	10-Year	15-Year	20-Year
1	33.33	20.00	14.29	10.00	5.00	3.75
2	44.45	32.00	24.49	18.00	9.50	7.22
3	14.81	19.20	17.49	14.40	8.55	6.68
4	7.41	11.52	12.49	11.52	7.70	6.18
5		11.52	8.93	9.22	6.93	5.71
6		5.76	8.93	7.37	6.23	5.28
7			8.93	6.55	5.90	4.89
8			4.45	6.55	5.90	4.52
9				6.55	5.90	4.46
10				6.55	5.90	4.46
11				3.29	5.90	4.46
12					5.90	4.46
13					5.90	4.46
14					5.90	4.46
15					5.90	4.46
16					2.99	4.46
17–20						4.46
21						2.25

service for only six months in the first year, which lowers the first-year write-off across the board. The IRS stipulated the double-declining balance method for assets with up to 10 years of life, and a variation of this method, the 150 percent declining balance method, for assets with a 15- and 20-year life.

Figure 3–8 shows the tax write-off patterns for the six different asset classes established by the IRS under the so-called accelerated cost recovery system (ACRS), using the percentage of the depreciable investment allowed as a deduction in each year.

The IRS permits a switch to straight-line depreciation in the latter years, when this becomes advantageous. These methods must be used if a company chooses to use accelerated depreciation for *tax* purposes, while *any* other method can be employed for bookkeeping and reporting. The specifics of the tax regulations applicable at the time of the analysis are best examined in the detailed materials provided by the Internal Revenue Service.

The Impact of Inflation

The extreme inflationary conditions in the United States beginning in the early 1970s resulted in significant distortions in many of the calculations we discussed. In recent years, inflationary trends have improved greatly in the major countries, to the extent that inflation is now considered relatively benign. Many other countries have, of course, had to deal with far more insidious levels of inflation for much longer periods of time, and some still do.

In the United States, the accounting profession and the Securities and Exchange Commission have expended much effort in developing new ways to account for and disclose the impact of changes in prices of goods and services and of fluctuating exchange rates that are due in part to inflation. However, the intricacies and arguments abundant in this difficult area are beyond the scope of this book. We are mentioning only a few of the basic mechanisms commonly employed to deal with price level changes where this is necessary to understand the impact on financial analysis. Thus, Chapters 2, 4, and 10 contain brief discussions of essential price level adjustments pertaining to the subjects of operating funds management, projections, and valuation. Appendix IV contains a discussion of the basic concepts underlying the inflation phenomenon.

In performance analysis, the main problem associated with inflation is the use of *historical costing* as a generally accepted accounting principle. The original cost of assets utilized in and charged to operations is reflected on the balance sheet. Depreciation and amortization reflect past values, which are often lower than current values. Financial statements of particularly heavily capitalized industries with long-lived depreciable assets and physical resources tend to reflect overstated profits and taxes, and understated asset values. This raises the issue of comparability of companies of different ages, and certainly of comparability of whole industries. Even short-term fluctuations in values will affect companies with high inventory turnover, such as wholesalers.

Another area of distortion affects the *viewpoint of the lender.* In inflationary times, the declining value of currency will affect borrowing/lending relationships, because eventual repayment will be made in less valuable dollars. Thus the lender would be at a disadvantage unless the interest rate contracted for is high enough to offset this risk. The dramatic rise in the 1970s and subsequent fall in the 1980s and early 1990s of short- and long-term interest rates in response to growing and waning inflationary pressures will remain in the memories of long-term lenders in particular.

Among the many methods used to deal with price level changes are replacement cost accounting, new forms of inventory valuation, and partial or full periodic restatement of financial reports. In fact, inflation has turned the deceptively simple accounting principle of matching costs and revenues into an economic and intellectual challenge. As yet, there are no consistent ways of appraising the difference between this type of recast statement and the original accounting statements. A recent ruling by the Financial Accounting Standards Board goes part way toward recasting financial statements for banks and financial institutions, asking that loans and investments be valued at current values. This raises a variety of issues that are far from resolved at the time of this writing.

Key Issues

The following is a recap of the key issues raised directly or indirectly in this chapter. They are enumerated here to help the reader keep the materials discussed within the perspective of financial theory and business practice.

1. Analysis of business performance is a complex process, which requires a clearly defined viewpoint, careful selection of appropriate measures, and an understanding of the interrelationships of the measures chosen.

2. The context of any analytical effort is critical to successfully addressing the issue or problem to be resolved by the analysis. Much of the thought process underlying an analysis should be directed to ensuring consistency between the objectives and the data sources and processes employed.

3. Although published financial statements are the most widely available source for financial analysis, the limitations inherent in their preparation (based on generally accepted accounting principles) require a basic understanding on the part of the user of how analytical results in the areas of performance and valuation can be distorted and what adjustments may be necessary.

4. There is no one measure or set of measures that fits every situation in which business performance is assessed. The choice is always dependent on the viewpoint and circumstances involved.

5. Performance analysis of a company or business unit is ultimately related to shareholder value creation. Therefore, past performance and future expectations have to be viewed at some point in terms of cash flow generation, investment returns, and operational effectiveness.

6. Many performance measures are related to each other in various ways, and sound analysis requires a thorough understanding of these linkages.

7. Comparative analysis of companies and business units is challenged by the frequent lack of truly comparable data, because of differences in product/service mix, accounting choices, size and age of the businesses, differences in the portfolio, and geographic scope. Industry statistics available from various sources often suffer from comparability issues as well.

8. Performance analysis is best performed as a dynamic process, using financial models where possible, to assess combinations of data and measures over time.

Summary

In this chapter, we discussed essential aspects of the main financial statements as a basis for appraising business performance, although we again established that true value creation is based on cash flow reasoning and criteria. With this background, we then demonstrated that the assessment of performance is made meaningful when seen from the points of view of the key groups interested in the company's success.

We chose to concentrate on the particular viewpoints of three groups—management, owners, and lenders—which are essential to the functioning of the business. The insights of these groups are used and expanded by others for their own particular needs. All three groups are concerned about the success of the business, each from its own standpoint.

It's management's prime duty to bring about stability, growth, and reliable earnings performance with the investment entrusted to it by the owners. We found that within the wide range of ratios displayed, the crucial test is the return on the capital employed in the business and its attendant effect on the value of the ownership stake, which will be discussed in more detail in Chapters 10 and 11. We also found that the ratios are linked by their common information base, and many are directly connected through the common use of certain elements. They are best interpreted when the business is viewed as a system of interdependent conditions responding to the decisions of management, and the specific impact of carefully defined value drivers. To this end, modeling and computer simulation are meaningful processes, because many individual ratios are, by their nature, only static tests that cannot do justice to the dynamics of a business.

Shortcomings in the analysis relate to the limitations of the accounting principles commonly used, and we strongly suggested that managers and analysts take an economic (cash flow) viewpoint for decision making, which will in the long run result in good accounting performance. Further distortions are introduced through price level changes stemming from inflation, currency fluctuations, and economic value changes. No definitive ways of compensating for these measurement problems have as yet been found to make financial analyses readily comparable and economically meaningful. As a result, the manager and analyst must use care and judgment at all times when dealing with performance assessment.

Analytical Support

A set of Excel-based templates (*Interactive Templates*) is available for download at no charge from the Web at www.mhhe.com/helfert11e. The second of these, "Ratios as a System: Key Ratios and Their Elements," activates the diagram of the interrelationship of ratios in Figure 3–5 on page 150. The template allows you to vary a given set of key assumptions about the investments, operations, and financing conditions of a sample company, and to observe the numerical changes resulting from these modifications on a graphic representation of ratio relationships. The template also contains a set of abbreviated financial statements linked to the ratio diagram, instantly displaying the results of any changes made. The template helps you explore and understand in depth the linkages within the ratio diagram and its accompanying financial statements, and to simulate and test the impact of any one, or a combination of modifications in financial policies, investment commitments, and price/volume/cost conditions.

Financial Genome, the advanced financial analysis software application described in Appendix I, is a fully integrated analytical and planning model for both the professional user and the business student. It's designed to develop a full set of financial ratios and relationships in addition to creating integrated financial statements from historical data inputs as well as for projections of financial performance. The software contains a five-year database (1996 to 2000) for 3M Corporation, matching the company's financial statements reproduced in this chapter. It also contains databases and project files with which to work Problems 2, 7, and 8 on pages 165 and 168.

Financial Genome is downloadable from the Web, using the unique code provided with this book. (See details in "Downloads" at the end of Appendix I, p. 479.)

Selected References

Anthony, Robert N. *Essentials of Accounting.* 5th ed. Reading, MA: Addison-Wesley, 1993.

Bandler, James P. *How to Use Financial Statements.* Burr Ridge, IL: Irwin Professional Publishing, 1994.

Brealey, Richard, and Stewart Myers. *Principles of Corporate Finance.* 5th ed. Burr Ridge, IL: Irwin/McGraw-Hill, 1996.

Dun & Bradstreet. *Industry Norms and Key Business Ratios* (annual). New York.

Merrill Lynch. *How to Read a Financial Report.* 7th ed. New York: Merrill Lynch, 1993.

Robert Morris Associates. *Annual Statement Studies.* Philadelphia.

Palepu, Krishna G.; Victor L. Bernard; and Paul M. Healy. *Business Analysis and Valuation: Using Financial Statements.* Cincinnati: Southwestern College Publishing, 1996.

Ross, Stephen; Randolph Westerfield; and Jeffrey Jaffe. *Corporate Finance.* 5th ed. Burr Ridge, IL: Irwin/McGraw-Hill, 1999.

Standard & Poor's. *Analysts' Handbook* (annual issues with monthly supplements). New York.

Troy, Leo. *Almanac of Business and Financial Ratios* (annual issues). Englewood Cliffs, NJ: Prentice Hall.

Weston, J. Fred; Scott Besley; and Eugene F. Brigham. *Essentials of Managerial Finance.* 11th ed. Hinsdale, IL: Dryden Press, 1997.

Self-Study Exercises, Problems, and Discussion Questions

Exercises and Problems (Selected Solutions Provided in Appendix VI)

1. Using the second interactive template, "Ratios as a System: Key Ratios and Their Elements," examine the ratio diagram, the key assumptions field, and the financial statements to become familiar with the structure of the template. (For help turn to the illustrative template in the "Read Me" tab). Examine the red explanation symbols to understand the contents of boxes and statements, especially the added blue boxes, which represent incremental details.

    a. Successively vary operational, investment, and financing assumptions and watch their impact on the diagram and the financial statements.

Note that the changes trigger movements throughout the system, as was the case in the business systems template. Check your understanding.

b. Develop a set of assumptions you would like to test and enter them into the key assumptions field. Observe the results in the various boxes on the diagram and in the financial statements. Try to improve the return on equity or the other ratios by varying individual assumptions, and note the relative impact on the results from different drivers. Check your understanding and discuss your findings.

2. Using Financial Genome, open one of the sample projects in the project files and create a Ratios Statement. Examine the contents and structure of this statement, which contains the ratios discussed in this book, grouped by the three decision areas. Click the (?) button to call forth the definitions of any of them to test your understanding. Alternatively, use the dictionary browser to define the ratios statement hierarchy, and obtain definitions of any ratio from the definition box.

3. Work the following exercises:

a. A company's net profit represents 11.4 percent of sales. What's the company's return on shareholders' investment if asset turnover is 1.34 and the capitalization is 67 percent of total assets? How would a faster asset turnover affect the result?

b. A company's gross margin on sales is 31.4 percent. Total cost of goods sold amounts to $4,391,300 and net profit is 9.7 percent of sales. What are the company's total assets if the ratio of sales to assets is 82.7 percent? What's the return on capitalization if current liabilities are 21 percent of total assets?

c. What's the change in a company's current ratio of 2.2:1 (current assets are $573,100) if the following actions are taken individually?

   1. Cash payment of $67,500 for accounts payable.
   2. Collection of $33,000 of notes receivable.
   3. Purchase of merchandise of $41,300 on account.
   4. Payment of dividends of $60,000, of which $42,000 has been shown as an accrued liability.
   5. Cash sale of machinery for $80,000, with a book value of $90,000 and accumulated depreciation of $112,000.
   6. Sale of merchandise on account, with a recorded cost of $73,500. Gross margin is 33 percent.
   7. Write-off of $20,000 in inventory as scrap; amortization of goodwill of $15,000.

d. From the data shown below, calculate the outstanding days' receivables and payables for the company, using the methods shown in the chapter. What's the inventory turnover, calculated in different ways? Discuss your assumptions.

Sales for three months	$437,500
Cost of sales	298,400
Purchases	143,500
Beginning inventory	382,200
Ending inventory	227,300
Accounts receivable	156,800
Accounts payable	69,300
Normal terms of sale	2/10, n/30
Normal purchase terms	n/45

4. The following data are available for three companies, A, B, and C, all stated in millions of dollars. Calculate the return on equity, return on net assets, return on sales, NOPAT, and the operating return on net assets.

   a. Which of the three companies has the best performance and why?

   b. Why is Company B showing a better ROE than Company A, even though its RONA is worse?

   c. Note the differences in RONA and in operating return on net assets. Which company is having the better results overall, A or B?

   d. A new investment proposed by a manager in Company C has a NOPAT return on net assets of 17 percent in the first year. Should this investment be considered?

   e. If Companies A and B were combined, what would be the impact on the results? Under what conditions would such a combination make sense?

   f. If Company A and C were combined, what would be the impact on the results? Under what conditions would such a combination make sense?

	A	B	C
Sales	$100	$100	$250
Net assets	120	180	125
Shareholders' equity	80	90	100
Long-term debt	40	90	25
Net profit after taxes	12	15	25
After-tax interest rates	2	5	1

5. From the following financial statements of the ABC Company for 2002 and 2003, prepare the full set of ratios and measures discussed in this chapter.

   a. Ratios from the viewpoint of management.

   b. Ratios from the viewpoint of owners.

   c. Ratios from the viewpoint of lenders.

   Comment on the changes experienced between the two years and on the significance of the results from the three points of view. Indicate what additional kinds of comparisons you'd like to make for this company (a high technology manufacturer) and the types of information you'd need.

   Financial Genome contains the historical data for this problem in a separate database. You can create the Ratios Statement from this information, which arranges the ratios according to the three decision areas of the business system. Supply additional data that you deem appropriate to enable the program to calculate ratios missing because of the limited data available in this example. Discuss your findings.

ABC COMPANY
Balance Sheets
December 31, 2002 and 2003 ($ millions)

	2002	2003
Assets:		
Current assets:		
Cash	$ 82.7	$110.9
Accounts receivable—net	92.6	146.2
Inventories	88.8	129.5
Prepaid expenses	2.8	6.2
Advances from government	5.3	2.8
Total current assets	272.2	395.6
Property, plant, and equipment	215.2	283.4
Less: Accumulated depreciation	101.2	119.6
Net property	114.0	163.8
Other assets	3.1	4.2
Total assets	$389.3	$563.6
Liabilities and Shareholders' Equity		
Current liabilities:		
Accounts payable	$ 43.4	$ 62.9
Accrued income tax	36.7	44.0
Accrued pension and profit sharing	27.1	38.4
Other accruals	21.9	31.2
Current portion of long-term debt	2.1	—
Total current liabilities	131.2	176.5
Debentures	—	94.0
Other long-term debt	7.8	4.1
Deferred income tax	5.2	7.6
Common stock ($1 par)	10.1	10.2
Paid-in surplus	25.1	27.2
Retained earnings	209.9	244.0
Total liabilities and shareholders' equity	$389.3	$563.6

ABC COMPANY
Income Statements for 2002 and 2003
($ millions)

	2002	2003
Net sales	$655.1	$872.7
Cost of goods and services*	460.9	616.1
Gross profit	194.2	256.6
Selling, general, and administrative expenses	98.3	125.2
Employee profit sharing and retirement	26.9	38.7
	125.2	163.9
Operating profit	69.0	92.7
Other income	1.1	1.8
	70.1	94.5
Interest paid	1.0	7.4
	69.1	87.1
Provision for income taxes	31.8	40.1
Net profit†	$ 37.3	$ 47.0

*Depreciation and amortization $28.2 $38.5
†Common dividends paid   5.5   12.9

6. Review the 10-year financial summary of 3M Corporation on pages 154–155 and analyze the company's performance over this period. What additional information would you like to have to develop a thorough assessment and comparison of 3M's situation? Discuss.

7. Using Financial Genome and the built-in database for 3M Corporation, develop a five-year historical perspective of balance sheets, income statements, cash flow statements, statements of change in shareholder equity, and ratio statements. Note that the last two years match the 3M statements reproduced in Chapters 1, 2, and 3. Examine the results and compare them to the materials and results in Chapter 3. You can temporarily override any numerical inputs (not calculated terms) on the financial statements and trace the effect on the statements and the ratio results (restore the overrides to the original database value by highlighting and pressing "return"). Test your understanding and comment on your findings.

8. Using Financial Genome, follow the process of entering data as described in the "help" system and create integrated sets of financial statements for companies of your choice. In particular, examine the Ratios Statement in each case. Analyze the results and select key measures that assist you in appraising the company's performance. Develop significant industry comparisons and comment on the relative position of your company samples.

Discussion Questions

1. Explain the relationships of the four basic financial statements. Which statement encompasses the results of all decisions? Why?

2. Why is return on shareholders' equity one of the most commonly used ratios? What are the implications of accounting changes and financial leverage on the meaning of this ratio?

3. What are the key factors that allow comparison of industry ratios to the ratios of an individual company? What factors make comparisons difficult?

4. List several accounting practices that can result in changes in the ratios that measure profitability. What's their effect?

5. List several accounting practices that can result in changes in the ratios that measure liquidity and debt exposure. What's their effect?

6. What measurement issues arise when two different divisions of a company are compared on the basis of management ratios, given widely divergent conditions in the age of the business, markets, and costs?

7. A commonly used ratio from the standpoint of the lender is "times interest earned." How meaningful is this ratio in assessing the quality of the indebtedness involved?

8. Does operating cash flow represent the majority of funds movements caused by operations? If not, why not?

9. What key questions would you ask if you were a banker reviewing a loan request from a small, rapidly growing company?

10. What's the impact of inflation on ratio analysis? What key distortions can be expected, and in which ratios?

11. What are the major problems encountered in the process of adjusting for inflation?

12. If you were general manager of a division, which key ratio would you choose to be evaluated on for your unit's financial performance, and why? What conditions would you stipulate?

CHAPTER 4

PROJECTION OF FINANCIAL REQUIREMENTS

Up to this point, we've discussed appraisal of performance and management of operating funds in the context of *past* decisions involving investments, operations, and financing. This chapter shifts the emphasis to a *forward* look, that is, forecasting likely future conditions, a critically important task in managing any business. We'll discuss the key concepts and techniques of projecting operating performance and expected financial requirements with which to support future operations. Such projections normally involve alternative plans developed for different sets of conditions, and testing of the sensitivity of the results to changes in key assumptions.

Projection of financial requirements is only part of the business planning process with which management positions the company's future activities relative to the expected economic, competitive, technical, and social environment. When business plans are developed, they are usually structured around specific goals and objectives cooperatively set by the organization and its subgroups. The plans normally spell out strategies and actions for achieving desired short-term, intermediate, and long-term results, with special attention to the need for creating shareholder value by exceeding the cost of capital in ongoing operations as well as sound new growth investments.

Eventually, such plans are quantified in financial terms, in the form of projected financial statements (pro forma statements) and a variety of operational budgets. Detailed cash budgets and cash flow statements are used to provide greater insight into the funding implications of the projected activities. Also, key ratios are usually calculated and presented. The concepts and techniques discussed in Chapters 2 and 3 are the necessary tools for this quantification.

The scope of this book allows us to focus only on the major methods and formats of financial projection. We cannot explicitly take into account the broader strategic planning framework through which the future direction of the company should be explored before any financial quantification can become fully meaningful. Nor can we go into the details of various statistical methods which are at times used to test and support the judgments involved in estimating future conditions.

Nevertheless, financial projection techniques by themselves can be useful simulations of the likely results of broad assumptions made by management about a variety of future conditions. The ease with which pro forma financial statements and cash flow projections can be developed makes them attractive as convenient approximations—which can then be refined with additional information and insights—especially as the number of alternatives for action is narrowed down.

Computer spreadsheets and planning models have become ubiquitous, and a growing selection of software packages offers financial simulation and projection capabilities. Many of these applications have helped reduce the drudgery of tracing investment, operational, and financing assumptions through the financial framework of a business. Although commercial software offerings differ in their specific orientation and degree of sophistication, they are all built around the basic concepts we'll be discussing in this chapter, as is the available advanced Financial Genome software described in Appendix I.

The most important requirement for making successful use of projection methods, however, is a solid understanding of basic financial techniques and relationships, because spreadsheets and analytical packages cannot remove the overriding need for judgment and consistency. Only with such understanding can the analyst take full advantage of their capabilities. Therefore, this book doesn't focus on the technicalities of how to use spreadsheets, but rather on explaining the financial concepts and techniques themselves, structured around our decisional context.

The main techniques of financial projection fall into three categories:

- Pro forma financial statements.
- Cash budgets.
- Operating budgets.

Pro forma statements, as the name implies, are projected financial statements embodying a set of assumptions about a company's future performance and funding requirements. Cash budgets are detailed projections of the specific periodic incidence of cash moving in and out of the business. Operating budgets are detailed projections of company-wide or departmental revenue and/or expense patterns, and they are subsidiary to both pro forma statements and cash flow statements.

All three projection categories involve organized arrays of financial and economic data for the purpose of assessing future performance and funds requirements. As we'll see, the three methodologies are also closely interrelated—a linkage that can be exploited to achieve consistent financial forecasts.

After discussing each category in detail, we'll examine basic financial modeling concepts and the use of sensitivity analysis for testing the impact of changes in critical assumptions underlying the financial projections, subjects we'll revisit in a broader context in Chapter 5.

Pro Forma Financial Statements

The most accessible, integrated overview of the future financial performance of a company can be obtained by developing a set of pro forma statements. These are merely an income statement and a related balance sheet extended into the future by a variety of assumptions. The pro forma income statement represents a broad operational outlook for the business, whereas the pro forma balance sheet reflects the anticipated cumulative impact of assumed future decisions on its financial condition. Both statements are prepared by taking the most readily available esti- mates of future activity and projecting, account by account, the assumed results and conditions. As we'll see, the approach is not based on detailed accounting transactions, but rather on a creative use of the financial statement framework as a structure on which to arrange future expectations.

Most of the time the third key statement, the pro forma cash flow statement, is prepared to add further insight by displaying the funds movements expected during the forecast period, arranged into our familiar categories of operations, in- vestments, and financing. As we saw in Chapter 2, cash flow statements provide the most dynamic view of the expected changes in the company's funding picture.

Pro forma projections can be prepared for any time frame and at any level of detail desired. In summarized form, these statements are one of the most widely used ways of quickly making estimates of funding needs. They are particularly fa- vored by bank loan officers, who must assess the creditworthiness of the client company from a total financial standpoint. Detailed operating plans aren't needed to construct complete pro forma statements, even though using the results of a for- mal planning process would increase the degree of precision. Instead, selected ra- tios and relationships can be employed as *forecast drivers* to produce statements that are entirely satisfactory, particularly as a first look. As we'll demonstrate, an important aspect of pro forma analysis is the ability to establish the company's net cash needs as of the future date for which the pro forma balance sheet is prepared.

To show how pro forma statements are developed, we'll use the example of a fictitious manufacturing company called XYZ Corporation. We've chosen a manufacturing company here because such statements tend to be more complex than those of service organizations, especially in the operations area, and thus provide an opportunity to show more interrelationships. XYZ Corporation makes and sells three different products, has a seasonal pattern with the low point occur- ring in December, and is currently profitable. The most recent actual results avail- able are for the third quarter of 2002. This initial set of data allows us to project ahead, but we can also ask management for additional information as needed. The pro forma projection is to be made for the last quarter of 2002, with the objective of determining both the level of profit for the quarter and the amount of additional funds that will be needed as of the end of the year. A quarterly pattern was chosen for this illustration because it permits us to consider seasonal changes in addition to simple period-to-period changes. We've also included an annual view, showing the estimated results for all of 2002, and a pro forma projection for the year 2003.

There's no difference in the basic principles for projecting either annual or quarterly periods—only the length of the time interval itself and the matching of the forecast drivers to the period.

Pro Forma Income Statement

We begin the process with the pro forma income statement for XYZ Corporation. The income statement is normally prepared first, because the amount of after-tax profit developed there must later be reflected in the pro forma balance sheet as a change in retained earnings, in order to ensure consistency between the two statements.

The starting point for the income statement, as shown on the first line in Figure 4–1, is a projection of the unit and dollar volume of *sales*. This can be estimated in a variety of ways, ranging from trend-line projection to detailed departmental sales forecasts by individual product, often built up from field estimates. In the absence of any other information we can, of course, make our own "guesstimates" based on past overall results. In the case of XYZ Corporation, we know that a seasonal pattern exists, and that sales can be expected to decline in the last quarter. On an annual basis, we are showing the estimated results for all of 2002, which include the projected last quarter, and a pro forma projection for 2003.

In the first column of Figure 4–1, we've reproduced the actual income statement for the third quarter of 2002. Dollar amounts are given for key revenue and cost elements, as well as a breakdown into percent of sales, or common numbers. In making the necessary series of assumptions for the fourth quarter, we'll use the third quarter experience as a guide, because we've been assured that the quarterly pattern over the years has been reasonably stable. For purposes of this illustration, we'll extensively use as forecast drivers the various expense ratios based on a percentage of sales, which is the most common and direct overall approach. However, we should emphasize that a more detailed buildup of assumed conditions from budgets and supporting data, as well as statistical analysis and probabilistic methodology can be used for a more refined approach to the process.

Company statistics from past years suggest that a drop of 18 to 20 percent in sales volume is normal during the fourth quarter. We'll take the midpoint of this range as a beginning assumption. After calculating a 19 percent drop in unit volume, we'll further assume that both prices and product mix will remain unchanged. It's possible, of course, to make different assumptions about volume, prices, and the mix of the three individual products in order to reflect specific insights or to test the sensitivity of operating profit to the impact of "what-if" questions. In our case, an inquiry to sales management will confirm that this set of assumptions about sales matches their own forecast.

In establishing the volume for the estimated full year 2002, we are told that units sold through 9/30/02 were 399,000, to which we can add the fourth quarter estimate of 111,000 units. With no change in price and mix, 2002 sales revenue

FIGURE 4–1

XYZ CORPORATION
Pro Forma Income Statements*
For the Quarter Ended December 31, 2002, and for the Years Ended December 31, 2002 and 2003 ($ thousands)

	Actual Quarter Ended 9-30-02		Pro Forma Quarter Ended 12-31-02		Estimated Full Year Ended 12-31-02		Pro Forma Year Ended 12-31-03		
Units sold**	137,000		111,000		510,000		550,000		Last quarter is seasonal low; past data show 18 to 20 percent decline from third quarter.
Sales	$12,650	100.0%	$10,250	100.0%	$47,100	100.0%	$52,250	100.0%	Projection for the quarter has 19 percent lower volume, same price and mix; pro forma year assumes 7.3 percent growth
Cost of goods sold:									
Labor	2,210		1,810		8,250		9,050		Continued at 21.5 percent of total cost of goods sold
Materials	2,045		1,680		7,675		8,400		Continued at 20 percent of total cost of goods sold
Overhead	5,685		4,660		21,315		23,350		Continued at 55.5 percent of total cost of good sold
Delivery	305		250		1,150		1,250		Continued at 3.0 percent of total cost of goods sold
Total cost of goods sold	10,245	81.0	8,400	82.0	38,390	81.5	42,050	80.5	
Gross margin	2,405	19.0	1,850	18.0	8,710	18.5	10,200	19.5	Margin reduced for the quarter by 1 percentage point due to inefficiencies; improvement for pro forma year
Expenses:									
Selling expense	875	6.9	825	8.0	3,340	7.1	3,550	6.8	Lower activity in last quarter; increase in pro forma year
General and administrative	585	4.6	600	5.9	2,215	4.7	2,350	4.5	Slight increase for quarter; improvement in pro forma year
Total expenses	1,460	11.5	1,425	13.9	5,555	11.8	5,900	11.3	
Operating profit (EBIT)	945	7.5	425	4.1	3,160	6.7	4,300	8.2	Quarter shows impact of slowdown; improvement for pro forma year
Interest	190	1.5	175	1.7	785	1.7	850	1.6	Based on outstanding debt and temporary borrowing
Profit before taxes	755	6.0	250	2.4	2,375	5.0	3,450	6.6	
Income taxes	272	2.2	90	0.9	855	1.8	1,250	2.4	Projected at 36 percent
Net income	483	3.8	160	1.5	1,520	3.2	2,200	4.2	
Dividends	100	0.8	0	0.0	300	0.6	400	0.8	No payment in last quarter; higher in pro forma year
Retained earnings	383	3.0%	160	1.5%	1,220	2.6%	1,800	3.4%	Carried to balance sheet
Depreciation effect added back	575		600		2,330		2,450		From fixed asset records (tax and book depreciation the same)
Net cash flow after dividends	958		760		3,550		4,250		
Add back tax-adjusted interest	122		112		502		544		
Add back dividends	100		0		300		400		
Cash flow from operations	$ 1,180		$ 872		$ 4,352		$ 5,194		

*For financial projection software, see "Analytical Support," p.199.

**399,000 units were sold between 1/1/02 and 9/30/02

will be $47,100,000. In the pro forma year 2003, sales management expects a 40,000 unit increase over 2002, with product mix and prices still unchanged, for total sales of $52,250,000.

Next we turn to *cost of goods sold.* The actual third quarter income statement provides details on the main components—labor, materials, overhead, and delivery—contained in cost of goods sold. The simplest approach to projection is to calculate the proportion of cost that each of these elements represents in the total cost of goods sold, and assume that the same proportions will hold during the fourth quarter.

We must also remember that the last quarter is the company's seasonal low point, and we can assume that overall production costs are likely to rise, because as operations slow down, some inefficiencies will likely occur. Without more data, we can probably assume a rise of something like 1 percentage point in the ratio of cost of goods sold to sales as a quick way to allow for the seasonal distortion. The dollar penalty of this assumption is a reduction in the gross margin by 1 percent of sales, or $102,500. We could, of course, test the impact of other levels of the cost of goods sold ratio, using the detailed cost breakdown (labor, materials, etc.) given in the third quarter income statement. If more precision were desired, specific assumptions could be made about each of these components. This is a basic form of sensitivity analysis—testing the impact on the outcome from changes in one or more key assumptions.

As was done in the case of sales, to make an estimate for the full year 2002, our cost of goods sold projection for the fourth quarter was added to the year-to-date amounts provided to us by management. Note that the gross margin percentage for the full year is above both the third and fourth quarters, because of better performance in the first two quarters. The projection for the year 2003 assumes unchanged annual performance at 19.5 percent.

The main expense categories can be estimated by examining again the actual statement for the third quarter. The figures provided there might simply be accepted and used as the base for our projection, or more detailed assumptions could be tested. For a quick first look, such an overall approach is usually acceptable. *Selling expense* is shown as $875,000. Given that the fourth quarter has lower sales activity, we can probably assume a small decrease, such as $50,000. A reduction fully proportional to the 19 percent drop in volume would not be realistic, however, given that many of the costs, such as base salaries of sales and marketing personnel, are essentially fixed in the near term. This assumption, when added to the results to date given to us by the finance staff, leads to a full year 2002 estimate of $3,340,000, and a projection for 2003 of $3,550,000, where higher sales efforts are assumed to support the increased volume.

Administrative expenses should be rounded off a little higher for purposes of our quarterly projection because of expected nonrecurring year-end outlays. Note that both expense elements now represent a higher proportion of sales than was true for the actual prior quarter. If there's reason to believe that this result seems out of line, it can, of course, be modified. But we must remember that even if historical patterns were available in great detail, our projection has to deal with the future, and the purpose of the exercise is to make the most realistic assumptions possible. These will, of course, remain assumptions until actual experience supersedes them. Including the fourth quarter figure, the estimate for all of 2002 becomes $2,215,000, again based on year-to-date information given us, and $2,350,000 for pro forma 2003.

As a result of all our assumptions, the fourth quarter *operating profit* falls by half a million dollars, and the profit ratio drops to almost one-half its former level. This is due mostly to the 19 percent drop in sales volume and the associated loss in profit contribution. This volume reduction represents $2.4 million of lost sales which, with a normal cost of goods sold ratio of 81 percent, would have contributed $456,000 to profit. Moreover, we assumed certain inefficiencies in operations and expected only a partial ability to reduce what are mostly fixed expenses. As stated before, this result can and should be examined against the best available experience to judge its appropriateness. For the year as a whole, operating profit is expected to amount to $3,160,000, while the year 2003 results are boosted to $4,300,000. This is due in part to the assumed volume increase of 40,000 units, and also because of the improvements in operating expenses as reflected in their lower percentages of sales compared with expected 2002 results.

Interest expense is charged according to the provisions of the company's outstanding debt, information which is provided to us by the finance staff for all the pro forma periods. The income statement will be complete once we calculate *income taxes* (assumed here at an effective rate of 36 percent) to arrive at *net income*. We note that net income for the quarter has dropped significantly in response to the slowdown in operations, while results for 2003 versus estimated 2002 are up by almost $700,000.

A further assumption needs to be made about *dividends* to arrive at *retained earnings* for the period, which will be reflected in the pro forma balance sheet. In XYZ Corporation's case, no dividends have been declared for the quarter, although payments already made during 2002 amount to $300,000. Dividends are expected to rise to $400,000 for the year 2003. As a last step, we've added back the depreciation effect for each of the periods, as well as tax-adjusted interest and dividends to calculate the *cash flow from operations*. As we recall from Chapter 3, this total is a quick approximation which we'll review later in the context of all other expected funds movements.

Pro Forma Balance Sheet

Armed with the data about expected operations, we can now develop the pro forma balance sheets at the end of 2002 and 2003, as illustrated in Figure 4–2. Again, we must make specific assumptions about each account, using the actual balance sheet data at the beginning of the forecast period and applying any additional information and judgments we can obtain from management. Fortunately, we have relative freedom to make and vary our estimates in this statement—except that there must always be complete consistency between any assumptions affecting *both* the income statement and the balance sheet. The objective is not

FIGURE 4–2

XYZ CORPORATION
Pro Forma Balance Sheets*
As of December 31, 2002, and December 31, 2003
($ thousands)

	Actual 9/30/02	Change	Pro Forma 12/31/02	Change	Pro Forma 12/31/03	
Assets						
Current assets:						
Cash	$ 1,450	$ −200	$ 1,250	$ 0	$ 1,250	Cash set at estimated minimum balance.
Accounts receivable	4,250	−1,200	3,050	450	3,500	Represents 30 days' sales (projected December sales)
Raw materials	1,500	0	1,500	100	1,600	Safety level; requirements purchased as needed
Finished goods	4,050	−750	3,300	500	3,800	Reduced production by 19 percent for quarter; up for 2003
Total current assets	11,250	−2,150	9,100	1,050	10,150	Drop from September to December 2002 reflects seasonal pattern
Fixed assets:						
Land	2,500	0	2,500	0	2,500	No change assumed
Plant and equipment	20,800	−1,500	19,300	1,750	21,050	Machine sold in last quarter 2002; cost $1,500, accum. depreciation $950; new equipment to be bought in 2003
Less: Accumulated depreciation	8,350	−350	8,000	2,450	10,450	Depreciation for quarter $600; less $950 reduction from sale; normal depreciation for 2003
Net plant and equipment	12,450	−1,150	11,300	−700	10,600	
Total fixed assets	14,950	−1,150	13,800	−700	13,100	
Other assets	1,250	0	1,250	200	1,450	No change in quarter; purchased patents in 2003
Total assets	27,450	−3,300	24,150	550	24,700	
Liabilities and Shareholders' Equity						
Current liabilities						
Accounts payable	1,120	−410	710	600	1,310	45 days' purchases from estimated pattern in Figure 4–4; increase for 2003
Notes payable	3,000	−1,500	1,500	−1,500	0	Scheduled repayments
Due contractor	3,400	−2,900	500	−500	0	Scheduled payments on building contract
Accrued taxes	1,250	−310	940	400	1,340	Payment for quarter $400; plus accrual of $90; net increase for 2003
Total current liabilities	8,770	−5,120	3,650	−1,000	2,650	
Long-term liabilities	8,500	0	8,500	0	8,500	No change assumed
Common stock	4,250	250	4,500	0	4,500	Sale of stock under option during quarter; none in 2003
Retained earnings	5,930	160	6,090	1,800	7,890	Retained earnings as calculated on income statement; net of dividends in 2003
Total liabilities and shareholder's equity	$27,450	$−4,710	$22,740	$ 800	$23,540	
Funds required		1,410	1,410	−250	1,160	"Plug" figure representing financing needs as of December 31; same amount as in Figures 4–3 and 4–4

*For financial projection software, see "Analytical Support," p.199.

accounting precision, of course, but rather to develop an indication of approximate funds needs three months hence and a look at the overall financial condition of the company at that time, as well as one year later.

We'll start the process with the first account, *cash,* and assume that three months hence, the company would need to keep only the minimum working balance in its bank accounts, and that this will also apply to 12/31/03. The information source for this figure ($1,250,000) is again the finance staff. In the absence of such specific data, we could assume a level of cash that is common among companies of this size. As we'll see later, the amount of cash on hand desired directly affects the amount of funds the company may have to borrow. Also, we must not forget that any cash balance maintained as an ongoing requirement on the balance sheet represents an investment like any other commitment of resources.

Next we turn to *accounts receivable.* If the company sells its products on terms of net 30, it can expect to have at least 30 days' sales outstanding; more, if some of its customers are late in paying. Given no abnormal delays in collections, the accounts receivable balance on the December 31 balance sheet should represent the sales for the whole month of December. However, we do not have exact December sales estimates, because our pro forma income statement for the quarter shows the last three months' sales combined, and we have only an annual sales estimate for 2003. As a simple shortcut, we could assume that one-third of the projected quarterly sales would be outstanding at the end of the fourth quarter, and one-twelfth of the annual sales outstanding on 12/31/03.

For XYZ Corporation, the figure for 12/31/02 would be one-third of the sales of $10,250,000 shown in Figure 4–1, or $3,417,000. But we learn after some discussion with sales management that in view of the seasonal low in December, the company's sales force projects the month's sales at only $3,050,000. This amount thus represents the 30 days of sales we can assume to be outstanding in the form of accounts receivable at the end of 2002, given normal collection experience. Similarly, the estimate for December sales in 2003 is given to us as $3,500,000.

Raw material inventory could be projected by using monthly withdrawal and purchase patterns, information that the company would be able to provide. However, manufacturing management informs us that for reasons of continuity, they like to keep $1,500,000 worth of raw materials on hand at all times, and frequent purchases are made as needed to maintain that level, which is assumed both for 2002 and 2003.

Finished goods inventory is likely to decline in concert with lower sales and production activity, and we have allowed for a 19 percent reduction. If we considered this an optimistic assumption, because of likely inefficiencies in adjusting production exactly to the seasonal low, a higher amount can, of course, be specified. This would necessarily mean, however, that a lesser amount of funds would be released from declining inventories. A somewhat higher figure is assumed for the end of 2003, reflecting the higher volume of sales in that year, net of the seasonal slowdown.

When we add up all our changes in the *current asset accounts,* we find that this total at the end of the fourth quarter is projected to decline by over $2 million, in effect releasing these funds for other uses in the company. Note that this pattern reflects the normal funds flow characteristics of seasonal operations, as demonstrated in Chapter 2. By the end of 2003, however, the higher sales volume will have caused an increase of about $1.0 million, requiring additional funding instead.

Fixed assets are affected by several events. While *land* remains unchanged, we are told that some machines will be sold during the last quarter. Their original cost was $1.5 million, against which $950,000 of depreciation has been accumulated. They are to be sold for their book value of $550,000, involving no taxable gain or loss. To reflect this transaction, the *plant and equipment* account on our pro forma balance sheet must be reduced by the original cost, while *accumulated depreciation* must be reduced by the $950,000 of past write-offs recorded there. This effectively removes all traces of the sold machinery from the company's books, while cash in the amount of $550,000 will have been received.

We also know from the pro forma income statement that the company's normal depreciation charges for the quarter will be $600,000. This amount has to be added to the accumulated depreciation account. As a net result of the two changes, accumulated depreciation will decline by $350,000. Overall, the combined effect of these fixed asset transactions will decrease the net plant and equipment account by $1,150,000.

During the year 2003, new equipment is expected to be purchased for $1,750,000, which must be added to the plant and equipment account. Depreciation charges for the year as calculated by the finance staff and shown on the pro forma income statement will amount to $2,450,000, and this figure must be added to the accumulated depreciation account. *Other assets* are assumed to be unchanged during the last quarter of 2002, but during 2003 some patents are expected to be purchased for $200,000.

On the liability side, *accounts payable* are expected to decline in response to lower activity in the final quarter. We're told that payables are mostly related to purchases of raw material. We could approximate accounts payable, which have payment terms of net 45, by assuming that because the pro forma income statement reflects 90 days of raw materials use, about one-half of this amount would be outstanding ($840,000). But we have additional inside information on the actual level of purchases scheduled (Figure 4–4 on p. 186), and are able to refine our assumption to show all of December's purchases ($460,000) and one-half of November's ($250,000) as total accounts payable outstanding at year end 2002 ($710,000). At the end of 2003, about $1.3 million are expected to be outstanding.

Other current liabilities must be analyzed in terms of specific payment schedules. We're informed that *notes payable* carry a provision for repayment of $1.5 million during the quarter, and for payment of the balance in the year 2003. Moreover, the account *due contractor* requires XYZ Corporation to make a payment of $2.9 million owed on construction in progress, which will become due in the final quarter, with the balance of $500,000 due in 2003. *Accruals* largely involve income tax obligations. We already know from the pro forma income statement that tax accruals projected for the quarter will be $90,000. We're also told that the company must make an estimated tax payment of $400,000 during the quarter. The two items cause a net reduction in accrued taxes of $310,000. During the year 2003, tax accruals are assumed to increase by $400,000 because of over-all higher tax obligations and payments. Note that with all these changes, total current liabilities are estimated to be reduced by $5.12 million by 12/31/02, a significant drain of funds during the quarter, with another $1.0 million net reduction occurring by 12/31/03.

Long-term liabilities are assumed to remain unchanged both during the quarter and during 2003, while the recorded value of *common stock* is expected to increase by $250,000, because stock options are about to be exercised in late 2002. Finally, *retained earnings* should increase by the amount of net profit (income) of $160,000 as calculated on the pro forma income statement for the quarter, and by the net amount after dividends of $1.8 million for the year 2003.

When we add up all these results, we find that neither of the pro forma balance sheets balances! However, this shouldn't be surprising because we didn't use double-entry bookkeeping to balance our calculations. Instead, we made a variety of independent assumptions about many of the accounts, taking care only to be consistent with related projections in the respective pro forma income statements. Having maintained this consistency, and given that we're reasonably satisfied with our assumptions, the balancing figure required to equalize assets and liabilities at the end of both periods will represent either the company's net *funds deficit* or *funds excess* as of the pro forma balance sheet date.

This *plug* figure, as it's often called, serves as a quick estimate of what additional indebtedness the company will face on the date of the statement, or what uncommitted funds it will have at its disposal. But the plug won't indicate what peaks and valleys in funds requirements might have occurred *during* each of the three months. These fluctuations could, of course, be found by generating intermediate balance sheets more frequently than every 90 days.

In other words, we could find any major variations in funding conditions by taking financial "snapshots" in more closely spaced intervals, such as months or even weeks. As we'll see shortly, however, preparing a detailed cash budget is a much more direct way of tracing the ups and downs of funding requirements within the forecast period. But before illustrating the detailed cash budget for XYZ Corporation, we need to discuss the further interpretation of balance sheet changes by means of a cash flow analysis, using the third financial statement commonly prepared in pro forma projections. This approach allows us to see the cash uses and sources individually, and to reconcile them with the cash balances on hand.

Pro Forma Cash Flow Statement

As we observed in Figure 4–2, some very significant changes took place between the beginning and ending balance sheets of the two forecast periods. A pro forma cash flow statement will help us highlight the cash movements caused by these changes and their impact on the company's financial condition. Using the techniques discussed in Chapter 2, we can take the changes in the respective balance sheets and selected information from the related income statements to construct the pro forma cash flow analysis shown in Figure 4–3.

FIGURE 4-3

XYZ CORPORATION
Pro Forma Cash Flow Statements*
For the Quarter Ended December 31, 2002, and the Year Ended December 31, 2003
($ thousands)

	Quarter Ended 12/31/02	Year Ended 12/31/03
Cash flow from operations:		
Net income	$ 160	$ 2,200
Depreciation effect	600	2,450
Changes in working capital:		
Decrease (increase) in receivables	1,200	−450
Decrease (increase) in raw materials	0	−100
Decrease (increase) in finished goods	750	−500
Increase (decrease) in payables	−410	600
Increase (decrease) in accruals	−310	400
Total changes in working capital	1,230	−50
Net cash flow from operations	1,990	4,600
Cash flow from investments:		
Purchase of new equipment	0	−1,750
Purchase of patent (other asset)	0	−200
Proceeds from sale of machines	550	0
Net cash flow from investments	550	−1,950
Cash flow from financing:		
Repayment of notes	−1,500	−1,500
Repayment of construction loan	−2,900	−500
Proceeds from stock options	250	0
Dividends paid	0	−400
Net cash flow from financing	−4,150	−2,400
Net cash flow	−1,610	250
Beginning cash balance	1,450	−160
Ending cash balance	−160	90
Minimum cash balance	$ 1,250	$ 1,250
Funding requirement as of December 31	1,410	1,160

*For financial projection software see "Analytical Support," p.199.

Reflecting prevailing practice, we've separated the various cash flow items into cash flow from operations, cash flow from investment, and cash flow from financing. It becomes quite obvious that the reduced operations of the last quarter of 2002 are expected to release a significant net amount of working capital ($1,230,000) of which $1.2 million comes from reduced accounts receivable alone. These working capital funds sources almost triple the basic operating cash flow (net income of $160,000 plus depreciation of $600,000) into a total cash inflow from operations of about $2.0 million.

In contrast, the growth assumed during all of 2003, affected by a similar seasonal pattern late in the year, will cause essentially unchanged working capital requirements. The higher net income, plus somewhat higher depreciation charges, will almost totally be available for funding other needs, as we'll see.

During the quarter, operating funds sources are far outweighed by significant funding needs in the financing area, however. To meet various financial obligations currently due, $4.4 million are scheduled for repayment. Of this total, the notes payable of $1.5 million represent repayment of seasonal funding, made possible by the significant release of working capital as the seasonal low approaches, while a sizable payment of $2.9 million is due the building contractor. Cash received from the sale of machinery and the exercise of stock options assists somewhat in this. But in the end there is a cash outflow of $1.61 million for the quarter, only slightly offset by the planned reduction in the minimum cash balance. The remainder to be financed is $1.41 million, as we already observed in the pro forma balance sheet of 12/31/02.

The conditions for the year 2003 are also affected by the repayment of notes ($1.5 million), and the balance due the contractor ($500,000) to be paid. In addition, there are significant investment outlays for machinery ($1.75 million) and patents ($200,000). Dividend payments of $400,000 require funding as well. In contrast to the fourth quarter pattern of the prior year, there is a net cash inflow of $250,000 for 2003, but in order to maintain the assumed minimum cash balance of $1.25 million, funding of $1.16 million must be obtained. Again, this is the same funds deficit we observed as the "plug" in the pro forma balance sheet of 12/31/03. It appears that for the foreseeable future XYZ Corporation will have to rely on financing of between $1.0 million and $1.5 million to carry out the planned activities in the operational, investment, and financing areas of its business system.

It should be clear by now that any changes in the various assumptions for the pro forma cash flow projections will directly affect the size of the funding gap. In fact, it's often very helpful to test the sensitivity of the projected conditions to variations in key assumptions, such as sales volume, pricing, collection patterns, and major cost deviations.

However, because we've looked at the fourth quarter of 2002 as a whole, the likely funding stresses falling within the three individual months of the quarter still haven't been dealt with. These occur because the gradual release of operating funds caused by the seasonal slowdown during the quarter will likely lag the decline in operating volume, as discussed in Chapter 2. As a consequence, the exact scheduling of repayments within the three-month period could cause significant temporary shortfalls. For example, if all repayments came due in October, the funding gap would be much higher during that month than what the pro forma statements suggest for the end of December. As we'll see shortly, only a detailed cash budget can reveal such hidden fluctuations.

To summarize, pro forma statements are a convenient and relatively simple way of projecting expectations about a company's performance. To create these statements requires maintaining consistent assumptions affecting both the income statement and the balance sheet, but otherwise, a great degree of subjective judgment is allowed. The ultimate balancing element in the pro forma balance sheet is the funds deficit or funds excess resulting from the conditions assumed. This "plug" figure will of course vary as assumptions are changed.

Pro forma cash flow statements help highlight the funds movements implied by changes in the balance sheet. Pro forma analysis is limited by the static nature of the balance sheet, which shows the funds deficit or excess only at a specific point in time, and not their ebb and flow. A more dynamic intraperiod analysis requires either generating several short-term pro forma statements at key decision points, or making the detailed budgetary forecast embodied in the cash budget.

Financial Genome, the advanced business analysis and planning software described in Appendix I, enables the user to create fully integrated pro forma statements as described here, including the use of forecast drivers, and to automatically derive the funds deficit or excess resulting from the assumptions used.

Cash Budgets

Cash budgets, or detailed cash flow projections, are very specific month-by-month or even week-by-week planning vehicles normally prepared by a company's finance staff. These budgets focus exclusively on scheduling the specific incidence of cash receipts and payments—as distinguished from the leads and lags embodied in the accrual accounting approach used by most enterprises. A financial analyst who develops a cash budget is very interested in observing the ongoing changes in the cash account as assumptions are made, with the objective of maintaining a level of cash sufficient to allow timely payments of all obligations as they become due. Consequently, the analyst must plan cash activity in very specific detail, reflecting the exact timing of the inflows and outflows of cash in response to planned operational, investment, and financing decisions.

As we'll see, cash budgets again indicate the level of any funds deficits or excesses. In fact, the amount at the end of the planning period will match exactly the funding need or excess shown on the pro forma balance sheet—if the cash budget was prepared with the same basic assumptions as those underlying the pro forma statements.

Cash budgeting is quite simple in principle. It's very similar to personal budgeting, where bills due are matched with receipts from paychecks, dividend checks, bank interest payments, and so on. This matching is necessary, period by period, to align funds requirements on the one hand, and cash available for payment on the other. Normally, the cash balance will fluctuate from day to day, week to week, month to month, whether a personal or company budget is involved. If a company's collections from credit sales tend to lag for weeks while wages and purchases must be paid currently, serious cash shortages can occur. (The concept of lags in relation to cash flow patterns was extensively demonstrated in Chapter 2.) Similarly, cash payments for nonrecurring items, such as outlays for capital equipment, might cause temporary funding problems that must be met. Given its focus and detail, the cash budget is the ultimate expression of cash flow analysis, because in the end, all funds movements wind up as changes in the cash balance.

When preparing a cash budget, a time schedule of estimated receipts and payments of cash must be laid out carefully. This schedule shows, period by period, the net effect of projected activity on the cash balance, leaving out accounting allocations such as depreciation, which do not represent cash flows. The selection of the time intervals covered by the cash budget depends on the nature of the business and the trade terms under which it operates. If daily fluctuations are likely to be large, as in the banking business, day-by-day projections are necessary. In other cases, weekly, monthly, or even quarterly projections will suffice.

Let's now return to the data of XYZ Corporation and prepare a monthly cash budget for the last quarter of 2002. This will increase our understanding of the company's cash flow patterns beyond what was provided by the pro forma analysis alone. Figure 4–4 presents some of the basic data of the company's operations regarding sales, production, and purchases. We show two months of actual activities *prior* to the last quarter, because (due to the nature of the credit terms for sales and purchases) the cash lag from these past months will influence the three months being projected. Also, we're again showing matching totals for the year ended 12/31/03, even though we've omitted the details behind these figures. Accordingly, we'll focus on the quarter in this discussion, knowing that the totals for the year 2003 were similarly derived.

The lag effect can be demonstrated clearly in the first item of the *cash receipts,* collection of *receivables.* On the assumption that the company's customers will continue to remit within the 30-day terms, cash receipts for any month should be the sales made in the prior month. In contrast, if there was a 60-day collection period, collections would represent the sales made two months earlier. Thus, any expected change in customer behavior or in credit terms themselves must be reflected in a different receipts pattern.

It's often helpful to draw a scale of time periods on which the days, weeks, or months of dollar sales are recorded when they first occur. Using this scale, any assumed collection experience can be simulated by "staggering" (i.e., delaying) the dollar receipts according to the appropriate number of days. For example, a schedule of sales and successful collections on 30-day credit terms would appear as follows:

	January	February	March	April	May	June
Credit sales	$25,000	$30,000	$40,000	$42,000	$35,000	$30,000
Collections	(Dec. sales)	$25,000	$30,000	$40,000	$42,000	$35,000

In XYZ Corporation, proceeds from the exercise of *stock options* and from the sale of used *machinery* have been budgeted in their respective months of incidence. The total cash receipts for each month show a diminishing pattern which lags behind the declining sales by one month. This gradual reduction in collections is moderated somewhat by the nonoperating proceeds from options and sale of used machinery.

As we turn to *cash disbursements,* we encounter another lag in the payments for *purchases* made on credit. Under the normal credit terms of 45 days extended to XYZ Corporation, we can assume that the company's payments will

FIGURE 4–4

XYZ CORPORATION
Sample Cash Budget for the Quarter Ended December 31, 2002 and for the Year Ended
December 31, 2003 ($ thousands)

	Aug.	Sept.	Oct.	Nov.	Dec.	Total for Quarter	Total for Year Ended 12/31/03
Basic data:							
Unit sales	48,000	46,000	42,000	36,000	33,000	111,000	550,000
Unit production	50,000	50,000	35,000	34,000	31,000	100,000	560,000
Change in units in inventory	2,000	4,000	−7,000	−2,000	−2,000	−11,000	10,000
Sales volume (on credit)	$4,450	$4,250	$3,850	$3,350	$3,050	$10,250	$52,250
Purchases (on credit)	$ 760	$ 740	$ 520	$ 500	$ 460	$ 1,480	$ 8,400
Cash receipts:							
Collection of receivables (prior month's sales)			$4,250	$3,850	$3,350	$11,450	$52,100
Proceeds from exercise of stock options			0	250	0	250	0
Proceeds from sale of machines at book value			0	0	550	550	0
Total cash receipts			4,250	4,100	3,900	12,250	52,100
Cash disbursements:							
Payment for purchases*			750	630	510	1,890	8,300
Production payroll (from operating budget)			560	545	500	1,605	9,050
Manufacturing expenses (from operating budget)			1,265	1,260	1,235	3,760	21,700
Selling and delivery expenses (from sales budget)			350	345	335	1,030	4,800
General overhead (from administrative budget)			200	200	200	600	2,350
Interest payment on debt			0	0	175	175	850
Principal payment on note payable			1,500	0	0	1,500	1,500
Federal tax payment			400	0	0	400	850
Payment on construction of new plant			0	2,000	900	2,900	500
Purchase of new equipment			0	0	0	0	1,750
Purchase of patent (other assets)			0	0	0	0	200
Dividends paid			0	0	0	0	400
Total cash disbursements			5,025	4,980	3,855	13,860	51,850
Net cash receipts (disbursements) for the peiod			−775	−880	45	−1,610	250
Cumulative net cash flow			$−775	$−1,655	$−1,610		
Analysis of cash requirements:							
Beginning cash balance			1,450	675	−205	1,450	−160
Net cash receipts			−775	−880	45	−1,610	250
Ending cash balance			675	−205	−160	−160	90
Minimum cash balance			1,250	1,250	1,250	1,250	1,250
Cumulative cash requirements			$ 575	$ 1,455	$ 1,410	$1,410	$1,160

*For the quarter, normal terms of 45 days are assumed. Payments represent one month's purchases prior to last 1.5 months (e.g., one-half of August's and one-half of September's payables are disbursed during October).

trail by 45 days. Consequently, purchases made in the second half of August and the first half of September will be paid for in October, with a similar pattern repeating itself in November and December. In other words, one month's worth of purchases staggered by 45 days will be paid in a given month. Under these conditions, a time scale with 15-day intervals will help illustrate the payment pattern.

Inasmuch as the last quarter of 2002 is projected to show a declining monthly pattern, on the basis of an assumed December seasonal low in sales and manufacturing activities, the staggered timing pattern shifts earlier, with somewhat higher cash receipts into a period of lower operating activity, for which reduced purchase and payroll payments are projected. As a result, net operational funds are released, but these are not sufficient to overcome the heavy debt repayments scheduled in October and November, and only in December is there barely a breaking even of net cash receipts and disbursements.

Had there instead been a rising volume of operations, more cash would have become tied up in working capital, requiring additional funding. In fact, we observed that effect in the pro forma results for 2003, where working capital was assumed to grow enough to offset the seasonal decline in the last quarter. Had the last quarter of 2002 also been a growth period, the cash budget would have reflected the lag effect of the lower activities of the earlier months, with staggered collections gradually rising, while growing manufacturing outlays required cash. It should be obvious by now that there is a critical need for careful cash budgeting in any business where operating levels, receipts, and payments tend to vary significantly.

Other cash disbursements (*payroll, manufacturing expenses, selling and delivery,* and *general overhead*) are shown here without lags, on the assumption that payments for these expenses and obligations will be made within the month they are incurred. This assumption could be slightly incorrect in the case of payroll disbursements and certain manufacturing expenses. Such items could indeed lag by one or two weeks. How precisely these lags are dealt with is a function of the relative size and importance of the cash flow issues they represent.

Production-related payments, such as payroll and raw materials purchases, are based on the declining pattern of production shown in the basic data section of Figure 4–4, which also reflects a gradual inventory reduction. Yet, in the pro forma income statement for the period, cost of goods sold assumptions were based on the pattern of *selling* activities, to make the projection a little easier. Thus, the pro forma income statement and the more detailed cash budget might differ because of different assumptions about sales and production. To ensure complete consistency, it's therefore necessary to determine carefully whether the pattern of production is projected on a different basis than the pattern of sales.

As an example of such a potential difference, it's entirely possible that the seasonal low could be used by management to build up inventories in advance of the expected resurgence of sales. If that were so, the inventory assumption for the pro forma balance sheet would have to be adjusted upward to show the buildup of inventories and the resultant additional funds deficit. The cash budget, in turn, would have to reflect the higher expenditures involved in producing for inventory.

Recognizing such differences in production and selling patterns is a key to refining the projection of company performance, and to making cash budgeting results consistent with the pro forma statements.

The final result of our cash budgeting exercise is a picture of the monthly cash effect of the operating plans on which it is based, and the net cash needs or excesses incurred each month. Note that the cash needs at the end of December 31, 2002 ($1.41 million), and December 31, 2003 ($1.16 million), exactly match the indications we received from the pro forma statements—which is not surprising, because we've used the same assumptions throughout.

Although our focus was on a manufacturing setting for our example, the same principles apply to the somewhat less complex conditions in a service business, or a retailing or wholesaling operation. Payrolls and leasing costs, for example, will loom much larger in a service business, while purchases, inventories, and credit terms take on greater importance in a retailing or wholesaling company. In a financial institution, short- and long-term investment changes will be significant, as will shifts in deposits and other liabilities, with operations focused on personnel and infrastructure costs. However, the process of developing assumptions for pro forma statements and cash budgets is very similar to what we've shown here. In all cases they must be based on the physical as well as financial levers and forecast drivers particular to each situation. The reader might recall our discussion in Chapter 2 about retailing and wholesaling examples.

To summarize, cash budgets lay out in specific detail the exact timing incidence of cash receipts and disbursements. Like household budgets, they allow us to watch for peaks and valleys in cash availability and to schedule additional financing or repayments as needed. Unlike pro forma statements (which are generally limited to the beginning and end of a specific period or to its total net effects), cash budgets can be drawn up for as many intervals as desired within the period to simulate the fluctuations in cash flow. Given the same assumptions in terms of the volume of production and sales, and the handling of receipts, payments, and credit, the cash budget and pro forma statements will agree in signaling the amount of funds deficit or excess at the end of the period covered.

Operating Budgets

The pro forma statements and cash budget we prepared for XYZ Corporation provide an overall view of the company's future performance. But in any sizable company, a whole hierarchy of more specific operating budgets is normally prepared. Operating budgets are essentially internal documents. As expressions of the details of ongoing operations, such budgets are linked closely to the organizational structure and to the type of performance measurement used by the particular company. They're part of the planning process we mentioned earlier, and are very useful as background for pro forma and cash flow projections when a higher degree of detail and accuracy is desired.

Most companies structure their operations into manageable parts, and for each of them an executive or manager is held responsible. The structure might be organized by *functions,* that is, sales, production, purchasing, and so on. In other cases, the organization might be composed of a set of smaller *profit centers,* each of which is expected to make a profit contribution to total company performance. Some activities might be grouped into *cost centers,* focusing the managers' attention on cost-effectiveness. More recently, cross-functional teams have been used for certain activities, with budget arrangements to match. Growing activity-based costing and analysis efforts, which we've mentioned before, have refined budgetary processes even as they caused rethinking and restructuring—and outsourcing—of certain activities in many companies. Even though there are countless variations of organizational structures, the principles of budgeting and financial projection are straightforward and commonly applicable.

Any projection of operating results must be done in a form that reflects the scope of the business unit involved. It must be related to the elements controllable by the responsible manager or team, and should be done on the same basis as the one with which the manager's performance is measured. These criteria obviously require that operating budgets be carefully designed to fit the particular unit's conditions and the management style of the company as a whole. This means that there'll be a great deal of difference in the approach taken by various companies, even in the same industry. There might even be differences within the same company in the operating budgets used for different organizational units and processes. A growing body of literature has recognized the positive contribution of so-called responsibility accounting for tracking managers' results, more recently expanded to include team management and process management concepts.

For purposes of our discussion, a few illustrations of basic operational budgeting will suffice. Among the various internal operating budgets routinely prepared by XYZ Corporation are the *annual sales budget by quarters* and a *quarterly factory budget.* The sales budget is designed to show the sales unit's projected contribution to total corporate profits, whereas the factory budget reflects expected output and the total costs incurred in producing the forecast volume. There are many other types of profit and expense budgets, but we'll limit our discussion to these two, showing how they're used to provide background information for the financial analyst preparing and analyzing pro forma statements and cash budgets. The principles employed in our examples are the same for any other kind of budgeting arrangement.

Sales Budget

As is shown in Figure 4–5, the sales manager must first project the level of *unit sales* expected in the market territories served by the business. The projection is made by major product lines. Most likely, this forecast will be built up from the individual judgments of the persons closest to current and potential customers. Economic conditions will likely be factored in, as will the impact of marketing strategies XYZ Corporation and its competitors are likely to employ.

FIGURE 4–5

XYZ CORPORATION
Sample Quarterly Sales Budget
For the Year Ended December 31, 2003
($ thousands)

	First	Second	Third	Fourth	Total
			Quarter		
Basic data:					
Unit sales (number of units):					
Product A	2,700	2,900	3,000	2,800	11,400
Product B	8,000	8,500	10,000	8,000	34,500
Product C	17,500	18,500	21,000	16,000	73,000
Price level (per unit):					
Product A	$ 145	$ 145	$ 150	$ 150	—
Product B	92	92	95	95	—
Product C	74	74	74	74	—
Number of salespersons	25	25	25	26	—
Operating budget ($000):					
Sales revenue	$2,423	$2,572	$2,954	$2,364	$10,313
Less: returns, allowances	25	26	28	24	103
Net sales	2,398	2,546	2,926	2,340	10,210
Cost of goods sold	1,916	2,051	2,322	1,868	8,157
Margin before delivery	482	495	604	472	2,053
Delivery expense	56	60	68	54	238
Gross margin	426	435	536	418	1,815
Selling expense (controllable):					
Salespersons' compensation	94	94	94	98	380
Travel and entertainment	32	32	32	33	129
Sales support costs	23	23	26	24	96
Total selling expenses	149	149	152	155	605
Gross contribution	277	286	384	263	1,210
Departmental period costs	18	18	18	18	72
Net contribution	259	268	366	245	1,138
Corporate support (transferred):					
Staff support	23	25	25	27	100
Advertising	50	50	75	50	225
General overhead	63	63	63	63	252
Total corporate support	136	138	163	140	577
Profit contribution (before taxes)	$ 123	$ 130	$ 203	$ 105	$ 561

Next the *price levels* for each product must be estimated. Prices commonly are a function of three factors:

- Industry pricing practices.
- The competitive environment.
- The cost-effectiveness of the company's manufacturing operations.

Once the price has been established, the *sales revenue* can be calculated. Then the *cost of goods sold* for the products transferred internally or possibly purchased on the outside must be determined. The difference between the revenue and cost is the *margin before delivery* achieved by the sales unit. Next are the projected *delivery costs* to the customers, if these are borne by the company. Controllable *selling expenses* include *compensation* of sales personnel, *travel and entertainment,* and *sales support costs.*

The result is the *gross contribution* from selling activities, which must be reduced by estimated *departmental period costs* (like rent, managers' salary, and other items that do not vary with short-term fluctuations in volume) to arrive at the *net contribution* provided by the department. After deducting allocated *corporate support costs,* which are staff support, advertising, and general overhead, the *profit contribution* for the period is established. In making all of these estimates, the sales manager can use past relationships and selected ratios, tempered by his or her judgment concerning changes in future conditions.

In our example, both basic data and dollar elements have been estimated and set out by the four quarters and the full year of 2003. There's nothing unique about the format we've selected here, because many different arrangements of such information are possible to suit any specific organization. Generally, a company prescribes the format for its managers to follow in preparing projected activity budgets, both to maintain a degree of uniformity and to lessen the accounting problem of consolidating the projections when preparing overall financial forecasts. From the standpoint of financial projection, the sales and contribution data in our example are the raw material which goes into the company's total operating plan.

Production Budget

The sales budget we just discussed is basically a projection of profit contribution. However, companies also must forecast for operations or activities that involve only costs or expenses. An example of this type of projection, a cost budget for a factory, is shown in Figure 4–6. This time the data are given for each month. We've included three months and the total for the quarter. The period shown is the second quarter, during which sales and production are expected to increase.

Again, the amount of detail included and the presentation format are chosen to suit the particular needs and preferences of the organization. This time we've arranged the headings and data to show that certain cost items (both direct and period costs) are under the control of the local manager. (Other costs, like allocated general overhead, are transferred in from corporate headquarters and thus are beyond the local manager's control.) This arrangement of data will also be useful if the operating plan serves as a control device with which to measure the unit's performance.

Both sales and cost budgets commonly include additional columns in which *actual* as opposed to *projected* figures are recorded. In addition, *variance* columns are frequently used to measure deviations from plan. We'll not go into

FIGURE 4–6

XYZ CORPORATION
Sample Production Budget
For the Quarter Ended December 31, 2003
($ thousands)

	April	May	June	Total
Basic data:				
Number of shifts (5-day week)	3	3	3	3
Days worked	20	21	22	63
Hourly employees per shift	33	33	33	33
Number of machines	35	35	34	—
Unit production:				
Product A	1,000	1,050	1,100	3,150
Product B	2,400	2,510	2,640	7,550
Capacity utilization	94%	94%	96%	95%
Downtime for repairs (hours)	0	36	0	36
Operating budget:				
Direct costs (controllable):*				
Manufacturing labor	$57,600	$60,500	$63,400	$181,500
Raw materials	53,800	56,400	59,200	169,400
Operating supplies	6,500	6,900	7,300	20,700
Repair labor and parts	7,300	12,400	6,500	26,200
Power, heat, light	4,200	4,500	4,800	13,500
Total direct costs	129,400	140,700	141,200	411,300
Period costs (controllable):				
Supervision	5,500	5,500	5,500	16,500
Support labor	28,500	28,500	28,500	85,500
Insurance, taxes	8,700	8,700	8,700	26,100
Depreciation	20,500	20,500	20,500	61,500
Total period costs	63,200	63,200	63,200	189,600
Total controllable costs	192,600	203,900	204,400	600,900
General overhead (allocated)	72,000	72,000	72,000	216,000
Total cost	$264,600	$275,900	$276,400	$816,900

*Where appropriate, unit costs can be shown.

such refinements here, because our examples were only meant to show the type of internal budgeting and projection used formally or informally in most organizations preparatory to developing an overall financial forecast.

Interrelationship of Financial Projections

It should be obvious by now that the various types of projection presented in this chapter are closely related. If all three forecasts—pro forma statements, cash budgets, and operating budgets—are based on the same set of assumptions about receipts and collections, repayment schedules, operating rates, inventory levels, and so on, they will all precisely fit together as illustrated in Figure 4–7.

FIGURE 4–7

Interrelationship of Financial Projections

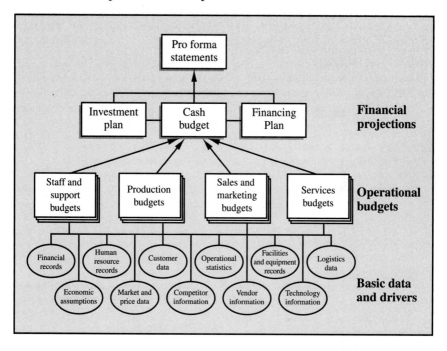

The financial plans and the projected funds deficit or excess will differ only if different assumptions concerning the various drivers affecting cash flows are used, particularly between the pro forma statements and the cash budget. It is easy to reconcile pro forma statements and cash budgets, however, by carefully thinking through the key assumptions to be made, one by one, and by laying out formats that contain sufficient detail and properly timed background data.

The diagram shows how the various operational budgets flow into a consolidated cash budget, which in turn is reinforced by specific data from the investment and financing plans. The combined information supports the pro forma statements at the top of the exhibit. Thus, pro forma statements are the all-encompassing expression of the expected conditions for the projected period. If we choose for planning purposes to develop a broad overall financial projection using pro forma statements directly (rather than building them up from the company's detailed plans and budgets), the results will in effect *imply* specific assumptions about all the other elements in the diagram.

We haven't yet discussed some of the other elements shown in Figure 4–7. *Investment plans (capital budgets)* are projections of new outlays for land, buildings, machinery and equipment, and related incremental working capital, as well as major outlays for new products and services, expanding markets, new technology, and so forth. They also contain plans to divest any of the company's assets. Acquisitions and divestitures of whole companies, lines of business, or activities are usually part of these projections.

We recall that XYZ Corporation made a minor reduction in its fixed assets by selling some used machines in 2002, and planned to purchase new equipment items in 2003. Also, a recently constructed plant was in the final stages of completion, as evidenced by the amount that had become due and payable to the contractor. This facility investment was already reflected on the actual balance sheet of September 30, 2002, largely supported by long-term debt raised earlier. Only the current payment due the contractor was properly scheduled as a pro forma cash disbursement. Given the size of the plant investment, the company might consider raising some additional long-term debt to fund the new facility, because our projections of ongoing operations show insufficient cash flow to pay off the contractor liabilities.

Financing plans are schedules of proposed future additions to or reductions in indebtedness or ownership funds during the forecast period. They might involve significant expansion or restructuring of a company's capital structure, depending on the projected capital requirements. XYZ Corporation planned no specific future financing, but provisions will have to be made for financing the sizable near-term funds need revealed with the help of our pro forma analysis, and to avoid straining current funds as the plant is paid off.

Staff budgets, as the name implies, are spending plans based on the expected cost of operating various support functions of a company, such as the finance organization, human resources, legal and governmental affairs, and so on. These budgets are prepared and used in the same fashion as other expense budgets, with personnel expenses usually being the largest element. *Services budgets* are spending plans representing such service activities as customer or technical support, delivery and communication, online services of various kinds, and so on. Budgetary categories will differ depending on the nature of the activity, of course.

Underlying the operating budgets and financial projections, Figure 4–7 shows a selection of key data sources, formal or informal, from which the relevant drivers of physical and financial activities can be derived. Whether they are made apparent or not, the structure of projections is supported by explicit or implicit assumptions about such basic data and conditions. In our example of XYZ Corporation we touched on a limited number of these areas, relying in all cases on information given to us by management—who would have to base their expectations on their understanding of all the conditions affecting their company.

A word about projection methodology should be added here. Any form of financial projection involves both an examination of past trends and specific assumptions about future behavior of the strategic and operational drivers and conditions affecting revenues, costs, expenses, and other receipts and payments. Past trend analysis can range from simple "eyeballing" of obvious patterns to applying a variety of statistical methods and probabilistic analyses to the available data in order to establish a trend line or curve as the basis for judging future conditions. The projection of key variables might start with such a trend, but hard, informed judgments about likely changes must override the temptation merely to extrapolate past conditions. The mathematical elegance of statistical methods and the ready access to electronic databases should not be allowed to supplant the effort of making realistic future assumptions about specific company and market conditions, industry performance, and the national and world economic outlook affecting the likely financial performance of the business. The past is only history and at best only a starting point for the process. The end-of-chapter references and Appendix III are information sources on forecasting techniques and other processes that will assist the analyst in technical and judgmental aspects of financial projection.

Financial Modeling

In recent years, software developed for financial modeling has vastly expanded the financial analyst's ability to explore the consequences of different assumptions, conditions, and plans. In principle, such software packages are mathematical representations and templates of key financial accounting relationships, ratios, and formats, supported by automatic subroutines that calculate, update, and display data and results in whatever form is desired. They draw on company databases and may also link to Internet-based published financial statistics. Although the degree of sophistication varies widely in these approaches, the underlying process is based on the very same steps and reasoning we discussed in this chapter.

The simplest form of financial modeling is found in the common use of spreadsheets to represent a particular set of relationships for analysis and manipulation. Here the analyst specifies the basic formulas and connections underlying the data and formats under review, but must take special care to maintain internal consistency. At the other extreme is a full-fledged financial model, usually developed by a company's staff in collaboration with software vendors, which encompasses many elements such as the company's accounting procedures, depreciation schedules, tax calculations, debt service schedules, debt covenants and restrictions, inventory policies, and so on. In most cases, the terms used, key assumptions, and output formats are "custom tailored" so that the model reflects the specific characteristics of a given company. This allows the analyst to calculate the projected results of the conditions expected by the company, examine several sets of assumptions, and assess alternative outcomes.

The major difference between the projection techniques we discussed earlier in this chapter and the use of computer models is only the degree of automation and support in the process. A cash budget, even if done by hand, is essentially a model of the cash flow patterns of the company. In constructing such a budget, the analyst must take into account corporate policies regarding accounting methods, tax reporting, and other detailed operating rules. These constraints also can be incorporated into a basic financial planning software package, or even a powerful modeling program. The main difference is that the computer can run different options and test the sensitivity to changes in key variables, while simultaneously tracking all important interrelationships much more easily and consistently than is possible when doing an analysis on a simple spreadsheet.

The financial modeling software available on the market is constantly evolving, and the reader should become familiar with the available offerings. In relative scope, the modeling packages range all the way from simple spreadsheet templates with which to calculate condensed pro forma statements to highly sophisticated representations of a company's financial accounting system, and to so-called enterprise models. In the last case, a generalized model is extensively refined by experts to reflect the company's specific situation. Some companies have developed models that not only will calculate the results of specific sets of assumptions, but also will contain optimizing routines that select the most desirable alternative investment and financing patterns according to criteria stipulated by management. Other models include statistical projection programs that can be used for initial trending of key variables from past experience. It's clearly beyond the scope of this book to detail the vast number of concepts and specialized techniques involved in the building and use of computerized financial models. However, the reader can refer to Appendix I, which describes Modernsoft, Inc.'s Financial Genome, an advanced financial analysis application downloadable for use in connection with this book and for general professional use.

Figure 4–8 depicts a broad overview of the major relationships represented in a full-fledged financial model, with linkages to internal and external databases. The central element is the software program that governs the calculations and displays, with the inputs coming from various sources and databases as needed, and the outputs grouped into our familiar categories of analysis, including special economic analyses and shareholder value calculations. Such analytical capability permits the use of clearly defined assumptions about corporate strategy and operational plans, backed by trend analysis of relevant historical internal data and external information, to develop meaningful, consistent statements and analyses. Once key drivers of performance and financial conditions are specified, the task of projecting financial statements, cash flow patterns, and valuation aspects is relatively straightforward, as is the use of extensive sensitivity analysis and scenario planning. Strategic plans for several years ahead, the impact of potential acquisitions or restructuring, or more near-term operational conditions can all be expressed in financial terms.

Sensitivity Analysis

As we mentioned, one of the advantages of financial modeling is the ability to perform sensitivity analysis with considerable ease. This approach involves selecting a few key performance drivers and altering them to determine the sensitivity of the result to such changes. For example, one of the key assumptions in our pro forma analysis of XYZ Corporation was the usual seasonal pattern of an 18 to 20 percent decline in sales volume in the last quarter. If there were reason to believe that a more serious drop might occur, the analyst could estimate the dollar decline in contribution from each additional 1 percent decrease in volume. Assuming all other conditions remain the same, that dollar decline would be the lost contribution from the units left unsold.

F I G U R E   4–8

Financial Modeling: An Overview of Key Interrelationships

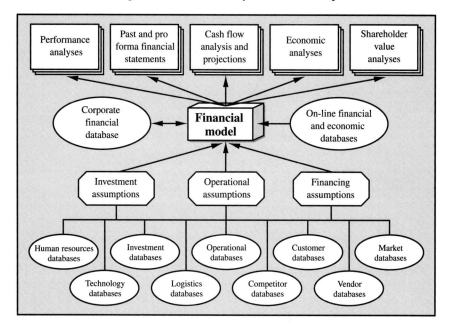

The impact on cash needs would be traced by adjusting after-tax profits, and by recognizing that there would be a change in working capital because sales levels are lower, except in inventory where the unsold units might remain. If prices were considered unstable, the impact of a series of assumptions about the effect of lower prices for one or all of the product lines could be tested. In every case, the critical issue would be the sensitivity of the cash needs to the changes in each of the three months. Clearly, many other tests could be applied and related to the altered result brought about by the change in any given assumption.

The key to this type of reasoning is the analyst's judgment as to which elements and key drivers in the operating and financial patterns being projected are most subject to variability. Then the task is to simulate how sensitive the desired result is to each change. Care must be taken to observe any interrelationships among the chosen variables. These interrelationships include the inverse impact of price changes on volume, and nonlinear conditions such as varying changes in some costs and certain activities in response to volume assumptions and load factors. Given such a range of results, the decision maker using the analysis can judge the risk of the proposed course and adjust operating and financial policies accordingly. A full-fledged financial model is not critical to applying such sensitivity tests. Even our simple pro forma statements and cash budgets can be modified easily on a spreadsheet to answer basic questions of this sort.

Nonetheless, with appropriate software, the analyst can examine many more possibilities and determine the impact of a far greater number of assumptions. Sensitivity tests can be performed on more than one variable simultaneously, and whole scenarios can be developed with the financial impact reflected in the output. We'll return to the topic of sensitivity analysis again in the chapters that follow.

Key Issues

The following is a recap of the key issues raised directly or indirectly in this chapter. They are enumerated here to help the reader keep the materials discussed within the perspective of financial theory and business practice.

1. Projecting the financial requirements of a business is a logical extension of financial statement preparation and cash flow thinking. It's the culmination of a set of planning assumptions that must be applied consistently in the process to ensure consistency among the different representations of the business provided by financial statements and cash budgets. Given such consistency, the common link among the displays will be the financing requirement identified.

2. The process of financial projections rests on explicit and implicit assumptions about the expected behavior of key drivers in the future periods under review. These can be derived from a detailed planning process including strategic direction, operational budgeting, and other key conditions affecting future performance, or they can be specified in broad terms for a quick assessment. The main issue is to think through the financial systems effects in all areas of the business.

3. Extrapolating past trends, and extending them with forecast drivers such as margin percentages, expense ratios, credit conditions, and asset turnovers should be considered only as a starting point, from which refinements must be made to allow for likely changes in future conditions. Such key forecast drivers should be specifically identified and reviewed carefully to ensure reasonableness.

4. Sensitivity analysis is a key requirement for thoughtful planning of financial requirements as well as of other projections involving future events. The impact on the final result from varying assumptions about individual variables considered key drivers must be tested to assist in judging the range of possible outcomes. Focusing on drivers with the most impact will tend to sharpen the analytical and decision-making process.

5. Whenever projections and plans are subject to uncertainty, especially if forecast periods are extensive, it's useful to develop alternative scenarios based on consistent assumptions about sets of key drivers under different potential conditions.

6. Financial modeling is an important activity which provides varying degrees of automatic linkage among key variables and output formats. It is not a substitute for judgment, however, because the underlying assumptions necessary for an analysis require thoughtful choices and insights, whether the model is highly evolved or merely a simple spreadsheet.

Summary

The principles of financial projection discussed in this chapter revolve around the use of *pro forma statements* and various types of *budgets*. We observed that financial projection is only part of the broader process of *business planning*. Financial projection can be expressed in the familiar form of financial statements and in many specifically tailored budget formats. The process is simple in that it represents an orderly way of sorting out the financial impact of investment, operating, and financing decisions. The process is difficult in that judgments about future conditions are fraught with uncertainty—as planning of any sort must be by its very nature.

Here, the use of *sensitivity analysis,* the calculation of the impact of alternative assumptions, can narrow the range of uncertainty. Financial projection basically is a form of modeling the future within the context of operational and policy constraints. To the extent that more detail and more options for future plans are desired, *financial modeling* can yield the significant benefits of speed and accuracy of calculation. Greater insights can be derived from such modeling, but the judgmental requirements for proper inputs and assumptions remain the same.

Analytical Support

The set of Excel-based templates (*Interactive Templates)* is downloadable at no charge from the Web at www.mhhe.com/helfert11e. The third of these, "Cash Budget Example: Projections and Key Drivers," provides a live layout of problem no. 7, the XYZ Company, shown on pp. 205-207 under Self-Study Exercises, Problems, and Discussion Questions. The template allows you to vary a set of key assumptions about the budgeting inputs of XYZ Company, and to observe the numerical changes resulting from these modifications on a series of supporting schedules and financial statements. The display helps you explore and understand in depth the linkages between budgeting drivers, the cash budget itself, and related financial statements.

Financial Genome, the advanced financial analysis software application described in Appendix I, is a full-fledged analytical and planning model for both the professional user and the business student. It is designed to create fully integrated pro forma financial statements as extensions of historical data or from direct forecast assumptions. The software contains a five-year database (1996 to 2000) for

3M Corporation, matching the company's financial statements reproduced in Chapters 1, 2, and 3, which can be used for practicing projections based on your assumptions. It also contains databases and project files with which to work Problems 8 and 9 on pages 207 and 208.

Financial Genome is downloadable from the Web, using the unique code provided with this book. See "Downloads Available" at the end of Appendix I, p. 479.

Selected References

Anthony, Robert N. *Essentials of Accounting.* 5th ed. Reading, MA: Addison-Wesley, 1993. (A classic.)

Brealy, Richard, and Stewart Myers. *Principles of Corporate Finance.* 5th ed. New York: McGraw-Hill, 1996.

Ross, Stephen; Randolph Westerfield; and Jeffrey Jaffe. *Corporate Finance.* 5th ed. Burr Ridge, IL: Irwin/McGraw-Hill, 1999.

Weston, J. Fred; Scott Besley; and Eugene Brigham. *Essentials of Managerial Finance.* 11th ed. Hinsdale, IL: Dryden Press, 1997.

Self-Study Exercises, Problems, and Discussion Questions

Exercises and Problems (*Selected Solutions Provided in Appendix VI*)

1. Complete the following exercises, based on these selected data about a company. Consider each exercise separately.

Total assets on 12-31-03	$2,750,000
Sales for the year 2003	9,137,000
Current assets on 12-31-03	1,315,000
Long-term debt on 12-31-03	210,000
Current ratio on 12-31-03	2.4:1
Cost of goods sold for 2003	83% of sales
Purchases during 2003	$5,316,000
Depreciation for 2003	174,000
Net profit after taxes for 2003	131,000
Income taxes for 2003	112,000

a. Currently, the company's accounts receivable outstanding are 18 days' sales. To meet competitive pressures in 2004; the company must extend credit to an average of 40 days' sales to maintain operations and profits at 2003 levels. No other changes are contemplated for the next year, and sales and operations are expected to continue at 2003 rates. What's the impact of this change in credit policy on corporate funds needs? Will the company have to borrow? What if credit had to be extended to 60 days? Discuss.

b. The inventory levels maintained by the company have averaged $725,000 during 2003 with little fluctuation. If turnover were to slow to seven times (average inventory vs. cost of goods sold) due to a switch to a consignment policy, what would the financial impact be? Assume no change in sales levels. What other changes are likely to take place, and how would these affect the company's financial stance? What if turnover rose to 11 times? Discuss.

c. Payment for purchases has been made under normal trade terms of 2/10, n/30 with discounting done as a matter of policy. Suppliers anxious for business are beginning to offer 2/15, n/45 terms, which will become universal during the coming year. What would the financial impact of this change be if the company were to follow its policy of discounting purchases? What trade-off has to be considered? Discuss.

d. If the company is planning capital expenditures of $125,000 and simultaneously is planning to pay dividends at the rate of 60 percent of net profits, what are the financial implications, assuming all other elements are unchanged?

e. If sales are expected to grow 10 percent for the following year, with all *normal* relationships under (*a*) through (*c*) unchanged, what financial considerations arise? How would the intentions of (*d*) look then? Discuss your findings.

2.   In September 2004, ABC Company, a manufacturing firm, was making budget plans for the 12 months beginning November 1, 2004. Projected sales volume was $4,350,000 as compared to an estimated $3,675,000 for the fiscal year ended October 31, 2004. The best estimates of the operating results for the current year are shown in the income statements. The projected increase in volume of operations was expected to bring improvements in efficiency, while at the same time some of the cost factors would continue to rise absolutely, in line with past trends. Following this statements are the specific working assumptions with which to plan financial results for the next year.

ABC COMPANY
Estimated Income Statement
For the Year Ended October 31, 2004
($ thousands)

	Amount	Percent
Net sales	$3,675	100%
Cost of goods sold:		
Labor	$919	25.0
Materials	522	14.2
Overhead	743	20.2

Depreciation	133	2,317	3.6	63.0
Gross profit		1,358		37.0
Selling expense	305		8.3	
General and administrative expenses	323	628	8.8	17.1
Profit before taxes		730		19.9
Income taxes		336		9.1
Net income		$ 394		10.8%

Assumptions for fiscal year 2005:

Manufacturing labor would drop to 24 percent of direct sales because volume efficiency would more than offset higher wage rates.

Materials cost would rise to 14.5 percent of sales because some price increases wouldn't be offset by better utilization.

Overhead costs would rise above the present level by 6 percent of the 2001 dollar amount, reflecting higher costs. Additional variable costs would be encountered at the rate of 11 percent of the incremental sales volume.

Depreciation would increase by $10,000, reflecting the addition of some production machinery.

Selling expenses would rise more proportionately, by $125,000, because additional effort would be required to increase sales volume.

General and administrative expenses would drop to 8.1 percent of sales.

Income taxes (federal and sate) were estimated at 46 percent of pretax profits.

Develop a pro forma income statement for the ABC Company and discuss your findings.

3. In December 2004, the DEF Company, a distributor of stationery products, was planning its financial needs for the coming year. As a first indication, the firm's management wished to have a pro forma balance sheet as of December 31, 2005, to gauge funds needs at that time. Estimated financial condition as of December 31, 2004, was reflected in this balance sheet:

DEF COMPANY
Estimated Balance Sheet
December 31, 2004

Assets	
Current assets:	
Cash	$ 217,300
Receivables	361,200
Inventories (pledged as security)	912,700
Total current assets	1,491,200
Fixed assets:	
Land, buildings, trucks, and fixtures	421,500
Less: Accumulated depreciation	217,300
Total fixed assets	204,200
Other assets	21,700
Total assets	$1,717,100

Liabilities and Net Worth

Current liabilities:

Accounts payable	$ 612,300
Note payable—bank	425,000
Accrued expenses	63,400
Total current liabilities	1,100,700
Term loan—properties	120,000
Common stock	200,000
Paid-in surplus	112,000
Retained earnings	184,400
Total liabilities and shareholders' equity	$1,717,100

Operations for the ensuing year were projected using the following working assumptions to plan the financial results:

Sales were forecast at $10,450,000, with a gross margin of 8.2 percent.

Purchases were expected to total $9,725,000, with some seasonal upswings in May and August.

Accounts receivable would be based on a collection period of 12 days, while 24 days' accounts payable would be outstanding.

Depreciation was expected to be $31,400 for the year.

Term loan repayments were scheduled at $10,000, while bank notes payable would be allowed to fluctuate with seasonal needs.

Capital expenditures were scheduled at $21,000 for trucks and $36,000 for warehouse improvements.

Net profits after taxes were expected at the level of 0.19 percent of sales.

Dividends for the year were scheduled at $12,500.

Cash balances were desired at no less than $150,000.

Develop a pro forma balance sheet and discuss your findings.

4. In September 2004, the BCD Company, a department store, was planning for cash needs during the last quarter of 2004 and the first quarter of 2005. The Christmas buying season always meant a considerable strain on finances, and the first planning step was development of a cash budget. The following data were available for this purpose:

Projected sales (half for cash, half charged on 90-day account):

October	$ 770,000	January	$650,000
November	690,000	February	580,000
December	1,010,000	March	720,000

Projected purchases (half on n/45; 40 percent on 2/10, n/30; 10 percent for cash):

October	$ 610,000	January	$320,000
November	535,000	February	450,000
December	290,000	March	480,000

Projected payments on purchases as of 9-30-04:

Due by October 10 (2% discount)	$ 60,000
Due by October 31 (net 45)	257,000
Due by November 15 (net 45)	113,000
Total	$430,000

Projected collections of receivables as of 9-30-04:

Due in October	$215,000
Due in November	245,000
Due in December	265,000
Total (bad debts negligible)	$725,000

Projected financial data:

Minimum cash balance required	$ 75,000
Beginning cash balance (October 1)	95,000
Mortgage payments (monthly)	7,000
Cash dividend due December 31	40,000
Federal taxes due January 15	20,000

Projected operations: salaries and wages average 19 percent of sales; cash operating expenses average 14 percent of sales.

Develop a monthly cash budget to show the seasonal funds requirements and discuss your findings.

5.   A newly formed space technology company, the ZYX Corporation, was in the early stages of planning for the first several months of operations. The initial capital put up by the founders and their associates amounted to 250,000 shares of $1 par value stock. Furthermore, patents estimated to be worth $50,000 were provided by two of the principals in exchange for 50,000 shares of common stock. Equipment costing $175,000 was purchased with the funds, and organization expenses of $15,000 were paid. Operations were to start February 1, 2004. Orders already in hand amounted to $1,400,000 of electronic devices, which at an estimated monthly output of $400,000 (sales value), represented almost four months' sales. More orders were expected from contacts made. Monthly operating expenses and conditions were estimated as follows:

Manufacturing labor	$ 60,000
Rent for building	18,500
Overhead costs	76,000
Depreciation	6,000
Amortization of patents	500
Selling and administrative expenses	55,000
Purchases of materials, supplies	125,000
Sale terms	n/30
Collection experience expected	45 days
Purchase terms	n/30
Raw materials inventory level	60,000
Finished goods inventory level	145,000
Prepaid expenses (average)	12,000
Accrued wages	1 week's
Accrued taxes (40% effective rate)	As incurred

If the company wanted to maintain a minimum cash balance of $40,000, what would the financial situation be after six months of operations? Develop pro forma statements and discuss the likely timing of any funding requirements. How are the next six months likely to affect this picture? Discuss your findings.

6. The ABC Supermarket's management expected the next six months (January 1, 2004, through June 30, 2004) to bring a variety of cash requirements beyond the normal operational outflows. A monthly cash budget was to be developed to trace the specific funds needs. The following projections were available for the purpose:

   a. Cash sales projected:

January	$200,000	April	$200,000
February	190,000	May	230,000
March	220,000	June	220,000

   b. Cost of good sold averages 75 percent of sales.
   c. Purchases closely schedule with sales volume. Payments average a 15-day lag behind purchases. December purchases were $168,000.
   d. Operating expenses projected:
   1. Salaries and wages at 12 percent of sales, paid when incurred.
   2. Other expenses at an average 9 percent of sales, paid when incurred.
   3. Rent of $3,500, paid monthly.
   4. Income tax payments of $2,000 due in January, March, and June, and $3,500 due in April.
   5. Cash receipts from sale of property at $6,000 per month, due in March, April, and May.
   6. Payments on note owed local bank due as follows: $3,000 in February and $5,000 in May.
   7. Repayments of advances to principals of the firm due at $3,000 each in January, March, and May.
   8. New store fixtures of $48,000 acquired, with four payments of $12,000 each due in February, March, April, and May.
   9. Old store fixtures with a book value of $4,500 scrapped, to be written off in January.
   10. Rental income from a small concession granted on the premises to begin at $300 per month in March.

   Develop a cash budget as requested and show the effect of the operations and other elements described above on the beginning cash balance of $42,500. The principals of the firm would like to keep a cash balance of not less than $20,000 at any one time. Will additional funds be required? If so, when? Discuss your findings.

7. **Note:** This problem is represented in a live layout in the Interactive Templates described earlier. The third template, "Cash Budget Example: Projections and Key Drivers" allows you to view and vary the necessary supporting schedules for developing your solution, and to observe the impact on the cash budget and other related statements.

   The XYZ Company, a fast-growing manufacturing operation, found its inventories in 2004 increasing faster than the growth in sales. (As additional territories and customers had been developed, production schedules were stepped up in an effort to provide excellent service levels.) Also, collections had deteriorated, and the company's receivables represented two months' sales compared to normal 30-day terms. Because both conditions caused considerable pressures on the company's finances, a change to a level production schedule was considered beginning October 1, 2004, to allow inventories to be worked off while still providing employment to the company's full-time workers. Also, more effort would be expended on collections. A six-month trial of the new policy was to be analyzed in September before implementation, and the following assumptions and data were provided:

a. Current sales and forecast:

August	$1,925,000	December	$2,450,000
September (est.)	2,050,000	January	2,625,000
October	2,175,000	February	2,750,000
November	2,300,000	March	2,850,000

b. Current purchases and forecast (terms n/45):

August	$750,000	December	$650,000
September (est.)	675,000	January	650,000
October	650,000	February	650,000
November	650,000	March	650,000

c. Collection period, current and forecast:

August 31	63 days	December 31	40 days
September 30 (est.)	60	January 31	40
October 31	50	February 28	40
November 30	50	March 31	40

d. Materials usage, beginning October: $825,000 per month.

e. Wages and salaries, beginning October: $215,000 per month, paid as incurred.

f. Other manufacturing expenses, beginning October: $420,000 per month, paid as incurred.

g. Depreciation: $43,000 per month.

h. Cost of good sold has consistently averaged 70 percent of sales.

i. Selling and administrative expenses: October and November 15 percent of sales; December and January, 14 percent of sales; and February and March, 12 percent of sales.

j. Payments on note payable: $750,000 each in November and February.

k. Interest due in January: $300,000.

l. Dividends payable in October and January: $25,000 each.

m. Income taxes due in January: $375,000.

n. Most recent balance sheet (estimated) is shown below.

XYZ COMPANY
Estimated Balance Sheet
for September 30, 2004
($ thousands)

Assets
Current assets:

Cash		$ 740
Accounts and notes receivable		3,975
Inventories:		
Raw materials	$ 2,725	
Finished goods	6,420	9,145
Total current assets		13,860
Plant and equipment	12,525	
Less: Accumulated depreciation	5,315	7,210
Other assets		1,730
Total assets		$22,800

Liabilities and Shareholders' Equity
Current liabilities:

Accounts payable	$ 1,050
Notes payable	4,120
Accrued liabilities	2,875
Total current liabilities	8,045
Long-term debt	5,250
Preferred stock	1,750
Common stock	5,000
Retained earnings	2,755
Total liabilities and shareholders' equity	$22,800

From the data given, develop a cash budget for the six months ended March 31, 2005, and pro forma statements for the quarters ended December 31, 2004, and March 31, 2005. Assume income taxes to be 50 percent, don't detail cost of goods sold, and assume no changes in accounts not specifically analyzed or projected here. What funds needs arise, and when? What if the collection speedup effort were unsuccessful and receivables stayed at 60 days? Discuss your findings about the policy changes being considered.

8. Using Financial Genome, develop an integrated set of pro forma financial statements for 3M corporation, based on the five-year annual historical database contained in the software. Carefully review the forecasting instructions in the software's help system, and build up a full set of forecast assumptions, using the Ratio Drivers Statement and/or inputting your assumptions on the projected statements themselves. Observe the changing funds deficit/excess on the projected balance sheets, and attempt to bring this to zero by making various financing assumptions. Comment on your observations.

9. Using Financial Genome, develop an integrated set of pro forma financial statements for a company of your choice, by first inputting a set of historical data and making sure they balance, and then building up your own assumptions as suggested in problem 8. Comment on your observations.

Discussion Questions

1. Because we can balance a pro forma balance sheet with a plug figure (funds deficit or surplus) representing borrowing or excess cash, must we be very careful to use accounting conventions? Explain.

2. Given the freedom one has to project pro forma balance sheets and plugging them in the end, what limitations are there to this ability? Explain.

3. Name the key assumptions that have to agree for both a pro forma balance sheet and the matching pro forma income statement in order to provide internal consistency.

4. Differentiate between a cash budget and a pro forma income statement.

5. Should depreciation ever appear on a cash budget? If not, does it have any direct impact anywhere?

6. Must a cash budget and a corresponding set of pro forma statements always tie together so that they can be reconciled?

7. Differentiate between an operating budget (sales, manufacturing, service) and a cash budget.

8. Is it permissible to show an increase in finished goods inventories on a pro forma balance sheet, while at the same time reflecting a production level less than current unit sales in the cost of goods sold area of the income statement?

9. In what ways is a pro forma cash statement helpful to understand projected conditions?

10. What is the proper basis for selecting forecast drivers for key elements? Is sales volume the key to forecasting, or are there other ways to build up projections? Under what circumstances?

11. What are the major forecasting tools that can be applied to developing appropriate financial planning assumptions?

12. Does an integrated set of pro forma statements fully represent the financial aspects of a business plan? What additional information might be desirable?

CHAPTER 5

DYNAMICS AND GROWTH OF THE BUSINESS SYSTEM

In Chapter 1 we characterized the business system as a dynamic growth model and described in broad terms the interrelationship of decisions, financial yardsticks, and management policies used in the pursuit of shareholder value creation. In the previous three chapters, we dealt with several specific aspects of financial management: the movement of cash through the system, the evaluation of the financial results of the system, and the projection of future financial requirements. We ended Chapter 4 with a broad description of financial modeling as a valuable assist in developing financial projections, after demonstrating basic pro forma and cash budgeting processes as common tools for financial planning. Now we need to return to our systems concept and become more specific about how some of the system's internal characteristics and dimensions affect changes in the cash flow patterns that lead to shareholder value creation.

There are two important subjects that so far we've touched on only briefly, but that are an integral part of understanding and modeling the business system, namely leverage and the potential for growth. The reader will recall that financial leverage and the funding potential with which to support growth were represented in the financing sector of the business system diagram. We also recognized the interplay of fixed and variable costs in the operational sector. At the time we briefly indicated the trade-offs and choices that could be made by management in dealing with these areas. Now it's time to integrate these concepts into a more thorough financial planning discussion that deals with the operational and policy drivers underlying the pro forma statements and cash budgets covered in the previous chapter.

We'll focus first on the concept of *leverage*—the impact of fixed elements on overall results—in two critical areas:

- Operating leverage
- Financial leverage

Here we'll explore in detail the impact of volume changes on profitability under a variety of assumptions about the nature and level of fixed elements in the company's cost pattern, and deal with their implications for structuring and managing the operational part of the system. Then we'll illustrate the impact of financial leverage on a company's profitability, and how the introduction of fixed interest charges into the financial system can both benefit a company's return and magnify the variability of these returns, based on a trade-off of risk versus return.

Last, we'll turn to an integrated modeling approach that'll demonstrate the drivers of growth in the system and their financial implications. Our focus will be on testing the financial impact of top-level policy changes in investment, operations, and financing. The vehicle for this process will be a basic financial growth model format, which in a highly summarized way allows us to visualize the interrelationship of the key financial dimensions and drivers affecting the performance and growth of the total business system. We'll cover the following concepts in detail:

- The basic financial growth model.
- Determining sustainable and affordable growth.
- The integrated financial plan.

The reader is encouraged to revisit the first section of Chapter 1, which describes the business system and its key linkages, many of which we'll test in this discussion. The broader concept of shareholder value creation will be dealt with extensively in Chapter 11.

Leverage

Leverage, as previously mentioned, refers to the often favorable, but at times problematic, condition of having within the overall cost pattern of the business system a stable element which supports a wide range of activity. *Operating leverage* simply means that part of the ongoing costs of a business are fixed over a broad range of operating volume. As a result, profits are boosted or depressed more than proportionally for given changes in sales volume. The phenomenon is positive as long as volume is increasing—but when volume turns down because of unfavorable market conditions, there can be a large negative impact on operating profit. Similarly, *financial leverage* occurs when a company's capital structure contains obligations with fixed interest rates. Earnings after interest and return on equity are boosted or depressed more than proportionally as volume and profitability fluctuate. However, there are differences in the specific elements involved and in the methods of calculation of each type of leverage. Both operating and financial leverage can be present in any business, depending on the choices made by management in structuring operations and the financing requirements, and the respective impact on net profit will tend to be mutually reinforcing. We need to understand the specific impact of leverage whenever it's encountered in a business, because it is an important element in the financial planning process.

Operating Leverage

Distinguishing between fixed and variable costs (those costs that vary with time and those that vary with the level of activity) is an old idea. This separation of costs by their behavior is the basis for *break-even analysis*. The idea of "breaking even" is based on the simple question of how many units of product or service a business must sell in order to cover its fixed costs before beginning to make a profit. Presumably, unit prices are set at a level high enough to recoup all direct (i.e., variable) unit costs and leave a margin of contribution toward fixed (period) costs and profit. Once sufficient units have been sold to accumulate the total contribution needed to offset all fixed costs, the margin from any additional units sold will become profit—unless a new layer of fixed costs has to be added at some future point to support the higher volume of activity.

Understanding this principle will improve our insight into how the operational aspects of a business relate to financial planning and projections. This knowledge is also helpful in setting operational policies, which, especially in a volatile business setting might, for example, focus on minimizing fixed costs through outsourcing of certain activities. But in a broader sense, it'll allow us to appreciate the distorting effect which significant operating leverage might exert on the measures and comparisons used in financial analysis.

A word of caution must be added here. There's nothing absolute about the concept of fixed costs, because in the long run, every cost element becomes variable. All costs rise or fall as a consequence of management policies and decisions, and can therefore be altered. As a result, the break-even concept must be handled with flexibility and judgment.

As we mentioned, introducing fixed costs to the operations of a business tends to magnify profits at higher levels of activity up to the point when another layer of fixed costs might be needed to support greater volume. This is due to the buildup of incremental contribution which each additional unit provides over and above the strictly variable costs incurred in producing it. Depending on the proportion of fixed versus variable costs in the company's cost structure, the total incremental contribution from additional units can result in a sizable overall jump in profit.

Analyzing a leveraged operating situation is quite straightforward. Once all fixed costs have been recovered through the cumulative individual contributions from a sufficient number of units, profits begin to appear as additional units are sold. Profits will grow proportionally faster than the growth in unit volume. Unfortunately, the same effect holds for declining volumes of operations, which result in a profit decline and accelerating losses that are disproportional to the rate of volume reduction. Operating leverage is definitely a double-edged sword!

We can establish the basic definitions as follows:

$$\text{Profit} = \text{Total revenue} - \text{Total cost}$$
$$\text{Total revenue} = \text{Volume (quantity)} \times \text{Price}$$
$$\text{Total cost} = \text{Fixed cost} + \text{Variable cost}$$

The formal way of describing leverage conditions is quite simple. We're interested in the effect on profit (I) of changes in volume (V). The elements that bear on this are the unit price (P), unit variable costs (C), and fixed costs (F). The relationship is:

$$I = VP - (VC + F)$$

This formula can be rewritten as:

$$I = V(P - C) - F$$

which illustrates that profit depends on the number of goods or services sold times the difference between unit price and unit variable cost—which is the contribution of every unit to the constant element, namely fixed costs.

As unit volume changes, the unit contribution (P - C) multiplied by the change in volume will equal the total change in profit. Under normal conditions, the constant, fixed costs (F) will remain just that. The relative changes in profit for a given change in volume will be magnified because of this fixed element.

Another way of stating the leverage relationships is to use profit as a percent of sales (s), one of the ratios developed in Chapter 3. Using the previous notation,

$$s = \frac{I}{VP}$$

and defining I in terms of the components, the formula becomes:

$$s = \frac{V(P - C) - F}{VP}$$

and slightly rewritten:

$$s = \left[1 - \frac{C}{P}\right] - \frac{F}{VP}$$

The relationship indicates that the profit/sales ratio depends on the contribution per unit of sales, less fixed costs as a percent of sales revenue. We observe that, to the extent fixed costs are present, they cause a reduction in the profit ratio. The larger F is, the larger the reduction. Any change in volume, price, or unit cost, however, will tend to have a disproportional impact on s because F is constant.

Now let's examine how the process works with some concrete examples. We'll use the cost/profit conditions of a simple business that has relatively high fixed costs of $200,000 in relation to its volume of output and variable costs per unit. The fixed costs are largely overhead and costs related to owning and operating the production facilities, including the depreciation effect. Our company has a maximum level of production of 1,000 units, and for simplicity, we assume there's no lag between production and sales. Units sell for $750 each, and variable costs of materials, labor, and supplies amount to $250 per unit. Every unit therefore provides a contribution of $500 toward fixed costs and profit.

Figure 5–1's *break-even chart* on the next page is a simple representation of the conditions just outlined. At zero volume, fixed costs amount to $200,000, and they remain level as volume is increased until full capacity has been reached. Variable costs, on the other hand, accumulate by $250 per unit as volume is increased until a level of $250,000 has been reached at capacity, for a total cost of $450,000. Revenue rises from zero, in increments of $750, until total revenue has reached $750,000 at capacity.

Where the revenue and variable cost lines cross (at 400 units of output), a break-even condition—no profit and no loss—has been reached. This means that the total cumulative revenue of $300,000 at that point is just sufficient to offset the fixed costs of $200,000, plus the total variable costs of $100,000 (400 units at $250 each). If operations increase beyond this point, profits are generated; at volumes of less than 400 units, losses are incurred. The break-even point can be found numerically, of course, by simply dividing the total fixed costs of $200,000 by the unit contribution of $500, which results in 400 units, as we expected:

$$\text{Break-even point } (I = \text{zero}): \frac{F}{P - C} = V$$

$$\text{Zero profit} = \frac{\$200,000}{\$500} = 400 \text{ units}$$

The most interesting aspect of the break-even chart, however, is the clear demonstration that increases and decreases in profit are not proportional. A series of 25 percent increases in volume above the break-even point will result in much larger percentage jumps in profit growth.

The relevant change data are displayed in the table under the chart. They show a gradual decline in the growth rate of profit from infinite to 51 percent. Similarly, as volume decreases below the break-even point in 25 percent decrements, the growth rate of losses goes from infinite to a modest 18 percent, as volume approaches zero. Thus, changes in operations *close* to the break-even point, whether up or down, are likely to produce *sizable* swings in earnings. Changes in operations well above or below the break-even point will cause lesser fluctuations.

We must be careful in interpreting these changes, however. As in any percentage analysis, the specific results depend on the starting point chosen and on the relative proportions of the components. In fact, managers will generally be much more concerned about the total dollar amount of change in profit than about percentage fluctuations. Moreover, it's easy to exaggerate the meaning of profit fluctuations unless they are viewed carefully in the context of a company's total cost structure and its normal level of operations.

Nevertheless, the concept should be clear: The closer to its break-even point a firm operates, the more dramatic will be the profit impact of volume changes. The analyst assessing a company's performance or making financial projections must attempt to understand where the level of its current operations is relative to normal volume and the break-even point, and then interpret the analytical results accordingly.

FIGURE 5-1

ABC CORPORATION
Simple Operating Break-even Chart*

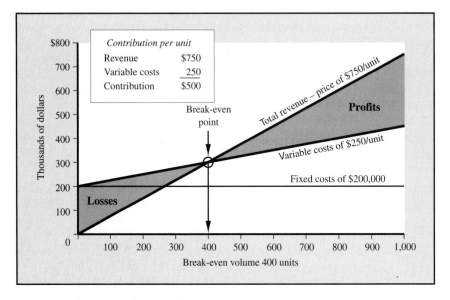

Profits and Losses as a Function of Volume Changes of 25 Percent

Volume	Increase	Profits	Increase
400	—	-0-	—
500	25%	$ 50,000	Infinite†
625	25	112,500	125%
781	25	190,500	69
976	25	288,000	51

Volume	Decrease	Losses	Increase
400	—	-0-	—
300	25%	$ 50,000	Infinite†
225	25	87,500	75%
169	25	115,500	32
127	25	136,000	18

*This diagram is available for download as an interactive template; see "Analytical Support," p. 240.
†infinite because the base is zero.

Clearly, the greater the relative level of fixed costs, the more powerful the effect of operating leverage becomes. Therefore, we need to understand this aspect of the company's cost structure. In capital-intensive industries, such as steel, mining, forest products, and heavy manufacturing, most of the costs of production are indeed fixed for a wide range of volumes. This tends to accentuate profit swings as companies move away from break-even operations.

Another example is the airline industry, which from time to time substantially increases the capacity of its flight equipment. The fixed costs associated with leasing and operating these expensive aircraft initially cause sharp drops in profit for many airlines. As business and private travel rise to approach the new levels of capacity, well-managed airlines experience dramatic improvements in profits, whereas marginal performers continue to suffer losses. In contrast, service industries, such as consulting firms, can directly influence their major cost—salaries and wages—by adjusting the number of employees as demand changes. Thus, they're much less subject to the effects of the operating leverage phenomenon. In many businesses, the use of temporary or contract employees has risen dramatically in recent years, reflecting the desire to reduce in part the more long-term obligations associated with regular employees.

As we mentioned before, in most situations management should assess whether there would be value in reducing the level of fixed costs through creative solutions such as outsourcing, partnering, and contract work arrangements that move the responsibility for fixed expense obligations elsewhere. Such assessments became a growing phenomenon in the 90s during the widespread efforts at corporate restructuring and reengineering. Naturally, there are trade-offs involved in such choices, such as giving up control over what might be important elements of value-creating activities.

There are three main elements management can influence in the operating leverage relationship:

- Fixed costs
- Variable costs
- Price

All three are in one way or another related to *volume*. We'll demonstrate the effect of changes in all three by varying the basic conditions in our example.

Effect of Lower Fixed Costs

If management can lower *fixed costs* through energetic reductions in overhead by using facilities more intensively, by contracting out part of its production, or through other restructuring of the company's activities, the break-even point might be lowered significantly. As a consequence, the boosting effect on profits will start at a lower level of operations. Figure 5–2 shows this change.

Note that reducing fixed costs by one-eighth has led to a corresponding reduction in break-even volume. It will now take one-eighth fewer units contributing $500 each to recover the lower fixed costs. From the table we can observe that successive 25 percent volume changes from the reduced break-even point lead to increases or decreases in profit that are quite similar to our first example in Figure 5–1. Reducing fixed costs, therefore, is a very direct and effective way of lowering the break-even point to improve the firm's profit performance.

FIGURE 5–2

ABC CORPORATION
Simple Operating Break-even Chart: Effect of Reducing Fixed Costs*
(reduction of $25,000)

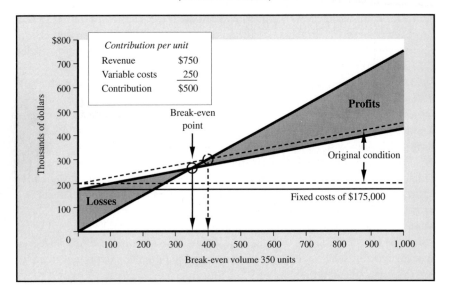

Profits and Losses as a Function of Volume Changes of 25 Percent

Volume	Increase	Profits	Increase
350	—	-0-	—
438	25%	$ 44,000	Infinite[†]
547	25	98,500	125%
684	25	167,500	69
855	25	252,000	51

Volume	Decrease	Losses	Increase
350	—	-0-	—
262	25%	$ 44,000	Infinite[†]
196	25	77,000	75%
147	25	101,500	32
110	25	120,000	18

*This diagram is available for download as an interactive template; see "Analytical Support," p. 240.
[†]Infinite because the base is zero.

Effect of Lower Variable Costs

If management is able to reduce the variable costs of production (direct costs), thereby increasing the contribution per unit, the action can similarly affect profits at

FIGURE 5–3

ABC CORPORATION
Simple Operating Break-Even Chart: Effect of Reducing Variable Costs*
(reduction of $25 per unit)

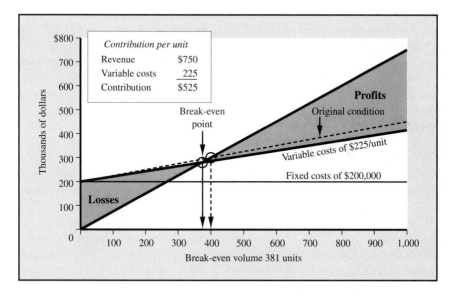

Profits and Losses as a Function of Volume Changes of 25 Percent

Volume	Increase	Profits	Increase
381	—	-0-	—
476	25%	$ 49,900†	Infinite‡
595	25	98,500	125%
744	25	167,500	69
930	25	252,000	51

Volume	Decrease	Losses	Increase
381	—	-0-	—
286	25%	$ 50,150	Infinite‡
215	25	87,125	75%
161	25	115,475	32
121	25	136,475	18

*This diagram is available for download in an interactive format; see "Analytical Support," p. 240.
†First 25 percent change not exactly equal due to rounding.
‡Infinite because the base is zero.

current levels and influence the movement of the break-even point itself. In Figure
5–3, we've shown the resulting change in the slope of the variable cost line, which
in effect widens the area of profits. At the same time, loss conditions are reduced.

However, the change in break-even volume resulting from a 10 percent change in variable costs is not as dramatic as the change experienced when fixed costs were lowered by one-eighth. The reason is that the reduction applies only to a small portion of the total production cost, because variable costs are relatively low in this example. (This illustrates the point we made earlier about always having to consider the relative cost proportions in this type of analysis.)

Only at the full capacity (1,000 units) does the profit impact of $25,000 correspond to the effect of the reduction of $25,000 in fixed costs in the earlier example. At lower levels of operations, lower unit volumes and the lesser impact of variable costs combine to minimize the effect. Nevertheless, the result is a clear improvement in the break-even condition, and a profit boost is achieved earlier on the volume scale. Again, 25 percent incremental changes are tabulated to show the specific results.

Effect of Lower Prices

Up to this point, we've concentrated on *cost* effects which are largely under management's control. In contrast, price changes are for the most part dependent on the firm's competitive environment. As a result, price changes normally affect the competitive equilibrium and will directly influence the unit volume a business is able to sell. Thus, it's not enough to trace the effect of raised or lowered prices on the break-even chart, but we also must anticipate the likely impact on volume resulting from the price change. In other words, raising the price could more than proportionally affect the unit volume the company will be able to sell competitively, and the price action could actually result in lower total profits. Conversely, lowering the price could more than compensate for the lost contribution per unit by significantly boosting the total unit volume that can be sold against competition.

Figure 5–4 demonstrates the effect of lowering the price by $50 per unit, a 6.7 percent reduction. Note that this change raises the required break-even volume by about 11 percent, to 444 units. In other words, the company needs to sell an additional 44 units just to recoup the loss in contribution of $50 from the sale of every unit.

For example, if the current volume was 800 units, with a contribution of $400,000 and a profit of $200,000, the price drop of $50 per unit would require the sale of enough additional units to recover 800 times $50, or $40,000. The new units required will, of course, provide the lower per unit contribution of $450.

Under these conditions, as many as 89 additional units ($40,000 ÷ $450) have to be sold at the lower price to maintain the $200,000 profit level, which represents a volume increase of 11 percent. Note that this results in a more than proportional change in unit volume (11 percent) versus the drop in price (6.7 percent). Price changes affect internal operating results, but they could have an even more pronounced and lasting impact on the competitive environment. If a more than proportional volume advantage—and therefore improved profits—can be obtained over a significant period of time after the price has been reduced, this could change the competitive situation to the company's advantage. Otherwise, if

FIGURE 5-4

ABC CORPORATION
Simple Operating Break-even Chart: Effect of Reducing Price*
(reduction of $50 per unit)

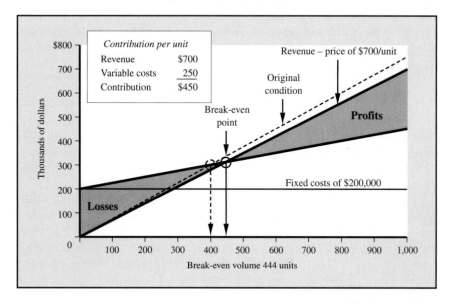

Profits and Losses as a Function of Volume Changes of 25 Percent

Volume	Increase	Profits	Increase
444	—	-0-	—
555	25%	$ 49,750†	Infinite‡
694	25	112,300	125%
867	25	190,150	69
1,084	25	287,800	51

Volume	Decrease	Losses	Increase
444	—	-0-	—
333	25%	$ 50,150†	Infinite‡
249	25	87,950	75%
187	25	115,850	32
140	25	136,000	18

*This diagram is available for download in an interactive template; see "Analytical Support," p. 240.
†First 25 percent change not exactly equal due to rounding.
‡Infinite because the base is zero.

price reductions can be expected to be quickly matched by other competitors, the final effect could simply be a drop in profit for everyone, because little if any shift in relative market shares would result. The airline price wars mentioned earlier are a prime example of this phenomenon.

This isn't the place to discuss the many strategic issues involved in pricing policy; the intent is merely to show the effect of this important factor on the operating area of the business system and to provide a way of analyzing likely conditions.

Multiple Effects on Break-Even Conditions

Up to now, we've analyzed cost, volume, and price implications and their impact on profit separately. In practice, the many conditions and pressures encountered by a business often affect these variables *simultaneously*. Cost, volume, and price for a single product might all be changing at the same time in subtle and often non-measurable ways. The analysis is further complicated when several products or services are involved, as is true of most major companies. In such cases, changes in the sales mix can introduce many additional complexities.

Moreover, our simplifying assumption to make production and sales simultaneous doesn't necessarily hold true in practice; the normal lag between production and sales has a significant effect. In a manufacturing company, sales and production can be widely out of phase. Some of the implications of this condition were discussed in Chapter 2, when we dealt with funds flow patterns caused by varying levels of operations, and in Chapter 4 when we examined the relationship of cash budgets and pro forma income statements.

So far we've also assumed that operating conditions were essentially *linear*. This allowed us to simplify our analysis of leverage and break-even conditions. A more realistic framework is suggested in Figure 5–5. The chart shows potential changes in both fixed and variable costs over the full range of operations. Possible price–revenue developments are also indicated. In other words, changes in all three factors affecting operating leverage are reflected at the same time.

Figure 5–5 on the next page further shows that the simple straight-line relationships used in Figures 5–1 through 5–4 are normally only approximations of the "step functions" and the gradual shifts in cost and price often encountered under realistic circumstances. Inflationary distortions arising over time also must be considered. A few examples of the possible changes and likely reasons are described below the diagram.

Target Profit Analysis

One application of operational leverage calculations is the use of target profit analysis as part of the planning process of a company. It takes into account the relative proportions of fixed and variable costs expected to occur in the company's system. Given projections of total fixed costs (F), estimates of variable costs (C), and expected price (P), the unit volume required to achieve any desired pretax target profit (TP) can be determined with the basic break-even formula:

FIGURE 5–5

ABC CORPORATION
Generalized Break-even Chart: Allowing for Changing Cost and Revenue Conditions

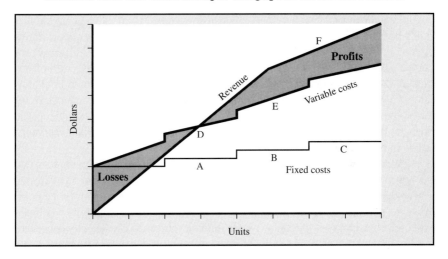

A. A new layer of fixed costs is triggered by growing volume.
B. A new shift is added, with additional requirements for overhead costs.
C. A final small increment of overhead in incurred because some operations require overtime.
D. Efficiencies in operations reduce variable unit costs.
E. The new shift causes inefficiencies and lower output, with more spoilage.
F. The last increments of output must be sold on contract at lower prices.

Volume for target profit:

$$V = \frac{F + TP}{P - C}$$

Similarly, if management wishes to test the level of variable costs (C) allowable for any desired pretax target profit (TP), with an estimated unit volume (V) and price (P) based on expected market conditions and projected fixed costs (F), the formula can be rewritten as:

Variable unit cost for target profit:

$$C = P - \frac{F + TP}{V}$$

The reader is invited to rewrite the formula for the required price to achieve a desired pretax profit, and also to determine the change required to put the formula on an after-tax basis. Calculations of this kind serve well to scope the dimensions of the planning process, but cannot be substituted for detailed analysis and projections as discussed in Chapter 4. The approach is helpful for analysts and managers to recognize in broad terms the implications of the company's operating leverage.

Financial Leverage

The concept of introducing an element of fixed cost into the financial system also applies to financial leverage. In the case of operating leverage, we saw that advantage can be gained from a fixed level of cost that serves a wide variety of volume conditions. With financial leverage, advantage is gained from the expectation that funds borrowed at a fixed interest rate can be used for investment opportunities earning rates of return higher than the interest paid on the funds. The difference, of course, accrues as profit to the owners of the business and boosts the return on equity, as seen in Chapter 3. Viewed superficially, the implication would be that as long as a company's investments consistently provide returns above this rate of interest, the augmented rate of return on equity would benefit the shareholders. The opposite would, of course, apply if the company earned returns on its investments below the rate of interest paid.

We remember, however, that the basic principle of value creation requires that the return on all investments already in place as well as on any future investments must exceed not only the interest paid on debt but also the expectations of the holders of the company's shares. Shareholder value can be created only if the combined cost of capital, representing all long-term funding sources, is consistently exceeded. We established this principle early on and will revisit it in detail in Chapters 8 and 11. This return requirement doesn't affect or alter the principles of leverage itself, but it forces us to think carefully about the minimum level of return with which resources have to be employed. Instead of considering the rate of interest as the threshold return, it's the overall cost of capital that must be met and exceeded.

Given that higher standard, however, the effect of financial leverage is still derived from the fixed nature of the interest charges relative to the overall return created, with the difference, positive or negative, accruing to the shareholders. The principle is simple: Using return on shareholders' equity as the criterion, the higher the proportion of debt—and its fixed interest charges—in the capital structure, the greater will be the leverage contribution to the return on shareholders' equity, for a given positive return achieved on the investments. Conversely, as achieved returns drop below the rate of interest (tax-adjusted), the fixed nature of the interest charges will begin to magnify the reduction in return on equity. The reader will recall the systems view diagram in Chapter 3, p. 150, which shows the connection of financial leverage to return on equity.

To illustrate the relationships further, Figure 5–6 shows the leverage effect on the return on equity measure under three different levels of return on net assets. All three curves are drawn with the assumption that funds can be borrowed at 4 percent per year after taxes. If the normal return before interest, after taxes on the company's capitalization is 20 percent (curve A), growing proportions of debt cause a dramatic rise in return on equity. This return jumps to infinity as debt nears 100 percent—obviously a dangerous extreme in capital structure proportions. Curves B and C show the leverage effect under more modest investment return conditions. While somewhat lessened, the return on equity still shows sharp increases as the proportion of debt rises. We haven't drawn the

FIGURE   5–6

ABC CORPORATION
Return on Equity as Affected by Financial Leverage
(after-tax interest on debt is 4 percent)

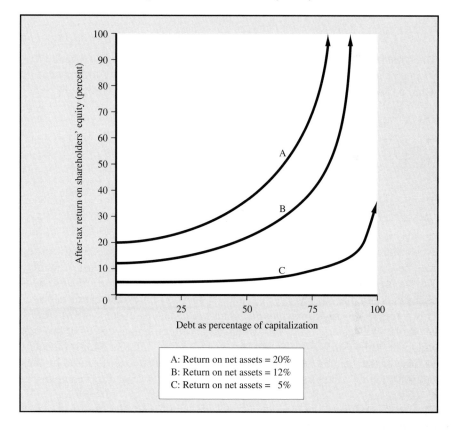

A: Return on net assets = 20%
B: Return on net assets = 12%
C: Return on net assets = 5%

downward sloping curves that would reflect a sharp plunge in negative return on equity when the return drops below 4 percent, the after-tax cost of interest. This effect is also suggested by the increase in the distances between curves A, B, and C at higher debt levels.

To express financial leverage relationships formally, we begin by defining the components, as we did in the case of operating leverage. Profit after taxes (I) now has to be related to shareholders' equity (E) and long-term debt (D). We also single out the return on shareholders' equity (R), and the return on capitalization (net assets) (r) before interest and after taxes, and the after-tax rate of interest (i). First we define the return on shareholders' equity as:

$$R = \frac{I}{E}$$

and the return on capitalization (the sum of equity and debt) as:

$$r = \frac{I + Di}{E + D}$$

We now restate profit (I) in terms of its components:

$$I = r(E + D) - Di$$

which represents the difference between the return on the total capitalization ($E + D$) and the after-tax cost of interest on outstanding debt (Di). We substitute this re-stated profit for I in our initial return on equity formula, which now reads:

$$R = \frac{r(E + D) - Di}{E}$$

and which can be further rewritten as:

$$R = r + \frac{D}{E}(r - i)$$

This formulation highlights the leverage effect, represented by the positive expression after r (i.e., the proportion of debt to equity), multiplied by the difference between the earnings power of net assets and the after-tax cost of interest. Thus, to the extent that debt is introduced into the capital structure, the return on equity is boosted as long as after-tax interest cost doesn't exceed earnings power. This is the *net leverage contribution,* which we displayed in our systems view of key ratios in Chapter 3 on p. 150. Companies with different degrees of leverage will, even if their earnings power is the same, achieve different returns on equity because of the specific net leverage contribution (or detraction) caused by their capital structures. Analysts must therefore be careful in making direct comparisons of ROE results.

When we apply the formula to one set of conditions that pertained to Figure 5–6, the results can be calculated as follows. Given $i = 4$ percent and $r = 12$ percent, if

(1) $D = 0$ and $E = \$100$, then R equals 12.0%

(2) $D = \$25$ and $E = \$75$, then R equals 14.7%

(3) $D = \$50$ and $E = \$50$, then R equals 20.0%

(4) $D = \$75$ and $E = 25$, then R equals 36.0%

In this illustration, we have four different debt/equity ratios, ranging from no debt in the first case to a 3:1 debt/equity relationship in the fourth case. Given an after-tax cost of interest of 4 percent, and the normal opportunity to earn 12 percent after taxes on net assets invested, the return on shareholders' equity in the first case is also 12 percent after taxes—because no debt exists, and the total capitalization is represented by equity.

As increasing amounts of debt are introduced to the capital structure, however, the return on equity is boosted considerably, because in each case, the return on investment far exceeds the cost of interest paid to the debt holders. This is, of course, demonstrated in the graph of Figure 5–6. The reader is invited to work through the opposite effect, that is, interest charges in excess of the ability to earn a return on the investments made with the funds.

We're also interested in the impact of leverage on the return on net assets, or capitalization (r), which we obtain first by reworking the formula

$$R = r + \frac{D}{E}(r - 1)$$

into

$$r = \frac{RE + Di}{E + D}$$

Given $i = 4$ percent and $R = 12$ percent, we can determine the minimum return on capitalization (r) necessary to obtain a return on equity of 12 percent, for

(1) $D = 0$ and $E = \$100$, then r equals 12%

(2) $D = \$25$ and $E = \$75$, then r equals 10%

(3) $D = \$50$ and $E = \$50$, then r equals 8%

(4) $D = \$75$ and $E = \$25$, then r equals 6%

This is a useful way of testing the expected return from new investments. The approach simply turns the calculation around by fixing the return on equity and letting the expected return on investment vary. The process is straightforward. Note that the required amount of earnings on net assets, or capitalization, drops sharply as leverage is introduced, until it begins to approach the 4 percent after-tax interest cost. It'll never quite reach this figure, however, because normally some amount of equity must be maintained in the capital structure to keep the company viable, and also the cost of debt will rise as lenders assess the risk of high debt levels.

Although it's simple to work out the mathematical relationships, the translation of these conditions into the appropriate financial strategies is much more complex. No management is completely free to vary the capital structure at will, and there are practical, as well as legal and contractual constraints, on any company to maintain some normalcy on the liability side of the balance sheet. Even though no absolute rules exist, the various tests of creditworthiness run the gamut of the ratios discussed in Chapter 4, particularly the measures oriented to the lenders' point of view.

With enlightened self-interest in mind, lenders will impose upper limits on the amount of debt capital to be utilized by any potential borrower. For manufacturing companies, the amount of long-term debt will normally range between 0 and 50 percent of their capitalization, whereas public utilities will range between 30 and 60 percent. Trading companies with highly liquid assets might have even higher debt proportions (carried to extremes by the now defunct Enron Corporation). At the same time, restructuring and corporate reengineering are shifting both capital requirements and debt levels in many instances. For example, outsourcing as part of corporate strategy might serve to reduce the need for capital, including debt, because part of the asset base is effectively transferred to suppliers. The vast increase in leveraged buyouts during the 1980s introduced far higher than normal levels of debt into the capital structures of many companies. In those cases, financial leverage is used to the ultimate extent, which also vastly increases the companies' exposure to the adverse effects of cash flow falling below expectations.

The most important issue around the use of financial leverage, however, relates to its impact on a company's overall market value. Financial theory has firmly established that introduction of financial leverage into an unleveraged capital structure will raise the market value of the company because of the change in total return to debt and equity holders—but only up to a point. The lift in market value is in fact a function of the corporate tax deductibility of the interest cost of debt, as demonstrated in Figure 5–7. As debt levels increase, the value of this favorable tax shield impact increases. Here we've assumed a total capital of $2.0 million, on which pretax operating earnings are 30 percent, or $600,000. With no debt, there are no interest charges and net income after taxes of 40 percent is $360,000. If instead we assume a 50 percent debt level, interest at 8 percent on $1.0 million amounts to $80,000, lowering taxable income and income taxes paid, thus dropping net income to $312,000. At 75 percent debt, we've assumed a higher interest rate of 10 percent, because of the greater financial exposure, and net income drops to $270,000.

Note, however, that XYZ Corporation's investors can claim potential distribution of after-tax income through the combination of dividends paid to the shareholders, and interest paid to the debt holders, a total which rises from $360,000 to $420,000 under the three conditions. As it turns out, the increase of $32,000 in potential distribution when moving from zero to 50 percent debt represents exactly the amount of taxes saved, because of the deductibility of interest (40 percent of $80,000). The increase of $60,000 in potential distribution when moving from zero to 75 percent debt likewise represents the tax savings of 40 percent on $150,000 of interest paid. Shown in the next set of figures is the result if income taxes didn't exist—and, as we might expect, there's no change in the distribution potential, regardless of the amount of leverage introduced, because the tax shield has disappeared. Naturally, in a no-tax environment the total available for distribution would be much higher; in fact it would remain at the level of EBIT, with the pattern of distribution again shifting gradually toward the holders of debt as leverage and risk increased.

We've demonstrated here in very basic terms that successful employment of financial leverage does in fact create higher overall returns, if all potential distributions are taken into account, because there is a true economic (cash flow) saving from employing fixed, tax-deductible interest in the capital structure. As we'll see in Chapter 11, the stock market does ascribe a higher market value to a company that is able to bring about an improved result from a cash flow standpoint.

There is a risk-reward trade-off, however. As the proportion of debt with its fixed requirements rises to levels at which the risk of nonperformance and even

FIGURE 5-7

XYZ CORPORATION
Impact of Leverage on Earnings and Distribution
($ thousands)

	Debt Proportion		
	0	50	75
Total capital	$2,000	$2,000	$2,000
Debt	0	1,000	1,500
EBIT @ 30% of capital	600	600	600
Interest expense @ 8% and 10%	0	80	150
Income before taxes	600	520	450
Income taxes @ 40%	240	208	180
Net income	360	312	270
Distribution of after-tax income:			
Dividends	360	312	270
Interest	0	80	150
Total income to investors*	360	392	420
Distribution of income assuming no taxes:			
Dividends	600	520	450
Interest	0	80	150
Total income to investors	$ 600	$ 600	$ 600

*Before personal income taxes.

bankruptcy looms ever higher, the expectations of shareholders and creditors will increasingly factor in the potential for difficulties, and the market value of the company will level off and even decline. The trade-off here is simply between the cash flow implications from the obtainable tax savings and the cash flow implications from financial stress and even failure. The "right" level of leverage will differ greatly among companies, industries, and management styles. Finding the optimal degree of leverage for a business requires a careful assessment of potential financial risks, which are a function of the variability of performance of the company's business system, the outlook for the markets served, competitive conditions, strategic positioning, and so on. In short, successful application of financial leverage is much more than a numerical exercise, and we'll return to it when discussing capital structure planning in Chapter 9. The reader is also referred to the various sources listed at the end of this chapter for further insights.

Our main interest for the rest of the chapter is in the demonstrable effect of financial leverage on the broader area of financial planning for a company. As such, it's only one of several aspects affecting overall performance. In the next section, we'll integrate the numerical aspects of financial leverage as well as other key factors into a broader financial plan.

Financial Growth Plans

Most managers aspire to building ever larger businesses, whenever the opportunities in the marketplace permit this. Typically, common shareholders also expect growing economic benefits to accrue from share ownership. As a consequence, profitable and sustainable growth within the competitive environment is one of the key strategic underpinnings of shareholder value creation, as we'll discuss in detail in Chapter 11. Thus it's not surprising that one important dimension of financial planning is continual assessment of the effects of growth on investment, operations, and financing. The choices of financial policy open to management have different impacts on the expected results, and therefore must be tested along with the operational aspects of the plans.

Management can set a variety of financial objectives and financial policies to direct and constrain the company's planning effort and the specific financial projections based on these plans. One of the most commonly used financial objectives is return on shareholders' equity, even though this measure is accounting based and not necessarily a direct indicator of value creation. We'll use it here to demonstrate the planning process. The objective of a specific return on shareholders' equity in turn is derived from underlying objectives about:

- Growth in earnings per share.
- Growth in dividends per share.
- Growth in total profits.
- Growth in shareholders' equity.
- Growth in market value.

None of these objectives can be used singly as an overall standard, of course. In fact, the strong emphasis in recent years on shareholder value creation and total shareholder return achieved has put many of the accounting-based measures into a secondary role. As we'll discuss and demonstrate in more detail in Chapters 10 and 11, shareholder value creation ultimately is based on cash flows and market expectations, whereas total shareholder return takes into account the combined return to the investor from dividends and changes in the market price of the stock. The accounting measures remain important, however, because they're conveniently derived from published financial statements, and can be visibly linked to financial policies. Foremost among these financial policies is the amount of financial leverage the company considers prudent, and subsidiary considerations are the related measures of creditworthiness that management will have to observe as constraints on its actions.

To demonstrate the buildup of an integrated financial plan that enables us to observe the effect of growth and its relationship to financial objectives and policies, we'll begin by selecting just one of the objectives named above to work through a simple conceptual model of a hypothetical company. The format of this model is the basic framework that we'll use later to build a more detailed integrated financial plan. It'll also serve to demonstrate the important concept of *sustainable growth*.

F I G U R E   5–8

Financial Growth Model: Three Different Policies($ Thousands)*

	Case I	Case II	Case III
Capital structure:			
Debt as percent of capitalization	0	50%	50%
Debt	0	$250	$250
Equity	$500	$250	$250
Net assets (capitalization)	$500	$500	$500
Profitability (after taxes):			
Gross return on net assets†	10%	10%	10%
Amount of profit	$ 50	$ 50	$ 50
Interest rate	0	4%	4%
Amount of interest	0	10	10
Profit after interest	$ 50	$ 40	$ 40
Disposition of profit:			
Dividend payout	0%	0%	50%
Dividends paid	0	0	20
Reinvestment of profit	$ 50	$ 40	$ 20
Financing:			
Additional debt	0	40	20
Funding potential	$ 50	$ 80	$ 40
Cash flow implications:			
Amount of after-tax profit	$ 50	$ 40	$ 40
Depreciation effect	25	25	25
Cash flow from operations	75	65	65
Dividends paid	0	0	20
Cash flow available for reinvestment	75	65	45
Additional debt	0	40	20
Total investment potential	$ 75	$105	$ 65
Results:			
Net return on net assets‡	10%	8%	8%
Return on equity	10%	16%	16%
Growth in equity§	10%	16%	8%

*This model is available for download in an interactive format; see "Analytical Support," p. 240.
†Profits before interest, after taxes related to net assets (capitalization).
‡Profits after interest and taxes related to net assets.
§Growth in recorded equity based on earnings reinvested after payment of dividends.

Basic Financial Growth Model

A simple way to demonstrate the interrelated elements that affect growth in the business system is to use the objective of growth in shareholders' equity, as recorded on the balance sheet. Not only is this particular element easy to calculate, but also it encompasses the effects of profit growth and dividend payout—apart from any changes caused by issuing new shares or repurchasing existing shares in the market.

Figure 5–8 represents this simplified financial model that allows us to trace the aspects affecting equity growth in a company, namely, leverage, profitability, earnings disposition, and financing. With its help, we can demonstrate the effect that different financial policies have on this objective. In fact, the model is a broad representation of our business system as discussed in Chapter 1.

Three cases have been worked out. The first represents an unleveraged company with $500,000 in equity, which pays no dividends and reinvests all of its profits in operations similar to its present activities. The second case shows the same company, but in a leveraged condition with debt at 50 percent of capitalization. In the third case, we take the conditions of the second case, but in addition assume a dividend payout of 50 percent of earnings. All other financial conditions are assumed to remain constant.

Let's trace through the data for Case I. Given a gross return on net assets (capitalization) of 10 percent after taxes, the amount of net profit generated for the year is $50,000, all of which is the basic funding potential that can be reinvested in the company's activities in the form of new investment for expansion, profit improvements, and so on.

The results of Case I are a net return on net assets (capitalization) after interest, which is zero in this example, of 10 percent, and a return on equity of 10 percent. The latter also represents a growth in equity of 10 percent during the period. This condition holds because all profits are retained in the business for reinvestment.

In Figure 5–9, we've calculated three additional periods of operations for the Case I company, without changing any of the assumptions. We can quickly observe that given stable policies and conditions, equity growth will indeed continue at 10 percent per year for periods 2 and 3, matched by growth in profit after interest.

Returning to Figure 5–8, we next examine the cash flow implications for Case I, which show that when the depreciation effect of $25,000 is added in, the total cash available for investment in fact is $75,000, without raising any additional debt. For purposes of this model we'll assume that this amount of depreciation is also reinvested, but in the form of equipment replacement necessary to maintain the profitability of the existing facilities. By this choice, therefore, the return on net assets of 10 percent is maintained. We've applied this approach to the additional periods of Figure 5–9 in every case.

Case II differs only with regard to the use of debt financing. Because $250,000 has been borrowed at 4 percent after taxes, $10,000 of after-tax interest must be deducted from the amount of profit earned on net assets, which reduces the amount available for reinvestment to $40,000. If management wishes to maintain its policy of a 50 percent debt level, an additional $40,000 can be borrowed, matching the increase in equity. This raises the funding potential for reinvestment to $80,000. From a cash flow standpoint, however, the total investment potential now is $105,000, because the depreciation effect must be added, as done in Case I.

Compared to Case I, the results have changed in several ways. Net return on net assets (capitalization) has dropped to 8 percent because interest charges were introduced. As we expected, however, the return on equity was boosted to 16 percent because of the financial leverage effect. Figure 5–9 again demonstrates that

FIGURE 5-9

Financial Growth Model Results of Three Different Policies Held Constant over Three Periods($ Thousands)*

	Case I			Case II			Case III		
	Period 1	Period 2	Period 3	Period 1	Period 2	Period 3	Period 1	Period 2	Period 3
Capital structure:									
Debt as percent of capitalization	0%	0%	0%	50%	50%	50%	50%	50%	50%
Debt	0	0	0	250.0	290.0	336.4	250.0	270.0	291.6
Equity	$500.0	$550.0	$605.0	250.0	290.0	336.4	250.0	270.0	291.6
Net assets (capitalization)	$500.0	$550.0	$605.0	$ 500.0	$ 580.0	$ 672.8	$500.0	$540.0	$583.2
Profitability (after taxes):									
Gross return on net assets†	10%	10%	10%	10%	10%	10%	10%	10%	10%
Amount of profit	$50.00	$55.00	$60.50	$ 50.00	$ 58.00	$ 67.28	$50.00	$54.00	$58.32
Interest rate	—	—	—	4%	4%	4%	4%	4%	4%
Amount of interest	0	0	0	10.00	11.60	13.46	10.00	10.80	11.66
Profit after interest	$50.00	$55.00	$60.50	$ 40.00	$ 46.40	$ 53.82	$40.00	$43.20	$46.66
Disposition of profit:									
Dividend payout	0%	0%	0%	0%	0%	0%	50%	50%	50%
Dividends paid	0	0	0	0	0	0	$20.00	$21.60	$23.33
Reinvestment of profit	$50.00	$55.00	$60.50	$ 40.00	$ 46.40	$53.82	$20.00	$21.60	$23.33
Financing:									
Additional debt (next year)	0	0	0	$ 40.00	$ 46.40	$53.82	$20.00	$21.60	$23.33
Funding potential (next year)	$50.00	$55.00	$60.50	$ 80.00	$ 92.80	$107.64	$40.00	$43.20	$46.66
Cash flow implications:									
Amount of after-tax profit	$50.00	$55.00	$60.50	$ 40.00	$ 46.40	$ 53.82	$40.00	$43.20	$46.66
Depreciation effect	25.00	28.00	31.00	25.00	30.00	36.00	25.00	27.00	29.00
Cash flow from operations	75.00	83.00	91.50	65.00	76.40	89.82	65.00	70.20	75.66
Dividends paid	0.00	0.00	0.00	0.00	0.00	0.00	20.00	21.60	23.33
Cash flow available for reinvestment	75.00	83.00	91.50	65.00	76.40	89.82	45.00	48.60	52.33
Additional debt	0.00	0.00	0.00	40.00	46.40	53.82	20.00	21.60	23.33
Total investment potential	$75.00	$83.00	$91.50	$105.00	$122.80	$143.64	$65.00	$70.20	$75.66
Results:									
Net return on net assets‡	10%	10%	10%	8%	8%	8%	8%	8%	8%
Return on equity	10	10	10	16	16	16	16	16	16
Growth in equity§	10	10	10	16	16	16	8	8	8
Growth in profit after interest	—	10	10	—	16	16	—	8	8

*This model is available for download in an interactive format; see "Analytical Support," p. 240.
†Profits before interest, after taxes related to net assets (capitalization) as a measure of operational return on assets.
‡Profits after interest and taxes related to net assets, as often shown in financial reports.
§Growth in recorded equity based on earnings reinvested after payment of dividends.

231

under these conditions, growth in equity can be similarly maintained at a level of 16 percent for periods 2 and 3, as long as all of the internally generated funds are reinvested in opportunities returning 10 percent, and matching amounts of debt funds are obtained and similarly invested.

The cash flow implications of Case II once more show that the total invest- ment potential is higher by the amount of depreciation, and we'll again assume that this amount will be reinvested to maintain the return on net assets, which was done in Figure 5–9. There we observe the faster growth in net assets in periods 2 and 3, because of the higher reinvestment, which is also supported by increasing amounts of new debt raised in each subsequent period to maintain the 50 percent debt proportion desired by management.

In Case III, the only change is the introduction of dividends. The assumed 50 percent payout reduces the internal funds available for reinvestment to only $20,000, and also reduces the available additional debt to $20,000, under the stated 50 percent debt policy. The funding potential from reinvestment has thus been re- duced to $40,000. This dividend action seriously affects our objective of growth in equity, which is now only half the level in Case II. From a cash flow standpoint, the total investment potential including the depreciation effect is now only $65,000. This figure is lower than in the other two cases, because of the combined impact of a high dividend payout and the more limited incremental debt. Periods 2 and 3 re- flect the continued lower growth induced by the new dividend policy.

The simple model framework in Figures 5–8 and 5–9 illustrates the effects of a combination of decisions about investment, operations, earnings disposition, and financing strategy. It permits easy analysis of changes, and testing of the sensitiv- ity of results in response to changed assumptions. Clearly we've oversimplified the conditions for purposes of demonstration, but refinements in the assumptions about such items as return on net assets, dividend payout ratios, and increments of addi- tional borrowing, will only be variations on the basic theme expressed here.

Sustainable Growth and the Sustainable Growth Equation

One of the key issues in planning the future successful growth of a company is to grapple with the inherent limitations and constraints of the business system. Limitations are such inherent aspects as the amount of assets required to support a given level of sales, which will depend greatly on the nature of the business model used. There are, of course, wide differences between service companies, trading companies, and manufacturing or natural resource companies, and the basic profitability of their activities. Among the constraints are the policies un- der which a management team operates, such as the degree of leverage to be employed, the readiness to issue new equity, or the dividend policy followed.

When it comes to establishing the potential for normal growth, we must make specific assumptions about the key limitations and policies, as we previ- ously did in our simple financial growth model. There we observed that growth in shareholders' equity in fact is a good surrogate for expressing growth potential un- der the stipulated assumptions. If we visualize a growing company under stable policies, increasing sales volume will require proportional increases in working capital, as well as proportional investments in fixed assets and other assets supporting the operations. The funding of these requirements has to come from two sources, ownership funds and debt. To the extent that profits are retained in the business, they build up recorded shareholder equity and this buildup, together with incremental debt, represents the funding potential for growth, as we first demonstrated in the business system model on page 8. Given stable policies and performance, the rate of increase in shareholders' equity will therefore represent the rate of expansion of the balance sheet necessary to support the growth.

If the company wished to grow faster than the growth in equity implied by stable policies, additional funds would have to be raised from new debt or new equity, thus changing one or more financial policy constraints. If the company wished to grow at a lower rate, some of the funding potential could be used to pay increased dividends, buy back outstanding shares, or retire debt instead of providing an expanded asset base, again changing some of the policy constraints. The concept of sustainable growth, therefore, is simply defined as the growth in the business that can be sustained by stable policies over a period of time, and it is reflected by growth in shareholder equity.

Let's now turn to a formal way of describing the drivers of growth and their relationships. Revisiting our simple growth model in Figures 5–8 and 5–9, we noted that in Case I, when no debt was employed and no dividends were paid, the following relationship held:

$$g = r$$

where g is growth in equity and r is the after-tax rate of return on capitalization. This equation simply expresses the fact that under these basic conditions, return on capitalization is *equal* to return on equity, and growth in equity is *equal* to return on equity.

In Case II, debt was introduced to the capital structure, and we therefore have to add the leverage effect to the formula to arrive at this expression of growth:

$$g = r + \frac{D}{E}(r - i)$$

where D is debt, E is equity, and i is the after-tax interest rate. Leverage, as we discussed earlier, is a direct function of these two elements:

- Proportion of debt in the total capital structure.
- Difference between the return on capitalization and the interest cost of debt funds, both after taxes.

Because in Case II all earnings are assumed to be reinvested, the rate of growth in equity must again be equal to the *return* on equity—which in this case is a combination of the return on net assets and the net contribution from leverage.

In Case III, the introduction of dividend payments slowed the growth in equity, because only the earnings retained could be reinvested. We now have to adjust each of the two components of the expression to reflect this change. The factor p stands for the proportion of earnings retained as a percentage of total earnings. The resulting equation is:

$$g = rp + \frac{D}{E}(r - i)p$$

We now have a generalized formula for the rate of growth in equity that can be sustained by a business if stable conditions and policies hold. It's called the *sustainable growth equation.*[1] If the business, over the long run, is managed within the following parameters, the growth in equity achieved will stabilize at the rate determined by the equation:

- Continually able to invest funds at the return indicated.
- Maintain the debt/equity proportion stable.
- Interest rates and the dividend payout ratio do not change.

The main driver of growth in the sustainable growth equation is the return on capitalization (r), which is the key indicator of the effectiveness with which working capital, fixed assets, and other assets funded by the capitalization are employed. Not surprisingly, the greater the return, the higher the growth potential. Next is the policy of earnings retention versus dividend payout. As we saw in Case III, sustainable growth can be significantly reduced if a high payout policy is pursued. Finally, the degree of financial leverage directly influences growth potential. The higher the successful use of leverage, the greater the growth potential—within the constraints of prudent financing, of course.

As changes in policies or conditions are introduced, however, the fluctuations in year-to-year performance can be severe. In fact, most companies are unlikely to operate for extended periods at a particular sustainable growth rate.

Another way of looking at sustainable growth is to multiply the profit margin on sales (profit after taxes P divided by sales S) (in percent), asset turnover (number of times), financial leverage (assets A divided by the beginning balance of shareholders' equity Eb) (number of times), and the retention rate (p) of earnings (in percent). These elements, of course, also underlie our earlier formulation, only the form of expressing them here has changed.

Our modified formula appears as follows:

$$g = \frac{P}{S}(\%) \times \frac{S}{A} \times \frac{A}{E_b} \times p\,(\%)$$

Now the drivers of growth reflect the focus on sales profitability, asset effectiveness in terms of turnover, the degree of leverage, and the retention of earnings. Again sustainable growth boils down to managing profitability, managing resource utilization, using leverage prudently, and choosing a sustainable dividend policy.

---

[1] This equation and its components are available as a model for download in an interactive format; see "Analytical Support," p. 240.

What are the implications of sustainable growth analysis? Clearly, a company in a fast-growing industry that is characterized by thin operating margins and high asset requirements isn't likely to be able to sustain its desired growth from internal sources alone, even if it pays out very little in dividends. The financial policies that management must consider will include expanding the equity base beyond retained earnings by issuing new shares, and using increasing leverage, especially if rapid growth in the early stages of the product/service life cycle is essential to attaining a strategic advantage. There are likely to be significant, repeated cash shortfalls during the growth period. In contrast, a company in a mature business setting might have a sustainable growth rate that exceeds its internal strategic growth needs, resulting in a buildup of excess cash. Management may have to reexamine its financial policies, consider higher dividends, share repurchases, and reduction of debt, unless other strategic opportunities can be found to employ the resources being created by its older products and services.

When doing trend analysis of past performance, it's useful to calculate the sustainable growth rate for the years examined and to compare the results to the actual year-to-year growth achieved. The differences will indicate whether the company has exceeded or lagged its growth potential, and a further check of the financial policies in place at the time will indicate whether significant changes were made in them or could perhaps be in the offing.

As we've stated before, however, growth in equity is only one of several different types of financial objectives. Figure 5–9 indicated that our basic model is applicable to testing other objectives, such as growth in earnings. As the last line of the "Results" section shows, growth in total earnings (profit after taxes) stabilizes at the same rate as growth in equity, when assuming our stable sets of policies. In fact, the formula used for growth in equity applies to this objective as well, because profit growth depends on the same variables.

Similar models can be developed for the variables affecting earnings per share, dividends per share, debt service, or any other financial area of the business. We won't attempt to go into detail about these, but rather let growth in equity and growth in earnings serve as examples. Creative use of spreadsheets is a natural assist in these types of analysis.

Integrated Financial Plan

We can now turn to an illustration of an integrated financial plan, which in concept and format is based on the models in Figures 5–8 and 5–9. This time, however, our focus is on taking a set of changing operating and financial assumptions and working them through the format, in a more realistic representation of the impact of the economic and competitive environment. As part of its strategy development, the XYZ Company is considering a number of modifications in its financial policies, and management wishes to study the impact of the combination of operating projections and policy modifications on its rate of growth and profitability over the

FIGURE 5–10

XYZ CORPORATION
Integrated Financial Plan*
Sample Five-Year Projection of Effect of Policy Changes ($thousands)

	Year 1	Year 2	Year 3	Year 4	Year 5
Capital structure:					
Debt as percent of capitalization	33.3%	43.0%	43.0%	50.0%	50.0%
Debt	$300.0	$ 470.7	$ 492.5	$ 688.9	$ 728.5
Equity	600.0	624.0	652.9	688.9	728.5
Net assets (capitalization)	$900.0	$1,094.7	$1,145.4	$1,377.8	$1,457.0
Profitability (after taxes):					
Gross return on net assets[†]	8%	7%	8%	8%	9%
Amount of profit	$ 72.0	$ 76.6	$ 91.6	$ 110.2	$ 131.1
Interest rate	4%	4%	4%	4.5%	4.5%
Amount of interest	$ 12.0	$ 18.8	$ 19.7	$ 31.0	$ 32.8
Profit after interest	$ 60.0	$ 57.8	$ 71.9	$ 79.2	$ 98.3
Disposition of profit:					
Dividend payout	60%	50%	50%	50%	40%
Dividends paid	$ 36.0	$ 28.9	$ 35.9	$ 39.6	$ 39.3
Reinvestment of profit	$ 24.0	$ 28.9	$ 36.0	$ 39.6	$ 59.0
Financing (next year):					
New debt, old ratio	$ 12.0	$ 21.8	$ 27.2	$ 39.6	$ 59.0
New debt, revised ratio	158.7	0	169.2	0	0
Funding potential	$194.7	$ 50.7	$ 232.4	$ 79.2	$ 118.0
Cash flow implications:					
Amount of after-tax profit	$ 60.0	$ 57.8	$ 71.9	$ 79.2	$ 98.3
Depreciation effect	40.0	46.0	50.0	65.0	72.0
Cash flow from operations	100.0	103.8	121.9	144.2	170.3
Dividends paid	36.0	28.9	35.9	39.6	39.3
Cash flow available for reinvestment	64.0	74.9	86.0	104.6	131.0
Additional debt	170.7	21.8	196.4	39.6	59.0
Total investment potential	$234.7	$ 96.7	$ 282.4	$ 144.2	$ 190.0
Results:					
Net return on net assets[‡]	6.7%	5.3%	6.3%	5.8%	6.8%
Return on equity	10.0%	9.3%	11.0%	11.5%	13.5%
Growth in equity[§]	4.0%	4.6%	5.5%	5.8%	8.1%
Earnings per share (100,000 shares)	0.60	0.58	0.72	0.79	0.96
Dividends per share	0.36	0.29	0.36	0.40	0.39

*This model is available for download in an interactive format; see "Analytical Support," p. 240.
[†]Profits before interest, after taxes related to net assets (capitalization).
[‡]Profits after interest and taxes related to net assets.
[§]Growth in recorded equity based on earnings reinvested after payment of dividends.

next five years. The resulting integrated financial plan in Figure 5–10 encompasses changes in debt proportions, return on net assets, interest cost (changing as debt proportions rise), and dividend payout.

One key benefit of displaying the interrelationships in this form is that any obviously inconsistent conditions will show up in the results. As undesirable effects occur, the analyst can explore them with more tenable assumptions and calculate the impact of such changes. Basic planning frameworks of this kind are fairly easy to construct on spreadsheets, and more inclusive financial models can be programmed to provide output of this kind.

XYZ Corporation has a total capitalization of $900,000 and starts with a debt proportion of 33.3 percent (every dollar of equity is matched by 50 cents of long-term debt). The current return on net assets after taxes but before interest is 8 percent, which provides a profit of $72,000. Interest after taxes requires $12,000, which leaves a net profit of $60,000.

With an assumed dividend payout of 60 percent, cash dividends of $36,000 are required, which leaves a balance of retained earnings of $24,000 for reinvestment in new assets. This is in addition to the amount of investment equivalent to depreciation, which we assume to be spent automatically to keep facilities in good repair. If the debt proportion of 33.3 percent in Year 1 were to be maintained, new debt of $12,000 supported by the increased equity could be incurred and used for new investment in Year 2.

In anticipation of major expansion plans, XYZ management has considered raising its debt proportion for Year 2 to 43 percent. This change would allow additional borrowing of $170,700, which is $158,700 beyond the increase of $12,000 that would be possible under the old debt proportion. (The total amount of new debt is found by simply letting the increased equity of $624,000 represent 57 percent of net assets for Year 2.) For simplicity, we've assumed that all changes take place at year-end.

The results for the first year show a net return on capitalization of 6.7 percent, a return on equity of 10 percent, and growth in equity of 4 percent. Earnings per share are $0.60 and dividends per share are $0.36. The influx of new funds at the beginning of Year 2 raises the company's capitalization to almost $1.1 million.

For Year 2, the assumption about returns is lowered to reflect some normal inefficiencies as the new funds are invested; the overall return on net assets is expected to be 7 percent. After making proper allowance for interest payments, profits after taxes are $57,800. The assumed reduction in dividend payout to 50 percent requires only $28,900—which leaves $28,900 for reinvestment. Under the existing debt proportion of 43 percent, this amount permits raising of $21,800 of new debt ($28,900 reinvested represents 57 percent of the increase in capital). These combined funds are added to the investment base for Year 3.

The process is repetitive as changes in policies are anticipated at the end of each year's operations. For example, we find a sizable new influx of capital in Year 4, as the debt proportion is again raised, this time to 50 percent. A small increase in the after-tax interest rate to 4.5 percent is assumed, because lenders will require higher interest as the capital structure becomes more leveraged and thus more risky. At the same time, however, the effectiveness of employing capital (after-tax return on net assets) has been left at 8 percent in Years 3 and 4, and only raised to 9 percent in Year 5, to allow some time for the new investments to become effective.

The results at the bottom of the table show some fluctuations in the net return on capitalization over the years, as either profitability or interest cost is
changed. The return on equity, however, after dropping in Year 2, rises steadily to
a sizable 13.5 percent in Year 5. Growth in equity jumps, after some intermediate
boosts, to about double the original 4 percent rate, that is, to 8.1 percent in Year 5.
Changes in total profit after interest are quite significant, as policy changes from
year to year take effect. Similarly, growth in earnings per share fluctuates while
dividends per share are somewhat diminished—showing little or no growth for
most years as funds are reserved for investment.

The results from such a model raise some realistic questions. For example,
it might not be prudent to change the dividend payout ratio in sizable steps as was
done here. We observe a drop in dividends per share of almost 20 percent in the
second year. In the absence of general economic problems, the corporation's directors might be very reluctant to make this change because a consistent dividend
pattern is generally considered desirable. The main reason is that dividends represent part of the total shareholder return the investors have come to expect. Therefore, the dividend payout ratio for Year 2 might be maintained near the original
level with the purpose of avoiding a drop in dividends per share. The dividend
payout ratio would be lowered only as total earnings rise sufficiently to permit
paying a level, or even growing, dividend.

At the same time, it might be useful to refine the assumptions about return
on net assets. We've used an overall percentage in this example. It would be more
realistic if, specifically taking into account the lag in expected returns on the new
investments, we split the analysis into

- Return on existing assets.
- Return on incremental assets.

Such a refinement might be particularly useful if a company were diversi-
fying its operations and would expect a significantly different return from some of
these new activities. More attention might also be paid to our current assumption
that an amount equal to depreciation will be reinvested without generating additional profits. A company with short life cycles of products or services, or one
that's consolidating some of its ongoing operations to free funds for redeployment
in more diversified lines of business, might not be willing to reinvest the equivalent of depreciation in old product lines. Dealing with capital expenditures as a
separate input would help clarify some of these questions.

The main purpose of this illustration is to show the usefulness of financial
planning in the context of the overall business system. By observing how the key
results respond to a variety of different inputs, the analyst can arrive at a set of assumptions and recommendations that fairly reflect management's desires and capabilities. Many more refined formats are, of course, possible.

Key Issues

The following is a recap of the key issues raised directly or indirectly in this chapter. They are enumerated here to help the reader keep the materials discussed within the perspective of financial theory and business practice.

1. The business system is a dynamic linkage of decisions, policies, and constraints, which must be considered as a whole when dealing with any subset of elements. Leverage in operations and financing has significant effects extending throughout the system, and these should be understood in specific terms as conditions are analyzed and changes are considered.

2. Operating leverage has both financial and strategic implications, because it cannot be separated from the trade-offs involved in pricing, cost effectiveness including outsourcing, and insights from activity-based analysis. It is intimately tied to all operational aspects of the business system, but also has implications for investment choices and financing considerations.

3. Use of financial leverage is a complex policy issue which not only relates to the specific impact of tax-deductible fixed interest charges on the return that is characteristic of the business, but requires fundamental understanding of the risk/reward trade-offs implicit in exposing a particular company to the risk of financial distress. Financial leverage thus is part of the policy mix that both enables successful performance and matches the management style of the company involved.

4. The ultimate purpose of using financial leverage is to enhance the overall market value of the firm, and as such the risk/reward trade-offs in the operational and competitive setting of the company have to be made explicit to find the optimum level.

5. Sustainable growth is a concept based on stable policies in investment, operations, and financing. Given the assumption of such stability, sustainability is subject to significant change as key conditions and constraints are altered. The sustainable growth concept can serve, however, as a yardstick against which the actual performance of a company can be held over time.

6. Financial modeling is useful in displaying the key drivers and results of assumed sets of conditions affecting growth. The degree of sophistication can vary widely; usually adequate ballpark estimates can be achieved with fairly basic sets of relationships. Integrated financial models will give more precise and interrelated results, but these also will be dominated by a limited set of key variables.

Summary

In this chapter we've attempted to integrate some key concepts discussed in the earlier parts of the book into the dynamic system framework established in Chapter 1. We added an expanded treatment of operating and financial leverage to demonstrate the important impact of fixed cost elements on changing operating conditions, and the risk/reward trade-off implicit in using debt financing. Through the use of a simplified financial growth model, we illustrated the need for consistency in setting operating and financial objectives and policies. We highlighted the various implications of growth, and developed the policy rationale for sustainable growth over time, given a stable set of conditions and choices. Finally, we applied the modeling approach to the needs and policies of a sample company and developed an integrated financial plan with which we tested the impact of planned changes in various key policies on the company's growth and performance.

In the end, the key test of financial analysis is the viability of the methods and results as predictors of future activity, which was a major point made in the earlier chapters. Often the optimal approach requires use of quite detailed and sensitive financial models of the business. Yet the outside analyst, and even insiders, often will be well served with simplified yardsticks and models which can sufficiently approximate solutions to planning alternatives. In this sense, the chapter draws together many of the points of earlier materials to give the reader an overall, albeit simplified, framework for analysis.

Analytical Support

A set of Excel-based templates (*Interactive Templates*) is downloadable at no charge from the Web at www.mhhe.com/helfert11e. The fourth of these, "Break-Even Model: Key Variables" activates Figures 5–1 through 5–4 in this chapter. The fifth template, "Sustainable Growth Model and Supporting Statements" activates the sustainable growth formula on page 234, integrating it with a linked representation of the business systems model of Chapter 1 and its related financial statements. The sixth template, "Policies Impacting Growth: Comparative Cases," activates Figure 5–8 on page 229. The seventh template, "Integrated Growth Model: Projecting Financial Results" activates Figures 5–9 and 5–10 on pages 231 and 236. In each case, the template allows you to vary a set of key assumptions and policies and to observe the numerical changes resulting from these modifications on graphic representations or abbreviated financial statements. You may also find it useful to revisit the first template, "The Business System—An Overview," which was described at the end of Chapter 1 and provides the perspective of an overall financial model.

Financial Genome, the advanced financial analysis software application described in Appendix I, is a fully integrated analytical and planning model for both the professional user and the business student. It is designed to create fully integrated financial projections as extensions of historical data or from direct forecast assumptions, as well as all related ratios and relationships. It also generates the key ratios important to the implications of growth. The software contains a five-year database (1996 to 2000) for 3M Corporation, matching the company's financial statements reproduced in Chapters 1, 2, and 3, which can be used for projection purposes. It also contains databases and project files which can be used for financial planning practice.

Financial Genome is downloadable from the Web, using the unique code provided with this book. See "Downloads Available" at the end of Appendix I, p. 479.

Selected References

Brealey, Richard, and Stewart Myers. *Principles of Corporate Finance*. 5th ed. Burr Ridge, IL: Irwin/McGraw-Hill, 1996.

Donaldson, Gordon. *Corporate Restructuring: Managing the Change Process from Within*. Boston: Harvard Business School Press, 1994.

Donaldson, Gordon. *Managing Corporate Wealth: The Operation of a Comprehensive Financial Goals System*. New York: Praeger, 1984. (A classic)

Donaldson, Gordon. *Strategy of Financial Mobility*. Boston: Division of Research, Graduate School of Business Administration, Harvard University, 1969. (A classic.)

Drucker, Peter F. "The Information Executives Truly Need." *Harvard Business Review*, January/February 1995.

Ross, Stephen; Randolph Westerfield; and Jeffrey Jaffe. *Corporate Finance*. 5th ed. Burr Ridge, IL: Irwin/McGraw-Hill, 1999.

Self-Study Exercises, Problems, and Discussion Questions

Exercises and Problems (*Selected Solutions Provided in Appendix VI*)

1. The ABC Corporation, a manufacturing company, sells a product at a price of $5.50 per unit. The variable costs involved in producing and selling the product are $3.25 per unit. Total fixed costs are $360,000. Calculate the break-even point and draw an appropriate chart.

   a. Calculate and demonstrate the effect of operating leverage by noting the profit impact of moving from the break-even point in 20 percent volume increments and decrements.

   b. Calculate and graph separately the impact of a 50 cent drop in price, a 25 cent increase in variable cost, and an increase of $40,000 in fixed cost.

   c. Draw a graph and discuss the implications if fixed costs increase $30,000 after 175,000 units of production, the average price drops to $5.25 per unit after 190,000 units are produced, and variable costs drop to an average of $3 after 150,000 units. How are the calculations for breakeven affected?

2. Using the template "Break-Even Model" Key Variables" in the Interactive Templates, observe the changes in the numerical and graphic results obtained from varying the key assumptions. Input the data from problem 1 (*a*) and (*b*) and check your results. Note the general purpose use of this template for any combination of assumptions under unchanging conditions.

3. Calculate the effect of financial leverage under the following two conditions:

   a. Interest rate is 5 percent after taxes; return on net assets is 8 percent after taxes.

   b. Interest rate is 6 percent after taxes; return on net assets is 5 percent after taxes.

   Develop the effect on return on equity in each case for debt as a percentage of capitalization at 0 percent, 25 percent, 50 percent, and 75 percent. Discuss.

4. From the following data provided on XYZ Company, develop the sustainable growth rate implied in every year's results, using the formula on page 234. Compare the sustainable growth rate to the actual growth achieved in sales and in shareholders' equity. (Sales in 1997 were $45,200, and shareholders' equity was $26,650.) Interest on debt is not shown separately and can be ignored for this purpose.

	1998	1999	2000	2001	2002	2003
Sales	$49,850	$58,120	$71,280	$75,690	$79,910	$83,170
Net assets	44,630	47,240	55,930	60,230	61,110	64,430
Shareholders' equity	29,730	33,500	41,300	49,360	55,510	62,090
Net profit after taxes	8,120	9,230	11,450	11,600	10,250	11,280
Dividends paid	3,000	3,600	3,960	3,960	4,150	4,650

   a. Observe the differences between calculated and actual growth rates, and explain how much the lower actual growth in the last three years affected the capital structure.

   b. What are the implications of the slowdown for future growth strategies? What specific ratios and relationships are important here?

   c. Would a higher dividend payout be desirable?

   d. How would a higher future growth be financed?

5. Using the template "Sustainable Growth Model and Supporting Statements" in the Interactive Templates, examine the red explanation symbols in the various boxes and statements to understand the structure of the template. Input the data for each year of problem 4 and observe the results on the formula as well as on the business system diagram and statements. Vary the assumptions to observe the impact of each and in combination. Comment on your findings.

6. Using the template "Policies Impacting Growth: Comparative Cases" in the Interactive Templates, examine the red explanation symbols to

understand the structure of the template. Vary the assumptions to observe the impact on the results and relationships in separate cases side by side. Develop extreme conditions to visualize the possibilities and implications of policy changes. Note the general purpose use of this template. Comment on your findings.

7. Using a spreadsheet, develop a five-year financial growth plan as presented in Figure 5–10 on page 236 for DEF Company, based on the following assumptions:

	Year 1	Year 2	Year 3	Year 4	Year 5
Net assets (000)	$1,500	—	—	—	—
Debt–equity	0.25:1	0.25:1	0.50:1	0.50:1	0.50:1
Depreciation effect (000)	$75	$78	$80	$90	$92
Return on net assets (after taxes)	8%	9%	10%	10%	10%
Interest rate (after taxes)	4.5	4.5	5.0	5.0	5.0
Dividend payout	⅔	⅔	⅔	½	½
Number of shares	200,000	—	—	—	—

a. Calculate all relevant financial results, such as earnings per share, return on equity, growth in equity, and growth in earnings. Discuss your assumptions and findings.

b. Demonstrate the sensitivity of earnings per share, return on equity, and growth in equity by varying the conditions in Year 5 as follows: debt/equity, 0.75:1, return on net assets, 11 percent; interest rate, 4.5 percent; and dividend payout, two-thirds. Discuss your findings.

8. Using the template "Integrated Growth Model: Projecting Financial Results" in the Interactive Templates, examine the red explanation symbols to understand the structure of the template. Vary the key inputs at will and observe the consequences of your changes throughout the diagram. What are the key implications and major policy changes? How free would a management team be to make such changes? Note the general purpose use of this template.

Discussion Questions

1. Derive a simple formula to express the break-even point in relation to volume and cost

2. What influence does depreciation, as a fixed cost, have on a company's break-even characteristics?

3. Draw parallels and distinctions between operating and financial leverage, and cite examples from your own experience.

4. Why isn't it likely, at the same time, to have high growth in equity and a high dividend payout? What other elements enter the picture?

5. What are the key levers management can apply to bring about high growth in equity?
6. What important growth areas can you name as modeling targets, and why are they relevant?
7. What are the cash flow implications of growing above or below sustainable growth?
8. Is it realistic to assume a continuous rollover of debt in the growth model? Are there any likely limitations?
9. What are the potential lags involved in attaining sustainable growth targets, such as were discussed in Chapter 2?
10. How does the growth model analysis relate to the business systems diagram in Chapter 1?
11. Which are the most important assumptions in a growth model?

CHAPTER 6

CASH FLOWS AND THE TIME VALUE OF MONEY

$\mathbf{T}$ hroughout this book we've referred to the primary business objective of creating shareholder value through successful economic decisions made by the company's managers. We've defined value creation in terms of a positive trade-off of cash generated versus cash given up when making investment, operating, and financing decisions. We've also made the point that the cash flows involved in most decisions have a future dimension. To properly analyze the implications of a decision, therefore, we need to understand how to measure, at a given point in time, future cash flows and their value to the decision maker. The techniques and indicators required for this purpose are relatively straightforward because of their basic mathematical nature—involving discounting and compounding methodologies—although their application and especially the interpretation of results require a deeper understanding of the context of the decision and the many judgments involved in developing the estimates and implications of the underlying data and the cash flows expected. The various techniques we'll discuss are fundamental to financial/economic decisions, whether these are made in a corporate context, in the financial markets, or by individuals dealing with investments or financial instruments of various kinds.

In this chapter we'll concentrate first on defining the basic concepts underlying the time value of money. Then we'll provide a review of the common components involved in structuring the pattern of investment analyses in the business setting, followed by a discussion of the major techniques and indicators employed in the economic analysis of cash flows. We'll illustrate the techniques by using simple examples. In Chapter 7 we'll focus on the broader context of business investment decisions, identify the issues and complexities encountered, and provide numerous illustrations of more complex cases. We'll discuss in some detail the derivation of the underlying data, and the interpretation of the results of the analysis. Finally, we'll take up the issue of risk and how to factor uncertainty into the analytical process.

The Time Value of Money

Given the future orientation of most decisions, the proper application of economic reasoning requires us to recognize the intimate connection between two elements:

- The specific timing of every cash inflow and outflow relevant to the decision.
- The combined value of all relevant cash flows at the point of decision.

It's a simple axiom that a dollar received today is worth more than a dollar received one year hence, because we forgo the opportunity of profitably investing today the future dollar for which we must wait. Similarly, spending a dollar a year later is preferable to spending it now, because it can earn a return in the meantime. Thus, in principle the time value of money is related both to the timing of any receipt or expenditure and to the individual's or company's opportunity to earn a return on funds invested.

Discounting, Compounding, and Equivalence

Common sense tells us that we won't be indifferent to two investment propositions that are exactly alike in all aspects except for a difference in timing of the future benefits. An investor will obviously prefer the one providing more immediate benefits. The reason, of course, is that funds available earlier give an individual or a company the opportunity to invest these funds and earn a return, be it in a savings account, a government bond, a loan, a new piece of equipment, a promotional campaign, or any one of a great variety of other economic possibilities. Having to wait for a period of time until funds become available entails an opportunity cost in the form of lost earnings potential, as well as uncertainty about the future.

Conversely, common sense also dictates that given the choice between making an expenditure now versus making the same expenditure some time in the future, it's advantageous to defer the outlay. Again, the reason is the opportunity to earn a return on the funds in the meantime. As we stated earlier, the time value of an amount of money, or a series of cash flows, is affected directly by the specific timing of the receipt or disbursement, and the level of return the investor or the business can normally achieve on invested funds.

A simple example will help illustrate this point. If a person normally uses a savings account to earn interest of 5 percent per year on invested funds, a deposit of $1,000 made today will grow to $1,050 in one year. (For simplicity, we ignore the practice of daily or monthly compounding commonly used by banks and savings institutions.) If for some reason the person had to wait one year to deposit the $1,000, the opportunity to earn $50 in interest would be lost. Without question, a sum of $1,000 offered to the person one year hence must be worth less today than the same amount offered immediately. Specifically, today's value of the delayed

$1,000 must be related to the person's normally chosen opportunity to earn a 5 percent return. Given this earnings goal, we can calculate the *present value* of the $1,000 to be received in one year's time as follows:

$$\text{Present value} = \frac{\$1,000}{1 + 0.05} = \$952.38$$

The equation shows that with an assumed rate of return of 5 percent, $1,000 received one year from now is the *equivalent* of having $952.38 today. This is so because $952.38 invested at 5 percent today will grow into $1,000 by the end of one year. The calculation clearly reflects the economic trade-off between dollars received today versus a future date, based on the length of time involved and the available opportunity to earn a return. If we ignore the issue of risk for the moment, it also follows that our investor should be willing to pay $952.38 today for a financial contract that will pay $1,000 one year hence. Under these assumed conditions, our investor should in fact find no difference between $952.38 today and $1,000 one year from now.

The longer the waiting period, the lower becomes the present value of a sum of money to be received, because for each additional period of delay, the opportunity to earn a return during the interval is forgone. Principal and interest left in place would have compounded by earning an annual return on the growing balance. As we already pointed out, the concept applies to outlays as well. It'll be advantageous to defer an expenditure as long as possible, because this allows the individual to earn a return during every period on the amount not spent plus any earnings left in place.

Calculating this change in the value of receipts or expenditures is quite simple when we know the time period and the opportunity rate of return. For example, a sum of $1,000 to be received at the end of five years will be worth only $783.53 today to someone normally earning a rate of return of 5 percent, because that amount invested today at 5 percent compounded annually would grow to $1,000 five years hence, if the earnings are left to accumulate and interest is earned on the growing balance each year.

The formula for this calculation appears as follows:

$$\text{Present value} = \frac{\$1,000}{(1 + 0.05)^5} = \frac{\$1,000}{1.27628} = \$783.53$$

The result of $783.53 was obtained by relating the *future value* of $1,000 to the *compound earnings factor* at 5 percent over five years, shown in the denominator as 1.27628—which is simply 1.05 raised to the fifth power. When we divide the future value by the compound factor, we have in effect *discounted* the future value into a lower *equivalent* present value.

Note that the mathematics are straightforward in achieving what we described in concept earlier: The value of a future sum is lowered in precise relationship to both the opportunity rate of return and the timing incidence. The opportunity rate of return in this example is our assumed 5 percent compound interest, while the timing incidence of five years is reflected in the number of times the interest is compounded to express the number of years during which earnings were forgone.

Naturally it's possible to calculate *future* values for today's values by multiplying the present value by the compound interest factor. If we take the conditions of the example just cited, we can derive the future value of $1,000 to be received in Year 5 from the present value of $783.53 as follows:

Future value = $783.53 \times (1 + 0.05)^5 = $783.53 \times 1.27628 = $1,000$

We refer to the calculation of present values as discounting, whereas the reverse process, the calculation of future values, is called compounding. These basic mathematical relationships allow us to derive the equivalent value of any sum to be received or paid at any point in time, either at the present moment, or at any specified future date.

The process of discounting and compounding is as old as money lending and has been used by financial institutions from time immemorial. Even though the application of this methodology to business investments is of relatively more recent vintage, techniques employing discounting and compounding have now become commonplace. Electronic calculators and ubiquitous computer spreadsheets with built-in discounting and compounding capability have made deriving time values and time-based investment measures a matter of routine.

Even though we recommend the use of calculator and spreadsheet programs to quickly arrive at time-adjusted cash flow results, we'll display in our examples the actual discount factors that are embedded in those routines in order to highlight their impact. These factors are taken from present value tables, which all analysts used before electronic means were available. Although these tables are no longer needed for making the actual calculations, they do provide a visual demonstration of the effect of discounting, which becomes ever more powerful the higher the rate and the longer the time period. Two of the tables are provided at the end of this chapter as a reference.

We can clarify a few points with the help of these tables. Table 6–I (p. 276) contains the factors that translate into equivalent present values a single sum of money received or disbursed at the end of any period, under different assumptions about the rate of earnings. They are based on this general formula:

$$\text{Present value of sum} = \frac{1}{(1 + i)^n}$$

where i is the applicable opportunity rate of return (also referred to as discount rate) and n is the number of periods over which discounting takes place. In effect, the table factors are compound interest factors divided into 1. The table covers a range from 1 to 60 *periods,* and discount rates from 1 to 50 percent. The rates are related to these periods, however defined. For example, if the periods represent years, the rates are annual, whereas if months are used, the rates are monthly. The present value of a sum of money therefore can be found by simply multiplying the amount involved by the appropriate factor:

$$\text{Present value} = \text{Factor} \times \text{Sum}$$

while the future value of any sum can be found by dividing the present value by the appropriate factor from the table:

$$\text{Future value} = \frac{\text{Present value}}{\text{Factor}}$$

Note that the present value results from our savings account example on pages 246–248 can be found in Table 6–II (p. 277) in the 5 percent column, lines 1 and 5, for the 1-year and 5-year illustrations, respectively. The same result for the first case can be obtained from a spreadsheet, by using the *npv* (net present value) function, entering 5 percent, and placing $1,000 in the first time period. The second result can be obtained again by using the *npv* function, entering 5 percent, zero values in periods 1 through 4, and $1,000 in period 5. Similarly, future values can be derived from a spreadsheet, by using the *fv* (future value) function, and entering the percentage rate, the number of time periods, and the present value into the appropriate openings.

The factors in Table 6–II, (p. 277), a variation of Table 6–I, allow the direct calculation of the present value of a *series* of equal receipts or payments occurring over a number of periods. Such even series of cash flows are called *annuities,* and occur mostly in connection with financial instruments, such as mortgages. The same result could, of course, be obtained by using Table 6–I and repeatedly multiplying the periodic amount with the appropriate series of successive factors and adding all of the results. Table 6–II directly provides a set of such additive factors, which allow obtaining the present value of an annuity in a single step, that is, multiplying the period receipt or payment by the appropriate factor:

$$\text{Present value} = \text{Factor} \times \text{Annuity}$$

For example, the present value of an annuity of $100 per year for seven years is $5.206 \times \$100$, or $520.60. Using a spreadsheet, we can obtain this result by selecting the *pv* (present value) function, entering 8 percent, and seven periods @ $100 per period, taking care to properly interpret the sign of the value displayed. The mathematical relationships embedded in the table and in the spreadsheet routine are represented by the annuity formula:

$$\text{Present value of annuity} = \frac{1}{i} - \frac{1}{i(1 + i)^n}$$

In practice one can choose many possible variations and refinements in timing, such as more frequent discounting (monthly or weekly), or assuming that the annuity is received or disbursed in weekly or monthly increments rather than at the end of the period, a distinction which is important for financial institutions. The use of the continuous flow option introduces a forward shift in timing that leads to slightly higher present values, both for single sums and annuities. Refinements such as daily discounting or compounding are commonly applied to financial instruments, such as mortgages, bonds, charge accounts, and so on, all of which involve specific contractual arrangements.

For the practical purpose of analyzing business investments, such refinements are not critical, because as we'll see, the inherent imprecision of many of
the estimates involved easily outweighs any incremental numerical refinement
that might be obtained. The normal settings of calculators and spreadsheet programs use the periodic discounting embodied in the formulas of the two tables at
the end of the chapter. This is quite adequate for most analytical needs in a business environment, but if more precision is sought, the optional settings in calculators and spreadsheets easily accommodate such refinements.

We'll now turn to the discussion of the basic analytical framework for business investments, and identify the critical components involved. Then we'll take up
one by one the commonly used measures for investment analysis, most of which
employ these discounting principles. We'll cover the basic rationale on which the
measures are based, and their applicability to business investment analysis, as well
as their shortcomings. Our illustrations and discussion will be built around simple
business investment projects, but their applicability to the broader variety of cash
flow–based investments and instruments will become obvious.

Because the economic analysis of business investments involves projecting
a whole series and pattern of incremental cash flows, both positive and negative,
and usually uneven, we need to apply time value adjustments to develop a consistent translation of these future flows into equivalent values at the point of decision. Figure 6–1 shows the pattern of cash flows connected with a typical
investment, consisting of an initial outlay, a series of positive benefits, an intermediate additional outlay, and ultimate recovery of part of the resources committed in the form of a terminal value.

All of these future cash flows have to be brought back in time to the present
point of decision by an appropriate methodology, in order to determine whether the
trade-off between the expected positive and negative cash flows is favorable. As
we've discussed, expressing future dollars in the form of *equivalent* present dollars
requires discounting. It's the basis for all the modern techniques of investment

---

F I G U R E   6–1 ──

Typical Cash Flow Pattern for a Business Investment

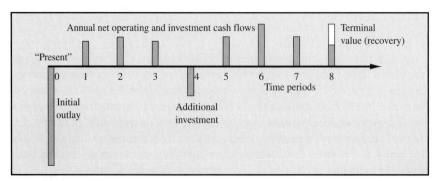

analysis and valuation discussed in this book. We'll return to describing the key tools employing the time value of money after we've discussed the basic layout and elements of the cash flow analysis.

Components of Investment Analysis

In essence, financial resources are invested for one basic reason: to obtain sufficient future economic returns to warrant the original outlay and any related future outlays, that is, sufficient cash receipts over the life of the project to justify the cash spent. This basic trade-off of current cash outflow against expected future cash inflow must be recognized by any of the analytical methods used in one way or another.

To judge the attractiveness of any investment, we must consider the following four elements involved in the decision:

- The amount expended—the *net investment.*
- The potential benefits—the *net operating cash inflows.*
- The time span of benefits—the *economic life.*
- Any final recovery of residual value—the *terminal value.*

A proper economic analysis must take these four elements into account to be able to determine whether or not the investment is worthwhile.

For Example

An outlay of $100,000 for equipment needed to manufacture a new product is expected to provide an after-tax cash flow of $25,000 over a period of six years, without significant annual fluctuations. Although the equipment will not be fully worn out after six years, it's unlikely that more than scrap value will be realized at that time because of technical obsolescence. The cost of removal is expected to offset this scrap value. The effect of straight-line depreciation over the six years ($16,667 per year) was correctly adjusted for in the annual cash flow figure of $25,000, having been added back to the expected net after-tax improvement in profits of $8,333.

Net Investment

The first element in the analysis, the net investment, normally consists of the gross capital requirements for new assets, reduced by any funds recovered from the trade or sale of any existing assets caused by the decision. Such recoveries must be adjusted for any change in income taxes arising from a recognized gain or loss on the disposal of existing assets.

The basic rule for finding the investment amount committed to the decision is to calculate the net amount of initial outlays and recoveries actually caused by the decision to invest. In our simple example, no funds are recovered at the decision point and therefore the net investment is the full outlay of $100,000.

When an investment is made to support a new product or service, or to provide an increased volume of existing products or services, any additions to working capital required by the increased level of sales also must be included in the analysis. Normally, any initial incremental working capital is added to the net investment, and future requirements or releases are shown as cash flows in the respective time periods. For our simple example this refinement is ignored, but in Chapter 7 we'll demonstrate how working capital increments are handled.

Further investment outlays might also become necessary during the life of the project, and might be foreseeable enough to be estimated at the time of analysis. If such future outlays are a potential consequence of the initial decision, they must be considered part of the current decision process, and reflected as cash outflows in the time periods when they are expected to occur. We'll also demonstrate examples which involve sequential investments in Chapter 7.

Net Operating Cash Inflows

The operational basis for defining the economic benefits over the life of the investment is the expected period-by-period *net change* in revenues and expenses caused by the investment, after adjusting for applicable income taxes and the effect of accounting elements such as depreciation to arrive at a cash flow basis. These incremental changes include such elements as operating savings from a machine replacement, additional profits from a new product line or a new service, increased profits from a plant expansion, or profits created by developing land or other natural resources. Generally, these changes will be reflected in the form of increased profit as reported in periodic operating statements, once the investment is in place and functioning. Our main focus, however, has to be on finding the estimated net impact on periodic cash flow, adjusted for all applicable taxes and for accounting elements like depreciation. They must be carefully defined as only the changes actually caused by the decision to invest, that is, only those cash inflows and outflows that are relevant to the situation. Later, we'll give examples of how such project cash flows are derived.

For our simplified illustration, we'll assume that the net annual operating after-tax cash inflow will be a level amount of $25,000 over the project's life. This figure represents the sum of estimated net after-tax profits of $8,333 to which is added the depreciation effect of $16,667. As we'll see later, introducing a variable pattern of periodic cash flows can significantly influence the analytical results. Level periodic flows are easiest to deal with, and are generally found in financial contracts of various kinds, but they are quite rare in the business setting. Uneven cash flows are more common and they make the analysis a little more complex—but such patterns can be handled readily for calculation purposes, as we'll demonstrate.

Economic Life

The third element, the time period selected for the analysis, is commonly referred to as the *economic life* of the investment project. For purposes of investment analysis, the only time period relevant to the decision is the economic life, as distinguished from the *physical* life of equipment, or the *technological* life of a particular process or service.

Even though a building or a piece of equipment might be perfectly usable from a physical standpoint, the economic life of the investment is finished if the market for the product or service has disappeared. Similarly, the economic life of any given technology or service is bound up with the economics of the marketplace—the best process is useless if the resulting product or service can no longer be sold. At that point, any resources still usable will have to be repositioned, which requires another investment decision, or they might be disposed of for their recovery value. When redeploying such resources into another project, the net investment for that decision would, of course, be the estimated recovery value after taxes.

In our simple example, we have assumed a six-year economic life, the period over which the product manufactured with the equipment will be sold. The *depreciation life* used for accounting or tax purposes doesn't normally reflect an investment's true life span, and in this case we've only made it equal to the economic life for simplicity. As we discussed earlier, such write-offs are based on standard accounting and tax guidelines, and don't necessarily represent the investment's expected economic usefulness.

Terminal (Residual) Value

At the end of the economic life an assessment has to be made whether any residual values remain to be recognized. Normally, if one expects a substantial recovery of capital from eventual disposal of assets at the end of the economic life, these estimated amounts have to be made part of the analysis. Such recoveries can be proceeds from the sale of facilities and equipment (beyond the minor scrap value assumed in our example), as well as the release of any working capital associated with the investment. Also, there are situations in which an ongoing value of a business, a facility, or a process is expected beyond this specific analysis period chosen. This condition is especially important in valuation analyses, which we'll discuss in Chapters 10 and 11. For our simple illustration no terminal value is assumed, but later we'll demonstrate the handling of this concept.

Methods of Analysis

We've now laid the groundwork for analyzing any normal business investment by describing the four essential *components* of the analysis. Our purpose was to focus on *what* must be analyzed. We'll now turn to the question of *how* this is done—the methods and criteria of analysis that will help us judge the economics of the decision.

How do we relate the four basic components—

- Net investment
- Operating cash inflow
- Economic life
- Terminal value

to determine the project's attractiveness? First we'll dispose quickly of some simplistic methods of analysis, which are merely rules of thumb that intuitively (but incorrectly) grapple with the trade-off between investment and operating cash flows. They are the *payback* and the *simple rate of return,* both of which are still used in practice occasionally despite their demonstrable shortcomings.

Our major emphasis will be on the measures employing the time value of money as discussed earlier, which enable the analyst to assess the trade-offs between relevant cash flows in equivalent terms, that is, regardless of the timing of their incidence. Those key measures are *net present value,* the *present value payback,* the *profitability index (benefit/cost ratio),* and the *internal rate of return (yield),* and in addition, the *annualized net present value.* We'll focus on the meaning of these measures, the relationships between them, and illustrate their use on the basis of simple examples. In Chapter 7, we'll discuss the broader context of business investment analysis, within which these measures play a role as indicators of value creation, and discuss more complex analytical problems. As part of this broader context, we'll also deal with risk analysis, ranges of estimates, simulation, probabilistic reasoning, and risk-adjusted return standards.

Simple Measures

Payback

This crude rule of thumb directly relates assumed level annual cash inflows from a project to the net investment required. Using the data from our simplified example, the calculation is straightforward:

$$\text{Payback} = \frac{\text{Net investment}}{\text{Average annual operating cash flow}} = \frac{\$100,000}{\$25,000} = 4 \text{ years}$$

The result is the number of years required for the original outlay to be repaid, answering the question, How long will it be until I get my money back? It's a rough test of whether the amount of the investment will be recovered within its economic life span. Here, payback is achieved in only four years versus the estimated economic life of six years. Recovering the capital is not enough, of course, because from an economic standpoint, one would hope to earn a return on the funds while they are invested.

Visualize a savings account in which $100 is deposited, and from which $25 is withdrawn at the end of each year. After four years, the principal will have been repaid. If the bank statement showed that the account was now depleted, the saver would properly demand to be paid the 4 or 5 percent interest that should have been earned every year on the declining balance in the account.

We can illustrate these basics of investment economics in Figure 6–2, where we've shown how both principal repayment and earnings on the outstanding balance have to be achieved by the cash flow stream over the economic life. We're again using the simple $100,000 investment, with a level annual after-tax operating cash flow. If the company typically earned 10 percent after taxes on its investments, part of every year's cash flow would be considered as normal earnings return, with the remainder used to reduce the outstanding balance.

The first row shows the beginning balance of the investment in every year. In the second row, normal earnings of 10 percent are calculated on these balances. In the third row are operating cash flows which, when reduced by the normal earnings, are applied against the beginning balances of the investment to calculate every year's ending balance.

The result is an amortization schedule for our simple investment that extends into the sixth year—requiring about two more years of annual benefits than the simple payback measure would suggest. If the project ended in Year 4, an opportunity loss of about $30,400 would be incurred, and in Year 5, the loss would be about $8,400. Only in Year 6 will the remaining principal balance have been recovered and an economic gain of about $15,700 achieved. As we'll see shortly, all modern investment criteria are based on the basic rationale underlying this example, with some refinements in the precise calculations used.

We can now quickly dispose of the payback measure as an indicator of investment desirability: It's insensitive to the economic life span and thus not a meaningful criterion of earnings power. It'll give the same "four years plus something extra" reading on other projects that have similar cash flows but 8- or

---

F I G U R E   6–2

Amortization of $100,000 Investment at 10 Percent

	Year 1	Year 2	Year 3	Year 4	Year 5	Year 6
Beginning balance	$100,000	$85,000	$68,500	$50,350	$30,385	$ 8,424
Normal company earnings @ 10%	10,000	8,500	6,850	5,035	3,039	842
Operating cash inflows of project	25,000	25,000	25,000	25,000	25,000	25,000
Ending balance to be recovered	85,000	68,500	50,350	30,385	8,424	−15,734
Simple payback (4 × $25,000)				Year 4		

10-year economic lives, even though those projects would be clearly superior to our example. The payback implicitly assumes level annual operating cash flows, and cannot properly evaluate projects with rising or declining cash flow patterns—although these are very common. It cannot accommodate any additional investments made during the period, or recognize capital recoveries at the end of the economic life.

The only situation where the measure has some applicability is in comparing a series of simple projects with quite similar cash flow patterns, but even then it's more appropriate to apply the economic techniques that are readily available on calculators and spreadsheets.

However, it's possible to make use of a refined concept of payback that is expressed in economic terms, but this measure requires the discounting process to arrive at the so-called *present value payback*. It's one of the indicators of investment desirability that build a return requirement into the analysis, and we'll discuss it in detail later.

Simple Rate of Return

Again, only passing comments are warranted about this simplistic rule of thumb, which in fact is the inverse of the basic payback formula. It states the desirability of an investment in terms of a percentage return on the original outlay. The method shares all of the shortcomings of the payback, because it again relates only two of the four critical aspects of any project, net investment and operating cash flows, and ignores the economic life and any terminal value:

$$\text{Return on investment} = \frac{\text{Average annual operating cash flow}}{\text{Net investment}} = \frac{\$25,000}{\$100,000}$$

$$= 25\%$$

What this result simply indicates is that $25,000 happens to be 25 percent of $100,000, because there's no reference to economic life and no recognition of the need to amortize the investment. The measure will give the *same* answer whether the economic life is 1 year, 10 years, or 100 years. The 25 percent return indicated here would be economically valid only if the investment provided $25,000 per year *in perpetuity*—not a very realistic condition!

Economic Investment Measures

Earlier, we described business investment analysis as the process of weighing the economic trade-off between current dollar outlays and future net cash flow benefits that are expected to be obtained over a relevant period of time. This economic valuation concept applies to all types of investments, whether made by individuals or businesses. The time value of money is employed as the underlying methodology in every case. We'll use the basic principles of discounting and compounding discussed earlier to explain and demonstrate the major measures of investment analysis. These measures utilize such principles to calculate the quantitative basis for making economic choices among investment propositions.

Net Present Value

The net present value (NPV) measure has become the most commonly used indicator in corporate economic and valuation analysis, and is accepted as the preferred measure in the widest range of analytical processes. It weighs the cash flow trade-off among investment outlays, future benefits, and terminal values in *equivalent* present value terms, and allows the analyst to determine whether the net balance of these values is favorable or unfavorable—in other words, the size of the economic trade-off involved relative to an economic return standard. From the standpoint of creating shareholder value, a positive net present value implies that the proposal, if implemented and performing as expected, will add value because of the favorable trade-off of time-adjusted cash inflows over outflows. In contrast, a negative net present value will destroy value because of an excess of time-adjusted cash outflows over inflows. As a basic rule one can say the higher the positive NPV, the better the value creation potential.

To use the tool, a rate of discount representing a normal expected rate of return first must be specified as the standard to be met. As we'll see, this rate is commonly based on a company's weighted average cost of capital, which embodies the return expectations of both equity and debt providers of the company's capital structure, as described in Chapter 8. Next, the inflows and outflows over the economic life of the investment proposal are specified and discounted at this return standard. Finally, the present values of all inflows (positive amounts) and outflows (negative amounts) are summed. The difference between these sums represents the net present value. NPV can be positive, zero, or negative, depending on whether there is a net inflow, a matching of cash flows, or a net outflow over the economic life of the project.

Used as a standard of comparison, the measure indicates whether an investment, over its economic life, will achieve the expected level of return applied in the calculation, given that the underlying estimates are in fact realized. Inasmuch as present value results depend on both timing of the cash flows and the level of the required rate of return, a positive net present value indicates that the cash flows expected to be generated by the investment over its economic life will:

- Recover the original outlay (as well as any future capital outlays or recoveries considered in the analysis).
- Earn the specified rate of return standard on the outstanding balance.
- Provide a "cushion" of economic value over and above meeting the minimum standard.

Conversely, a negative net present value indicates that the project is not achieving the return standard and thus will cause an economic loss if implemented. A zero NPV is value neutral. Obviously, the result will be affected by the level of benefits assumed, the specific timing pattern of the various cash flows, and the relative magnitudes of the amounts involved.

Another word should be said at this point about the discount rate applied as a rate of return standard. From an economic standpoint, it should be the rate of return an investor normally enjoys from investments of similar nature and risk, as we explained in our discussion of the time value of money. In effect, this standard represents an opportunity rate of return. In a corporate setting, the choice of a discount rate is complicated both by the variety of investment possibilities and by the types of financing provided by both owners and lenders. The corporate return standard normally used to discount business investment cash flows should reflect the minimum return requirement that will provide the normally expected level of return on the company's investments, under normal risk conditions.

The most commonly employed standard is based on the overall corporate *cost of capital,* which takes into account shareholder expectations, business risk, and leverage. As we've mentioned before, shareholder value can be created only by making investments whose returns exceed the cost of capital. Therefore, the actual standard established by a company will often be set above the cost of capital, reflecting a specific management objective to achieve returns higher than the cost of capital. Sometimes a corporate return standard is separated into a set of multiple discount rates for different lines of business within a company, in order to recognize specific risk differentials. We'll deal with these concepts in greater depth in Chapters 7 and 8. For purposes of this discussion, we'll assume that management has chosen an appropriate return standard with which to discount investment cash flows, and we'll focus on how present value measures are used to assess potential investments on an economic basis.

As a first step, it's generally helpful to lay out the pertinent information period by period to give us a proper time perspective. A horizontal time scale matching spreadsheet patterns should be used, on which the periods are marked off, as Figure 6–3 shows. Positive and negative cash flows are then inserted as arrows at the appropriate positions in time, scaled to the size of the dollar amounts. Note that the time scale begins at point 0, the present decision point, and extends out as far as the project's economic life requires. Any events that occurred prior to the decision point (shown as negative periods) are not relevant to the analysis, unless the decision specifically causes a recovery of past expenditures, such as the sale of old assets.

To illustrate the process, let's return to the simple investment example used earlier in the chapter. We'll show the numerical information as a table in Figure 6–4. Note the similarity in approach to the simple amortization process we used in Figure 6–2 (p. 255). Figure 6–4 demonstrates that the pattern in our sample net investment of $100,000, with six annual benefit inflows of $25,000 from Year 1 through Year 6, results in a net present value of almost $16,000. This assumes that our company considers the relatively low rate of 8 percent after taxes a normal earnings standard. The total initial outflow will have been recovered over the six-year period, while 8 percent after taxes will have been earned all along on the declining investment balance outstanding during the project life. The positive net

F I G U R E 6–3

Generalized Time Scale for Investment Analysis

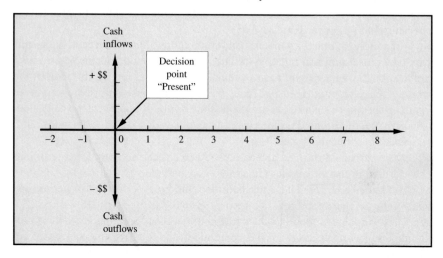

F I G U R E 6–4

Net Present Value Analysis at 8 Percent*

	Totals	Year 0	Year 1	Year 2	Year 3	Year 4	Year 5	Year 6
Investment outlay								
(outflow)	$−100,000	$−100,000	0	0	0	0	0	0
Benefits (inflows)	150,000	0	$25,000	$25,000	$25,000	$25,000	$25,000	$25,000
Present value								
factors @ 8%†		1.000	0.926	0.857	0.794	0.735	0.681	0.630
Present values of								
cash flows	15,575	−100,000	23,150	21,425	19,850	18,375	17,025	15,750
Cumulative present								
values		−100,000	−76,850	−55,425	−35,575	−17,200	−175	15,575
Net present value								
@ 8%	$ 15,575							

*This model is available for download in an interactive format; see "Analytical Support", p. 272

†From Table 6–I (p. 276), which assumes benefits occur at year-end. Because the inflows are level, we could instead use an annuity factor of 4.623 from Table 6–11 (p. 277) for an identical result.

present value shows that a value creation of about $15,600 in equivalent present value dollars can be expected if the cash flow estimates are correct and if the project does live out its full economic life.

In the simple payback concept we discussed earlier, we referred to the recovery of the original investment plus "something extra." The critical difference between simple payback and net present value, however, is the fact that net present value has a built-in return requirement in addition to full recovery of the investment. Thus, the value "cushion" implicit in a positive net present value is truly a calculated economic value gain that goes beyond satisfying the required return standard. In fact, we can see from the cumulative present value line that if the project performs as expected, the cash flows are sufficient to recover the principal and earn 8 percent by the end of period 5, where the cumulative present value is very close to zero.

If a higher earnings standard had been required, say 12 percent, the results would be those shown in Figure 6–5. The net present value remains positive, but the size of the value creation has dramatically decreased to only $2,800. We would expect such a decrease, because at the higher discount rate, the present value of the future cash inflows must decline, with all other circumstances unchanged. Note that this time the present value payback requires almost the full six years.

At an assumed earnings standard of 14 percent, the net present value shrinks even further. In fact, it is transformed into a negative result ($25,000 $\times$ 3.889 $-$ $100,000 = -$ $2,775). These results reflect the great sensitivity of net present value to the choice of earnings standards, especially at higher rates.

The cumulative present values row in the two sets of calculations illustrates the importance of the length of the economic life of the investment. We can observe that the time required for the cumulative present value to turn positive (and thus achieve a present value payback) was lengthened as the earnings standard was raised. At 8 percent, the economic life had to last about five years for the switch to occur (the net present value after the benefits of Year 5 is almost zero), whereas at 12 percent, most of the sixth year of economic life was necessary for a positive turnaround (approximately $10,000 of negative present value remaining at the end of Year 5 has to be recovered from the benefits of Year 6). At 14 percent more time than the economic life was required to achieve a positive net present value, making the project uneconomic.

F I G U R E   6–5

Net Present Value Analysis at 12 Percent[*]

	Totals	Year 0	Year 1	Year 2	Year 3	Year 4	Year 5	Year 6
Investment outlay (outflow)	$−100,000	$−100,000	0	0	0	0	0	0
Benefits (inflows)	150,000	0	$ 25,000	$ 25,000	$ 25,000	$ 25,000	$ 25,000	$25,000
Present value factors @ 12%[†]			1.000	0.893	0.797	0.712	0.636	0.567	0.507
Present values of cash flows	2,800	−100,000	22,325	19,925	17,800	15,900	14,175	12,675
Cumulative present values		$−100,000	$−77,675	$−57,750	$−39,950	$−24,050	$−9,875	$ 2,800
Net present value @ 12%	$ 2,800							

[*]This model is available for download in an interactive format; see "Analytical Support," p. 272

[†]As in Figure 6–4, we could use 4.112 times $25,000 from Table 6–II, p. 277.

In our example we assumed a level operating cash inflow of $25,000. Uneven cash flow patterns have a notable impact on the results, although the method of calculation remains the same. The net present value approach can, of course, accommodate any combination of cash flow patterns without difficulty. The reader is invited to test this, using a cash inflow pattern that rises from, say, $15,000 to $40,000, and one that falls from $40,000 to $15,000, each totaling $150,000 over six years. When using a spreadsheet, the reader can select the NPV function, specify the discount rate, enter the cash flows from Year 1 through 6, and subtract the net investment from the result to arrive at the net present value.

Net present value is a direct measure of value creation as well as a screening device that indicates whether a stipulated minimum return standard, such as the cost of capital, can be met over an investment proposal's economic life. We stated before that when net present value is positive, there is potential for a return in excess of the standard and therefore, economic value creation. When net present value is negative, the minimum return standard and capital recovery cannot be achieved with the projected cash flows. When net present value is close to or exactly *zero,* the return standard has just been met. In this case the investment will be value neutral. All of these conditions, of course, hold only on the assumption that the cash flow estimates and the projected life will in fact be achieved. The graphic representation of net present value in Figure 6–6 demonstrates the three outcomes.

Although net present value is the most frequently used tool in evaluating investment alternatives, it doesn't answer all of our questions about the economic attractiveness of capital outlays. For example, when comparing different projects, how does one evaluate the respective size of the value creation calculated with a given return standard, particularly if the investment amount differs significantly? Also, to what extent is achieving the expected economic life a factor in such comparisons?

F I G U R E   6–6

A Representation of Net Present Value

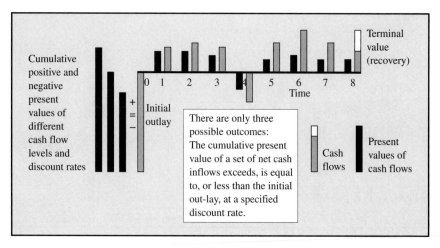

Furthermore, how does one quantify the potential errors and uncertainties inherent in the cash flow estimates, and how does the measure assist in investment choices if such deviations are significant? Finally, one can ask what specific return the project will yield if all estimates are in fact realized? Further measures and analytical methods are necessary to answer these questions, and we'll show later how a combination of techniques helps narrow the choices to be made.

Present Value Payback

We've already referred to this measure during our discussion of net present value. As we saw, the concept establishes the *minimum life* necessary for an investment to operate as expected, and still meet the return standard of the present value analysis, a break-even condition in value creation. In other words, present value payback is achieved at the specific point in time when the cumulative positive present value of cash benefits equals the cumulative negative present value of all the cash outlays—in fact, a zero net present value condition. It's the point in the project's economic life when the original investment has been fully amortized and a return equal to the built-in return standard has been achieved on the declining balance—the point at which the project becomes economically attractive and can begin to create value. Figure 6–7 provides a visual representation of this concept similar to the one for net present value.

Recall that in Figures 6–4 and 6–5, we included a row for the cumulative net present value of the project. It served as a visual check for determining the point at which net present value turned positive. The present value payback for our example, using a discount rate of 8 percent, was about five years, whereas a 12 percent standard required almost six years, just about the full economic life of the investment. The minimum time needed to recover the investment and earn the return standard on the declining balance of the investment, when compared to the economic life, is also a way of expressing the potential risk of the project. The

---

FIGURE 6–7

A Representation of Present Value Payback

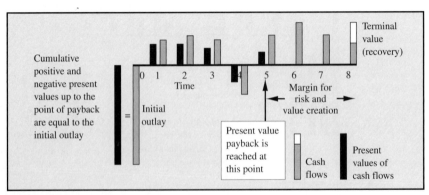

measure doesn't specifically address the nature of the risk, but merely identifies any remaining part of the economic life as an overall risk allowance. One can then judge whether the risk entailed in the combination of the key drivers of the project—or any one key variable in particular—is likely to outweigh the cushion of safety implied in the additional time the project might operate once it has passed the present value payback point. Remember, however, that the measure focuses only on the life span of the project, assuming implicitly that the estimated annual operating conditions will in fact continue to be achieved.

When uneven and more complicated cash flow patterns are projected, a condition we'll examine later, the minimum life test of the present value payback again requires a year-by-year accumulation of the negative and positive present values, as was done in simplified form in Figures 6–4 and 6–5.

If a project is a straightforward combination of a single outlay at point zero and expected level annual operating cash inflows, in effect representing an annuity, the analysis is especially simple and can, of course, be done readily on a calculator or spreadsheet. To illustrate the concept, however, we'll again make use of our present value tables, this time using the annuity factors in Table 6–II to quickly identify the present value payback. The following relationship is utilized:

$$\text{Present value} = \text{Factor} \times \text{Annuity}$$

We're looking for the condition under which the present value of the outflows is exactly equal to the present value of the inflows. Inasmuch as the net investment (outflow) must be recovered by the inflows, we can change the formula to:

$$\text{Net investment} = \text{Factor} \times \text{Annuity}$$

Because we know the level of the annuity, which is represented by the annual operating cash inflows, we can find the factor that satisfies the condition:

$$\text{Factor} = \frac{\text{Net investment}}{\text{Annuity}}$$

For our machine example, we can calculate the following results: $100,000 ÷ $25,000 = 4.0. We can look for the closest factor in the 8 percent column of Table 6–II. The answer lies almost exactly on the line for period 5 (3.993), which indicates that the project's minimum life under the assumed operating conditions must be five years to achieve the standard 8 percent return. If the standard is 12 percent, the minimum life has to be approximately 5⅔ years (an interpolation between 3.605 and 4.112).

The test for present value payback (minimum life) at any given return standard thus becomes one more factor in assessing the margin for error in the project estimates. It sharpens the analyst's understanding of the relationship of economic life and acceptable performance, and is a much improved version of the simple payback rule of thumb. The measure is a useful companion to the net present value criterion. It does not, however, address specific risk elements and in fact leaves weighing of any favorable difference between minimum and economic life to the decision maker's judgment.

Profitability Index (BCR)

After calculating the net present values of a series of projects, we might be faced with a choice that involves several alternative investments of different sizes. In such cases, we cannot ignore the fact that even though the net present values of the alternatives might be close or even equal, they involve initial funds commitments of widely varying amounts.

In other words, it does make a difference whether an investment proposal promises a net present value of $1,000 for an outlay of $10,000, or whether in another case, a net present value of $1,000 requires an investment of $25,000—even if we can assume equivalent economic lives and equivalent risk. Although both projects will create value if implemented successfully, the value creation in the first case is a much larger fraction of the net investment, which makes the first investment clearly more attractive, given that all other conditions are comparable.

The profitability index is a formal way of expressing this relationship of benefits to cost, a ratio which also is called the *benefit cost ratio (BCR):*

$$\text{Profitability index} = \frac{\text{Present value of operating inflows } (\textit{benefit})}{\text{Present value of net investment outlays } (\textit{cost})}$$

The present values in this formula are the same amounts we used earlier to derive the net present value, although then we subtracted inflows from outflows. In the case of the profitability index, the question is simply: How much in present value is being created for each dollar of net investment outlay?

The two cases we cited above would yield the following results:

$$1. \text{ Profitability index} = \frac{\$11,000}{\$10,000} = 1.10$$

$$2. \text{ Profitability index} = \frac{\$26,000}{\$25,000} = 1.04$$

The higher the index, the better the project. As we expected, the first project is much more favorable, given the assumption that all other aspects of the investment are reasonably comparable. If the index is 1.0 or less, the project is just meeting or even below the minimum return standard used to derive the present values. An index of exactly 1.0 corresponds to a zero net present value and no value creation. Our simple machine example has a profitability index of 1.16 at 8 percent in Figure 6–4 ($115,575 ÷ $100,000), and 1.03 at 12 percent in Figure 6–5 ($102,800 ÷ $100,000).

The profitability index provides results that directionally are consistent with the net present value measure. It's based on the same inputs but differs in format, focusing on the relative size of the trade-off. When used in conjunction with net present value, it provides additional insight for the analyst or manager. As already mentioned, it allows us to choose between investment alternatives of differing magnitudes. But it still leaves several points unanswered, and there are some theoretical issues involved that we'll point out later.

Internal Rate of Return (IRR, Yield)

The concept of a "true" return yielded by an investment over its economic life, also referred to as the *discounted cash flow return,* or *DCF,* was briefly mentioned in our earlier discussion of net present value. The internal rate of return is simply the unique discount rate that, when applied to both cash inflows and cash outflows over the investment's economic life, provides a zero net present value—that is, the present value of the inflows is exactly equal to the present value of the outflows. Stated another way, if cash flow estimates are achieved, the principal of an investment will be amortized over its specified economic life, while earning the exact return implied by the underlying discount rate. Figure 6–8 visually presents the dimensions of this measure.

The project's IRR might coincide with the return standard desired, might exceed it, or might fall short of the standard. These three conditions parallel those of net present value. One of the attractions of the internal rate of return for many practitioners is its ease of comparison with the return standard, and/or the cost of capital, being stated in percentage terms.

Naturally, the result of a given project will vary with changes in the economic life and the pattern of cash flows. In fact, the internal rate of return is found by letting it become a variable that is dependent on cash flows and economic life. In the case of net present value and profitability index, we had employed a specified return standard to discount the investment's cash flows. For the internal rate of return, we switch the problem around to find the specific discount rate that makes cash inflows and outflows exactly equal.

We can again employ our basic formula (Present value = Factor × Annuity) if the project is simple enough to involve a single investment outlay and only level annual cash inflows. The formula can then be expressed as follows:

$$\text{Factor} = \frac{\text{Present value (net investment)}}{\text{Annuity}}$$

FIGURE   6–8

A Representation of Internal Rate of Return (IRR, Yield, DCF)

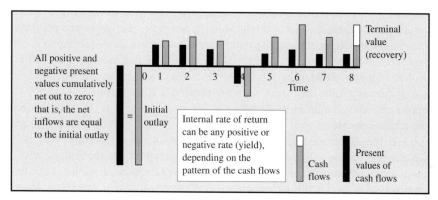

The factor then can be located in the present value table for annuities (Table 6–II). Because the economic life is a given, we can find the rate of return by moving along the proper period row to the column containing a factor that approximates the formula result. Obviously, the result can be quickly obtained using a programmed calculator or a spreadsheet (using the IRR function and specifying the cash flows by period), but again we're showing the details here to improve our understanding of the underlying mechanics.

To illustrate, our earlier investment example has a factor of 4.0 ($100,000 ÷ $25,000). On the line for period 6 in Table 6–II we find that 4.0 lies almost exactly between 12 percent (4.112) and 14 percent (3.889). Approximate interpolation suggests that the result is about 13 percent. (The precise result from a spreadsheet is 12.98 percent.)

When a project involves a more complex cash flow pattern, a trial-and-error approach is implied. Successive application of different discount rates to all cash flows over the investment's economic life can be made until a reasonably close approximation of a zero net present value has been found. We observed this effect in our earlier example, when the net present value declined as the discount rate was raised from 8 to 12 percent (see Figures 6–4 and 6–5). Again, programmed calculators and computer spreadsheets will arrive at the result directly, once the cash flows have been specified for all the periods involved.

As a ranking device for investments, the internal rate of return isn't without problems. First, there's the mathematical possibility that a complex project with many varied cash inflows and outflows over its economic life might in fact yield two different internal rates of return. Although a relatively rare occurrence, such an inconvenient outcome is caused by the specific pattern and timing of the various cash inflows and outflows.

More important, however, is the practical issue of choosing among alternative projects that involve widely differing net investments and that have internal rates of return inverse to the size of the project (the smaller investment has the higher return). A $10,000 investment with an internal rate of return of 50 percent cannot be directly compared to an outlay of $100,000 with a 30 percent internal rate of return, particularly if the risks are similar and the company normally requires a 15 percent earnings standard. Although both projects exceed the desired return and thus create value, it might be better to employ the larger sum at 30 percent than the smaller sum at 50 percent, unless sufficient funds are available for both projects to be undertaken. If the economic life of alternative projects differs widely, it might similarly be advantageous to employ funds at a lower rate for a longer period of time than to opt for a brief period of higher return. This condition applies if a choice must be made between two investments, both of which exceed the return standard.

It should be apparent that the internal rate of return, like all other measures, must be used with some caution. Because it provides the analyst with a unique rate of return inherent to each project, the IRR of an investment permits a ranking of potential alternatives by a single number and by a direct comparison to the return standard. In contrast, the net present value method builds in a specified earnings standard reflecting the company's expectations from such investments, and the ranking is based on relative present value creation in dollar terms.

When the internal rates of return of different projects are compared, there's also the implied assumption that the cash flows thrown off during each project's economic life can in fact be reinvested at their unique rates. We know, however, that the company's earnings standard usually is an expression of the long-run earnings power of the company, even if only approximate. Thus managers applying a 15 or even 20 percent return standard to investments must realize that a project with its own internal rate of return of, say, 30 percent, cannot be assumed to have its cash flows reinvested at this unique higher rate. Unless the general earnings standard is quite unrealistic, funds thrown off by capital investments can only be expected to be reemployed over time at this lower average rate.

This apparent dilemma does not, however, invalidate the internal rate of return measure, because any project will certainly yield its calculated internal rate of return if all conditions hold over its economic life, regardless of what is done with the cash generated by the project. Therefore, it's appropriate to rank projects by their respective IRRs.

In the last part of Chapter 7, we'll return to a comparative overview of all measures and develop basic rules for their application. The reader is invited to turn to the references listed at the ends of this chapter and Chapter 7 for more extensive discussions of the many theoretical and practical arguments surrounding the use of present value techniques, particularly in the case of the internal rate of return.

Annualized Net Present Value

Another useful way of employing the annuity principle of discounting is to estimate how much of an annual shortfall in operating cash inflows would be permissible over the full economic life of a project, while still meeting the minimum return standard. We know that the net present value calculation normally results in either a cumulative excess or a cumulative deficiency of present value benefits vis-à-vis the net investment. We also know that if the net present value is positive, the amount can be viewed as value creation in excess of the cost of capital, if that is the standard employed. This figure also can be considered, at least in part, as a cushion against any estimating error contained in future cash inflows, especially when the discount rate has been set much higher than the cost of capital.

Unless a project has highly irregular annual flows, it's often useful to transform the positive net present value at the decision point into an *equivalent annuity* over the project's economic life. Such an annual equivalent, representing the allowable margin of error, can then be directly compared to the original estimates of annual operating cash inflow. This is possible because the net present value has in effect been "reconstituted" into a series of level cash flows on the same basis as the estimates themselves, that is, in the form of annual cash flows unadjusted for time value. To illustrate, we can transform the net present value shown in Figure 6–4, $15,575, into an annuity over the six-year life by simply using the familiar present value relationship:

$$\text{Present value} = \text{Factor} \times \text{Annuity}$$

or by using the annuity routines in calculators and spreadsheets, choosing the *pmt* (payment) function and specifying the discount rate, the number of periods, and the present value to be recovered. Because we're interested in finding the annuity represented by the net present value, and wish to do so over a known economic life and at a specified discount rate—which is the earnings standard employed in the net present value calculation in the first place—we can transform the annuity formula as follows:

$$\text{Annuity} = \frac{(\text{Net}) \text{ present value}}{\text{Factor}}$$

Our example has the following result:

$$\text{Annuity} = \frac{\$15,575}{4.623} = \$3,369$$

The annual operating cash inflows were originally estimated to be $25,000. Given the result above, the actual cash flow experienced could be lowered by about $3,400 per year, and the project would still meet the minimum standard of 8 percent, but obviously not create value. Note, however, that the investment would have to operate at that lower level of cash flows over its full economic life for this value-neutral condition to be true.

In this case, the shortfall allowance directly translates into a permissible downward adjustment of estimated operating cash inflows by 22 percent. We must remember from page 251, however, that the annual cash flow consists of an estimated after-tax operating profit of $8,333, to which depreciation of $16,667 has been added back. In view of this sizable depreciation allowance—which is not subject to uncertainty—the relevant permissible reduction applies to the after-tax profit alone. The adjustment reduces the after-tax profit to about $5,000 ($8,333 − $3,369 = $4,964), which amounts to a hefty 40 percent! As we can see, this type of analysis represents a more direct approach to judging the allowable variation in the key estimates than did the present value payback, which focused on the time period instead of the cash flow estimates.

Annualization can be more generally applied as a very practical and quick preliminary "scoping" of the attractiveness of a tentative investment proposal that has not yet been fleshed out in detail. This method turns the normal investment analysis around by finding the approximate annual operating cash flow required to justify an estimated capital outlay, at a time when specific operating benefits have yet to be determined. Given an estimate of the economic life and an earnings standard, we can employ the formula

$$\text{Operating cash flow} = \frac{\text{Net investment}}{\text{Factor}}$$

to find the annual cash flow equivalent that, on average, will be the minimum target benefit. We can, of course, readily use electronic means to make this transformation directly by again applying the *pmt* function and entering the discount rate, the number of periods, and the investment to be amortized.

We must be careful, however, to interpret this figure properly. Because by definition it's an after-tax cash flow, the result has to be correctly adjusted for the assumed annual depreciation in order to transform it into the minimum pretax operating improvement necessary to justify the outlay. The process simply involves working backward through the analysis, using the knowledge that cash flow consists of the sum of after-tax operating profit and annual depreciation. We can apply the approach to our example from Figure 6–4.

First, we find the target cash flow benefits over six years at 8 percent, using the appropriate factor from Table 6–II or obtaining them directly from a spreadsheet, using the *pmt* function and entering 8 percent, 6 periods, and the $100,000 present value:

$$\frac{\$100,000}{4.623} = \$21,631$$

Next we transform this required after-tax cash flow into its equivalent pretax operating improvement:

After-tax cash flow	$21,631
Less: Depreciation	16,667
After-tax profit	$ 4,964
Tax at 34% of *pretax* profit	$ 2,557
Pre-tax profit	$ 7,521
Add back depreciation	16,667
Minimum pre-tax operating improvement	$24,188

Thus, our investment has to provide a minimum of about $24,200 in direct operating improvements such as lower costs, incremental revenues, and so on. Clearly, this method provides a quick look at the amount of pretax profit benefits required and allows the decision maker to think about the likely potential of the investment to achieve them. In other words, annualization applied in this way is a useful tool for making a first assessment of the chances that an investment will be in the ballpark.

Applying Time-Adjusted Measures

As we stated earlier, the practice of discounting and compounding is inextricably connected with the services and instruments of the financial community worldwide. In our discussion we have concentrated on the use of discounting and compounding methodologies for the more specific purpose of analyzing business investments, defining the four key parameters of such investments and demonstrating the major tools used in the process. It should be clear to the reader, however, that minor rethinking of the key inputs as defined here will make the analysis process generally applicable to analyzing financial instruments, contracts, and any situation which involves cash flow trade-offs extending from the present into the future. In fact, we've used simple analogies to financial instruments in our discussion, and also indicated that the process would be present again in the valuation discussions in the final chapters of the book. The general applicability of discounting and compounding is also apparent from the general wording contained in calculator and spreadsheet routines, which are structured to handle any problem that involves present values, future values, payments, receipts, time periods, and rates for discounting and compounding.

As we also mentioned, applying the methodology is relatively easy once a degree of comfort has been acquired in understanding the basic mathematics and relationships. Manipulating data within the various frameworks can become quite routine. The real challenge in the application of time-adjusted methodologies relates to framing the problem, establishing the relevant data, defining the key risk factors, and interpreting the results. Chapter 7 illustrates many of these challenges. Business investments generally are more complex in these aspects than straightforward contracts and financial instruments, and the skills acquired from studying the materials in this chapter will provide a sound basis for handling the process in the many other areas to which it applies.

Key Issues

The following is a recap of the key issues raised directly or indirectly in this chapter. They are enumerated here to help the reader keep the analysis tools and methods within the perspective of financial theory and business practice.

1. Decisions involving trade-offs between present and future cash flows are a common occurrence in any business. They require a consistent framework for analyzing these cash flows at the point of decision in equivalent terms.

2. Discounting and compounding methodologies use basic mathematical relationships to integrate timing, monetary returns, and cash flow amounts into a value framework. They are not a substitute for judgment, however, only numerical assists.

3. Business investment analysis requires careful definition of the key inputs and variables underlying the cash flow pattern, which involves an understanding of the expected changes brought about by the decision, independent of accounting methodology, adjusted for tax implications, and fitted to the economic life span. Economic analysis of investment decisions must be based on differential revenues and costs in the form of cash flows that are caused by the decision, and not on changes that are merely due to accounting conventions.

4. The major investment measures are designed to take into account the timing of inflows and outflows of an investment and relate to

economic attractiveness to defined return expectations. Simple rules of thumb violate these criteria, and the ease of spreadsheet analysis has made the use of economic measures fully accessible to any interested person.

5. Creating shareholder value through economic returns above the cost of capital is the key criterion in business investment analysis, and the net present value and IRR measures can be used to test the analytical results for this outcome.

6. Testing for potential leeway in achieving lesser cash flow returns while still meeting or exceeding the standard used in the analysis is a useful application of economic payback and annualization, although care must be taken in the interpretation of such modifications.

7. Although all economic measures discussed here directionally give the same reading of desirability, using only one measure in isolation can lead to misinterpretation of project desirability, depending on such elements as project size, interdependence, and funding limits.

8. Analytical techniques can provide ranges of results as well as quantitative insights of considerable sophistication, but they can't supplant qualitative business judgments that must deal with the broader context of strategy and risk assessment.

9. The use of discounting and compounding in the financial and economic environment is far broader than its specific application to business investments as described here; however, business investments represent the most complex set of conditions because of the uncertainty of estimates and the need to integrate projects into business strategy.

Summary

In this chapter, we've presented the basic analytical framework for business investment analysis within the context of the key parameters required for most business applications. Even though the material dealt largely with the time value of money and the specific techniques used to analyze the cash flow trade-offs in examples of simple business investments, we made the point repeatedly that the most critical aspect of the process was thoughtful attention to defining the parameters of net investment, net operating cash flows, economic life, and terminal value before any quantitative techniques are applied.

We discussed the importance of dealing with the net effect of the investment decision on future cash flows, that is, to focus on the relevant changes attributable to the decision. We pointed out the importance of deriving cash flows adjusted for accounting allocations, of recognizing the tax shield effect of write-offs such as depreciation, and generally dealing with the net after-tax cash impact of net investment, operating cash flows, and any terminal recoveries.

After introducing the basic mathematics of time adjustment through discounting and compounding, we presented a step-by-step approach to the various tools of analysis. We discarded as uneconomic the simple rules of thumb still being used at times, and demonstrated how the major economic tools, net present value, discounted payback, internal rate of return, and annualization all gave indications of whether value was created in excess of the cost of capital, albeit in different form. We laid out a common format for analysis, and related this visual representation to the internal routines of calculators and spreadsheets. Working through a series of simple examples, we provided the reader with the ability to perform the key numerical aspects of investment analysis. But we cautioned that numerical results were only one input to the broader management task of selecting investment projects in a strategic context with defined corporate objectives and goals, and with the ultimate purpose of creating shareholder value, and indicated that the next chapter will be devoted to viewing business investment analysis in this broader, judgmentally more difficult, setting.

Analytical Support

A set of Excel-based templates (*Interactive Templates*) is downloadable at no charge from the Web at www.mhhe.com/helfert11e. The eighth of these, "Present Value Model: Calculating Cash Flows and Key Measures," is a general purpose tool which activates the present value analyses of Figures 6–4 and 6–5 on pages 259 and 260 in this chapter, and all similar analyses in Chapter 7. The template allows you to vary a set of key assumptions about investment outlays, cash flow benefits, depreciation patterns, tax rates, and discount rates of any investment project. You can observe the numerical changes resulting from these modifications on the key measures and on a graphic representation of the cash flow patterns.

Financial Genome, the advanced financial analysis software application described in Appendix I, p. 479 does not contain present value routines at this point.

Selected References

Brealey, Richard, and Stewart Myers. *Principles of Corporate Finance.* 5th ed. Burr Ridge, IL: Irwin/McGraw-Hill, 1996.

Grant, Eugene L., et al. *Principles of Engineering Economy.* 8th ed. New York: Wiley, 1990. (A classic.)

Ross, Stephen; Randolph Westerfield; and Bradford D. Jordan. *Fundamentals of Corporate Finance.* 4th ed. Burr Ridge, IL: Irwin/McGraw-Hill, 1998.

Thorndike, David. *The Thorndike Encyclopedia of Banking and Financial Tables, 1995 Yearbook.* Boston: Warren, Gorham & Lamont, 1995.

Weston, Fred; Scott Besley; and Eugene Brigham. *Essentials of Managerial Finance.* 11th ed. Hinsdale, IL: Dryden Press, 1997.

Self-Study Exercises, Problems, and Discussion Questions

Exercises and Problems (*Selected Solutions Provided in Appendix VI*)

1. Calculate the following exercises, using both the present value tables and a spreadsheet, and check your results.

    a. Present value of $1,500 to be paid in Year 7, with a return standard of 12 percent.

    b. Future value of $678 in Year 7, compounded at 12 percent.

    c. Future value of $1,250 in Year 11, compounded at 8 percent.

    d. Present value of $300 per year received for nine years, with a return standard of 18 percent.

    e. Future value of $675 per year for 16 years, compounded at 5 percent (use spreadsheet).

    f. Convert principal of $50,000 today into a five-year annuity at 6 percent.

2. Using the template "Present Value Model: Calculating Cash Flows and Key Measures" solve the following problem:

    An investment proposition costing $60,000 is expected to result in the following after-tax cash inflows over seven years:

Year	
1	$10,000
2	15,000
3	15,000
4	20,000
5	15,000
6	10,000
7	5,000

    a. Calculate the net present value at 10 percent and at 16 percent.

    b. Determine the internal rate of return (yield) of the proposition.

    c. If the annual cash flows were an even $13,000 per year for seven years, what would be the net present value at 10 percent?

    d. What level of annual cash flows would be required to yield at 16 percent return?

    e. How would the results of (*a*) and (*b*) change if there were a capital recovery of $10,000 at the end of Year 7?

    f. How would the result of (*d*) change if there were a capital recovery of $10,000 at the end of Year 7?

3. Using both the present value tables and a spreadsheet, solve the following problem:

After careful analysis of a number of possible investments, the trustee of a major estate is weighing the choice between two $100,000 investments considered to be of equal risk. The first (a) will provide a series of eight year-end payments to the estate of $16,500 each, whereas the second (b) will provide a single lump sum of $233,000 at the end of 11 years. Which proposition provides the higher yield? If the normal return experienced by the estate of investments of this risk category is 6 percent, which investment is preferable? Should the pattern of cash flows be a consideration here, and how would this affect the choice? Ignore taxes and discuss your findings.

4. After having spent and written off against expenses of past periods an estimated $1,150,000 of R&D funds on a new product, the ABC Company must decide whether to invest a total of $1,500,000 in a large-scale initial promotional and advertising campaign to bring the product to market. The campaign will be conducted over a twelve-month period, and all costs will be charged off as expenses in the current year. The effect of the campaign is an estimated average incremental profit of $450,000 per year for at least the next five years, before taxes and without the initial promotional costs. The likely pattern of profits is estimated to be $250,000 in the first year, $450,000 in the second, $750,000 in the third, $500,000 in the fourth, and $300,000 in the fifth year.

Assume that income taxes on incremental profits are paid at the rate of 36 percent and that the company normally has the opportunity to earn 14 percent after taxes. Calculate the various measures of investment desirability, first on the average profit and then on the annual pattern expected. Determine the simple payback and return on investment, average return, net present value, present value index, present value payback, annualized net present value, and internal rate of return (yield).

What's the effect of the R&D expenditures on these results? Discuss your findings.

5. In an effort to replace a manual operation with a more efficient and reliable automatic process, the DEF Company is considering the purchase of a machine that will cost $52,800 installed and has an expected economic life of eight years. It will be depreciated over this period on a straight-line basis for both book and tax purposes, with no salvage value foreseen. The main benefit expected is a true reduction in costs due to the elimination of an operator position and less materials spoilage. There will be some additional costs such as power, supplies, and repairs. The net annual savings are estimated to be $12,100, and the machine will be scrapped at the end of its life.

Assume that income taxes on incremental profits are paid at the rate of 36 percent and that normal opportunities return 12 percent after taxes. Calculate the simple payback and return on investment, average return, net present value, present value index, present value payback, annualized net present value, and internal rate of return (yield). Discuss your findings.

Discussion Questions

1. Define the difference between present value payback and annualized net present value.
2. What's the difference between an annualized net present value and an annuity?
3. What's the connection between present value and future value?
4. Why is the profitability index an indicator of performance? What does it depend on?
5. Why is a zero net present value useful as an indicator of performance? What does it depend on?
6. What's the connection between net present value, internal rate of return, and present value payback? What do they have in common?
7. How important is it to lay out a specific timing pattern of future cash flows, and why?
8. What are the most important issues affecting the cash flow data being used in a present value analysis?

TABLE 6-I

Present Value of Single Sum of $1 Received or Paid at End of Period

Period of Receipt or Payment	1%	2%	4%	5%	6%	8%	10%	12%	14%	15%	16%	18%	20%	22%	24%	25%	26%	28%	30%	35%	40%	45%	50%
1	0.990	0.980	0.962	0.952	0.943	0.926	0.909	0.893	0.877	0.870	0.862	0.847	0.833	0.820	0.806	0.800	0.794	0.781	0.769	0.741	0.714	0.690	0.667
2	0.980	0.961	0.925	0.907	0.890	0.857	0.826	0.797	0.769	0.756	0.743	0.718	0.694	0.672	0.650	0.640	0.630	0.610	0.592	0.549	0.510	0.476	0.444
3	0.971	0.942	0.889	0.863	0.840	0.794	0.751	0.712	0.675	0.658	0.641	0.609	0.579	0.551	0.524	0.512	0.500	0.477	0.455	0.406	0.364	0.328	0.296
4	0.961	0.924	0.855	0.823	0.792	0.735	0.683	0.636	0.592	0.572	0.552	0.516	0.482	0.451	0.423	0.410	0.397	0.373	0.350	0.301	0.260	0.226	0.198
5	0.951	0.906	0.822	0.784	0.747	0.681	0.621	0.567	0.519	0.497	0.476	0.437	0.402	0.370	0.341	0.328	0.315	0.291	0.269	0.223	0.186	0.156	0.132
6	0.942	0.888	0.790	0.746	0.705	0.630	0.564	0.507	0.456	0.432	0.410	0.370	0.335	0.303	0.275	0.262	0.250	0.227	0.207	0.165	0.133	0.108	0.088
7	0.933	0.871	0.760	0.711	0.665	0.583	0.513	0.452	0.400	0.376	0.354	0.314	0.279	0.249	0.222	0.210	0.198	0.178	0.159	0.122	0.095	0.074	0.059
8	0.923	0.853	0.731	0.677	0.627	0.540	0.467	0.404	0.351	0.327	0.305	0.266	0.233	0.204	0.179	0.168	0.157	0.139	0.123	0.091	0.068	0.051	0.039
9	0.914	0.837	0.703	0.645	0.592	0.500	0.424	0.361	0.308	0.284	0.263	0.225	0.194	0.167	0.144	0.134	0.125	0.108	0.094	0.067	0.048	0.035	0.026
10	0.905	0.820	0.676	0.614	0.558	0.463	0.386	0.322	0.270	0.247	0.227	0.191	0.162	0.137	0.116	0.107	0.099	0.085	0.073	0.050	0.035	0.024	0.017
11	0.896	0.804	0.650	0.585	0.527	0.429	0.350	0.287	0.237	0.215	0.195	0.162	0.135	0.112	0.094	0.086	0.079	0.066	0.056	0.037	0.025	0.017	0.012
12	0.887	0.788	0.625	0.557	0.497	0.397	0.319	0.257	0.208	0.187	0.168	0.137	0.112	0.092	0.076	0.069	0.062	0.052	0.043	0.027	0.018	0.012	0.008
13	0.879	0.773	0.601	0.530	0.469	0.368	0.290	0.229	0.182	0.163	0.145	0.116	0.093	0.075	0.061	0.055	0.050	0.040	0.033	0.020	0.013	0.008	0.005
14	0.870	0.758	0.577	0.505	0.442	0.340	0.263	0.205	0.160	0.141	0.125	0.099	0.078	0.062	0.049	0.044	0.039	0.032	0.025	0.015	0.009	0.006	0.003
15	0.861	0.743	0.555	0.481	0.417	0.315	0.239	0.183	0.140	0.123	0.108	0.084	0.065	0.051	0.040	0.035	0.031	0.025	0.020	0.011	0.006	0.004	0.002
16	0.853	0.728	0.534	0.458	0.394	0.292	0.218	0.163	0.123	0.107	0.093	0.071	0.054	0.042	0.032	0.028	0.025	0.019	0.015	0.008	0.005	0.003	0.002
17	0.844	0.714	0.513	0.436	0.371	0.270	0.198	0.146	0.108	0.093	0.080	0.060	0.045	0.034	0.026	0.023	0.020	0.015	0.012	0.006	0.003	0.002	0.001
18	0.836	0.700	0.494	0.416	0.350	0.250	0.180	0.130	0.095	0.081	0.069	0.051	0.038	0.028	0.021	0.018	0.016	0.012	0.009	0.005	0.002	0.001	0.001
19	0.828	0.686	0.475	0.396	0.331	0.232	0.164	0.116	0.083	0.070	0.060	0.043	0.031	0.023	0.017	0.014	0.012	0.009	0.007	0.003	0.002	0.001	
20	0.820	0.673	0.456	0.377	0.312	0.215	0.149	0.104	0.073	0.061	0.051	0.037	0.026	0.019	0.014	0.012	0.010	0.007	0.005	0.002	0.001		
21	0.811	0.660	0.439	0.359	0.294	0.199	0.135	0.093	0.064	0.053	0.044	0.031	0.022	0.015	0.011	0.009	0.008	0.006	0.004	0.002	0.001		
22	0.803	0.647	0.422	0.342	0.278	0.184	0.123	0.083	0.056	0.046	0.038	0.026	0.018	0.013	0.009	0.007	0.006	0.004	0.003	0.001			
23	0.795	0.634	0.406	0.326	0.262	0.170	0.112	0.074	0.049	0.040	0.033	0.022	0.015	0.010	0.007	0.006	0.005	0.003	0.002	0.001			
24	0.788	0.622	0.390	0.310	0.247	0.158	0.102	0.066	0.043	0.035	0.028	0.019	0.013	0.008	0.006	0.005	0.004	0.003	0.002				
25	0.780	0.610	0.375	0.295	0.233	0.146	0.092	0.059	0.038	0.030	0.024	0.016	0.010	0.007	0.005	0.004	0.003	0.002	0.001				
26	0.772	0.598	0.361	0.281	0.220	0.135	0.084	0.053	0.033	0.026	0.021	0.014	0.009	0.006	0.004	0.003	0.002	0.002	0.001				
27	0.764	0.586	0.347	0.268	0.207	0.125	0.076	0.047	0.029	0.023	0.018	0.011	0.007	0.005	0.003	0.002	0.002	0.001	0.001				
28	0.757	0.574	0.333	0.255	0.196	0.116	0.069	0.042	0.026	0.020	0.016	0.010	0.006	0.004	0.002	0.002	0.002	0.001	0.001				
29	0.749	0.563	0.321	0.243	0.185	0.107	0.063	0.037	0.022	0.017	0.014	0.008	0.005	0.003	0.002	0.002	0.001	0.001	0.001				
30	0.742	0.552	0.308	0.231	0.174	0.099	0.057	0.033	0.020	0.015	0.012	0.007	0.004	0.003	0.002	0.001	0.001	0.001	0.001				
35	0.706	0.500	0.253	0.181	0.130	0.066	0.036	0.019	0.010	0.008	0.006	0.003	0.002	0.001									
40	0.672	0.453	0.208	0.142	0.097	0.046	0.022	0.011	0.005	0.004	0.003	0.001	0.001										
45	0.639	0.410	0.171	0.111	0.073	0.031	0.014	0.006	0.003	0.002	0.001	0.001											
50	0.608	0.372	0.141	0.087	0.054	0.021	0.009	0.003	0.001	0.001	0.001												
60	0.550	0.305	0.095	0.054	0.030	0.010	0.003	0.001															

1. To find present value (PV) of fixture amount: PV = Factor × Amount.
2. To find future amount representing given PV: Amount = PV/Factor.
3. To find period given future amount, PV, and yield: Factor = PV/Amount; locate in column.
4. To find yield given future amount, PV, and period: Factor = PV/Amount; locate in row.

TABLE 6–II

Present Value of $1 per Period Received or Paid at End of Period (Annuity)

Number of Periods	1%	2%	4%	5%	6%	8%	10%	12%	14%	15%	16%	18%	20%	22%	24%	25%	26%	28%	30%	35%	40%	45%	50%
1	0.990	0.980	0.962	0.952	0.943	0.926	0.909	0.893	0.877	0.870	0.862	0.847	0.833	0.820	0.806	0.800	0.794	0.781	0.769	0.741	0.714	0.690	0.667
2	1.970	1.942	1.886	1.859	1.833	1.783	1.736	1.690	1.647	1.626	1.605	1.566	1.528	1.492	1.457	1.440	1.424	1.392	1.361	1.289	1.224	1.165	1.111
3	2.941	2.884	2.775	2.722	2.673	2.577	2.487	2.402	2.322	2.283	2.246	2.174	2.106	2.042	1.981	1.952	1.923	1.868	1.816	1.696	1.589	1.493	1.407
4	3.902	3.808	3.630	3.545	3.465	3.312	3.170	3.037	2.914	2.855	2.798	2.690	2.589	2.494	2.404	2.362	2.320	2.241	2.166	1.997	1.849	1.720	1.605
5	4.853	4.713	4.452	4.329	4.212	3.993	3.791	3.605	3.433	3.352	3.274	3.127	2.991	2.864	2.745	2.689	2.635	2.532	2.436	2.220	2.035	1.876	1.737
6	5.795	5.601	5.242	5.075	4.917	4.623	4.355	4.111	3.889	3.784	3.685	3.498	3.326	3.167	3.020	2.951	2.885	2.759	2.643	2.385	2.168	1.983	1.824
7	6.728	6.472	6.002	5.786	5.582	5.206	4.868	4.564	4.288	4.160	4.039	3.812	3.605	3.416	3.242	3.161	3.083	2.937	2.802	2.508	2.263	2.057	1.883
8	7.652	7.325	6.733	6.463	6.210	5.747	5.335	4.968	4.639	4.487	4.344	4.078	3.837	3.619	3.421	3.329	3.241	3.076	2.925	2.598	2.331	2.108	1.922
9	8.566	8.162	7.435	7.108	6.802	6.247	5.759	5.328	4.946	4.772	4.607	4.303	4.031	3.786	3.566	3.463	3.366	3.184	3.019	2.665	2.379	2.144	1.948
10	9.471	8.983	8.111	7.722	7.360	6.710	6.145	5.650	5.216	5.019	4.833	4.494	4.192	3.923	3.682	3.571	3.465	3.269	3.092	2.715	2.414	2.168	1.965
11	10.368	9.787	8.760	8.307	7.887	7.139	6.495	5.937	5.453	5.234	5.029	4.656	4.327	4.035	3.776	3.656	3.544	3.335	3.147	2.752	2.438	2.185	1.977
12	11.255	10.575	9.385	8.863	8.384	7.536	6.814	6.194	5.660	5.421	5.197	4.793	4.439	4.127	3.851	3.725	3.606	3.387	3.190	2.779	2.456	2.196	1.985
13	12.134	11.343	9.986	9.393	8.853	7.904	7.103	6.424	5.842	5.583	5.342	4.910	4.533	4.203	3.912	3.780	3.656	3.427	3.223	2.799	2.468	2.204	1.990
14	13.004	12.106	10.563	9.898	9.295	8.244	7.367	6.628	6.002	5.724	5.468	5.008	4.611	4.265	3.962	3.824	3.695	3.459	3.249	2.814	2.477	2.210	1.993
15	13.865	12.849	11.118	10.379	9.712	8.559	7.606	6.811	6.142	5.847	5.575	5.092	4.675	4.315	4.001	3.859	3.726	3.483	3.268	2.825	2.484	2.214	1.995
16	14.718	13.578	11.652	10.838	10.106	8.851	7.824	6.974	6.265	5.954	5.669	5.162	4.730	4.357	4.033	3.887	3.751	3.503	3.283	2.834	2.489	2.216	1.997
17	15.562	14.292	12.166	11.274	10.477	9.122	8.022	7.120	6.373	6.047	5.749	5.222	4.775	4.391	4.059	3.910	3.771	3.518	3.295	2.840	2.492	2.218	1.998
18	16.398	14.992	12.659	11.690	10.828	9.372	8.201	7.250	6.467	6.128	5.818	5.273	4.812	4.419	4.080	3.928	3.786	3.529	3.304	2.844	2.494	2.219	1.999
19	17.226	15.678	13.134	12.085	11.158	9.604	8.365	7.366	6.550	6.198	5.877	5.316	4.844	4.442	4.097	3.942	3.799	3.539	3.311	2.848	2.496	2.220	1.999
20	18.046	16.351	13.590	12.462	11.470	9.818	8.514	7.469	6.623	6.259	5.929	5.353	4.870	4.460	4.110	3.954	3.808	3.546	3.316	2.850	2.497	2.221	1.999
21	18.857	17.011	14.029	12.821	11.764	10.017	8.649	7.562	6.687	6.312	5.973	5.384	4.891	4.476	4.121	3.963	3.816	3.551	3.320	2.852	2.498	2.221	2.000
22	19.660	17.658	14.451	13.163	12.042	10.201	8.772	7.645	6.743	6.359	6.011	5.410	4.909	4.488	4.130	3.970	3.822	3.556	3.323	2.853	2.498	2.222	2.000
23	20.456	18.292	14.857	13.489	12.303	10.371	8.883	7.718	6.792	6.399	6.044	5.432	4.925	4.499	4.137	3.976	3.827	3.559	3.325	2.854	2.499	2.222	2.000
24	21.243	18.914	15.247	13.799	12.550	10.529	8.985	7.784	6.835	6.434	6.073	5.451	4.937	4.507	4.143	3.981	3.831	3.562	3.327	2.855	2.499	2.222	2.000
25	22.023	19.523	15.622	14.094	12.783	10.675	9.077	7.843	6.873	6.464	6.097	5.467	4.948	4.514	4.147	3.985	3.834	3.564	3.329	2.856	2.499	2.222	2.000
26	22.795	20.121	15.983	14.375	13.003	10.810	9.161	7.896	6.906	6.491	6.118	5.480	4.956	4.520	4.151	3.988	3.837	3.566	3.330	2.856	2.500	2.222	2.000
27	23.560	20.707	16.330	14.643	13.211	10.935	9.237	7.943	6.935	6.514	6.136	5.492	4.964	4.524	4.154	3.990	3.839	3.567	3.331	2.856	2.500	2.222	2.000
28	24.316	21.281	16.663	14.898	13.406	11.051	9.307	7.984	6.961	6.534	6.152	5.502	4.970	4.528	4.157	3.992	3.840	3.568	3.331	2.857	2.500	2.222	2.000
29	25.066	21.844	16.984	15.141	13.591	11.158	9.370	8.022	6.983	6.551	6.166	5.510	4.975	4.531	4.159	3.994	3.841	3.569	3.332	2.857	2.500	2.222	2.000
30	25.808	22.396	17.292	15.372	13.765	11.258	9.427	8.055	7.003	6.566	6.177	5.517	4.979	4.534	4.160	3.995	3.842	3.569	3.332	2.857	2.500	2.222	2.000
35	29.408	24.999	18.665	16.374	14.498	11.654	9.664	8.176	7.070	6.617	6.215	5.539	4.992	4.541	4.164	3.998	3.845	3.571	3.333	2.857	2.500	2.222	2.000
40	32.835	27.355	19.793	17.159	15.046	11.925	9.779	8.244	7.105	6.642	6.234	5.548	4.997	4.544	4.166	3.999	3.846	3.571	3.333	2.857	2.500	2.222	2.000
45	36.094	29.490	20.720	17.774	15.546	12.108	9.863	8.282	7.123	6.654	6.242	5.552	4.998	4.545	4.166	4.000	3.846	3.571	3.333	2.857	2.500	2.222	2.000
50	39.196	31.424	21.482	18.256	15.762	12.234	9.915	8.304	7.133	6.661	6.246	5.554	4.999	4.545	4.167	4.000	3.846	3.571	3.333	2.857	2.500	2.222	2.000
60	44.955	34.761	22.623	18.929	16.161	12.376	9.967	8.324	7.140	6.665	6.249	5.555	5.000	4.545	4.167	4.000	3.846	3.571	3.333	2.857	2.500	2.222	2.000

1. To find present value (PV) of series of equal receipts or payments: PV = Factor × Annuity. 2. To find annuity representing given PV: Annuity = PV/Factor.

3. To find number of periods to recover investment: Factor = Investment/Annuity; locate in column.

4. To find yield of annuity given investment: Factor = Investment/Annuity; locate in row.

CHAPTER 7

ANALYSIS OF INVESTMENT DECISIONS

The decision to invest resources is one of the key drivers of the business financial system, as we established in Chapter 1. Sound investments that implement well-founded strategies are essential to creating shareholder value, and they must be analyzed both in a proper context and with sound analytical methods. Whether the decision involves committing resources to new facilities, a research and development project, a marketing program, additional working capital, an acquisition, or investing in a financial instrument, an economic trade-off must be made between the resources expended now and the expectation of future cash flow benefits to be obtained. Analyzing this trade-off is essentially a valuation process that makes an economic assessment of a combination of positive and negative cash flow patterns. The task is difficult by nature because it deals with future conditions subject to uncertainties and risks—yet this basic valuation principle is common to all investments, large and small.

In this chapter, we'll examine in some detail both the key conceptual and practical aspects of investment decisions, using the analytical techniques described in Chapter 6. In Chapters 8 and 9, we'll address the related issues of financing costs and the choice among financing alternatives. In Chapters 10 and 11, we'll expand on these concepts and demonstrate how the process applies to valuing a business and to the creation of shareholder value. From time to time, we'll introduce applicable portions of managerial economics and financial theory. In keeping with the scope of this book, however, we'll avoid the esoteric in favor of the practical and useful. At the end of each chapter, we'll summarize, as before, the key conceptual issues underlying the analytical approaches covered, both as a reminder and as a guide for the interested reader in exploring the references listed.

The analysis of decisions about new investments (as well as the opposite, disinvestments) involves a particularly complex set of issues and choices that must be defined and resolved by management. We'll discuss these in several categories:

- Strategic perspective.
- Decisional framework.
- Refinements of investment analysis.
- Application of economic measures.

Because business investments, in contrast to operational spending, are normally long-term commitments of resources, they should always be made within the context of a company's explicit strategy. In fact, investment in the absence of a sound strategy is an invitation to economic ruin. An effective approach to value creation cannot be built on retroactively trying to make sense out of sunk resource commitments. In addition, the financial analysis underlying the decisions and the trade-offs involved must be carried out within a consistent economic framework of accepted conceptual and practical guidelines.

As we discussed in Chapter 6, most business investment projects have several key components of analysis in common. These must be understood and made explicit, as well as comparable, in order to arrive at a proper choice among different investment alternatives, as we'll demonstrate on the basis of more complex examples. Finally, the economic nature of the process requires that the analytical methods supporting the decisions focus on the true cash flow impact of the investment or disinvestment and must be properly interpreted.

We'll take up each area in turn, emphasizing in greater detail the analytical components and methodologies. Once we've demonstrated the fundamental concepts, we'll introduce certain specialized aspects of the analytical process, such as sensitivity analysis, simulation, and the broader issues of dealing with risk. Some comments about related topics will follow, and we'll close with a checklist of key issues affecting investment analysis.

Strategic Perspective

Investments in land, productive equipment, buildings, natural resources, research facilities, product development, employee development, marketing programs, working capital, acquisitions, and other resource deployments made for future economic gain represent physical expressions of a company's strategy—which management must carefully develop and periodically reevaluate. Investment choices should always fit into the desired strategic direction the company wishes to take, with due consideration of:

- Expected economic conditions.
- Outlook for the company's specific industry or business segment.
- Competitive position of the company.
- Core competencies of the organization.

An almost infinite variety of business investments is available to most firms. It doesn't matter how the resource commitment is reflected on the company's books, whether in the form of an asset or as an expense for the period—the critical point is that the outlay is being made with an expectation of future returns. A company might invest in new facilities for expansion, expecting that incremental profits from additional volume will make the investment economically desirable. Investments might also be made for upgrading worn or outmoded facilities to improve cost-effectiveness. Here, savings in operating costs are the justification.

Some strategies call for entering new markets, which could involve setting up entirely new facilities and associated working capital, or perhaps a major repositioning of existing facilities through rebuilding or through sale and reinvestment. In a service business, expansion strategies could involve significant employee training outlays and electronic infrastructure investments. Other strategic proposals might involve creating a new business model of Internet connectivity, or establishing a research program, justified on the basis of its potential for developing new products or processes. Business investment also could involve significant promotional outlays, targeted on raising the company's market share over the long term and, with it, the profit contribution from higher volumes of operation. At times, acquiring a company whose product or service lines fit into the company's strategy, or purchasing a supplier to integrate the technology base, might be appropriate. At other times, partnering or outsourcing part of the company's product or service offerings might create additional value.

These and other choices are conceived continuously by the organization. Typically, lists of proposals are examined during the company's strategic planning process within the context and constraints of corporate and divisional objectives and goals. Then the various alternatives are narrowed down to those options that should be given serious analysis, and periodic spending plans are prepared which contain those capital outlays that have been selected and approved.

The many steps involved in identifying, analyzing, and selecting capital investment opportunities—as well as opportunities for divestiture—are collectively known as capital budgeting. This process includes everything from a broad scoping of ideas to very refined economic analyses. In the end, the company's capital budget normally contains an acceptable group of projects that individually and collectively are expected to provide economic returns meeting long-term management goals in support of shareholder value creation.

In essence, capital budgeting is like managing a personal investment portfolio. In both cases, the basic challenge is to select, within the constraint of available funds, those investments that promise to yield the desired level of economic rewards in relation to the degree of acceptable risk. The process thus involves a series of conscious economic trade-offs between exposure to potential adverse conditions and the expected profitability of the investments. As a general rule, the higher the profitability, the higher the risk exposure. Moreover, the choice among alternatives in which to invest the usually limited funds available invariably involves opportunity costs, because committing to one investment can mean rejecting others, thereby giving up the opportunity to earn perhaps higher but riskier returns.

In an investment portfolio, cash commitments are made in order to receive future inflows of cash in the form of dividends, interest, and eventual recovery of the principal through sale of the investment instrument—which over time might have appreciated or declined in market value. In capital budgeting, the commitment of company funds is made in exchange for future cash inflows from incremental after-tax profits and from the potential recovery of a portion of the capital invested, or from the value of a going business at the end of the planning horizon.

However, the analogy carries only so far. In a typical company, managing business investments is complicated by the need not only to select a portfolio of sound projects, but also to implement them well and to operate the facilities, service functions, or other new resources deployed with quality and cost effectiveness. In addition, analyzing potential investments in a business context is far more complex than selecting among stocks and bonds because the outlays often involve multiple expenditures spread over a period of time and a wide variety of operational cash flows that are expected over the economic life. Examples are constructing and equipping a new factory, or the gradual building up of a service business and its infrastructure.

Determining the economic benefits to be derived from the outlay is even more complex. An individual investor generally receives specific contractual interest payments or regular dividend checks. In contrast, a business investment typically generates additional profit contributions from higher volume, new products and services, or cost reduction. The specific incremental cash flow from a business investment might be difficult to identify, because it's intermingled in the company's financial reports with other accounting information. As we'll see, the analysis of potential capital investments involves a fair degree of economic reasoning and projection of future conditions that goes beyond merely using normal financial statements.

If we follow the analogy between a capital budget and an investment portfolio to its logical conclusion, capital budgeting would ideally amount to arraying all business investment opportunities in the order of their expected economic returns, and choosing a combination that would meet the desired portfolio return within the constraints of risk and available funding. The theoretical concepts that have evolved around these issues rely heavily on portfolio theory, both in terms of risk evaluation and in the comparison between investment returns and the cost of capital incurred in funding the investments.

These concepts are highly structured and depend on a series of important underlying assumptions. Not easy to apply in practice, they continue to be the subject of much learned argument. In simple terms, the theory argues that business investments—arrayed in declining order of attractiveness—should be accepted up to the point at which incremental benefits equal incremental cost, given appropriate risk levels. The economic attractiveness is most frequently expressed via the amount of net present value created.

This theory encounters several problems when applied in a practical setting. First, at the time the capital budget is prepared, it's simply not possible to foresee all investment opportunities, because management faces a continuously revolving planning horizon over which new opportunities keep appearing, while known opportunities might fade as conditions change even more rapidly. In recent times the speed of change in the business environment has increased dramatically.

Second, capital budgets are generally prepared only once a year in most companies. As various timing lags are encountered, actual implementation can be delayed or even canceled, because circumstances often change.

Third, economic criteria, such as the cost of capital and return standards based thereon, are merely approximations. Moreover, they are not the sole basis for the investment decision. Instead, the broader context of strategy and its attendant risks, the competitive environment, the ability of management to implement the investment, organizational considerations, and other factors come into play as management weighs the risk of an investment against the potential economic gain. Thus there is nothing automatic or simple in arriving at decisions about the stream of potential investments that are continuously surfaced within a business organization.

In this chapter, we'll explore the decisional framework and apply the analytical techniques discussed in Chapter 6 to the decision process for analyzing and choosing business investments. We won't delve into the broader conceptual issues of capital budgeting and portfolio theory, except to point out some of the key issues. Readers wanting more information on these topics should check the references at the end of the chapter. The important question of the cost of capital as related to capital budgeting will be taken up in the next chapter. Then, Chapter 9 will cover analytical reasoning behind the choice among types of potential funding sources for capital investments.

Decisional Framework

Effective analysis of business investments requires that both the analyst and the decision maker be very conscious of and specific about the many dimensions involved. We need to set a series of ground rules to ensure that our results are thorough, consistent, and meaningful. These ground rules cover:

- Framing the issue.
- Nature of the investment.
- Estimates of future costs and benefits.
- Incremental cash flows.
- Relevant accounting data.
- Sunk costs.

A good rule of thumb to keep in mind is that of the total time and effort required to analyze a business investment, at least 85 percent should be spent on meeting the important requirements of framing the issue and refining the elements of the decision, and only 15 percent on various forms of "running the numbers." Because of the ease with which our spreadsheets can calculate data, however, there is the strong temptation to develop numerical approaches before proper framing has been done. Thus, unfortunately, the proportions of effort are often reversed in practice, resulting in potentially costly omissions of insight and clarification.

Framing the Issue

We should begin any evaluation by stating explicitly what the investment is supposed to accomplish. Carefully defining the problem to be solved, or the opportunity to be exploited by the investment and identifying any potential alternatives to the proposed action are critically important to proper analysis. This elementary point is often overlooked, at times deliberately, when the desire to proceed with a favorite investment project overrides sound judgment.

In most cases, at least two or three alternatives are available for achieving the purpose of an investment, and careful examination of the specific circumstances might reveal an even greater number. The simple diagram in Figure 7–1 can help us visualize the key options for deciding on which alternatives to pursue in an investment proposal.

For example, the decision of whether to replace a machine nearing the end of its useful life at first appears to be a relatively straightforward "either/or" problem. The most obvious alternative, as in any case, is to do nothing, that is, to continue patching up the machine until it falls apart. The ongoing, rising costs likely to be incurred with that option are compared with the expected cost pattern of a new machine when we decide whether or not to replace it. But the alternative of doing nothing always exists for any investment project, and sound analysis requires that its implications be tested before proceeding.

But there are some not-so-obvious alternatives. Perhaps the company should stop making the product or providing the service altogether! This "go out of business" option should at least be considered—painful as it might be to think about—before new resources are committed.

The reasoning behind this seemingly radical notion is quite straightforward. Although the improved efficiency of a new machine or a whole new service infrastructure might raise this particular operation's economic performance from poor to average, there might indeed be alternatives elsewhere in the company that would yield greater returns from the overall funds committed. By going ahead with the investment, an opportunity cost from losing a higher return option might be incurred. In the interest of shareholder value creation, it might indeed be better to redeploy all existing resources now devoted to the product or service instead of prolonging its substandard performance through an incremental investment that viewed strictly by itself might be quite acceptable.

Moreover, even if the decision to continue making a product is economically sound under prevailing conditions, there still are several additional alternatives open to management. Among these, for example, are replacement with the same machine, or with a larger, more automated model, or with equipment using an altogether different technology and manufacturing process—or outsourcing the manufacture and thereby avoiding the investment.

FIGURE 7–1

Alternatives for a Business Investment Decision

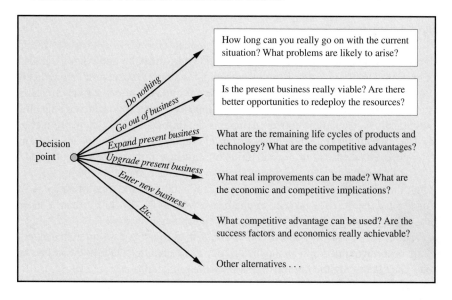

It's crucial to select the appropriate alternatives for analysis and to structure the problem in such a way that the analytical tools are applied to the real issue to be decided. For decisions of major strategic importance, formal processes are available which use the disciplines of decision theory to aid in structuring the issue and in establishing an array of creative alternatives (see end-of-chapter references). As a general rule, however, no investment should be undertaken unless the best analytical judgment allows it to clear the basic hurdles implied in the first two branches of the decision tree in Figure 7–1.

Nature of the Investment

Most business investments tend to be independent of each other; that is, the choice of any one of them doesn't preclude also choosing any other—unless there are insufficient funds available to do them all. In that sense, they can be viewed as a portfolio of choices. The analysis and reasoning behind every individual decision will be relatively unaffected by past and future choices.

There are, however, circumstances in which investments compete with each other in their purpose so that choosing one will preclude the other. Typically, this arises when two alternative ways of solving the same problem are being considered. Such investment projects are called mutually exclusive. The significance of this condition will become apparent when we discuss some of the specific examples later on. A similar condition can, of course, arise when management sets a strict limit on the amount of spending, often called capital rationing, which will preclude investing in some worthy projects once others have been accepted. This situation is quite common, because companies will more often than not find their funding potential limited, whether due to debt proportions that already are at target levels, fluctuations in profitability, or exercising caution in preserving cash flow for yet unspecified needs.

Another type of investment involves sequential outlays beyond the initial expenditure. For example, any major capital outlay for plant and equipment also might entail additional future outlays for major maintenance, upgrading, and partial replacement some years hence. These future outlays—to which the company is committing itself by the initial decision—must be formally considered when the initial analysis is made. Another example is the introduction of a new product or service with high growth potential, where additional working capital and perhaps future capacity expansions are a natural consequence of the decision to proceed.

The most logical evaluation of such investments comes from taking into account the whole pattern of major outlays recognizable at the time of analysis. If this isn't done, such a project might be viewed more favorably than a more straightforward one, because a number of future negative cash flows have been left out of the cash flow pattern. Moreover, if the project is chosen, management could become trapped into having to approve these unanticipated future outlays as they arise later—on the argument that these incremental funds are clearly justifiable because the project is "already in place." Although that argument might be true given the earlier decision, the fact remains that the project originally was not judged on its full implications, and under those conditions might not have been justifiable to begin with. This type of incrementalism invariably causes undesirable economic results.

Future Costs and Benefits

As we stated earlier, one of the key principles in making investment decisions is that the economic calculations used to justify any business investment must be based on projections and forecasts of future revenues and costs. It's not enough to assume that the past conditions and experience, such as operating costs or product prices, will continue unchanged and be applicable to a new venture. Although this might seem obvious, there's a common human temptation to extrapolate past conditions instead of carefully forecasting likely developments. We must at all times remember that the past is at best a rough guide, and at worst irrelevant for analysis.

The success of an investment, whether the time horizon is 2, 5, 10, or even 25 years, rests entirely on future events and the uncertainty surrounding them. It therefore behooves the analyst to explore as much as possible the likely changes from present conditions in the key variables relevant to the analysis. If potential deviations in several areas are large, it might be useful to run the analysis under different sets of assumptions, thus testing the sensitivity of the quantitative result to changes in particular variables, such as product volumes, prices, key raw material costs, and so on. (Recall our references to this type of analysis in earlier chapters.)

This task has been eased with the availability of software packages specifically designed for comprehensive sensitivity analysis, yet even basic spreadsheets make the effort of testing a variety of assumptions about key variables quite manageable.

The uncertainty of future conditions affecting an investment is the cause of the risk of not meeting expectations and being left with an insufficient economic return or even an economic loss—the degree of risk being a function of the relative uncertainty about the key variables of the project. Careful estimates and research are often warranted to narrow the margin of error in the predicted conditions on which the analysis is based, although removing all risk is clearly a futile endeavor. Because the basic rationale of making investments relies on a conscious economic trade-off of risk versus reward, as we established earlier, the importance of explicitly addressing key areas of uncertainty should be obvious. Identifying key variables also will be helpful in judging the actual performance of the project after implementation. This is because tracking of these elements is usually much easier than trying to reconstruct the full scope of the incremental project from the overall accounting data flow into which it has been merged.

Incremental Cash Flows

The economic reasoning behind any capital outlay is based strictly on the incremental changes which result directly from the decision to make the investment. In other words, the test question must always be: What is different between the current state of affairs and the new situation introduced by the decision? The differences will be reflected in the form of

- Incremental investment.
- Incremental revenues.
- Incremental costs and expenses.

Moreover, proper economic analysis recognizes only cash flows, that is, the after-tax cash effect of positive or negative funds movements caused by the investment. Any accounting transactions related to the decision but not affecting cash flows are irrelevant for the purpose.

The first basic question to be asked is: What additional investment funds will be required to carry out the chosen alternative? For example, the investment proposal can, in addition to the outlay for new equipment, entail the sale or other disposal of assets that will no longer be used. Therefore, the decision might actually free some previously committed funds. In such a case, it's the net outlay that counts, after any applicable incremental tax effects have been factored in.

Similarly, the next question is: What additional revenues will be created over and above any existing ones? If an investment results in new revenues, but at the same time causes the loss of some existing revenues, only the net impact, after applicable taxes, is relevant for economic analysis.

The third question concerns the costs and expenses that will be added or removed as a result of the investment. The only relevant items here are those costs, including applicable taxes, that will go up or down as a consequence of the investment decision. Any cost or expense that is expected to remain the same before and after the investment has been made is not relevant for the analysis.

These three basic questions illustrate why we refer to the economic analysis of investments as an incremental process. The approach is relative rather than absolute, and is tied closely to carefully defined alternatives and the differences between them. The only data relevant and applicable in any investment analysis are the differential investment funds commitments as well as differential revenues and costs caused by the decision, all viewed in terms of after-tax cash flows.

Relevant Accounting Data

Investment analysis in large part involves the use of data derived from accounting records, not all of which are relevant for the purpose. Accounting conventions that don't involve cash flows must be viewed with extreme caution. This is true particularly with investments that cause changes in operating costs. Therefore we must distinguish clearly between those cost elements that in fact vary with the operation of the new investment and those which only appear to vary. The latter are often accounting allocations which might change in magnitude but do not necessarily represent a true change in costs incurred.

For example, for accounting purposes, general overhead costs (administrative costs, insurance, etc.) might be allocated on the basis of a chosen fixed level of operating volume expressed in units produced. At other times, direct labor hours are the basis for allocation. In the former case, the accounting system will charge a new machine, which has a higher output, with a higher share of overhead than it charged the machine it replaces.

Yet it is likely that there was no actual change in overhead costs that could be attributed to the decision to substitute one machine for the other. Therefore, the reported change in the allocation is not relevant for purposes of economic analysis. The analyst must constantly judge whether there has been a change in the true cash outlays and revenues—not whether the accounting system is redistributing existing costs in a different way. A sound rule that helps prevent being trapped by allocations is to avoid unit costs whenever possible and to perform the analysis on the basis of annual changes in the various cost categories expected to be caused by the investment decision.

We should point out that the growing use of activity-based costing, which we mentioned earlier, is a very positive development insofar as determining relevant data for economic analysis is concerned. Essentially a system which expresses the economic costs and benefits of activities, product lines, and organizational units, activity-based analysis and accounting establishes a flow of information that directly relates to economic choices and trade-offs. Based on a careful assessment of the physical flow of activities, the data collected and stored in the system are in most cases representative of the type of information that must be stipulated when analyzing the changes in revenues and costs brought about by a business investment. The nature of cost assessments and economic allocations is much more transparent than in customary cost accounting systems, although the need for judgment in selecting appropriate data still remains.

Sunk Costs

There's a common temptation to include in the analysis of a new investment all or some portion of outlays that occurred in the past, expenditures that perhaps were incurred preparatory to making the new commitment being considered. No basis in economic analysis exists, however, that would justify such backtracking to expenditures that have already been made and that are not recoverable in part or as a whole. Past decisions simply do not count in the economic trade-off underlying a current investment decision. The basic reason for this is that such sunk costs, even if they are connected in some way to the decision at hand, simply cannot be altered by making the investment now.

If, for example, significant amounts had been spent on research and development of a new product in excess of original plans, the current decision about whether to invest in new facilities to make the product should in no way be affected by those sunk costs. Perhaps the earlier decision to do research and development in retrospect turned out to be less rewarding than expected because of such overspending, and shouldn't have been made at the prior decision point. But now the only relevant question is: If the new investment required to exploit the results of such past research appears economically justified on its own merits from future benefits, should it be undertaken at the present time? There's nothing that can be done about sunk costs, except to learn from any mistakes made.

Another, more specialized situation arises, however, when an incremental productive investment is added to a group of operating facilities, all of which are supported by a large past investment in infrastructure, such as power generation, shipping docks, service networks, and so on, which is not fully utilized at this point. The infrastructure might have been sized to allow for the addition of several future operating investments before the infrastructure itself has to be expanded. In such a case, it'll be relevant to make an economic allocation of an appropriate share of the cost of the existing infrastructure as part of the investment, and to do the same with other similar alternative productive investments, if the strategy of the company calls for continued expansion in the foreseeable future. In contrast, if the current operating investment proposal were the only remaining planned addition, the infrastructure in place would be irrelevant and sunk in the true sense of the word, because no other use of the excess capacity was envisioned. Somewhat differently, if the productive investment triggered another round of infrastructure expansion as part of a long-term growth strategy, a share of such infrastructure would have to be considered part of the productive investment requirements, with other portions allocated to any other current or future expansion investments planned. Again, the effort here must be to judge the specific investment proposition on its full set of implications, and to view the specific proposition within the larger context of the company's strategy and future plans, which is part of the task of framing the issue.

Economic decisions are always forward-looking and must involve only those things that can be changed by the action being decided. This is the essential test of relevance for any element to be included in the analysis.

Refinements of Investment Analysis

We'll now turn to some more realistic and complex examples in order to refine various aspects of both the components of analysis and the methodology itself. No new concepts or techniques will be introduced here; instead, some expanded practical examples will help us work through the implications of many of the points that so far we've only mentioned in passing. As we go through the projects step by step, the essentials of economic investment analysis should become firmly implanted in your mind.

At this point, we'll stress once more that it's always essential as the first step in any economic analysis to carefully define the problem in all of its aspects. From this flows the rationale for deriving the net investment, operating cash flows, the economic life, and any terminal values. Once these detailed aspects have been properly established and understood, the actual calculation of the appropriate yardsticks becomes almost automatic, as we'll see in the examples we're about to discuss.

A Machine Replacement Example

A company is analyzing whether to replace an existing five-year-old machine with a more automatic and faster model. Acquiring a new machine of some sort is viewed as the only reasonable alternative under the circumstances, because the product fabricated on the equipment is expected to continue to be profitable for at least 10 years. Moreover, the markets served could absorb additional output beyond the current capacity, as much as one-third more than the present volume.

The old machine is estimated to have at most five years' life left before it becomes physically worn out, whereas the new machine will operate acceptably for 10 years before it has to be scrapped. The old machine originally cost $25,000 and has a current book value of $12,500, having been depreciated straight-line at $2,500 per year. It can be sold for $15,000 in cash to a ready buyer.

The new machine will cost $40,000 installed. Also to be depreciated straight-line over 10 years, it will likely be salable at book value if it is disposed of prior to the end of its physical life. It has an annual capacity of 125,000 units (compared to the present equipment's 100,000-unit ceiling), and it will produce at lower unit costs for both labor and materials. In fact, the new machine will involve slightly lower total labor costs because of fewer setups, releasing the required time of the skilled mechanic for other productive tasks in the plant. One operator will run the machine as before. Materials usage will be reduced because of a lower level of rejects. The company expects no difficulty in selling the additional volume at the current price of $1.50, and will incur only modest incremental selling and promotional expense in the process.

Such a set of conditions is both common and fairly realistic except for the stable long-term market conditions we've assumed—yet the same analytical principles do apply in a shorter time frame. As we analyze this project, we'll expand on several aspects of economic capital investment analysis and draw generalized conclusions where appropriate.

Net Investment Refined

Net investment has been defined as the net change in cash committed to a project as a result of the investment decision. Two specific changes in cash flow must be considered in this case: (1) the initial outlay of $40,000 for the new machine, which is a straightforward cash commitment, and (2) the recovery of cash from the sale of the old machine.

Because the sale of the old machine is a direct consequence of the decision to replace it, the release of these funds is relevant to the analysis. The amount received, however, will have to be adjusted below the $15,000 cash value because the capital gain realized on the sale is a taxable event. We recall that the book value was only $12,500; thus the company will be taxed on the difference of $2,500. For simplicity, we'll assume that the applicable tax rate is the full corporate income tax rate of 34 percent, resulting in an incremental tax outlay of $850.

We now have all the components of the initial net investment figure relevant for this example:

Cost of the new machine	$40,000
Cash from sale of old machine	(15,000)
Tax payable on capital gain	850
Net investment	$25,850

In this economic analysis, we don't recognize the remaining book value of the old machine, except for its brief role in the income tax calculation. As we've observed before, any funds expended in the past are irrelevant because they are sunk, and we're interested only in the changes caused by the current decision. Therefore, the proceeds from the equipment sale and the incremental tax due on the capital gain are the only relevant elements.

Had the old machine not been salable despite its stated book value of $12,500, the only item of relevance would be the tax savings on the capital loss incurred with this condition. Although there might be a temptation to include the loss of sizable book values in such analyses, doing so would confuse accounting with cash flow economics.

The net investment shown represents the difference between current cash movements, both in and out, that are direct consequences of the investment decision. If we assume that the decision caused working capital (incremental receivables and inventories less incremental payables) to rise in support of the expected higher sales volume, any funds committed for this purpose would also become relevant for our analysis. Similarly, if the current decision were expected to directly cause further capital outlays in later years, such amounts would have to be recognized in the analysis. In our second example, we'll demonstrate how incremental working capital and sequential investments are handled.

Operating Cash Inflows Refined

As we established before, operating cash inflows are the net after-tax cash changes in revenue and cost elements resulting from the investment decision. In our replacement example, we must first carefully sort out the expected conditions to identify relevant differential revenues and costs. Each element should be tested as to whether the decision to replace will make a cash difference in operating conditions. The decision to replace has three significant effects:

- The new machine will bring about greater efficiency that should result in operating savings vis-à-vis the old machine.

- The additional volume of product produced will provide an incremental profit contribution, if we assume that sales efforts will be successful.

- There'll be a tax impact from the change in the amount of depreciation charged against operations.

The calculations in Figure 7–2 illustrate how to deal with these elements in three clearly labeled successive stages.

Stage 1: Operating Savings. Operating savings for the existing level of output (100,000 units) are found by simply comparing the annual costs of operating the two machines at that volume. Although each requires one operator, the new machine will incur $1,000 less in setup costs because the time of the skilled mechanic involved can be employed elsewhere in the plant. We were also told earlier that the new machine uses materials more efficiently, and this attribute will save about $2,000.

Overhead changes, in contrast, are not relevant for this comparison, because overhead costs are represented by *allocations* at the rate of 120 percent of direct labor. The fact that direct labor cost has declined does not automatically mean that spending on overhead has changed. The only change is in the basis of allocation, which in this case happens to be a lower labor cost against which an unvarying percentage rate is applied. Clearly, the plant manager and the office staff still receive the same salaries, and other overhead costs are not affected.

Only if the decision to replace directly caused an actual change in overhead spending, such as higher property taxes, insurance premiums, additional maintenance, and technical and other staff support, would a change have to be reflected in the calculation. Under those conditions, we'd estimate the annual overhead expenditures before and after the installation of the new machine, and calculate the differential cost to be included in the analysis, just as we did for the other differential operating cash inflows.

Whenever we're comparing operating costs, it's usually more appropriate to use annual totals rather than to rely on per unit figures. The latter could cause the analyst to inadvertently apply accounting allocations, which as a rule are irrelevant

FIGURE 7–2

Differential Benefit and Cost Analysis

	Old Machine	New Machine	Relevant Annual Differences
1. Operating savings from current volume of 100,000 units:			
Labor (operator plus setup)	$ 31,000	$ 30,000	$ 1,000
Material	38,000	36,000	2,000
Overhead (120% of direct labor)	37,200	36,000	—*
	$106,200	$102,000	$ 3,000
2. Contribution from additional volume 25,000 units sold at $1.50 per unit		$ 37,500	
Less:			
Labor (no additional operators)		—	
Material cost at 36¢/unit		(9,000)	
Additional selling expense		(11,500)	
Additional promotional expense		(13,000)	$ 4,000
Total savings and additional contribution			$ 7,000
3. Differential depreciation (additional expense; for tax purposes only)	$ 2,500	$ 4,000	$(1,500)
Taxable operating improvements			5,500
Income tax at 34%			1,870
After-tax profit improvement			3,630
Add back depreciation			1,500
After-tax operating cash flow			$ 5,130

*Not relevant, because it represents an allocation only.

for this type of economic analysis—even though they are necessary and appropriate for cost accounting (determining cost of goods sold, inventory values, price estimating, and so on) in line with generally accepted accounting principles.

Stage 2: Contribution from Additional Volume. Now we're ready to determine the incremental contribution from the increased output. This change must be counted as an additional benefit from the decision to replace, because the old machine had a ceiling of 100,000 units of production. The additional sales revenue of $37,500 from the extra 25,000 units available for sale at $1.50 each is relevant, as are any additional costs which can be attributed to the higher sales volume.

We know that the existing operator is able to produce the higher output, and thus there will be no additional labor cost. The higher volume will require additional materials, however, which are charged at the usage rate of the more efficient machine, that is, 36 cents per unit, or $9,000. We've also been told that additional selling and promotional expenses of $24,500 will be incurred to move the higher volume, and these are relevant as well. The combination of operating savings and incremental product contribution totals $7,000.

Stage 3: Differential Depreciation. The only remaining relevant item is the tax impact of differential depreciation. As we discussed in Chapters 1 and 2, depreciation as such is not relevant to cash flows. For purposes of our analysis, it merits attention only because depreciation is tax deductible. Remember that because depreciation charges normally reduce income tax payments, they're called a tax shield. If an investment decision causes higher or lower depreciation charges than before, such a difference must be reflected as a change in the tax shield.

For our replacement example, the differential depreciation for the next five years will be $1,500, an increase due to the higher cost basis of the new machine. We're assuming that straight-line depreciation also is used for tax purposes, to keep the calculations simple.

As is shown in Figure 7–2, the analysis results in taxable operating improvements of $5,500, an incremental tax of $1,870, and a change in after-tax profit of $3,630. The applicable tax rate normally is the rate a company would be paying on any incremental profit. As the final step, the differential depreciation is added back to arrive at the after-tax operating cash flow of $5,130.

In following these steps, we have correctly reflected a tax reduction due to the differential depreciation, but then removed depreciation itself from the picture to leave us with the economic cash effect of the investment.

We could have obtained the same result by doing the analysis in two phases: (1) determining the tax on the operating improvement before depreciation, and (2) directly determining the tax shield effect of the differential depreciation. This would appear as shown below, and as we might expect, the result is exactly the same.

Operating improvement before depreciation	$7,000
Tax at 34%	2,380
After-tax operating improvement	$4,620
Tax shield at 34%* of depreciation of $1,500	510
After-tax operating cash flow	$5,130

*Each dollar of depreciation provides a tax shield of $1 times the applicable tax rate.

Unequal Economic Lives

In Chapter 6, we defined economic life as the length of time over which an investment yields economic benefits. Now we find that a complication has been introduced because of the expected difference in the physical lives of the two machines. Inasmuch as the old machine is assumed to wear out in 5 years, whereas the new one will last for 10 years, with no change in the market for the product assumed, the two investments are comparable only over the next 5 years. After that, the original alternative no longer exists, and a new decision will have to be made at that point in any case. The situation is illustrated in Figure 7–3.

Differential revenues and costs can be defined only as long as both alternatives exist together. After 5 years, the old machine will be gone, which means that we can't analyze the situation beyond 5 years without making some assumptions about the remaining life of the new machine. While we have assumed that the

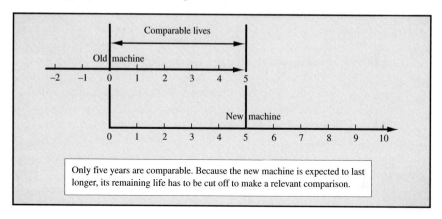

FIGURE 7-3

Overlapping Economic Life Spans

Only five years are comparable. Because the new machine is expected to last longer, its remaining life has to be cut off to make a relevant comparison.

product is likely to be salable for at least the total 10-year life of the new machine, the economic comparison for the current replacement decision can be made only over the 5 years the two alternatives have in common.

There are two ways of handling this problem. First, we can cut off the analysis at the end of Year 5 and assign an assumed recovery value to the new machine at that point, because it should be able to operate well for another 5 years. This terminal value estimate must be counted as a capital recovery in Year 5, that is, its present value should be recognized as a cash flow benefit. This approach is widely used in practice, and usually, as a simplifying assumption, the amount of terminal value is considered to be at least the amount of the remaining book value. But if the asset's value is quite predictable (as is the case with automobiles or trucks), the estimated sales value (adjusted for any tax consequences) is entered in the present value analysis as a cash flow benefit.

An alternative way of dealing with the problem is to assume that the old machine will be replaced by a new one in Year 5, and that a similar replacement will be made in Year 10 when the current new machine wears out. This approach involves a great deal of sequential guessing about possible replacement options 5 and 10 years hence. Moreover, in spite of such extra analytical effort, the economic lives of the two machines still will not be the same. Admittedly, the power of discounting will make the estimates of the later years almost immaterial. On balance, unless there are compelling reasons to develop such a series of replacement assumptions, the cutoff analysis described earlier is far more straightforward and less fraught with judgmental traps.

Capital Additions and Recoveries

The treatment of terminal values deserves a few more comments here. It's quite common for larger projects to require a series of additional capital outlays over time, and eventually provide likely recoveries of at least part of these funds. As a practical matter, any increments of capital committed or recovered must be entered in the present value framework as cash outflows or cash inflows at the point in time when they are expected to occur. This also applies to incremental working capital commitments, which must be shown as outflows when incurred, and which can be assumed to be recovered in part or in total at the end of the economic life of the project.

In our replacement example, we've made no provision for additional working capital in order to keep the problem focused on the other basic refinements. The assumed terminal value of the new machine after five years, however, is to be treated as a capital recovery and entered as a positive cash inflow at the end of Year 5. For simplicity, we'll assume that its economic value (realizable through sale or trade) will be equal to its book value. This would amount to $20,000 ($40,000 less five years' depreciation at $4,000 per year), with no taxable capital gain or loss expected.

We'd have to modify this amount, of course, if circumstances indicated a higher or lower value because of changes in technology or other conditions. Book value is frequently used because it's easy to do, causes no taxable gains or losses, and also because the need for precision in terminal values is diminished by the exponential impact of discounting in later years.

Analytical Framework

With all the basic data at hand, we now can lay out the framework for a present value analysis. We'll assume a 10 percent return standard and again set up the figures in a table. The results, as displayed in Figure 7–4, indicate a sizable net present value of $6,013—assuming, of course, that all of our assumptions are borne out in fact! It suggests that the replacement is desirable, at least on a numerical basis.

As in Chapter 6, we've laid out the cash flow analysis with the present value factors displayed. Using a spreadsheet will, of course, give the same result when the NPV function is applied at 10 percent to the cash flows of Years 1 through 5 (including the year-end recovery), and the net investment of Year 0 is subtracted from the result.

Note that the analysis is affected significantly by the assumed recovery of the book value of $20,000 in Year 5, which amounts to a present value inflow of $12,420. In effect, this terminal inflow reduces the investment, when viewed over the five-year span, to only $13,430 in present value terms as can be determined in row 4 of the analysis by netting the present values of the investment cash flows. Remember, economic analysis requires that the recovery value must be counted as a cash benefit at the end of Year 5, even though there might be no intention of actually selling the machine at that point.

This value inclusion is relevant because the company would have the option of selling the machine at the end of Year 5 and thereby realizing this economic value. After the five years are over, the alternative of selling could, of course, be compared with the alternative of recommitting the realizable value of $20,000 in order to preserve the profitable business at the level of 125,000 units. But these latter considerations deal with a future set of decisions and therefore are not relevant today.

The profitability index (BCR) of the project is positive, as we might expect from the sizable net present value of about $6,000. Dividing $13,430 (net investment of $25,850 less recovery of $12,420) into the operating benefits of $19,443 results in an index of 1.45, which should give the project a favorable ranking against an implied average return of only 10 percent from the company's investment opportunities. Because of the uncertainty implicit in establishing a terminal value, many analysts prefer to express the profitability index by relating the original net investment of $25,850 to the total of all inflows, that is, operating cash flows of $19,443 and capital recoveries of $12,420. In our example, this alternative result would be $31,863 ÷ $25,850 = 1.23, again a very favorable showing even when this more stringent test is applied. Although one could argue for and against either method, consistent application of one of them will be satisfactory.

The internal rate of return has to be found by trial and error when using the present value tables, both for the single sums and for the five-year annuity, because the capital recovery at the end of Year 5 complicates an otherwise straightforward annuity. The analysis can be handled as shown in Figure 7–5. The trial at 15 percent indicates a positive net present value of $1,286, which at 16 percent is reduced to $466. Thus, the precise result lies somewhat above 16 percent. Again, we've used the present value tables of Chapter 6 to illustrate the process, and the reader can confirm the exact result of 16.6 percent by using the *irr* function on a spreadsheet and entering the total cash flow pattern over the five-year period.

A simple risk analysis can be carried out by calculating the present value payback (minimum life) and the annualized net present value. For the former, we must cumulate the present values of operating cash inflows until they approximate the net investment of $25,850, as was made visible in the cumulative present values of Figure 7–4. A quick scanning of the sixth row shows that this will not happen until Year 5, when the terminal value of $20,000, discounted to $12,420, is required to turn the net present value positive. If we are reasonably certain that the machine will be salable as assumed here, we could argue that this terminal value

---

FIGURE 7-4

Present Value Analysis of a Machine Replacement*

	Totals	Year 0	Year 1	Year 2	Year 3	Year 4	Year 5	Year-end 5
Net investment outlay and recovery	$ −5,850	$ −25,850	0	0	0	0	0	$20,000
Operating cash inflows	25,650	0	$ 5,130	$ 5,130	$ 5,130	$ 5,130	$ 5,130	0
Present value factors @ 10%		1.000	0.909	0.826	0.751	0.683	0.621	0.621
Present values of investment cash flows	−13,430	−25,850	0	0	0	0	0	12,420
Present values of operating cash flows	19,443	0	4,663	4,237	3,853	3,504	3,186	0
Cumulative present values		$ −25,850	$ −21,187	$ −16,949	$ −13,097	$ −9,593	$ −6,407	$ 6,013
Net present value @ 10%	$ 6,013							
Profitability index (BCR) @ 10%	1.45/1.23							

*This model is available for download in an interactive format; see "Analytical Support," on p. 319.

should be subtracted from the net investment first. Under this assumption, the net present value payback would occur very early in Year 4. As a general rule, it is advisable not to count on terminal values in such a precise fashion, given that technological and competitive conditions are always subject to change even during a few years' time.

A minor technical question arises here as to whether we should bring the assumed recovery at the end of Year 5 forward in time nearer the payback point to obtain a more precise calculation of minimum life. This would involve a process of iteration, because not only would the present value of the recovery rise, but the sales value of the machine would also be higher in earlier years. Such a refinement normally is not called for even though it can be handled readily by altering the magnitudes on the spreadsheet or by a simulation routine.

The annualized net present value can be found when we divide the net present value in Figure 7–4 by the 10 percent annuity factor in Year 5 from Table 6–II on page 277, or $6,013 ÷ 3.791, which amounts to $1,586 per year. On a spreadsheet, we would use the *pmt* function and specify the 10 percent discount rate, the five periods, and the net present value to obtain this amount. All other aspects being equal, the project would still meet the minimum standard of 10 percent if the annual operating cash inflows over the five years dropped from $5,130 to only $3,544, a possible shrinkage of over 30 percent. If we remove the depreciation tax shield of $510 from this test, the allowable drop in the pure after-tax operating improvement could be better than 34 percent ($1,586 against $4,620) to arrive at a value-neutral result. Remember, however, that under these conditions the project would just meet the return standard, but not create additional shareholder value, even if all the modified cash flows are in fact achieved.

Another way of interpreting the net present value amount from a risk standpoint is to ask how sensitive the result would be to a reduced expected capital recovery at the end of Year 5. The answer to a value-neutral condition can be found readily by reconstituting at the end of Year 5 a dollar amount that has the equivalent present value of the value creation of $6,013. To find this future

---

Present Value Analysis to Find Internal Rate of Return[*]

	Totals	Year 0	Year 1	Year 2	Year 3	Year 4	Year 5	Year-end 5
Investment outlay and recovery	$−5,850	$−25,850	0	0	0	0	0	$20,000
Operating cash inflows	25,650	0	$5,130	$5,130	$ 5,130	$5,130	$5,130	0
Present value factors @ 15%		1.000	—	—	3.352 (annuity)		—	0.497
Present values of cash flows		−25,850	—	—	17,196	—	—	9,940
Net present value @ 15%	1,286							
Present value factors @ 16%		1.000	—	—	3.274 (annuity)		—	0.476
Present values of cash flows		$−25,850	—	—	$16,796	—	—	$ 9,520
Net present value @ 15%	$ 466							
Internal rate of return	16.6%							

[*]This model is available for download in an interactive format; see "Analytical Support," p. 319.

dollar amount, we simply divide the net present value of $6,013 by the single sum factor given in Table 6–I on page 276 for 10 percent in period 5, which is 0.621, to obtain a required amount of $9,684. On a spreadsheet, we would use the FV function and specify the 10 percent discount rate, the five periods, and the net present value of $6,013 to obtain the same result. We can see that if the expected recovery of $20,000 were reduced by about $10,300, the project would still earn the 10 percent standard (at a zero net present value), given that all the other conditions hold.

Although perhaps a little complex, the step-by-step process we've just completed has exposed most of the basic practical issues encountered in the methodology of investment analysis. Let's turn to another illustration which adds the handling of working capital as well as successive investments.

A Business Expansion Example

The cash flow patterns in Figure 7–6 reflect the kinds of commitments and recoveries normally associated with a major business expansion. In the early life of the project, we find not only an outlay for facilities, but also a buildup of working capital during the first and second years. Additional equipment outlays are required during Years 4 and 6, while recoveries of equipment and working capital are made as the economic life comes to an end in Year 8. All cash flows are assumed to represent the expected incremental revenues and expenses caused by the decision to invest, and they have been adjusted for tax

---

F I G U R E   7–6

Present Value Analysis of Complex Expansion Project ($ thousands)[*]

	Totals	Year 0	Year 1	Year 2	Year 3	Year 4	Year 5	Year 6	Year 7	Year 8
Equipment outlays and recovery[†]	$–130,000	$–130,000	0	0	0	$–15,000	0	$–10,000	0	$25,000
Working capital outlays and recovery[‡]	–10,000	0	$–25,000	$–20,000	0	0	0	0	0	35,000
Operating cash inflows	270,000	0	20,000	40,000	$40,000	$40,000	$50,000	$50,000	$20,000	10,000
Total project cash flows	130,000	–130,000	–5,000	20,000	40,000	25,000	50,000	40,000	20,000	70,000
Present value factors @ 12%		1.000	0.893	0.797	0.712	0.636	0.567	0.507	0.452	0.404
Present values of investment cash flows		–130,000	–22,325	–15,940	0	–9,540	0	–5,070	0	24,240
Present values of operating cash flows		0	17,860	31,880	28,480	25,440	28,350	25,350	9,040	4,040
Present values of total cash flows		–130,000	–4,465	15,940	28,480	15,900	28,350	20,280	9,040	28,280
Cumulative present values		$–130,000	$–134,465	$–118,525	$–90,045	$–74,145	$–45,795	$–25,515	$–16,475	$11,805
Net present value @ 12%	11,805									
Profitability index (BCR) @ 12%	1.09									
Internal rate of return	13.9%									
Present value payback @12% (requires part of capital recovery)	Year 8									

---

[*]This model is available for download in an interactive format; see "Analytical Support," p. 319.

[†]Additional depreciation on investments in Years 4 and 6 has been reflected in the cash flows.

[‡]Assume loss in liquidation of $10,000.

consequences along the lines we discussed in our first example. The periodic operating cash flows show a growth stage, a peak in the middle years, and decline toward the end.

No new concepts are required for us to deal with this investment example. As we know from Chapter 2, new working capital additions (incremental inventories and receivables less new trade obligations) represent a commitment of resources just as definite as an expenditure for buildings and equipment, except that no depreciation write-off is involved. If all inventories and receivables are expected to be successfully liquidated at the end of the economic life, these funds (net of payables) will become a cash inflow at that point, a capital recovery. If we assume some fraction of this investment to be not salable or uncollectible, the figure must be lowered accordingly.

Additional capital expenditures for equipment during the life of the project are simply recognized as cash outflows when incurred. We must take care, however, to reflect the additional depreciation pattern in each case as additional tax shields during future operating periods and we can assume that this was done in the cash flows shown. Of course, it's quite easy to lay out these patterns over time in successive series. The uneven cash flows of this project present no problems when we use spreadsheets or calculators to find the net present value of the overall cash flow pattern and derive directly the other measures listed. For the present value payback, the present values for each period must be calculated and accumulated period by period. But to demonstrate the background structure of the calculations, we've again employed the present value tables to show the actual factors involved.

As was shown in Figure 7–6, the expected result of the project is a positive net present value of almost $12 million. The profitability index is about 1.1, while the internal rate of return is approximately 14 percent, and present value payback is not achieved until Year 8, requiring about one-half of the terminal recovery. These results leave little margin for error. When we annualize the net present value, the result suggests that the annual operating cash inflows can be reduced by $11,815 ÷ 4.968, or at most, by about $2.4 million per year.

We've gone about as far as we can to carry out the quantitative financial aspects of the analysis with the data at hand. The various judgments leading to the final decision call for much more insight into the nature of the product, the technology, the requirements and outlook of the marketplace, the competitive setting, and so on. As we outlined in the first section of this chapter, we cannot overemphasize the importance of those areas for any well-informed business investment decision.

Mutually Exclusive Alternatives

So far we've dealt with individual investment projects without regard to the broader question of how these projects fit into the whole range of possibilities open to a company. We've assumed that our examples were independent investment projects that could be evaluated and ranked against other independent projects. At times, however, managers face the issue of evaluating projects that are not independent of each other. Such is the case with sets of different alternatives which might be available for achieving the same purpose. These are called mutually exclusive alternatives, because if one is chosen, the others are eliminated by that very decision.

Analyzing such a situation is merely a special case of economic analysis which uses the same underlying concepts as before but emphasizes incremental reasoning. To illustrate, let's first take the simple case of a choice between continuing a current process through relatively high maintenance outlays versus an up-front expenditure to replace the equipment, which entails low maintenance costs and a significant terminal value. Next, we'll take up the issue of choosing between a full-fledged, state-of-the-art solution to a facility upgrade versus an economy solution with lower capital costs and somewhat lower benefits, each of which can serve the purpose equally well. Finally, we'll discuss three individually feasible alternatives of investing in facilities and working capital to produce and sell a modified product and compare the economic implications of the choice.

Maintain versus Replace

This issue involves the often encountered trade-off of carrying on an operation by maintaining supporting equipment at significantly higher cost levels than would be required for new items, but forgoing the near-term outlay of funding new equipment. The decision must be seen within a larger context of market and technological change, and also withstand the question of whether maintenance of current equipment will in fact ensure an uninterrupted flow of quality products or services. Our example in Figure 7–7 assumes that over a five-year horizon maintenance expenditures will rise from $40,000 in Year 1, until in Year 3 a partial overhaul of $100,000 becomes necessary in addition to $80,000 in regular maintenance, after which maintenance expenditures will settle back to earlier levels.

FIGURE 7–7

Comparison of Maintain Versus Replace: I. Maintain[*]

	Totals	Year 0	Year 1	Year 2	Year 3	Year 4	Year 5
Maintenance expenditures	$−350,000	0	$−40,000	$−60,000	$−180,000	$ −30,000	$ −40,000
Tax rate			36%	36%	36%	36%	36%
After-tax cost	−224,000	0	−25,600	−38,400	−115,200	−19,200	−25,600
Depreciation tax shield	0	0	0	0	0	0	0
Total project cash outflows	−224,000	0	−25,600	−38,400	−115,200	−19,200	−25,600
Present value factors @ 12%		1.000	0.893	0.797	0.712	0.636	0.567
Present values of cash outflows		0	−22,861	−30,605	−82,022	−12,211	−14,515
Cumulative present values		0	$−22,861	$−53,466	$−135,488	$−147,699	$−162,214
Net present value cost @ 12%	$ −162,214						
Annualized net present value cost @ 12%	$ −45,000						

[*]This model is available for download in an interactive format; see "Analytical Support," p. 319.

FIGURE 7–8

Comparison of Maintain Versus Replace: I. Replace*

	Totals	Year 0	Year 1	Year 2	Year 3	Year 4	Year 5
Equipment outlay and recovery	$ −300,000	$ −400,000	0	0	0	0	$ 100,000
Maintenance expenditures	−50,000	0	$ −8,000	$ −9,000	$ −10,000	$ −11,000	−12,000
Tax rate			36%	36%	36%	36%	36%
After-tax cost	−32,000	0	−5,120	−5,760	−6,400	−7,040	−7,680
Depreciation tax shield ($80,000 × .36)	144,000	0	28,800	28,800	28,800	28,800	28,800
Total project cash flows (incl. recovery)	$ −188,000	−400,000	23,680	23,040	22,400	21,760	121,120
Present value factors @ 12%		1.000	0.893	0.797	0.712	0.636	0.567
Present values of cash flows		−400,000	21,146	18,363	15,949	13,839	68,675
Cumulative present values		$ −400,000	$ −378,854	$ −360,491	$ −344,542	$ −330,703	$ −262,028
Net present value cost @ 12%	$ −262,028						
Annualized net present value cost @ 12%	$ −72,689						

*This model is available for download in an interactive format; see "Analytical Support" on p. 319.

The replacement alternative shown in Figure 7–8 requires a current outlay for equipment of $400,000, which still will be worth $100,000 (tax-adjusted) at the end of Year 5, and which will be depreciated straight-line over five years. Maintenance costs rise slowly from $8,000 in Year 1 to $12,000 in Year 5.

It so happens that total cash outlays and recoveries are equal for both alternatives over the five years at $350,000 each, but with significant timing differences. A return standard of 12 percent has been stipulated, and the two alternatives are assumed to be the only feasible options of dealing with this situation.

Both analyses lay out the cash flow patterns in our now familiar format, focusing on the respective net present value cost, both in total and on an annualized basis. As they are two different ways of achieving the same objective, it's possible to use this cost focus. Note the significant impact of the tax shield effect of depreciation in the second alternative, which turns annual cash flows positive. If we assume that either alternative will serve the product/service requirements equally well, the first alternative is far superior from an economic standpoint, representing about $100,000 less in present value cost. As we mentioned, the critical question, however, relates to whether in fact the first alternative will be able to perform to expectations, especially if heavy maintenance and the Year 3 overhaul were to cause business interruptions and lower volume and quality. The difference in net present value cost of the second alternative could be viewed as broad insurance against such potential disruptions, but it might be useful to try to quantify the cost of potential interruptions directly in analyzing the first alternative.

Full-Fledged Versus Economy Solution

Another example of mutually exclusive alternatives is the often encountered situation where a full-fledged solution to a facility improvement or expansion, or for support equipment like computer systems, will create value by comfortably exceeding the return standard. On closer examination there might, however, be an economy solution which for significantly lower capital outlays and somewhat lower benefits creates even more value. Once these alternatives are stipulated and analyzed, the economic results clearly point to the economy version, and an incremental analysis demonstrates the value destruction caused by the additional capital outlay required in the full-fledged version. The practical issue in such a scenario is that because the full-fledged version easily meets the standard, the economy version might not even be analyzed and surfaced. The reason for this is simply that the full-fledged version also satisfies the less tangible but often encountered desire to have the latest in design, all possible "bells and whistles," and an extra margin of performance, most of which might not be relevant to the specific solution sought.

The analysis of the full-fledged version in Figure 7–9 shows a seven-year project with an outlay of $11.5 million, a recovery of $1.0 million in Year 7, and level annual benefits of $4.0 million before taxes. For simplicity we've assumed level cash flows and straight-line depreciation over seven years, and the capital recovery in Year 7 is a net value after taxes. The company's return standard is 14 percent, and as the analysis shows, the project has a net present value of about $2.2 million, a profitability index of 1.2, and will be paid back in present value terms between Year 5 and Year 6, depending on the treatment of the recovery in Year 7. Thus, this project appears quite favorable.

When we analyze the economy alternative in Figure 7–10, however, an even more favorable result emerges. For an outlay of only $8.75 million, and a smaller recovery of $0.75 million, benefits are expected to be 10 percent less at $3.6 million per year. But when the analysis is completed, the net present value is higher by about $1.0 million, the profitability index rises to 1.36, and the IRR jumps to 25 percent. Payback is achieved between Years 4 and 5. If thorough examination of the situation suggests that the objectives of the project can in fact be met by the economy alternative, this version is clearly superior.

FIGURE 7–9

Comparing Alternatives: Full-Fledged Solution ($ thousands)[*]

	Totals	Year 0	Year 1	Year 2	Year 3	Year 4	Year 5	Year 6	Year 7
Equipment outlay and recovery	$-10,500	$-11,500	0	0	0	0	0	0	$1,000
Annual benefits	28,000	0	$ 4,000	$ 4,000	$ 4,000	$ 4,000	$4,000	$4,000	4,000
Tax rate			36%	36%	36%	36%	36%	36%	36%
After-tax benefits	17,920	0	2,560	2,560	2,560	2,560	2,560	2,560	2,560
Depreciation tax shield ($1,500 × .36)	3,780	0	540	540	540	540	540	540	540
Total project cash flows (including recovery)	11,200	$-11,500	3,100	3,100	3,100	3,100	3,100	3,100	4,100
Present value factors @ 14%			1.000	0.877	0.769	0.675	0.592	0.519	0.456	0.400
Present values of cash flows		-11,500	2,719	2,384	2,093	1,835	1,609	1,414	1,640
Cumulative present values		$-11,500	$-8,781	$-6,397	$-4,305	$-2,470	$-861	$ 553	$2,193
Net present value @ 14%	$ 2,193								
Profitability index (BCR) @ 14%	1.19								
Internal rate of return	19.9%								
Present value payback @ 14%	Year 6								

*This model is available for download in an interactive format; see "Analytical Support," p. 319.

Comparing Alternatives: Economy Solution ($ thousands)*

	Totals	Year 0	Year 1	Year 2	Year 3	Year 4	Year 5	Year 6	Year 7
Equipment outlay and recovery	$ −8,000	$−8,750	0	0	0	0	0	0	$ 750
Annual benefits	25,200	0	$ 3,600	$ 3,600	$ 3,600	$3,600	$3,600	$3,600	3,600
Tax rate			36%	36%	36%	36%	36%	36%	36%
After-tax benefits	16,128	0	2,304	2,304	2,304	2,304	2,304	2,304	2,304
Depreciation tax shield ($1,150 × .36)	2,898	0	414	414	414	414	414	414	414
Total project cash flows (including recovery)	11,026	−8,750	2,718	2,718	2,718	2,718	2,718	2,718	3,468
Present value factors @ 14%		1.000	0.877	0.769	0.675	0.592	0.519	0.456	0.400
Present values of cash flows		−8,750	2,384	2,090	1,835	1,609	1,411	1,239	1,387
Cumulative present values		$−8,750	$−6,366	$−4,276	$−2,442	$−832	$ 578	$1,818	$3,205
Net present value @ 14%	$ 3,205								
Profitability index (BCR) @ 14%	1.36								
Internal rate of return	25.0%								
Present value payback @ 14%	Year 5								

*This model is available for download in an interactive format; see "Analytical Support," p. 319.

To illustrate the value impact of choosing the full-fledged version over the economy alternative, we've prepared a differential analysis in Figure 7–11, by calculating the differences in the outlays and benefits, and deriving the present value measures from these. The results clearly show that the incremental outlay of $2.75 million achieves only $0.4 million per year incremental benefits, causing a negative net present value of about $1.0 million, with all other measures indicating a bad investment. The trade-off is clearly a poor one, and this simple example again illustrates the critical importance of defining all relevant alternatives for a project early on, to ensure that a company's resources are deployed with the highest possible value creation potential in net present value terms.

Comparing Alternatives: Differential Analysis ($ thousands)*

	Totals	Year 0	Year 1	Year 2	Year 3	Year 4	Year 5	Year 6	Year 7
Equipment outlay and recovery	$ −2,500	$−2,750	0	0	0	0	0	0	$ 250
Annual benefits	2,800	0	$ 400	$ 400	$ 400	$ 400	$ 400	$ 400	400
Tax rate			36%	36%	36%	36%	36%	36%	36%
After-tax benefits	1,792	0	256	256	256	256	256	256	256
Depreciation tax shield ($350 × .36)	882	0	126	126	126	126	126	126	126
Total project cash flows (including recovery)	174	$−2,750	382	382	382	382	382	382	632
Present value factors @ 14%		1.000	0.877	0.769	0.675	0.592	0.519	0.456	0.400
Present values of cash flows		−2,750	335	294	258	226	198	174	253
Cumulative present values		$−2,750	$−2,415	$−2,121	$−1,863	$−1,637	$−1,439	$−1,265	$−1,012
Net present value @ 14%	$ −1,012								
Profitability index (BCR) @ 14%	0.63								
Internal rate of return	1.46%								
Present value payback @ 14%	none								

*This model is available for download in an interactive format; see "Analytical Support," p. 319.

Comparing Different Scenarios

Carrying the analysis of the previous example a little further, we can take a more general case in which three potential ways of achieving the implementation of a new product investment have been identified, analyzed, and quantified. Each alternative will achieve the purpose over the next seven to eight years, and the company's return standard is 14 percent. The first alternative represents existing technology, the second a more costly but advanced process, and the third provides higher capacity as well as the advanced process. Let's assume further that both the quality of the estimates and the uncertainty about the outcomes are the same in all three cases—which is not quite realistic but simplifies our example here.

The key dimensions of the three alternatives are presented as follows:

Alternative	Net Investment	Annual Inflows	Terminal Value
(1) Standard	$500,000	$112,000	$150,000
(2) Advanced	600,000	128,000	150,000
(3) Expanded	750,000	169,000	200,000

The three major investment measures were calculated and appear as follows:

Alternative	Net Present Value (NPV)	Internal Rate of Return (IRR)	Profitability Index (BCR)
(1) Standard	$40,256	16.3%	1.08
(2) Advanced	8,864	14.4%	1.01
(3) Expanded	54,672	16.1%	1.07

The first observation is that all three alternatives meet the company standard by every measure, although to different degrees. The issue is to select the best of the three alternatives, however, and we have to contend with somewhat different signals. From a net present value standpoint, alternative 3 is clearly best, while the IRR and BCR results favor alternative 1.

We must remember that the objective of successful investment is to create an economic trade-off that will increase shareholder value. Because only one alternative can be chosen, this would argue for alternative 3 with the highest net present value. But alternative 3 is also the most expensive one, and its creation of value per dollar invested (BCR) is somewhat less than alternative 1.

A useful way of thinking through the purely economic aspects of mutually exclusive alternatives is again to examine the incremental benefits obtained as one moves from the least expensive to the most expensive, as we did in the prior example. In this situation, the incremental investment for alternative 2 is $100,000, but it reduces net present value from $40,256 to $8,864. This clearly is not desirable, and the lower IRR and BCR measures for alternative 2 confirm this. Going from alternative 1 to alternative 3, however, results in an incremental investment of $250,000, which improves net present value by $14,416. This incremental investment certainly exceeds the company standard of 14 percent, because its IRR can be calculated at 15.7 percent. This result is not quite as attractive as alternative 1 with an IRR of 16.3 percent—but then the question becomes whether the company has any other projects that might give a return better than 15.7 percent. If not, alternative 3 should be favored, assuming that all other judgmental aspects are comparable among the three alternatives—especially that the higher volume of business can in fact be counted on.

Many other factors, of course, will have to be considered for a final decision, such as the relative technological and operational risks of the alternatives, issues of implementation, and market aspects. What we've shown here is the interpretation of the economic results alone to illustrate their use in assessing value creation.

Dealing with Risk and Changing Circumstances

Throughout this discussion we have dealt with estimates of future costs and benefits largely as givens. In practice, estimates are more often than not proved wrong by actual experience—in either direction. When projects are performing better than expected, all is well. When actual results are disappointing, however, economic analysis becomes important if it is possible to terminate the project in midstream. Such an option is particularly important if a project contains another decision point for additional investment.

Figure 7–12 illustrates such a situation, where the first four years of the project's life have passed with disappointing results, and management is faced with whether or not to fund the second investment phase. The cardinal rule of economics to remember here is that past investments and cash flows are sunk, and that only present and future cash flows affect the decision to continue or quit. The economic trade-off, therefore, is between

- The net present value of the additional investment and the revised future cash flows on the one hand, and
- Any recovery value of the investment in place on the other.

If no additional investment is required, the trade-off is between the present value of expected future cash flows and the recovery value. In either case, the view taken must extend from the decision point onward into the future.

The same argument can be made when a company is faced with the decision to produce a product or service after having spent much more than planned on research and development. We touched on this issue earlier in our discussion of sunk costs. With hindsight, the past decision to invest in the total project was a poor one, because had this higher level of research spending been anticipated, the total project would not have met the return standard. But the current decision to proceed with funding the follow-on production stage might very well remain a sound economic choice, if the estimates about future price, volume, and cost continue to be favorable.

The weight of past mistakes cannot be allowed to suppress sound current judgment, which must be based on only relevant factors, that is, present and future conditions which can be affected by a current decision. At the same time, it should be obvious that management must be careful not to create a series of

FIGURE   7–12

Actual Results Lower than Expected—New Decision Required

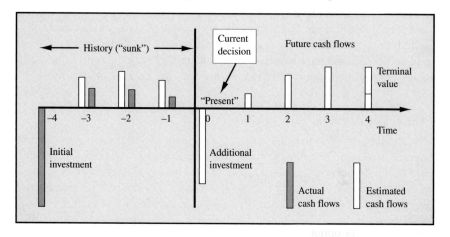

sunk costs through a pattern of such investments, each of which as a whole turns out to be unsatisfactory because of early overruns—despite the attractiveness of later stages. Remember, sunk costs were future costs at one time, and should have been properly estimated and refined when they were relevant to the initial decision.

Specifying Risk

The estimates used to analyze business investments are inevitably uncertain because they are dealing with future conditions. As we stated before, business investments involve risk because of the uncertainties surrounding the key variables used. The analyst who prepares the investment calculations and managers who use these results for decision making must allow for a whole range of possible outcomes. Even the best estimates can go wrong as events unfold, yet decisions always have to be made in advance of the actual experience.

The analytical and judgmental challenge is to assess the risk inherent in the key variables of the investment proposal. Such risk analysis can take many forms. In earlier chapters, we mentioned sensitivity analysis as a formal means of testing the impact of changes in key assumptions. This process can be very informal, such as back-of-the-envelope reasoning, or it can involve systematically working through the impact of assumed changes in revenues, operating savings, costs, size of outlays, recovery of capital, and so on, either singly or in combination, and testing the impact on the results. We've also discussed using two of the present value measures, the present value payback and the annualized net present value, as simple risk assessment tools, which allow the user to test the impact of overall changes in periodic cash flows and terminal recoveries.

Earlier we briefly mentioned a more specific approach which involves using differing scenarios based on ranges of estimates, either for the total cash
flows, or for individual key variables making up the cash flows. This method allows the decision maker to examine the most optimistic and pessimistic cases as
well as the most likely figures, and it is far superior to single-point estimating, especially for significant investments. We'll first discuss the use of ranges of estimates, and their refined application in probabilistic simulation in more detail
below. Finally, we'll touch on the subject of risk-adjusted rates.

Ranges of Estimates

Risk can be defined as the degree of variation in the actual versus estimated cash
benefit levels of an investment. The wider the possible deviations, the greater the
risk. Therefore, using a range of estimates is a more direct approach to investment
risk analysis. It might not be necessary to do this for all types of investments, however, because degrees of risk vary widely among business and financial investments, as do the relative importance and magnitude of the investments themselves.

For example, the risk involved in holding a U.S. government bond is very
small indeed, because default on the interest payments and ultimate repayment of
principal is extremely unlikely. Therefore, the range of possible benefits from the
bond investment is narrowly focused on the contractual payments—in effect no
range at all. In contrast, the risk of a business investment for a product or service
is a function of the whole range of possible benefit levels that can go from very
positive cash flows to negative loss conditions. The uncertainty surrounding these
outcomes poses a challenge to the analyst and the decision maker.

The "single-point" estimates of annual cash flow projections we've used so
far are the expected results based on the best judgment of the analyst and the type
of information available. In effect, they amount to an average of the possible outcomes, implicitly weighed by their respective probabilities. By introducing a
range of high, low, and expected levels of annual cash inflows and outflows, the
analyst can employ a form of sensitivity analysis to indicate the consequences of
expected fluctuations in the annual results—and thus the degree of risk. At times,
past experience can provide clues to the range of future outcomes, but essentially, the projection of future conditions has to be judgmental and based on specific forward-looking estimates. The impact of changes in key variables on, say,
net present value also can be shown in graphic form in diagrams displaying the
impact on the total result for each variable on a scale, which allows the decision
maker to assess, for example, how important the relative impact of a change in
price is compared to changes in key cost elements. A number of analytical computer programs have such built-in capabilities, and graph the results in bar charts
that show the relative size of the change induced by modifying each variable.

The decision maker must assess the likelihood that the range of estimated
outcomes fairly expresses the characteristics of the project, and decide whether
the expected outcome is sufficiently attractive to compensate for the possibility
that the actual results might vary as defined. Risk assessment in essence comes

down to how comfortable the decision maker is with the possibility of experiencing adverse results—that is, a very personal risk preference or risk aversion. Stipulating a range helps the responsible person or group visualize the possible extremes in the expected results.

Business Investments as Options

When we discussed sequential investments earlier, our examples involved stages of commitments, such as research and development followed by implementation, or different stages of supporting a product or service expansion. We were looking at these stages in retrospect. At times, however, companies face strategic investment choices which offer sequential commitments and thus the option to abandon a project if at an early stage it becomes clear that the overall concept is a failure. Recognizing, during the initial analysis, the points in a complex project's pattern where the option to abandon exists and planning to act on the results after implementation can help reduce the impact of value destruction as expressed by changes in net present value.

For example, if a company wishes to invest in applying a new technology, recognizing that the chance of success is limited to say, 60 percent, it will be useful to develop a comparative analysis which includes the option to abandon early in the economic life, given that results are unacceptable. Two scenarios can be drawn up, one specifying the cash flow pattern given success, the other specifying the cash flow implications of failure. Weighting the cash flows by their respective probabilities, and discounting the expected cash flows at the return standard applicable to the type of business, the expected net present value can be determined, as shown in Figure 7–13. Without the option to abandon, as shown in the top portion of the analysis, the negative expected net present value is far larger than when the option to abandon is considered in the bottom portion. Note that there is a ramp-up of cash flow benefits if the project is successful, and a leveling out of negative cash flows in the unsuccessful situation. Viewed by itself, the success alternative provides a significant positive net present value of $103 million, as shown below the first alternative, but given the high chance of failure this is obviously not a realistic picture. The probability-weighted expected net present value reflects the risk/reward trade-off situation better.

Clearly, it's unlikely that the unsuccessful alternative would be maintained for its seven-year life, and accordingly, the option to abandon has been included in Year 3, with provision for a recovery of some of the initial investment built in. Note also that we have used a fairly high return standard of 18 percent, reflecting the risky nature of the business. Many managers would probably raise this hurdle even higher given the uncertainty, but this brings up the issue of doubly adjusting for risk in both the cash flows and the discount rate. We'll discuss multiple standards later.

The decision makers still face the question of whether this uncertain investment fits their risk preferences, that is, whether a chance of 60 percent success is sufficient for the first, modest investment stage. But they might want to consider another option in the form of a potential large expansion stage in the second year,

FIGURE 7–13

Investing in New Technology ($ Millions)

Stage 1 Investment Without Option to Abandon	Totals	Year 0	Year 1	Year 2	Year 3	Year 4	Year 5	Year 6	Year 7
After-tax cash flows if successful	$ 440	$-250	$ 70	$ 80	$ 90	$ 100	$ 110	$ 120	$ 120
After-tax cash flows if unsuccessful	-860	-250	-110	-90	-90	-80	-80	-80	-80
Weighted cash flows—success 60%	164	-250	42	48	54	60	66	72	72
Weighted cash flows—failure 40%	-494	-250	-44	-36	-36	-32	-32	-32	-32
Expected cash flows	-80	-250	-2	12	18	28	34	40	40
Present value factors @ 18%		1.000	0.847	0.718	0.609	0.516	0.437	0.370	0.314
Present values of cash flows		-250	-2	9	11	14	15	15	13
Cumulative present values		$-250	$-252	$-243	$-232	$-218	$-203	$-188	$-175
Expected net present value @ 18%	-175								
Net present value if succcessful @ 18%	103								
With Option to Abandon									
After-tax cash flows if successful	$ 440	$-250	$ 70	$ 80	$ 90	$ 100	$ 110	$ 120	$ 120
After-tax cash flows if unsuccessful	-390	-250	-110	-90	60	0	0	0	0
Weighted cash flows—success 60%	164	-250	42	48	54	60	66	72	72
Weighted cash flows—failure 40%	-306	-250	-44	-36	24	0	0	0	0
Expected cash flows	108	-250	-2	12	78	60	66	72	72
Present value factors @ 18%		1.000	0.847	0.718	0.609	0.516	0.437	0.370	0.314
Present values of cash flows		-250	-2	9	48	31	29	27	23
Cumulative present values		$-250	$-252	$-243	$-196	$-165	$-136	$-109	$-87
Expected net present value @ 18%	$ -87								

FIGURE 7–14

Investing in New Technology ($ millions)

Stage 2 Investment Given Success of Stage 1	Totals	Year 0	Year 1	Year 2	Year 3	Year 4	Year 5	Year 6	Year 7
After-tax cash flows if successful	$ 1,700	0	0	$-1,000	$ 400	$ 500	$ 600	$ 600	$ 600
After-tax cash flows if unsuccessful	-1,350	0	0	-1,000	-450	-300	400	0	0
Weighted cash flows—success 90%	1,430	0	0	-1,000	360	450	540	540	540
Weighted cash flows—failure 10%	-1,035	0	0	-1,000	-45	-30	40	0	0
Expected cash flows	1,395	0	0	-1,000	315	420	580	540	540
Present value factors @ 18%		1.000	0.847	0.718	0.609	0.516	0.437	0.370	0.314
Present values of cash flows		0	0	-718	192	217	253	200	170
Cumulative present values		0	0	$ -718	$-526	$-309	$ -56	$ 144	$ 313
Expected net present value @ 18%	$ 313								

given that the technology has been proven workable in the first year. The chances of success at that point will have dramatically improved, and the larger follow-on investment could be viewed as a 90 percent success bet. Such a set of conditions is very typical in high technology companies, where initial investments in new advances can lead to significant exploitation of the full potential, once a smaller-scale project has proved out. Note in Figure 7–14 the sizable investment in Year 2, followed by rising cash flow benefits.

The risk of failure was built into the analysis at 10 percent, and the expected cash flow and net present value results appear quite favorable, because the decision can be held off until success has been achieved in the first stage. Viewed by itself this analysis indicates an expected net present value of $313 million. But because the decision on the first stage has to be made in Year 0, we must adjust the net present value for the combined stages of the whole project by taking the expected net present value of the first stage of -87 million (with the option to abandon built in), and add to it 60 percent of the expected net present value of the second stage (0.6 × $313) or $188 million, for a total expectation of $101 million.

Using the option to abandon reduced the negative results of the first stage significantly, and adding the deferrable option to expand made the whole project attractive from a net present value standpoint, even though the individual outcomes of the two stages remain subject to the probabilities assigned to them. Thus this type of analysis has provided a clearer picture of the dimensions of the risk/reward trade-offs involved.

Probabilistic Simulation

A more refined approach to risk assessment consists of estimating ranges or probabilities not only for the total annual cash flows, but also for the individual key variables that make up these cash flows. Probability distributions are then assigned to the likelihood of the outcomes for each of the variables. A number of the variables are usually interdependent, such as changes in price causing changes in volume, and it is helpful to define such interdependencies and build them into the analysis. The possible outcomes of the project can then be simulated by running many iterations on the computer. The method is an extension of sensitivity analysis in that the potential changes in many variables are evaluated both simultaneously and relative to each other.

The result is a range of possible annual cash inflows in the form of a probability distribution, or even a range of net present values or internal rates of return arrayed by probability. Such a risk profile allows the decision maker to think about the relative attractiveness of a project in terms of statements such as, "chances are 9 out of 10 that the project will meet the minimum standard of 10 percent," or, "there is a probability of 60 percent that the net present value of the project will be at least $1.0 million or better." Cumulative probability distributions such as those shown in Figure 7–15 can be drawn up as an assist. The relative ease with which such simulations can be carried out does not eliminate the many practical issues involved in assigning specific probability distributions to the individual variables in the first place, or ease the problem of interpreting the final results. There are a number of commercial simulation models available to spreadsheet users, which permit doing this type of analysis to various degrees of complexity.

As we said before, judging both the likelihood of an event and one's own attitude toward the risk expressed in this fashion is a highly personal response that often defies precise quantification. The amount of risk a decision maker will accept is largely a matter of personal experience and preference. In addition, investment decisions in a business setting are as much a function of complex personal and group dynamics as they are dependent on the pure analytical results, the quality of presentation, and examination of specific economic data.

FIGURE 7–15

Cumulative Probability Distribution for Two Projects

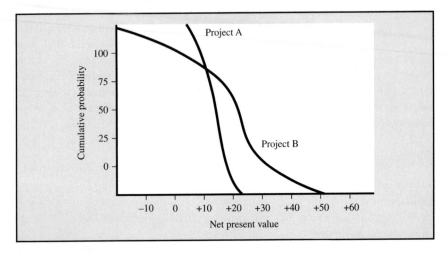

Risk-Adjusted Return Standards

Another way of adjusting for risk is to modify the return standard itself to include a risk premium where warranted. Such a standard is called a risk-adjusted discount rate (RADR). In a sense, the concept is quite simple—the greater the risk, the higher the return desired from the investment. Also, this reasoning is intuitively attractive to business decision makers, because the process parallels the way we think about personal investments. At the same time, however, letting the return standard be the main expression of riskiness deals only indirectly with the true source of risk, that is, the uncertainty about the investment cash flows themselves and the specific key variables they contain. Also, the higher discount rate applies over the total life span, whereas specific risks may occur at different points in the time pattern. This makes choosing a risk-adjusted rate fairly subjective.

It's usually preferable to expend considerable thought and analysis on understanding and evaluating the riskiness of the cash flows and the key drivers implicit in them, to avoid applying arbitrarily high return standards to specific projects or businesses. Decision theory can be employed to develop the so-called certainty equivalent (C-E) of a project, using decision trees and the probabilistic methodology mentioned earlier. The certainty equivalent, a concept closely related to expected value, is the value a decision maker would be willing to trade off for the probability distribution defined in the project. This is a fairly sophisticated process and requires techniques that go beyond the scope of this book. The references at the end of this chapter provide further insight.

Investments in businesses subject to wide profit swings and competitive pressures should command a significant premium above the return standard, while fairly predictable businesses might find a lesser return acceptable. This is no different from recognizing the basic risk/reward trade-off implicit in the premiums commanded by interest-bearing financial instruments, depending on the degree of risk involved, ranging from essentially risk-free government bonds to so-called junk bonds. Remember also that the corporate cost of capital, the basic minimum standard for value creation, has a built-in allowance for not only the market risk, but also the specific risk implicit in a company's business. This is discussed in detail in Chapter 8.

When multiple return standards are employed, it's done on the assumption that a diversified company can use different standards which, in combination, will ensure an appropriate overall return to the shareholders and also fairly reflect the risk exposure of the individual lines of business. We'll return to the basis for earnings standards in Chapter 8, and discuss both the conceptual and practical issues involved.

When to Use Investment Measures

During our discussion of the investment measures in Chapter 6, and while using them with different examples in this chapter, we cautioned the reader about various shortcomings and issues of interpretation. We'll now review and expand some of these caveats. Basically, investment analysis measures exist to help analysts and managers determine whether a project meets the return standard established for the business and thereby satisfies the basic value creation criterion of exceeding the company's cost of capital. Also, they assist in ranking the relative desirability of a group of proposals during the capital budgeting process. If the projects being considered are independent of each other, the time-adjusted measures of net present value, profitability index, discounted payback, and internal rate of return will singly or in combination properly reflect the projects' relative economic attractiveness and result in an appropriate ranking sequence, although in practice the net present value criterion is the most commonly used and accepted measure.

Shown in Figure 7–16 is a comparative view of the consistent readings of net present value, internal rate of return, and present value payback as applied to three types of independent projects. Project A exceeds the company standard, project B falls short of the standard, and project C just meets the standard. In every case, each measure gives an economic reading that indicates the proper ranking of the project.

As we demonstrated earlier, uneven lives of capital investments pose complications that are handled by adjusting the analysis to equalize the time spans for purposes of comparison. This can be done by truncating the life of a project with an assumed recovery of funds from disposal at an earlier point, as in our replacement example in Figure 7–3, or by extending the shorter alternative by assuming repeated investment. Mutually exclusive projects with different lives also can be compared by annualizing their net present values over their respective economic lives to determine their respective annual equivalent benefits or cost. This process simply calls for dividing the net present value by the relevant annuity factor, or for using calculator or spreadsheet routines.

F I G U R E   7–16

Investment Measures Applied to Three Projects

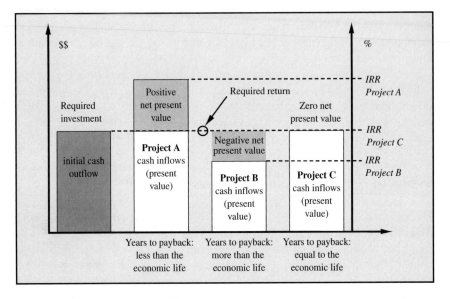

For mutually exclusive projects, the profitability index (BCR) will normally give a fair assessment, but the choice has to be considered in terms of the relative size and length of the commitment as well—the risk/reward trade-off. As we discussed earlier, a larger investment with a somewhat lower profitability index and yield might be preferable to a smaller investment, if both alternatives show benefits well above normal. If a company's identified projects exceed the limits of its funding potential, however—a fairly common condition—management has to apply what is called capital rationing. This involves spending the company's limited funds on the best selection of projects from the larger list of acceptable projects. Here the investment measure used must provide an economic ranking, that is, optimize the benefits obtained from the investment dollars spent. Essentially, the company should choose that group of projects within the budget limit that will generate the highest aggregate net present value.

To do this, projects can be ranked in declining order of their profitability index until the budgeted amount has been exhausted. This amounts to maximizing the present value benefits achieved per dollar of investment, because investment funds are the limiting factor. This concept ties closely to the principles of shareholder value creation, as will be discussed in more detail in Chapter 11. In practice, however, capital budgets are rarely so precise that truly attractive projects that were initially rejected for lack of funds or that appeared during the budget period could not at least be considered at another point in time.

Let's also remember that there should be nothing automatic about the use of any of the investment measures. The seemingly precise results achieved with present value calculations can tempt us to "let the numbers decide." Many more elements have to be weighed in even fairly straightforward projects, as we observed at the beginning of the chapter and hinted at in our examples. Besides the obvious constraints imposed by uncertainty in the economic estimates, management also must consider competitive, technical, human, societal, and other constraints within the company's strategic context, before significant investment or divestment decisions are made.

Some Further Considerations

Several specialized aspects of business investment analysis have been mentioned only briefly so far. A detailed treatment would go beyond the scope of this book. Yet, for completeness, we'll add some further comments on how the choice of leasing affects the economic analysis of an investment, on the impact of accelerated depreciation on present value analysis, and on the impact of inflation. Finally we'll once more put into perspective the degree of accuracy warranted in the calculations.

Leasing—A Financing Choice

Leasing is a popular means of obtaining a wide variety of capital assets for businesses as well as individuals, in exchange for making a pattern of periodic payments. For our purposes, however, the main point to consider is that leasing represents merely one form of financing, as we'll discuss in Chapter 9. Therefore, it's only after economic investment analysis has shown a project to be acceptable that alternative ways of financing should be considered. This principle is consistent with the business systems approach we've taken, where we clearly separated the decisions on investment, operations, and financing. Although financing for business investments should come from appropriate sources—matching their long-term nature—the specific alternatives of financing, including leasing, must remain independent from the economic justification of the investment itself.

All along we've viewed investment analysis as a cash flow trade-off which is independent of the compensation paid for the funds that finance the asset. The cost of capital or a return standard related to it automatically takes into account the expectations of the various providers of capital for appropriate compensation. If such an economic analysis is favorable, a separate test can then be applied to determine whether the company is better off leasing or owning the assets involved. This involves comparing various funding methods, where the question clearly becomes "lease versus buy" not "invest versus not invest." A number of specialized software applications exist, which permit analysts and managers to make the necessary calculations and tests for comparing financing alternatives. Because of the special complexities involved in these analytical methods, the reader is directed to the references at the end of the chapter for more information.

Accelerated Depreciation

For simplicity, we've used straight-line depreciation in our examples to derive the tax shield effect of depreciation charges as they affect economic analysis. However, we've also referred to the accelerated write-offs allowed under the Internal Revenue Code (see Chapter 3, p. 160), which are periodically modified by Congress. Rather than focus on any one of the several methods permitted, we'll make only a few generally applicable comments.

Remember, when doing investment analysis we're interested in depreciation, whatever pattern it might take, only insofar as it changes the tax expenditures of the company and thereby provides a tax shield. From a present value standpoint, accelerated depreciation provides an advantage because it moves the favorable tax impact of the write-offs forward in time. In other words, in the early years of a project, the tax shield effect on cash flows will be greater than with straight-line write-offs.

Similarly, shorter lives permitted by the ever-changing Internal Revenue Code will also place more tax benefits into the early stages of a project. Project benefits will be increased in the present value context, assuming, of course, that the company has sufficient taxable profits to take advantage of higher early write-offs. The calculations required to take account of accelerated depreciation in economic investment analysis can be handled easily with computer spreadsheets, just as any other uneven cash flow pattern can be accommodated.

The reader is encouraged to seek out the most current information published by the IRS to ascertain the proper depreciation class and write-off patterns for the assets being analyzed, and also to be aware of the particular tax management circumstances of the company that might affect its election of write-off patterns for tax purposes.

Inflation and Investment Analysis

The most important point to remember about the impact of inflation on investment analysis is the need for consistency between the measures used and data being analyzed. As we'll see in the next chapter, company return standards are commonly based on the weighted cost of capital. This cost specifically embodies inflation expectations both in the interest rate ascribed to debt, and the investors' return expectations on which the cost of shareholder equity is based.

The analysis of business investment projects should therefore be carried out with revenue and cost estimates that contain the same inflation expectations as the return standard employed. In other words, reasonable assumptions about price level changes affecting every part of the investment cash flow analysis should be built in, in order to make the discounting process meaningful. For example, using a return standard which contains an inflation allowance to discount constant dollar projections would give a result biased against the project. Similarly, using a constant dollar return standard to discount inflated cash flows would unduly improve the project's measures. The reader is referred to Appendix IV on inflation for a more detailed discussion of the underlying concepts.

Accuracy

At all times we must remember that the great precision implied by the mathematical basis of the investment analysis tools should be viewed with extreme caution. As we've pointed out before, the very nature of cash flow estimates—to which these tools are applied—is uncertain because the estimates are based on expectations, forecasts, projections, and sometimes plain guesses. Only rarely does the analyst deal with contractual sums, such as interest or lease payments, and even these are subject to a degree of uncertainty. Therefore it makes no sense to generate deceptively precise results or to allow highly specific numerical rankings to take on undue importance.

In our examples, we've been more precise than needed. Our intention was mainly to give the reader enough specific details to be able to follow the various methods step by step. In practice, liberal rounding of calculations (and certainly the final results) is highly advisable to keep the mathematical process from overwhelming the realistic business judgments required.

Keeping accuracy in proper perspective is even more important when we realize that the power of discounting is such that even widely different estimates for distant time periods can be so severely reduced in present value terms that they have relatively minor effects on the final result. A glance at the present value tables will confirm the rapid shrinkage of factors as discount rates rise and periods are more remote.

Key Issues

The following is a recap of the key issues raised directly or indirectly in this chapter. They are enumerated here to help the reader keep the analysis tools and methods within the perspective of financial theory and business practice.

1. Framing of investment decisions within the broader context of strategy, alternative solutions, capital constraints, and uncertainty—over an appropriate time horizon—is the critical prelude to economic analysis and to the use of analytical techniques, and this framework is also inextricably involved in the final decision process.

2. Business investment decisions are made continuously within the larger context of business strategy. This context evolves over time, and the portfolio of potential investments never remains constant or visible in its entirety.

3. The trade-off between outlays and benefits must be made with the objective of increasing shareholder value, that is, the return standards employed in measuring this trade-off must reflect the earnings potential and risks expected from a given business.

4. Shareholder expectations are incorporated into relevant return yardsticks through the concept of the weighted cost of capital, which reflects the expected level of future compensation to all providers of capital, but which must be exceeded for value creation.

5. To permit an economic judgment to be made, investment measures must take into account the timing of inflows and outflows of an investment and relate economic attractiveness to defined return expectations.
6. Economic analysis of investment decisions must be based on differential revenues and costs in the form of cash flows that are caused by the decision, and not on changes that are merely due to accounting conventions.
7. At times, economic allocations of existing or potential infrastructure must be made to the investment analysis, if the proposal over the economic life requires a portion of infrastructure that could be committed to other current or future alternatives.
8. Risk is inherent in all estimates of future conditions because of the uncertainty about most variables affecting an investment project. It must be expressed consistently in developing the expected cash flows, their potential range, and in applying the investment measures. Sensitivity analysis is a key aspect of business investment analysis of any significant size.
9. Inflation and specific price changes in revenues and costs can complicate both the estimating process and the level of the investment standards, and they must be handled consistently.
10. Capital budgets in practice are neither absolute ceilings on the amount of investments for a company, nor automatically affected by purely quantitative project ranking.
11. Financing patterns affect both the capability to make business investments and management's risk tolerance because of the impact of financial leverage and the need to cover fixed obligations.

Summary

In this chapter, we've presented the basic analytical framework for investment analysis in the broad context of capital budgeting. The strategic backdrop of this activity was highlighted before we illustrated the use of the time-adjusted measures with a variety of realistic examples.

All along we've stressed, however, that the most critical aspect of the process was thoughtful structuring of the problem in all of its dimensions before any quantitative techniques are applied. We discussed the need to define the problem, including development of relevant alternatives, careful preparation of all relevant data about the investment and the changes in the operating conditions introduced by the decision, and any capital recoveries—all done in an economic cash flow context. We found conceptual problems in all of these aspects, particularly in the use and meaning of the investment measures themselves. Working through increasingly complex examples, we provided the reader with a basic ability to perform investment analysis. But we cautioned that numerical results were only inputs to the broader management task of strategic positioning of the business—the selection and matching of appropriate long-term capital commitments with appropriate funding sources, within the framework of defined corporate objectives and goals, and with the ultimate purpose of creating shareholder value.

Analytical Support

A set of Excel-based templates (*Interactive Templates*) is downloadable at no charge from the Web at www.mhhe.com/helfert11e. The eighth of these, "Present Value Model: Calculating Cash Flows and Key Measures," is a general purpose tool which activates the present value analyses of Figures 7–4 through 7–11 in this chapter, and all similar analyses in Chapter 6. The template allows you to vary a set of key assumptions about investment outlays, cash flow benefits, depreciation patterns, tax rates, and discount rates of any investment project. You can observe the numerical changes resulting from these modifications on the key measures and on a graphic representation of the cash flow patterns.

Financial Genome, the advanced financial analysis software application described in Appendix I, p. 479, does not contain present value routines at this point.

Selected References

Aggarwal, R., ed. *Capital Budgeting under Uncertainty: Advances and New Perspectives.* Englewood Cliffs, NJ: Prentice Hall, 1991.

Bierman, Harold Jr., and Seymour Smidt. *The Capital Budgeting Decision.* 8th ed. New York: Macmillan, 1992. (A classic.)

Brealey, Richard, and Stewart Myers. *Principles of Corporate Finance.* 5th ed. Burr Ridge, IL: Irwin/McGraw-Hill, 1996.

Dixit, Avinash K., and Robert S. Pindyck. "The Options Approach to Capital Investment." *Harvard Business Review,* May–June 1995.

Garrison, Raymond H., and Erick W. Noreen. *Managerial Accounting.* 8th ed. Burr Ridge, IL: Irwin/McGraw-Hill, 1997.

Grant, Eugene L., et al. *Principles of Engineering Economy.* 8th ed. New York: Wiley, 1990. (A classic.)

Hertz, David B. "Risk Analysis in Capital Investment." *Harvard Business Review,* September–December 1979. (A classic.)

McNamee, Peter, and John Celona. *Decision Analysis with Supertree.* 2d ed. South San Francisco, CA: Scientific Press, 1990.

Perlman, Kalman I. *The Leasing Handbook.* Chicago and Cambridge, England: Probus, 1992.

Weston, Fred; Scott Besley; and Eugene Brigham. *Essentials of Managerial Finance.* 11th ed. Hinsdale, IL: Dryden Press, 1997.

Self-Study Exercises, Problems, and Discussion Questions

Exercises and Problems (*Selected Solutions Provided in Appendix VI*)

1. Using a spreadsheet, solve the following problem:

   The XYZ Corporation's strategy includes the periodic introduction of a new product line, which involves investments in R&D, promotion, plant, equipment, and working capital. Now the company has readied a new product after an expenditure of $3.75 million on R&D during the past 12 months. The decision to be made is whether to invest $6.3 million for production of the new line. The economic life of the product is estimated at 12 years, while straight-line depreciation will be taken over 15 years. At the end of 12 years, the equipment's book value is expected to be recovered through sale of the machinery. Working capital of $1.5 million must be committed to the project during the first year, and $1.25 million of this amount is expected to be recovered at the end of the 12 years. An expenditure of $1 million for promotion must be made and expensed in the first year as well.

   The best estimate of profits before depreciation, promotion expenses, and income taxes is $1.9 million per year for the first three years, $2.2 million per year for the fourth through eighth years, and $1.3 million per year for Years 9 through 12. Assume that income taxes on incremental profits are paid at the rate of 36 percent and that the company normally earns 12 percent after taxes on its investments. Calculate the various measure of investment desirability. Which of these best indicates the project's attractiveness? Should the company plan to develop similar opportunities by spending research and development funds? How much margin for error exists in this project? Discuss your findings.

2. After developing the relevant data inputs, use both a spreadsheet and the template, "Present Value Model: Calculating Cash Flows and Key Measures," to solve the following problem:

   The ZYX Company has found that after only two years of using a new machine for a semiautomatic production process, a more advanced and faster model has arrived on the market, which not only will turn out the current volume of products more efficiently but will allow an increased output of the item. The original machine had cost $32,000 and was being depreciated straight-line over a 10-year period, at the end of which time it would be scrapped. This machine's market value currently is $15,000, and a buyer is interested in acquiring it.

   The advanced model now available costs $55,500 installed, and because of its more complex mechanism is expected to last eight years. A scrap value of $1,500 is considered reasonable. The current level of output of the old machine, now running at capacity, is 200,000 units per year, which the new machine would boost by 15 percent. There's no question in the minds of the sales management that this additional output could be sold. The current machine produces the product at a unit cost of 12 cents for labor, 48 cents for materials, and 24 cents for allocated overhead (at the rate of 200 percent of direct labor). At the higher level of output, the new machine would turn out the product at a unit cost of 8 cents for labor (because a less skilled operator can handle the process), 46 cents for materials (because of less spoilage), and 16 cents for allocated overhead. Differences in other operating costs, such as power, repairs, and supplies, are negligible at both volume levels.

If the new machine were run at the old 200,000-unit level, the new operator would be freed for a proportional period of time for reassignment in other operations of the company. The additional output is expected to be sold at the normal price of $0.95 per unit, but additional selling and promotional costs are expected to amount to $5,500 per year.

Assume that income taxes are paid at the rate of 36 percent and that the company normally earns 16 percent after taxes on its investments. Calculate the various measures of investment desirability and select those that are most meaningful for this analysis. What major considerations should be taken into account in this decision? Discuss your findings.

3. The GSB Corporation, a high-technology company, is adding a product/service combination which it expects to exploit over a seven-year period. Incremental electronic and other equipment required will be $100,000 at the start, with a follow-up investment in Year 3 of $25,000. Working capital commitments will be $25,000 at the start, with annual increments as sales rise rapidly and finally tail off. Year 1 will require $4,000, Years 2 and 3 $5,000 each. Year 4 $6,000, and Year 5 $2,000. The equipment will be depreciated for tax purposes on the seven-year ACRS pattern (see Chapter 3, Figure 3–6, p. 160) (percentages: 14.29; 24.49; 17.49; 12.49; 8.93; 8.93; 8.93; 4.45) and taxes are paid at the rate of 36 percent. It is expected that a net recovery from the equipment investments will amount to $8,000 after tax adjustments in Year 7, and a partial recovery of inventories and receivables will amount to $32,000.

Operating profits after taxes, but before depreciation, are expected to be $15,000 in the first year, followed by this pattern over the remaining six years: $25,000; $40,000; $65,000; $45,000; $30,000 and $20,000.

The project will require infrastructure support valued at about $16,000 represented by a portion of facilities already in place that could be used for other purposes, at least over the next three years.

The company has set a return standard of 15 percent for its investments. Lay out the cash flow patterns, including the depreciation tax shield effect as a separate benefit, and calculate the various measures of investment desirability. Comment on the results and consider how these would be affected if the infrastructure portion were to be considered. What are the implications of this issue? Discuss your findings.

4. The UVW Company, a small but growing oil company, was about to invest $275,000 in drilling development wells on a lease near a major oil field with proven reserves. Since other companies were also drilling in the vicinity, the volume of the flow of oil expected couldn't be predicted except within wide limits. Nevertheless, some oil would be obtained for a period of 12 years, in the best judgment of the geologists. After careful evaluation of the market and distribution aspects, company management decided that the major uncertainty lay in the physical yield, with lesser risk in the other areas. Consequently, an assessment was made of the range of aftertax cash flows (after considering depletion, depreciation, etc.) at various levels of production, and the likelihood of occurrence of these levels was estimated. There was believed to be a 5 percent chance that the cash flow would be $15,000 per year over the life of the project, a 15 percent chance that it would be $35,000, a 40 percent chance that it would be $45,000, a 25 percent chance that it would be $50,000, and a 15 percent chance that it would be $60,000 per year. It was expected that oil would flow at any given level for the full life of the project, although there was the risk that the wells could run dry sooner. Would this be a worthwhile project if the company normally earned 10 percent after taxes? What considerations are critical? Discuss your findings.

Discussion Questions

1. Define the difference between cash flows, differential costs, and relevant costs.
2. Why should we study the various alternatives before making a capital investment decision?
3. Are sunk costs always to be ignored in capital investment analysis? Can't such a practice lead to financial difficulties?
4. Do past investments in large support facilities count when considering production investments that will make use of this unused capacity? How does one frame the problem in this case?
5. Do accounting allocations ever become relevant in investment analysis?
6. Why is it necessary to adjust for uneven lives in alternative capital investments when discounting reduces the importance of future cash flows anyway?
7. Is it possible to make an annual capital charge for working capital in a capital investment proposal, in lieu of specifying an outflow for the amount of working capital at point zero and an inflow for its recovery at the end of the past year?

8. Differentiate between capital budgeting and capital investment analysis. Which additional questions need to be resolved in the former?

9. Which aspects of capital investment analysis and capital budgeting lend themselves to modeling?

10. What are the key strategic issues surrounding business capital investment?

CHAPTER 8

COST OF CAPITAL AND BUSINESS DECISIONS

A common theme of this book is to view business decisions as economic cost/benefit trade-offs, designed ultimately to create value for the shareholders. Up to this point, however, we've focused mainly on the *economic benefits* obtained from investing in and operating a business. Now we'll deal in more specific terms with the *economic costs* associated with business decisions.

For example, during our discussion of financial leverage in Chapter 5, we encountered the special profit impact that is caused by the cost of long-term debt funds. We demonstrated how such fixed-cost obligations introduce magnified earnings fluctuations at different levels of profitability. In Chapters 6 and 7, we referred to the overall cost of long-term capital as a main criterion by which to judge the desirability of business investments. We established that only projects providing a time-adjusted cash flow return above the cost of capital will create value for the company's shareholders.

In this chapter, we'll discuss in greater detail the cost of various types of capital employed in a business, examine how this cost is measured, and in what form and for which purposes this economic reality should affect business decision making. We'll begin by sketching out the types of decisions for which cost of capital considerations are important. Then we'll discuss the cost of the different types of capital used, including operating funds, long-term debt, and shareholder equity (preferred stock and common equity).

Given the specific costs of each of these types of capital, we'll derive an approach to determining the overall corporate weighted cost of capital, and discuss the use of this cost concept in relation to the various return standards for business investments. We applied the cost of capital-based standards to the examples in Chapters 6 and 7, and we'll use them again in Chapters 10 and 11. As usual, the chapter will end with a list of key issues.

Decisional Context

The decisional context we've used all along stresses the interrelationship of investment, operations, and financing. We observed that, over time, most management decisions cause cash movements in one form or another. However, we didn't deal directly with the sources of the various types of funds employed in managing the system's cash flows, and did not dwell on their respective costs.

The dynamics of the business system require that funds be available at any time—temporarily or permanently—from a variety of sources, provided internally or externally. Key internal sources are cash flows from profitable operations or shifts in existing funds commitments. Key external sources are borrowing or raising new equity. Because the basic purpose of investing in, operating, and financing a business is to increase the economic value of the owners' stake over time, management decisions should create economic value for the shareholders by generating after-tax results that are higher than the cost of all the supporting capital inputs. This point was made repeatedly throughout the book, and we'll now take up in detail the main aspects of the cost aspect of this trade-off.

Investment Decisions

In Chapter 6 we discussed the various economic measures used to judge the desirability of an investment, and in Chapter 7 we demonstrated their use in a variety of investment decisions and trade-offs. All of these measures had in common the basic requirement that a project provide an economic return. This implies that the capital investment and all costs must be recovered, including an appropriate compensation to the providers of the various types of funds committed to the project. We also established that minimum standards for investments had to be set high enough to compensate both for the project's specific risk and for the opportunity loss of forgoing the returns from any alternative uses of the funds invested. Such alternative investments in the company's normal activities or in new initiatives were similarly assumed to adequately compensate both shareholders and lenders for providing their capital. We then suggested that the company's overall cost of capital, when used as a minimum standard for the economic desirability of investments, implicitly embodied all of these requirements, and value would be created if a project's cash flow performance exceeded the company's cost of capital.

The analytical methods discussed in Chapters 6 and 7 purposely did not, however, directly include any financing costs; rather, the cash outflows and inflows as defined represented only investment outlays on the one hand, and incremental after-tax operating benefits and capital recoveries on the other. These cash flows were then discounted at a return standard that implicitly allowed for the recovery of all actual costs and opportunity costs combined. Importantly, we didn't take into account the cost of the specific funds to be used for financing the project, instead letting at all times a broad overall standard represent the combined cost of all types of funding employed by the company.

FIGURE 8–1

Long-Term Funds Commitments versus Long-Term Sources

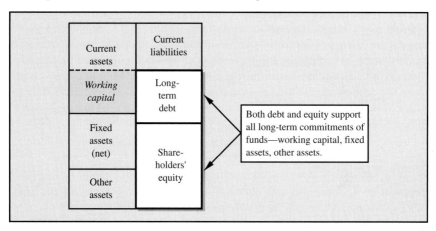

Accordingly, the economic results from a business investment have to be sufficiently attractive to justify allocation of part of the various long-term funds available to the company, because business investments generally have a fairly long-term economic life span. Here we must recognize an important principle, derived from our discussion of the business system in Chapter 1: Normally, the funds for new investments come from a pool of different sources, none of which can or should be specifically identified with any particular project under review. Instead, any funds used for investment purposes represent the mix contained in the pool, and therefore should carry the overall cost of the company's long-term funding, as suggested by Figure 8–1. There we see the basic combination of debt and equity, in whatever proportions management deems an appropriate level, supporting working capital, fixed assets of all types, and any other assets employed by the company.

Given the long-term nature of commitments for working capital, facilities, technology, and so forth, these investments are normally backed by the long-term capital structure of a company. This structure may employ different degrees of leverage and a whole range of financial instruments, and it may change over time as the company's business patterns develop. The important point is that the long-term pool of funds is the relevant source of funding—not any particular increment of financing which the company may be using at a given point in time to augment its capital structure. Therefore, the weighted cost of capital measure, which we'll discuss shortly, is the most significant criterion of cost in the capital budgeting and investment analysis context.

Operating Decisions

The time horizon for operating decisions is generally shorter than that of the typical business investment. Nonetheless, operational funds movements, such as increases or decreases in trade credit—both used and extended—and swings in cash balances and accruals as described in Chapter 2 do involve costs, both in the form of out-of-pocket charges and opportunity costs. For example, a near-term decision to take purchase discounts might involve significant economic benefits when weighed against the cost of any incremental borrowing necessary to take advantage of the discount. Cash management decisions to minimize bank balances can eliminate the opportunity costs inherent in idle funds. In fact, there are myriad circumstances in which near-term decisions can cause or eliminate the cost of employing funds, because these decisions are often directly linked to incremental sources that entail specific costs. We'll discuss some of these shortly.

Financing Decisions

There are costs connected with obtaining financing and compensating providers of various sources of funds, both short term and long term, which must be considered by management in making any financing decision. Clearly, using any type of funds entails an economic cost to the company in one form or another. One of management's obligations is to develop a pattern of funding that both matches the risk/reward profile of the business and is sufficiently adapted to meeting the evolving needs of the company. At the same time, the use of long-term funds entails meeting the expectations of creditors, and meeting or preferably exceeding the expectations of the providers of equity funds, the company's shareholders. We'll discuss the major financing choices and the framework for analyzing them in the next chapter.

Cost of Operating Funds

In the course of operations, a business commonly carries many types of debt, including trade obligations (in the form of accounts and notes payable), short- and intermediate-term credit, notes payable to banks or individuals, tax accruals owed various government agencies, wages due employees, payments due on installment purchases, and lease obligations. For all types of debt, including long-term obligations in the company's capital structure, the specific cost of borrowing can be determined rather easily. Normally, debt arrangements carry stated interest provisions that call for interest payments during the debt period, at its end, or as an advance deduction from principal. The last of these provisions is called discounting. In all cases, the specific cost of debt is simply the direct cost of the interest commitment.

We also must remember that under current IRS taxation guidelines, interest payments of all kinds are tax deductible for corporations. Because of this feature, the net cost of interest to corporations (at least for those with sufficient profits to be liable for taxes or able to apply tax-averaging provisions) is the annual interest multiplied by a factor (f) of 1 minus the applicable tax rate.

For example, if a corporation pays 8 percent per year on the principal of a note and its effective tax rate (t) for any incremental revenue or cost is 34 percent, the net annual effective interest cost (i) of this note will be:

$$f = 1 - t$$
$$f = 1 - 0.34 = 0.66$$
$$i = 8\% \times 0.66 = 5.28\% \text{ (after taxes)}$$

Tax deductibility effectively reduces the cost of debt to a net amount after the prevailing tax rate is applied, if the company is in a position where changes in net income affect the amount of taxes due. This tax advantage might also be enjoyed by individuals in some circumstances, such as in the case of home mortgage interest deductions. However, the specific cost of other forms of capital (such as dividends on preferred stock) is not tax deductible for corporations at this time, as we'll see later.

We can define operating debt as short- or intermediate-term revolving obligations incurred in the ordinary daily operations of most businesses. Some of these debt funds are provided by creditors free of charge for short periods, under trade terms generally accepted in the industry or service sector in which the company operates.

Foremost in this category are accounts payable, which are the amounts owed vendors for goods or services purchased. Depending on the terms of the purchase agreement, the company being billed for goods and services can hold off payment for 10 or 15 days, or as long as 45 or even 60 days. In the interim, it can make use of the funds without incurring any specific cost. Recall from Chapter 2 that such trade credit is in fact a significant funds source that is rolled over continuously, and that grows or declines with the volume of operations.

In many cases, suppliers offer their customers a discount for early payment. For example, the supplier's terms might provide for a 2 percent reduction in the invoice amount if payment is received within 10 days (2/10) or 3 percent within 15 days (3/15) of the date of the invoice. This practice, common in many business sectors and reflecting applicable conditions, allows the customer effectively to reduce the original cost of the goods or service by the specified discount. The incentive is intended to speed up the vendor's collections and thus reduce the level of the vendor's funds tied up in customer credit.

If the buyer lets the discount period lapse, however, the invoice amount becomes due and payable in full at the end of the period specified (n/30, n/45, and so on), although in practice these terms are rarely observed with precision. Failure to take advantage of the trade discount, and thereby prolonging the time during which the buyer can make alternative use of the funds, results in a definite opportunity cost. Although often ignored, this cost can be quite sizable.

For instance, if the credit terms are 2/10, n/30, the cost of using the funds for the extra 20 days amounts to a loss of 2 percent of the invoice amount, or an annual rate of 36 percent! The calculation is quite simple:

$$\frac{360 \text{ days}}{20 \text{ days}} \times 2\% = 36\% \text{ (before taxes)}$$

In effect, the company loses, as taxable income, the cash discount it would otherwise have earned. To arrive at the net cost, the cash discount must be reduced by the taxes that would have been paid on the lost income. If we assume taxes to be 34 percent, the net cost for using the creditor's funds for the extra 20 days amounts to

$$1 - 0.34 = 0.66$$
$$2\% \times 0.66 = 1.32\% \text{ (after taxes)}$$

The annualization is calculated as

$$\frac{360 \text{ days}}{20 \text{ days}} \times 1.32\% = 23.76\% \text{ (after taxes)}$$

This cost is obviously very high, especially when compared to the after-tax cost of the prime interest rate, which is the rate normally charged large corporations of impeccable credit rating—or even relative to the after-tax cost of much higher interest rates smaller companies pay to borrow operating funds.

Some companies, especially small and rapidly growing enterprises, make it a practice to use accounts payable as a convenient source of credit, often unilaterally exceeding the outside limits of credit terms by significant periods. The longer the funds are kept, of course, the lower the specific cost of accounts payable becomes, as trade creditors normally do not charge interest unless the receivable has to be renegotiated. In extreme cases, trade creditors might force the customer to convert unpaid amounts into notes payable due on specific dates, with or without interest. This is usually done—albeit reluctantly—by vendors who wish to establish a somewhat stronger claim against a troubled customer's resources.

It's clearly a poor practice for any borrower to violate stipulated trade credit terms, both from the standpoint of business reputation and continuing creditworthiness. Prospective creditors will take such tardy performance into account when evaluating the customer's credit history, inasmuch as such information is readily available from the databases of credit rating agencies. This is an implicit economic cost which must be considered in addition to the specific monetary cost incurred with trade credit.

Another form of operating debt includes short-term notes and installment contracts, where interest is either charged ahead of time or added to the amount of principal stated in the contract. For example, a one-year, $1,000 note which carries an interest rate of 9 percent will provide the debtor with only $910 in ready cash if the note is "discounted" by deducting the interest in advance. The effective cost before taxes is higher than the stated interest, because the company is in effect paying $90 for the privilege of borrowing $910 for one year:

$$\frac{\$90}{\$910} = 9.89\% \text{ (before taxes)}$$

The adjustment for income taxes is handled exactly as shown in the previous example.

In the case of an installment contract for, say, $1,000 payable in four equal quarterly installments, with annual interest of 10 percent on the original balance, the effective cost of interest is far higher than stated, because decreasing amounts of principal will be outstanding over the term of the contract as the quarterly payments amortize the principal, while providing interest on the rapidly declining balance. The precise cost of 15.7 percent can be easily determined with a calculator or a spreadsheet, using the present value approach discussed in Chapter 6.

We can use an averaging process as a quick method of determining the approximate effective cost. Over the term of the contract, the amount of principal will decline from $1,000 to zero, with the average outstanding balance of roughly one-half this range, or $500. The contractual interest was 10 percent on $1,000, or $100, one-quarter of which was added to each of the four payments. When we relate the total interest paid to the average amount of funds used by the borrowing company during the term of the contract, the approximate cost doubles, as follows:

$$\frac{\$100}{\$500} = 20\% \text{ (before taxes)}$$

The actual result of 15.7 percent is lower because in our example interest in effect is also paid on the installment basis. (The adjustment for income taxes is the same as before.) If the contract ran for more than one year, the interest cost must be annualized, that is, the amount of interest must be allocated to the specific time period involved to derive the true cost per year, which is the normal period of comparison. More complex financial arrangements are normally handled with present value techniques. The computerized systems used by banks and other lending institutions routinely calculate the payments and charges precisely, and they are legally bound to disclose the effective cost of the arrangement on an annualized basis. The simple averaging technique shown earlier is useful as a quick check in many circumstances, including personal finance, to approximate the effective cost of credit for rough initial comparisons.

The discussion so far has focused on the specific cost of operational debt, which can range from zero to substantial annual rates of interest. This specific cost is not the only aspect of debt, however. As already mentioned in earlier chapters, repayment of the loan is required, which commits part of the company's future cash flows to that purpose. The obligation to repay the loan principal in a timely fashion forces the financial manager to forecast and plan cash receipts and disbursements with care. The projections could indicate that refinancing might be desirable when the amount becomes due. The basic techniques of making cash flow projections as discussed in Chapter 4 are applicable here.

Another element of the burden of debt, as already mentioned, is the impact various forms of debt obligations have on a company's creditworthiness in relation to current and future funding requirements. In other words, the balance between owners' equity and other people's money might become precarious and forestall borrowing of any kind for some time until the company has worked itself out from under its debt obligations. Highly debt-leveraged operations can be costly, both in terms of the risk of not meeting obligations as they fall due, and in having to turn to much more expensive sources of credit or equity funds as additional needs arise.

Cost of Long-Term Debt

Most companies employ at least some form of long-term debt obligation to support part of their permanent financing needs arising from major capital outlays, growth of operations, or replacement of other types of capital. This type of debt becomes integral to the long-term capital structure of the company. Examples are bonds of various types issued by a company and traded in the financial markets and long-term borrowing arrangements with banks and other financial institutions.

As we'll discuss in Chapter 9, management must make well-planned decisions when determining an appropriate level of debt in the capital structure, weighing the cost, risk, and debt service involved relative to the prospective uses of the funds. Long-term debt commitments by their very nature have a much more lasting impact on a company's situation than do short-term, working capital, financing, or intermediate-term loans.

The specific cost of long-term debt is expressed in the stated annual interest rate of the financial instrument involved. For example, a 9 percent debenture bond, which is an unsecured (no specific assets are pledged) general debt obligation of the company, has a specific after-tax cost of

$$9\% \times (1 - 0.34) = 5.94\%$$

if we assume that the company is able to take advantage of the interest deduction. An incremental tax rate of 34 percent was used. In addition, we'll assume that the bond had been sold at a price that nets the company its par value (face value). The stated annual interest rate (coupon rate) of a bond is based on the par value, that is, 100 percent of the principal due at a specified future date—regardless of the actual proceeds received by the issuing company. These proceeds often vary because marketable debt securities are generally sold at the best possible price obtainable in the market through underwriters who take some or all of the risk of marketing the issue for a small percentage of the gross receipts. Legal and registration expenses also are borne by the company. Therefore, depending on the issue price, which is related to prevailing interest yields and the quality of the company's credit rating, the company might actually receive net proceeds at a discount (below par value), or it might receive a small premium over par.

In either case, the specific cost has to be adjusted to take the actual proceeds into account. The effect is similar to the short-term loan discussed earlier, on which the interest was due in advance and which therefore entailed a specific cost somewhat higher than the stated rate. If we assume that instead of 100 percent of par value, the company received 95 percent for its debentures after all expenses and commissions, the effective after-tax cost with a 9 percent coupon rate is as follows:

$$9\% \times (1 - 0.34) \times \frac{1}{0.95} = 6.25\%$$

Apart from the specific cost of interest, long-term debt also again involves repayment of the principal. There are many types of repayment provisions, generally structured to fit the nature of the company and the type of risks the debt holder visualizes. Periodic repayment requirements can be met through a sinking fund set aside for that purpose and held in trust by a depository institution. Partial or full principal payments due at the end of the lending period are called balloon payments.

The basic point to remember is that debt instruments, even if long term, must in some form and at some time be repaid, or at least rolled over into new debt. The cost of this repayment is implicit in the need to carefully plan future cash flows, and also to consider the ability to achieve future refinancing if the funds needs are likely to continue or even grow. Recall the discussion of funds projections in Chapter 4.

Another implicit cost of long-term debt involves the nature and degree of restrictions normally embodied in the debt agreement (indenture). Such provisions can limit management's ability to use other forms of credit (e.g., leasing), might specify minimum levels of some financial ratios (e.g., working capital proportions or debt burden coverage), or might limit the amount of dividends that can be paid to shareholders. At times, specific assets might have to be pledged as security. Any set of such provisions carries an implicit cost in that it limits management's freedom of choice in making decisions. The greater the perceived risk of the indebtedness, the greater the restrictions are likely to be. One of the effects can be a reduction in the ability to grow through new investment, which can lead to lost opportunities from a market and strategic standpoint. Profitable growth depends, of course, on appropriate funding policies and options, as we discussed in the sustainable growth discussion of Chapter 5.

The rationale for debt restrictions was presented in the discussion of financial ratios from the point of view of lenders (Chapter 3). Not to be overlooked is the introduction of financial leverage into the capital structure, as discussed in Chapter 5. The implicit cost of this condition again depends on the degree of risk exposure caused by specific company and industry conditions.

Cost of Shareholders' Equity

Preferred Stock

This form of equity ownership is conceptually at the midway point between debt and common stock. Although subordinated to the various creditors of the corporation, the preferred shareholder has a claim on corporate earnings that ranks ahead of the common shareholders' position up to the amount of the stated preferred dividend. In liquidation, the preferred shareholders' claims are satisfied prior to the residual claims of the holders of common stock.

The specific cost of preferred stock is normally higher than that of debt with a similar quality rating. Because of the near-equity status of preferred stock, preferred dividends as of this writing are not tax deductible for the issuing corporation and are therefore an outflow of after-tax funds. For instance, an 11 percent preferred stock, issued at par (net of expenses), costs the corporation 11 percent after taxes. For each dollar of dividends to be paid on this preferred stock, the corporation must therefore earn, before taxes:

$$\$1.00 \times \frac{1}{1 - 0.34} = \$1.52$$

as compared to $1 for every dollar of interest paid on a long-term debt obligation. Where the 9 percent bond in the previous section had an after-tax cost of 5.94 percent, the 11 percent preferred stock has an after-tax cost of 11 percent. The stated dividend rate of a preferred stock therefore is directly comparable to the tax-adjusted interest rate of a bond.

We can easily compare the cost to the company of long-term debt and preferred stock if we assume that they were issued at prices that result in proceeds exactly equal to the par (face) value. When proceeds do not equal par value, as often happens because of market conditions, the cost must be based on the proceeds to obtain the effective cost as discussed above.

The additional implicit cost of preferred stock lies in the fact that it is a security senior to common stock, and the dividend claims of its holders rank ahead of common dividends. In addition, the essentially fixed nature of preferred dividends (they can be omitted only under serious circumstances) introduces a degree of financial leverage with varying earnings levels. Preferred stock being closer in concept to owners' equity than to debt, however, makes the implicit costs of its encumbrances far less serious than those of debt.

Common Equity

The holder of common shares is the residual owner of the corporation, with a claim extending to all assets and earnings not subject to prior claims. Common shareholders provide long-term funds with the expectation of being rewarded with both dividends and an increase in the economic value of their shares. This value accretion consists of the combined impact of (it is hoped) growing earnings and growing dividends on the market value of the shares. In turn, the market value is impacted by general economic conditions and by risks specific to the industry and to the individual company. We have already referred to the concept of total shareholder return (TSR) as an expression of this dual expectation of dividends and share price appreciation. In other words, in the case of common stock, we are dealing with more variables, while contractual provisions for compensation, such as coupon interest or the stated preferred dividend rate, are absent. As a result, the specific cost of common equity requires a more complex evaluation than we encountered with either debt or preferred stock.

The cost of common equity has to be viewed in an opportunity framework. The investor has provided funds to the corporation expecting to receive the combined economic return of dividends declared by the board of directors and future appreciation in market value. The investment was made—presumably on a logical basis—because the level and nature of the risk embodied in the company and its business reasonably matched the investor's own risk preference. In addition, the investor's expectations about earnings, dividends, and market appreciation were considered satisfactory.

The investor made this choice, however, by forgoing other investment opportunities. Moreover, the commitment was made under a condition of uncertainty about future results, because the only hard data available to any investor are past performance statistics. Therefore, measuring the cost of the shareholders' funds to the corporation is a challenge that must address investor expectations about the risk/reward trade-off executed by investing in this opportunity. In other words, the company must strive to compensate the shareholder with an economic return implicit in its past performance, but most important in its future outlook, and relative to the potential returns from peer companies and from the stock market as a whole.

Several approaches to measuring the cost of common equity are used in practice; all involve many assumptions and quite a bit of judgment. The greatest difficulty lies in finding a specific linkage with the collective risk/reward judgments continuously made in the security markets, judgments that drive the market value of the common shares. We'll discuss two major methods:

1. The dividend approach.
2. The risk assessment approach based on the capital asset pricing model (CAPM).

The dividend approach is fairly straightforward; in effect it directly values expected future streams of dividends. But it is limited by highly simplifying assumptions. The risk assessment method, in contrast, approximates shareholder return expectations by adding to a "normalized" rate of return on securities in general, a calculated numerical risk premium that is company-specific. As we'll see, it's the only approach that arrives at an economic return for the specific security relative to average yields experienced in the securities markets.

Dividend Approach to Cost of Common Equity

A way of dealing with at least one of the measurable benefits obtained by the shareholder is to use annual dividends to estimate the cost of common equity. Originally developed by Myron Gordon, it is appealing inasmuch as cash dividends represent the most visible periodic compensation to the shareholder. As a cash flow method, it parallels the measures for the other forms of capital. Yet the approach suffers from serious oversimplification, because companies vary greatly in their rate of dividend payout, and the method does not specifically address the effect of reinvestment of retained earnings. Remember, common shareholders are the residual owners of all earnings not reserved for other obligations, and dividends paid are usually only a portion of the earnings accruing to common shares.

In its simplest form, the dividend approach to the cost of equity is the same as the dividend yield, which we discussed as one of the measures from the owners' point of view in Chapter 3:

$$\text{Dividend yield} = \frac{\text{Annual dividend per share}}{\text{Average market price per share}}$$

Our formula appears as follows:

$$k_e = \frac{dps}{P}$$

where

$$k_e = \text{the cost of common equity}$$
$$dps = \text{the projected dividend per share}$$
$$P = \text{the current market price per share}$$

Introducing estimated growth in dividends into the formula is an improvement that implicitly recognizes the effect of reinvestment on the value received by shareholders. The assumption here is that over time, successful reinvestment of retained earnings will lead to growing earnings and thus growing dividends. The mathematics of the formula allow us simply to add the assumed rate of growth in dividends to the equation shown above. We begin with the dividend yield and add a stable percentage rate of dividend growth (g) to simulate the overall expectations of the shareholders:

$$k_e = \frac{dps}{P} + g$$

The difficulty, however, lies in determining the specific dividend growth rate, which must be based on our best assumptions about future performance, tempered by past experience. Many estimating processes can be used. In Chapter 5, we discussed the concept of sustainable growth, which assumed stable investment, payout, and financing policies. This might yield clues to the growth rate that would be appropriate for the dividend approach, but the process really requires projecting expected future dividend policies as set by the company's directors. If significant changes in dividend policy can be expected, the analyst might want to modify the approach, making a series of year-by-year assumptions and in effect, calculating a composite of future dividend growth patterns from these yearly forecasts.

A word about taxes is necessary here. In the dividend approach, we're dealing with after-tax cash flows from the company's viewpoint. Common dividends, like preferred dividends, are not tax deductible and must be paid out of after-tax earnings. No adjustment is therefore necessary in the result to make it comparable with the after-tax cost of debt and preferred stock.

The shareholder is judging the opportunity to earn an economic return on the same basis. However, interest and dividends are taxable income to the recipient. Because personal tax conditions vary greatly, one more adjustment is necessary from the investor's point of view to assess investment options objectively. Yet the business analyst cannot perform the calculation for the shareholder without knowledge of the individual's tax status. Consequently, the only working assumption we can make in this context is that most investors are subject to some taxation; we can arrive at financial results that are consistent up to the point at which the individual investor must calculate the personal tax impact.

Risk Assessment Approach to Cost of Common Equity

As we said earlier, the risk assessment method doesn't rely on specific estimates of present and future earnings or dividends. Instead, a normal market return is developed from published data on financial returns and yields, which is adjusted by a company-specific risk premium or discount. The rationale is based on the assumption that a company's cost of equity in terms of shareholder return expectations is related to the relative risk of its common stock. The greater this relative risk, the greater the premium—in the form of an additional economic return over and above a normalized return—that should be expected by an investor. This approach makes intuitive sense and also can be demonstrated statistically.

At any time, the securities markets yield a spread of rates of return ranging from those on essentially risk-free government securities at the low end of the scale (4 to 7 percent), to the sizable returns from highly speculative securities, including high-yield but risky junk bonds (15 to 18 percent or more). The risk/return trade-off inherent in the many classes of security investments is reflected in this spread. Risk is defined as the variability of returns inherent in the type of security, whereas return is defined as the total economic return obtained from the security, including both interest or dividends and changes in market value.

A number of specific methods have been developed over the years to express the risk premium concept of return on common equity—which reflects the cost of common equity to the corporation—as a methodology both theoretically acceptable and practically usable. Although no individual method is totally satisfactory in these terms, the most widely accepted is the capital asset pricing model (CAPM). We'll discuss some of its salient features here, but the conceptual and theoretical underpinnings are extensive and far beyond the scope of this book. The reader is encouraged to explore the references at the end of the chapter for more extensive treatments of the evolution, theory, and validation of the CAPM.

Three elements are required in applying the capital asset pricing model approach, and each must be estimated carefully:

- Level of return from a risk-free investment.
- Level of return from securities of average risk.
- Expression of relative risk of the company's securities.

The first element is a judgment about the basic return of a security from which all risk has been excluded. The purpose is to find the lowest part of the range of yields currently experienced in the securities markets as the starting point from which to build up the higher, risk-adjusted return specific to the particular common stock. Long-term U.S. government obligations are commonly used as a surrogate for such a risk-free return. The yields on U.S. government obligations are widely quoted and accessible, both for the present and for historical periods. For our purposes, current yields can be used, possibly adjusted for expected changes, such as the inflation outlook during the next several years. Precision is not possible here, and reasonable approximations supported by the analyst's judgment are quite workable.

The second element is an estimate of the return from a comparable type of security of average risk. This is needed because the CAPM approach develops a specific adjustment for the relative riskiness of the particular security as compared to an average or baseline. For our purposes, we can use an estimate of the total expected return for the Standard & Poor's 500 Index, a broad-based measure of the price levels of the common stocks of 500 widely traded companies. Such projections of the total return—a combination of dividends and market appreciation—that is expected from the companies represented in the index are frequently made by security analysts and published in financial services and newsletters (see Appendix III). While the S&P 500 Index provides a broad-based estimate of return, more specific indexes could be chosen. Again, the analyst must exercise judgment in using projections of future economic returns. The main point is to obtain a reasonable approximation of the average return from average investments of the type being evaluated.

The third element required is an expression of relative risk, which is based on the variability of returns of the particular security being analyzed. The definition of risk is very specific in the CAPM approach, and this has caused some controversy. Risk is not defined as total variability of returns, but rather, as the covariance of the particular stock's returns with those of assets of average risk. The assumption here is that an investor does not focus on the total variability of return experienced with each individual security, but rather on how each security affects the variability of the total return from the portfolio held by the investor. Note, however, that significant changes in a company's capital structure will tend to affect the company's relative risk as well as its covariance with the portfolio.

Risk, therefore, is a very relative concept in the CAPM, and its specific definition might not be acceptable to everyone. We'll ignore the arguments for and against this risk definition in our discussion, and concentrate instead on how risk is recognized in the CAPM approach to arrive at a company-specific return. This risk measure, in the form of the covariance of an individual stock's returns with that of the portfolio of stocks of average risk, is called beta (β). It is found by linear regression of past monthly total returns of the particular security against a baseline such as the S&P 500 Index. Financial data services like *Value Line* list the current β for publicly traded securities as a matter of course.

How are these three elements combined to arrive at an expected return and the company's cost for a particular equity security? As we stated earlier, the CAPM method defines the cost of common equity as the combination of the risk-free return and a risk premium that has been adjusted for the specific company risk.

The CAPM formula is

$$k_e = R_f + \beta(R_m - R_f)$$

where

k_e = the cost of equity capital
R_f = the risk-free return
β = the company's covariance of returns against the portfolio
R_m = the average return on common stocks

The company's β is expressed as a simple factor that is used to multiply the difference between the expected return on the average portfolio and the expected risk-free return. This difference, of course, equals the risk premium inherent in the portfolio. The β factor adjusts this average risk premium to reflect the individual stock's higher or lower relative riskiness. β goes above 1.0 as the relative risk of the stock exceeds the average, and drops below 1.0 when the relative risk is less than average.

The calculation itself is quite simple, whereas deriving the inputs is not, as we've already observed. To illustrate, let's arbitrarily choose a risk-free rate of return of 6.5 percent, an S&P 500 return estimate of 11.5 percent, and a company with a fairly "risky" β of 1.4. The cost of equity in this hypothetical example would be

$$k_e = 6.5\% + 1.4(11.5\% - 6.5\%) = 13.5\%$$

composed of the risk-free return of 6.5 percent plus the calculated company-specific risk premium of 7.0 percent, for a total of 13.5 percent.

A large number of issues surface when the CAPM or related measures are used to derive the cost of securities. One of these, already mentioned, is the quality of the estimate of both the risk-free return and the average return on a portfolio of common stocks. Although the return on long-term U.S. government securities is a reasonable surrogate for the former, estimating an average portfolio return is fraught with conceptual problems. If β is the sole indicator of relative risk, the nature of the portfolio against which covariance is measured is clearly important. Broad averages such as the S&P 500 might or might not be appropriate under the circumstances. Also, there is the problem of using past data, particularly for variability of returns, in estimating the future relationships that indicate shareholder expectations. Finally, there is the issue of the effect of changes in a company's financial leverage.

Consequently, the results of these calculations, as with most types of financial analysis, should be used with caution and a great deal of commonsense judgment.

Inflation

So far we've been talking about the cost of capital without specific reference to the impact of inflation. We could do this because no adjustment is in fact needed. The risk-free return on a government bond does implicitly allow for the expected level of inflation, inasmuch as expectations about future inflationary conditions affect the yield from such securities. When inflation abates, the yields decline— as occurred dramatically in the mid-1980s, in the early 1990s, and again in 2001. When inflation expectations rise, so do bond yields. The same is true of the yields from other financial instruments.

If no inflation existed, risk-free returns would probably be in the range of 3 to 4 percent, the basic interest rate. In fact, not just the CAPM, but all the measures of cost of capital we've been discussing include expected inflationary effects in that estimates of future returns take these expectations into account. The spectrum of returns ranging from risk-free bonds to those on speculative securities also is consistent in reflecting the effects of inflation.

To summarize, it should be obvious by now that the cost of common equity, apart from the specific method of calculation, is generally higher than the cost of interest-bearing securities or preferred stocks. As we said at the beginning of this section, the residual claim represented by common shares involves the highest risk/reward trade-off. Thus returns expected of common shares are higher, which in turn, must translate into the highest cost of capital from the corporation's standpoint. This fact will become even more important when we examine the alternative choices of financing new funds requirements, the subject of the next chapter.

Weighted Cost of Capital

Having determined the specific costs of the various types of capital individually, we now have all the specific cost inputs needed to make some of the funding decisions listed earlier. But because most companies use more than one form of long-term capital in funding investments and operations, and because the mix of sources used for long-term financing can change over time, it's necessary to examine the cost of the company's capital structure as a whole. The result we're looking for is a cost of capital figure that is weighted to reflect the mix of the various capital sources used as a matter of policy. It encompasses the cost of compensating long-term creditors and preferred shareholders in terms of the specific provisions applicable to them, and of rewarding the holders of common stock in terms of the risk-adjusted return they expect.

Several issues have to be resolved in determining an overall corporate cost of capital. The first is generating appropriate costs for the different types of long-term capital employed, which we have already done conceptually. The second is a decision about the weights, or proportions, of each type of capital in the structure to be analyzed. The third is the question of whether to apply market values versus book values of the various categories of capital in arriving at the weighting.

It's only then that we can calculate a weighted cost of capital that is meaningful for the intended purpose.

Cost Choices

First to be resolved is the question of whether it is relevant to consider the past costs of existing securities in a company's capital structure, or alternatively, the incremental costs involved in adding newly issued securities. Quite often the debt and preferred stock section of the balance sheet lists a whole array of past issues, many of which carry interest or dividend rates that differ significantly from current experience. Obligations that are 5, 10, or 15 years old likely carry stated costs that are no longer relevant today. Moreover, the various methods of arriving at the cost of common equity were based on future expectations, which are not necessarily consistent with past debt or preferred costs. To solve this dilemma, we must again apply the principle established early in this book: The purpose of the analysis always determines the choice of data and methodology.

Normally, the key purpose of calculating a weighted cost of capital is for use in decisions about new business investments, serving as a standard of return that will adequately compensate all providers of capital. Unless a company undergoes significant restructuring, the funds for new capital commitments are likely to come from current internal cash flow, augmented by new debt, new equity, or both. This is an incremental condition, because the choices for adding new investments are still being made. Consequently, the cost of capital measure most appropriate here is based on the expected incremental costs of the various forms of capital employed by the company. As we already know, past decisions on investments and financing are sunk costs, and not relevant here.

Weighting the Proportions

As already mentioned, we're deriving a weighted cost that reflects the normal proportions of the different types of capital in a company's capital structure. Again, significant issues arise. The current capital structure as reflected on the balance sheet is the result of past management decisions on funding both investments and operations. The question to be asked here is whether the types and proportions of capital in this structure are likely to hold in the future, that is, whether they match the strategic plans of management. The intended capital budget supporting the company's future strategy, particularly when calling for sizable outlays, might indeed cause significant shifts in the long-term financing pattern. Also, management might choose to make gradual modifications to its financial policies which, over time, can cause sizable adjustments in the capital structure. (Recall the discussion in Chapter 5 of the impact of policy changes.)

In other cases, management might well be satisfied with the current proportions of the company's capital structure as a long-term objective. Yet the incremental capital required from time to time is normally raised in blocks limited to one form of security, that is, debt, preferred stock, or common equity. Therefore, in the near term, any one type of capital might be emphasized more than the long-term proportions desired would suggest. Capital must be raised in response to market conditions, and the choice of which type is appropriate at any given point is based on a series of considerations that we'll explore in the next chapter.

The analyst has to resolve the dilemma caused by such divergences with judgment. Given the fact that a company's conditions never remain static in the long run, the choice of capital structure proportions has to be a compromise intended to approximate the conditions relevant for purposes of analysis. Precision becomes secondary to common sense. Current proportions are a good starting point, but should normally be modified by specific assumptions about the future direction of the company's long-term financing. It also might be useful to generate a range of assumptions to bracket the findings, which as we know is a form of sensitivity analysis.

One common way of dealing with the issue of weights is to identify a "target" level of debt versus equity, which management identifies as a longer-term objective, even though near-term fluctuation might occur. This is done to relate the cost of capital to the strategic direction of the company, and also to avoid introducing fluctuations in the cost of capital measure which, after all, is to serve as a long-term gauge for value creation. But even this approach of necessity rests on assumptions and judgments.

Market versus Book Values

The weights to be assigned to different types of capital are going to be clearly different if we choose to apply current market values as contrasted with the stated values on the right-hand side of the balance sheet. Again, we must be guided by the purpose of the analysis to decide which value is relevant. If we're interested in a criterion against which to judge expected returns from future investments, the most common use of the cost of capital, we should use the current market values of the various types of capital of the company, because these values reflect the expectations of both creditors and shareholders. The latter certainly didn't invest in the book value of common equity, which usually differs significantly from the current share value as traded in the market. Further, it is management's obligation to meet the expectations of the shareholders in terms of the future economic value to be created by investments and operations, and to compensate creditors out of future earnings. Stated book values, as we observed before, are static and not responsive to changing performance or values.

The choice of market values also complements the use of incremental funding in that both are expressed in current market terms. The market value of common equity automatically (and implicitly) includes retained earnings as reported on the balance sheet. Although some believe that retained earnings bear no cost, this is a misconception. In fact, retained earnings represent part of the residual claim of the shareholders, even if they are imperfectly valued on the balance sheet because of required accounting conventions.

In this area, there are again conceptual issues and arguments that can be raised for and against market value weights. One of these has to do with a company that is experiencing financing requirements rather different from the historical pattern reflected in its capital structure. There it can be argued that a book value approach might be more suitable. Again, we must leave the in-depth exploration of these concepts to the reader, because they go beyond the scope of this book.

Calculating the Weighted Cost of Capital

Let's now turn to a simplified example of calculating a weighted cost of capital for a hypothetical company. This will allow us to demonstrate the basic mechanics of what we now understand to be a process that involves a great deal of judgment. We'll use the condensed balance sheet of ABC Corporation in Figure 8–2, augmented by some additional data and assumptions.

The company has three types of long-term capital, that is, long-term debt, preferred stock, and common equity. We assume that it could issue new bonds at an effective cost of 8.5 percent, and new preferred stock at an effective cost of 10 percent, based on proceeds from expected pricing in the market and after applicable underwriting and legal expenses. Note that these current costs are below the rates the company has been paying on its long-term capital as stated in the balance sheet, and it would most likely be prudent for management to consider refinancing at currently prevailing lower rates. ABC's common stock is currently trading between $63 and $67, and the most recent earnings per share were $4.72. Dividends per share last year were $2.50. The company's β, as calculated by security analysts, is 1.1, a fairly average risk. We further assume that the estimated risk-free return is 6.5 percent, and the best available forecast for the total return from the S&P 500 is 13 percent.

Overall company prospects are assumed to be satisfactory, and security analysts are forecasting normal growth in earnings at about 8 percent. Given this background, it's possible to calculate a weighted cost of capital. As we proceed, the choices to be made will be highlighted.

F I G U R E   8–2 ———————————————————————————————

ABC CORPORATION
Condensed Balance Sheet
($ thousands)

Assets		Liabilities and Net Worth	
Current assets	$27,500	Current liabilities	$9,500
Fixed assets (net)	35,000	Bonds (10%)	12,000
Other assets	1,500	Preferred stock (12%)	6,000
Total assets	$64,000	Common stock (1.0 million shares)	10,000
		Retained earnings	26,500
		Total liabilities and shareholder's equity	$64,000

The respective costs of the three types of capital employed can be derived as shown below. Note that we are employing the incremental cost of funds in each case, rather than the past costs as reflected in the balance sheet, where outstanding bonds carry a rate of 10 percent and preferred stock a dividend rate of 12 percent. The calculations for each type of capital appear as follows, using the methods discussed earlier:

Long-term debt: $k_d = 8.5\% \times (1 - 0.34) = 5.61\%$ after taxes

Preferred stock: $k_p = 10.0\%$ after taxes

Common equity: $k_e = 6.5\% + 1.1\,(13.0\% - 6.5\%) = 13.65\%$ after taxes

The cost of debt was based on the effective cost of 8.5 percent and adjusted for taxes, while the effective cost of preferred stock required no tax adjustment. The CAPM was used for the common equity calculation. The CAPM figure of 13.65 percent can be compared to the less satisfactory answer obtained using the dividend approach, which provides an alternative lower result. This is a function of the current dividend rate and the expected dividend growth rate:

$$\text{Common equity: } k_e = \frac{\$2.50}{\$65} + 8.0\% = 11.85\% \text{ after taxes}$$

It's not uncommon to find that the two approaches to determining the cost of equity provide rather different results, because the data and assumptions going into the calculations are not comparable. We already highlighted the most significant issues when we discussed each measure earlier.

The weights to be used in calculating the corporate cost of capital depend both on the relative stability of the current capital structure and the relevance of market values to the results. Let's assume that management is satisfied with the current capital structure as its target level and is likely to raise funds in the same proportions over time. Let's further assume that the existing bonds of the company are currently trading at 117⅝ (a $1,000 bond with a coupon rate of 10 percent is worth a premium price of about $1,176.50, in view of the decline in bond yields), while the existing preferred stock with a $12 dividend rate is trading at 120 because of the decline in preferred yields (each share with a nominal value of $100 is currently worth about $120.00).

As Figure 8–3 shows, the following proportions result when we list both book value and market value for each type of capital. Depending on the way management assesses its future needs, the proportions could remain as shown in the table, or they could be altogether different.

Assuming that no significant change is foreseen, we can calculate the weighted cost of capital for both the market and book value (Figure 8–4). The results don't differ materially in this case. Differences would become significant only after more than one percentage point.

Given that all the assumptions and choices needed to make the calculations involve some margin of error, the results should be liberally rounded off in all cases before the measure is used as a decision criterion. We can say that under the stipulated conditions for ABC Corporation, the weighted cost of incremental capital is approximately 11.5 to 12 percent.

FIGURE 8-3

Capital Structure of ABC Corporation

	Book Value	Proportion	Market Value	Proportion
Bonds	$12,000	22.0%	$14,118	16.4%
Preferred stock	6,000	11.0	7,200	8.3
Common equity	36,500	67.0	65,000	75.3
Totals	$54,500	100.0%	$86,318	100.0%

FIGURE 8-4

Weighted Cost of Capital for ABC Corporation

	Book Value Weighting			Market Value Weighting		
	Cost	Weight	Composite	Cost	Weight	Composite
Bonds	5.61%	0.22	1.23%	5.61%	0.164	0.92%
Preferred stock	10.00	0.11	1.10	10.00	0.083	0.83
Common equity	13.65	0.67	9.14	13.65	0.753	10.28
Totals		1.00	11.47%		1.000	12.03%

If the measure is used to judge the expected return from new investments, it should be viewed as a minimum standard of return from investments with comparable risk characteristics. The weighted cost of capital becomes the discount rate to determine net present values as discussed in Chapter 7. Remember, it represents the boundary between projects that create value and those that destroy value for the shareholders.

Cost of Capital and Return Standards

We've stated all along that the basic purpose of deriving a weighted cost of capital was to find a reasonable criterion for measuring new investments. This amounts to establishing a level of return high enough to compensate all providers of funds according to their expectations. By definition, projects with a positive net present value when their cash flows are discounted at this return standard would create economic value for the shareholders in the form of growing dividends and market appreciation.

However, using the weighted cost of capital for this purpose warrants further discussion. In this section, we'll examine more closely the notion of using the measure as a *cutoff rate,* and then discuss the question of projects in different *risk categories.* We'll also review the problem of the *multibusiness* firm, in which a variety of business risks are combined. Finally, we'll touch on the issue of modified standards using *multiple discount rates*. In all of these areas, a balance has to be found between the theoretically desirable and the practically doable.

Cost of Capital as a Cutoff Rate

In a *single-business company* with fairly definable risk characteristics, the weighted cost of capital as calculated here can serve as a cutoff rate in assessing capital investment projects ranked in declining order of economic desirability. If consistent analytical methods and judgments are applied to projecting the project cash flows, and if the risks inherent in the projects are similar and have been consistently estimated and tested through sensitivity analysis, then acceptance or rejection can be decided with this minimum return standard built into the net present value calculations. We're assuming that the company can finance all the projects being considered at the same incremental cost of capital and without significantly changing the capital structure.

The weighted cost of capital works well in this idealized condition because the risk premium built into the measure, the proportions of the sources of new funds, and the range of risks embodied in the projects are all consistent with each other as well as the business risk inherent in the company. When some of these conditions change, however, managerial judgment must be exercised to modify the cost of capital and its application.

One common problem, even in the single-business firm, is the real possibility that the amount of potential capital spending will exceed readily available financing to some degree. If the list of projects contains many investments that more than meet the standard, they might be attractive enough for management to modify the company's capital structure to accommodate them—if the management team has the capacity to implement all of them. Then the weighted cost of capital will likely change.

Increasing leverage might introduce additional risk, thus exerting upward pressure on the cost of both debt and equity. A significant increase in the equity base will result in near-term dilution of earnings per share, thus affecting the market value of the stock and possibly the β of the company's common stock as judged by security analysts. Although the changes might be manageable, the point is that the process of business investment and the selection of appropriate standards is never a static exercise.

Another practical issue is management's attitude toward taking business risks. Knowing that the analyses underlying business investment projects contain many uncertainties, management might wish to set the cutoff rate arbitrarily higher than the weighted cost of capital. This is done to allow for estimating errors—and even for deliberate bias in the preparation of the estimates, which is not at all uncommon in most organizations where managers compete for funds. There also might be a desire to play it safer in view of the limited reliability of the return standard itself. This adjustment, however, shouldn't be considered a substitute for using the best possible analytical effort and decision analysis tools to sharpen and test the cash flow patterns underlying the investment proposals. As we observed in Chapters 6 and 7, risk and uncertainty are a function of the many variables of an investment, which must be understood, quantified, and subjected to sensitivity analysis before appropriate return standards are applied to expected outcome.

From a conceptual standpoint, using cutoff rates significantly higher than the cost of capital might cause opportunity losses, because potentially worthwhile projects are likely to be rejected. From a practical standpoint, however, it might be prudent to leave a margin for error by adding some points to the cost of capital before using it as a cutoff rate. Of course, it's still possible at any time to reach below such a higher standard if a project has many other strategic or operational advantages that mitigate the effects of its marginal economic performance. But care must be taken to judge the impact of cutoff rates on the behavior of managers both in sponsoring risky projects and in potentially biasing their analyses to fit the higher standard expected. It's possible that over time the risk profile of the company's portfolio could be altered.

Finally, we must reiterate that capital budgeting and project selection are not merely numerical processes. Even in the most tightly focused single-product company, where all levels of management have firsthand knowledge about the intricacies of the business and its competitive setting, the decision process is always a combination of judgments affected by personal preferences, group dynamics, and the pressures of organizational realities.

Risk Categories

By definition, the weighted cost of capital represents a company's unique relative risk and particular capital structure. Yet, in a sense, this is misleading because even in the single-business company, different investment projects do involve different degrees of risk. Normally, a company encounters a variety of classes of investments ranging from replacement of equipment and facilities to expansion in existing markets, and beyond that to ventures into new products or services, or into entirely new markets, as well as into new technology.

The degree of risk inherent in these classes of investments will differ, sometimes materially, even though the products and services involved are within the scope of a single industry with a definable overall risk. Replacement of physical assets to continue serving a proven market where the company holds a strong position is far less risky and permits more reliable estimates of cash flow benefits than entering a new domestic or even international market.

A common way of handling such divergences is to set a higher discount standard for projects that are perceived to be riskier. A hierarchy of minimum rates of return can be established, somewhat arbitrarily, that ranges upward from the weighted cost of capital cutoff point. For example, if the weighted cost of capital is, say, 12 percent, that standard can be applied to ordinary replacements and expansion in markets where the company has a position. A standard of 14 or 15 percent can be applied to entering related markets, whereas a risky new venture might be measured at a premium standard of even 20 percent or higher.

As we demonstrated earlier in discussing the power of discounting, particularly at the higher rates, the chances of riskier projects being acceptable will be severely tested under such conditions. Yet a demanding risk/reward trade-off standard might be appropriate if management's risk preferences are quite conservative.

On the other hand, it's often argued—particularly in a single-business company—that the weighted cost of capital implicitly embodies the whole range of risks normally encountered while participating and growing in that business. Consequently, one can even stipulate that the range of discount standards should be grouped around the weighted cost of capital. In effect, this allows the less risky projects to be discounted at a return standard below the weighted cost of capital, whereas riskier ones would be tested at or above that level. When all projects are combined, the result should be an average return at or above the weighted cost of capital.

This approach would require, however, that the proportions of projects being approved in the various risk classes be carefully monitored to ensure that the overall average will achieve the desired result over time. Otherwise, the company could encounter significant deviations from expected performance. Moreover, we must remember that shareholder value can grow only if investment returns exceed the cost of capital in the long run.

An additional practical issue tends to support raising the return standards for the different classes of capital projects. Every company faces a certain percentage of capital expenditures that yield no definable cash flow benefits. Among these are mandated outlays for environmental protection, investments for improved infrastructure of facilities, and expenditures for office space and equipment.

A strong argument can be made that funds required for these purposes must in fact be economically carried along by the expected cash flow benefits obtained from all other productive investments. By definition, therefore, the total amount of capital invested should provide a return sufficient to meet or exceed the weighted cost of capital. If some part of the capital budget is economically neutral, the returns from the economically positive projects will have to be higher to make up for such "nonproductive" investments. If management chooses to adjust its return standards for this condition, the modification will likely involve a fair degree of judgment about the mix and characteristics of the expected project portfolio.

Our discussion has gone beyond the purely analytical aspects of the subject and we've pointed out many practical issues involved in choosing and using economic measures for business decisions, of which discount standards are only one form. It's important to remember that the actual procedures employed by a company are likely to allow for a fair degree of judgmental override of the quantitative results of any financial analysis. This includes the specific return standards for capital investments, which are likely to be modified from time to time, to assist not only in project-specific economic assessment, but also in shifting the strategic emphasis between classes of investments. Senior management must, of course, continuously monitor and guide the pattern of investments they wish to undertake so that shareholder expectations are met. The pattern of investments suggested by the economic analyses and the return standards can and should be modified to fit the changing strategic direction of a company.

Cost of Capital in Multibusiness Companies

The issues involved in setting appropriate return standards become even more complex when a company has several divisions or subsidiaries engaged in rather different businesses and markets that vary greatly in their risk characteristics. Although it's possible to calculate an overall cost of capital for the company with the help of a β that reflects the company's covariance of consolidated returns with the market return, it's far more difficult to derive equivalent cost of capital standards for the individual operating divisions. Most commonly, a multibusiness company has a single capital structure that supplies funds for the various businesses. Therefore, capital cannot be apportioned to the different risk categories on the basis of individual cost of capital standards that employ specific betas and debt ratings. These would be available only if the divisions were autonomous companies whose shares are traded in the securities markets.

The approach often used under such conditions is to estimate a series of surrogate costs of capital based on costs for independent companies that are comparable to the various businesses, if that's at all possible. From this background, a group of individual standards can be developed for the multibusiness company—modified with a great deal of judgment—that are similar to the array of risk categories in a single-business company.

Obviously, the apportionment of capital in a multibusiness setting also is complicated by the practical issue of divisional managements competing for limited funds while having to meet different standards. Corporate management must be very careful first to establish broad allocations of funds to the various operating divisions that match the desired corporate strategic emphasis, after having valued the respective business strategies in an overall portfolio sense. Then projects can be ranked within those individual blocks of allocated funds according to the different discount rates, and decisions can be made to accept or reject specific investments.

A predictable consequence of such an approach, however, is the dilemma of having to refuse specific higher-return (and perhaps higher-risk) opportunities in one division, whose overall allocation is exhausted, in favor of lower-return (and perhaps lower-risk) opportunities in another division. This dilemma has to be resolved by the corporate management team, who is responsible for developing and monitoring the strategic direction of the total company, including the desired business risk profile of the company's portfolio. The main point to remember is that top management needs to shape the company's overall capital investment portfolio in line with shareholder expectations, so that the sum of the parts can be expected to meet or exceed the corporate weighted cost of capital standard.

As we'll discuss in Chapter 11, the cost of capital also is used to determine whether individual lines of business in a diversified company are contributing to or detracting from shareholder value creation. Here the point is to test past and prospective overall cash flows from each business unit as a whole in relation to a minimum cash flow return standard based on the cost of capital.

Multiple Rate Analysis

One additional technical observation should be made here. Some practitioners argue for applying different discount rates to different portions of the cash flow pattern of a *single* project when calculating the measures of economic desirability, in order to reflect the relative riskiness of the various elements of the project. In effect, this is one more risk adjustment beyond the risk premium already inherent in a particular discount standard. For example, an investment can be separated into elements that carry a business risk, such as products or services, and elements that carry an investment risk, like land or other resources underlying the former. There are many variations of this approach, although it's not widely used in practice.

It should be apparent that because of the uncertainties inherent in project analysis and the complexities of establishing several standards, multiple rate analysis might not be warranted in most normal business investment situations. At the same time, different standards might indeed be necessary in assessing specialized projects, such as real estate investments, complex leasing proposals, natural resources investments, and other uniquely structured cash flow proposals. Such special conditions can involve financial contracts integral to the projects themselves, or require economic judgments about rather different stages in a given project.

In those cases, it is appropriate to discount portions of project cash flows at rates that reflect their contractual nature, as compared with other portions of the cash flow pattern that are subject to the uncertainties of operating in the business environment. These analytical refinements are too specific to be covered here, but are dealt with in the reference materials listed at the end of the chapter.

Key Issues

The following is a recap of the key issues raised directly or indirectly in this chapter. They are enumerated here to help the reader keep the techniques discussed within the perspective of financial theory and business practice.

1. The specific costs to a company of various types of indebtedness and preferred securities are readily apparent in the tax-adjusted cash obligations incurred, but it's difficult to measure the secondary costs implicit in debt service, credit rating, and market assessment.

2. Determining the cost of equity capital is intricately linked to the risk/reward expectations of the financial markets, because the cost of equity must be expressed in terms of an expected economic return for the shareholders of the company.

3. Simple surrogates for the cost of equity capital, such as earnings and dividend models, suffer both from variability of underlying conditions, which can distort their results, and from conceptual shortcomings.

4. The conceptual link established by modern financial theory between general financial market expectations and the value of an individual company's equity securities remains an approximation based on a series of simplifying assumptions.

5. The use of a company-specific risk factor (β) to adjust average return expectations is a valid theoretical concept, but both definition and measurement of this factor remain open to disagreement and continue to pose practical problems.

6. The development of a weighted cost of capital raises significant questions regarding not only the elements composing the various costs, but also the weights to be used and the concept of measuring incremental funding.

7. The use of a weighted cost of capital in setting business investment return standards is conceptually useful for projects within a company's normal range of risk, but the measure might need modification for business investments of dissimilar risk.

8. The theory of finance continues to evolve, but as new concepts are introduced and refined in the decision-making process, careful linkages to both data sources and the organization have to be established in order to make practical application both understandable and feasible.

9. Objective analytical approaches to business investment assessment are only one important input in the choices management must make. Individual and group attitudes, preferences, and judgments exert significant influences over interpretation and decision processes in the areas of investment, operations, and financing.

10. The precision implied in the calculations of economic measures like cost of capital or net present value must be tempered by the knowledge that the data and assumptions underlying them are potentially subject to a wide range of error.

Summary

In this chapter, we sketched out the rationale for determining the costs of various forms of financing as an input in making different types of financial decisions. We found that the specific cost of debt, both short term and long term, was relatively easy to calculate, given the nature of the contracts underlying it in most cases. The same was true for preferred stock. We also found that the fixed nature of the obligations incurred with debt and preferred stock raised a host of secondary considerations that exact an economic cost from the company in terms of debt service and restrictive covenants. Establishing the cost of common equity was particularly challenging because of the residual claim common shareholders have on the company, and because of their risk/reward expectations, which are reflected in the market's valuation of the shares.

After discussing techniques for calculating the respective costs of the three basic types of financing, and pointing out the theoretical and practical caveats, we developed the weighted cost of capital as an input to investment analysis. It was characterized as the dividing line between projects that added value and those that destroyed value for the shareholders. We found that use of the weighted cost of capital as a minimum standard for discounting investment cash flows is affected by the way project and business risks are interpreted within the corporate portfolio, and by the attitudes of corporate decision makers. At the same time, we found the approximate weighted cost of capital to be a conceptually appropriate target around which to build a series of return standards befitting a particular company's range of businesses and the investments and risks connected with them.

Analytical Support

The set of Excel-based templates (*Interactive Templates*), which is downloadable at no charge from the Web at www.mhhe.com/helfert//edu does not contain a template for cost of capital calculations as discussed in this chapter.

Financial Genome, the advanced financial analysis software application described in Appendix I, is a fully integrated analytical and planning model for both the professional user and the business student. It is designed to develop a full set of financial ratios and relationships, in addition to creating integrated financial statements from historical data inputs as well as for projections of financial performance. It is capable of developing and displaying the cost of capital of a company in various forms, calculated automatically from appropriate input data as well as databases. The software contains a five-year database (1996 to 2000) for 3M Corporation, matching the company's financial statements reproduced in this chapter, which can be used to display a full range of financial indicators and to determine the company's cost of capital.

Financial Genome is downloadable from the Web, using the unique and restricted code provided with this book. (see "Downloads" at the end of Appendix I, p. 479).

Selected References

Brealey, Richard and Stewart Myers. *Principles of Corporate Finance.* 5th ed. Burr Ridge, IL: Irwin/McGraw-Hill, 1996.
Ross, Stephen A.; Randolph W. Westerfield; and Jeffrey Jaffe. *Corporate Finance.* 5th ed. Burr Ridge, IL: Irwin/McGraw-Hill, 1999.
Weston, J. Fred; Scott Besley; and Eugene Brigham. *Essentials of Managerial Finance.* 11th ed. Chicago: Dryden Press, 1997.

Self-Study Exercises, Problems, and Discussion Questions

Exercises and Problems *(Selected Solutions are Provided in Appendix VI)*

1. The GHI company has three types of capital in its capital structure:

   Long-term debt at 10%. (Current yield is 8%.)
   12% preferred stock. (Current yield is 10%.)
   Common stock with a book value of $67.50 per share.

Currently, the company's common stock is trading in the range of $75 to $82; the most recent closing price was $77. The most recent annual earnings per share were $9.50, while dividends paid over the past year were at the rate of $4.50 per share. The company's earnings have been growing on average about 7 percent per year. *Value Line* lists the company's β at 1.25, while the risk-free return is estimated to be 7 percent. Forecasts for returns from the S&P 500 are currently about 13 percent. Calculate the specific cost of capital for each type of capital of GHI Company. Assume a tax rate of 36 percent. Discuss your findings.

2. The KLN Company has the following capital structure:

	Proportion	Existing Conditions	Current (Incremental)
Long-term debt	$250	11% average rate	8% yield
Preferred stock	50	12% stated rate	9% yield
Common equity	400	—	Price range $45–$60
(10 million shares)			(Recent price $50)
Total capitalization	$700		

The company's β is currently estimated at 1.2, while the risk-free return is considered to be 5.5 percent. The most recent estimate of the return from the S&P 500 is 13.0 percent. Develop the weighted average cost of capital for KLN Company for both the existing conditions (original costs) and incremental conditions. Use both a book value and a market value weighting for each case, as well as management's target ratio of 42 percent debt and 58 percent equity, with preferred stock eliminated. Assume a tax rate of 36 percent. Discuss your findings and the range of results achieved.

3. Using Financial Genome and its database for 3M Corporation, develop the company's cost of capital in the various forms discussed in this chapter. Stipulate the company's β and any other necessary assumptions as inputs to this process. Discuss your findings.

Discussion Questions

1. Why can't we speak of "*the* cost of capital" as an absolute figure?
2. What indirect costs can be ascribed to a long-term loan or to a convertible debenture?
3. Why are shareholder expectations important in developing the cost of common equity when the company has no control over the behavior of the stock market?
4. If beta (β), as defined in the CAPM, isn't a fully satisfactory measure of risk, what alternative concepts can you suggest?
5. How important is the choice of weights in developing the weighted cost of capital as a minimum return standard?

6. If weighted cost of capital is a useful standard with which to assess prospective returns from new capital investments, how should the return on existing investments be judged?

7. If a company's financial policies are changing (e.g., the use of leverage increases), does this mean its return requirements must change also?

8. If you were president of a multidivision company with rather different businesses, how would you answer the argument that some divisions use lower return standards than others?

9. How critical is it that a capital investment project exactly meet the weighted cost of capital standard? What questions would you ask?

10. What major elements would you consider in developing a broad allocation of capital to the rather different divisions of a company? Which would be most important?

CHAPTER 9

ANALYSIS OF FINANCING CHOICES

$\mathbf{L}$et's now turn to analyzing the third aspect of the three-part decisional systems context introduced in Chapter 1: investment, operations, and financing. We'll concentrate on the choices available in arranging a company's long-term financing, while setting aside the incremental operational funds sources used routinely by companies in line with practices in a particular industry or service, and broadly discussed in Chapter 2. We choose this focus because, as we observed earlier, the nature and pattern of long-term funding sources are intricately connected with the types of business investments made and are critical to the growth, stability, or decline of operations. Indeed, management must fund its strategic business design with an appropriate mix of capital sources that will assist in bringing about the desired increase in shareholder value.

This chapter will deal with the key considerations in assessing the basic financing options open to management. Because the choice among long-term debt, preferred, and common equity is blurred by a bewildering array of modifications and specialized instruments in each category, we'll discuss only the main characteristics of the three basic types of securities. Because our emphasis is on quantitative analysis, we must keep in mind that many other considerations enter into these choices. For example, the specific type of business and the industry in which it operates will affect the long-term capital structure chosen at various stages of a company's development, as will the preferences and experiences of senior management and the board of directors. These aspects cannot be adequately covered within the scope of this book.

We'll begin with a broad framework for analysis that defines the key areas to be analyzed and weighed in choosing sources of long-term financing. Next, we'll look at the techniques of calculating the impact on a company's financial performance resulting from the introduction of new capital supplied by each of the three basic sources. Then we'll turn to a graphic representation of these results, the range of earnings (EBIT) break-even chart, in order to demonstrate the dynamic impact that funds choices have on changing company conditions. After touching on leasing as a special source, we'll briefly discuss capital structure proportions and list the key issues involved in the area of funds choices.

Framework for Analysis

Several key elements must be considered and weighed when a company is faced with raising additional (incremental) long-term funds. We'll take up the five most important ones in some detail:

- Cost
- Risk exposure
- Flexibility
- Timing
- Control

This discussion is intended to serve as a conceptual checklist to ensure that the most important considerations have been covered in the choice of long-term financing.

Cost of Incremental Funds

One of the main criteria for choosing from among alternative sources of additional long-term capital is the cost involved in obtaining and servicing the funds. In Chapter 8, we discussed in detail the specific and implicit costs a company incurs in using debt, preferred stock, or common equity.

As a general rule, we found that funds raised with various forms of debt are least costly in specific terms, in part because the interest paid by the borrowing company is tax deductible under current U.S. laws. The actual rate of interest charged on incremental debt will depend, of course, on the credit rating of the company and on the degree of leverage introduced into the capital structure by the new debt, as discussed in Chapter 5. In other words, the specific cost will be affected not only by current market conditions for all long-term debt instruments, but also as a function of the company-specific risk as perceived by lenders, underwriters, and investors. As we mentioned at the time, other costs are also implicit in raising long-term debt, including legal and underwriting expenses connected with the issue, and the nature and severity of any restrictions imposed by the creditors.

The stated cost of preferred stock is generally higher than debt, partly because preferred dividends are not tax deductible, and partly because preferred stock has a somewhat weaker position on the risk/reward hierarchy. Holders of these shares expect a higher return to compensate for their ownership risk. The comparative specific cost of preferred stock is relatively easy to calculate. The dividend level is clearly defined, and legal and underwriting costs incurred at the time of the issue are reflected in the net proceeds to the company. However, at times a variety of specific provisions can involve implicit costs to the company.

In Chapter 8 we found that determining the cost of common equity turned out to be a fairly complex task. It involved constructing a theoretical framework within which to assess the risk/reward expectations of the shareholder. Direct approaches (shortcuts) to measuring the specific cost of common equity were found wanting because they didn't address the company's relative risk as reflected in common share values. We had to use a more integrated framework that involved some surrogates and approximations to arrive at a practical result, based on the theoretical model.

The cost of common equity based on the CAPM approach could be directly compared to the specific costs of debt and preferred stock, and it also could be used to arrive at a weighted overall cost of the company's capital structure. As we'll see shortly, however, increasing common equity in the capital structure by issuing new shares involves additional considerations. The incremental shares dilute earnings per share, require additional and even growing dividends where these are paid, and also change the capital structure proportions. These effects introduce implicit economic costs or advantages into the funding picture.

Risk Exposure

If we use variability of earnings as a working definition of risk, we find that a company's risk is affected by the specific cost commitments, such as interest on debt or dividends on preferred shares, that each funding source entails. These commitments introduce financial leverage effects in the company's earnings performance, or will heighten any financial leverage already existing. As we discussed in Chapter 5, the use of instruments involving fixed financial charges will widen the swings in earnings as economic and operating conditions change.

Given the responsibility for providing holders of common shares with growing economic value, management must therefore expend much thought and care in determining the appropriate mix of debt and equity in the company's capital structure. This balance involves providing enough lower-cost debt to boost the shareholders' returns, but not so much debt as to endanger shareholder value creation during periods of low earnings, to arrive at a mix of capital sources carefully tailored to industry and company conditions.

The ultimate risk, of course, is that a company will not be able to fulfill its debt service obligations. The proportion of debt in the capital structure, and similarly, the proportion of preferred stock, affects the degree of risk of partial or total default. Analyzing risk exposure is based on establishing a historical pattern of earnings variability and cash flows from which future conditions are projected. These must take into account the extent to which a company's strategy is changing, any shifts in exposure to the business cycle, shifting competitive pressures, and potential operating inefficiencies.

Clearly, company-specific risk (earnings variability) and the company's ability to service its debt burden are intimately related to the particular characteristics of the business or businesses in which the company operates. Moreover, they're affected by general economic conditions—apart from management's ability to generate satisfactory operating performance.

The degree of financial leverage advisable and prudent will therefore vary greatly among different industries and services, and also will depend on the firm's relative competitive position and maturity stage. A new business entails a far different risk exposure for the creditor than does the established industry leader, apart from specific industry conditions.

Flexibility

The third area we must consider is the question of flexibility, defined here as the range of future funding options that remain open once a specific alternative has been chosen. As each increment of financing is completed, the choice among future alternatives might be more limited during the next round of raising capital. For example, if long-term debt obligations are chosen as a major funding source, the level of total debt in the capital structure, restrictive covenants, encumbered assets, and other constraints that impose minimum financial ratios might mean that the company can use only common equity as a future source of capital for some time ahead.

Flexibility essentially requires forward planning. Careful consideration must be given to matching strategic plans and corporate financial policies. Potential acquisitions, expansion, and diversification all are affected by the degree of flexibility management has in choosing appropriate funding, and by the funds drain resulting from servicing debt commitments or preferred dividends. To the extent possible, management must coordinate its planned future cash flows and investment patterns with the pattern of successive rounds of financing that will support them. Being in a situation where future funds sources are limited to only one option because of present commitments can pose a significant problem. Changing conditions in the financial markets for different types of securities might make this single option unappealing or even unavailable when funds needs become critical.

Timing

The fourth element in choosing long-term funding is the timing of the transaction. Timing is important in relation to the movement of prices and yields in the securities markets. Shifting conditions in these markets affect the specific cost a company incurs with each option, in the form of the stated interest rate on new debt or the preferred dividend rate carried by new preferred stock, as well as in terms of the net proceeds to be received from each of the alternatives. Therefore, the timing of the issue will affect the cost spread between the several funding alternatives available. Also, specific market conditions might in fact either preclude or distinctly favor particular choices.

For instance, in times of depressed stock prices, bonds might prove to be the most suitable alternative from the standpoint of both cost and market demand. Inasmuch as the proceeds from any issue depend on the success of the placement—public or private—of the securities, the conditions encountered in the stock or bond markets can seriously affect the choice. Potential uncertainty in financial markets is therefore a strong argument for always maintaining some degree of flexibility in the capital structure.

Control

Finally, the degree of ownership control of the company held by existing share-holders is an important factor as funding choices are considered. Obviously, when new shares of common stock are issued to new shareholders, the effect is a dilu-tion of both earnings per share and the proportion of ownership of the existing shareholders. Such dilution becomes a significant issue for the owners of compa-nies that could be subject to potential takeovers. In the past decade, the issue of control has been raised to new heights in the many battles over control during the corporate merger and acquisition boom.

Even if debt or preferred stock is used as the source of long-term funding, existing shareholders can be affected indirectly because restrictive provisions and covenants might be necessary to obtain bond financing, or because concessions must be made to protect the rights of the more senior preferred shareholders.

Dilution of ownership is a very important issue in closely held corporations, particularly new ventures. In such situations, founders of the company and/or the major shareholders generally exercise full effective control over the company. Issuing new shares will dilute both control over the direction of the company and the key shareholders' ability to enjoy the major share of economic value growth from successful performance. Dilution of earnings and possible retardation of growth in earnings per share brought about by diluting common equity owner-ship is, of course, not limited to closely held companies. Rather, it's a general phenomenon that we'll discuss shortly.

Finally, dilution of control and earnings is a major consideration in convert-ibility, a feature found in certain bonds and preferred stocks. This provision allows conversion of the security into common stock under specified conditions of tim-ing and price. In effect, such instruments are hybrid securities, because they rep-resent delayed issues of common stock at a stipulated price higher than the market value of the common stock at the time the convertible bond or preferred stock is issued. We mentioned this feature in earlier chapters in terms of its effect on fi-nancial ratios, particularly when discussing the concept of diluted earnings per share, and we'll return to it later in this chapter.

Control becomes an issue in convertible financing options because the eventual conversion of the bond or preferred stock will add new common shares to the capital structure and thus cause dilution. The ultimate effect is just like a di-rect issue of new common stock.

The Choice

It should be clear from this brief résumé of the considerations involved that any decision about alternative sources of long-term funding can't be based on cost alone, even though cost is a very important factor and must be analyzed early in the decision-making process. Unfortunately, there are no hard-and-fast rules spelling out precisely how the final decision should be made, because the choice depends so much on the conditions prevailing in the company and in the securities markets at the time, and on the preferences of the board and senior management. The best approach is to consider carefully the five areas we've just presented and to examine the pros and cons of each as an input to the decision. Needless to say, one very significant consideration is the effect of each funding source on a company's future earnings performance. In the section that follows, we'll examine methods of calculating this effect.

Techniques of Calculation

For purposes of illustration, we'll employ the basic statements of a hypothetical company, ABC Corporation. The company is weighing alternative ways to raise $10 million to support the introduction of a new product. After analyzing the corporation's current performance, we'll successively discuss the impact on that performance level caused by introducing long-term debt, preferred stock, and common equity, in equal amounts of $10 million each. We'll focus on the implications of financing alternatives on the company's reported earnings, but will also test the cash flow implications of the choices to be made.

ABC's abbreviated balance sheet is shown in Figure 9–1. The company currently has one million shares of common stock outstanding, with a par value of $10 per share. From the company's income statement (not shown), we learn that ABC Corporation has earned $9 million before taxes on sales of $115 million in the most recent year. Income taxes paid amounted to $3.06 million, an effective rate of 34 percent.

Current Performance

We begin our appraisal of the current performance of ABC Corporation by calculating the earnings per share (EPS) of common stock. Throughout the chapter, this format of calculating EPS and related measures will be used. It's a step-by-step analysis of the earnings impact of each type of long-term capital.

First, we'll establish the earnings before interest and taxes (EBIT), a measure we discussed in Chapter 3. From that figure we must subtract a variety of charges applicable to different long-term funds. The first of these is interest charges on long-term debt. Normally short-term interest can be ignored unless it's a significant amount, because we assume—given the temporary nature of short-term obligations that arise from ongoing operations—that the related interest charges have been properly deducted from income before arriving at the EBIT figure.

The calculations of earnings per share are shown in Figure 9–2. A provision is made in the table for both long-term interest and preferred dividends. No amounts are shown for these, however, because our hypothetical company at this

FIGURE 9-1 ————————————————————————————————————

ABC CORPORATION
Balance Sheet
($ millions)

Assets		Liabilities and Net Worth	
Current assets	$15	Current liabilities	$7
Fixed assets (net)	29	Common stock	10
Other assets	1	Retained earning	28
Total assets	$45	Total liabilities and shareholders' equity	$45

FIGURE 9-2 ————————————————————————————————————

ABC CORPORATION
Earnings per Share Calculation
($ thousands, except per share figures)

Earnings before interest and taxes (EBIT)	$9,000
Less: interest charges on long-term debt	-0-
Earnings before income taxes	9,000
Less: Income taxes at 34%	3,060
Earnings after income taxes	5,940
Less: Preferred dividends	-0-
Earnings available for common stock	$5,940
Common shares outstanding (number)	1 million
Earnings per share (EPS)	$5.94
Less: Common dividends per share	2.50
Retained earnings per share	$3.44
Retained earnings in total	$3,440

point has neither long-term debt nor preferred stock outstanding. The calculations result in earnings available to common stock of $5.94 per share. From that figure we must subtract $2.50, which represents a cash dividend voted by the board of directors. We find that this fairly high level of dividend payout (between 40 and 50 percent of earnings) has been maintained for many years, impacting ABC's financing flexibility somewhat. The company's earnings have steadily grown by about 4 percent on average over the past decade. The stock is widely held and traded, and currently commands a market price ranging from about $38 to $47, which means it's trading at roughly seven to eight times earnings. The latest security analyst's report suggests a β of 0.9, while the risk-free rate of return is judged to be 6.5 percent, and the expected stock market return from the S&P 500 is forecast at 14.0 percent.

Long-Term Debt* in the Capital Structure

As debt is introduced into this structure, both the financial condition and the earnings performance of ABC Corporation are significantly affected. To raise the $10 million needed to fund the new product, management has found that it's possible, as one alternative, to issue debenture bonds. Debentures are not secured by any specific assets of the company; instead they're issued against the company's general credit standing. These bonds, under assumed market conditions, will carry an interest (coupon) rate of 11.5 percent, will become due 20 years from date of issue, and will entail a sinking fund provision of $400,000 per year beginning with the fifth year. The balance outstanding at the end of 20 years will be repaid as a balloon payment of $4 million. The company expects to raise the full $10 million from the bond issue after all underwriting expenses, in effect receiving the par value.

Once the new product financed with the proceeds has been successfully introduced, the company projects incremental earnings of at least $2.0 million before taxes. Little risk of product obsolescence or major competitive inroads is expected by management for the next 5 to 10 years, because the company has developed a unique process protected by careful patent coverage.

We can now trace the impact of long-term debt on the company's performance, observing both the change in earnings and dividends, and the specific cost of the newly created debt itself. (A fairly high interest rate and preferred dividend were chosen for this illustration to make the impact of the choices more visible in the graphic analysis shown later.) We'll analyze two contrasting conditions:

- The immediate impact of the $10 million debt without any offsetting benefits from the new product.

- The improved conditions expected once the investment has become operative and the new product has begun to generate earnings, probably after one year.

The results of the two calculations are shown in Figure 9–3. The instantaneous effect of adding debt is a reduction of the earnings available for common stock. This is caused by the stated interest cost of 11.5 percent on $10 million of bonds, or $1,150,000 before taxes. Earnings after interest and taxes drop by $759,000 as compared to the initial conditions in Figure 9–2. This earnings reduction represents, of course, the after-tax cost of the bond interest, or $1,150,000 times $(1 - 0.34)$.

As a consequence, earnings per share decline to $5.18, a drop of 76 cents, or an immediate dilution of 12.8 percent from the prior level. This change is purely due to the incremental interest cost which, on a per share basis, amounts to the same 76 cents, that is, the after-tax interest of $759,000 divided by 1 million

---

*We are limiting our discussion and examples to ordinary long-term debt instruments recorded on the balance sheet. Discussion of the use of off-balance sheet financing through a variety of creative and often risky arrangements of the kind which brought the Enron Company down in late 2001 is left to specialized texts.

F I G U R E   9–3

ABC CORPORATION
Earnings per Share with New Bond Issue
($ thousands, except per share figures)

	Before New Product	With New Product
Earnings before interest and taxes (EBIT)	$9,000	$11,000
Less: Interest charges on long-term debt	1,150	1,150
Earnings before income taxes	7,850	9,850
Less: Income taxes at 34%	2,669	3,349
Earnings after income taxes	5,181	6,501
Less: Preferred dividends	-0-	-0-
Earnings available for common stock	$5,181	$ 6,501
Common shares outstanding (number)	1 million	1 million
Earnings per share (EPS)	$ 5.18	$ 6.50
Less: Common dividends per share	2.50	2.50
Retained earnings per share	$ 2.68	$ 4.00
Retained earnings in total	$2,681	$ 4,001
Original EPS (Figure 9–2)	$ 5.94	$ 5.94
Change in EPS	−0.76	+0.56
Percent change in EPS	−12.8%	+9.4%

shares. In Chapter 8 we discussed the stated annual cost of debt funds, defined as the tax-adjusted rate of interest carried by the debt instrument. Assuming an effective tax rate of 34 percent in our example, the stated cost of debt for ABC Corporation is therefore 7.59 percent. We also explained in Chapter 8 that the specific annual cost of debt is found by relating the stated annual cost to the actual proceeds received. If these proceeds differ from the par value of the debt instrument, the specific annual cost of the debt will, of course, be higher or lower than the stated rate.

In the case of ABC Corporation, we assumed that net proceeds were effectively at par, and therefore the specific cost of ABC's new debt is also 7.59 percent, a figure which we'll compare with the specific cost of the other alternatives for raising capital.

When we turn to the second column of Figure 9–3, we find that the assumed successful introduction of the new product will more than compensate ABC Company for the earnings impact of the interest paid on the bonds. In other words, the investment project is earning more than the specific cost of the debt employed to fund it. After-tax earnings have risen to $6,501,000, a net increase of $561,000 over the original $5,940,000 in Figure 9–2. As a consequence, earnings per share rose 56 cents above the original $5.94, an increase of almost 10 percent.

By more than offsetting the total after-tax interest cost of the debentures of $759,000, the successfully implemented new investment is projected to boost the earnings of the common shares. Incremental earnings of $1,320,000 ($2 million pretax earnings less tax at 34 percent) significantly exceed the incremental cost of $759,000. Therefore, the investment—if ABC's earnings assumptions prove realistic—apparently has provided an increment of economic value. In effect, the financial leverage introduced with the debt alternative is positive.

Yet, several questions might be asked. For example, suppose the investment earned just $759,000 after taxes, exactly covering the cost of the debt supporting it and maintaining the shareholders' position just as before in terms of earnings per share. Would the investment still be justified? Would this mean that the investment was made at no cost to the shareholders?

At first glance, one might believe this, but a number of issues must be considered here. First of all, no mention has been made of the sinking fund obligations which will begin five years hence and which represent a cash outlay of $400,000 per year. Such principal payments are not tax deductible and must be paid out of the after-tax cash flow generated by the company. Thus, debt service (burden coverage) will require 40 cents per share over and above the interest cost of 76 cents per share, for a total of $1.16 per share. The $400,000 will no longer be available for dividends or other corporate purposes, because it is committed to the repayment of debt principal. If we suppose that earnings from the investment exactly equaled the interest cost of the debt, how would the company repay the principal? At what point are the shareholders better off than they were before?

There's an obvious fallacy in this line of discussion. It stems from the use of accounting earnings to represent the benefits of the project and comparing these to the after-tax cost of the debt capital used to finance it. This isn't a proper economic comparison, as we demonstrated in Chapters 6 and 7. Only a discounted cash flow analysis can determine the true economic cost/benefit trade-off. We could say that the project was exactly yielding the specific cost of the debt capital associated with it only if the net present value of the project was exactly zero when we discount the incremental annual cash flows at 7.59 percent.

This result would then represent an internal rate of return of 7.59 percent, a level of economic performance that would scarcely be acceptable to management. Yet even under that limited condition, the project's cash flows (as contrasted to the accounting profit recorded in the operating statement) would have to be higher than the $759,000 after-tax earnings required to pay only the interest on the bonds. This must be so because under the present value framework of investment analysis, the incremental cash flows associated with a project must not only provide the specified return but also amortize the investment itself, as we saw in Chapters 6 and 7.

Let's now return to the real purpose of this analytical framework. Our analysis is clearly *not* designed to judge the desirability of the investment; we must assume that this has been adequately done by management. Instead, we're interested only in which alternative form for financing the approved investment is most advantageous for the company under the specific circumstances presented. In this context, the impact of each alternative on the company's earnings is one of several aspects considered when deciding on new funding.

In the case of debt, which under normal conditions is the lowest-cost alternative, we would indeed expect a financial leverage effect in favor of the shareholder. When the project was chosen, it must have met a return standard based approximately on the weighted cost of capital—a return which is far higher than the cost of debt capital alone. In summary, the introduction of debt immediately dilutes earnings per share, but this impact is followed by a boost in earnings per share when the project's reported accounting earnings exceed the interest cost as reflected in the company's income statement. Also, the company must allow for the future sinking fund payments from a cash flow planning standpoint, because beginning with the fifth year, 40 cents per share of the company's cash flow will be committed annually to repayment of principal.

It's generally useful to examine the implications of these facts under a variety of conditions, that is, the risk posed by earnings fluctuations in both the basic business and in the new products' incremental profit contribution, which all along we've assumed to be successful. We'll take such variations into account later.

Preferred Stock in the Capital Structure

ABC Corporation could also meet its long-term financing needs with an alternative issue of $10 million of preferred stock, at $100 per share, which carries a stated dividend rate of 12.5 percent. For simplicity, we'll again assume that the net proceeds to the company will be equivalent to the nominal price of $100, after legal and underwriting expenses. Figure 9–4 analyzes the conditions before and after implementation of the new product investment.

This time we find a more severe drop in the earnings available for common stock, because of the impact of the preferred dividends of $1.25 million per year. Not only is the stated cost (as well as the specific cost, given that the net proceeds were again at par) of the new preferred stock higher by one full percentage point than the stated cost of the bonds, but also the dividends paid on the preferred stock are not tax deductible under current laws. In fact, we're dealing with an alternative which costs, in comparable terms, 12.5 percent after taxes versus 7.59 percent after taxes for the bonds.

Therefore, the immediate dilution in earnings with the preferred issue is $1.25 per share, or 21 percent, when compared to the initial situation. Over time, as the earnings from the new product are realized, the eventual increase in earnings per share amounts to only 7 cents, or a slight improvement of 1.2 percent. The $1.25 million annual commitment of after-tax funds for dividends leaves very little room for any net gain in reported profit from the earnings generated by the investment—which we know are estimated as $2 million before taxes and $1,320,000 after taxes.

In this situation, the assumed conditions allow for very limited financial leverage. Only little more than a 1 percent rise in earnings per share is achieved over the starting level, whereas the fixed after-tax financing costs have nearly

FIGURE 9–4

ABC CORPORATION
Earnings per Share with New Preferred Stock Issue
($ thousands, except per share figures)

	Before New Product	With New Product
Earnings before interest and taxes (EBIT)	$9,000	$11,000
Less: Interest charges on long-term debt	-0-	-0-
Earnings before income taxes	9,000	11,000
Less: Income taxes at 34%	3,060	3,740
Earnings after income taxes	5,940	7,260
Less: Preferred dividends	1,250	1,250
Earnings available for common stock	$4,690	$ 6,010
Common shares outstanding (number)	1 million	1 million
Earnings per share (EPS)	$ 4.69	$ 6.01
Less: Common dividends per share	2.50	2.50
Retained earnings per share	$ 2.19	$ 3.51
Retained earnings in total	$2,190	$ 3,510
Original EPS (Figure 9–2)	$ 5.94	$ 5.94
Change in EPS	−1.25	+0.07
Percent change in EPS	−21.0%	+1.2%

doubled when compared to the bond alternative. Earnings per share would be unchanged if the product were to achieve minimum earnings in the amount of the pretax cost of preferred dividends:

$$\frac{\$1,250,000}{(1 - 0.34)} = \$1,894,000$$

At that level, the incremental earnings from the new product would just offset the incremental financing cost—a break-even situation. Note that the sizable earnings requirement of almost $1.9 million is two-thirds larger than the $1,150,000 pretax interest cost with the bond alternative.

Common Stock in the Capital Structure

A new issue of common stock as the third alternative for raising $10 million has an even more severe impact on earnings. Let's assume that ABC Corporation will issue 275,000 new shares at a net price to the company of $36.36 after underwriters' fees and legal expenses are met. Such a discount from the current market price of $40 should help ensure successful placement of the issue. The number of

FIGURE 9–5

ABC CORPORATION
Earnings per Share with New Common Stock Issue
($ thousands, except per share figures)

	Before New Product	With New Product
Earnings before interest and taxes (EBIT)	$9,000	$11,000
Less: Interest charges on long-term debt	-0-	-0-
Earnings before income taxes	9,000	11,000
Less: Federal income taxes at 34%	3,060	3,740
Earnings after income taxes	5,940	7,260
Less: Preferred dividends	-0-	-0-
Earnings available for common stock	$5,940	$ 7,260
Common shares outstanding (number)	1.275 million	1.275 million
Earnings per share (EPS)	$ 4.66	$ 5.69
Less: Common dividends per share	2.50	2.50
Retained earnings per share	$ 2.16	$ 3.19
Retained earnings in total	$2,752	$ 4,072
Original EPS (Figure 9–2)	$ 5.94	$ 5.94
Change in EPS	−1.28	−0.25
Percent change in EPS	−21.5%	−4.2%

shares outstanding thus increases by 27.5 percent over the current one million shares. Figure 9–5 shows the impact on earnings in the same way as was done for the other two alternatives.

We observe that immediate dilution is a full $1.28 per share, a drop of 21.5 percent, which is the highest impact of the three choices analyzed. Common stock, in terms of this comparison, is the costliest form of capital—if only because it results in the greatest immediate dilution in the earnings of current shareholders.

Moreover, there also will be an annual cash drain of at least $687,500 in after-tax earnings from the 275,000 new shares, if the current $2.50 annual dividend on common stock is maintained. Further, we can project that this cash drain could grow at the historical earnings growth rate of 4 percent per year. This assumption will hold if the directors continue their policy of declaring regular cash dividends at a fairly constant payout rate from future earnings that continue growing. For the present, the pretax earnings required to cover the $2.50 per share dividend amount to:

$$\$2.50 \times 275,000 \text{ shares} = \$687,500 \text{ (after taxes)}$$

$$\frac{\$687,500}{(1 - 0.34)} = \$1,042,000 \text{ (before taxes)}$$

We can directly compare this earnings requirement of about $1.05 million to the alternative bond requirement of $1.15 million and the preferred stock requirement of $1.90 million. From both an earnings and a cash planning standpoint, these amounts and the differences between them are clearly significant.

The effect of immediate dilution of earnings is only part of the consideration. There will be the second-stage effect of continuing dilution, because in contrast to the other two types of capital, the new common shares created represent an ongoing residual claim on corporate earnings on a par with that of the existing shares. Thus the rate of growth in earnings per share experienced to date will be slowed in the future, merely because more shares will be outstanding—unless, of course, the earnings provided by the investment of the proceeds are superior in level and potential growth to the existing earnings performance.

When we turn to the second column of Figure 9–5, it's apparent that despite the incremental earnings from the new product, a net dilution of earnings per share in the amount of 25 cents, or 4.2 percent, will in fact continue. The contribution of the new product to reported earnings wasn't sufficient to meet the earnings claims of the new shareholders and maintain the old per share earnings level. The negative impact on earnings of the common stock alternative thus is greater than the earnings generated by the new capital raised.

Up to this point, we've dealt with the earnings impact of common stock financing. To find a first rough approximation of the specific cost of this alternative, we can establish as a minimum condition the maintenance of the old earnings per share level, and relate this to the proceeds from each new share of common stock. The current EPS of $5.94 (Figure 9–2) and the proceeds of $36.36 result in a cost of about 16 percent:

$$\frac{\$5.94}{\$36.36} = 16.34\% \text{ (after taxes)}$$

Recall from the discussion in Chapter 8, however, that using accounting earnings in measuring the cost of common equity is not appropriate. If we employ the dividend approach to find the specific cost of the incremental common stock, as discussed in Chapter 8, we must relate the current dividend per share to the net price received, and add prospective dividend growth. We know that the company has experienced fairly consistent growth in earnings of 4 percent per year, and we'll assume that, given a constant rate of dividend payout, common dividends will continue to grow at the same rate. The result is a cost of about 11 percent:

$$\frac{\$2.50}{\$36.36} + 4.0\% = 10.9\%$$

As we stated in Chapter 8, however, the dividend approach is limited in concept and usefulness. Therefore, let's now use the background data provided to test the specific cost of capital for ABC's common equity with the CAPM approach explained in Chapter 8.

The resulting cost of common equity, k_e, is approximately 13.25 percent when we put into the CAPM formula the risk-free return R_f of 6.5 percent, the β of 0.9, and the expected average return R_m of 14 percent, represented by the S&P 500 estimate :

$$k_e = R_f + \beta (R_m - R_f)$$
$$k_e = 6.5\% + 0.9 (14.0\% - 6.5\%)$$
$$k_e = 13.25\%$$

This result is the most credible one for judging the specific cost of the common stock. It can be compared to the specific cost of the bonds of 7.59 percent, and that of the preferred stock of 12.5 percent.

Clearly, the common equity alternative is the most expensive source of financing, and we have already established that the dilution effect is also serious. In addition, the cash flow requirements for paying the current dividend of $2.50 per share plus any future increases in the common dividend have to be planned for. Because it's difficult to keep all of these quantitative aspects visible in our deliberations, let's turn to a graphic representation of the various earnings and dilution effects to compare the relative position of the three alternatives.

Range of Earnings Chart

We've referred several times to changes in the earnings performance of the company and the different impact the three basic financing alternatives have under varying conditions. The static format of analysis we've used so far doesn't readily allow us to explore the range of possibilities as earnings change, or to visualize the sensitivity of the alternative funding sources to these changes. It would be quite laborious to calculate earnings per share and other data for a great number of earnings levels and assumptions. Instead, we can exploit the direct linear relationships that exist between the quantitative factors analyzed.

A graphic break-even approach can be used to compare the earnings impact of alternative sources of financing. In this section, we'll show how such a model, keyed to fluctuations in EBIT and resulting EPS levels, can be employed to display important quantitative aspects of the relative desirability of the choices available. As we'll see, the break-even model allows us to perform a variety of analytical tests with ease.

To begin with, we've summarized the data for ABC Corporation in Figure 9–6. Variations in these data can then be displayed graphically in a simple break-even chart which shows earnings per share (EPS) on the vertical axis and EBIT on the horizontal axis. This EBIT chart allows us to plot on straight lines the EPS for each alternative under varying conditions, and to find the break-even points between them.

Commonly, one of the reference points is the intersection of each line with the horizontal axis, that is, the exact spot where EPS is zero. These points can be found easily by working the EPS calculations backward, that is, starting with an

FIGURE 9-6

ABC CORPORATION
Recap of EPS Analyses with New Product
($ thousands, except per share figures)

	Original	Debt	Preferred	Common
EBIT	$9,000	$11,000	$11,000	$11,000
Less: Interest	-0-	1,150	-0-	-0-
Earnings before taxes	9,000	9,850	11,000	11,000
Less: Taxes at 34%	3,060	3,349	3,740	3,740
Earnings after taxes	5,940	6,501	7,260	7,260
Less: Preferred dividends	-0-	-0-	1,250	-0-
Earnings available for common stock	$5,940	$ 6,501	$ 6,010	$ 7,260
Common shares outstanding (number)	1 million	1 million	1 million	1.275 million
Earnings per share (EPS)	$ 5.94	$ 6.50	$ 6.01	$ 5.69
Less: Common dividends per share	2.50	2.50	2.50	2.50
Retained earnings per share	$ 3.44	$ 4.00	$ 3.51	$ 3.19
Retained earnings in total	$3,440	$ 4,001	$ 3,510	$ 4,072
Change from original EPS		−12.8%	−21.0%	−21.5%
Final change in EPS		+9.4%	+1.2%	−4.2%
Specific cost		7.59%	12.5%	13.25%

FIGURE 9-7

ABC CORPORATION
Zero EPS Calculation
($ thousands, except per share figures)

	Original	Debt	Preferred	Common
EPS	-0-	-0-	-0-	-0-
Common shares	1 million	1 million	1 million	1.275 million
Earnings to common	-0-	-0-	-0-	-0-
Preferred dividends	-0-	-0-	$1,250	-0-
Earnings after taxes	-0-	-0-	1,250	-0-
Taxes at 34%	-0-	-0-	644	-0-
Earnings before taxes	-0-	-0-	1,894	-0-
Interest	-0-	$1,150	-0-	-0-
EBIT for zero EPS	-0-	$1,150	$1,894	-0-

F I G U R E   9–8

ABC CORPORATION
Range of EBIT and EPS Chart*

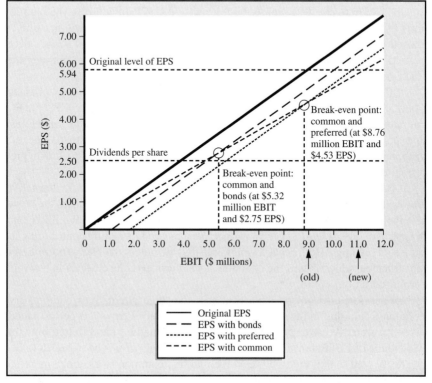

*This model and its subsidiary calculations in Figures 9–1 to 9–7 is available for download in an interactive format; see "Analytical Support," p. 384.

assumed EPS of zero and deriving an EBIT that just provides for this condition. The calculation is shown in Figure 9–7 for the original situation and for each of the three alternatives. The data in Figures 9–6 and 9–7 give us sufficient points with which to draw the linear functions of EPS and EBIT for the various alternatives, as shown in Figure 9–8.

We can quickly observe that the conclusions about the earnings impact of the alternatives we drew from the two EBIT levels previously analyzed, $9 million and $11 million, hold true over the fairly wide range of earnings presented. That is, every alternative considered causes a significant reduction in earnings per share relative to the original condition.

There's a major new observation, however. Under the common stock alternative, the slope of the EPS line is different. In fact, the line for common stock intersects both the debt and the preferred stock lines at different points in the graph. The latter two lines are parallel with each other and also with the line representing the original situation, both appearing to the right of the original line. The lesser slope of the common stock line is easily explained. Introducing new shares of common stock results in a proportional dilution of earnings per share at all EBIT levels. As a consequence, the incremental shares cause earnings per share to rise less rapidly with growth in EBIT. In contrast, the parallel shift by the debt and preferred stock lines to the right of the original line is caused by the introduction of fixed interest or dividend charges, while at the same time the number of common shares outstanding remains constant over the EBIT range studied.

The significance of the two intersections should now become apparent. They are break-even points at which, for a given EBIT level, the EPS for the common stock alternative and one of the other two alternatives are the same. Note that the break-even point of common stock line with the bond alternative occurs at about $5.3 million EBIT, while the break-even point of common stock with preferred stock occurs at about $8.8 million EBIT.

Below about $5.0 million EBIT, therefore, the common stock alternative causes the least EPS dilution, whereas above $9 million EBIT, it causes the worst relative dilution in EPS. Recall that ABC's current EBIT level is $9 million, and is expected to be at least $11 million once the new product is fully contributing its projected earnings. Both break-even points thus lie below the likely future EBIT performance, which makes the common stock alternative the costliest in terms of earnings dilution.

Therefore, it's not possible to assess the three alternatives without first defining a "normal" range of EBIT for the company's expected performance, given that relative earnings effects of the three alternatives are different over the wide range of EBIT shown. If future EBIT levels could in fact be expected to occur fairly well within the two break-even points, common stock looks more attractive than preferred stock from the standpoint of EPS dilution, but worse than debt. If EBIT can be expected to grow and move fairly well to the right of the second break-even point, as is almost certain in the case of ABC Corporation, new common stock is not only least attractive from the standpoint of EPS dilution, but will remain so.

All of these considerations depend, of course, on unchanging assumptions about the terms under which the three forms of incremental capital could be issued. If we can expect any of these terms to change significantly, such as the offering price of the common stock, or the terms of the bond, an entirely new chart must be drawn up, or we must at least reflect any possible discontinuities in cost or proportions of the alternatives as EBIT levels change.

The intersections between the EPS lines that represent the EBIT break-even points for the common stock alternative with the other two choices can be calculated easily. For this purpose, we formulate simple equations for the conditions underlying any intersecting pair of lines. EPS are then set as equal for the two alternatives, and the equations are solved for the specific EBIT level at which this condition holds.

To illustrate, let's first establish the following definitions:

E = EBIT level for any break-even point with the common stock alternative.

i = annual interest on bonds in dollars (before taxes).

t = tax rate applicable to the company.

d = annual preferred dividends in dollars.

s = number of common shares outstanding.

The equation for any of the EPS lines can be found by substituting known facts for the symbols in the following generalized equation:

$$\text{EPS} = \frac{(E - i)(1 - t) - d}{s}$$

We can now find the EBIT break-even levels for bonds and common stock at the point of EPS equality. For this purpose, we fill in the data for the two expressions and set them as equal:

Bonds		*Common*
$\dfrac{(E - \$1,150,000)0.66 - 0}{1,000,000}$	$=$	$\dfrac{(E - 0)0.66 - 0}{1,275,000}$

When we solve for E we obtain the following result:

$$0.66E - \$759,000 = \frac{0.66E}{1.275}$$

$$0.842E - \$967,725 = 0.66E$$

$$E = \$5,317,000$$

This break-even level of $5.32 million can easily be verified graphically in Figure 9–8. When the same approach is applied to the preferred and common stock alternatives, the following result emerges:

Preferred		*Common*
$\dfrac{(E - 0)0.66 - \$1,250,000}{1,000,000}$	$=$	$\dfrac{(E - 0)0.66 - 0}{1,275,000}$

$$0.66E - \$1,250,000 = \frac{0.66E}{1.275}$$

$$0.842E - \$1,593,750 = 0.66E$$

$$E = \$8,757,000$$

Again, the chart can be used to verify the break-even level of $8.76 million.

We also can use the EBIT chart to show the impact of different assumptions about common dividends on the three alternatives. For example, the horizontal line at $2.50 in the chart represents the current annual common dividend. Where this line intersects any alternative EPS line we can read off the minimum level of EBIT required to supply this dividend. Similarly, it's possible to reflect in the chart the earnings requirements for sinking funds or other regular repayment provisions. In effect, such annual provisions commit a portion of future earnings for this purpose.

We can develop the effect of these requirements by carrying the calculations one step further and arriving at the so-called uncommitted earnings per share (UEPS) for each alternative after provision for any repayments. We simply subtract the per share cost of such repayments (that require after-tax dollars) from the respective EPS of the alternative thus affected, and redraw the lines in the chart. The result will be a parallel shift of the affected line to the right of its prior position.

For example, the sinking fund requirement of $400,000 per year in the bond alternative would represent 40 cents per share, and the new line for bonds would move to the right by this amount over its whole range. Similarly, the intersection at the zero EPS point, currently $1,150,000 EBIT, would move right to a zero UEPS point of $1,756,000. This shift reflects the sinking fund requirement of $400,000 per year, which translates into an incremental pretax earnings requirement of $400,000 ÷ (1 − 0.34), or $606,000. In this case, the UEPS line for bonds would move very close to the EPS line for preferred stock in Figure 9–8.

By now the usefulness of this framework for a dynamic analysis of the earnings impact of various financing alternatives should be clear. The reader is invited to think through the implications of the variety of tests that can be applied. It's possible, for example, to determine the minimum EBIT level under each alternative that would cover the current common dividend of $2.50 per share, while assuming a variety of different payout ratios, such as 50 percent or 40 percent. For example, with an assumed 50 percent payout, EPS would have to be $5. A horizontal line would be drawn at the $5 EPS level, and its intersection with the lines of the various alternatives would represent the minimum EBIT levels for the $2.50 dividend. The analyst would have to assess the likelihood of EBIT declining to this level, and judge whether this endangers the current dividend payout. Other tests can be applied, of course, depending on the particular circumstances of the company.

While we've concentrated on the implications for recorded accounting earnings involved in the choice, it should be clear that the framework also can be used to work through the cash flow implications of each of the results, by translating the respective EBIT levels into equivalent cash flow from operations, as discussed in Chapters 2 and 3. This would bring the analysis closer to the valuation concepts we'll take up in the final chapter—recognizing that cash flows are the ultimate drivers of company performance and value. Among the extra steps required are calculating the tax shield effect of depreciation and depletion write-offs, elimination of other accounting adjustments, and recognition of new investment requirements. A spreadsheet analysis can of course be used to make the multiple calculations required.

Again we must emphasize, however, that any one specific EBIT chart works only under fixed assumptions about proceeds and stable rates of interest and preferred dividends. If there's reason to believe that any of the key assumptions might change, the EPS lines on the graph must be adjusted. Obviously, any changes in the relative costs of the various alternatives will also have an effect. As the spread between the alternatives increases, for example, the differences in earnings impact will widen, and thus the distance between the parallel lines will increase. This simply reflects the fact that imposing higher-cost fixed obligations depresses EPS.

Enlarging the amount of capital issued also has an effect, because the slope of the line is determined by the amount of leverage already present in the existing capital structure. In other words, if there's already some debt and preferred stock in the capital structure, the basic EPS would rise and fall much more sharply with changes in EBIT. Any increases in the fixed-cost alternatives would simply magnify this leverage. At the same time, the slope of the EPS line for common equity is governed by the relative number of shares issued, which in turn is related to the degree of earnings dilution, as demonstrated in the example.

Financial planning models or spreadsheet analyses can be used to enhance the basic framework demonstrated here. The point to remember, however, is that the process in essence quantifies the relative impact of the alternatives on reported accounting earnings. This effect is but one of the many factors that have to be weighed in making funding choices. As we mentioned in the beginning of this chapter, the conceptual and practical setting for the eventual decision is far more inclusive than this graphic expression of respective break-even conditions suggests. Strategic plans for the future, risk expectations, market factors, the specific criteria we listed, and current company conditions all have to enter the final judgment.

The Optimal Capital Structure

A great deal of theoretical and practical effort continues to be expended on determining the optimal mix of different long-term capital sources in a company's capital structure. This book is not the place to explore the many intricate conceptual issues involved, but some discussion is in order. We've referred many times to the fact that financial decision making involves a series of economic trade-offs as well as the personal judgments and risk preferences of the key managers and directors. Such is the case with the design and modification of capital structure proportions, which ultimately must be judged in terms of their support of value creation over time.

One of the key trade-offs is risk versus reward. Introducing leverage into a capital structure will, as we've observed before, tend to lower the overall cost of capital because of the least-cost aspect of debt (due to the tax deductibility of interest, as discussed in Chapter 8). This is not a static condition, however, because as we've mentioned, increasing amounts of debt expose the company to greater risk of earnings (and cash flow) variability, as well as potential default on the principal. Theoretical models of finding the optimal cost of capital take into account the dynamics of changing proportions of debt, preferred stock, and equity. Many studies have shown that, as a general rule, the cost of capital will tend to be lowest at debt proportions of around one-third versus two-thirds of equity in various forms. The specific risk characteristics of the company and its industry clearly will affect this general result. The evidence also shows that the overall cost of capital generally moves in a relatively narrow band between the extremes of leverage conditions, usually no more than two percentage points. But as we said before, the specific cost involved in financing is but one of many other considerations entering the complex trade-offs in capital structure planning.

One of the key considerations in shaping the capital structure is the relative growth performance and outlook of the company. Empirical studies have shown that fast-growing companies tend to create superior value through a capital structure with a conservative debt level, allowing them to maintain flexibility in accessing financial markets. This is generally accompanied by low dividend payout and emphasis on internal funds sources in financing growth. Additional equity is raised only when absolutely necessary to maintain profitable growth, whereas new debt is limited by relatively modest leverage targets. Overall, the focus must be on funding successful investments to sustain the growth pattern without excesses in funding choices, and exceeding the expectations of the market in implementing them.

In contrast, slow-growing companies that generate sizable cash flows can create superior value by disposing of the excess cash through share repurchases, reducing the equity base. Here the trade-off is simply between the quality and risk of perceived reinvestment opportunities on the one hand, and the impact of returning excess cash to the shareholders on the other. Given that attractive internal investment opportunities tend to be limited in slow-growth situations, it might be economically advantageous to increase financial leverage even further and borrow funds for more share repurchases. The effect will generally be a rise in the value of the stock as fewer shares are left outstanding, and because of the proportional lessening of the dividend payments. Such a policy will not be sustainable in the long run, of course, because at some point the equity base will shrink to insignificance and expectations about future cash flows will diminish as the company's productive resources are used up.

It should be added here that the effect of restructuring and the more successful performance achieved by many companies in the first half of the 1990s have led to a definite shift toward more conservative capital structures with the notable exception of complex, partially hidden debt structures in certain companies, of which the failed Enron is a prime example. Strong cash flows obtained from disposals of underperforming businesses and leaner ongoing operations have often been applied to reducing the temporarily inflated debt proportions of many companies. This was in part a reaction to the heavy—at times extreme—use of leverage especially during the 1980s, which apart from greater risk exposure had not been justified by the results of the investments made with these funds. At the same time, imprudent acquisitions at premium prices can seriously impair a company's capital structure through increased leverage.

The drive to create shareholder value in the past decade has included a rethinking of sustainable capital structure proportions in relation to business performance and outlook and not just from the standpoint of minimizing the cost of capital. Ultimately, of course, we must view the optimal capital structure in the broad context of our business system model as discussed in Chapter 1. It cannot be separated from the investment, operational, and financing variables we identified in all parts of the system.

Some Special Forms of Financing

Our earlier discussion focused on the very basic choice between debt, preferred stock, and common stock, setting aside the many variations often found in these instruments as well as in other specialized forms of financing. We'll now briefly cover several more specialized areas of financing choices, namely leasing, convertible bonds and preferred stocks, rights offerings, and warrants.

Leasing

We've referred to leasing at several points in this book. Leasing is a special form of financing that gives a business access to a whole range of assets, from buildings to aircraft and rail cars, and from automobiles to computers, without having to acquire these items outright. The lessee pays an agreed-upon periodic fee for use of the asset, set at a level that covers the lessor's ownership costs, financing and tax expenses, and also provides an economic return to the lessor. Lease contracts and provisions can vary widely, but they fall into two basic categories:

- Operating leases
- Capital (financial) leases

An *operating lease* essentially reflects the pure choice of leasing rather than owning. The lessee can use the asset for a specified period, usually less than the physical life, assumes none of the risks of ownership or technical obsolescence, and can replace or upgrade the asset while the lessor assumes the task of disposing of the used items. The latter provision is particularly appealing in the case of computers or technical equipment. The lessee, in effect, incurs only a tax-deductible periodic expense, while the lessor receives a stream of taxable payments against which are offset the ownership costs as well as any services provided the lessee. The lessor enjoys the tax shield effect of depreciation, and must decide what to do with the used asset at the end of the lease term.

A *capital lease* essentially represents a form of long-term financing, because title to the asset will be transferred to the lessee at the end of the lease term, directly or via a nominal purchase option. The specific choice to be made lies in the nature of the financing arrangement, viewed as a trade-off between a long-term debt issue supporting immediate ownership versus a leasing contract providing eventual ownership. The lease obligation, just like debt, is fixed, and the lease payment is based on recovering the value of the asset for the lessor and the cost of any other services provided. Long-term lease contracts, particularly for buildings, can extend over many years and thus become, in fact, part of a company's financial structure.

The impact of a lease on a company's financial statements differs between the two major types. Operating leases enter the income statement via tax-deductible lease costs, but do not affect the balance sheet directly, even though the lease contract usually extends over several periods. Instead, if operating leases are material in the cost structure of the company, a footnote disclosing the current and future annual lease totals is required to accompany the financial statements, indicating the size of this "off-balance sheet" obligation. Because ownership remains with the lessor, the assets involved are not reflected on the balance sheet of the lessee.

In contrast, capital leases are reflected in a company's financial statements on the balance sheet, where the asset involved is recorded, and offset on the liability side by the capitalized value of the lease payments. In effect, a capital lease has a recorded impact quite similar to a secured loan arrangement, and the total lease obligation is viewed as debt along with any conventional long-term debt arrangements. The periodic lease payments are included as an operating expense in the income statement. Under current accounting rules, any lease which has just one of the following four attributes must be considered a capital lease and recorded on the balance sheet:

- Ownership is transferred to the lessee before expiration of the lease.
- The lessee can purchase the asset for a low price upon expiration of the lease.
- The lease term is for at least 75 percent of the asset's economic life.
- The present value of the lease payments is at least 90% of the asset's value.

From a tax standpoint, the periodic lease payments made by the lessee are tax deductible, whereas the tax shield effect of depreciation remains with the lessor, offset against taxable lease payments collected. The IRS is very specific about distinguishing between genuine leases and installment purchases or secured loans in order to allow a tax deduction of the lease payment by the lessee.

As we might expect, any company that leases a significant portion of its assets has less flexibility in its financing choices. The effect is the same as that of a large outstanding long-term debt. Also, fixed leasing charges introduce a degree of leverage into the company's operations that is quite comparable to leverage resulting from other sources, as discussed in Chapter 5.

Because leasing involves a choice of owning versus leasing, or leasing versus borrowing, the basic analytical process should be based on a comparison of the respective tax-adjusted cash flows. Using the present value techniques of Chapters 6 and 7, the analyst can develop comparative cash flow patterns for the alternatives involved. One of the basic patterns is the analysis of the cost of ownership, from which a break-even lease payment can be calculated, as shown in Figure 9–9. A seven-year life has been assumed for an equipment investment, with recovery of the residual book value at the end of Year 7. Maintenance and support costs are growing slightly as the equipment ages, and accelerated depreciation has been used to calculate the tax shield effect.

FIGURE 9–9

Present Value Analysis of Cost of Ownership ($ thousands)

	Year 0	Year 1	Year 2	Year 3	Year 4	Year 5	Year 6	Year 7
Cost of equipment and recovery	$–100,000	0	0	0	0	0	0	$ 4,450
Maintenance, insurance, support costs	0	$–15,000	$–15,000	$–16,000	$–16,000	$–17,000	$–17,000	–18,000
Tax rate		36%	36%	36%	36%	36%	36%	36%
After-tax cash cost	0	–9,600	–9,600	–10,240	–10,240	–10,880	–10,880	–11,520
Depreciation tax shield*		9,146	15,674	11,194	7,994	5,715	5,715	–3,430
Operating cash outflows	0	–454	6,074	954	–2,246	–5,165	–5,165	–14,950
Present value factors @ 12%	1.000	0.893	0.797	0.712	0.636	0.567	0.507	0.452
Present values of equipment cash flows	–100,000	0	0	0	0	0	0	2,011
Present values of operating cash flows	0	–406	4,841	679	–1,429	–2,928	–2,619	–6,758
Present values of total cash flows	$–100,000	$ –406	$ 4,841	$ 679	$ –1,429	$ –2,928	$ –2,619	$ –4,746
Net present value @12%								$–106,608
Annualized net present value @ 12%								–23,360
Pretax equivalent lease payment @ 36% tax rate								36,500

*Based on seven-year accelerated depreciation percentages (14.29%; 24.49%; 17.49%, 12.49%; 8.93%; 8.93%; 8.93%; 4.45% residual).

The net present value cost at 12 percent of owning the equipment is about $107,000, which can be converted into an annualized equivalent cost of $23,360, as was discussed in Chapter 7 (on a spreadsheet, use the *pmt* function, specifying the discount rate, the number of periods, and the present value). Assuming that the lessor has similar ownership costs, the minimum lease payment required to earn the lessor a 12 percent cash flow return would be the pretax equivalent of $36,500 per year. From the lessee's standpoint, this lease payment represents a break-even level between leasing and owning, from which any significant deviation would have to be evaluated. Similar analyses can be developed for other potential alternatives, always being careful to lay out cash flows and tax implications properly.

There are many considerations involved in the choice of leasing versus ownership beyond the purely financial trade-offs. Very important, the analysis of leasing as a financing choice can come only *after* the cash flow economics of the investment project itself have indicated that it will indeed add value to the company. Thereafter, leasing can properly be considered as merely one form of financing. We'll not deal with the specific cash flow implications of the many types of leasing arrangements available, because they are too specialized and complex to be covered here. But we must recognize that leasing often involves an economic cost, because especially in operating lease arrangements the lessor must be compensated for providing, financing, servicing, and replacing the asset. By definition, leasing charges must be high enough to make leasing attractive for the lessor as the investor in the asset. At the same time, the lessor is often able to use economies of scale in acquiring and servicing the assets, an attribute that might favorably affect the cost of leasing, as is the case with major equipment leasing companies, for example.

In the comparative analysis of the final choice between leasing and ownership we have to weigh such elements as the periodic expense to the lessee, any technological advantages from being able to use the latest in facilities and equipment, services received as part of the contract, the flexibility of not being tied down by ownership, and the impact on the company's financial position. As in all financial analyses, the choice is based on both quantifiable data and management judgment. In some industries, leasing is part of the normal way of doing business. For example, in wholesaling, warehouses are commonly leased, and in the transportation industry, leasing of rolling stock, trucks, and aircraft prevails. In other areas, the choice of leasing is wide open and depends on the financing alternative that is considered advantageous at the time.

Convertible Securities

As we stated earlier, convertibility into common shares is a feature sometimes added to issues of bonds or preferred stocks for reasons of marketability and timing. The essence of convertibility is simply that the issuing company is in effect able to sell common shares at prices higher than those prevailing at the time the bond or preferred stock is issued. This is due to the fact that the conversion price for the common stock it represents is set at an expected future level, based on the company's value growth experience and expectation.

The conversion price is the basis for the conversion ratio set for the bond or preferred issue. For example, a new $100 convertible preferred might have a conversion ratio of 3, that is, each share of preferred stock is convertible into three shares of common stock. This represents a conversion price of $33.33 per common share, while the company's shares might currently be trading in the $25 to $27 range. The difference between current price and the conversion price is called the conversion premium. The same approach applies to bonds, which are usually denominated in thousand-dollar units.

Given the expectation that the company's common stock will in time exceed the conversion price, the bond or preferred stock will trade at values that reflect both the underlying interest or dividend yield, and the conversion value itself. Initially the stated interest or yield will predominate, but when common share prices begin to exceed the conversion price, the price of the bond or preferred stock will be boosted to reflect the current market value of the underlying common shares. This is the point at which conversion becomes increasingly attractive to the investor. If share prices remain below the conversion price, however, the conversion value will always be the floor value for the bond or preferred—while the actual price will depend on the yield provided by the stated interest rate or the preferred dividend.

Given the potential attraction of conversion to the investor, the issuing company usually pays a somewhat lower rate of interest or preferred dividend on these instruments. To limit the time period over which these securities are outstanding, the company can usually force conversion—once the market price of common stock has reached the conversion price—by exercising the call provision (the right of the company to redeem all or part of the issue) included in most convertible issues. This provision is usually based on a predetermined price close to the conversion price.

Convertibility adds a number of considerations to the three basic choices discussed earlier. Because successful convertible issues eventually result in an increase in common shares, the delayed impact on control, earnings per share, and the amount of future common dividends must be taken into account in the analysis. The graphic display used earlier can be applied by showing this alternative in two forms:

- The convertible bond or preferred as a straight bond or preferred.
- The additional common shares from eventual conversion.

As long as significant convertible issues remain outstanding, companies are required to calculate diluted earnings per share, as discussed in Chapter 3.

Stock Rights

A so-called rights offering is a form of common stock financing that minimizes the dilution of existing shareholders' proportional holdings. Also referred to as a privileged subscription, such an offering, provides to each existing shareholder a proportional number of rights to purchase a specified number of new common shares from the company at an advantageous subscription price during a limited time period, after which the rights expire. The number of rights issued matches the number of shares of common stock outstanding, and a defined number of rights are necessary to purchase each share of new stock. Rights are issued as special certificates and are often traded in the securities markets.

To illustrate, if the XYZ Company has one million common shares outstanding and wishes to sell 250,000 new shares, one million rights will be issued to existing shareholders with the provision that four rights are required to purchase a new share of stock at the subscription price. If the subscription price is $30, and the current market price is $40, a shareholder has to surrender four rights and $30 to the company to receive one share currently worth $40.

A company is attracted to this course of action because, apart from limiting the potential for dilution of control, it is a direct appeal for funds to a group of investors already familiar with its history and outlook. If so inclined, a shareholder will exercise the rights by purchasing directly from the company the number of shares specified at the set subscription price. If the shareholder isn't interested, the rights can be sold as such, because they'll reflect the value differential between the subscription price and the market price of the stock. We'll return to determining the value of rights to the investor in Chapter 10.

The analytical implications of this alternative are quite similar to those of a public offering, which we assumed to be the case earlier in the chapter. The subscription price might differ somewhat from the price the underwriters provide in a public offering, but otherwise the analysis will parallel the common stock alternative we explored.

Warrants

Warrants are a form of corporate security that entitles the holder to purchase a specified number of common shares at a fixed exercise price over a stated period of time. Some warrants have no expiration date. They are issued as an added incentive for investors to purchase a new public issue of bonds, or a private placement of loans or bonds. Sometimes warrants are issued as part of an offering of common stock. The proportion of warrants issued with the new offering will vary depending on the exercise price and the degree of incentive desired to move the new debt issue into the hands of investors. Warrants are attached to these new securities as part of the offering, but in most cases, they can be detached by the holder and sold separately if desired. Numerous warrants are traded at any time in the securities markets.

In effect, a warrant gives the holder the option to buy common stock if it's advantageous to do so, for example, if the exercise price is below the market price. Just as in the case of rights, when a warrant is exercised, the funds go directly to the company. Because warrants, in contrast to rights, are valid for relatively long time periods, there is the potential for earnings dilution from unexpired warrants. Companies with significant numbers of warrants outstanding must calculate diluted earnings per share, just as in the case of convertible issues outstanding (Chapter 3).

The main implication for analysis of a new debt offering with attached warrants is the need to recognize the potential funds inflow from new shares as warrants are exercised, and the earnings dilution from these shares. Our graphic analysis has to be modified to allow for the combination of these effects. We'll return to the value of warrants in Chapter 10.

Key Issues

The following is a recap of the key issues raised directly or indirectly in this chapter. They are enumerated here to help the reader keep the analysis techniques discussed within the perspective of financial theory and business practice.

1. The choice among different types of long-term financing is inextricably connected with the business strategy of a company. The final choice must match the risk/reward characteristics inherent in both strategy and financing, and should support value creation over the long term.

2. The cost of different types of capital is only one element on which a decision about new funding is based. Whereas debt is generally the lowest-cost alternative (due to tax deductibility of interest) and

common equity the highest-cost alternative, the need to build and maintain an appropriate balance in the capital structure often overrides the cost criterion.

3. Several noncost elements, such as risk, flexibility, timing, and shareholder control as well as management preferences, have to be weighed in relation to both changing market conditions and the company's future policies.

4. New financing at times might represent a significant proportion of the existing capital structure. How these funds are raised can cause shifts away from a firm's ideal target capital structure. Because a block of one form of long-term capital was chosen at one point in time, management might be limited in the choices for the next round of financing. To compensate for this imbalance, a compromise mix of funds might have to be used.

5. The specific provisions of a new issue of securities are generally tailor-made for the situation. Investment bankers, underwriters, and management collaborate to negotiate the design and price of a financial instrument that reflects market conditions, the company's credit rating and reputation, risk assessment, the company's strategic plans, and current financial practices.

6. As a company's capital structure changes, so does its weighted cost of capital. However, temporary shifts resulting from adding blocks of new capital should not affect the return standards based on cost of capital, unless there is a deliberate and permanent change in the company's policies.

7. New common equity has the long-term effect of diluting both ownership and earnings per share. This is true whether the new shares are directly issued or brought about by conversion of other securities, or by exercise of warrants. The decision as to whether to issue new common shares, therefore, must be closely tied to the expected results from the strategic plans in place. It also involves weighing the advantages of introducing new permanent equity capital into the capital structure.

8. Leasing as a form of financing is based on a series of cash flow and operational trade-offs that must be weighed in relation to both the company's capital structure and its business direction. It cannot serve as a means of justification for obtaining the asset involved; only economic analysis is the appropriate foundation for adding investments.

Summary

In this chapter we've reviewed both the decisional framework and some of the techniques used to analyze the different types of long-term funds. We focused on the three basic alternatives open to management: long-term debt, preferred stock, and common equity, leaving the discussion of the many specialized aspects of funding instruments to be pursued in the reference materials at the end of the chapter.

We found that the choice of financing alternatives is a complex mixture of analysis and judgment. Several areas of consideration were highlighted. We reviewed the cost to the company, the relative risks, and the issues of flexibility, timing, and control with respect to the various funding sources. We found that many of the aspects involved in choosing types of capital went beyond quantifiable data.

We also focused on the impact of each financing alternative on the reported earnings of a company, and then developed a break-even graph relating EPS and EBIT. This simple model allowed us to test visually the earnings impact of the alternatives over the whole dynamic range of potential earnings levels. The graph suggested the potential use of broader financial models or computer spreadsheets with which to simulate more fully the impact of alternative financing packages or changing conditions. Very important, we pointed out that the optimal capital structure is not a function of earnings impact alone, but the result of weighing the key characteristics of the business and its performance and longer-term outlook to arrive at a mix that will sustain value creation.

We briefly examined the key aspects of other specialized forms of financing, convertible securities, rights, warrants, and leasing and suggested the kind of analytical considerations applicable to these modified conditions.

Analytical Support

A set of Excel-based templates *(Interactive Templates)* is downloadable at no charge from the Web at www.mhhe.com/helfert11e. The ninth of these, "Impact of Financing Choices: Range of EBIT and EPS Chart," activates the EPS break-even diagram of ABC Corporation in Figure 9–8 on page 371, as well as all subsidiary calculations displayed in Figures 9–1 through 9–7. The template allows you to vary a set of key assumptions about the investments, operations, and financing conditions, and to observe the numerical changes resulting from these modifications on the graphic representation and statements. The display helps you explore and understand in depth the linkages within the EPS diagram and its accompanying financial statements, and to stimulate and test the impact of your assumptions.

Financial Genome, the advanced financial analysis software application described in Appendix I, is a fully integrated analytical and planning model for both the professional user and the business student. It is designed to develop a full set of financial ratios and relationships in addition to creating integrated financial statements from historical data inputs as well as for projections of financial performance. The software creates earnings per share and other indicators as a matter of course, and can be used to simulate the integrated impact of financing changes when in the forecasting mode.

Financial Genome is downloadable from the Web, using the unique and restricted code provided with this book (see details in "Downloads" at the end of Appendix I, p. 479).

Selected References

Brealey, Richard, and Stewart Myers. *Principles of Corporate Finance*. 5th ed. New York: McGraw-Hill, 1996.

Hull, John. *Options, Futures and Other Derivative Securities*. New York: Prentice Hall, 1993.

Ross, Stephen; Randolph Westerfield; and Jeffrey Jaffe. *Corporate Finance*. 5th ed. Burr Ridge, IL: Irwin/McGraw-Hill, 1999.

Weston, J. Fred; Scott Besley; and Eugene Brigham. *Essentials of Managerial Finance*. 11th ed. Chicago, IL: Dryden Press, 1997.

Self-Study Exercises, Problems, and Discussion Questions

Exercises and Problems *(Selected Solutions Are Provided in Appendix VI)*

1. The ABC Corporation is planning the financing of a major expansion program for late 2003. Common stock has been chosen as the vehicle, and the 50,000 shares to be issued in addition to the 300,000 shares outstanding are to bring estimated proceeds of $5 million. The current price range of common stock is $120 to $140 per share. The new program is expected to raise current operating profits of $14.7 million by 18 percent. The company's capital structure contains long-term debt of $10 million, with an annual sinking fund provision of $900,000 to begin in 2004 and interest charges of 11 percent. The most recent estimated operating statement of the company, which includes the additional profit, appears as follows:

ABC CORPORATION
Pro Forma Income Statement
For the Year Ended December 31, 2004 ($ thousands)

Net sales	$66,000
Cost of goods sold*	42,000
Gross profit	24,000
Selling and administrative expenses	9,300
Operating profit	14,700
Interest on debt	1,100
Profit before taxes	13,600
Income taxes (34%)	4,600
Net income	$ 9,000

*Includes depreciation of $2,250.

The company's β was calculated at 1.4, while the risk-free return was estimated to be 8 percent, and the expected return from the stock market 14.5 percent.

   a. Develop an analysis of earnings per share, uncommitted earnings per share, and cash flow per share, and show the effects of dilution in earnings.
   b. Develop the same analysis for an alternative issue of $5 million of 10 percent preferred stock, and an alternative issue of $5 million of 9 percent debentures due in full after 15 years.
   c. Develop the specific comparative cost of capital for all three alternatives and discuss your findings.

2. XYZ Corporation is planning to raise an additional $30 million in capital, either via 240,000 shares of common stock at $125 per share net proceeds, or via 300,000 shares of 9 percent preferred stock. Current earnings are $12.50 per share on one million shares outstanding, $2.5 million in interest is paid annually on existing long-term debt, and dividends on existing preferred stock amount to $1.5 million per year. The current market price is $140 per share, the β is 1.2, and risk-free return is 8 percent. The expected return from the stock market is 13 percent.
   a. Develop the specific cost of capital for each alternative and show calculations (long form). Assume income taxes are 46 percent.
   b. Develop the point of earnings per share equivalence between the common and preferred alternatives. Assuming a common dividend of $8 per share, calculate the EPS/dividends per share break-even point for the common stock alternative.
   c. Assuming EBIT levels of $10 million, $15 million, $22.5 million, and $33.75 million, demonstrate the effect of leverage with the preferred stock alternative, by graph and calculation. Discuss your findings. Use the template for Figure 9–8 to check your analysis.

3. The DEF Company was weighing three financing options for a diversification program that would require $50 million and provide greater stability in sales and profits. The options were as follows:
   a. One million common shares at $50 net to the company.
   b. 500,000 shares of 9.5 percent preferred stock.
   c. $50 million of 8.5 percent bonds (entailing a sinking fund provision of $2 million per year).

   The current capital structure contained debt on which $1 million per year was paid into a sinking fund and on which interest of $1.2 million was currently paid. Preferred stock obligations were dividends of $1.8 million per year. Common shares outstanding were two million, on which $2 per share was paid in dividends. The current market price range was $55 to $60, and the company's β was 1.2. The risk-free rate of return was 7.5 percent, while expectations about the returns from a portfolio of stocks were 14 percent. EBIT levels had fluctuated between $22 million and $57 million, and earnings before interest and taxes from diversification were expected to be about $8 million. The most recent EBIT level of the company had been $34 million.

Assume that proceeds to the company after expenses would equal the par value of the securities in the second and third alternatives; also, disregard the obvious exaggerations in the relationships that were made for better contrast. Income taxes are 36 percent.

Develop a graphic analysis of the data given and establish by calculation the earnings per share, uncommitted earnings per share, dilution, specific costs of capital, break-even points, dividend coverage, and zero earnings per share. Discuss your findings. Use the template for Figure 9–8 to check your analysis.

4. Using Financial Genome and its database for 3M Corporation, develop an integrated projection based on your assumptions, including significant business investment outlays, and test the impact on key variables from using different financing choices to fund the cash requirements. Discuss your findings.

Discussion Questions

1. List the key conditions that would affect the relative importance of the areas of cost, risk exposure, flexibility, timing, and control.
2. Why is it important to look ahead to the potential next stage of financing when deciding the choice among current alternatives for new funds?
3. Relate the weighted cost of capital of a company to the costs of the respective alternatives for incremental funds. Are they based on the same reasoning?
4. How does the immediate dilution of earnings caused by alternative ways of raising additional funds relate to the return standards required for new investments?
5. Why are calculations of the comparative cost of alternative financing choices based on the proceeds and not on the face value?
6. What are the key assumptions underlying the EBIT chart, and under what conditions is it necessary to redraw the lines?
7. How does prospective inflation affect the choice among alternative methods of raising additional funds?
8. When leasing is an alternative, what are the key considerations that would make it attractive? How does the analysis of leasing options relate to present value concepts?
9. Is there such a thing as an optimal long-term capital structure, and should blocks of incremental capital be tailored to fit such a structure?
10. Within a reasonable range of debt/equity proportions, is debt always to be preferred over equity? Why? What are the key considerations that enter into this analysis?

CHAPTER 10

VALUATION AND BUSINESS PERFORMANCE

Throughout this book, we've stressed that managers must primarily focus their decision making about investments, operations, and financing on the creation of economic value for the company's shareholders. Now let's put shareholder value into a broader context by examining the key concepts of value and relating them to successful business performance. Earlier we discussed such categories as the recorded values reflected in a company's financial statements, the economic values represented by the cash flows generated through capital investments, and the market value of shares or debt instruments. In each case, value was viewed in a specific context of analysis and assessment, but not necessarily against the full dynamics of management strategies and decisions that underlie the performance of any business.

We'll discuss the meaning of value in a variety of common situations where valuation is required. We'll not only define several concepts of value in more precise terms, but also once again use some of the now familiar analytical approaches that can be applied to the process of valuation. Foremost among these, of course, is the present value analysis of future cash flows (the main subject of Chapters 6 and 7), which is the common underpinning of modern valuation principles and shareholder value creation. In the final chapter we'll integrate the various concepts into an overview of value-based management, returning to the systems approach first discussed in Chapter 1 and using it to provide a consistent perspective of successful value creation.

We'll begin here with some basic definitions of value as found in business practice. Next, we'll take the point of view of the investor assessing the value of the main forms of securities issued by a company, and the point of view of the creditor judging the value of the company's obligations. Finally, we'll discuss the key issues involved in valuing an ongoing business as the basis for determining whether shareholder value is being created—the principal objective of modern management. As we've emphasized throughout this book, the linkage between cash flows and the creation of economic value is the ultimate expression of success or failure of business decisions in the areas of investment, operating, and financing. Recognition of this linkage spurred the wave of takeovers and restructuring activities of the 1980s—essentially a reassessment of the effectiveness with which resources were employed by target companies—leading to redeployment of those resources in alternative ways expected to generate higher cash flows and returns to the shareholders. But the recent failure to recognize these basic linkages at the turn of this century led to the enormous bubble and subsequent deflation in the dot-com business valuations, as well as in highly leveraged companies which were based mostly on speculation and the naive belief in a "new paradigm" of value creation.

Definitions of Value

It'll be useful to refresh our memory briefly about the different types of value we've encountered so far, and to state as clearly as possible what they represent and for what purposes they might be appropriate. In this enumeration we'll demonstrate that only some of these concepts are really useful for what we now understand to be the economic task of value creation in a business setting.

Economic Value

This concept, used throughout the book as the relevant term for shareholder value creation, relates to the basic ability of an asset—or a claim—to provide a stream of after-tax cash flows to the holder. Such cash flows can be generated through earnings, or contractual payments, and/or partial or total liquidation at a future point. As earlier chapters stated, economic value is essentially a cash flow trade-off concept. The value of any asset is defined as the amount of cash a buyer is willing to give up now—its present value—in exchange for a pattern of future expected cash flows. Therefore, economic value is very much a future-oriented concept. It's determined by estimating and assessing prospective future cash flows, including proceeds from the ultimate disposal of the asset itself. Remember that past costs and expenditures caused by prior decisions are sunk costs and thus irrelevant from an economic standpoint.

As we'll see, economic value underlies some of the other common concepts of value because it's based on a trade-off logic that is quite natural to the process of investing. Calculating economic value is not without practical difficulties, however. Recall that a representative discount rate (cost of capital or return standard) has to be selected and applied to the expected positive and negative cash flows over a defined period of time. The cash flows themselves are often difficult to estimate, and they might also include specific assumptions about any recoverable cash from liquidation, or about any ongoing value remaining at the termination point of the analysis. The process in effect determines today's equivalents of the cash flow amounts expected to occur in different parts of the time dimension, based on a great deal of judgment.

Recall also the need for careful risk assessment, both in determining the cash flow pattern and time frame itself and in setting the appropriate return standard. In other words, economic value isn't absolute; it's the result of the relative risk assessment of future expectations. In fact, economic value is closely tied to individual risk preferences, because different individuals will arrive at different valuation results because of their varying perceptions of risk. Yet, whether or not these aspects are made explicit in a given situation, the principle of economic value is at the core of all business decisions on investment, operating, and financing.

Market Value

Also referred to as fair market value, this is the value of any asset, or collection of assets, or going business, when traded in an organized market—or negotiated between private parties—in an unencumbered transaction without duress. The various securities and commodities exchanges are examples of organized markets, as are literally thousands of regional and local markets and exchanges, including the emerging Web-based market sites, that enable buyers and sellers to find mutually acceptable values for all kinds of tangible and intangible assets. Market value is, of course, also established through transactions between individuals when no organized market is conveniently available.

Again, there's nothing absolute in market value. Instead, it represents a momentary consensus of two or more parties. In a sense, the parties to a transaction adjust their respective individual assessments of the asset's economic value sufficiently to arrive at the consensus. The market value at any one time can therefore be subject to the preferences and even whims of the individuals involved, the psychological climate prevalent in an organized stock exchange, the heat of a takeover battle, significant industry developments, shifts in economic and political conditions, and so forth. Moreover, the volume of trading in the asset or security will influence the value placed on it by buyers and sellers.

Despite its potential variability, market value is generally regarded as a reasonable criterion in estimating the current value of individual balance sheet assets and liabilities, as contrasted with their recorded value. It's frequently used in inventory valuation and in capital investment analysis where future recovery values have to be estimated. On a larger scale, mergers and purchases of going concerns are also based on market values negotiated by the parties involved. As was the case with economic value, there are practical problems associated with establishing market value. A true market value can be found only by actually engaging in a transaction. Thus, unless the item is in fact traded, any market value assigned to it remains merely an estimate, which will tend to shift as conditions change and the perceptions of the parties are altered.

But even if market quotations are readily available, certain judgments apply. For example, popular common stocks traded on the major exchanges have widely quoted market prices, yet frequently there are significant price fluctuations even within a day's trading, and the volume of shares changing hands might vary greatly—affecting the relevance of these quotations for all other, nontraded shares outstanding. Also, overall market movements will affect individual stocks. Thus market value based on many similar transactions can be established only within a given range, which in turn, is tied to the trading conditions of the day, week, or month. For items that are traded infrequently or in relatively small numbers, estimating a realistic transaction value can become even more difficult. Yet the fact remains that market value is one of the most significant value concepts used in financial/economic analysis. It's closely related to economic value, because it ultimately is based on the parties' expectations about future cash flows to be derived from the asset or business involved.

Book Value

Recall from Chapter 1 that the book value of an asset or liability is the stated value as reflected on the balance sheet, which has been recorded and at times modified according to generally accepted accounting principles. Although book value is handled consistently for accounting purposes, it usually bears little relationship to current economic value. It's a historical value that, at one time, might have represented market value, but the passage of time and changes in economic and market conditions increasingly distort it. Assets of a long-term nature are particularly subject to changes in economic value over time. The frequently quoted book value of common shares, which represents the shareholder's proportional claim on the composite net result of all past transactions in assets, liabilities, and operations, is especially subject to distortion. Because it is a residual amount, it is affected by all past and present accounting adjustments, required set-asides for contingencies, as well as by those limited actual value changes which have to be recognized under the increasingly complex GAAP rules. Its usefulness for economic analysis is therefore questionable under most circumstances.

Liquidation Value

This value relates to the special condition when a company needs to liquidate part or all of its assets and claims. In essence, it's an abnormal situation where time pressures and even duress distort the value assessments made by buyers and sellers. Under the cloud of impending business failure or intense pressure from creditors, management will find that liquidation values generally are considerably below potential market values. The setting for the negotiations is adversely affected by the known disadvantage under which the selling party must act in the transaction. As a consequence, liquidation value is really applicable only for the limited purpose intended. Nevertheless, it's sometimes used to value assets of unproved businesses as a more realistic basis for analysis than to estimate highly uncertain cash flow patterns when testing such aspects as creditworthiness.

Breakup Value

A variation of liquidation value, breakup value is related to corporate takeover and restructuring activities, as discussed on page 455. On the assumption that the combined economic values of the individual segments of a multibusiness company exceed the company's value as an entity—because of inadequate past management or current opportunities that were not recognized earlier—the company is broken up into salable components for disposal to other buyers. Any redundant assets, such as excess real estate, are also sold for their current values.

Note that breakup value is usually realized on business segments with ongoing operations, and less frequently through forced liquidation of individual assets supporting these business segments, as would be the case in a bankruptcy sale, for example. Any redundant assets not required for ongoing operations might, of course, be liquidated as such. Estimates of breakup value are a critical element in the analysis preceding takeover bids.

Reproduction Value

This is the amount that would be required to replace an existing fixed asset in kind. In other words, it's the like-for-like replacement cost of a piece of equipment, facility, or other similar asset. Reproduction value is, in fact, one of several yardsticks used in judging the worth of the assets of an ongoing business. Determining reproduction value of specific assets is an estimate largely based on engineering judgments.

There are several practical problems involved. The most important is whether the fixed asset in question could, or would, in fact be reproduced exactly as it was constructed originally. Most physical assets are subject to some pattern of technological obsolescence with the passage of time, in addition to physical wear and tear. This is especially true in the case of computer equipment where rapid technological improvement renders physically perfect machines obsolete within a year or two. There's also the problem of estimating the currently applicable cost of actually reproducing the item in kind. For purposes of analysis, reproduction value often becomes just one checkpoint in assessing the market value of the assets of a going business.

Collateral Value

This is the value of an asset that is used as security for a loan or other type of credit. The collateral value is generally considered the maximum amount of credit that can be extended against a pledge of the asset. With their own security in mind, creditors usually set the collateral value lower than the market value of an asset. This provides a cushion of safety in case of default, and the risk preference of the individual creditor will determine the magnitude of the often arbitrary downward adjustment. Where no market value can be readily estimated, the collateral value is set on a purely judgmental basis, the creditor being in a position to allow for as much of a margin of safety as is deemed advisable in the particular circumstances.

Assessed Value

This value concept is established in local governmental statutes as the basis for property taxation. The rules governing assessment practices vary widely, and might or might not take market values into account. Use of assessed values is limited to raising tax revenues, and therefore such values bear little relationship to the other value concepts.

Appraised Value

Appraised value is subjectively determined and used when the asset involved has no clearly definable market value. An effort is usually made to find evidence of transactions that are reasonably comparable to the asset being appraised. Often used in transactions of considerable size—especially in the case of commercial or residential real estate—appraised value is determined by an impartial expert accepted by both parties to the transaction, whose knowledge of the type of asset involved can narrow the gap that might exist between buyer and seller, or at least can establish a bargaining range. The quality of the estimate depends on the expertise of the appraiser and on the availability of comparable situations. Again, individual ability and preference enter into the value equation. Only rarely will different appraisals yield exactly the same results, and ranges of value are used at times.

Going Concern Value

This concept applies economic valuation to a business in operation. A company viewed as a going concern is expected to produce a series of future cash flows that the potential buyer must value to arrive at a price for the business as a whole. Note that the same concept applies to valuing whole business segments of a company when its breakup value is established, as discussed earlier. Apart from the specific valuation techniques used, which we discuss on page 409, the concept requires that the business be viewed as a "living system" of investments, operations, and financing rather than a mere collection of assets and liabilities, and that a suitable time period for projection and analysis is chosen.

Recall our earlier strong emphasis on the fact that economic value is created by a positive trade-off of future cash flows for present commitments and outlays. As we'll see in Chapter 11, the going concern value is useful when comparative cash flow analyses, singly and in combination, are developed for setting value-based management goals and for acquisitions and mergers. Going concern value also enters such cash flow analyses as the final estimate at the end of the analysis period, where it represents the ongoing value of the business in relation to future performance beyond the period under review. In these types of analyses going concern value may also be called residual value, or terminal value, which refers to its positioning as a future value estimate at the end of the analysis period. The continuing challenge to the analyst is to properly judge and weigh this future value as well as the overall pattern of estimated cash flows.

Shareholder Value

As we've stated repeatedly, shareholder value is created when the cash flow returns generated from existing and new investments consistently exceed the cost of capital of the company. It represents the total increase in the economic value of the business over time. This value in turn is reflected in the form of a growing periodic total return to shareholders as measured by the combination of dividends and capital gains or losses achieved, which can be compared to overall market returns or the returns achieved by selected peer companies or industry groupings. Shareholder value, the ultimate expression of corporate success, is closely tied to cash flow trade-offs and return expectations that are the basis of economic value. We'll discuss the concept in more detail in Chapter 11.

In summary, we've discussed a number of value definitions. Some are specialized yardsticks designed for specific situations. Many are directly or indirectly related to economic value. We've again defined economic value as the present value of future cash flows, discounted at the investor's risk-adjusted standard. As we know, this value concept is broadly applicable as the underpinning of shareholder value creation, and we'll use it extensively as we examine various decision areas where value measures are needed.

Valuing Securities

As in Chapters 5, 8, and 9, we'll concentrate here only on the three main types of corporate securities—bonds, preferred stock, and common stock—in discussing the techniques involved in assessing value and yield. For our purposes, we'll define value as the current attractiveness of the investment to the investor in present value terms, while yield represents the internal rate of return (IRR) earned by the investor on the price paid for the investment. We'll briefly discuss major provisions stipulated in the basic securities types insofar as they might affect their value and yield. The techniques covered should appear quite familiar to the reader because they closely relate to the various analytical approaches presented in Chapters 6 and 7.

Bond Values

Valuing a bond is normally fairly straightforward. A typical bond issued by a corporation is a simple debt instrument. Its basic provisions generally entail a series of contractual semiannual interest payments, defined as a fixed rate based on the bond's stated par (face) value (usually $1,000). The legal contract, or indenture, promises repayment of the principal (nominal value) at a specified maturity date a number of years in the future. The two basic characteristics, defined interest payments and repayment stipulations, are encountered in most normal debt arrangements. Complicating aspects are sometimes found in provisions such as conversion into common stock at a predetermined exchange value, or payment of interest only when earned by the issuing company. We review some of these specialized features on page 399.

A bond's basic value rests on the investor's assessment of the relative attractiveness of the expected stream of future interest receipts and the prospect for eventual recovery of the principal at maturity. Of course, there's normally no obligation for the investor to hold the bond until maturity because most bonds can be traded readily in the securities markets. Still, the risk underlying the bond contract must be considered here in terms of the issuing company's future ability to generate sufficient cash with which to pay both interest and principal. The collective judgment of security analysts and investors about the issuing company's prospects influences the price level at which the bond is publicly traded, which is further affected by prevailing interest rates in the U.S. and also in international economies. Moreover, the bond is likely to be rated by financial services like Moody's and Standard & Poor's and placed in a particular risk category relative to other bonds.

To determine a bond's value, we must first calculate the present value of the interest payments received up to the maturity date and add to this the present value of the ultimate principal repayment. You'll recognize this method as comparable with the process of calculating the present value of business investment expenditures shown in Chapter 6. The discount rate applied is the risk-adjusted interest rate that represents the investor's own standard of measuring debt investment opportunities within a range of acceptable risk. For example, an investor with an 8 percent annual interest return standard would value a bond with a coupon interest rate of 6 percent annually significantly lower than its par value. The calculation is shown in Figure 10–1. The investor's annual standard of 8 percent is equivalent to a semiannual standard of 4 percent, a restatement for purposes of calculation that's necessary to match the semiannual interest payments paid by most bonds.

The resulting value, $832.89, represents the maximum price our investor should be willing to pay—or the minimum price at which the investor should be willing to sell—if the investor normally expects a return (yield) of 8 percent from this type of investment. This particular bond should therefore be acquired only at a price considerably below (at a discount from) par. Note that the stated interest rate on the bond is relevant only for determining the semiannual cash receipts in absolute dollar terms.

The actual valuation of the bond and the cash flows it represents therefore depend on the investor's opportunity rate (return standard). In other words, the desired yield determines the appropriate price, and vice versa. This relationship also applies, of course, to the market quotations for publicly traded bonds. The quoted price, or value, is a function of the current yield collectively desired by the many buyers and sellers of these debt instruments, which in turn is based on general interest rate conditions.

If our investor were for some unrealistic reason satisfied with the very low annual yield of only 4 percent from holding the same bond (equivalent to 2 percent per six-month period), the value to the investor would rise considerably above par, as shown in Figure 10–2. Under these assumed conditions, the investor should be willing to pay a premium of up to $212.43 for the $1,000 bond, because

F I G U R E   10–1 ──────────────────────────────────────

Bond Valuation with Return Standard of 6 Percent per Year

Date of analysis:	July 1, 2003
Face value (par) of bond:	$1,000
Maturity date:	July 1, 2017
Bond interest (coupon rate):	6% per year
Interest receipts:	$30 semiannually

	Total Cash Flow	Present Value Factors, 4 Percent*	Present Value
28 receipts of $30 over 14 years (28 periods)	$ 840	16.663 (× $30)	$499.89
Receipt of principal 14 years hence (28 periods)	1,000	0.333	333.00
Totals	$1,840		$832.89

*From Tables 6–I and 6–II (end of Chapter 6, pp. 276 and 277), respectively.

F I G U R E   10–2 ──────────────────────────────────────

Bond Valuation with Lower Return Standard of 4 Percent per Year

	Total Cash Flow	Present Value Factors, 4 Percent*	Present Value
28 receipts of $30 over 14 years (28 periods)	$ 840	21.281 (× $30)	$ 638.43
Receipt of principal 14 years hence (28 periods)	1,000	0.574	574.00
Totals	$1,840		$1,212.43

*From Tables 6–I and 6–II (end of Chapter 6, pp. 276 and 277), respectively.

the personal return standard is lower than the stated interest rate. If the investor's own standard and the coupon interest rate were to coincide precisely, the value of the bond would, of course, exactly match the par value of $1,000.

In fact, the quoted market price of any bond will tend to approach the par value as it reaches maturity, because at that point, the only representative value will be the imminent repayment of the principal—assuming, of course, that the company is financially able to pay as the amount becomes due.

Bond Yields

A related but common task for the analyst or investor is the calculation of the yield produced by various bonds, when quoted prices differ from par value. The key to this analysis again is the relationship of value and yield as discussed above, and the technique used is a present value calculation that in effect determines the internal rate of return (IRR) of the cash flow patterns generated by the bond over its remaining life.

The method is identical to that used for assessing the cash flows of any business investment proposal. The key difference in the data is that the individual investor's calculations are based on pretax cash flows that must be adjusted in each case by the investor for his or her personal tax situation. Other minor differences are the cash incidence in a semiannual pattern, and the form in which bond prices (the net investment) are quoted. Published prices are normally stated as a percentage of par. For example, a bond quoted at 103⅜ has a price of $1,033.75. The change to decimal trading in process in early 2001 has made these quotations easier to handle.

Bond yield tables have long been employed to determine a bond's internal rate of return, or yield. Although today's computers and calculators have specialized financial routines that make direct calculation a simple matter, we'll nevertheless take a quick look at a yield table, mainly to help the reader understand the examples by visual inspection of the relationships. In essence, bond yield tables are finely graduated present value tables that list the whole potential range of stated interest rates, subdivided into fractional progressions of as little as ½₂ of a point. They're far more detailed than the present value tables used in Chapters 6 and 7.

For example, Figure 10–3 is a small segment of such a yield table, in this case for a bond with a coupon interest rate of precisely 6 percent. The columns show the number of six-month periods remaining in the life of the bond, and the rows display the yield to maturity. The yield to maturity simply refers to the yield obtained by the investor if the bond were actually held until its par value is repaid at the maturity date. If the investor were to sell at an earlier date, the market price of the bond received at that time would be substituted for par value in calculating the return. As a result, the yield achieved for the period up to the date of sale might differ from the yield to maturity if the bond is trading above or below par. We can quickly find the bond's yield to maturity at any given purchase price in the bond yield tables. Conversely, it's also possible to find the exact price (value) that corresponds to any particular desired yield to maturity. Our example of the 6 percent bond used in the previous section (Figure 10–2) is represented on the 4 percent yield line and in the 28-period column of the bond yield table segment reproduced in Figure 10–3. Bond yield tables provide a visual impression of the progression or regression of prices and yields which is, of course, purely based on their mathematical relationship, as discussed in Chapter 6. A calculator or spreadsheet program goes through the same steps and formulas as were used to generate the tables.

In summary, bond yield calculations involve a fairly straightforward determination of the internal rate of return of future cash flows generated by the bond investment at a known present price. As in the case of a business capital investment,

FIGURE 10–3

Bond Yield Table: Sample Section for a 6 Percent Return

	Price Given Years or Periods to Maturity					
Yield to Maturity	13 Years (26 periods)	13½ Years (27 periods)	14 Years (28 periods)	14½ Years (29 periods)	15 Years (30 periods)	15½ Years (31 periods)
3.80%	1.224 043	1.230 661	1.237 155	1.243 528	1.249 782	1.255 919
3.85	1.218 284	1.224 709	1.231 012	1.237 196	1.243 263	1.249 215
3.90	1.212 559	1.218 793	1.224 907	1.230 904	1.236 787	1.242 557
3.95	1.206 868	1.212 913	1.218 841	1.224 654	1.230 354	1.235 944
4.00	1.201 210	1.207 068	1.212 812*	1.218 443	1.223 964	1.229 377
4.05	1.195 585	1.201 260	1.206 821	1.212 273	1.217 616	1.222 853
4.10	1.189 993	1.195 486	1.200 868	1.206 142	1.211 310	1.216 375
4.15	1.184 434	1.189 747	1.194 952	1.200 051	1.205 046	1.209 940
4.20	1.178 908	1.184 043	1.189 073	1.193 999	1.198 823	1.203 549
4.25	1.173 414	1.178 374	1.183 230	1.187 985	1.192 642	1.197 201

*This example was used in Figure 10–2 (slight difference due to rounding of present value factors). Note that prices are given in the form of a seven-digit multiplier, which is applied against a $1,000 par value.

a trade-off of current outlays for future cash flows under conditions of uncertainty is involved. Yield and value are mathematically related and this relationship can be utilized to locate either result in preset bond yield tables, or to solve the analysis directly with a programmed calculator or spreadsheet.

Bond Provisions and Value

The simple value and yield relationships discussed so far are, of course, affected by the specific conditions surrounding the company and its industry, and also by additional provisions in the specific bond indenture itself. The issuer's ability to pay must be assessed through careful analysis of the company's earnings pattern and projections of expected performance. The techniques discussed in the early chapters of this book are helpful in this process. Ability to pay is a function of the projected cash flows and how well these flows cover debt service of both interest and principal. Sensitivity analysis based on high and low estimates of performance can be useful here, as can more sophisticated analytical modeling.

Variations in the bond indenture also will affect the value and the yield earned. To illustrate, we'll refer only to the major types of bond variations here. Mortgage bonds are secured by specific assets of the issuing firm. Because of this relationship, the bondholders have a cushion against default on the principal. This reduces the risk for the investor, and accordingly the coupon interest rate offered with mortgage bonds might be somewhat lower than that of unsecured debenture bonds, resulting in a reduced yield to the investor. Income bonds are at the other extreme on the risk spectrum because not only are they unsecured, but they also pay interest only if the earnings of the company reach a specified minimum level. Their coupon interest rate and yield level will be correspondingly high.

Convertible bonds, as we already observed, add the attraction of the holders' eventual participation in the potential market appreciation of common stock for which the bond can be exchanged at a set price. Therefore, the coupon rate of interest can be set at a somewhat lower level than that of a straight bond. In Chapter 9 we noted that the value of convertible bonds is affected by

- The market's assessment of the likely performance of the common stock.
- The gap between the stipulated conversion price and the current price of the common stock.
- The coupon interest it pays semiannually.

Normally, the conversion price is set higher than the prevailing market value of the common stock at the time of issue, to allow for expected value growth of the common stock over time. Conversion is essentially at the investor's discretion when found advantageous, although the indenture usually stipulates a time limit. Moreover, the issuing company usually has the right to call the bonds for redemption at a slight premium price after a certain date, thus forcing the investor to act. As common share prices approach and surpass the conversion price, the bond's value will rise above par because of the growing value of the equivalent common shares it represents.

A more recent phenomenon in the bond markets is the use of so-called junk bonds, extensively promoted by some investment bankers to support company takeovers that use very high levels of debt, or for leveraged buyouts by groups of managers or investors that similarly rely on extremely high financial leverage to finance the purchase of the company involved. These securities are in effect subordinated to (ranking below) the claims of other creditors in case of default and are sold under often highly risky circumstances, because the amount of indebtedness involved in some of these transactions exceeds what are normally considered prudent levels. The yields provided by these unsecured instruments are usually commensurate with the high risk perceived by investors, and defaults are not uncommon.

Many other modifications and provisions are possible to tailor bonds of various types to the needs of the issuing company and to the prevailing conditions in the securities markets. Numerous variations in bond provisions and their impact on value and yield call for careful judgments that go beyond the direct analytical techniques we discussed. We repeat that the calculations described are but the starting point, and no hard-and-fast rules exist for mechanically weighing all aspects of bond valuation. In the final analysis, value and yield must be adjusted with due regard to the investor's economic and risk preferences, in line with the specific objectives in owning debt instruments. The references at the end of the chapter cover these aspects in greater detail.

Preferred Stock Values

By its very nature, preferred stock represents a middle ground between debt and common equity ownership. The security provides a series of cash dividend payments, but normally has no specific provision (or expectation) for repayment of the par value of the stock. However, at times preferred stock carries a call provision, which allows the issuing company to retire part or all of the stock during a specific time period by paying a small premium over the stated value of the stock.

Although the investor enjoys a preferential position over common stock with regard to current dividends and also to recovery of principal in the case of liquidation of the enterprise, preferred dividends might in fact not be paid if the company's performance is poor, a decision made by the board of directors. Such an event will, of course, adversely affect the value of the stock.

Preferred dividends, like common dividends, are declared at the discretion of the board of directors and, if missed currently, might not be made up in future periods, unless the preferred issue carries specific legal requirements to the contrary. Such provisions, for example, might call for cumulating past unpaid dividends until the company is in a position to afford declaring dividends of any kind. At other times, particularly in new companies, preferred stocks might carry a participation feature, which requires the board of directors to declare preferred dividends higher than the stated rate if earnings exceed a stipulated minimum level. But these two special situations are infrequent.

The task of valuing preferred stock, therefore, has to be based on less-definite conditions than was the case with bonds, because the only reasonably certain element is the stated annual dividend, which was originally set as a percentage of stated value. For example, an 8 percent preferred stock usually refers to a $100 share of stock which is expected to pay a dividend of $8 per year, most likely in quarterly installments, a pattern normally matching that for common stocks. The investor is faced with valuing this stream of prospective cash dividends. If the price paid for a share of preferred stock was $100, and the stock is held indefinitely, the yield under these circumstances would be 8 percent, assuming that the company is likely to be able to pay the dividend regularly.

If the price paid was more or less than the stated value, the yield could be found by relating the amount of the dividend to the actual price per share:

$$\text{Yield} = \frac{\text{Annual dividend per share}}{\text{Price paid per share}}$$

If the investor could expect to sell the stock at $110 five years hence, the exact yield of this combination of expected cash flows can be determined by using either present value techniques or the shortcut methods discussed in the section on bonds.

However, estimating a future recovery value involves a good deal of conjecture. In contrast to bonds, preferred shares have no specific maturity date or par value to be paid at maturity. The actual price of a preferred stock traded in the securities markets depends both on company performance and on the collective value the securities markets place on the given preferred issue. In turn, this price level reflects the risk/reward trade-off demanded for the whole spectrum of investments at the time. The value range will depend not only on the respective risk premiums assigned to individual securities, but also on the inflationary expectations underlying the economy that are reflected in the risk-free rate to which risk premiums are added. Value might be a little easier to estimate if the stock carries a mandatory call provision applicable at a specific future date and price, especially if the date of analysis is close to that time.

When we look at preferred stock values from the viewpoint of investing, we should use the investor's own return standard to arrive at the maximum price the investor should be willing to pay for the stock, or the minimum price at which the investor should be willing to sell. We simply relate the stipulated dividend rate to our investor's required return—relevant for the level of risk implicit in the preferred issue—to arrive at the answer. If the return standard were 9 percent against which to test the 8 percent preferred, we would determine the investor-specific value as follows:

$$\text{Value per share} = \frac{\text{Stated dividend rate}}{\text{Required return}} = \frac{0.08}{0.09} = \$88.89$$

If the investor were satisfied with only a 7 percent return, the value would be:

$$\text{Value per share} = \frac{0.08}{0.07} = \$114.28$$

The judgments that remain to be made, of course, relate to any uncertainty in the future dividend pattern, and any likely material change in the future value of the stock, either because of changing market conditions or because of a scheduled call for redemption at a premium price.

Preferred Stock Provisions and Value

As in the case of bonds, there are many modifications in the provisions of preferred stocks that can affect their value in the market. We mentioned earlier that some preferred stocks, particularly in newly established companies, contain a participation feature, which entitles the preferred holder to higher dividends, if corporate earnings exceed a set level. This feature can favorably affect the potential yield, and thus the valuation of the stock, depending on the prospects that the company will in fact reach this higher earnings level.

A much more common feature, similar to some bonds, is convertibility, the possibility of changing the preferred ownership position into that of common stock, as discussed in Chapter 9. As in the case of convertible bonds, however, the value of this feature can't be calculated precisely. Yet as the price of common stock reaches and exceeds the stated conversion price, the price of the convertible preferred stock will tend to reflect the market value of the equivalent number of common shares. Before this point is reached, the convertible preferred stock's value will largely be considered the same as a regular preferred, and based essentially on the stated dividend. Convertibility is generally accompanied by a call provision, at a premium price, which enables the company to force conversion when conditions are advantageous.

In summary, the challenge of preferred stock valuation also goes beyond the simple techniques we have shown. In the end, decisions should be made only after careful assessment of the relative attractiveness of the specific features and conditions surrounding a particular company's preferred stock, and its place in the desired range of the risk/reward spectrum of the individual or institutional investor.

Common Stock Values

The most complex valuation problem is encountered when we turn to common stock, because by definition common stock represents the residual claim of owners on the total performance and outlook of the issuing corporation. We found this to be true when we examined the cost of capital from the point of view of the corporation in Chapter 8.

Common stock valuation is especially difficult because shareholders carry full ownership risks, yet have residual claims on both assets and earnings only after all other claims have been satisfied. Thus, an investment in common stock involves sharing both risks and rewards. This heightens the uncertainty about potential dividend receipts and any future gain or loss in recovering the price paid for the shares. As a consequence, measurement techniques have to deal with variables subject to a high degree of judgment.

The rewards of successful common stock ownership are two-fold: cash dividends (and sometimes additional stock distributions in lieu of cash), and growth in market value from growing earnings, whose underlying cash flows are reinvested by management in total or in part. The key driver of market value is the past and prospective cash flow performance of the company, which is the basis for potential appreciation (or decline) of the stock's market price and resulting capital gains or losses. We've stated many times that shareholder value creation depends on the combination of dividends and capital gains or losses achieved over time, expressed in the form of total shareholder return, or TSR. As we observed in Chapter 8, there are many practical and theoretical issues surrounding the interpretation and measurement of these elements. Here we'll focus on ways of developing reasonable approximations of common share values, and similarly, show approximations of the yield an investor derives from a common stock investment.

Earnings and Common Stock Value

The quickest—if simplistic—way to approach the valuation of a share of common stock is to estimate the likely future level of earnings per share, and to capitalize these earnings at an appropriate earnings multiple (price/earnings ratio) that reflects expectations about the company and its industry:

Value per share = Earnings per share × Price/earnings ratio

There are, of course, serious shortcomings in using projected accounting earnings as a measure of shareholder expectations. Because ultimately all economic value derives from cash flows, using the surrogate of earnings per share can't capture the full impact on value. Moreover, the approach is static unless any potential growth or decline in earnings is built in. Finally, there remains the basic problem of forecasting the earnings pattern itself, both for the company and its industry.

A more specific, cash-based approach to estimating common share value is to capitalize expected dividends. The size, regularity, and trend in dividend payout to shareholders has an important effect on the value of a share of common stock, being one of the elements of shareholder value creation. Yet there's also a degree of uncertainty about the receipt of any series of future dividends. Not only will such dividends depend on the ability of the company to perform successfully, but also any dividends paid are declared at the discretion of the corporate board of directors.

No general rule applies in this area—dividend policies can range from no cash payment at all to regular payments of 75 percent or more of current earnings. At times, dividends paid might even exceed current earnings, because the company is unwilling to cut the current dividend per share during a temporary earnings slump. Most boards of directors see some value in a consistent pattern of dividend payments, and major adjustments in the size of the dividend, up or down, are made very reluctantly.

The approach to valuation via dividends involves projecting the expected dividends per share and discounting them by the return standard appropriate for the investor. Several major issues arise here.

First, the current level of dividends paid is likely to change over time. For example, in a successful, growing company dividends, as well as earnings, are likely to grow. The problem is to make the projection of future dividends realistic, even though past performance is the only available guide. If a company has been paying a steadily growing dividend over many years, an extrapolation of this past trend might be reasonable. But this pattern must be tempered by subjective judgments about the outlook for the company and its industry. Companies with more erratic patterns of earnings and dividends, however, pose a greater challenge, as do young growth companies which pay no dividends at all in the early stages of their life cycle.

The second issue is the method of calculation. The most common format is the so-called dividend discount model, or dividend growth model, which appears below in its simplest form. The formula is a restatement of the dividend approach we used as one way of calculating the cost of equity in Chapter 8. In that approach, we defined the cost of common equity as the ratio of the current dividend to the current market price plus the expected rate of growth of future dividends. Here, instead of solving for the cost of equity, which is the investor's expectation of return, we solve for the value, or price, of the stock:

$$\text{Value per share} = \frac{\text{Current dividend}}{\text{Discount rate (Investor's expectation of return)} - \text{Dividend growth rate}}$$

This particular formula is based on the idea that the value of a share of stock is the sum of the present values of a series of growing annual dividend payments, discounted at the investor's return expectation for this class of risk. The formula also permits using the less realistic assumption of a constantly declining dividend. But either way it implies an ongoing series of payments in perpetuity, and it also implies a constant annual rate of growth or decline in the dividend payment.

Note, however, that this model would give an invalid answer for a company paying dividends expected to grow as fast or faster than the discount rate, because then the denominator would become zero or even negative. Clearly, under such a happy condition, the investor's return expectation should be reexamined and raised, or the stock should be considered as being outside the investor's risk/ reward spectrum.

The dividend discount model is related mathematically to an annuity formula (see Chapter 6) which assumes a constant growth rate and constant discount rate. The valuation it provides implicitly includes any appreciation in the stock's future market value as management reinvests the retained portion of the growing earnings. This condition holds because in the model, the market value of the stock at any future time is defined as the present value at that point of the ensuing stream of growing dividends.

The simplifying assumption of a constant rate of growth in dividends can be modified if a more erratic pattern of future dividends is expected. The calculation then becomes a present value analysis of uneven annual cash flows up to a selected point in the future. If the analyst wishes to assume that the dividend growth rate will stabilize at some future time, the basic formula can then be inserted and its result discounted to the present. Remember, however, that forecasting a precise pattern of dividends is problematic under most circumstances, and the analyst is forced to look for reasonable approximations.

The dividend discount model (and earnings multiples) does not take into account the general trends and specific fluctuations in the securities markets. Obviously, the market value of specific shares can't be independent of movements in the securities markets as a whole, which are caused by economic factors like inflation, industry conditions, taxation, political events, disruptions and myriad other factors. Therefore, the economic returns a company achieves on the assets invested tend to be recognized in the relative market value of its shares, that is, relative to share values of its peers and within the context of overall market movements. Moreover, the value of a company's shares reflects the collective performance assessments by security analysts, institutional and individual investors, and the resulting demand for, or lack of interest in, those shares. Although very important, these considerations are beyond the scope of this book.

Common Stock Yield and Investor Expectations

In Chapter 3, we presented two simple yardsticks for measuring the owners' return on investment in common stock. One of these was the earnings yield, a simple ratio of current or projected earnings per share to the current market price. The other was the inverse relationship, the so-called price/earnings ratio. As we pointed out, these simple ratios are static expressions based on readily available data and should only serve as temporary rough indicators of the real investor's yield created by a company's economic performance, that is, the cash flow pattern generated and projected.

The two yardsticks are useful mainly for a comparative analysis of companies or industry groupings, but must be supplemented by more insights if the analyst wishes to approximate the actual economic yield of a stock. Any serious examination of value or yield relative to the expectations of the shareholder should use more sophisticated techniques, such as the capital asset pricing model (CAPM, discussed in Chapter 8), which take into account market risk, specific company risk, portfolio considerations, and investors' risk preferences.

A third measure, most important for measuring shareholder value creation, is total shareholder return, or TSR, as we discussed in Chapter 3. This is an expression of the actual yield achieved over a period of time when a share of stock is acquired at the beginning of the period and sold at the end. The combination of dividends received during the period and the gain or loss achieved from the change in the share price is then related to the initial investment, as reflected in Figure 10–4 on the next page. This calculation, which is published widely for publicly held companies in statistical compilations such as the Fortune 500 represents a direct approach to measuring the yield for the investor.

Yield, of course, is a function of the risk exposure chosen by an investor. A great deal of research has improved our understanding of the relative performance of common stocks within the broad movements of the security markets. This has resulted in refined definitions of the systematic risk underlying a diversified portfolio of stocks traded and the unsystematic (avoidable) risk of a particular security. As we discussed in Chapter 8, the CAPM relates the relative risk of a security to the risk of the market portfolio through a calculated factor, β, which indicates the difference in the risk characteristics of the stock versus the risk characteristics of the portfolio. The β factor is applied to the market portfolio's overall risk premium, defined in terms of the historical trend in returns earned over and above the risk-free return from the safest type of investment, such as long-term U.S. government bonds.

Thus the expected yield of a particular common stock is the sum of the risk-free return and a risk premium, which is the risk premium earned in the total portfolio of stocks, adjusted by the inherent riskiness β of the particular security. We described the formula in Chapter 8:

$$\text{Yield} = R_f + \beta \, (R_m - R_f)$$

where

R_f = the risk-free return.
β = the particular stock's covariance of variability in returns (the specific measure of riskiness).
R_m = the average return expected on common stocks.

Fortunately, as we've mentioned, the β for publicly traded companies is published routinely in financial services such as *Value Line*. Current indications of the risk-free rate prevalent at the time and estimates of the return from groups of common stocks are also available in published sources.

F I G U R E   10–4

Total Shareholder Return—the Components

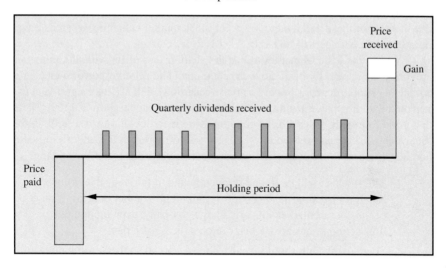

We've only touched on some of the techniques used to determine value and yield for common stocks. Much more practical and theoretical insight is needed to deal confidently with the complex issues involved. The references listed at the end of this chapter provide more information.

Other Considerations in Valuing Common Stock

The book value per share of common stock is often quoted in financial references and company reviews. As we observed before, this figure represents the recorded residual claim of the shareholder as stated on the balance sheet. Book value is an accumulation of past transactions and values and does not reflect current economic value, which is based on potential earnings or dividends. It's only under unusual circumstances that book value per share will be reasonably representative of anything approximating the economic value of a share of common stock. This might be true, for example, if a company has either just been started, or is about to be liquidated. Under normal conditions, however, book value per share will tend, over time, to become increasingly remote from current values, because under current accounting rules, positive changes in the values of existing assets are rarely, if ever, reflected on the books. The book to market ratio discussed in Chapter 3 is used as a rough indicator of this divergence, and a book value that is close to or even exceeding market value might suggest that the issuing company is underperforming, a situation that could invite takeover attempts by aggressive investors or corporations.

Market values of common stocks have been treated very lightly in our discussion, because a book on financial analysis techniques is not the place in which to explore the complex workings of the securities markets themselves. Earlier we established the principle that in the broadest sense the stock market bases value on expected future cash flows, which are implicitly discounted by a rate of return reflecting the current outlook for the economy and the market as a whole. Key factors driving this rate of return are inflation expectations and projected tax rates. A rise in either of these will tend to lower the stock market valuation, whereas lower inflation and tax rates will boost it.

Within the general market trends the share prices of individual companies are similarly driven by cash flow expectations. The relative performance of a company's shares depends largely on these cash flows, but also to a significant extent on the trading pattern and volume of the particular stock. Suffice it to say here that if the following several basic conditions are met, quotations of a stock in the securities markets can reasonably be assumed to represent the underlying economic value based on the current and prospective performance of a company.

- The stock should be traded frequently and in fairly sizable volume. Small transactions between a few individuals cannot be a fair indication of the overall market value of a large company, even though the transaction prices are properly quoted on a given day.

- Share ownership should ideally be widespread so that trading does not involve moving large blocks of shares between a small number of interested parties.

- The stock should be publicly traded on one or more stock exchanges, or be part of the increasingly important NASDAQ market.

Even if all of these conditions are met, the market value of a stock at any point might not necessarily reflect the true potential of the company. External factors, such as changes in the economy, publicity about the company and its industry, or takeover attempts, can affect the price at which the stock is traded. To help them understand this context, analysts will study the range within which market values have moved. Preferably this is done over at least one year and usually longer. Analysts will chart the behavior of specific share prices relative to market averages and composite averages for the industry peer group, using current databases for the process. Historical data and charting of key variables of publicly held companies are available on-line from a large variety of service providers (see Appendix III).

As we'll see on p. 411 when we discuss the valuation of a total company, there's also a difference between (1) valuing individual shares, (2) valuing the fraction of a company's shares traded normally in the stock market on a daily basis, and (3) the value of all shares at a given point of time. In most cases, partial trading can be viewed as establishing the value of minority holdings, that is, the value of partial positions in the company's equity—which is what current quotations represent. When it comes to valuing the total equity of a company, however, for example in the case of an acquisition, experience has shown again and again that the market price of recent partial trading and the value of the total enterprise in play for acquisition can differ widely, usually leading to a premium for the total company. The basic reason is that an acquisition transaction dramatically narrows the number of parties involved in trading, significantly increases the volume of shares traded, and introduces competitive bidding to realize synergistic and other advantages envisioned by the acquirers.

Valuing a Business

Managers, investors, analysts, and investment bankers need to know how to measure the value of a business as an ongoing entity. Whether it's a multibusiness global corporation, any of its individual operations, or a small single-business company, there are many occasions when obtaining a current valuation is necessary. The most obvious need arises when an acquisition of a company or a line of business is being considered, or when two companies plan to merge. The wave of acquisitions, mergers, and hostile takeovers in the past decade involved thousands upon thousands of such valuations.

A similar type of valuation is useful when a company, for purposes of internal restructuring, disposes of certain product lines, operating divisions, or past acquisitions. The buyers might be other companies, groups of investors, or even the existing management, who might want to acquire the division financed through a leveraged buyout (a purchase based on using a high proportion of debt in excess of normal capital structure proportions). Regardless of the form of the purchase, sale, or restructuring, both the buyer and the seller need to arrive at a reasonable approximation of the economic value of the company or line of business as a going concern.

Another important use of business valuation—related to the ones mentioned—stems from the growing recognition of value-based management as the critical focus for successful performance. Managing for shareholder value has become a key strategic objective for many corporate managers. Most successful companies measure economic value creation in one form or another for the company as a whole and for its major businesses, and reward the management team accordingly. In this context, the business is periodically valued with various techniques to determine progress against planned performance, and to set the appropriate incentive compensation awards. We'll discuss value-based management in more detail in Chapter 11, where we'll review the broad implications of shareholder value creation—the concept with which we began the book.

At this point we'll first briefly discuss the concepts of valuing the shareholders' equity of a company, and then take up the more inclusive and common process of valuing the company as a whole. In each case, we'll use cash flow techniques which apply to most valuation situations.

Valuing the Equity

In its most basic form, the value of the shareholders' equity of a company can be calculated by estimating the future cash flows accruing to the shareholders. The process is quite comparable to the business investment techniques we developed in Chapter 7. In essence, the value of the stake of the shareholders in the company is (1) the present value of the total pattern of expected common dividends to be received, carefully choosing an analysis period that is reasonable for the type of industry (3 to 5 years for fast-changing industries like high technology firms, and 10 to 15 years for resource-based industries like forest products or oil); plus (2) the present value of the expected worth of the equity at the end of the analysis period.

We can express this definition in a simple formula:

$$VE = PV \text{ (expected cash dividends)} + PV \text{ (value of equity at end of period)}$$

Note that these cash flows are expectations, just like the ones encountered in all types of business investments. We also encounter again the problem of companies that do not pay dividends, a situation which removes one part of the analytical approach and forces the analyst to rely mostly on assumptions about future equity values at the end of the analysis period. Under any circumstance, establishing the likely value of the equity at the terminal point of the analysis raises the complex subject of ongoing, or residual, values which we'll discuss in more detail shortly. Note also that this approach differs from the dividend discount model in that it establishes a definite time period and substitutes a direct estimate of the future value of the equity at the end of the period versus the simple assumption about a perpetually growing dividend from the present onward.

The calculation is carried out by discounting the expected pattern of annual dividends and the assumed value of the ending equity value at the company's cost of equity capital, which reflects the risk to the owners of the equity. This cost is not the weighted average cost of capital, which is based on a combination of debt and equity in the company's capital structure, but it reflects the higher cost of the equity alone. The pattern of estimated dividend cash flows can rise or decline, depending on the specific assumptions made by the analyst. Similarly, the estimate of the ending value of the total equity might be based on a variety of assumptions, ranging from a simple dividend or earnings multiple to a detailed assessment of the company's competitive viability.

The attempt to focus specifically on the value of the company's equity, however, blurs the contribution received from the successful use of leverage. Remember, the dividend cash flow to shareholders is made possible not only through successful investment of equity funds, but also from earnings that exceed the cost of long-term financing employed in the capital structure. In fact, the important theme established early in the book was that the economic success of any company had to come from exceeding the weighted overall cost of capital in all of its present and future investments—by effectively and consistently employing the pool of funds provided by its total capital structure. As we'll demonstrate in the next section, it's far more useful and common to approach valuing shareholders' equity by first valuing the company as a whole and then deriving the value of the equity portion of the capital structure from this result.

Valuing the Total Company

We now turn to a discussion of the most commonly used approach for valuing a company as a whole, which, as before, employs the principles of discounting expected cash flows but does so with reference to the conditions in the total business system. In other words, overall business performance is projected under assumed conditions and transformed into a cash flow pattern. Once this pattern has been used to establish a company valuation, the value of the shareholders' equity can be derived by simply removing the value of the other segments of the capital structure, as we'll demonstrate shortly.

To arrive at the total value of the company, also called firm (enterprise) value, we must transform its past and projected overall earnings performance into a net cash flow framework, just as if we were calculating the desirability of a capital investment project as discussed in Chapters 6 and 7. This framework requires choosing an analysis period, developing periodic cash flows, and estimating the residual company value at the end of the period. We should emphasize here that residual values in valuation analysis take on a much more important role than do terminal values in basic business investment projects. Business investments tend to generate cash flows over their economic lives at levels that usually allow recovery of the investment and earnings at or above the cost of capital within the analysis period, with residual values providing some extra benefits. In company valuations—because of the long-term nature of most business enterprises—the cash flows generated during the analysis period generally are quite insufficient to provide an adequate return, and the ongoing or residual value is a critical factor in establishing company value and performance. This is especially true of fast-growing companies, which require significant funding during their growth phase, with extensive cash flow generation deferred until much later periods. The dot-com phenomenon was an extreme example of such growth situations, especially because expectations about both operations and residual values far exceeded reality. The importance of ongoing values places great emphasis on the quality of estimates made at the terminal point in the valuation framework, and we'll discuss several approaches in some detail after our examination of periodic cash flow elements.

Free Cash Flow

The particular cash flow concept generally employed for valuation purposes is so-called free cash flow (also called cash flow to capitalization), which is defined as the net amount of the following key elements in each period:

- Operating profit before interest, after taxes (EBIAT).
- Depreciation and amortization expense and other noncash items in operating profit.
- Funds required or released by changes in working capital.
- Funds required or released by capital investments, acquisitions, and disinvestments.
- Adjustments for any significant nonoperating revenues or expenses.

This cash flow concept in effect represents the cash available to the company in each period for compensating investors and creditors *after* all ongoing strategic investment needs of the business have been met. It's a specialized approach specifically intended for this type of analysis, although in practice one can find some differences in the exact definition of free cash flow as applied to particular situations. Note that our definition parallels the basic principles we employed in Chapters 6 and 7, where the total cash flow pattern assumed for a business investment was developed independent of any compensation to the providers of the funds (interest and dividends), because the cost of capital used for discounting embodied the weighted average of shareholder and creditor expectations.

As in any comprehensive financial planning project, many assumptions must be made about key variables while making sure that internal consistency is maintained. Although it's possible to do quick valuation analyses in a highly summarized form, more satisfactory results can be achieved by using an integrated planning model, such as the Financial Genome software described in Appendix I, to develop an expected performance pattern and financial structure as inputs to the final valuation approach.

Let's explore some of the key issues implicit in the derivation of free cash flow, where a variety of judgments are involved. The starting point for developing projections of operating earnings (EBIAT) is to establish periodic revenue forecasts and gross margin assumptions. Future revenue patterns and margins must be viewed rationally within the strategic position of the company and its market. Just assuming continuous growth, especially at a high rate, may not be realistic given certain conditions like specific market position, product/service cycles, technological change, and so forth. Yet revenue assumptions are critical because they normally are considered the key driver for establishing working capital needs, new capital investment, and operational requirements in the analysis. Similarly, gross margin assumptions have to be tempered against the competitive environment, especially in high technology markets where rapid change can erode pricing in short order.

Assumed operating expenses—including expected depreciation and amortization expense—are then subtracted from gross margin. In their simplest form, these projections can be made in relation to sales revenue, but a more detailed set of assumptions about key operating expense elements will help refine the analysis. Note that interest expense is not considered here, because it is neither an operating expense nor relevant to the analysis. The effective tax rate is then applied to this operating profit to derive EBIAT, earnings after taxes but before interest.

The next step is to add back depreciation, amortization, and other noncash items. A shortcut method for establishing depreciation levels is to charge a level percentage of the assumed prior year's depreciable asset balance, thus allowing for periodic capital additions and reductions. A more detailed approach would track the staggered buildup of capital assets and develop related depreciation expenses for each period to improve the result. In either case, allowance has to be made for the planned changes in the plant, property, and equipment base—as well as separately in intangible assets for purposes of amortization of goodwill and other write-offs—and for consistency with the operating expense assumptions.

Expected net changes in working capital will depend on the level of operations and assumed working capital management effectiveness. Such changes can, of course, involve cash outflows as well as inflows, and as such should always be correctly reflected as subtractions or additions. The key forecast driver is usually sales revenue, and working capital changes can simply be tied to sales growth or decline, using a percentage relationship. More refined analyses will take into account applicable operational drivers and specific expectations about working capital management to improve the result.

Expected net capital requirements for funding the company's strategy are important inputs to the analysis in support of any anticipated changes in operations. They include spending on new property, plant, and equipment, major programs such as research and development projects, and also planned acquisitions. Such needs will be reduced by any planned disposals of existing assets, or divestment of lines of business, all adjusted for income tax implications. Therefore, net capital requirements again may be cash outflows or inflows, because they are a combination of funds needs and releases. A quick analysis often ties investment changes to changes in sales revenue as the driver, whereas a more refined approach identifies specific strategic changes in the investment base for each period as they are expected to occur. As we established in Chapter 2, a company expecting little growth may simply replace assets at the level of depreciation, fast-growth companies may need significant funding, and declining companies can release cash.

Finally, any significant nonoperating earnings or expenses after applicable taxes, such as investment income, or restructuring costs, should be recognized and eliminated in the period they occur, that is, by subtracting nonoperating income and adding back nonoperating expenses. As we'll see, the valuation approach separately adjusts for the value of nonoperating assets, such as cash, marketable securities, and other nonoperating assets, thus separating such elements from operating performance.

The net result of these calculations is periodic free cash flow, the first of the two key inputs to the analysis structure. Next we'll turn to the important subject of residual or ongoing value at the end of the analysis period, examining a variety of approaches that can be used in the process.

Ongoing (Residual) Value

Developing an ongoing or residual value of a company at the terminal point of the valuation analysis in principle corresponds to the terminal value concept used for business investment projects as discussed in Chapters 6 and 7. By definition, this ongoing value should be the sum of the present values of all future cash flows from that point on. Given the weight and importance of this element, however, it is usually advantageous to use several alternative approaches to calculate a range of possible values to be used. Not all approaches will fit every circumstance, of course, but as in any projection task, varying the assumptions and testing the range of outcomes are beneficial.

The most common ways of deriving ongoing or residual values for company valuation can be defined as follows. Note that the first four are going concern concepts, whereas the last applies to a business being dissolved at the terminal point of the analysis:

- Assume that the final analysis year's cash flows will continue at the same level.

- Assume that there is cash flow growth which will continue at a specific annual rate.

- Apply a price/earnings ratio to the after-tax earnings of the final analysis year.

- Use the assumed book value of the capitalization at the terminal point.

- Assume liquidation of the company's assets at the terminal point.

The first approach is likely the most popular way of dealing with the problem. It's also simple to calculate, because it represents a perpetuity (an annuity without end), which can be valued by simply dividing the cash flow by the discount rate (see Chapter 6 on discounting methodology). For example, a company with a cost of capital of 12 percent and free cash flow of $100,000 in the final year would have the ongoing value:

$$\$100,000 \div 0.12 = \$833,333$$

Given our assumption of no growth in future years, capital needs to support future operations will level off at the rate of depreciation, and changes in working capital will likely be minimal. The free cash flow figure used for this calculation at the terminal point may need to be adjusted to reflect this level condition, especially if the analysis in prior years assumed either growth or decline in operations and allowed for funding of these changes. A no-growth condition not only means an easy calculation, but also implies that the company will level off in its performance to earning the cost of capital on any new investments. This stable state is a more conservative approach than the perpetual growth assumption, and in many cases reflects a competitively sustainable condition.

The second approach assumes that growth will continue at a specific rate in perpetuity. In this case the so-called perpetual growth formula can be applied, which divides the expected annual free cash flow in the final analysis year by the cost of capital less the growth rate:

$$\text{Ongoing value} = \frac{\text{Free cash flow}}{k_w - g}$$

In our earlier example, if the company expected cash flows to grow at 7 percent, the result would be:

$$\$100,000 \div (0.12 - 0.07) = \$2,000,000$$

Note that this formulation by its very nature must apply only to growth rates lower than the cost of capital, because the result becomes meaningless when growth is equal to or in excess of the cost of capital. At the same time, assuming perpetual growth carries with it the hazard of overestimating the company's ability to gain and maintain a sustainable competitive advantage forever, regardless of market conditions or technological change. Given the power of compounding, even relatively modest growth rates over a long enough period of time thus may lose touch with reality. At times it might be reasonable to assume a declining cash flow pattern that reflects competitive and technological uncertainty, which would alter the formula on the previous page into adding the rate of decline to the cost of capital in the denominator, instead of subtracting the growth rate, thus lowering the resulting ongoing value. Again practicality must prevail here, because perpetual decline rapidly compounds into oblivion.

The third approach attempts to avoid the difficulty of forecasting cash flows beyond the end of the chosen analysis period and instead uses a shortcut for deriving the ongoing value. It applies a price to earnings multiple that might be warranted at the terminal point, that is, multiplying EBIAT in that year by 8, 12, or 15 times. The specific multiple chosen will depend on the nature of the business and the trends in the industry it represents. It's also possible to test the reasonableness of the multiple with current conditions in the company, with the somewhat tenuous assumption that these conditions will also hold in the future. In this case, the most recent historical EBIAT is related to the current market value of the total capitalization of the company, that is, the market value of the equity and debt combined, and the multiple is applied to the estimated EBIAT at the terminal point.

The fourth method of establishing ongoing value is simply using the estimated book value of the capitalization at the terminal point. It's a much less satisfactory shortcut than the earnings multiple, for all the reasons we discussed in earlier chapters about the divergence of book values and economic values. Using this approach in effect requires modeling the financial statements throughout the analysis period to arrive at a terminal balance sheet from which the book value of the debt and shareholders' equity can be determined. This can, of course, be done through approximate shortcuts, or by using a detailed planning model, but in either case it'll provide only a rough indication of residual value.

The final approach is a special case, which assumes that the company has reached the end of its economic life. Liquidation value of the company's assets is usually based on an assessment of the recorded values of working capital, fixed assets, and other elements like valuable intangibles (such as patents or software). It requires a final balance sheet to establish the recorded values built up during the analysis period, and judgments as to what proportion of each major category can be recovered. If the usual liquidation losses are expected, appropriate income tax adjustments should be made to reflect only the net amounts realized. The total amount assumed to be recovered from all asset sales then enters the calculation as the residual value.

A Basic Valuation Analysis

Once all the cash flow elements have been estimated, they can be assembled in the form of a spreadsheet model as shown in the generalized format of Figure 10–5, which parallels the one used for the various examples in Chapter 7. We have used a simple illustration of a hypothetical company which has a current capital structure of $26 million in long-term debt (market value $28 million), $5 million in preferred stock (market value the same), and $44 million of shareholders' equity, for a total capitalization of $75 million. 1.1 million common shares are outstanding, which are currently traded at $65 (total market value $71.5 million), while book value per share is $40. The company's EBIAT for the year just ended was $8.7 million, and on the company's balance sheet there are nonoperating assets (cash, marketable securities, and investments) of $5 million.

The analysis format of the model follows the sequence we described earlier. The assumed figures project modest revenue growth, leveling off in Year 4, and declining slightly thereafter. Gross margin is changing somewhat over the period, and EBIAT grows gradually from the actual $8.7 million but reflects the drop in revenue in later years. Assumed funding requirements for working capital follow this pattern, including a small reduction in working capital in the final year. Business investment exceeds depreciation in the growth phase, but levels off to near or below that amount in the latter years. Depreciation is broadly estimated, whereas nonoperating elements are minor.

The resulting periodic free cash flow, or cash flow to capitalization, represents the cash available to the company to support its obligations to all providers of the long-term funds, that is, the payment of interest and dividends, potential repayment of debt, or even repurchase of its own shares. In our example this cash flow is gradually rising in the last 3 years, because of the combination of operational performance and changing funding needs which in part offset each other. This pattern is discounted at an assumed cost of capital of 12 percent and the present values are accumulated.

The ongoing value assumption we've used here is 12 times EBIAT, which is the same as the one pertaining at present, because the company is assumed to grow only modestly before leveling off. The company's current capital structure has a book value of $75 million, and a market value of $104.5 million ($28 + $5 + $71.5), which represents about 12 times current EBIAT of $8.7 million. At 12 times EBIAT in Year 6 the ongoing value amounts to about $110.6 million (a present value of $56 million when the PV factor of 0.507 is applied). Note that this amount represents about two-thirds of the total present value in the analysis, quite a typical illustration of the importance of residual values.

Other residual values should be tried to obtain a range of potential outcomes, but tested against the likely circumstances. Under a level growth assumption, the final year's free cash flow would be divided by the 12 percent cost of capital rate assumed. As we mentioned, the last year should be examined to determine if it is representative of a stable condition, that is, no new funding in excess of depreciation would be required. In our example, a slight decline pattern was assumed, which resulted in a release of some working capital and investment

F I G U R E   10–5

F I G U R E   10–5

Business Valuation Model ($ thousands)*

	Results					
	Year 0	Year 1	Year 2	Year 3	Year 4	Year 5	Year 6
Sales revenue		$140,000	$150,000	$160,000	$170,000	$165,000	$160,000
Gross margin percent		33%	33%	35%	35%	34%	34%
Gross margin		46,200	49,500	56,000	59,500	56,100	54,400
Less: Operating expenses		29,000	31,000	35,000	38,000	40,000	40,000
Operating profit		17,200	18,500	21,000	21,500	16,100	14,400
Tax rate		36%	36%	36%	36%	36%	36%
Income taxes		6,192	6,660	7,560	7,740	5,796	5,184
EBIAT (earnings before interest, after taxes)		$ 11,008	$ 11,840	$ 13,440	$ 13,760	$ 10,304	$ 9,216
Add back: Depreciation and other noncash items		6,500	7,000	7,500	8,500	8,500	8,000
Less: Net new working capital		−1,200	−2,300	−2,500	−2,000	0	1,000
Less: Net new capital investments		−7,500	−8,000	−12,000	−9,000	−8,000	−7,000
Add/less: Nonoperating items (after taxes)		500	−300	600	−800	−500	200
Free cash flow		$ 9,308	$ 8,240	$ 7,040	$ 10,460	$ 10,304	$ 11,416
Ongoing value at end of analysis period (12 times EBIAT)		—	—	—	—	—	110,592
Present value factors @ 12%		0.893	0.797	0.712	0.636	0.567	0.507
Present values @ cost of capital		8,311	6,569	5,011	6,648	5,847	61,864
Cumulative present values	$ 94,249	$ 8,311	$ 14,880	$ 19,891	$ 26,539	$ 32,386	$ 94,249
Firm value from operations	$ 94,249						
Nonoperating assets (cash, marketable securities, etc.)	5,000						
Total firm value	$ 99,249						
Less: Market value of outstanding long-term debt	28,000						
Value of total shareholders' equity	$71,249						
Less: Market value of outstanding preferred stock	5,000						
Value of common shareholders' equity	$66,249						
Common shares outstanding	1,100,000						
Value per common share (1,100,000 shares)	$60.23						

*This model is available for download in an interactive format; see "Analytical Support," p. 424.

outlays less than depreciation. A figure closer to EBIAT, adjusted for nonoperating elements would be more representative of stable conditions, or in our case, approximately $9.4 million ($9.2 million + $0.2 million). When divided by 12 percent, the result is only $78.3 million, with a present value of about $40 million, or $16 million less than the present value ($56 million) of our assumed 12 times EBIAT of $110.6 million. A perpetual growth assumption would have to be applied to a final free cash flow adjusted from a decline to a growth mode, more in the area of $10 to $11 million. Divided by the factor of (0.12 − 0.6), the residual value would range between $166 and $183 million, changing the present value result significantly.

After discounting the pattern of free cash flows at the cost of capital (12 percent in our example) the resulting net present value should be a reasonable approximation of the operational value of the company. Note that the nonoperating assets of $5 million were added to the operational firm value to arrive at the total firm value of $99.2 million. After subtracting the market value of debt and preferred stock, the value of common equity is $66.2 million, or $60.23 per share. Note that in this example the market price warranted by the assumptions made is almost $5.00 less than the current market quotations, implying an erosion of value over time. If the no-growth assumption for the residual value ($78.3 million) is used, the warranted value per share drops to $45.34 per share, whereas under the 6 percent growth assumption (approximately $170 million) the value per share jumps to $87.60. It's not unusual to find such sizable ranges of outcomes in what amounts to a quantification of future expectations, not historical data. The quality of the result depends, of course, on the quality and reasonableness of the estimates that were used in deriving it. One should always employ extensive sensitivity analysis to test the likely range of outcomes, using different combinations of inputs, different discount rates, and especially different estimates of the ongoing value. The model in Figure 10–5 can be used as a template for this purpose.

It'll be useful to demonstrate visually how the firm value developed by this present value analysis relates to the company's capital structure. What we've developed by discounting the net cash flow stream and the assumed ongoing value, plus nonoperating assets, is the approximate fair market value of the company's overall capitalization. Figure 10–6 demonstrates that the total recorded value of a business is the sum of its working capital, fixed assets, and other assets, which are financed by the combination of long-term debt and equity. The present value approach has enabled us to express this accounting value in current economic terms—a present value which might be higher or lower than the recorded values on the balance sheet, and which also depends, of course, on all the assumptions implicit in the cash flow forecasts, including the important ongoing value. Only by coincidence will the two values be precisely equal, because as we discussed in Chapter 1, recorded values on the balance sheet reflect historical transaction values, which tend to become obsolete with the passage of time.

We've now achieved a direct valuation of the company's common equity by means of an economic (cash flow) approach which is conceptually superior to the simpler devices discussed in the common stock section of this chapter, although subject to the range of assumptions and judgments underlying it. This approach is the basis for much of the analytical work underlying modern security analysis, where the use of cash flow analysis has begun to overshadow most other methodologies.

In a multibusiness company, the approach can be refined by developing operating cash flow patterns for each of the business units, and discounting these individual patterns at the corporate cost of capital. If the businesses differ widely in

FIGURE   10–6

Present Value of Business Cash Flows and the Capital Structure

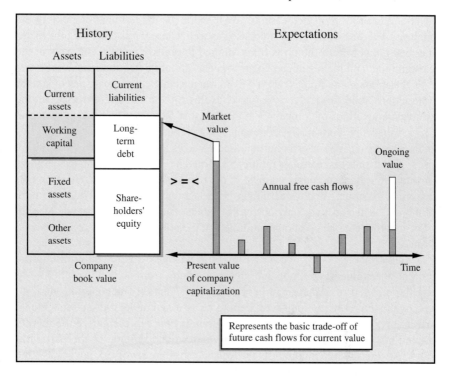

their risk/reward conditions, one can apply different discount standards that reflect these differences, as discussed in Chapter 8. In recent years, testing the present value of individual business units' cash flow patterns to determine the relative contribution to the total value of the corporation has become widely accepted.

Yet, given the nature of the estimates underlying the analysis, there's nothing automatic about the use of such values in an actual transaction involving the sale of a company or any of its parts. Different analysts and certainly buyers and sellers will use their own sets of assumptions in developing their respective results. There should also be efforts to test the analytical results against comparable transactions, to the extent these are available and relevant.

The actual value finally agreed upon in any transaction between a buyer and a seller will depend on many more factors, not the least of which are the differences in assessing business risk and in the return expectations of the parties involved, as well as in the negotiating stance and skills used by them. We'll return to the subject of valuation of a company or combination of companies within the context of shareholder value creation in Chapter 11.

Using Shortcuts in Valuing an Ongoing Business

In the previous example, an earnings multiple based on EBIAT was used to derive the ongoing value of the business. This multiple simply indicated what a particular level of current or projected earnings was "worth" at the termination point of the analysis. After-tax earnings are often used as well. Closely related to the price/earnings ratio, this rule of thumb is often applied to quickly value a company at the present time, and the result can be an "opener" in initial negotiations. Never precise, the earnings multiple is derived from rough statistical comparisons of similar transactions, and from a comparative evaluation of the performance of the price/earnings ratios of companies in the industry. Other multiples encountered at times, especially with smaller companies or new businesses, include multiples of sales, or even derived sales volumes based on an estimated customer group.

When an actual earnings multiple is turned into a ratio of estimated earnings to value, it provides a rough estimate of the rate of return on the purchase or selling price—assuming that the earnings chosen are representative of what the future will bring. When taken as only one of the indicators of value within a whole array of negotiating data, the earnings multiple and the related crude rate of return have some merit.

Other shortcuts in valuing an ongoing business involve determining the total market value of common and preferred equity from market quotations—in itself somewhat of a challenge in view of stock market fluctuations—and adjusting this total for any long-term debt to be assumed in the transaction. One issue involved in this approach is the question of how representative the market quotations are depending on the trading pattern and volume of the particular stock. At times, when no publicly traded securities are involved, the book value of the business is examined as an indicator of value. Needless to say, the fact that recorded values don't necessarily reflect economic values can be a significant problem.

All of these results can at one time or another enter into the deliberations, but considerable judgment must be exercised to determine their relevance in the particular case. In most situations, the discounted cash flow approach will be the conceptually most convincing measure, despite the difficulties of estimating the cash flow pattern in specific terms.

Specialized Valuation Issues

Rights and Warrants

In Chapter 9 we discussed the main aspects of rights and warrants from the perspective of the issuing company. We'll now turn briefly to illustrating the value of these specialized forms of financing to the investor.

Rights values arise from the fact that these securities entitle the holder to purchase additional common shares of the company at a price often significantly below the prevailing market price. For example, an investor holding five common shares has received five rights that represent the opportunity to purchase one new share of common stock at $30. The current market value of the existing common stock is $40.

Our investor's initial position is as follows:

Number of shares	5
Number of rights	5
Value of 5 shares @ $40	$200
Subscription price	$ 30

After exercising the rights and paying $30 to the company, the shareholder's position will be:

Number of shares	6
Value of investment	$230.00
Investment per share	$ 38.33
Value of a right	$ 1.67 (old value − new value)

The market value of the company's shares after all rights have been exercised will in fact tend to approximate $38.33, because the new shares were offered at a significant discount, in the ratio of one new share for each five old shares held. When a rights offering is announced, the shares of the company will trade *cum rights* from the effective date (holder-of-record date) until the specified date at which the stock becomes *ex rights*. At that time, the decline in price reflecting the value of the now separate rights will take place.

The value to the investor of each right is therefore the proportional discount provided by the rights offering, as related to the ratio of old and new shares. Rights are often traded in the market at the approximate level of the calculated value. Both the value of common stock ex rights, and the value of rights themselves will, of course, be influenced by general movements in the securities markets that are independent of the particular company's circumstances.

Warrants have value directly related to the market price of the common shares of the company. Unlike rights, warrants are not issued proportionally to all common shareholders, but are most frequently attached to issues of new debt and occasionally to new issues of common. Moreover, warrants tend to have expiration dates far longer than rights, and in some cases have no expiration at all. In effect, warrants are options entitling the holder to purchase a new share of common at a fixed exercise price for an extended period of time.

The value of the warrant therefore will be directly related to the difference between the exercise price and the expected market value of the common during the usually lengthy exercise period. If the common stock continually trades at or below the exercise price, the value of the warrant will approach zero as the expiration date draws near and no change is foreseen. If the market value of the common rises above the exercise price, and especially if it's expected to grow in the future during the remainder of the exercise period, the value of the warrant will rise in concert.

Options

Given the rapid increase in the importance of options trading in the money and securities markets, at least some brief reference should be made to this highly specialized form of investing and the basic valuation aspects involved. Rights and warrants as discussed above are in effect options extended by the issuing company to purchase additional shares at a set price, and we saw how the interplay of the trend in the company's market price, the exercise price, and the exercise period affected the value of these instruments. The broader concept of options refers to a form of security which permits the holder to buy or sell an asset at a specified price for a specified period of time. Options to buy are named *call options,* and options to sell are named *put options.* The underlying asset's specified price is called the exercise or strike price, and the date at the end of the exercise period is its maturity. Options can be purchased in the option markets for a price, called the premium. It reflects, at the time of purchase, the value of the privilege to buy or sell the asset involved under the conditions specified, in light of the current expectations about future movements in the value of the asset.

Options are a way to guarantee the amount of a purchase or sale under uncertain future conditions for a relatively small current investment, but the value of this opportunity rises and falls with the movements in the market price of the asset. A put option to sell stock at a given price will become worthless if the market price matches or falls below the strike price as the maturity date arrives, although it can become quite valuable when the reverse is true. Similarly, a call option to purchase a foreign currency at a certain value to the dollar will grow in value as the market quotations exceed the strike price, and lose value as they drop lower, expiring worthless. Options can be useful in taking a position in a stock or other asset for a partial investment, with the opportunity to leverage a significant return on this investment if the option speculation is successful, while limiting a potential loss to the premium paid. Options are also ideal hedging devices, used by investors and corporate managers to offset exposure in currency or securities with matching options that "bet the other way."

The specific valuation techniques dealing with options and the many risk/reward patterns and trade-offs are too specialized to cover in this space. They are based in large part on the Black Scholes valuation formulas that established the analytical foundation. Apart from detailed texts on the subject, there are software models available to assist in the analysis of options. and the interested reader should turn to the references at the end of the chapter.

Key Issues

The following is a recap of the key issues raised directly or indirectly in this chapter. They are enumerated here to help the reader keep the techniques discussed within the perspective of financial theory and business practice.

1. The concept of value is not independent of the purpose for which it is used, and its definition and meaning can vary widely with respect to the conditions and circumstances to which it is applied.
2. The value of a security is a function of the expectations about future performance placed upon it, which can be individual judgments as well as collective judgments representing a market.
3. Investors approach the valuation of an investment proposition in terms of their individual risk preferences and thus will differ widely in assessing the attractiveness of an investment.
4. Although the securities markets provide momentary indications, the relative value of a share of common stock in the market at any time is a combination of future expectations, residual claims, and assessments of general and specific risk, subject to economic and business conditions and the decisions of management and the board of directors. It's also affected by the breadth of trading in the security.
5. Valuation techniques are essentially assessment tools that attempt to quantify available objective data and estimates. Yet such quantification will always remain in part subjective, and in part impacted by forces beyond the individual parties' control.
6. Valuation of a security or a business is distorted by the same elements that distort other types of financial analysis: price-level changes, accounting conventions, economic conditions, market fluctuations, and many subjective intangible factors.
7. Validation of results achieved from valuation projects ultimately has to await actual performance in the future; this is why the importance of sound judgments at the time of the analysis cannot be overstated.

Summary

In this chapter, we've brought together a whole range of concepts and basic techniques to provide the reader with an overview of how to value assets, securities, and business operations. To set the stage, we discussed key definitions of value, and then took the viewpoint of the investor assessing the value of the three main forms of securities issued by a company. After covering both value and yield in these situations, we expanded our view to encompass the valuation of an ongoing business. Our purpose was to find basic ways of setting the value in transactions such as sale of a business, restructuring, or the combination of companies in the form of a merger or acquisition.

We found that methods were available for deriving such values, but that the specific assumptions and the background of the transaction added many, often complex, dimensions to the basic calculations. We demonstrated the valuation of a business specifically in cash flow terms, and showed how a company's equity can be valued on the basis of cash flow expectations, quite similar to the business investment analysis we discussed in Chapter 7. Ultimately, value will always remain partially subjective and will be settled in an exchange between interested parties—but managing effectively for economic performance and value will always remain the basic obligation of management.

Analytical Support

A set of Excel-based templates *(Interactive Templates)* is downloadable at no charge from the Web at www.mhhe.com/helfert11e. The tenth of these, "Business Valuation Model: Calculating Cash Flows and Value of the Firm," is a general purpose tool which activates the model in Figure 10–5 on page 417. The template allows you to vary a set of key assumptions about the future performance of a company, and to observe the numerical changes resulting from these modifications on the value of the firm and its shareholders' equity.

Financial Genome, the advanced financial analysis software application described in Appendix I, is a fully integrated analytical and planning model for both the professional user and the business student. It is designed to develop a full set of integrated financial statements from historical data inputs as well as for projections of financial performance. It can automatically derive accounting measures as well as common cash flow inputs to valuation analysis. The software contains a five-year database (1996 to 2000) for 3M Corporation, matching the company's financial statements reproduced in this chapter. It can be used to develop projected statements and free cash flow for 3M Corporation as an input to the valuation template to test assumptions about 3M's value.

Financial Genome is downloadable from the Web, using the unique and restricted code provided with this book (see details in "Downloads" at the end of Appendix I, p. 479).

Selected References

Brealey, Richard, and Stewart Myers. *Principles of Corporate Finance.* 5th ed. Burr Ridge, IL: Irwin/McGraw-Hill, 1996.

Copeland, Tom; Tim Koller; and Jack Murrin. *Measuring and Managing the Value of Companies.* 2nd ed. New York: Wiley, 1995.

Cornell, Bradford. *Corporate Valuation: Tools for Effective Appraisal and Decision Making.* Burr Ridge, IL: Business One Irwin, 1993.

Jones, Gary E., and Dirk Van Dyke, *The Business of Business Valuation.* Burr Ridge, IL: McGraw-Hill, 1998.

Pratt, Shannon P. *Valuing a Business: The Analysis and Appraisal of Closely Held Companies.* 3rd ed. Burr Ridge, IL: Irwin/McGraw-Hill, 1995.

Rappaport, Alfred. *Creating Shareholder Value.* Revised ed. New York: Free Press, 1998.

Ross, Stephen; Randolph Westerfield; and Jeffrey Jaffe. *Corporate Finance.* 5th ed. Burr Ridge, IL: Irwin/McGraw-Hill, 1999.

Weston, Fred; Scott Besley; and Eugene Brigham. *Essentials of Managerial Finance.* 11th ed. Hinsdale, IL: Dryden Press, 1996.

Self-Study Exercises, Problems, and Discussion Questions

Exercises and Problems *(Selected Solutions are Provided in Appendix VI)*

1. Using the present value tables at the end of Chapter 6 (p. 276) or a spreadsheet, develop the value (price) of bonds with the following characteristics:

   a. A bond with a face value of $1,000 carries interest of 8 percent per year, paid semiannually. It will be redeemed for $1,075 at the end of 14 years. At what price would the bond yield a return of 6 percent? At what price a return of 9 percent?

   b. A bond with a face value of $1,000 carries interest of 8.5 percent per year, paid semiannually. It's callable at 110 percent of face value beginning October 1, 2013, and will be redeemed (unless called) on October 1, 2025. What price on October 1, 2003, would yield a prospective investor a return of 6 percent? What price would yield 9 percent? (Use interpolation.)

2. Using a calculator or spreadsheet, develop the yield (return) of two bonds with the following characteristics:

   a. A bond with a face value of $1,000 carries interest at 7 percent per year, paid semiannually on January 15 and July 15. It will be redeemed at 110 percent on July 15, 2017. The market quotation on July 15, 2003, is 124⅛. What's the approximate yield to an investor who purchases the bond on this date? What's the exact yield given in an appropriate bond table?

   b. A bond with a face value of $500 carries interest at 8 percent per year, paid annually. It will be redeemed at par on March 1, 2014. The bond was purchased on August 20, 2003, for $487.50, including accrued interest. What's the approximate yield? What's the exact yield, using an appropriate bond table or a spreadsheet?

3. Develop and discuss the value of individual rights to subscribe to shares of stock under the circumstances of (*a*) and (*b*), and calculate the subscription price in (*c*).

   a. A company is offering its common stockholders the right to subscribe to one share of common at $65 for each 12 shares held. At the time of the offering, the common is trading at $89. What's the likely market value of the common going to be after the offering period (ex rights)?

   b. A company is offering its common stockholders the right to purchase one share of 7 percent convertible preferred at $82 for each six shares of common stock held. A reasonable expectation is that the preferred will be trading at $105, once issued. What would the rights value be if the offer were made for each four shares of common held?

   c. If the value of a right is expected to be $2, and the market price is expected to be $123 after exercise of the rights, what's the subscription price under a subscription ratio of 11:1?

4. The following information is available about two different common stocks, Company A and Company B:

	Company A	Company B
Earnings per share	$2.50	$7.25
Dividends per share	1.00	5.00
Growth in earnings	8%	4%
Price range	$26–$20	$60–$56
Beta (β)	1.3	0.8
Risk-free return	7.0%	7.0%
Expected return, S&P 500	13.5%	13.5%

   On the assumption that the companies' earnings growth rates will continue, develop an estimate of the value of the common stock and its yield for each. Discuss.

5. The following estimates about the next five years' performance of GHI Company have been provided to you. Based on this information and the current data available to you, calculate the firm value of the company as a going business, assuming that weighted cost of capital of 12% is the relevant standard, and also establish the value of the shareholders' equity. Using the template for Figure 10–5, develop the cash flow valuation with alternative ongoing value estimates, and compare the results against other yardsticks of value. What additional information would be helpful here? Discuss.

GHI Company Projections
($ millions)

	Year 1	Year 2	Year 3	Year 4	Year 5
Projected operating earnings (after taxes, before interest)	$2.7	$2.9	$3.2	$3.6	$4.0
Projected investments	0.7	2.1	1.5	1.5	2.0
Projected working capital changes	0.4	0.3	0.5	0.6	0.4
Projected depreciation	1.0	1.3	1.5	1.6	1.8
Projected dividends	1.2	1.3	1.5	1.6	1.9

The ongoing value at the end of the period is estimated at between 10 and 12 times earnings. The company's operating earnings for the past year were $2.5 million. The price/earnings ratio for GHI Company's industry is currently 11.0. Current nonoperating assets are $2 million, long-term debt outstanding is $12.2 million, and the current book value of the capitalization is $23.5 million. As an alternative to the ongoing value multiple, assume (*a*) that 6 percent growth in free cash flow can be expected for the foreseeable future and (*b*) that no future growth in free cash flow can be expected. Assume that the free cash flow in year 6 will be $3.6 million. The estimated book value of the capitalization at the end of year 5 is $28.5 million.

6. The MNO Company's stock was closely held, and the volume of stock traded over the counter represented only a small fraction of the total shares outstanding. You've been asked to develop as many valuation approaches as possible in preparation for the disposition of a 25 percent block of common stock held by the estate of one of the founders. The estate's executor will be interested in the various viewpoints that can be taken in arriving at a fair value.

    Listed below is the most recent balance sheet as of 12/31/2003, a five-year history of selected data including the first quarter of 2004, as well as a projection of selected data for the following five years. Assume a cost of capital of 10 percent, and the free cash flow in Year 6 as equal to Year 5.

    Using the template for Figure 10–5, develop a variety of valuation approaches based on book values, liquidation values, market values, past trends, and projections, taking into account redundant assets and the limited trading volume of the stock. Stipulate your assumptions and suggest additional information you would consider necessary for making your recommendation. Discuss your findings.

    Financial Genome contains a more detailed database for MNO, which can be used to develop alternative projections and valuations.

MNO COMPANY
Balance Sheet, December 31, 2003
($ thousands)

Assets

Current assets:

Cash	$ 230	(working balance, $150)
Marketable securities	415	(held for payment of taxes and investment in equipment)
Accounts receivable	525	(94% collectible, net of expenses)
Inventories	815	(quick disposal value two-thirds of book, normal sale 95%)
Total current assets	1,985	
Fixed assets	1,715	(quick sale value $225, replacement value, $2,500)
Less: Accumulated depreciation	820	
Net fixed assets	895	
Prepaid expenses	40	(insurance, licenses, etc.)
Goodwill	175	(based on previous acquisitions)
Organization expense	20	(legal fees, taxes)
Total assets	$3,115	

Liabilities and Shareholders' Equity

Current liabilities:

Accounts payable	$ 370	($350 current, $20 overdue)
Notes payable	125	(due 60 days hence)
Accrued liabilities	290	(wages, interest, etc.)
Accrued taxes	150	(income taxes, withholding)
Total current liabilities	935	
Mortgage payable	175	(80% of fixed assets as security)
Bonds, net of sinking fund	520	(unsecured)
Deferred income taxes	55	
Reserve for self-insurance	110	(contingency surplus reserve)
Preferred stock	300	(7% preferred, 3,000 shares)
Common stock	525	(52,500 shares, $10 par)
Capital surplus	110	(excess paid in for common)
Retained earnings	385	(accumulated earnings less dividends)
Total liabilities and shareholders' equity	$3,115	

MNO COMPANY
Key Past Performance Data

	1999	2000	2001	2002	2003	3-31-04*
Net profit after taxes (000)	$92	$110	$126	$139	$118	$34
Nonoperating income after taxes	8	11	14	9	19	5
Depreciation	62	63	66	70	72	19
Earnings per share	1.75	2.10	2.40	2.65	2.25	0.64
Dividends per share	1.20	1.60	1.60	1.80	1.80	0.45
Market price, high	31⅜	33¼	39⅞	34⅛	29¾	30⅞
Market price, low	13⅞	19¾	23⅝	22⅛	19¼	19⅜
Market price, average	22⅝	26½	31¾	28⅛	24½	25⅛
Industry price/earnings ratio	14.0	15.0	16.0	12.0	11.0	12.0

*Quarter.

MNO COMPANY
Five-Year Projection

	2004	2005	2006	2007	2008
Net profit after taxes (000)	$125	$130	$140	$140	$150
Nonoperating income after taxes	10	11	12	12	12
Interest expense after taxes	28	28	30	30	30
Depreciation	75	70	70	65	65
Earnings per share	2.38	2.48	2.67	2.67	2.86
Dividends per share	1.80	1.80	2.00	2.00	2.20
New investment	$ 50	$ 60	$ 60	$ 70	$ 80
Increase in working capital	20	20	25	25	30
Industry price/earnings ratio for the period			12.0		

7. Using Financial Genome and its database for 3M Corporation, develop a set of projections with your own assumptions about future performance of 3M, and derive valuations for the company. You can employ the built-in forecast drivers for the projection process, and utilize the specialized output statements to derive free cash flow and other valuation inputs. Discuss your findings.

Discussion Questions

1. Differentiate between economic value and market value. Are both concepts absolute in their meaning?
2. Is value merely in the eye of the beholder or can conditions be quantified sufficiently to allow for truly objective choices?
3. Discuss the relationship between yield and value. Are both concepts based on the same conditions?

4. Is it possible to allow specifically for the effect of such provisions as participation, convertibility, callability, and other special covenants in valuing preferred stocks or bonds?

5. Why should we attempt to value an ongoing business via a specific cash flow analysis when in the end the decision is based on many other factors as well?

6. Although the ongoing value is critical to the results of cash flow valuation analysis, it is fraught with uncertainty. How can this issue be dealt with satisfactorily?

7. Does it really make sense to assume cash flows in perpetuity, whether growing, level, or declining?

8. List major considerations affecting valuation in an inflationary environment.

9. With the growing availability of specialized software, will valuation likely become more quantified? Will this improve the quality of the analyses?

10. If there's so much uncertainty in estimates of future cash flows, why does it make sense to apply ever more sophisticated valuation concepts and formulas?

CHAPTER 11

MANAGING FOR
SHAREHOLDER VALUE

$\mathbf{W}$e now return to the primary concept we established at the beginning of this book, namely, that the basic obligation of the management of any business is to make investment, operating, and financing decisions that will enhance shareholder value over the long term. Our discussion of valuing business cash flows strongly suggested that management should periodically reexamine the company's policies and strategies to test whether its basic obligation of creating shareholder value is in fact being met. We recall that increasing shareholder value depends on making new investments that exceed the cost of capital—an expression of investor expectations—as well as managing all existing investments for cash flow results that similarly exceed investor expectations.

The most beneficial aspect of the growing emphasis on shareholder value creation over the past decade has been the widespread rediscovery of management fundamentals—even if at times under threat of dismissal by hostile raiders. Despite the periodic lapses of economic discipline exemplified in the recent dot-com bubble, there has been real progress made with the prospect of more to come. Growing numbers of corporate managers, in the U.S. and in other parts of the world, are tackling the critical task of creating value for their shareholders. They are doing this by reexamining the structure and functioning of their company as a whole and by placing greater emphasis on making their decisions, large and small, on the basis of sound economic trade-offs. The basic imperative of requiring that all investments earn above the cost of capital has been rediscovered as a practical—even if difficult to achieve—goal. Vast efforts at restructuring, increasing cost-effectiveness, making disinvestments and acquisitions, and developing value-based processes, data flows, measures, and incentives are being carried out in the name of shareholder value creation. In fact, testing the efficiency with which all resources are employed and defining the relative contribution from various business segments with an objective "outside" orientation has become commonplace in many companies. One could argue that this approach should really have been commonplace all along, because of the long-established fact that all business decisions have an economic basis—whether this is recognized or not. A number of specialized measures and valuation methodologies have emerged in support of value-based management principles, which we'll discuss later in this chapter.

Shareholder Value Creation in Perspective

Before we turn to a detailed discussion of value-based measurement techniques, it'll be useful to revisit the business system as shown in Figure 11–1 to provide an overall perspective for the various analytical processes presented in this book, and to review their relationship to shareholder value creation. Two additional overview perspectives which follow in Figures 11–2 and 11–3 also will help set the stage for this chapter.

As the upper part of the diagram shows, companies focusing on shareholder value will tailor their analytical processes and physical implementation to achieve economic (cash flow) returns above the cost of capital on new investments as well as on existing investments, making sure that return goals are set at appropriate levels and in the proper economic context. We recall the discussion of Chapters 6, 7, and 8 in which the principles and the measures supporting this approach were presented. One of the key issues to be faced in this area, however, is the dichotomy between the economic analysis of new investments, where expected cash flow patterns can be judged in an incremental fashion, and the analysis of the existing investment base, where normal accounting data and recorded values are the main source of information. It is here where much of the development of value-based methodologies has taken place, in an effort to close the conceptual gap between cash flow economics and ratio-based conventional analysis.

The midsection of the diagram reflects our familiar set of operational trade-offs, which should be made with long-term cash flow generation in mind, and always within the value creation context. Excellent product and service offerings, competitive advantage, and cost-effectiveness are the underlying driving forces, but the many decisions supporting daily activities require not only an analytical understanding of their cash flow impact, but also measures and incentives that reinforce economic decision making. Again, the increasing emphasis on value-based management is fueling a shift away from accounting-based methodology toward cash flow frameworks. We encountered some of this trend in our discussion of the analytical approaches of earlier chapters, and we'll expand on the measures and their implications later in this chapter.

The bottom part of the diagram deals with the financing aspects of value creation, where we recognize the many trade-offs we've encountered in Chapters 5, 8, and 9. Companies with a value orientation consciously manage these trade-offs for long-term cash flow generation, and view the disposition of profits and the target dimensions of the capital structure as critical supportive elements in their strategic planning. Choices that affect dividend payout, changes in leverage, repurchase of shares, and funding of future opportunities are made against the

FIGURE 11–1

Shareholder Value Creation in a Business System Context*

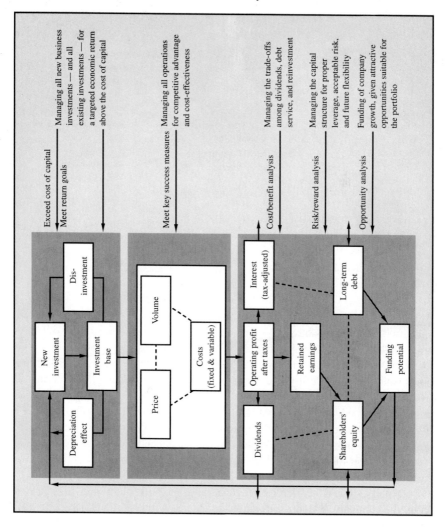

*This model is available for download in an interactive format; see "Analytical Support," p. 467.

criterion of value creation. The trade-offs chosen here can at times significantly affect the direction of the company's strategy.

Another overview of the integration of financial, strategic, and operational activities supporting shareholder value creation is provided in Figure 11–2. Here we see the core concept of earning returns in excess of the cost of capital surrounded by the key management activities, starting at the top with the evaluation

FIGURE 11–2

Shareholder Value Creation in a Management Context

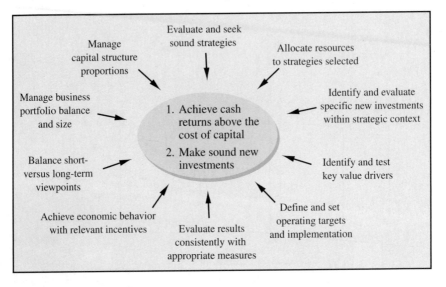

and selection of sound strategies, leading to broad resource allocation and the analysis of specific business investments. In this area the analytical tools of Chapters 6 and 7 come into play. This is followed by the identification of those elements and variables that drive value creation, which form the basis for operational targets and the measures by which performance is gauged. Here the materials of Chapters 2, 3, and 4 have relevance. Next is the critical area of designing incentives for managers to act in an economic fashion, and to support a long-term view of decision making. We've not focused on such incentive programs because they are beyond the scope of this book. However, financial and other measures selected for the purpose must reinforce the economic (cash flow) orientation we have stressed throughout.

Finally, there's the broad strategic issue of the portfolio of activities carried on by the company, which is intimately connected with the capital structure proportions and trade-offs. Here the materials in Chapters 5, 8, 9, and 10 are the appropriate background.

Let's now turn to a final summary overview of the major elements of shareholder value creation and their relationship to the three areas of management decisions: investments, operations, and financing. The diagram in Figure 11–3 will be useful in tying together the various concepts we've discussed. It's designed to assist the reader in visualizing the linkage between management decisions and shareholder value. The diagram shows the three basic types of decisions on the left and identifies their key impacts on the cash flows that are the drivers for creating value. The combination of investment and operating decisions generates

FIGURE   11–3

Shareholder Value Creation in a Cash Flow Context

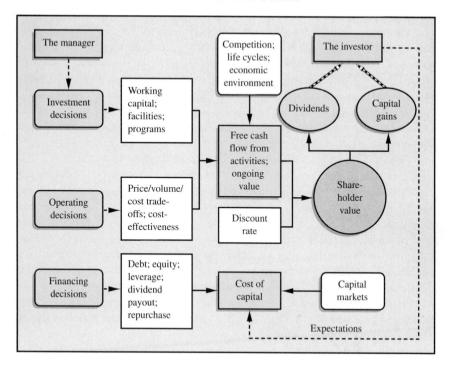

cash flow from operations after taxes, or free cash flow, whereas the financing decisions influence the capital structure and the level of the weighted cost of capital
of the company. Applying the cost of capital—which of course reflects expected
investor returns—as a discount rate to the free cash flow and ongoing value determines the total shareholder value, as discussed in Chapter 10. At the same time,
product life cycles, competition, and many other influences affect the size and
variability of these projected cash flows. In turn, the capital markets influence the
investor's return expectation.

Alternatively, the right side of the diagram shows that shareholder value
also can be viewed in the form of total shareholder return (TSR), which we know
to be the combination of cash dividends and realized capital gains, when seen
through the eyes of the shareholder. This investor viewpoint is inseparable from
the basic driving force of the business—cash flow patterns—because it is positive
free cash flow that will permit the company to pay dividends in the first place, and
also will boost the market value of the shares, enabling the investor to realize capital gains. Naturally, it's possible to create value by minimizing dividends and
reinvesting all funds in soundly based opportunities. The value increase would
then come from capital appreciation, assuming successful implementation and

expected growth in cash flow performance. Conversely, under conditions where sound new opportunities are not available, it might be best for the shareholders that the company repurchase shares rather than invest in mediocre business projects to avoid destroying value.

What are the implications of the three overviews we've just presented? Note that we've once more returned to a systems view of the corporation, driven by the same three basic management decisions, but stressing even more the cash flow patterns that are the economic underpinning of performance and value. All financial analysis techniques and methodologies discussed in this book are ultimately related to the business system and its strategic context as viewed here and in Chapter 1, and it's important that the analytical use of any measure, or a combination of measures, be judged in this sense.

The basic message of managing for shareholder value is nothing more than management's obligation to base all of its investment, operating, and financing decisions on an economic—cash flow—rationale, and to manage all resources entrusted to its care for superior economic returns. Over time, consistency in this approach will generate growing shareholder value, and relative growth in share price performance. If this sounds fundamental, it's intended to be, because the challenge for the 21st century is competitive survival through managing better in a world arena—where economic fundamentals are gaining dominance over ideology. Financial/economic analysis in its many forms, as introduced in Chapter 1 and specifically explained in the remainder of this book, is an essential toolkit for analytically oriented persons of any viewpoint, as they judge the financial/economic performance and outlook of any business.

The Value-Creating Company

Although we've concentrated on the requirements for creating economic value through economic management, let's reflect briefly on what the broader, key attributes of a successful company are. The value-creating company can be defined as an organization in which management has achieved integration of the interests and actions of its key stakeholders, that is, shareholders, managers, employees, customers, suppliers, creditors, and the community. As Figures 11–1 and 11–2 suggested, this integration is based on managing—through sound decision making—the business system and the many economic trade-offs implicit in this system. Such a company achieves, as nearly as possible, an optimization of the system's performance over time, driven by a sound business model, strategies with a sustainable competitive advantage, and superb operational execution, supported by an appropriate, balanced capital structure. This should result in achieving positive cash flows as well as expectations of future cash flow patterns that exceed the cost of capital. In turn, this will provide superior returns to shareholders, superior rewards for managers and employees, excellence in customer satisfaction, first-rate performance and loyalty from suppliers, and superior credit relations. Financial/economic analysis, properly applied, plays a key role in every one of these aspects, but to ensure ongoing success, the following three critical areas—*relevant decision information, economic incentives,* and *total systems management*—must be part of the management philosophy and processes at all times.

Relevant Decision Information

No sound decisions are possible in a business setting without relevant information being available to the decision maker. This axiom applies to all types of decision situations, whether large or small. The value-creating company has established reliable information sources as well as access to this information, to enable persons at all levels to make rational trade-offs whenever they are faced with an issue to be decided. This requires several supportive management practices:

- Sharing of relevant information.
- Decision support by the finance organization.
- Distinction between accounting and economic data.

Sharing   The first practice is a deliberate management attitude of sharing. Too often old-economy companies have fostered a climate in which information and knowledge are limited to those "in the know," while new-economy companies often have been too busy to even develop appropriate information flows. The principle here is one of delegation, of entrusting people at all levels with relevant data that will help them make sound decisions in the interest of value creation. This fits well with the modern management concepts of flat organizations and empowered employees. Empowerment begins with knowledge and is expanded by targeted training, which includes understanding the nature and relevance of financial/economic data, and is further reinforced by a climate of trust.

Decision Support   The second practice defines the support role of the finance organization in the company. If sharing of information and its appropriate application are to succeed, the finance organization must be proactive, because they are the basic supervisors of transactions and data collection, sponsors of internal information and accounting systems, and guardians of financial information. Again we're describing a mind-set, a shifting away from the primary attitude of control and stewardship—which historically has been the orientation of accounting professionals—to an attitude of business adviser and facilitator of decision support. The significance of this shift cannot be overemphasized. The value-creating company looks upon its qualified finance organization as business consultants, working closely with line managers—our economic managers—and bringing to bear their insights and access to information in order to empower the decision makers up and down the line to make appropriate trade-offs. This is an educational function as well as a support role, because even when information is shared, it's necessary to explain the meaning and relevance of the financial/economic data, and to assist the nonfinancial personnel in the appropriate use of decision criteria and tools. At the same time, as we observed in Chapter 1, nonfinancial managers must not simply delegate the analytical aspects of their economic decisions to the experts, because understanding the principles involved as well as being clear about the nature of the trade-offs is part of the overall effectiveness of the enlightened modern manager.

Accounting versus Cash   The third practice is related to the first two, and also echoes an important theme mentioned earlier and carried throughout this book. The value-creating company has managed to draw a clear distinction between the two points of view with which financial information is gathered and interpreted, namely, the accounting viewpoint and the economic decision viewpoint. The blurring between these two, which is too often found in financial analysts' commentary and security analysts' reports can lead senior management to pursue results in accounting terms, such as managing quarterly earnings results and expectations, when in fact cash flows are increasingly being recognized as the real key to building value. The value-creating company encourages internal decision making on the basis of managerial economics and cash flow data, tasking the finance organization to develop decision rules and decision information and provide support that clarifies the economic trade-offs to be made.

In this process, such a company certainly doesn't ignore the basic requirements of financial accounting and reporting, which are still the mainstay of published financial information. But the company actively promotes—in parallel fashion—viewing its performance in cash flow terms, and embraces appropriate shareholder value techniques of the kind described in the last part of this chapter. As top management sends clear signals that decision making must be economic and cash trade-off oriented, it also requires that the accounting implications are to be recognized as a separate view. At times, divergent near-term accounting impacts might have to be explained in external communications, if a strategic move is at stake which could depress current reported earnings but promises strong cash flow results over time. The value-creating company does this as a matter of course, confident in the integrity of its decision-making processes, and communicating clearly why financial accounting cannot express the true economic results, given its different orientation.

In short, the value-creating company has established a corporate climate in which all decisions and all actions are viewed as economic trade-offs, and which fosters access to and sharing of carefully developed, relevant information, decision rules, and tools in a collaborative fashion. Because the common objective is value creation for the long term, such a supportive climate for decision making is the vital underpinning of success.

Economic Incentives

One of the critical attributes of the value-creating company is the degree of attention paid to providing appropriate near-term and long-term incentives to its managers and employees. As we mentioned earlier, there should be a true cause-and-effect relationship between incentives and results. If a company's incentives are based on some of the common, broad accounting measures such as return on equity, or return on assets, or even earnings per share, there is a real risk that decisions, large and small, will suffer from the economic disconnect and time lag inherent to these measures. Although the complex subject of management incentives is beyond the scope of this book, we believe the principles involved are the same basic economic choices that affect financial analysis and planning.

Therefore, both near-term and long-term incentive programs should be built on a careful set of measures designed to reinforce shareholder value creation. Because value creation depends on consistent cash flow generation in excess of the cost of capital, incentives chosen will tend to reward results from consistent cash flow–based decision making. Targets are set and measured with yardsticks as close as possible to cash. As we said earlier, this approach is directly applicable in the operational area, where the cause-and-effect relationship between incentives and results can be found in fairly basic targets, such as volume goals in sales or production, carefully calibrated against quality standards and relative contribution from products and services, or cost effectiveness standards that encourage enhanced performance within required service and quality levels. Here we're not talking merely about managing budgetary variances, but about setting specific subgoals within a broader set of systematic expectations, accompanied by open communication about the fit of these subgoals into the overall strategic context. The process in effect focuses on identifiable and measurable value drivers, which we mentioned earlier.

In the strategic area, long-term incentives should primarily be based on the cash flow expectations from specific plans, whether for a product or service sector in the business, or for the company as a whole. In essence, incentives are founded on the ability to bring about the cash flow streams committed to in strategic plans, and rewards appropriately fluctuate in response to such performance. The value-creating company structures true incentives, that is, underperformance causes a tangible penalty, while excellence is well rewarded. In addition, there is great emphasis on long-term performance to avoid the temptation to make decisions that enhance short-term results to the detriment of shareholder value creation.

Total Systems Management

As our earlier overviews demonstrate, the most important attribute of a successful, value-creating company is its deliberate emphasis on managing the company and its parts as a total system. In simple terms, this means that there is coherence and positive, economic reinforcement reaching across all operational, investment, and financing activities. The pattern of strategies and policies chosen is well matched with the purpose and core capabilities of the company and its stakeholders. Senior management constantly monitors and reinforces this systems view through its feedback and actions, and stands ready to remedy any conflicting actions that could detract from the aim to optimize the overall system. Every major decision, whether affecting operational execution, investments, acquisitions, or disinvestments, or financing choices and funding sources, is made within the systems context to ensure that all implications and linkages are considered and the appropriate trade-offs established. Decision rules and practices for day-to-day decisions are calibrated to reflect the systems view as well.

To achieve such integration of corporate purpose, strategies, policies, activities, and decision-making is not an easy task. Only a few companies experience it fully and consistently, but it is here where the attributes of the economic manager we discussed in Chapter 1 can be applied most effectively. It requires constant vigilance and communication, as well as very consistent management behavior with responses that match this image. The rewards to shareholders, managers, and other stakeholders are obvious, when value creation at the levels of, say, General Electric is considered. Every management team must ask itself from time to time whether it is managing the system entrusted to it by the shareholders in a coherent systems manner, and financial/economic analysis as we discuss it in this book is a critical component supporting this integrated approach.

Evolution of Value-Based Methodologies

Over the last two decades, a number of value-based methodologies have evolved and are gaining increasing acceptance. Their basic aim is to link performance expressed in past and expected cash flow patterns or their surrogates to the market value of a company as a whole and to the relative price level of its common shares. They have become popular within the context of value-based management processes, and various consulting firms use these approaches to establish a firm connection between management actions and shareholder value results. Moreover, such programs relate cash flow thinking and results to management incentive pay. They are designed to provide a coherent set of economic principles that should guide a company's planning processes, investment policies, financing choices, operational decisions, and management incentives toward increasing shareholder value, as displayed earlier in our overviews.

The change in thinking underlying these processes is exemplified in the simple diagram of Figure 11–4, which displays the significant shift in emphasis as reflected in the way corporate performance is being measured.

Prior to the 1980s, management emphasis in the majority of situations tended to be on achieving consistently high profit margins. The asset base necessary to support operations was of secondary importance, almost an afterthought, as indicated by the separation border. The idea was that if margins were high enough, asset recovery and returns would take care of themselves, as would funding of new investment needs for rapid growth. Needless to say, companies applying this way of thinking did not make the best use of invested funds, and asset effectiveness was problematic. In the 80s the emphasis shifted toward growth of profits in absolute terms, again with a focus on the operating statement and less attention paid to asset effectiveness. With some luck, sufficient profit growth would support existing and new investments, but this mind-set still left asset effectiveness open to real questions.

It wasn't until the 90s that formal closure began between the asset base and operating profits, usually in the form of a percent return of profits on assets, expressed in a variety of ways. Although recorded values and accounting-based

FIGURE 11-4

The Changing Emphasis in Corporate Performance Measures

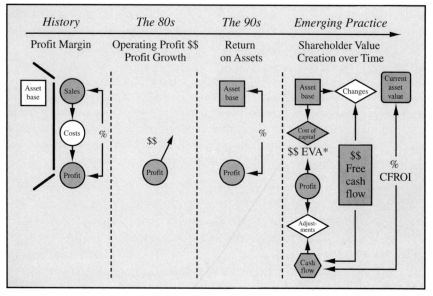

*EVA is a registered trademark of Stern Stewart & Co.

profit could introduce distortions and use of short-term returns as a goal could lead to less than optimal new investment actions, combining assets and profitability was a significant step toward a more integrated way of judging results and making new decisions. As more economic and integrated measures began to be used in practice, growing efforts were made to deal with the shortcomings of accounting-based thinking, and to provide more meaningful signals to managers at all levels. Shareholder value creation was introduced and was based on a variety of adjusted data representing the asset base and operating results.

One key element was the rediscovery of the cost of capital (which first appeared in economic literature around 1890!) as a key criterion for judging performance. The concept of economic profit was defined as the excess of adjusted earnings over the cost of the adjusted resources supporting them. Another key element was the rediscovery of cash flow as the driver of value, whether in the form of free cash flow for judging a whole company, or net cash flows for investment proposals. Various cash flow measures gained importance, among them cash flow return on investment (CFROI) in a variety of forms. The common theme during this evolution was the belated recognition that any business entity is in fact an economic system which has to be judged over a reasonable time horizon with performance and value criteria that reflect and encourage the cash flow trade-offs underlying management decisions, incentives, execution, and results.

A Review of Key Measures

At this point we'll review in broad terms the key performance and value measures encountered in current business practice, and comment in more detail on several of the emerging tools that support shareholder value creation. We've grouped the measures into earnings, cash flow, and value categories, and will take up each area in sequence.

Earnings Measures

The five measures in this area are the traditional ways of stating earnings or relating earnings to different expressions of invested capital, which we discussed in Chapter 3. They are being supplanted increasingly by cash flow and value-based measures, especially for internal planning, analysis, and evaluation purposes. We list them here more for completeness than for their current relevance.

- Earnings per share (EPS) is accounting net income after taxes divided by the number of shares outstanding.

- Return on investment (ROI) is accounting profit divided by the book value of the investment supporting the operations, both defined in a variety of ways.

- Return on net assets (RONA), or return on capitalization, is after-tax accounting operating profit (NOPAT) divided by the book value of total assets less current liabilities.

- Return on capital employed (ROCE) is accounting operating profit (NOPAT) over the book value of assets supporting the operations.

- Return on equity (ROE) is accounting net income after taxes divided by the book value of shareholders' equity.

EPS, one of the most commonly quoted indices of performance, which we discussed in several places in this book, has declined from its former preeminence. Although still tracked by security analysts as an indicator of near-term performance, and used in simple valuation situations via the earnings multiple, EPS expresses only the income side of the accounting spectrum. Moreover, it is subject to the many rules of accounting that have moved performance data further and further away from cash flow. In addition, the number of shares outstanding will fluctuate even more in these days of share buybacks, and will affect the level and trend of this measure.

ROI is the simplest way of expressing the profitability of asset use, and in its unadjusted form remains a basic accounting measure, not an expression of economic performance. The accounting earnings reflect many noncash charges and additions, whereas the book value of the investment is a recorded value, not a current economic value. It might be useful as an approximation, but can often be unreliable because of the nature of accounting data, as we mentioned in Chapter 3.

RONA has become fairly popular, using a more focused operating profit related to the net assets, or capitalization, as recorded on the balance sheet. It still suffers from some of the same accounting issues as ROI, especially in the valuation of the asset base.

ROCE is a further modification, focusing on operating profit and operating assets, but with similar accounting issues remaining. Mostly applied to internal goal setting, it helps make asset utilization a performance issue, at least near term. It does not, however, relate well to economic measures used in judging new investments, nor does it assist in making day-to-day decisions on an economic basis.

ROE is the relationship of accounting net profit to the recorded residual ownership claim of the common shareholders, a recorded value buffeted by a whole host of set-asides, reserves, and reclassifications. Still widely quoted and at times used in goal setting, the measure by its very nature cannot reflect the economic performance of a company. Apart from the usual accounting issues it's also affected by the financial leverage employed by a company. Besides the measure's shortcomings for internal use, the leverage distortion makes peer comparisons more difficult, when capital structures vary.

Cash Flow Measures

The more recent approaches to performance and value measurement are invariably based on cash flow analysis, with much emphasis placed on removing accounting allocations and noncash adjustments to arrive at cash provided by operations and cash invested to support the operations. They relate closely to commonly used economic criteria like net present value and internal rate of return, thus linking the economic approach to new investments with the assessment of ongoing operations. We've discussed many of these already in earlier chapters, and will take up the most current ones later in this section.

- Free cash flow is operating cash flow (net income after taxes plus depreciation and amortization, and usually adjusted to remove interest expense), less new business investments (including changes in working capital) plus dispositions of assets.

- Cash flow return on gross investment (ROGI) is operating cash flow (net income after taxes plus depreciation and amortization) divided by gross assets (before accumulated depreciation).

- Cash flow return on investment (CFROI) is the internal rate of return over the life of the investment, based on operating cash inflows, cash investment outflows, and cash recoveries. It involves a variety of adjustments to arrive at operating cash flows and the cash value of the asset base involved, as we'll demonstrate.

- Total shareholder return (TSR) is the yield to the investor from shares held over one or several periods, calculated from the combination of dividends and change in share value.

- Total business return (TBR) is the internal rate of return from a business unit or unlisted company over one or several periods from the combination of cash flows and change in capital value. It involves a variety of adjustments to develop beginning and ending values of the business.

Free cash flow has become a commonly accepted concept, useful as an economic criterion for periodic results, but, even more important, representing a key element in the valuation of companies and their parts, as well as in strategic planning analyses.

ROGI at times serves as a simple substitute for a periodic economic return, relating operating cash flows to recorded operating assets—which have been "grossed up" by adding back accumulated depreciation to provide a rough surrogate for current values of the asset base. It can be a useful approximation to a more rigorous cash flow analysis in many situations, but could introduce some distortions because in effect it relies on the original cost of assets of different ages as an indicator of current value.

CFROI, in its most sophisticated form, is an economic return developed for the company or its parts, representing an internal rate of return over the average life of the operating assets involved. It's directly comparable to the cost of capital, and to the results from cash flow–based new investment analyses. The methodology requires a series of adjustments and several conceptual constructs, as we'll discuss later.

TSR has become a popular concept, used and published widely, because it expresses the annual return achieved by an investor from holding a company's shares over a specified period of time, based on dividends and change in market value. It links to a company's cost of capital calculation as an expression of the shareholder expectations to be considered in establishing the cost of equity capital.

TBR is a parallel measure to CFROI, designed to measure the internal rate of return of business units or other entities, based on free cash flow and estimates of the beginning and ending values of the entity, much like the analysis of an investment project as presented in Chapter 7.

Value Measures

The seven value measures listed here similarly reflect the evolution from simple multiples to present value cash flow concepts. Again we've discussed several of the basic measures in earlier chapters, but later we'll go into more detail about the most important ones for current value-based management practice.

- Earnings multiples are based on total income after taxes or EPS multiplied by a judgmental factor. They are related to the price/earnings ratio, which is often employed as a guide for the factor used.

- Cash flow multiples are a modification of earnings multiples, using total income after taxes plus depreciation and amortization, or the same on a per share basis, multiplied by a judgmental factor.

- Economic profit, or economic value added (EVA*), is the difference between operating profit after taxes (NOPAT) and a capital charge, which is based on the cost of capital times the net operating assets employed. It's also expressed as the change in economic profit from period to period. The measure requires a variety of adjustments to operating profit and the asset base, as we'll see.

---

*EVA is a registered trademark of Stern Stewart & Co.

- Market value added (MVA) is the difference between the book value of the total invested capital and the market value of the various forms of capital. It requires a variety of adjustments to the recorded values and a careful judgment about how representative current share values are.

- Cash value added (CVA) is the difference between the required annual cash flow to amortize an investment (using the cost of capital as the discount factor), and the actual cash flows generated, expressed as a present value differential.

- Shareholder value (SHV), as we know, is the present value of the estimated future free cash flows over the planning period, discounted at the company's cost of capital, plus the present value of the ongoing value of the business, plus any nonoperating assets (such as marketable securities and other investments), less the amount of long-term debt outstanding. It represents the present value of shareholders' equity under the assumed conditions.

- Shareholder value added (SVA) is the change in total shareholder value, either from period to period or over a longer planning time span, using the process of calculating shareholder value (SHV) as described above for each data point.

Earnings multiples are still a popular way of establishing a "ball park" figure for the value of a business, even though accounting earnings are subject to many potential distortions from an economic standpoint.

Cash flow multiples represent an effort to reflect operating cash flows, even though in their simplest form only depreciation and amortization are added back. Again, they are useful mainly as first estimates before applying more sophisticated techniques.

EVA, the concept popularized by Stern Stewart & Co., is a form of economic profit derived from the excess (or deficit) of operating earnings after subtracting the cost of capital of the assets employed. With a variety of adjustments to both operating profit and the asset base, this approach can be used to track changes in value creation from period to period, and to establish a valuation of the company. Economic profit is not a new principle, because in its basic form it simply states that a company or a business unit is adding value when after-tax earnings before interest are higher than the weighted cost of capital of the resources employed in the creation of these earnings.

MVA is an expression of the value created by a business in excess of the amount of the invested capital as shown on the balance sheet, on a periodic basis as well as over a longer time span. Given that the base is recorded capital, a variety of adjustments are required to make the measure meaningful.

CVA establishes the economic value created, in cash flow terms, over and above the cash flows required to recover the capital employed in a business, using the cost of capital as a standard. It closely parallels the net present value criterion and it is consistent with internal investment analyses.

SHV is, of course, the familiar concept of letting expected cash flows represent the present value of shareholders' equity as a measure of value creation of the total company. Discussed in Chapter 10, this model of value representation underlies much of the value-based management activity extant in modern corporate America.

SVA has become a useful addition to the concept of total shareholder value, because of the importance of establishing trends in value creation when assessing corporate strategic plans and their impact over a period of time. It's also used in assessing the value creation potential from combinations and acquisitions.

Economic Profit and CFROI

We'll now discuss, in a little more detail, two of the most popular measures currently in use in value-based management processes. As we've stated before, economic profit (EVA™) represents a yardstick for measuring whether a business is earning above the cost of capital of the resources (capital base) it employs. The calculation is a straightforward subtraction of the cost of capital from net operating profit:

$$EVA = NOPAT - Ck$$

where

$NOPAT$ = operating profit after taxes (adjusted).
C = capital base employed (net of depreciation).
k = weighted average cost of capital.

Note that the formula as stated relies on reported earnings and the recorded capital base supporting these earnings, not on cash flows. In effect, EVA is determined by subtracting from operating earnings a capital charge for the book value of the money invested in the company by owners and creditors. For a business unit, the capital charge is usually based on the net assets employed. At first glance, EVA therefore appears to be more of an accounting-based than an economic measure. In practice, however, Stern Stewart & Co. makes a large series of adjustments when working with client companies. These adjustments are made to calibrate the measure more closely to an economic cash flow basis, in an effort to parallel the economic valuation concepts we discussed earlier (see the references at the end of the chapter). Moreover, the EVA approach is applied not only to measuring current performance but also to measuring new investments and to developing incentive compensation.

What are some of the key adjustments used in applying the EVA concept? Starting with the accounting statements of a company, the first step is to derive an adjusted NOPAT, and the second is the development of the relevant capital base. The major adjustments in the NOPAT and capital base calculations occur in the following areas:

- Operating lease expenses.
- Major research and development expenses.

- Major advertising and promotion expenses.
- Inventory value adjustment (LIFO).
- Deferred income taxes.
- Goodwill amortization.
- Separation of nonoperating assets.

In the case of operating leases, an adjustment becomes necessary because there's a preference for showing the unrecorded value of the leased assets as part of the capital base, and removing the imputed interest expense on these leased assets from the income statement. The lease payments are capitalized on the balance sheet, with an offsetting matching liability, and the capital value is amortized over the appropriate time period. This amortization expense is then subtracted from earnings in arriving at NOPAT.

The effects of research and development as well as advertising and promotion expenditures incurred in a given period often extend into future periods, although current accounting rules require that the total expense be charged to the period in which it was incurred. The adjustment to NOPAT involves removing these expenses from the income statement, capitalizing them as part of the capital base, and amortizing them over an appropriate time period. This periodic amortization, a smaller amount, is then subtracted from earnings in arriving at NOPAT.

Inventory values under LIFO can, over time, become understated because the recorded cost of the earlier items in inventory remains unchanged, while recent additions are charged into cost of goods sold. To adjust for this disparity, inventories on the balance sheet are restated to current higher values, with an offsetting increase to earnings. This adjustment also is referred to as adding back the change in the LIFO reserve.

Deferred income taxes, as we discussed in earlier chapters, arise from timing differences between taxes due on corporate tax returns and those reflected on the books. In an effort to represent the cash taxes actually paid during a period, the change in deferred taxes is added or subtracted in the revised NOPAT calculation.

Finally, where sizable goodwill amounts are carried on the balance sheet, the periodic amortization reflected on the income statement is reversed so that earnings are higher. Goodwill remains unchanged on the balance sheet, on the assumption that this asset is a permanent part of the capital base.

In most cases, the net effect of these adjustments will result in a somewhat higher NOPAT and an expanded capital base, but not necessarily in proportion to their impact on the EVA calculation.

How is the result of the EVA calculation to be interpreted? There are two ways of looking at the outcome. The first is an absolute determination of whether periodic earnings have exceeded or fallen short of earning the cost of capital. The second interpretation tracks the change from period to period, to reflect the amount of value creation. For example, let's assume that in 2002 a company fell short of earning the cost of capital by $200 million, but in 2003 achieved a positive economic profit of $50 million. Under the first interpretation, economic profit was highly negative in 2002, and positive in 2003. Under the second interpretation, the company's management created $250 million of economic profit between 2002 and 2003, by having reversed the negative results of 2002 into positive territory in 2003. From a value-based management standpoint, both interpretations are used, the first usually for goal setting in operations, planning, and investment, and the second as an incentive to bring about constructive change. As we'll see shortly, such economic profit analyses are best viewed over several periods, because they are modified accounting results and thus subject to some of the same period-to-period distortions as unadjusted accounting measures.

CFROI, the most sophisticated and empirically grounded methodology for value-based management, was developed over many years of statistical analysis by the former HOLT Value Associates, now functioning both as a part of The Boston Consulting Group and separately as Holt Value Associates LP. This cash flow–based approach, originally intended as an analytical guide for portfolio managers, is based on translating a company's financial results through a variety of adjustments into a current-dollar cash flow return on investment (CFROI) measure, which expresses the company's economic performance. This concept, when applied to expected cash flows and combined with projected growth in the company's asset base, can then be used in a proprietary analytical model to calculate the company's market value. The HOLT model recognizes the adjusted cash flow contributions from existing assets and combines them with new investment cash flows, all on a comparable economic basis. This culminates in the concept of *cash value added (CVA)*, which amounts to finding the economic value created by successful business strategies and investments over and above earning the cost of capital on a discounted cash flow basis.

In effect, the HOLT model transforms a company's financial data into a consistent series of economic "project" cash flows that, when discounted at an empirically derived investor's return standard (generalized cost of capital for the market as a whole), permits calculation of the relative market value of the company's capitalization. In most cases, the calculated share values not only track very closely with historical price patterns but also become predictors for an expected market value based on a company's strategic plans—if the assumed plan cash flows are realized in the future, of course. The model is a highly integrated and sophisticated application of the economic cash flow principles we've discussed throughout this book (see the references at the end of the chapter for additional reading).

The CFROI performance measure itself can be illustrated by the diagram in Figure 11–5, where the data are taken from the financial statements of a company after a variety of adjustments, some similar to the ones we described for the EVA process. In contrast to EVA, however, the approach is strictly cash flow based, and the data are adjusted to a current-dollar basis. Note that the diagram is a present value analysis of the current value of the gross investment in the company, a level cash flow projection over 12 years, the average asset life assumed, and the value of nondepreciating assets recovered at the end of 12 years.

FIGURE   11–5

A CFROI Perspective ($ thousands)

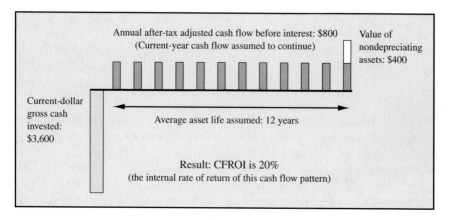

In this example, the result is an internal rate of return of 20 percent, which represents the cash flow return earned by the company in the current year. The reason the cash flow pattern was extended over the assumed average life of the assets and a recovery was provided is simply that the CFROI concept is designed to parallel the familiar new project economics cash flow patterns we discussed in Chapters 6 and 7. There we emphasized that the economic life and any recoveries must be taken into account to be able to calculate an internal rate of return. The CFROI result expresses only the performance for the year under analysis. The CFROI for the next year would be based on that year's cash flows, extended over the assumed asset life, using asset values adjusted as necessary for the current investment as well as for the assumed capital recovery at the end, and the process is repeated for ensuing years.

The adjustments underlying the data in Figure 11–5 are made in three areas. The first involves transforming accounting net income into a gross cash annual flow. The following changes were made:

Accounting net income:	$425
Add back depreciation effect, other noncash charges	200
Add back tax-adjusted interest expense	75
Add back tax-adjusted operating lease expense (see below)	50
Adjust for inventory valuation (LIFO reserve)	40
Adjust for inflation	10
Current dollar gross cash flow:	$800

When appropriate, adjustments to add back unusual advance expenditures on research and promotion also are made. Note the inflation adjustment, which currently is not large in U.S. companies, but can be significant in other economies.

The second area involves transforming recorded assets into a current cash value investment base. The following changes were made:

Recorded total assets:	$3,125
Add back accumulated depreciation to arrive at original cost	950
Adjust gross fixed assets for current dollar value	575
Capitalize operating leases to show imputed asset value	350
Subtract non-interest-bearing liabilities	(1,100)
Subtract goodwill	(300)
Current dollar gross cash investment:	$3,600

Note that the adjustment to transform the original cost of fixed assets into a current-dollar equivalent is a significant amount, which is based on choosing appropriate inflation measures. Non-interest–bearing liabilities, such as accounts payable, accruals, taxes payable, and other noncontractual liabilities, are subtracted to arrive at a modified net asset figure. Important is that goodwill is subtracted as irrelevant to the economics of this calculation, because the fixed asset adjustment to current values stands as a surrogate for goodwill arising from the premium paid for purchased assets.

The third area involves the development of a cost of capital standard in real (noninflationary) terms, which is based on a real risk-free interest rate, a real stock market premium, and a real interest cost of debt. The HOLT methodology uses a market-based cost of capital in those terms, rather than a company-specific cost of capital as discussed in Chapter 8, on the assumption that individual company risk (β) is expressed in the expected cash flow performance.

As we mentioned earlier, the CFROI calculation is one of the measures used in the HOLT methodology to judge whether a company is performing above the cost of capital in any given period. Because it's a strictly cash-based measure, CFROI is directly comparable to the cost of capital criterion. CFROI reappears in the HOLT methodology as part of an overall performance profile which links CFROI performance, past and projected investment growth, and competitive impact into a valuation framework that expresses past and prospective share price performance. The competitive impact is recognized in the form of a fade effect (reducing extraordinary results over time as unsustainable), and is incorporated into the judgment about the ongoing value of the business. We've given only a brief overview of this highly integrated methodology here; for more information the reader should turn to the references at the end of the chapter.

How can we compare economic profit and CFROI with some of the other measures? The table in Figure 11–6 is a highly simplified example of how the various approaches apply in the case of a company with an initial investment of $12 million, including $2 million of working capital, level net operating profit after taxes (NOPAT) of $825,000, and an economic life of eight years. We'll assume that no additional investments are required, that the working capital will be recovered in Year 8, and that all excess cash is paid out to the owners. In a real situation there would be more complex conditions, but for purposes of illustration this stripped-down example will provide acceptable indications.

FIGURE 11-6

An Illustration of Economic Profit, CFROI, and Earnings Measures ($ thousands)*

Economic Profit Analysis	Year 0	Year 1	Year 2	Year 3	Year 4	Year 5	Year 6	Year 7	Year 8
Book value of fixed investment (beginning)	—	$10,000	$ 8,750	$ 7,500	$ 6,250	$ 5,000	$ 3,750	$ 2,500	$ 1,250
Working capital	—	2,000	2,000	2,000	2,000	2,000	2,000	2,000	2,000
Total book value	—	12,000	10,750	9,500	8,250	7,000	5,750	4,500	3,250
Cost of capital	—	10%	10%	10%	10%	10%	10%	10%	10%
Capital charge @ 10%	—	$ 1,200	$ 1,075	$ 950	$ 825	$ 700	$ 575	$ 450	$ 325
NOPAT	—	825	825	825	825	825	825	825	825
Economic profit (EVA)	—	−375	−250	−125	0	125	250	375	500
Net present value of economic profits @ 10%	–0–								
Cash Flow Return on Investment Analysis									
NOPAT	—	825	825	825	825	825	825	825	825
Add back depreciation effect	—	1,250	1,250	1,250	1,250	1,250	1,250	1,250	1,250
Operating cash flow generated	—	2,075	2,075	2,075	2,075	2,075	2,075	2,075	2,075
Initial investment	12,000	12,000	12,000	12,000	12,000	12,000	12,000	12,000	12,000
Cost of capital		10%	10%	10%	10%	10%	10%	10%	10%
Capital charge @ 10%		1,200	1,200	1,200	1,200	1,200	1,200	1,200	1,200
Capital amortization @ 10%		875	875	875	875	875	875	875	875
Terminal recovery of working capital		0	0	0	0	0	0	0	2,000
Total cash flow required	$−12,000	$ 2,075	$ 2,075	$ 2,075	$ 2,075	$ 2,075	$ 2,075	$ 2,075	$ 4,075
Present value of future cash flows	12,000								
Net present value @ 10%	–0–								
Other Measures									
ROE		6.9%	7.7%	8.7%	10.0%	11.8%	14.3%	18.3%	25.4%
ROCE/RONA		6.9	7.7	8.7	10.0	11.8	14.3	18.3	25.4
ROGI		17.3	17.3	17.3	17.3	17.3	17.3	17.3	17.3
CFROI		10.0	10.0	10.0	10.0	10.0	10.0	10.0	10.0

*This model is available for download in an interactive format; see "Analytical Support," p. 467.

First we show an economic profit analysis, in which a cost of capital charge of 10 percent is applied to the declining book value of the investment base. This charge is offset against the level annual NOPAT of $825,000. Note that during the first three years the economic profit is negative, with breakeven achieved in Year 4, and with growing positive amounts in the remaining years. Given that we've assumed a level annual NOPAT, this pattern is not surprising, because the capital charge is being applied every year to a declining investment base. When we use a 10 percent discount rate to the individual annual economic profit results, the net present value is 0, suggesting that in this simplified example the company is earning exactly its cost of capital.

The same result is achieved when we proceed with a basic CFROI analysis as shown in the middle of the table. First we move from accounting NOPAT to a periodic operating cash flow by adding back the noncash depreciation effect, arriving at a level $2.075 million. This parallels the approach we used with new investment projects, as described in Chapters 6 and 7. Moving on, we find that in this instance the investment base does not decline, because we are recovering the initial cash investment from future cash flows via a level capital charge plus a level capital amortization. The former is simply a 10 percent charge against the initial investment base. The second, in effect, represents an annuity that will build up to a future value of $12 million at 10 percent in Year 8, an amount sufficient to recover the initial investment. Note that the combined capital charge and capital amortization are exactly equal to the operating cash flow of $2.075 million, indicating that the internal rate of return of this business is exactly 10 percent.

The major difference between the economic profit and the cash flow return approaches is the respective periodic patterns and their interpretation. Note that the end results are the same, namely a net present value of zero and an internal rate of return of 10 percent. The meaning of the periodic elements as shown, however, is quite different, because in the case of economic profit we're observing an adjusted accounting profit as well as a declining capital base as reflected on the books of the company. In the case of CFROI we are dealing with after-tax cash flows in every instance that over time provide a recovery of the investment and a cash flow return of 10 percent. The economic profit pattern shares the distortion inherent in accounting return measures, which is caused by the depreciation effect. CFROI provides a level reading because the depreciation effect has been canceled out. Accordingly, in interpreting economic profit movements over time this effect must be taken into account when, for example, judging the impact of new investments that will temporarily depress the results of early years. Similarly, goal setting in profit plans has to be done with proper attention to the accounting implications.

At the bottom of Figure 11–6 we've listed the results for two common accounting measures, return on equity (ROE) and return on capital employed (ROCE). In this example they are equivalent, because we haven't used any financial leverage, and they show the rapidly rising pattern that is also inherent in economic profit. The third measure, return on gross investment (ROGI), shows a level result, because we know that this is a simple surrogate for cash flow return. Note, however, that ROGI here is significantly higher than the true cash flow

FIGURE   11–7

The Divergence of Accounting and Cash Flow Measures

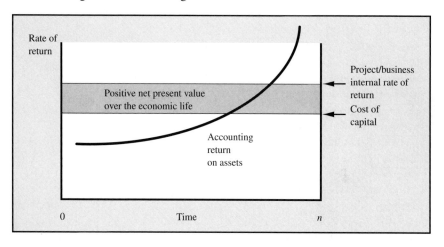

return we've calculated, an illustration of how such shortcuts can give distorted results. Figure 11–7 shows in symbolic form the basic divergence of accounting and cash flow measures over time on a new business or investment project. Typically, the accounting return rises sharply as depreciation reduces the capital base, while the cash flow return over the period is positive and level, with a positive net present value over the life span of the analysis.

Another way of showing the separation of accounting measures and economic results is displayed in Figure 11–8, the left portion of which we encountered in Chapter 3 (p. 150) during our discussion of the interrelationship of ratios. This time we're contrasting the family of accounting ratios that build up to the return on equity with a symbolic diagram of the shareholder value creation principles just discussed. Note the conceptual separation of the two approaches, but also note that the basic performance drivers on the far left of the diagram are indeed the same for accounting results and for cash flow generation.

This is a critical insight, because the issue facing companies as they move toward shareholder value creation is how to reach across this barrier and link the basic performance drivers to near-term and long-term management decisions. This requires performance measures and incentives that will ensure long-term cash flow results. To a large extent, the accounting ratios and measures in the center of the diagram can be a distraction if they remain the main focus of management attention, because it can be shown that if cash flow results are indeed the foremost management goal, over time the accounting results will tend to fall in line. But the reverse is not necessarily true. A glance at the listings of the best-performing companies in the Fortune 500 ranked by shareholder return and by various accounting measures will tend to confirm that superior shareholder value creation over time is reflected in strong accounting results.

FIGURE 11–8

Another View of Accounting versus Cash Flow Performance*

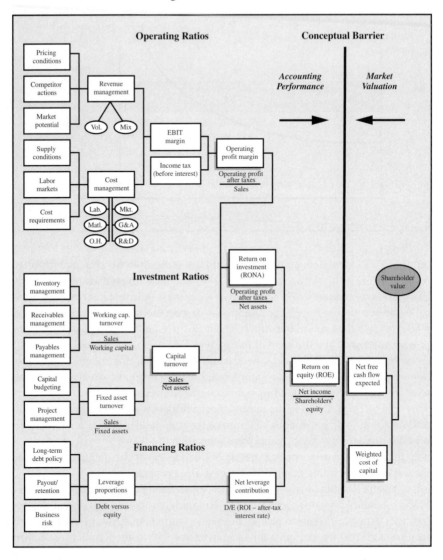

*This model is available for download in an interactive format; see "Analytical Support," p. 467.

This brief overview of the value-based measures in current use was intended to provide enough of an insight for the reader to recognize the principles, and to encourage further study of the much more extensive and specialized references listed. Every one of the economic measures discussed has advantages and drawbacks. This is especially true in the complexities of implementation and in the process and attitudinal changes required to move from existing methodologies and thought patterns to an organizational culture that enhances shareholder value creation. For these reasons the results from value-based management efforts vary significantly from company to company, but in the aggregate the new concepts are making a significant contribution to better management decisions and corporate performance.

Creating Value in Restructuring and Combinations

One of the ways management attempts to create shareholder value is through changing the structure of the organization or combining the company with other entities to achieve greater efficiency, placing more emphasis on core activities, a broader business base, greater mass in a given line of business, and so on. The 1990s witnessed unprecedented activity in restructuring, reengineering, and streamlining, as well as record levels of mergers and acquisitions not only in the U.S. but worldwide. Records were set both in numbers and in the size of the combinations, such as the Daimler-Chrysler and Exxon-Mobil combinations, and the more recent AOL–TimesWarner merger. Despite the popularity of such efforts, a variety of retrospective studies have shown that mergers and acquisitions create shareholder value only in a surprisingly small proportion of the cases, because of the premium prices usually paid, and the difficulties both in melding disparate organizations and achieving expected synergies. Restructuring and reengineering have a better track record, as management or takeover teams focus on running existing businesses better, and eliminating activities not related to core capabilities. We'll discuss only some of the more common concepts of financial analysis relative to this topic, suggesting that the reader turn to the references for coverage of the highly specialized and voluminous techniques and methodologies involved.

Restructuring and Value

The opportunity to restructure arises from the perception—by management or by interested outside parties—that a *value gap* exists between the value actually being created by a company and the potential value achievable under changed circumstances. In simple terms, this value gap is the difference between the present value of the company's projected cash flows under existing conditions, and the present value of a different and usually higher cash flow pattern expected from the restructured company. The attraction for the acquirer in a corporate takeover is to realize the potential benefits implicit in the perceived value gap. Depending on the circumstances, the value gap can at times support sizable premiums in the price bidding usually encountered in takeover situations. However, the final result frequently creates a reverse value gap, because an excessive premium was paid in the heat of the contest. Moreover, unanticipated difficulties are often encountered in implementing changes in managing the combined entity and ultimately in adapting the corporate cultures, which are necessary steps in realizing the greater portion of the benefits envisioned.

It's beyond the scope of this book to develop all aspects of the rationale and the special considerations and techniques employed by corporate takeover specialists, leveraged buyout consultants, and investment bankers. We cannot cover the large variety of equity and debt instruments, including junk bonds with premium yields, which are used to achieve the restructuring of large and small companies. Instead, we'll briefly discuss the economic rationale and basic analytical approach to determining the value gap. For this purpose, the most common reasons that explain the value gap should be listed first.

Underperformance by parts or all of a company is likely to be the most important cause of lowered values. In thousands of situations, the historical record and projected performance by existing management using existing strategies and policies can be used to demonstrate that performance is inferior to that of appropriate peer companies. Such a record is usually directly reflected in relative share price levels. Whether restructuring is initiated by the board of directors from within, or through friendly or hostile initiatives by outsiders, the aim is to raise lagging performance and cash flow expectations. Revision of business strategies, improved cost-effectiveness and technology, reduction of unnecessary expenses, and more aggressive management of the company's resources are commonly used to achieve such results.

Disposal of selected lines of business is an extension of the improvement strategies mentioned above. Here the considerations might involve the sale of poorly performing segments and reinvestment of the proceeds in more promising parts of the company. An alternative use of such funds can be the distribution to owners in the form of special dividends—or the repurchase of the company's shares in the market, which in recent years has become an increasingly popular way of creating value with excess cash. Successful lines of business can also be sold with the idea of realizing the economic gains from such "stars," and using the proceeds to fund potential successes remaining in the company's portfolio. Another aspect of such a sale is to focus management attention more sharply on lines of activity it can competently manage for long-term success. Not to be overlooked is the fact that from an acquirer's point of view, proceeds from the sale of part of a company can help finance the acquisition transaction itself.

Eliminating redundant assets is often used as a means of freeing economic value that tends to remain hidden, involving such assets as unused real estate, financial investments, and even excessive amounts of cash bearing only minimal returns. Restructuring analysis in effect focuses on separating those economic values that are necessary to carry on the desired activities from those that can be "cashed in" as not relevant to the core purposes of the new company.

It should be clear that the point of view of restructuring—whether done externally or internally—is to develop, in essence, a breakup value of the company, carefully examining each business unit and all major operating and nonoperating assets held. The next step is to look for ways of not only improving operating cash flows but also realizing the economic values of resources that can be stripped away without affecting the chosen direction.

From an analytical standpoint, the approach is quite similar to the present value cash flow valuation discussed earlier. The main difference is that a set of estimates is used, which identifies specific enhancements in the cash flow pattern, as well as disposal values from businesses or from redundant resources.

If our earlier analysis can be stated as

$$\text{Value} = PV\,(\text{Free cash flow} + \text{Ongoing value})$$

the restructuring approach can be stated as

$$\text{Value} = PV\,(\text{Free cash flow} + \text{Ongoing value}) + PV\,(\text{Enhancements})$$
$$= PV\,(\text{Disposal proceeds} - \text{Cash flow lost from disposals})$$

and the value gap will be the difference between the two results, the specifics of which are developed using the present value patterns discussed in Chapters 8 and 10. A key attraction to the external restructurer is, of course, obtaining control of the higher cash flows expected from the process.

It should be noted that two other aspects enter the picture. First, if a company changes hands in a restructuring, the depreciation basis for the assets involved is usually increased because of the higher values involved in the transaction, which under the purchase method of accounting are then recorded on the combined set of books at the new level. A portion of this recorded value increase translates directly into a stream of future cash flows because of the tax shield effect of depreciation. For example, if the acquired company's depreciable assets have a book value of $500 million, but are written up to $650 million because of the premium paid during the acquisition, the acquiring company will gain the cash value of the tax shield on the $150 million depreciation differential during the remaining life of the assets. If the company's effective tax rate is 40 percent, a total of $60 million in cash flow, spread over the remaining asset lives, will be created, assuming the company has sufficient earnings to take advantage of these write-offs. The present value of this cash flow pattern is a direct offset to the price premium the acquiring company is paying. In effect, the U.S. government is helping finance the transaction in such cases.

Second, if the restructuring introduces higher financial leverage, as is often the case, the impact on the accounting return on shareholders' equity can be favorable, even though the cash flow pattern might be adversely affected in the near term because of significant interest charges. As the risk exposure increases, expectations about the company's likely performance can shift, affecting the valuation of the future cash flows downward as higher discount rates must be employed to value the expected cash flow pattern. The key to success in restructuring, as in any significant change introduced to a business organization, lies in the implementation—and it's here that the track record of existing management or that of the new group involved will be scrutinized by analysts to gauge the likelihood of realizing the expected benefits.

Combinations and Synergy

Another form of restructuring is found in the combination of two or more hitherto independent companies. The rationale often claimed for acquisitions and mergers is that synergy between the entities will bring real economic benefits. Although empirical studies have cast serious doubt on whether business combinations are as mutually beneficial as hoped, it's tempting to assume that joining two separate businesses, particularly in the same industry, will tend to bring about some operating, resource, or market efficiencies. Examples might include the potential of fully engaging partially utilized manufacturing facilities or warehousing space; eliminating duplicate delivery systems or service networks; and consolidating certain activities, such as marketing and selling, support staff, and administration. Many of these benefits also are expected when complementary companies or even those in different businesses are combined. In recent years there's been increasing emphasis on combining already large businesses into huge entities, with the argument that success in industries such as automobiles, oil, banking, aerospace and defense, and communications depended in part on having critical mass and market strength, with attendant benefits in such areas as vendor relationships and global product/service patterns.

The impact of synergy can be felt in two major ways. The more specific benefits are identifiable cash flow improvements, for example, lower expenses that result from consolidation and reduction of facilities and staffs, and higher contribution from improved market position and coverage. The expected levels of these cash flow benefits must be estimated when an acquisition or merger is considered. Such estimates will, of course, vary in quality depending on how quantifiable the various opportunities for improvement are. There also are likely to be the kinds of tax shield and leverage effects we discussed in the previous section. All of these elements are then combined in the cash flow analysis pattern on a before-and-after basis to test for value creation.

A more general benefit is the expected impact on share price caused by the hoped-for cash flow improvements. This is ultimately where shareholder value improvement is recognized. The stock of the combined company might become more attractive to investors and thus achieve a higher market price, reflecting the benefits of the combination. Security analysts and the investment community generally expect combinations that are considered synergistic to result not only in a more profitable company, but possibly one poised for faster growth, with a stronger market position, or subject to lesser earnings fluctuations as the cycles of the individual businesses offset each other. The expectations implicit in this reassessment and successful implementation may in time improve the total shareholder return achieved.

Possible profit improvements resulting from a business combination can be analyzed to the extent they are quantifiable. To do this, the analyst uses two sets of pro forma statements. One set shows the projected net profits and cash flow patterns from each company separately, while the other reflects the combined company and includes the envisioned improvements. These statements then become the basis for comparative ratio analysis and for calculating the value of the individual companies and the combined entity with various methods. Once the cash flow patterns have been determined from this analysis, the various present value measures we've discussed can be applied.

At times it can be useful to determine separately the present value of all the synergistic cash flow benefits that were identified. This present value then can be used as a rough guide as the terms of the merger are being negotiated, because the value of realistic synergy expectations should be considered in setting the value premium the acquirer has to pay. In the end, however, the basis for valuation is likely to be a combination of present value analyses, rules of thumb, earnings and share price considerations, and a variety of tangible and intangible factors.

Combinations and Share Values

When an exchange of common stock is involved in an acquisition or merger agreement, as is true in many cases, the valuation challenge is extended. The economic valuation of the cash flow patterns, in which performance and synergistic expectations are expressed on an economic basis, should be the basis from which the parties proceed. The issue then becomes one of translating those valuation results into the medium of currently traded shares as valued in the stock market. This process requires arriving at a mutually acceptable interpretation of the respective values of the two different securities, as well as finding an appropriate ratio of exchange based on these shares. One aspect of this exchange is the usually significant premium (between 15 and 25 percent is the usual range) paid over what might be considered an initial fair economic value of the acquired company. While in the end a numerical solution is applied, the underlying values and the premium will be the result of extensive negotiation and a certain amount of "horse trading."

As the two stocks are valued, any differences in the quality and breadth of trading in the securities markets can be an important factor. If, for example, a large, well-established company acquires a new and fast-growing company, the market value assessment of the acquirer's stock is likely to be more reliable than that of the candidate, whose stock might be thinly traded and unproved, or might reflect excessive speculation. But even if they had comparable market exposure, the inherent difference in the nature and performance of the two companies might exhibit itself in, among other indicators, a pronounced difference in price/earnings ratios. In effect, this means one company's performance is valued less highly in the market than the other's by this measure. This difference will tend to influence valuation of the stocks and the final price negotiated—apart from the specific cash flow expectations that have been developed for economic valuation.

We'll demonstrate just a few key calculations needed to arrive at the basis of exchange from this standpoint, using a simplified example. Let's assume that Acquirer Corporation and Candidate, Inc., have the following key dimensions and performance data at the time of their merger negotiations:

Key Data	Acquirer Corporation	Candidate, Inc.
Current earnings	$50 million	$10 million
Number of shares	10 million	10 million
Earnings per share	$ 5.00	$ 1.00
Current market price	$60.00	$15.00
Price/earnings ratio	12.0	15.0

Negotiations between the management teams have reached a point where, after Candidate has rejected several offers, Acquirer now considers a price premium of about 20 percent over the current market value of Candidate's stock necessary to close the deal. This calls for an exchange ratio of $18 ÷ $60, or about 0.3 shares of Acquirer stock for each share of Candidate stock. The impact on Acquirer's accounting results is as follows, at the combined current levels of earnings that include no synergistic benefits:

Acquirer Corporation

Combined earnings	$60 million
Number of shares (10.0 + 3.0 million)	13 million
New earnings per share	$ 4.62
Old earnings per share	$ 5.00
Immediate dilution	$ 0.38

Under these conditions, Acquirer suffers an immediate dilution of 38 cents per share from the combination. Yet the fact that the stock of Candidate has a higher price/earnings ratio suggests that the smaller company enjoys desirable attributes and expectations about them, which might include high growth in earnings, a technologically protected position, and so on.

Acquirer must therefore consider two points. First, are the earnings of Candidate likely to grow at a rate that will close the gap in earnings per share relatively quickly, aided by any synergistic benefits available now? Second, is the inclusion of Candidate likely to change the risk/reward characteristics of the combined company so as to improve the price/earnings ratio—and thus help overcome the dilution in the accounting results?

In our example, the earnings gap to be filled is 13 million shares times 38 cents, or almost $5 million in annual earnings—just to return to the current level of Acquirer's earnings per share. How much in synergistic benefits can be expected? Perhaps the ratio of exchange has to be reconsidered in this light. But will the smaller company even be interested in being acquired at less than a 20 percent premium over market, a not uncommon inducement?

Note that if we assume a reversal of the price/earnings ratios in the example, both the terms of the offer and the reported performance of the combined companies will change dramatically. At 15 times earnings, the price of Acquirer will be $75 per share, while at 12 times earnings, Candidate will trade at $12 per share. Given a 20 percent acquisition premium for Candidate's stock, the exchange ratio will be $14.40 ÷ $75, or 0.192 shares of Acquirer for each share of Candidate. This calls for 1.92 million new shares of Acquirer, and the new earnings per share will amount to $60,000,000 ÷ 11,920,000 shares, or $5.03 per share, a slight net improvement even before any synergistic benefits are considered. In this changed situation, both parties will be better off immediately in their recorded results, simply because we assume the price/earnings ratios to be reversed. It's possible, of course, that a company acquired at a premium—which has caused the combined earnings per share to drop initially—might more than offset the gap with higher growth and synergistic benefits later. This will depend on the relative sizes of the two companies as well as on the value and exchange considerations discussed.

We've given but one simplified example, and therefore only a quick glimpse of the nature of these earnings-based deliberations involved in exchanges of stock, which usually are superimposed on the detailed cash flow economics used in valuing the companies. Note that this viewpoint deals with but one of the many issues underlying the valuation process in mergers and acquisitions. However, it's this concept that receives the most public attention in the financial community, because it deals with the visible effect of the deal on the companies' current financial statements and share data. But to ensure that expectations about shareholder value creation are reasonable, merger transactions must always go beyond earnings dilution issues to careful projections of the separate and combined earnings and cash flow patterns, and an assessment of the likely market response into the foreseeable future. Again the reader is encouraged to turn to the specialized literature on mergers and acquisitions to expand on the simple indications we've provided here.

Integration of Value Analysis

We've covered a large variety of value concepts and valuation approaches in the prior chapter and in this current discussion, ranging all the way from simple rules of thumb to economic cash flow models. We've used some illustrative examples from time to time in applying the formulas, but also have recognized that valuation is one of the more difficult areas of financial analysis that must be practiced with complex integrative situations. Such detailed case examples go beyond the scope of this book, but they can be readily found in more extensive finance texts and case books, such as we've listed at the end of each chapter.

To round out our discussion, we'll touch on a series of key judgmental areas that are commonly encountered in the valuation process, and provide a broad framework within which to view the practice. Some of these elements have come up in earlier discussions, but we believe that the reader might find it useful to have an overview context summarized in this fashion as we complete this final chapter. We'll address the following points:

- Perspectives in valuation.
- Dealing with expectations.
- Choosing the time period.
- Developing the pattern.

- Estimating ongoing values.
- Using comparables for validation.
- Results and negotiation.

Perspectives

No value judgment can be derived without a proper perspective on the nature of the issue being addressed. In Chapter 10 we presented a variety of definitions of value, each of which was based on a particular perspective that made it relevant. But even within a particular category, such as deriving the economic value of a business, there are different perspectives that must be defined and understood before the methodology and analytical framework are chosen. For example, are we establishing the value of equity for purposes of an exchange of shares, or are we determining the total business value? Are we attempting to value a business unit in order to set incentive plan targets for its management? Is the purpose of the analysis to establish a negotiating basis for a contested acquisition, or are we contemplating the sale of a successful business unit? In every case there will be differences not only in the specific inputs and even the methodology chosen, but also in the interpretation of the results. It also matters greatly whether there are parties involved with widely differing views of value, such as groups negotiating a merger. There is simply no generalized analytical or negotiation pattern that can serve all purposes, although in every one of these situations, an effort at economic cash flow analysis in one form or another should be undertaken to establish a sound basis. Let's remember that valuations, although more complex than most other decisions, do involve economic trade-offs—a concept we established early on and applied throughout this book.

As we've observed before, solid preparatory thinking to frame an analytical task is much more important than the application of the tools themselves. This is particularly true in business valuation analysis, because most issues in this area usually have to be viewed within a very complex framework and against a strategic background. When a business entity is valued in part or as a whole, the judgments required extend directly or indirectly to the relevant success factors that drive the business—with a future-oriented mind-set.

Expectations

These are the basis for most valuation approaches, because it's fair to say that the economic value of an object or a business entity reflects the future benefits to be obtained from owning it. These benefits, whether stated in the form of earnings, cash flows, or expected recoveries, always will be estimates of future, uncertain events that are subject to both specific and general risk exposure. We've encountered this principle in earlier chapters, and observed that, depending on the importance of the analytical task, a degree of sensitivity analysis should be performed to scope the impact of changes in variables and in the expected risk patterns. Given the importance of valuing businesses as a whole or in major segments, the need for at least developing ranges of estimates should be obvious. This requires that the drivers behind earnings and cash flows be understood and the major variables be tested for changes in projected conditions. It's simply not sufficient just to project current earnings or cash flow levels and to hope that these are indicative of the future.

Time Period

The period chosen for a business valuation most often depends on the nature of the activity in which the company or unit being analyzed is engaged. There also might be a time horizon specific to a situation, such as a planned strategic change or a limited life cycle because of expiring patents. The changes occurring in many products and services in high technology industries are so frequent and extensive that time horizons of more than three years can be quite unrealistic. In cyclical industries, the time horizon should extend for at least one business cycle, whereas multibusiness companies with a portfolio mix of ascending, declining, and new venture business units can likely be valued over a five- to eight-year period. The main point is that the time horizon has to be a function of the economic circumstances, not the apparent neatness and convenience of a 5- or 10-year pattern. One of the important judgments involved is which values to assign to assets or a going business at the end of the period, as we've observed before, and we'll summarize this area shortly.

Cash Flow Pattern

The economic valuation process depends greatly on establishing a realistic pattern of expected cash flows, just as we discussed in Chapters 6 and 7 for business investments. It's critical that the earnings stream expected during the time period under analysis not only reflect the ongoing operations of the company or business unit, but also adjust for planned strategic investments, divestments, potential synergies from combinations, major research outlays, and planned restructuring. In other words, the pattern of inflows and outflows should represent, as closely as possible, a strategic plan for the business under review.

Just as important is the need to be consistent in the adjustments for accounting processes, such as depreciation, amortization, and other elements that might or might not affect cash flows. This includes the tax shield benefits that can arise from revaluing assets in the case of a purchase, among others. In most analyses, the data will be expressed in a form closely related to free cash flow, while in simpler situations earnings-based approaches can be used.

It's good practice to base the analysis on cash flows early on in the process. This allows the analyst to deal consistently with the cash-in, cash-out trade-offs that underlie value, which can then be alternatively tested and expanded to consider the impact of accounting implications through earnings-based analyses, and against any shortcut approaches that appear reasonable in the context.

Ongoing Values

This aspect of value analysis is probably the least comfortable for analysts to deal with. The ongoing or terminal value at the point where the analysis is truncated on the time scale is in itself a business valuation of a continuing operation—but several years removed from the present. Obviously, the shorter the time period, the more this value can affect the result because of the time-value effect of discounting. But more important is the issue of how to set a realistic figure, when the pattern of expected cash flows leading up to this value was difficult enough to establish. In earlier chapters we discussed using price/earnings ratios, capitalizing the last year's cash flows (perpetuity assumption), using some operational rules of thumb, or employing growth formulas.

Any one of these processes doesn't substitute for the careful judgment required to assess, from a broad strategic standpoint, whether the company or business unit will indeed be viable at the end of the analysis. Is it realistic to assume steady growth, continued competitive strength, and repeated technological success? For example, it's probably a sound assumption that a level of performance far above a company's peers cannot be sustained indefinitely, because competitive pressures will inevitably moderate results. The analyst must address these issues during the valuation process and not let the convenience of simple rules of thumb or multiples take over. Ending values also are an area where ranges of estimates and sensitivity analysis should be employed, to scope the possible variations and their impact on the results.

Comparables

Part of the analytical challenge is the calibration of the results obtained against available real-world experience. In other words, the value derived from a thorough analysis of a particular company or business unit should be tested against comparable companies or business units as a matter of course. In fact, it's sound practice to attempt to calibrate the major assumptions used during the process of developing the time pattern and ending values. At the same time, we must be realistic about the amount and quality of data available for this purpose, and about the differences that invariably affect the matching of the subject company or business unit with peers.

The very effort of developing comparable values and indicators, however, forces the analyst to be thoughtful about the realism of the assumptions used in the analysis. If profit margins, growth rates, investment patterns, and research outlays differ materially from comparable companies, the resulting cash flow pattern should be assessed critically. Furthermore, comparable companies or businesses are likely to be competitors, and trying to bring their dimensions into the analysis necessarily introduces a strategic perspective. Finally, if the valuation results are to be used in negotiation, there's every reason to believe that comparables will be brought up in one form or another.

Negotiations

Inevitably, negotiations affect the extent and direction of any valuation process. Although objectivity for any analytical task is a worthwhile goal, the pressure of securing an advantageous negotiation position at the outset and during the deliberations will spur the parties to interpret the data and results from this perspective. Here the notion of using ranges as well as minimum and maximum acceptable results becomes commonplace. The practical implication for analysis is simply that the perspective of the analyst must change in order to take into account the tactics and strategies employed by the parties involved. The analysis likely should be made from more than one viewpoint. Analytical tools will usually be similar, but it's also to be expected that the parties will emphasize those approaches that favor their position. This shouldn't be surprising, because as we've said many times, financial/economic analysis is not a freestanding activity, but intricately related to the specific needs and issues surrounding it and affected by the vagaries of human judgment.

Key Issues

The following is a recap of the key issues raised directly or indirectly in this chapter. They are enumerated here to help the reader keep the techniques discussed within the perspective of financial theory and business practice.

1. Managing for shareholder value goes far beyond selection of appropriate measurements. It requires an integrated set of management processes tying together strategy, investment analysis, operational effectiveness, financial management, and evaluation and compensation—a systems approach to sound management.

2. The challenge of shareholder value creation can be stated simply: consistently exceeding the cost of capital in the performance of existing and new investments. However, bringing about value creation is the result of the very complex task of managing all aspects of the business system well.

3. Measures that gauge and reinforce shareholder value creation tend to reach beyond accounting results, because they should tie to the expectations of a cash flow–driven market. Accounting results will usually follow in time when decisions on investments, operations, and financing are driven by cash flow considerations—not the other way around.

4. There's no one single measure or value-based approach that is or should be the obvious choice for every management team. Significant trade-offs are encountered in the areas of complexity, changing the organization's mind-set, the degree of improvement likely, and precision of the process chosen. Measures must be judged within the framework of the capabilities of the total business system.

5. Valuation of businesses undergoing restructuring or combinations is only in part an economic cash flow exercise; there are many dimensions of expressing value and exchange parameters that fall back on accounting data and even purely judgmental aspects.

6. Proper framing of valuation tasks requires a critical set of judgments that are common to all economic investment deliberations. Effort spent early on this aspect will pay off in improved validity and relevance of the results.

7. Valuing a business for sale or purchase is one of the most complex tasks an analyst can undertake. It calls for skills in projection of earnings and cash flows, assessment of risk, strategic insight, and interpretation of the impact of combining management styles, operations, and resources.

8. Although accounting analyses are typically a significant part of the valuation process, especially in public transactions like mergers and acquisitions, the economic base established by cash flow approaches is critical to successful decision making.

9. Shareholder value is the ultimate result of successful investments, operations, and financing carried out by management within an economic framework. However, the link between a company's current and prospective performance in these areas and the market value of its common stock at a particular time is not necessarily direct or directly measurable, because of the combination of forces acting on the stock market.

Summary

In this final chapter, we came full circle by again taking a systems approach to managing effectively, and we placed the relevant analytical techniques in proper perspective within this larger setting of the value-creating company. We began with an overview of the value implications of managing the business system well, and provided further overviews of the many relationships of management processes and management decisions to the basic goal of shareholder value creation.

We then reviewed the evolution of selected financial measures in their movement toward cash flow–based concepts, and placed them in the same perspective. We brought the more conventional measures covered in Chapter 3 together with the newer concepts applied in current value-based practice, and described the more common adjustments required for them as well as their meaning. A comparative example was used to show the different implications of the measures, and we pointed to the need for further study and analysis to deal with the refinements implied in value-based approaches.

Restructuring and combinations were covered in the broader context of cash flow analysis and the economic trade-offs involved, supplemented by the most important implications of earnings-based results as they affect exchanges of shares and reported financial data.

Finally we returned to the need for defining the judgmental dimensions of valuation analysis, a theme we had touched upon in earlier chapters, indicating that inasmuch as business valuation is a highly complex matter going beyond the analytical measures themselves, a clear understanding of these judgmental aspects is critical.

Ultimately, valuation must always remain partly subjective, and where appropriate it will be settled in an exchange between interested parties. However, establishing, targeting, and implementing the company's investments, operations, and financing for economic performance and shareholder value will always be the basic obligation of management.

Analytical Support

A set of Excel-based templates (Interactive Templates) is downloadable at no charge from the Web at www.mhhe.com/helfert11e. The first of these, "The Business System—An Overview," was described at the end of Chapter 1, and you are encouraged to revisit it now, because it provides the broad perspective of this summary chapter. The tenth template, "Business Valuation Model: Calculating Cash Flows and Value of the Firm," is a general purpose tool which activates the model in Figure 10–5 on page 417 and it also applies to the valuation discussion in this chapter. The template allows you to vary a set of key assumptions about the future performance of a company, and to observe the numerical changes resulting from these modifications on the value of the firm and its shareholders' equity. The final template, "Comparing Economic Measures: An Illustration of Economic Profit, CFROI, and Earnings," activates the comparative analysis in Figure 11–6 on page 451, and allows you to test the impact on the different measures of changes in your assumptions. At the same time you can observe the divergence of accounting and cash flow measures in the related graph of Figure 11–7 on page 453.

Financial Genome, the advanced financial analysis software application described in Appendix I, is a fully integrated analytical and planning model for both the professional user and the business student. It is designed to develop a full set of integrated financial statements as well as special economic analysis statements from historical data inputs as well as for pro forma projections of financial performance for purposes of performance evaluation and valuation approaches. The software contains a five-year database (1996 to 2000) for 3M Corporation, matching the company's financial statements reproduced in Chapters 1, 2, and 3.

Financial Genome is downloadable from the Web, using the unique and restricted code provided with this book (see details in "Downloads" at the end of Appendix I, p. 479).

Selected References

Brealey, Richard, and Stewart Myers. *Principles of Corporate Finance.* 5th ed. Burr Ridge, IL: Irwin/McGraw-Hill, 1996.

The Boston Consulting Group. *Value-Based Management: A Framework for Managing Value Creation.* Chicago: The Boston Consulting Group, 1993. (Holt Value Concepts.)

Copeland, Tom; Tim Koller; and Jack Murrin. *Measuring and Managing the Value of Companies.* 2nd ed. New York: Wiley, 1995.

Johnson, Roy E. *Shareholder Value—A Business Experience.* Boston, MA: Butterworth/Heinemann, 2001.

Knight, James A. *Value-Based Management: Developing a Systematic Approach to Creating Shareholder Value.* Burr Ridge, IL: Irwin/McGraw-Hill, 1998.

Madden, Bartley J. *Cash Flow Return on Investment (CFROI) Valuation: A Total Systems Approach for Valuing the Firm.* Butterworth/Heinemann, 1999. (Holt Value Concepts.)

Martin, John D., and J. William Petty. *Value Based Management.* New York: The Financial Management Association Survey and Synthesis Series, 2000.

McTaggart, James M.; Peter W. Kontes; and Michael C. Mankins. *The Value Imperative.* New York: Free Press, 1994.

Pratt, Shannon P. *Valuing a Business: The Analysis and Appraisal of Closely Held Companies.* 3rd ed. New York: Irwin/McGraw-Hill, 1995.

Rappaport, Alfred. *Creating Shareholder Value.* Revised ed. New York: Free Press, 1998.

Ross, Stephen; Randolph Westerfield; and Jeffrey Jaffe. *Corporate Finance.* 5th ed. Burr Ridge, IL: Irwin/McGraw-Hill, 1999.

Stern, Joel M.; John S. Shiely; and Irwin Ross. *The EVA Challenge: Implementing Value-Added Change in an Organization.* New York: Wiley, 2001.

Stewart, G. Bennett, III. *The Quest for Value.* New York: Harper Business, 1991. (Stern Stewart & Co. EVA concepts.)

Weston, Fred; Scott Besley; and Eugene Brigham. *Essentials of Managerial Finance.* 11th ed. Hinsdale, IL: Dryden Press, 1996.

Self-Study Exercises, Problems, and Discussion Questions

Exercises and Problems *(Selected Solutions are Provided in Appendix VI)*

Because this overview chapter is designed to integrate the concepts discussed throughout this book and introduces some newer valuation methodologies that are largely based on proprietary models, exercises and problems have been kept to a minimum.

1. From the limited data provided below, assess the impact of a potential merger on two companies:

    Company A has a price/earnings ratio of 12.0, with current EPS of $8, a dividend of $2, and a market price range of $90 to $100, with a recent price of $98. Ten million shares are outstanding.

    Company B has a price/earnings ratio of 20.0, and is growing at twice the 6 percent rate of Company A. Its current EPS are $3, it pays no dividend, and its market price is ranging between $45 and $70. One million shares are outstanding.

Company A is assessing the impact of a potential offer to Company B at a price of $65, as compared to Company B's current price of $54. What basic information would you require to develop a cash flow valuation of each company, and how would potential synergy enter the analysis?

Calculate the appropriate measures to show the effect of these terms on the financial accounting picture and discuss potential implications. If you had access to more information, what specific elements would you like to have in order to improve your insights? Discuss your findings.

2. Using the template "Comparing Economic Measures: An Illustration of Economic Profit, CFROI, and Earnings," vary the key assumptions and observe the impact of these changes on the different measures and the graph. What limitations are inherent in this comparison, and what additional information would be useful to have in interpreting the example? Discuss your findings.

3. Using Financial Genome and its database for 3M Corporation, develop a detailed analysis and projection (based on your assumptions) of the company's past and expected performance. Use as many of the built-in analytical statements as you deem appropriate to improve your insights. What valuation assessments can you make? Is the company creating shareholder value? What additional information would you like to have? Discuss your findings.

Discussion Questions

1. Value-based management has been popularized in recent years. In what ways does it differ from basic management principles?
2. Why is it necessary to take a systems approach to creating shareholder value? Does it not depend on many individual decisions made over time?
3. List major considerations in establishing a value-based system of management. What elements beyond value-based performance and planning measures are necessary for success?
4. Cash-based measures are becoming more and more predominant in modern management. Do these measures have any drawbacks, and can (or should) they really replace accounting measures?
5. What is the difference between economic profit and cash value added? Does EVA™ relate to accounting measures? Does cash value added relate to accounting measures?
6. Comment on the divergence of cash flow and accounting measures. What practical implications do you see when these measures are used for performance evaluation?

7. Why does ROGI (return on gross investment) generally give a higher reading than CFROI?

8. If price/earnings ratios are important in setting the ratio of exchange in a merger based on a share swap, how can such a volatile measure give reasonable indications of value?

9. Synergy is often an argument for making business combinations, but it's hard to measure and achieve. Why?

10. Why is it important to establish a proper framework for economic analysis, whether it is used for a normal business investment or an acquisition?

11. Why do mergers and acquisitions remain so popular when empirical evidence shows that many of them are not economic and in fact destroy shareholder value?

APPENDIX I

Financial Analysis Using Financial Genome

A special six-months time-limited educational version of the advanced financial analysis, statement generation, and business planning software application Financial Genome is available for a free download, when using the unique and restricted code provided with this book (see "Downloads" on page 479). The software is based on patented knowledge-based technology developed by Modernsoft, Inc. and is structured around the business systems concept discussed in this book. This unique add-in for Excel 2000 (or later) running on Windows 98/NT4/2000/XP, or later is a professional application which empowers the user to do financial analysis and pro forma projections with ease, speed, and accuracy. While adding a complete, documented financial knowledge structure to spreadsheets, Financial Genome maintains full flexibility, and is far more intuitive to use than conventional spreadsheets.

Financial Genome easily accommodates widely different business analytical needs and projections. It links together a comprehensive, knowledge-based financial dictionary of terms and relationships, an analytical engine, and database access. The built-in financial knowledge ensures internal consistency, avoidance of spreadsheet errors, convenient data access, ready project setup, and true analytical and formatting flexibility. The internal help system at any time allows the user to view the definitions of financial terms, and their relationships to formulas and statements. The software reflects the structure and definitions of financial analysis concepts and tools discussed in this book.

The application contains an example database to get started, and a five-year database for 3M Corporation which ties to the company's statements reproduced in the early chapters of this book. The software is accompanied by a series of interactive templates and graphic displays that relate directly to the various diagrams and analytical layouts covered in this book, designed to allow the user to trace the effect of varying assumptions. Financial Genome and the separate set of interactive templates also serve as learning tools, reinforcing the insights gained from reading this book and other financial literature. Learning is enhanced by the transparent structure and capabilities of the application, which allows the user to check understanding of terms and relationships on the fly, as well as through experimenting with the graphic displays in the accompanying templates. Figure I–1 provides an overview of Financial Genome's system.

Financial Genome as a Financial Analysis and Planning Tool

This professional software enables the user to accomplish the following tasks with some of its capabilities depending on the specific edition of Financial Genome.

FIGURE I–1

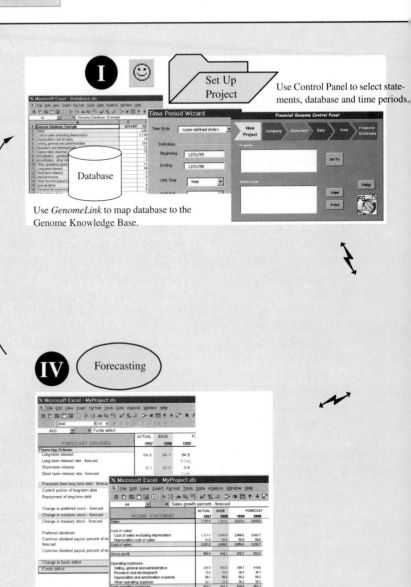

Use Control Panel to select statements, database and time periods.

Use *GenomeLink* to map database to the Genome Knowledge Base.

Forecast with built-in *forecast drivers* (ratio-driven). Funding requirements automatically calculated.

The *Financial Genome* System

By Modernsoft Inc. (*www.modernsoft.com*)

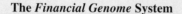

 II Design Statements

MyStatement	1993
Sales	
Cost of sales excluding depreciation	
Depreciation cost of sales	
Cost of sales	

Knowledge Base

Dynamically linked, internally consistent.

Choose from any of 350 financial terms and eleven customizable financial statements in the *Financial Dictionary*.

Financial Dictionary Browser

INCOME STATEMENT	Sales
BALANCE SHEET	COST OF SALES SECTION
CHANGE IN SHAREHOLDERS EQUITY	Gross profit
CASH FLOW STATEMENT	OPERATING EXPENSE SECTION
RATIOS STATEMENT	INCOME SECTION
BUSINESS PERFORMANCE ANALYSIS	DIVIDENDS SECTION

Browse Dictionary | Search | Explain Term | Insert Term

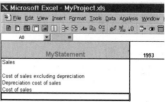 **III** Retrieve and Input Data

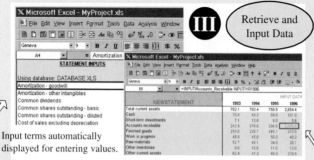

Input terms automatically displayed for entering values.

Database

Manually enter values (or override database values) on any sheet.

Data automatically re-trieved from database.

- Input a typical set of financial data about a business from spreadsheets, databases, or direct input, as well as access built-in sample databases.
- Manipulate selected data for free-form analysis.
- Create a wide range of financial reports and special statements.
- Do fully integrated financial pro forma forecasting and planning.

All of this can be done without the need to create formulas or relationships, or identifying spreadsheet cell locations. At the core of the application is the *Financial Dictionary*, which contains over 350 common financial terms, statements, and ratios, as well as the built-in knowledge of all the relationships between the terms and statements, and the formulas underlying them. Once a set of input data is entered into the program, or a database is accessed, the application ensures full consistency as the analysis proceeds, because statements, ratios, and special analytical views are created automatically. All calculated terms are prepared by the application from the individual inputs, which ensures accuracy. Assumptions and data values can be changed at the user's option.

A full range of features allows customization of the analysis by changing term names and statement formats, expanding or collapsing details, creating new relationships, changing time frames and databases, and so forth. At any point the user can display the definitions and relationships underlying any term or statement used, and access the complete built-in help system for further background information.

The following capabilities are available for the Financial Genome user to perform financial analysis as described in this book or in other financial texts:

- Display selected financial data individually or in any combination, and perform financial analysis using the built-in relationships or creating new ones:

    Use a familiar spreadsheet structure to display and manipulate data or groups of data.

    Keep track of the data necessary for the analysis on an automatic input statement.

    Choose annual, quarterly, or monthly time periods.

- Map data from spreadsheets or databases to Financial Genome:

    After mapping, freely use the data as an internal database for analysis.

    Create internal databases from ad hoc analyses.

- Automatically create the following standard financial statements:

    Income statement.

    Balance sheet.

    Cash flow statement.

    Statement of changes in shareholders' equity.

- Automatically create a special statement listing the typical assumptions used for financial forecasts:

  Forecast drivers for use in developing an integrated financial plan.

  Display of matching historical data for these forecast drivers.

- Ability to create financial forecasts and integrated financial plans:

  Use the built-in forecast drivers for making key assumptions.

  Override with and/or add own assumptions.

- Automatically create the following special performance statements:

  Ratios statement (all major financial ratios grouped by the three decision areas).

  Performance analysis statement displaying key performance measures.

- Automatically create the following economic analysis statements:

  NOPAT analysis for deriving economic profit.

  Capital base analysis for deriving economic profit.

  Cost of capital analysis by category and various weighted proportions.

  Economic profit analysis combining all of the above.

- Ability to modify built-in terms, statements, sections of statements, and free-form analyses:

  Rename, itemize, and duplicate individual terms.

  Move terms and groups of terms on the sheet.

  Expand and collapse statement detail.

  Modify groupings, names, headings.

  Customize formatting for printing.

- Ability to override any data input or user assumptions:

  Can modify conditions.

  Can perform what-if analysis.

  Can return to original database values at any time.

- Ability to change databases and timing:

  Switch to new database.

  Manually override data.

  Change analysis time periods.

- Ability to access Excel's many features for data manipulation and formatting:

  Financial formulas and relationships.

  Cell formatting, outlining, colors, highlighting, and so on.

- Ability to print out analyses and retain projects:

    Format print output as desired.

    Print statements as can be done from any Excel spreadsheet.

    Save project files for future access and use.

These capabilities allow the user to do professional financial analysis on typical sets of data, with the assurance that there will be accuracy and internal consistency as long as the input data themselves are correct. The analytical process can be applied to funds flow analysis as described in Chapter 2, the performance analysis of Chapter 3, the projections of Chapter 4, the growth conditions of Chapter 5, the cost of capital analyses of Chapter 9, and the financing options of Chapter 10, and fully integrated projections as inputs to valuation analyses in Chapters 10 and 11. Because the interrelationships of the business system are embodied in Financial Genome, it has capability to develop a consistent and fully integrated set of financial statements, views, and performance analyses.

The process of analysis is based on the familiar look and feel of the Excel application, but it's driven by a sophisticated underlying knowledge structure and Modernsoft Inc.'s patented *FinGen* technology. An intuitive control panel and a set of special tools are provided, which expand the standard Excel capabilities and tool bars.

Financial Genome and the Interactive Templates as Learning Devices

Financial Genome contains a fully integrated help system that allows the user at any time to display not only the definitions of terms but also their relationships to other terms and their place in the analytical structure. Thus it's possible to check one's understanding of the underlying concepts step by step as the analysis proceeds. When automatic financial statements or collections of terms like ratios are called forth by the user, it's similarly possible to check and display the underlying structure for any term or group of terms, thus reinforcing the learning process. The user can learn by doing individual analytical tasks, checking the progress as desired, and also can learn by investigating the background and meaning of automatically calculated data, ratios, and statements. All definitions and terminology are closely aligned with the materials in this book, and the help system incorporates definitions selected from this book.

The separate, downloadable Interactive Templates downloadable without charge are integrated with this book and designed as live and visual learning devices, allowing the user to trace the impact of changing assumptions on financial statements, analytical layouts, and key conceptual diagrams as discussed in this book. There are templates for all the major diagrams and displays, designed both for learning and also for application in a professional setting when appropriate. A chapter-by-chapter description of the use of the Interactive Templates and Financial Genome follows:

Chapter 1:   The business system in Figure 1–4 on page 8 is the key diagram that also reappears with the growth model templates of Chapter 5. The interactive template for the business system contains live cells for every element, which display the changing conditions and allow the user to interact and modify at will. A list of key assumptions drives the template, and the results are also reflected on a linked balance sheet, income statement, and cash flow statement. In addition, a live bar graph displays the changes in funds uses and sources. The user's input assumptions cover key operating, investment, and financing decisions and policies, and the template functions as a closed system that responds to any one or a combination of changes. By toggling between assumptions and results, the user can trace the impact of the changing cash flows implicit in all parts of the structure and enhance the understanding of the dynamics of the business system.

Chapter 2:   Financial Genome has the built-in capability to create fully integrated and consistent cash flow statements automatically from spreadsheet input data or databases.

Chapter 3:   The full ratio structure underlying the performance analysis in this chapter is automatically created by Financial Genome, and the user can request and display any single ratio, group of ratios, or a complete ratio statement from the underlying data. Definitions are available instantly. An interactive template provides a visual representation of the impact on return on equity from changes in the underlying drivers. Based on the systems view of key ratios and their elements in Figure 3–5 on page 150, the template allows the user to trace simultaneous changes in all elements affected by a change in assumptions. A linked balance sheet, income statement, and cash flow statement accompany the diagram to give the user the corresponding impact on the financial statements.

Chapter 4:   The pro forma analysis discussed here is integral to Financial Genome, which in the forecasting mode can create a full set of integrated pro forma financial statements, ratios, and performance analyses based on the user's assumptions about forecast drivers and expected conditions. It automatically provides financial closure by identifying the fund need or excess under any set of assumptions the user wishes to try. An interactive template based on problem 4–7 illustrates the interrelated conditions for developing a cash budget, requiring a variety of assumptions to be derived first. The template assists the user in building up a set of conditions over a six-month period, including sales forecasts and collection of receivables, inventory movements based on purchasing patterns, and changes in accruals. The template accepts key assumptions, displays staggered collection patterns, account receivable patterns, an inventory analysis, and accrued liability changes. All of these are linked to live displays of the cash budget, pro forma income statement, and balance sheet, and together provide an internally consistent set of results that culminate in the cumulative cash flow for the period. Changing any or several of the assumptions allows the user to visualize the impact on cash requirements and on the financial statements.

Chapter 5:   The business dynamics of this chapter are supported by four inter-active templates, each of which allows interactive simulation of changes in policies and operational decisions. The first template illustrates operational break-even analysis, based on Figure 5–1 on page 214, where changes in price, variable costs, and fixed cost can be traced on a live graph. The second template displays the sustainable growth equation on page 234 with live cells, and is linked to the analytical format of the financial growth model in Figure 5–8 on page 229. Also linked to this model is a live representation of the business system of Figure 1–4 on page 8, together with a balance sheet, an income statement and cash flow statement, and a bar graph illustrating changes in uses and sources. This complete model allows the user to study growth conditions and to view them from all major viewpoints. The third template, a companion to the second template, allows the user to establish different sets of financial and investment policies in the growth model format of Figure 5–9 on page 231, and to view a series of different cases side by side. The fourth template is an interactive representation of the five-year projection of conditions and policies of Figure 5–10 on page 236, which the user can vary at will and study the impact of different assumptions on the results.

Chapters 6 and 7:   The present value analysis concepts and structures are supported by a general-purpose interactive template which allows the user to input any desired return standard, cash flow pattern, depreciation tax shield, capital investments and recoveries, and to obtain the results of all present value measures, displayed in the spreadsheet format used in both chapters (see pages 259 and 260, and 297 to 304). The template is accompanied by a bar graph display showing the size of movements in investment and operational cash flows, and the depreciation tax shield.

Chapter 8:   The cost of capital calculations are directly supported by Financial Genome's built-in capability to develop the cost of capital for each element of the capital structure and to develop weighted average costs based on market values, book values, and target proportions. The user is required only to provide the necessary inputs requested by the software.

Chapter 9:   Financing choices are supported by an interactive template that calculates and displays graphically the range of EBIT and earnings per share (EPS) conditions discussed in the chapter. The user can vary the conditions underlying different financing alternatives and observe the impact on the balance sheet and on the separate calculations of EPS and zero EPS. A live graph based on Figure 9–8 on page 371 displays the varying conditions. The impact of different financing choices is also implicit in the forecasting results obtained with Financial Genome.

Chapter 10:   Business valuation as discussed here is directly supported by the forecasting capabilities of Financial Genome, which can derive both accounting measures and ratios as well as cash flow inputs such as EBIT, NOPAT, free cash flow, and others. A general purpose valuation interactive template modeled on

Figure 10–5 on page 417 allows the user to calculate the free cash flow valuation of a company, based on projections of revenues, costs, taxes, depreciation, changes in working capital, investment changes, and an estimate of the ongoing value of the business. It is based on the same spreadsheet format as the general purpose present value template for Chapters 6 and 7.

Chapter 11:   Shareholder value management covers an overview of key measures, including proprietary approaches, which cannot be replicated as discussed here. A basic CFROI calculation can be developed using the present value template, while a comparison of measures can be viewed interactively in the special template based on Figure 11–6 on page 451. Financial Genome has the built-in capability to calculate economic profit, among other indicators, from integrated forecasts on the basis of the user's inputs and assumptions, to assist in valuation analyses.

Although primarily designed as educational tools, the interactive templates can also serve the professional user to demonstrate, for example, the results of policy choices. The general purpose templates like the present value analysis and business valuation structures can be used for many practical applications. As a result, Financial Genome, together with the Interactive Templates, assists both the student and the practitioner in performing financial analysis better, faster, and with greater insight.

Downloads

- This book contains a unique and restricted code number which entitles the reader to a free download of the special six-month time limited educational version of Financial Genome from the book's McGraw-Hill website www.mhhe.com/helfert11e. This website also contains separate downloadable files for a Quickstart Guide and a Graphic Tutorial for Financial Genome.

- After expiration of the special version's use period, the reader can upgrade to the then current commercial version at a discount from the list price by visiting Modernsoft's website: www.modernsoft.com, locating the download page and following the instructions of the special discount arrangement. The unique and restricted code number provided with this book is again required for authorization. Permanent use of the software is achieved after paying by credit card and registering as instructed.

- The download of Financial Genome requires a minimum of five megabytes of disk space. System requirements are Microsoft Excel 2000 and later and Windows 98/NT4/2000/XP and later (only U.S. English versions in all cases).

- The Interactive Templates can be downloaded without charge as a separate file from the book's McGraw-Hill website www.mhhe.com/helfert11e.

APPENDIX II

Glossary of Key Terms and Concepts*

Accelerated depreciation Patterns of *depreciation* write-offs that place larger proportions into the early years of an *asset*'s book life, rather than into the later years, either for accounting or for tax deduction purposes.

Accounting earnings The difference between recognized *revenues* and *expenses* during an accounting period, based on generally accepted accounting principles.

Accounts payable (payables) Obligations owed to trade creditors and suppliers as incurred in the normal course of business; also called *trade credit.*

Accounts payable days A translation of *accounts payable* into the days of average purchases outstanding at a point in time; used as an indicator of the effectiveness with which *trade credit* is employed.

Accounts receivable (receivables) Obligations owed by customers and other parties as incurred in the normal course of business.

Accounts receivable days A measure of the credit quality of *accounts receivable,* which expresses outstanding receivables as days' sales outstanding in terms of average daily sales; can be compared with the *credit terms* under which sales were made.

Accruals Recognition of *revenues* or *expenses* when earned or incurred, without regard to the actual timing of the cash transactions; used in the accrual method of accounting.

Accumulated depreciation The total of past periodic depreciation charges applicable to depreciable assets carried on a company's *balance sheet,* shown as a deduction from gross property, plant, and equipment.

Acid test A stringent measure of *liquidity* relating current cash *assets* (cash, cash equivalents, and receivables) to *current liabilities.*

Activity-based analysis A form of *economic analysis* that develops the specific *costs* and *benefits* generated by an activity, product line, or business segment, based on the physical processes and resource requirements underlying each subpart.

Aftertax cash flow Cash generated from *operations* or from an *investment* net of income taxes, derived by adding back noncash charges like *depreciation* to aftertax earnings.

Aftertax value Net *revenue,* net *cost,* or net *investment* after adjusting for the effect of applicable income taxes.

Allocation An assignment or distribution of *costs* or *revenues* to products, activity centers, or other entities using a common basis.

Amortization A periodic charge reflecting the decline in the recorded value of an *intangible asset* over a specified number of years.

Annualized net present value The transformation of a *net present value* into an equivalent series of annual cash flows over the life of the project, used in judging the proposal's margin of *risk.*

Annuity A uniform series of payments or receipts over a specified number of periods.

Asset A physical or intangible item of value to a company or an individual.

Asset turnover An expression of the effectiveness with which *assets* generate sales, defined as the ratio of *net sales* to total assets.

Balance sheet A *financial statement* reflecting the recorded values of all *assets, liabilities,* and *owners' equity* at a point in time.

---

* Items shown in italics are defined separately.

481

Balloon payment   A significant *principal* payment due at the end of the term of a financial obligation.

Bankruptcy   A legal process of disposing of the *assets* of a business or individual to satisfy creditors' claims in total or in part, and protecting the debtor(s) from further legal action.

Benefit (cost/benefit)   The positive element in an *economic trade-off* which relates *economic earnings* to *economic costs* in an *investment, operating*, or *financing* decision.

Beta (β)   A calculated form of expressing the specific (systematic) risk of a company's *common stock* relative to the stock market as a whole. (Cf. *volatility*.)

Bond   A financial instrument representing a form of corporate *long-term debt* issued to investors; a variety of different types of bonds exist.

Bond rating   A published ranking of a *bond* developed by financial organizations to express its relative soundness on a defined scale.

Book value   The recorded value of an *asset* or *liability* as reflected in the *financial statements* of a company or individual.

Book value of equity   The recorded value of *owners' (shareholders') equity* on a company's *balance sheet*, representing the owners' residual claim on the *assets*.

Break-even analysis   Determining the level of sales at which a company will just recover *fixed* and *variable costs*; a zero-profit condition.

Breakup value   The value realized from separating the parts of a multibusiness company and disposing of them individually.

Burden   The combination of *interest* charges and current *principal* payments required by a financial obligation.

Burden coverage   The ratio of periodic *income* before taxes to the corresponding amount of *burden*, adjusted for income taxes; a test of the ability to service a *debt* obligation.

Business risk   The risk inherent in the expected *cash flows* from *investments* and *operations*, apart from the risk inherent in the form of *financing* used.

Business system   A dynamic representation of the key elements and relationships governing *investments, operations*, and *financing* of a business entity. (Cf. *financial model*.)

Call provision   A provision permitting the issuing company to redeem in part or in total a *bond* or *preferred stock* issue at a date determined by the company.

Capital   The total amount of long-term *funds* committed to an enterprise in the form of ownership *equity* and long-term *debt*.

Capital asset pricing model (CAPM)   An analytical approach to calculating the cost of *shareholders' equity*, using a *risk-free interest rate*, a *risk premium* (market premium), and a company-specific risk assessment *beta (β)*.

Capital budget   A selected group of *investment* projects approved in principle for implementation, pending individual approval, and related closely to a company's business strategies.

Capital expenditures   Expenditures made during a stated period for investments in new *fixed assets*, for the purpose of replacement, expansion, or new business opportunities.

Capital investment   A relatively long-term commitment of funds to a project expected to generate positive net *cash flows* over time.

Capitalization   The sum of all long-term sources of *capital* of a company, also derived by subtracting *current liabilities* from total *assets*.

Capital rationing   The allocation of limited *investment* funds to a selection of investment projects smaller than all currently acceptable projects; a fairly common condition.

Capital structure   The relative proportions of different sources of *capital* used in the long-term funding of the *investments* and *operations* of a company.

Cash   The amount of readily available currency owned by a company at a stated period in time.

Cash accounting   A method of accounting in which *revenues* and *expenses* and all other transactions are recognized when cash changes hands, in contrast to the *accrual* method of accounting.

Cash budget   A periodic projection of cash receipts and cash disbursements over a specified length of time. (Cf. *cash flow forecast.*)

Cash flow   The positive (inflow) or negative (outflow) movements of cash caused by an activity over a specific period of time.

Cash flow analysis   An economic method of analysis that employs the positive (inflow) and negative (outflow) movements of cash caused by an activity to determine the relative desirability of the activity; usually involves *discounted cash flow* methodology.

Cash flow cycle   The periodic movement of cash through an enterprise, caused by *investment, operating,* and *financing* decisions.

Cash flow forecast   A periodic forecast of cash movements through an enterprise, recognizing sources and uses of funds.

Cash flow from operations   Cash generated or used by the operations of a business over a specified period of time; usually derived by adjusting aftertax *net profit* for *noncash* charges and *noncash* receipts.

Cash flow return on investment (CFROI)   The relationship of operational *cash flows* to the cash value of the assets employed in generating them. In its most sophisticated form, it employs present value techniques.

Cash flow statement   A *financial statement* listing the cash impact of the activities of a business over a specified period of time, separating the *cash flows* into the areas of *operations, investments,* and *financing.* (Cf. *funds flow statement.*)

Cash value added (CVA)   A form of *net present value* analysis expressing the increase in present value caused by a business investment, a strategic plan, or the operations of a business unit.

Collection period   The average number of days over which *accounts receivable* are outstanding, either in total or by defined categories; a measure of the effectiveness with which customer *credit* is managed.

Common dividends   The total amount of dividends paid to a company's *common* shareholders in the form of cash or stock.

Common shares (common stock)   Securities representing a direct ownership interest in a corporation and a residual claim on the *assets.*

Common shares outstanding—basic   The number of *common shares* of a company issued and actually outstanding at a point in time, used in calculating *earnings per share—basic.*

Common shares outstanding—diluted   The number of *common shares* of a company issued and actually outstanding at a point in time, plus the number of shares potentially outstanding from exercise of stock options, rights and warrants, and securities convertible into common shares, used in calculating *earnings per share—diluted.*

Common-size financial statements   A ratio analysis of *balance sheets* and *income statements* in which all elements are represented as a percentage of *assets* or *net sales,* respectively. Used in analyzing trends and in comparing statements from different companies.

Comparables   Selected *assets* or business entities chosen by analysts to establish comparability with an asset or business being valued; used in determining the *fair market value* in the absence of market transactions.

Compounding   The process of calculating the growing value of a sum of money over time, caused by the periodic interest earned and by the reinvestment of such interest.

Constant-dollar analysis The adjustment of financial magnitudes for inflation to reflect a common dollar value basis (using dollar values of a specified point in time), and the use of these adjusted values in accounting or *economic analysis.*

Consumer price index (CPI) An index provided by the U.S. government that represents the periodic change in the cost of a selected group of items purchased by consumers; used as a measure of *inflation.*

Contribution analysis A method of analysis that determines the relative excess of revenue over variable costs of product lines, business segments, and activities, and judges the contribution made toward meeting *fixed costs,* overhead, and *profits.*

Contribution margin The excess (or deficit) of revenue over the variable costs of products or services, at times also the excess (or deficit) of revenue over the total cost of products or services *(cost of goods or services sold).*

Conversion ratio The stated number of *common shares* or other securities into which a *convertible security* may be exchanged.

Conversion value The *market value* represented by the *common shares* or other *assets* into which a *convertible security* may be exchanged.

Convertible security A financial security that may be exchanged at the option of the holder into another security or *asset* with a prescribed *conversion ratio.*

Cost The transaction value at which an *asset* was acquired; also, any periodic *expense* recognized against matching periodic *revenue.*

Cost of capital (weighted average cost of capital, hurdle rate) The weighted average of the aftertax cost to a company of all forms of long-term financing used; employed as a minimum standard for the return to be earned on new *investments.*

Cost of debt The *cost* to a company of employing *debt,* developed from the aftertax interest charges of various forms of debt.

Cost of equity The *cost* to a company of employing *common shareholders'* funds, developed from the investors' expectations about the return from holding such shares, usually in the form of the combination of dividends and capital gains.

Cost of goods (services) sold (cost of sales) The total of all *costs* and *expenses* incurred in producing, or acquiring, goods or services for sale.

Cost of preferred stock The *cost* to a company of employing *preferred shareholders'* funds, developed from the pretax preferred dividend required by preferred holders.

Coupon rate The stated interest rate specified on the interest coupons attached to *bonds,* as contrasted with the *yield* obtained on a bond, which relates the coupon rate to the *market value* of the bond.

Covenant Provision in the *bond* agreement specifying restrictions or other requirements that the issuer has to observe to maintain the bond's *credit* rating.

Coverage Relationship of fixed requirements, such as interest or *burden* connected with *debt,* to operating income before or after taxes. (Cf. *times interest earned; times burden covered.*)

Credit (creditworthiness) The recognized ability of an individual or company to assume indebtedness with the prospect of properly servicing such *debt.*

Cumulative effect of accounting changes The aftertax effect of changes in accounting methods used by a company, shown as a line item in the *income statement* and used in arriving at *net income.*

Cumulative preferred stock A form of *preferred stock* that carries the provision that any unpaid dividends accumulate for later payment, and must be paid in full before common dividends may be declared.

Current asset Any *asset* on the *balance sheet* with a short-term expectation of being turned into cash, such as *cash, receivables,* and inventories; usually considered as having a one-year time horizon or less.

Current-dollar accounting   The adjustment of historical financial magnitudes for inflation to reflect current-dollar values (adjusting for price changes) and the use of these adjusted values in accounting or economic analysis. (Cf. *constant-dollar analysis.*)

Current liability   Any *liability* on the *balance sheet* with a short-term maturity, usually payable within one year, such as *accounts payable* and accrued taxes.

Current portion of long-term debt   The proportion of a long-term *liability* that is due and payable within one year.

Current ratio   A common measure of *liquidity* that relates the sum of *current assets* to the sum of *current liabilities.*

Current-value basis   The restatement of the recorded values of selected *assets* in current-dollar terms to reflect price changes. (Cf. *current-dollar accounting.*)

Cutoff rate   The minimum *rate of return* (*hurdle rate*) that *capital investment* projects have to meet, usually based on the *cost of capital* or a judgmentally adjusted standard.

Cyclical variations   The impact on a company's *funds flows* from the operational changes caused by business cycles.

Days' sales   A measure of the credit quality of *accounts receivable*, which expresses outstanding receivables in terms of average daily *sales*; can be compared with the *credit* terms under which sales were made.

Debt (liability)   An obligation to pay amounts due (and interest if required) under specified terms, or to provide goods or services to others.

Debt to assets   A ratio relating outstanding *debt* obligations (usually *long-term debt* but at times all types of debt) to total *assets*; used as a measure of *financial leverage*. (Cf. *debt to equity.*)

Debt to capitalization   A ratio relating *long-term debt* to a company's *capitalization*; used as a measure of *financial leverage*

as found in the *capital structure*. (Cf. *debt to equity.*)

Debt to equity   A ratio relating outstanding *debt* obligations (usually *long-term debt* but at times all types of debt) to *shareholders' equity*; used as a measure of *financial leverage.*

Default   Failure to make a payment on a *debt* obligation when due.

Deferred charges   A provision recorded on the *balance sheet* to reflect expenses incurred, but applicable to future accounting periods.

Deferred income taxes   A provision for income tax *liabilities* or income tax *assets* recorded on the *balance sheet*, arising from timing differences between recognized tax liabilities in a company's accounting system and tax liabilities reported to the tax authorities.

Deflation   A decline in general price levels. (Cf. *inflation.*)

Depreciation   The decline in an *asset*'s value, from use or obsolescence, that's recognized in the accounting system and for income tax purposes as a periodic allocation (*write-off*) against income of a portion of the original *cost* of the *asset*. (Cf. *accelerated depreciation; noncash item.*)

Dilution   The proportional reduction of *earnings per share* or *book value* per share from an increase in the number of shares outstanding, either from a new issue or from conversion of *convertible securities* outstanding.

Discounted cash flow   The *discounting* methodology employed in determining the economic attractiveness of *capital investment* projects, which reduces the value of future cash receipts or payments.

Discounted cash flow rate of return (DCF)   The rate of return (*yield*) that equates a project's cash inflows and outflows over its economic life; also called *internal rate of return.*

Discounting   The process of calculating the reduced value of a future sum or series of sums of money in proportion to the opportunity of earning interest and the distance in time of payment or receipt. (Cf. *compounding; present value.*)

Discount rate   The rate of return or standard used in calculating the *present value* of future *cash flows*, using the *discounting process.*

Disinvestment   The act of disposing of assets or whole business segments, caused by a reassessment of the strategic fit of these assets; the opposite of *investment.*

Dispositions   The net value received from the sale of operations, lines of business, or divisions of a company during a stated period.

Diversification   The process of investing in a number of unrelated or partially interrelated *assets* or activities to achieve a more stable performance of the business *portfolio.*

Dividend coverage   Relationship of the amount of common and/or preferred dividends to aftertax *earnings* of a company; a test of the ability of the company to pay the current level of dividends.

Dividend discount model   A valuation method for *common stock* that employs the *present value* of expected future dividends and any change in the expected level of dividends.

Dividend payout   A ratio relating the amount of dividends distributed to the aftertax *earnings* of a corporation to derive the percentage of *earnings* paid to shareholders.

Dividend yield   The current return to shareholders from dividends received over a specified period, derived by dividing dividends per share by the current average market price of the *stock.* (Cf. *yield.*)

Dynamic analysis   A method of analyzing business decisions that incorporates the effect of likely changes in key variables, as contrasted with fixed assumptions. (Cf. *sensitivity analysis.*)

Earnings (income, net income, profit, net profit)   The difference between all recorded

revenues and all related *costs* and *expenses* for a specified period, using generally accepted accounting principles.

Earnings before interest and taxes (EBIT)   An expression of a company's earning power before the effects of financing and taxation; used in a variety of *financial analyses.*

Earnings per share (EPS)   The proportional share of a corporation's *earnings* that can be claimed by each share of *common stock* outstanding, derived by dividing aftertax earnings after payment of preferred dividends by the average number of common shares outstanding during the period. (Cf. *earnings per share— basic.*)

Earnings per share—basic   A company's earnings per share calculated on the basis of the average of all common shares actually outstanding. (Cf. *common shares outstanding—basic.*)

Earnings per share—diluted   A company's earnings per share calculated on the basis of the average of all common shares actually outstanding at a point in time, plus the number of shares potentially outstanding from exercise of stock options, rights and warrants, and securities convertible into common shares. (Cf. *common shares outstanding—diluted.*)

Earnings yield   The current return to shareholders from *earnings* recorded for a specified period, derived by dividing periodic earnings by the *stock*'s current or average market price. (Cf. *yield.*)

Economic analysis   The development of the economic impact of a business decision that determines the actual *trade-off* between *economic costs* and *benefits* in a cash flow framework independent of accounting conventions.

Economic benefit   The consequence of a decision that causes an ultimate increase in present and future *cash flows.*

Economic cost   The consequence of a decision that causes an ultimate reduction in present and future *cash flows.*

Economic earnings (loss)   The net result of a *trade-off* between *economic benefits* and *economic costs*.

Economic life   The time over which a current or future *investment* can be expected to provide *economic benefits*, which is independent of the physical life of any *assets* involved.

Economic profit   The amount of aftertax net operating profit (NOPAT) earned on the capital base supporting the activity relative to the company's *weighted average cost of capital* applied to the capital base.

Economic return   A measure of the earnings power of an *investment* in terms of net *cash flows* generated by the *capital* committed. (Cf. *discounted cash flow*.)

Economic trade-off   The comparison of the *economic benefits* and *economic costs* caused by a business decision using a cash flow framework.

Economic value   The *net present value* of all future *economic benefits* and *costs* expected from an existing or prospective *investment*.

Economic value added (EVA™)   A form of expressing the value created by investing in projects whose returns exceed the company's *cost of capital*. The simplest way is to show the difference between annual *profits* (or *cash flow*) and the cost of the assets employed. The concept is also applied to the companies and divisions as a whole.

Enterprise value (firm value)   The *net present value* of all estimated future *cash flows* to be generated by a business.

Equity (owners' equity, net worth, shareholders' equity)   The recorded ownership claim of common and preferred shareholders in a corporation as reflected on the *balance sheet*. Also defined as total *assets* less all *liabilities*.

Equivalence   A point of indifference at which the *present value* of future *cash flows* reflects the return expectations of a prospective investor.

Expected   return   (expectation)   A weighted average of alternative outcomes of an *investment*, using the respective probabilities as weights.

Expense   A periodic offset against *revenue* recognized under generally accepted accounting principles, representing either a direct cash outlay or an *allocation* or *accrual* of past and future outlays.

Extraordinary items   The aftertax impact of *costs* or *revenues* encountered on a nonrecurring basis outside the normal operations of a company during a stated period.

Fair market value (FMV)   The price for an *asset* on which two rational parties with sufficient information would agree in the absence of negotiating pressure.

Financial Accounting Standards Board (FASB)   The official rule-making institute of the accounting community, which is privately funded by the profession.

Financial analysis   The process of determining and weighing the financial impact of business decisions.

Financial flexibility   The ability to maintain alternative choices for raising additional *capital* while preserving a *capital structure* appropriate to the risks and conditions of a company's business.

Financial Genome   A professional software application by Modernsoft, Inc., designed for financial analysis, statement preparation, and financial planning.

Financial growth plan   A model of future financial flows that tracks the results of key *investment, operational*, and *financing* dimensions under a variety of assumptions about strategies, policies, and business conditions.

Financial leverage   The magnifying (or diminishing) effect on *return on equity* from the use of *debt* in the *capital structure*, caused by introducing fixed interest charges against the returns obtained from the incremental funds invested. (Cf. *operating leverage*.)

Financial model   The representation in a computer program of key financial dimensions of a business system for purposes of simulating the impact of management decisions. (Cf. *financial growth plan*.)

Financial statements   Key periodic statements prepared under generally accepted accounting principles, which represent the financial condition of a company (*balance sheet*), the operating results (*income statement*), the changes in *funds flows* (*cash flow statement*), and the changes in *owners' equity* (*statement of changes in shareholders' equity*).

Financing   The provision of *funds* from internal or external sources to support the *investments* and *operations* of a business.

First-in, first-out (FIFO)   A method of accounting for inventory in which the oldest item is assumed to be used or sold first. (Cf. *last-in, first-out*.)

Fixed assets   Any tangible *asset* on the *balance sheet* considered to have a life or usefulness for a business in excess of one year, such as land, buildings, and machinery. (Cf. *current asset*.)

Fixed costs   Any *cost* that doesn't vary with changes in the volume of operations over time.

Fixed-income security   Any security that provides an unchanging stream of interest or dividends to the holder over its life.

Foreign exchange exposure   The potential loss from an unexpected change in currency exchange rates affecting *investments* or *operations*.

Free cash flow   The net *cash flow* available to a company after providing for all acceptable new *investments* to support its strategy, before any dividend payments or changes in *financing*.

Fully diluted earnings per share   *Earnings per share* which are calculated on the assumption that all outstanding *convertible securities* and *warrants* have been converted into the appropriate number of common shares, raising the denominator and reducing *earnings per share*.

Funds   A general term denoting means of payment, often equated with cash.

Funds flow (cash flow)   The movement of *funds* of all types through a business over time, ultimately resulting in changes in *cash*.

Funds flow statement   A *financial statement* prepared to display the *funds* movements in a business over a specified period of time, separated into sections on *operations, investment, financing*, and cash balances. (Cf. *cash flow statement*)

Going-concern value   The *net present value* of the expected future *cash flows* generated by a business from its normal operations. (Cf. *economic value; enterprise value*.)

Goodwill   A category of intangible asset representing the excess paid over recorded values for acquisitions. It is generally amortized over specific time periods.

Gross margin   The difference between *net sales* and *cost of goods sold* (or *cost of services provided*), generally expressed as a ratio of this difference divided by net sales.

Growth/decline variations   The impact on a company's *funds flows* from the operational changes caused by growth or decline in the volume of business.

Hedge   A strategy to neutralize the risk of an *investment* by engaging in offsetting contracts whereby potential gains and losses will cancel each other.

Historical cost principle   An accounting principle requiring the recording of transactions and the maintenance of recorded values at the actual level incurred, regardless of any subsequent changes in the value of the *assets* or *liabilities* involved.

Hurdle rate   A minimum standard for the return required of an *investment*, used in selecting from alternative investment choices.

Income   The difference between the *revenues* and the matching *costs* and *expenses* for a specified period. (Cf. *earnings*.)

Income statement (operating statement, profit and loss statement)   A *financial statement* reporting the periodic *revenues* and matching *costs* and *expenses* for a specified period, and deriving the *income* for the period.

Incremental analysis   A method of analysis that focuses on the impact of changes caused by a business decision.

Inflation   An increase in general price levels, the opposite of *deflation*.

Inflation premium   The increased *return on investment* required to compensate the holders for expected *inflation*.

Insolvency   The condition where an individual's or company's *liabilities* exceed the realizable value of the *assets* held.

Intangibles   A category of asset representing intangible values such as patents, software, and *goodwill* from acquisitions. These are generally amortized over specific time periods.

Interest coverage   Relationship of periodic interest expense to operating *income* before or after taxes, used to judge a company's ability to pay interest charges. (Cf. *times interest earned*.)

Internal rate of return (IRR)   The *discount rate* that equates the cash inflows and cash outflows of an *investment* project, resulting in a *net present value* of zero. (Cf. *rate of return; yield*.)

Inventory turnover   A ratio that relates ending inventory or average inventory to the *cost of goods sold* for a specified period of time; used in judging the effectiveness with which inventories are controlled.

Inventory valuation   Any adjustment to recorded inventory values to correct for differences between historical *costs* and current prices, also affecting *cost of goods sold*.

Investment(s)   The commitment of *funds* for purposes of obtaining an *economic return* over a period of time, usually in the form of periodic *cash flows* and/or a *terminal value*.

Investment value   The value of a *convertible security* based strictly on its characteristics as a *fixed-income security*, without regard to its conversion provision.

Junk bond   Any *bond* issued by corporations with risk characteristics higher than what's normally rated as investment-grade risk (normal risk exposure).

Last-in, first-out (LIFO)   A method of accounting for inventory in which the newest item is assumed to be used or sold first. (Cf. *first-in, first-out*.)

Leasing   The process of contracting for the use of *assets* owned by others over a specified period of time, in exchange for a stipulated pattern of periodic payments.

Leverage   The magnifying effect from volume changes on *profits* caused by fixed elements in a company's *cost* structure, or the magnifying effect from profit changes on *return on equity* caused by *fixed-cost debt* obligations in the *capital structure*. (Cf. *financial leverage; operating leverage*.)

Leveraged buyout (LBO)   The acquisition of a business by investors using a high percentage of *debt* carried by the business itself.

Liability   An obligation to pay a specified amount or to perform a service; at times also the recognized potential obligation to pay or perform a service (contingent liability).

Liquid asset   An *asset* that can be rapidly converted into cash without suffering a significant reduction in value, usually classified as a *current asset*.

Liquidation   The process of terminating a business entity by selling its *assets*, paying off its *liabilities*, and distributing any remaining cash to its owners.

Liquidation value   The estimated value of a business based on *liquidation* of its *assets*.

Liquidity   The degree to which a company is readily able to meet its current obligations from *liquid assets*. (Cf. *acid test; current ratio*.)

Long-term debt   Any *debt* obligation of a company with a maturity of more than one year.

Managerial economics   The methodology underlying the analysis and resolution of the *economic (cash flow) trade-offs* involved in making management decisions.

Marginal costs (revenues)   Increments of *costs* and *revenues* attributable to changes in a variable affecting an issue being decided.

Market to book value   The relationship between the current market price of *common stock* and its recorded *book value*, a ratio often used in judging the performance of a company's *stock*.

Market value   The value of an *asset* as determined in an unconstrained market of multiple buyers and sellers, such as a securities exchange.

Market value added (MVA)   The difference between the recorded value of a company's *capitalization* and the current market value of the securities representing it.

Market value of equity   The combined value of all *common shares* of a company at current market prices. (Cf. *book value of equity*.)

Market value of firm   The *market value* of a company's *equity* plus the market value of its *debt*.

Minority interest   A small portion of shareholders' equity held by outsiders in a corporate entity acquired by a company.

Monetary asset   Any *asset* defined in terms of units of currency, such as *cash* and *accounts receivable*.

Multiple hurdle rates   A set of minimum return standards in a company that are used to judge the desirability of *investments* in activities or lines of business with widely different risk characteristics.

Mutually exclusive alternatives   Alternative *investments* for achieving the same objective, of which only one can be undertaken.

Net assets   Total *assets* less *current liabilities*, as recorded on the *balance sheet*.

Net assets turnover   An expression of the effectiveness with which assets generate *sales*, defined as the ratio of sales to *net assets*, on an average or ending value basis.

Net income (loss)   The difference between periodic *revenues* and matching *costs* and *expenses*. (Cf. *earnings; net profit; profit*.)

Net income available for common dividends   *Net income* adjusted for any *preferred* dividends declared during the period, representing the residual claim of the *common* shareholders.

Net investment   The commitment of new *funds* to an *investment* project, net of any funds recovered due to the decision to make the investment, adjusted for tax implications.

Net operating profit after tax (NOPAT)   Net profit from operations before *interest* and nonoperating income or expenses, adjusted for applicable income taxes. Used in a variety of ratios and valuation concepts.

Net present value (NPV)   The difference between the *present values* of cash inflows and outflows from an *investment*, representing the net gain or loss in value expected from the investment relative to the earnings standard applied.

Net profit   The difference between periodic *revenues* and matching *costs* and *expenses*, after applicable income taxes. (Cf. *earnings; net income; profit*.)

Net property, plant, and equipment   The residual recorded value of *property, plant and equipment*, after deducting the amount of applicable *accumulated depreciation* to date.

Net sales   Total *revenue* from sales for a specified period, less adjustments such as returns, allowances, and sales discounts.

Net worth   The recorded value of *shareholders' equity* on the *balance sheet*.

Nominal amount   Any quantity not adjusted for changes in the purchasing power of the currency in which it's recorded. (Cf. *real amount*.)

Noncash item   An *expense* or *revenue* recognized in the accounting process that doesn't represent a *cash flow* during the period, such as *depreciation* or unrealized income or gains.

Notes payable   Debt obligations representing trade or other credit extended to a company, generally interest-bearing commitments.

Ongoing value   The value of a business or activity that is assumed to be continuing at the termination point of a discounted cash flow analysis for valuation purposes, also referred to as *terminal value.*

Operating cash flow   The net *cash flow* generated by the operations of a business during a specified period, usually on an aftertax basis and adjusted for all noncash accounting elements such as depreciation and amortization.

Operating funds   *Funds* required to support current operations, such as the various *working capital* items.

Operating leverage   The magnifying (or diminishing) effect of volume changes on *profits* caused by the *fixed costs* in the company's operations.

Operating statement (income statement)   A *financial statement* reporting the *revenues* and matching *costs* and *expenses* for a specified period, and deriving the *net income.*

Operational analysis   The various methods of analyzing the specific and comparative aspects of a company's operating performance.

Operations   The activities in a company that support the basic purpose of the business, generating *revenues* and managing related *costs* and *expenses* for profitable results.

Opportunity cost   *Economic benefits* forgone by selecting one alternative course of action over another.

Opportunity rate of return   A rate of return standard reflecting the long-term level of returns expected in a business, often based on a company's *cost of capital.*

Option   A contractual opportunity to purchase or sell an *asset* or security at a predetermined price, without the obligation of doing so.

Over-the-counter market (OTC)   A market network among security dealers that permits electronic trading of securities not listed on a formal securities exchange.

Owners' equity   The recorded value of *preferred* and *common* shareholders' claims against the *assets* on a company's *balance sheet*; also, the proprietors' recorded claims in the case of an unincorporated business or partnership. (Cf. *equity; shareholders' equity.*)

Paid-in capital   The recorded amount of *capital* provided by shareholders on the *balance sheet*, as contrasted with *retained earnings.*

Par value   The *nominal* value established by the issuer of a security, as contrasted with the *market value* of the security. In the case of a *bond*, the issuing company contracts to pay the par value at maturity.

Payables   See *accounts payable.*

Payables period   A translation of *accounts payable* into the days of average purchases outstanding at a point in time; used as an indicator of the effectiveness with which *trade credit* is employed.

Payback period   The period of time over which the *cash flows* from an *investment* are expected to recover the initial outlay.

Perpetuity   A series of level periodic receipts or payments (*annuity*) expected to last forever.

Plug figure   A common term used to represent an unknown variable in a financial analysis, such as the amount of *financing* required in a pro forma projection. (Cf. *pro forma statement.*)

Portfolio   A set of diverse *investments* held by an individual or a company.

Preferred stock   A special class of capital stock, usually with a dividend provision, that receives a form of preference over *common stock* in its claims on *earnings* and *assets*.

Prepaid expenses　The portion of any expenses paid during a stated period but applicable to future periods, shown as a *current asset* on the *balance sheet*.

Present value　The value today of a future sum or series of sums of money, calculated by *discounting* the future sums with an appropriate discount rate.

Present value payback　The point in the *economic life* of an *investment* project at which the cumulative *present value* of *cash inflows* equals the present value of the cash outflows.

Price to earnings (P/E)　The relationship of the market price of a share of *stock* to the most recent *earnings per share* over 12 months; used as a rough indicator of what investors are willing to pay for $1 of a company's *earnings*.

Principal　The original amount of a loan or *bond*, also called face value, on which the rate of interest to be paid is based.

Private placement　The sale of securities to a selected group of investors rather than through a public offering.

Profit　The difference between periodic *revenues* and matching *costs* and *expenses*. (Cf. *earnings; net profit*.)

Profitability index (benefit/cost ratio, BCR)　A measure of *investment* desirability, defined as the *present value* of all cash inflows expected over the *economic life* of a project divided by the present value of the cash outflows.

Profit center　An organizational segment of a business in which *revenues, costs*, and *expenses* can be recognized separately, allowing the activity to be managed for *profit* performance.

Pro forma statement　A projected *financial statement* reflecting the financial impact of a set of assumed conditions for a specified future period.

Projection　A forecast of the quantitative implications of a set of assumed conditions.

Provision for income taxes　The amount of income taxes recognized as an expense for a stated period on the *income statement,* as distinguished from the amount of income taxes reported to the tax authorities. Any difference is due to differences in the timing and pattern of revenues and expenses reported for tax purposes, and this amount is recognized as *deferred income taxes* on the *balance sheet.*

Public issue (public offering)　The sale of newly issued securities to the public through underwriters. (Cf. *private placement.*)

Purchasing power parity　A condition in which commodities in different countries cost the same amount when prices are expressed in a given currency, due to expected adjustments in foreign exchange rates.

Quick ratio (acid test)　A stringent measure of *liquidity* relating current cash *assets* (cash, cash equivalents, and *receivables*) to *current liabilities.*

Quick sale value　The value of an asset or business when assumed to be sold under hurried conditions, resulting generally in a lower valuation than *market value.*

Range of earnings chart (EBIT chart)　A graphic representation of the related changes in *earnings before interest and taxes (EBIT)* and *earnings per share* under various financing alternatives.

Rate of return　The level of *earnings* attained or expected from an *investment* over a period of time. (Cf. *yield.*)

Ratio analysis　The use of a variety of ratios in analyzing the financial performance and condition of a business from various viewpoints, such as managers', owners', and creditors'.

Real amount　Any quantity that has been adjusted for changes in the purchasing power of the currency in which it's recorded. (Cf. *nominal amount.*)

Realized income   *Earnings* or gains that are recognized as the result of a transaction, as contrasted with earnings or gains that exist on paper only.

Receivables   See *accounts receivable.*

Recovery value (terminal value)   The value of any *assets* or future *profits* expected to be realized at the end of the *economic life* of an *investment,* net of taxes.

Redundant assets   Any *assets* held by a company that don't contribute returns appropriate for the lines of business principally engaged in; these are candidates for *disinvestment* (divestiture).

Relevant costs   Identifiable *cost* or *expense* elements that are expected to change in response to a decision being analyzed.

Relevant revenues   Identifiable *revenue* elements that are expected to change in response to a decision being analyzed.

Reserves   Portions of *shareholders' equity* set aside on the *balance sheet* in recognition of contingencies and potential *liabilities.*

Retained earnings (earned surplus)   The cumulative amount of past and current *earnings* retained and reinvested in a corporation, instead of being distributed to shareholders in the form of dividends.

Return on assets (ROA or ROAE)   The relationship of annual aftertax *earnings* to total *assets* (average or ending balance), used as a measure of the productivity of the assets a company employs to generate the earnings. At times aftertax earnings are adjusted for interest to eliminate the impact of *financing.*

Return on capitalization (invested capital) (ROC)   The relationship of annual *earnings* before interest, after taxes to the *capitalization* (average or ending balance); used as a measure of the productivity of a company's invested *capital* regardless of the amount of *financial leverage* employed. (Cf. *return on net assets.*)

Return on equity (net worth) (ROE)   The relationship of annual aftertax *earnings* to the recorded *shareholders' equity.* Used as a measure of the effectiveness with which shareholder funds have been invested.

Return on investment (ROI)   The relationship of annual aftertax *earnings* to the *book value* (average or ending balance) of the *asset,* business, or *profit center* generating these earnings. Used as a measure of the productivity of the *investment.* (Cf. *return on assets.*)

Return on net assets (RONA)   The relationship of annual *earnings* before interest, after taxes to total *assets* less *current liabilities* (*net assets*) (average or ending balance), used as a measure of the productivity of a company's invested *capital* regardless of the amount of *financial leverage* employed. (Cf. *return on capitalization.*)

Revenue (sales)   The recorded incidence of a sale of goods and/or services as recognized in the accounting system.

Risk-adjusted return standard (discount rate, hurdle rate, cost of capital)   A minimum *discount rate* that has been adjusted upward to include a specified risk premium.

Risk allowance   A provision for risk in an analysis, such as lowering a project's expected *cash flows* or using a *risk-adjusted return standard.*

Risk analysis   A process of integrating risk dimensions into an analysis, such as using *sensitivity analysis* or modeling outcomes that have been adjusted by probabilistic methods.

Risk aversion   A subjective unwillingness to accept a given level of risk unless a significant *economic trade-off* can be realized.

Risk-free interest rate   The assumed *yield* obtainable on a guaranteed security in the absence of *inflation,* generally represented by U.S. Treasury bonds.

Risk premium (market premium)   The increased return required from an *investment* to compensate the holder for the level of risk involved, generally represented by the difference between expected returns from a stock market portfolio and the risk-free interest rate. It is used as an input in determining the cost of *shareholders' equity* when calculating the cost of capital.

Sales (revenue)   The recorded incidence of a sale of goods and/or services as recognized in the accounting system.

Sales per employee   The ratio of annual sales to the number of employees (average or ending) as an expression of the effectiveness with which human capital is employed.

Seasonal variations   The impact on a company's *funds flows* from the operational changes caused by seasonal business conditions.

Secured creditor   A creditor whose claim is backed by the pledge of a specified *asset*, the proceeds of which will go to the creditor in case of *liquidation*.

Securities and Exchange Commission (SEC)   The regulatory body established by the federal government to oversee securities markets.

Senior creditor   Any creditor with specific claims on *income* or *assets* that rank ahead of that of general (unsecured) creditors.

Sensitivity analysis   The process of testing the impact on the results of an analysis from changes in one or more of the input variables.

Sequential outlays   One or more future *investment* outlays expected during the *economic life* of an investment project, which should be taken into account in judging the project's overall desirability.

Shareholders' equity   The recorded value of the residual claims of all shareholders as reflected on the *balance sheet*.

Shareholder value   The economic value created by successfully investing in activities whose returns exceed the company's *cost of capital*, which will cause growth in *total shareholder return*.

Share price appreciation   The change in the *market value* of preferred and common shares over time.

Share repurchases (stock buyback)   The purchase by a company of its own shares in the market, using available funds to reduce the number of shares outstanding versus investing those funds internally or paying an increased dividend.

Shelf registration   The filing, under *SEC* rules, of a general-purpose prospectus outlining possible financing plans for up to two years, to speed up the actual issue when the timing is considered appropriate.

Short-term liabilities   *Debt* obligations due within 12 months of the date of a *balance sheet*. Generally listed under *current liabilities*.

Simulation   The process of modeling the potential outcomes of a financial plan or *investment* proposal, taking into account alternative assumptions about key variables and policies, and calculating the results using computer programs. (Cf. *sensitivity analysis*.)

Sinking fund   A separate pool of cash, often held in trust, into which periodic payments are made for the future redemption of an obligation.

Solvency   The condition of an individual or company in which obligations can be paid when due.

Sources and uses statement   A *financial statement* that separates all *funds* inflows and outflows for a given period of time, derived from changes in *balance sheet* accounts and supplemented with *operating statement* data. (Cf. *cash flow statement*.)

Spot market   A market in which prices of securities or commodities are determined for immediate transactions.

Spread   The difference between the issue price of a new security and the net amount received by the issuing company, caused by underwriting commissions and *expenses*. Also, the difference between the *cost of capital* and the returns achieved on an *investment*.

Stock   General term used in referring to *common stock*; also applied to *preferred stock*.

Stock market risk premium   The premium in return to the investor governed by the risk of investing in the stock market versus risk-free long-term government bonds. Used in calculating the cost of capital. (Cf. *risk premium.*)

Stock option   A contractual arrangement allowing selected corporate employees to purchase a specified number of shares at a set price within a specified period of time; used as an incentive for key personnel.

Straight-line depreciation   A pattern of *depreciation* write-offs that charges level amounts during the *asset*'s book life, for either accounting or tax deduction purposes.

Subordinated creditor   A creditor whose claim is specifically designated as ranking below the claims of other creditors of a company.

Sunk cost   A past outlay of *funds* that can't be recovered or changed by a current or future decision, and which is therefore irrelevant in the analysis of future actions.

Sustainable growth rate   The rate of growth in *equity* or sales volume that a company can maintain without changing its *return on assets, asset turnover, debt to equity*, and *dividend payout*, and while keeping its *capital structure* proportions at their current levels.

Synergy   The assumed *economic benefits* to be obtained from a successful combination of two businesses due to increased efficiency, economies of scale, and mutual reinforcement of business effectiveness.

Tax shield   The impact on a company's income tax obligations from a change in a tax-deductible expense, such as *depreciation* or interest, defined as the amount of change times the applicable tax rate. It assumes that the company has sufficient taxable income to offset the change in the *expense.*

Terminal value (recovery value)   The value of any *assets* or future *cash flows* expected to be realized at the end of the *economic life* of an *investment*, net of taxes.

Time lags   The elapsed time between the recorded incidence of a transaction and its actual cash impact.

Times burden covered   The relationship of the amount of debt *burden* during a period to *earnings* before interest and taxes. Used as a measure of a company's ability to service its *debt.*

Times interest earned   The relationship of the amount of periodic interest expense to *earnings* before interest and taxes. Used as a measure of a company's ability to make regular interest payments.

Time value of money   The *discounted* or *compounded* value of a sum of money over a specified period of time, using a specified discount or compound rate. (Cf. *present value.*)

Total shareholder return (TSR)   The *economic return* to shareholders in the form of dividends and capital gains or losses from *share price appreciation* or decline realized during a specified period.

Trade credit   Credit extended to a company in the course of normal business operations by its suppliers. (Cf. *accounts payable.*)

Trade-off   The process of judging the relative advantage or disadvantage from making a decision that involves identified *economic benefits* and *costs*, generally in a cash flow framework.

Trade payables   Amounts owed to a company's suppliers of goods and services. (Cf. *accounts payable.*)

Transfer price   An internally established price level at which units of a company trade goods or services with each other.

Treasury stock   The value stated at acquisition cost of a company's own common shares which were purchased in the stock market and are held in safekeeping for future use. Shown as a subtraction from *shareholders' equity* on the *balance sheet.*

Trend analysis   A method of analysis that applies judgmental or statistical methods to historical series of data for the purpose of judging performance or making informed projections of future conditions.

Uncommitted earnings per share (UEPS) *Earnings per share* adjusted for the effect of future *sinking fund* payments and other repayment provisions, used in judging alternative financing possibilities.

Underwriter Investment banker or a group (syndicate) of investment bankers used by a corporation in marketing new securities issues to the public, guaranteeing a specific price to the issuing company. (Cf. *public issue.*)

Unrealized income (gain) *Earnings* or gains that are recognized on paper without the benefit of a transaction, as contrasted with earnings or gains that are realized through actual transactions. (Cf. *realized income.*)

Variable cost Any *cost* or *expense* that varies with operating volume over a specified period. (Cf. *fixed costs.*)

Volatility The risk introduced by past and expected fluctuations in a company's *earnings*, often expressed as B (*beta*).

Warrant A financial instrument issued to investors giving them the option to purchase additional shares at a specified price. Usually issued in connection with a new security issue.

Weighted average cost of capital Overall *cost of capital* derived by weighting the respective *costs* of different parts of a company's *capital structure* by their proportions.

Working capital (net working capital) The difference between *current assets* and *current liabilities* as recorded on the *balance sheet*, representing the amount of *operating funds* that is financed by the company's *capital structure.*

Working capital cycle The periodic transformation of *working capital* components into cash inflows and outflows.

Working capital turnover The relationship of sales to average *working capital* expressed as the number of times *working capital* is turned over during the period. It is an indicator of the effectiveness with which *working capital* is managed.

Write-offs Accounting entries that allocate portions of past outlays into appropriate operating periods, such as *depreciation* and *amortization.*

Yield The *rate of return* earned by an *investment*'s cash inflows and outflows during a specified period. (Cf. *internal rate of return.*)

Yield to maturity The *internal rate of return* earned by a *bond* when held to maturity.

APPENDIX III

Financial Information and On-Line Sources

Although this book's orientation is techniques of financial analysis, many uses of the tools we've discussed suggest the need for information beyond that stipulated or available directly. Successful application of financial analysis requires that you be familiar with at least the main sources of financial information, and how to obtain the necessary inputs for your analysis. For this reason, we've devoted this appendix to a brief review of common data sources; where required we've also given some guidance for interpreting the financial data presented. Information sources listed here will give you the background to make more sophisticated decisions about company performance, new financing, temporary borrowing, investments, credit, capital budgeting, and so on.

The rise of the Internet has literally opened a world of data sources and up-to-the-minute information to anyone willing to browse among the exploding number of websites being made available. These sources complement, continuously update, and expand what used to be limited to the printed page in newspapers, magazines, and reference books. Accordingly, we'll address both on-line and printed sources where appropriate within the major topics covered in this appendix, while realizing that the fast-changing environment of data access will render this presentation partially obsolete in a relatively short time. The on-line sources are listed first, with brief explanations of the contents that can be accessed; more detailed descriptions are provided with the print sources.

Several of the major search engines currently available offer access to a broad range of financial information. Foremost among these at the time of this writing is Yahoo Finance, which provides up-to-the-minute summary information on U.S. and international financial market data, stock and other securities quotations, individual company stock data and charts, financial news, and much more. Infoseek, Lycos, Excite, and Google each offer a selection of financial data, news, and a variety of information for individuals and businesses, as well as links to a large number of information sites on financial offerings by colleges and universities. It's generally useful to browse these extensive sites, searching for "finance" to see firsthand the type of information available.

Yahoo: www.finance.yahoo.com

Infoseek: www.infoseek.com

Lycos: www.lycos.com

Excite: www.excite.com

Google: www.google.com

In keeping with the nature of this book, this overview is meant only as an introduction to sources of current financial, periodic financial, and background company and business information. The reader is encouraged to search both the Internet as well as depository libraries for information relevant to specific inquiries, using the special catalog and information links of the latter.

Current Financial Information

The common way to keep abreast of financial developments has long been to scan the daily financial pages of national, metropolitan, and regional newspapers. The most complete and widely read financial coverage is found in *The Wall Street Journal* (www.dowjones.com) and *The New York Times* (www.nytimes.com) which contain detailed information on securities and commodity markets; news, feature articles, and statistics on economic and business conditions; news and earnings reports for individual companies; dividend announcements; currency, commodity, and trading data; and a great deal of coverage of international business and economic conditions. Major U.S. and Canadian dailies also carry key financial and economic data, but their coverage and emphasis vary greatly. Smaller and regional papers often provide only selected highlights tailored to the area and the readership. As we'll show, most of this information can be found on the Internet through the various service sites now available on-line.

The bulk of the materials shown in the financial pages involve securities transactions and current financial data. This information isn't entirely self-explanatory. We'll describe the meaning of some of the abbreviations and symbols used in *The Wall Street Journal* listings for stock transactions, bond transactions, and other key financial data. Other newspapers generally present data in a fairly comparable fashion, but in less detail.

Stock Quotations

On-Line Stock Market Data

Major on-line sources for current information about individual securities prices, trading volumes, and averages include the following exchange sites:

NYSE: www.nyse.com

NASDAQ: www.nasdaq.com and www.nasdaq-online.com

These sites provide current market averages, indexes, and trading data, as well as securities quotations, paralleling many of the listings found in the financial pages, but offering easy and immediate access.

On-Line Company Data

A growing number of websites make available up-to-date company information in a variety of formats, including charts of share price movements and other data. Many of these require subscriptions to obtain highly detailed company analyses, but most offer brief profiles and highlights for free. Again we suggest that the interested reader browse these sites to gain a sense of what information is available:

Bloomberg.com: www.bloomberg.com

Corporate Information Research Site: www.corporateinformation.com

Fortune 500 Companies: pathfinder.com/fortune

Hoover's Online: www.hoovers.com

Security APL Quote: www.secapl.com

Stockmaster: www.stockmaster.com

Stock Selector: www.stockselector.com

Stock Smart: www.stocksmart.com

Wall Street Research Network: www.wsrn.com

Wright's Investor Service: www.wisi.com

Zack's Investment Research: www.zacks.com

Printed Stock Market Data

Transactions executed on organized exchanges—New York Stock Exchange (NYSE), American Stock Exchange (AMEX) (which is now part of NASDAQ), and several regional exchanges—and the rapidly growing electronic network of the National Association of Securities Dealers (NASDAQ) are listed the following day in the financial pages of most newspapers. The format is generally comparable, although the detail provided and the number of companies covered will vary.

Daily trading statistics for the NYSE, AMEX, and NASDAQ are summarized under two overall headings, Stock Market Data Bank and The Dow Jones Averages, whereas composite transactions of individual securities are listed alphabetically by company. The Stock Market Data Bank shows the movement of the major indexes, that is, the Dow Jones averages, The New York Stock Exchange index, Standard & Poor's indexes, the NASDAQ Stock Market index, and a selection of other indexes. These are reflected in terms of the daily high, low and close, the net change, the change over the past 12 months, and the change from last year-end. Next is a listing, by a major exchange, of the most active issues, the price percentage gainers and losers, volume percentage leaders, and a summary of issues traded, advances, declines, new highs, new lows, and so on, as well as hourly volumes of trading on the NYSE. The Dow Jones Averages are graphed over six months with daily ranges, covering the 30 industrials, the 20 transportation stock, and 15 utility stocks. These summaries provide an overview of the market's mood and direction.

The various stock price averages and indexes are popular and important clues to the stock market's behavior in general. They're calculated daily and in most cases continuously from on-line databases. The averages are followed by analysts, investors, and financial managers who interpret market movements to decide on purchase or sale of securities, or to assess various types of new securities. Because the various averages involve a selected and relatively small number of stocks, their upward or downward movement over time isn't necessarily a predictor of the likely movement of any particular stock or of the overall market.

As we've discussed in Chapters 9 and 10, there are many factors underlying the value and market position of a particular security, the most important being the current and prospective operating circumstances of the company and the cash flows generated in response to these. The market's atmosphere and general economic conditions will certainly influence the particular stock's behavior, but we must caution against the adage that a "rising tide lifts all ships in the harbor" (a gross oversimplification of stock market behavior). The limitations of stock indexes are those of averages in general, which can only be broad indicators of a likely trend against which all particulars of a security have to be compared.

The most commonly quoted and publicized stock price averages are the Dow Jones averages of 30 industrial, 20 transportation, and 15 utility stocks, and the composite average of all those 65 securities. The Dow Jones Industrial Average contains the most well-known companies in the United States, such as IBM, General Motors, General Electric, 3M, Coca-Cola, and Procter & Gamble. Because it's heavily weighted toward these "blue chip" securities—many of which have performed less strongly than newer and more fashionable companies—the Dow Jones average isn't particularly applicable for analysis of securities of lesser-known companies, specialized "growth situations," Internet companies, and conglomerates.

The New York Times average of 50 stocks includes 25 transportation issues and 25 industrial stocks. This average is also somewhat weighted in favor of blue chips. The Standard & Poor's averages—composite indexes of 425 industrial stocks, 50 utilities, and 25 transportation companies, and a combination of all these averages in the S&P 500—are more broadly based and more closely approximate the average price level of all stocks listed on the New York Stock Exchange, because the S&P 500 includes about one-quarter of the issues actively traded there.

The NASDAQ composite average is a broad sampling of the many issues traded electronically through a wide network of security dealers. These quotations have achieved growing recognition over the past decade and represent a vast grouping of new, emerging, and fast-growing securities as well as securities of large numbers of smaller, well-established companies.

Because stock transactions are electronically tracked, the current level of the various averages is always available almost instantaneously during the trading day. Continuous adjustments are made for stock splits, stock dividends, and many changes in the corporate structure of the companies in the index. Some references at the end of this appendix detail how the indexes are calculated.

Individual stock quotations from the NYSE are generally presented in a tabular, common format. The various columns show the high and low achieved during the past 52 weeks, the name of the company, the stock exchange symbol, the annual dividend, the current dividend yield, the price/earnings ratio, the day's volume of trading in hundreds of shares, and the high, low, and closing price for the day. The quotations are accompanied by a large number of symbols and footnotes to provide further insight for the reader. For example, the notation "e" next to a company's dividend indicates that a dividend was declared but that there is no regular dividend rate. The letter "g" next to a company's name indicates that dividends are paid in Canadian dollars, while the stock is traded in U.S. dollars and no dividend yield is shown. If a preferred stock is traded, the symbol "pf" is added right after the name. The symbol "s" next to the high for a stock indicates a stock dividend or split, while the "n" with a company's name indicates a stock newly issued in the past 52 weeks. An upright black arrow at the beginning of the line indicates that a new 52-week high has been reached, whereas an inverse arrow indicates a new low.

The symbol "vj" ahead of the name indicates a state of bankruptcy and that no dividend is paid, and the letter "m" signals that the dividend was omitted during the past 52 weeks. Finally, "wt" with a company's name designates the issue as a warrant (trading separately from its related stock), whereas a new stock "wi" is trading on a "when issued" basis. Many other symbols refer mostly to dividend exceptions, and all are explained in the footnotes to the listing, as are the definitions of the listing categories themselves.

Individual listings of stock transactions in The Wall Street Journal are supplemented by various summaries of overall trading figures in the Stock Market Data Bank, which shows such statistics as the day's most active stocks. The Diary for the past two trading days covering the NYSE and NASDAQ/AMEX shows the number of issues traded, advancing and declining issues, volume leaders, leaders in price gains and declines, and so forth.

Quotations of transactions on the AMEX are printed in a similar format. Transactions on regional exchanges, such as the Pacific Stock Exchange in San Francisco and the Midwest Stock Exchange in Chicago, are often listed together with the most important quotations on the major Canadian stock exchanges in Toronto and Montreal. These transactions are usually quoted in less detail. Normally, only the number of shares traded, the high and low prices, and the closing prices with changes from the previous close are listed. At times, the quotations are limited to volume and closing prices only.

Quotations of transactions in the fast-growing NASDAQ market follow the basic format of the NYSE, except that notations indicating special conditions are incorporated into the four- or five-letter listing symbol. If a fifth letter is used, its special meaning is keyed to a symbol explanation below the NAS-DAQ listing. For example, the letter "F" indicates a foreign stock, whereas an "A" indicates a Class A stock. A huge volume of securities is traded in the NASDAQ system outside the organized exchanges, in an auction market consisting of hundreds of security dealers and individuals in all parts of the country. They're electronically linked via extensive computer networks, in an amazingly flexible arrangement which allows trading between prospective buyers and sellers of such securities as government bonds, state and municipal bonds, stocks and bonds of smaller and newer companies, bank stocks, mutual funds, insurance companies, small issues, and infrequently traded issues. A special listing of NASDAQ Small-Cap Issues is devoted to mostly new companies with a relatively small capitalization. Because of the limited trading in these stocks, the listing is confined to the name, the annual dividend, the volume traded in hundreds of shares, the last transaction price, and the change from the prior level.

Foreign Exchanges

Some of the larger newspapers carry limited quotations from major foreign stock exchanges. Trading of internationally recognized securities on the Paris, London, Tokyo, or Frankfurt stock exchanges is reported in the currency of the country involved. At times, the financial pages may contain current stock averages for foreign countries, supplemented by accounts of major activities there. *The Wall Street Journal* presents the Dow Jones World Stock Indexes, which reflect market trends in major regions of the world. Closing prices and changes from the prior trading day are provided for many industrial groupings and for major regions such as the United States, the Americas, Europe, and Asia-Pacific.

Mutual Funds

Mutual funds are professionally managed investment pools. A share of a mutual fund represents an investment in a portfolio of different securities, which may be oriented toward a variety of investment objectives such as earnings or capital appreciation. These funds have gained in importance in recent years, and mutual fund trading is quoted in most major newspapers. Price ranges are provided by the National Association of Securities Dealers (NASDAQ) and can be found on the NASDAQ website listed earlier.

The quotes normally show the investment objectives incorporated in the name of the specific fund under the heading to the management company, defined in many categories, including capital appreciation (CAP) and growth and income (G&I) for stock funds, short-term (BST) and high-yield taxable (BHI) for taxable bond funds, and intermediate-term (IDM) and high-yield municipal (HYM) for municipal bond funds. Next is given the net asset value per share (NAV), followed by the net change in NAV from the previous day. Finally, the total return is provided in percent for the year to date.

A variety of mutual fund indexes developed by Lipper are quoted to show daily trends in major categories, such as growth funds, small company growth funds, and gold funds, as well as bond indexes for different funds such as world income or general municipals.

Options

Options (which are essentially contracts to buy or sell a security on a future date and at a stipulated price) are traded on various exchanges and are listed in terms of closing prices for "puts" (sales prices) and "calls" (purchase prices) for several months in the future. This specialized market has grown rapidly in recent years as has the market for commodity futures, which similarly represent contracts for future sales and purchases of certain commodities and are quoted in the financial pages.

Option quotations provide the option and strike price, the expiration date, volume of trades during a given day, and the last trade in dollars plus fractions. The 40 most active contracts the exchange traded on are identified, as are the net change from the prior trading day, the closing price, and the "open interest" (options outstanding) from the prior trading day.

Bond Quotations

The three major types of bonds—corporate, state and municipal, and federal government—represent a huge market involving both the organized exchanges and the NASDAQ market. In fact, the overwhelming majority of government bonds of both types are traded in the NASDAQ market, while the majority of corporate bond issues are traded on the stock exchanges.

The first column lists the abbreviated name of the issuing company, accompanied by the coupon interest rate and the maturity date indicated by the last two digits of the year. Next is shown the current yield, followed by the volume traded in thousands of dollars (most bonds are denominated at $1,000 each), the closing price, and the net change from the prior trading day's closing price. The most important difference to remember vis-à-vis stock quotations is that bond prices are quoted in percentages of par value, expressed in fractions no smaller than one-eighth of a percent, although the switch to decimal quotations in early 2001 is beginning to change this practice. The symbols used with individual bond quotations parallel those discussed earlier. For example, "cv" indicates that the bond is convertible into common stock, and the price will reflect the share values of the common represented by each bond. The symbol "cld" indicates that the bond has just been called for redemption, while "dc" refers to a bond selling at a deep discount. The symbol "na" indicates that there is no interest accrual, usually associated with a bond from which investors expect little interest recovery beyond the principal due.

A slightly different method is used to list current quotations for government agency bonds and miscellaneous securities traded over the counter. We find that these securities are listed in terms of bid and asked quotations, which represent the price desired for purchase or sale on the trading day but don't necessarily denote specific transactions. Another important difference reflected in this example is the custom of quoting prices in percentage of par value, this time stated in terms of fractions of a percent in 32ds of a point. Thus, a quote of 141:07 means a price of 1,410 7/32 percent or $1,412.19 per $1,000 of par value. The final column shows the yield to maturity, which reflects the return on investment earned at the current price if the bond is held to its maturity date and redeemed at par.

U.S. government securities as well as other debt instruments will be affected by the general outlook for interest rates. U.S. government securities will tend to yield a lower return than most corporate and other public bonds, because the likelihood of default is extremely remote and the purchaser is normally looking for a safe investment with an assured long-term or short-term yield. Also, they generally are exempt from state income taxes.

As we found in the case of the stock market quotations, bond market listings are supplemented by a variety of reports on the volume of trading, bonds averages, summaries of advancing and declining conditions, highs and lows for the year, and so on. Again, these provide the investor with a general feel for the daily movements of the bond markets and interest rate conditions. The most commonly used averages are the Dow Jones Bond Averages (20 bonds, including 10 public utilities and 10 industrials), Merrill Lynch Corporate Debt Issues, and Lehman Brothers U.S. Securities Indexes. Bond averages are calculated in percentages of par, as were the quotations themselves.

Other Financial Data

Most papers list, in one form or another, so-called leading, coincident, and lagging business and economic indicators—such as indexes of industrial production, freight car loadings, prices, output in the automotive industry, and steel production—both in feature stories and in tabular form. When supplemented by reports of earnings and dividend declarations of individual corporations, news about corporate management, analysis and announcement of new financing, and industry analysis, this information can provide a broad background for financial analysis.

Among the more specialized data in the financial pages are listings of transactions in the commodities markets. Commodities include a great variety of basic raw materials such as cotton, lumber, copper, and rubber as well as foods such as coffee, corn, and wheat. The best-known exchange for commodity trading is the Chicago Board of Trade. More specialized exchanges include the New York Cotton Exchange or international exchanges such as the London Metal Exchange. Commodities may be traded on a spot basis; that is, the commodity is purchased outright at the time. Commodities futures are also traded. These are contracts to buy or sell a commodity at a specified price at some point in the future. The commodities market is far too varied to describe here, but we should take a quick look at how commodities are quoted.

The information on commodities trading provided by most sources usually involves opening and closing transactions as well as highs and lows for the trading day and the season. Changes from the previous trading day are also often listed. A variety of indexes are available, such as the Dow Jones Spot Index, Dow Jones Futures Index, and Reuters United Kingdom Index. A company whose operations depend to a large extent on raw materials traded in a spot or futures market can be severely influenced by fluctuations in spot or futures prices. Because fluctuations in commodities markets can be severe, traders in these markets often hedge. This involves arrangements to both buy and sell the same commodity, which will "cover" the trader for shifts in prices. References at the end of this appendix provide detailed information on commodities trading.

Foreign Exchange

Most newspapers list the major currencies of the world in equivalents of U.S. dollars. Normally the quotations represent selling prices of bank transfers in the United States for payment abroad, and quotations are given for the current trading day as well as for the previous day. Also, prices for foreign bank notes are often quoted in equivalents of U.S. dollars on both buying and selling bases.

Financial and Economic Information

Apart from the current financial data contained in daily newspapers, a wealth of information is provided by various financial, economic, and business periodicals. Furthermore, readily available reference works contain periodic listings and analyses of financial information oriented toward the investor and financial analyst. The advent of the computer has made possible the rapid collection and analysis of company and economic data, and current information can now be obtained on-line through database access or in hard copy on a timely basis. The most important sources of periodic financial and business information are discussed next.

Business and Economic Magazines

Major Periodicals

For general business coverage, *Business Week* (www.businessweek.com) remains one of the most useful and widely read publications. The magazine covers current developments in business and economics, both national and international. It analyzes major events and reports on individual companies, stock markets, labor, business education, and so on, with a selective listing of economic indicators as well as a special index of business activity.

For more detailed coverage of stock quotations, security offerings, banking developments, and financial, industrial, and commodity trends, the *Commercial and Financial Chronicle* is the most comprehensive print source available. *The Wall Street Transcript* (twst.com) analyzes securities from a great variety of individual companies, on both a financial and economic basis, and assesses the technical indications of stock market charts. It discusses major corporate presentations to security analysts about past performance and future plans, and features roundtable discussions on industry groups by security analysts.

Barron's (www.barrons.com) covers business trends in terms of individual companies as well as major industries, and provides much information about corporate securities. The section "Stock Market at a Glance" is a useful and detailed picture of the securities markets. *Fortune* magazine (pathfinder.com/fortune) offers biweekly comments on national economic trends. It profiles major U.S. and international executives in addition to giving detailed articles on industry, company, and socioeconomic trends. The magazine's annual listing and ranking of the Fortune 500 (the best-performing U.S. companies) and similar listings of banks and major foreign companies are useful references, also obtainable from the magazine's website.

Semimonthly *Forbes* magazine (www.forbes.com) takes the investor's viewpoint, providing detailed and searching analyses of individual companies and their managements. The annual January issue, which reviews the performance of major U.S. industries, is an excellent source of information on industry trends and ranks companies by a series of criteria.

For an international outlook, the weekly British magazine *The Economist* (www.economist.com) surveys international and United Kingdom developments in politics, economics, and business, and also discusses U.S. developments and business conditions in depth, supplemented by special features. It can be considered an international *Business Week*, as can *World Business*.

Economic and business trends are covered in considerable detail in publications of major commercial banks such as the *National City Bank Monthly Letter* and *New England Letter* of the First National Bank of Boston. The various Federal Reserve banks' general bulletins and regional bulletins contain regional economic data, and the St. Louis Federal Reserve Bank has an especially useful website (stls-frb.org/fred) which contains economic data series and a wide variety of statistics.

The bimonthly *Harvard Business Review* (hbsp.harvard.edu), a highly regarded forum for discussion of management concepts and tools, includes financial insights from practitioners and academicians for an extensive worldwide readership of business executives. Several other major business schools publish journals of similar orientation, and most of these can be found on websites specific to the journal or to the university.

Dun's Review presents trade indexes, data on business failures, and key financial ratios in addition to articles about industry and commerce. *Nation's Business*, a publication of the U.S. Chamber of Commerce, presents general articles on business subjects. The *Federal Reserve Bulletin* contains much statistical data on business and government finances, both domestic and international. The *Survey of Current Business* also provides extensive business statistics.

Detailed stock exchange quotations and data about many unlisted securities (those not traded on a recognized exchange), foreign exchange, and money rates are contained in the *Bank and Quotation Record*. The quarterly *Journal of Finance* presents articles on finance, investments, economics, money, and credit, including international aspects of these topics.

Other Periodicals

Many specialized periodicals are published by trade associations and banking, commercial, and trading groups too numerous to mention. Also useful are the great variety of U.S. government surveys and publications, statistical papers provided by the United Nations and its major agencies, and the various analyses and reviews in academic journals. The end of this appendix lists several books that provide detailed guidelines on and descriptions of the type of information available from various sources.

Listed below are some major periodicals that deal directly with, or relate to, corporate finance. Many other relevant publications are also available. Some publications are specialized and oriented toward a specific community of interest; others deal with financial conditions in foreign countries. The titles are largely self-explanatory:

Banker's Magazine	*Journal of Banking and Finance*
CFO Magazine	*Journal of Commerce*
Corporate Financing	*Management Accounting*
Credit and Financial Management	*Managerial Finance*
Finance	*Mergers and Acquisitions*
Financial Analysts Journal	(U.S. and British editions)
Financial Executive	*National Tax Journal*
Financial Management	*Shareholder Value*
Financial World	*World Financial Markets*

Other Background Information

Annual Reports

The most commonly used reference source about the current affairs of publicly held corporations is the annual report furnished to shareholders, supplemented by briefer quarterly reports. The formats used by individual corporations vary widely from detailed coverage (that may even include current corporate, industry, and national issues) to a bare minimum disclosure of financial results. Nevertheless, the annual report is generally an important direct source of financial information. Because the disclosure requirements of the Securities and Exchange Commission

(SEC), the recommendations of the accounting profession, and state laws have become more and more demanding over time, the analyst can usually count on annual reports presenting a fairly consistent set of data. Annual reports can be obtained directly from the companies by looking up their addresses in the websites listed earlier, or from services provided by newspapers and periodicals, such as *The Wall Street Journal,* which indicate which company's reports are available in its stock quotation columns.

Financial Manuals and Services

Most current financial and economic information is now available through various on-line services and information subscription services. This includes information available in published manuals and services. The most popular and best-known set of these is provided by Moody's (www.moodys.com), with Standard & Poor's (www.standardpoors.com) a close second. Moody's publishes several volumes: *Industrials, Banks and Finance, Insurance, Public Utilities, Transportation, Municipals, Government, OTC* (over the counter), and *International.* These manuals are published each year and contain up-to-date key historical data, financial statements, securities price ranges, dividend records, and debt ratings for a large number of companies, including practically all publicly held corporations. Moody's manuals are updated through semiweekly supplements with detailed cross-references.

Moody's *Quarterly Handbook* gives one-page summaries of key financial and operating data for major publicly held corporations. Furthermore, Moody's weekly stock and bond surveys analyze market and industry conditions. Besides its semiweekly *Dividend Record,* a semimonthly *Bond Record* contains current prices, earnings, and ratings of most important bonds traded in this country.

Standard & Poor's publications include the *Standard Corporation Records.* This financial information about a large number of companies is published in looseleaf format and is updated through daily supplements. A useful S&P publication, the *Analysts Handbook,* provides industry surveys with key financial data on individual companies and some industries. Standard & Poor's other services include several dealing with the bond market, weekly forecasts of the security markets, securities statistics, and a monthly earnings and stock rating guide. Standard and Poor's also provides the *Compustat* service, which makes available in electronic form highly detailed up-to-date company statistics for analysis purposes.

Financial services similar to Moody's and Standard & Poor's are provided by Fitch's *Corporation Manuals* and by more specialized manuals such as Walker's *Manual of Unlisted Stocks.* An almost overwhelming flow of information, judgments, and analyses of individual companies from an investor's standpoint is provided by the major brokerage houses. Furthermore, services available to individuals on a subscription basis provide up-to-date financial analyses and evaluations of individual companies and their securities. The most important among these services are *Value Line* (www.valueline.com), *United Business Service, Babson's,* and *Investor's Management Sciences.* The *Value Line* investment survey provides ratings and reports on companies, with selections and opinions for the investor, whereas *Investor's Management Services* concentrates on providing a great deal of standardized statistical information as the basis for making analytical judgments. *Dun & Bradstreet's* (www.dnb.com) credit information services help in evaluating small or unlisted companies.

Business to Government Reporting

More specific details about company operations can often be found in the annual statement that corporations must file with the SEC in Washington, D.C. This information is filed on Form 10-K and supplemented by quarterly 10-Q reports. Furthermore, when a corporation wants to issue new securities in significant amounts or alter its capital structure in a major way, the detailed proposal that must be filed with the SEC, the *prospectus*, is generally a more complete source of company background data than is the normal annual report. It will cover the history of the company, ownership patterns, directors and top management, financial and operating data, products, facilities, and information regarding the intended use of the new funds. Most of these publicly filed reports are now available on-line via the SEC's "Edgar" service (www.sec.gov/edgarhp.htm). If a company is closely held (most of the shares are held by founders, their families, and key employees) or too small to be listed by the key financial services, information about its financial operations can often be obtained from the corporation records departments of the states in which the company does business. Again, these reports are open to the public for inspection.

Trade Associations

Trade associations, which number in the hundreds, are a prime source of information about their respective industries. A great deal of statistical information is available annually or more often and covers products, services, finances, and performance criteria applicable to the industry or trade group. Often financial and performance data are grouped by types and sizes of firms to make overall statistics on the industry more applicable to a particular operation. Trade associations include the American Electronics Association, Automotive Parts and Accessories Association, and the American Paper Institute, to name but a few. Sources for listings and addresses of these associations and their publications can be found in the references at the end of the appendix or on-line through the Yahoo search engine.

Econometric Services

Many forecasts of U.S. and international economic conditions are available to the financial analyst. Based on econometric models developed by a variety of academic institutions and economic advisory services, these forecasts of the U.S. economy and more recently of other countries' economies as well can provide valuable clues regarding the likely movement of the economy within which financial conditions must be viewed. Among the widely quoted and used econometric models are those developed by the Wharton School at the University of Pennsylvania, Data Resources Inc., and Chase Econometric Associates. Many corporations subscribe to such forecasting services and use the projections in their operational and financial planning. Increasingly, corporate and academic economists are testing their own assumptions about economic trends with the help of econometric models. Another feature of these services is the growing variety of on-line databases containing a vast array of statistical and financial information for immediate access.

Although we've merely touched on the major sources of specific or general information on financial business affairs, the reader is encouraged to make use of the sources discussed as well as the references at the end of this appendix. In addition, a great deal of information is available from various business libraries in corporations, colleges, and universities as well as from local institutions. The problem facing a financial analyst, whether student or professional, isn't a lack of data; rather, it's selecting what's truly relevant.

Selected References

Fabozzi, Frank J., and Franco Modigliani. *Capital Markets*. Upper Saddle River, NJ: Prentice Hall, 1996.

Ibbotson, Roger G., and Rex A. Sinquefield. *Stocks, Bonds, Bills and Inflation*. Chicago: Ibbotson Associates. (Annual yearbook.)

Lehmann, Michael B. *The Dow Jones–Irwin Guide to Using* The Wall Street Journal. Burr Ridge, IL: Dow Jones–Irwin, 1990.

Novallo, Annette. *Information Industry Directory*. 14th ed. Detroit: Gale Research, 1993.

Pierce, Phyllis S., ed. *The Dow Jones Averages 1885–1990*. Burr Ridge, IL: Business One Irwin, 1991.

Virtual Finance Library, Ohio State University (www.cob.ohio-state.edu/dept/fin/overview.htm).

Way, James, ed. *Encyclopedia of Business Information Sources*. 9th ed. Detroit: Gale Research, 1992.

APPENDIX IV

Basic Inflation Concepts

Throughout this book we've referred to inflation's distorting effects on financial decisions and analysis. In this appendix, we'll offer a brief commentary on the basic nature of the often misunderstood phenomenon of inflation. Financial transactions are carried out and recorded with the help of a common medium of exchange, such as U.S. dollars. Variations in this medium will affect the numerical meaning of these transactions. But we know that underlying the transactions are economic trade-offs; that is, values are given and received. We must be careful not to confuse changes in economic values with changes in the medium used to effect and account for these transactions. We'll examine the ramifications of this important distinction in several contexts below.

Price Level Changes

The economic values of goods and services invariably change over time. The reason for this is as basic as human nature: The law of supply and demand operates, in an uncontrolled market environment, to increase the value of goods and services that are in short supply, and to decrease the value of those available in abundance. This shift in relative values takes place even in a primitive barter economy that doesn't utilize any currency at all. The ratio of exchange of coconuts for beans, for example, will move in favor of coconuts when they're scarce, and in favor of beans when these are out of season.

Many seasonal agricultural products go through a familiar price cycle, beginning with their temporary unavailability, on to the first arrivals in the marketplace, and eventually to an abundance before they become unavailable again. This phenomenon is not limited to seasonal goods, however. Natural resources go through cycles of availability, be it from the need to set up the expensive infrastructure to exploit new sources as old ones expire, or from extreme concerted actions such as OPEC's moves to limit production in the 1970s and 80s that caused world oil prices to surge because of the cartel's control of over half the world's production. As alternative sources of oil and other energy were stimulated by the high prices, the cartel's power began to wane, hastened by inevitable squabbles among the member countries trying to look out for their own interests—and oil prices settled on a much lower, more sustainable level.

We know that the economic value of manufactured goods is similarly subject to the law of supply and demand. For example, as new technology emerges in the market, such as the first digital watches or compact disk players, or successive waves of innovation in electronic chips and other components, the price commanded by the early units will be well above the prices charged later on, after many suppliers have entered the market and competed for a share of industrial or consumer demand. The same is true of all goods and services for which there are present or potential alternative suppliers, domestic or international.

Our point here is that the economic value underlying personal, commercial, and financial transactions is determined by forces that are largely independent of the monetary expression in which they're recorded. As we'll see, an analysis of price level changes ideally should separate the change in price levels caused by shifts in economic value from those caused by changes in the currency itself. Accurate separation of the two is difficult in practice, but necessary for understanding the meaning of financial projections.

Monetary Inflation

Another phenomenon affecting transaction values is any basic change in the purchasing power of the currency. There are many reasons underlying the decline or strengthening of a currency's value as a medium of exchange. One of the most important factors causing inflationary declines in purchasing power is the amount of currency in circulation relative to economic activity. If the government raises the money supply faster than required to accommodate the growth in economic activity, there will literally be more dollars chasing relatively fewer goods and services, and thus the stated dollar prices for all goods and services will rise—even though the basic demand for any specific item may be unchanged.

This description is oversimplified, of course. A great many more factors affect currency values. One of these is the impact of government deficits and the way they are financed. Another is the value of the dollar relative to other currencies and the impact of exchange rates on international trade. In addition, international money flows and investment in response to more attractive investment opportunities cause shifts in the values of national currencies over and above the effects of the individual countries' fiscal and economic conditions. Union negotiations, wage settlements, and cost of living adjustments in wages, pensions, and Social Security are also related to changing currency values. Every nation's central bank—the Federal Reserve Bank in the case of the United States—is vital in the process because its policies affect both the size of the money supply and the level of interest rates. These in turn affect government fiscal policies, business activity, international trade and money flows, and so forth. And ultimately, serious declines in the value of a currency can also affect the basic supply and demand of goods and services, as, for example, when customers and businesses buy ahead to beat anticipated price increases.

The point here isn't to systematically analyze inflation and its causes, but rather to make the basic distinction between economic and monetary changes influencing price levels. Suffice it to say that price level changes due to monetary effects are largely the ones that distort economic values of personal and commercial transactions. If monetary conditions remained stable (that is, if the amount of currency in circulation always matched the level of economic activity), price level changes would reflect only changes in economic values—something we've agreed is at the core of management's efforts to improve the shareholders' economic condition. Because monetary stability is an unrealistic expectation; however, the challenge remains to make the analysis of the actual conditions affecting prices and economic values truly meaningful.

Nominal and Real Dollars

Business and personal transactions are expressed in terms of *nominal* dollars, also called current dollars, that reflect today's prices, unadjusted or altered in any way. For accounting purposes, nominal dollars are used every day to record transactions. However, when dollar prices change over time, the amounts recorded in the past no longer reflect current prices, either in terms of the underlying economic values or in terms of the value of the currency at the moment.

To deal with changes in the value of the currency, economists have devised *price indexes* intended to separate, at least in part, monetary distortions from fluctuations in economic value. Such an index is constructed by measuring the aggregate change in the prices of a representative group of products and services as a surrogate for the change in the value of the currency. Yet we already know that any goods and services chosen for this purpose are themselves also subject to changes in supply and demand, apart from mere currency fluctuations. But there's no direct way to measure changes in currency values as such. Inevitably, therefore, the price index approach involves mixing demand/supply conditions and currency values, and the only hope is that the selection of goods and services employed in a given index is broad enough to compensate somewhat for the underlying demand/supply conditions.

The *consumer price index*, a popular index of inflation, is calculated in this fashion. It's based on frequent sampling of the prices of a "market basket" of goods and services purchased by U.S. consumers, including food, housing, clothing, and transportation. The composition and weighting of this basket is changed gradually to reflect changing habits and tastes, although there is much room for argument about how representative and up-to-date the selection is. Another popular index applicable to business is the *producer price index*, based on a representative weighted sampling of the wholesale prices of goods produced. Other indexes deal with wholesale commodity prices and a variety of specialized groupings of products and services.

The broadest index in common use is applied to the gross national product as a whole, the *GNP deflator*, which expresses the price changes experienced in the total range of goods and services produced in the U.S. economy. Based on broad statistical sampling, the current level of the GNP deflator is announced frequently throughout the year in connection with other economic statistics about business and government activity. All of these indexes are prepared by calculating the changes in prices from those of a selected base year, which is changed only infrequently to avoid having to adjust comparative statistical series whenever the base year is changed.

The price indexes are used to translate nominal dollar values in government statistics and business reports into *real dollar values*. This involves converting nominal dollar values to a chosen standard so that past and present dollar transactions can be compared in equivalent terms. For example, to compare this year's performance of the economy to that of last year, we may choose to express current economic statistics using last year's dollars as the standard. Last year's dollars are then called real, and today's data are expressed in these real terms. To do this, we simply adjust today's dollars by the amount of inflation experienced since last year. If inflation this year was 3 percent over last year as expressed in the GNP deflator, every nominal dollar figure for this year would be adjusted downward by 3 percent. The result would be an expression of this year's results in terms of real dollars, which are based on the prior year.

A real dollar is thus simply a nominal dollar that has been adjusted to the price level of a particular stated base year, using one of the applicable price indexes. The base chosen can be any year, as long as past or future years are consistently stated in terms of the currency value for the base year. In fact, real dollars are often called *constant dollars*, a name that simply recognizes that they're derived from a constant base. The process of adjustment has the following effect: During inflationary periods, the real dollars for the years preceding the base year will be adjusted upward, whereas the real dollars of future years will be adjusted downward. The reverse is true, of course, if the period involves deflation instead.

To illustrate, let's assume that the following price developments took place during a five-year period. We're using the producer price index (PPI). This index was constructed on the basis of Year 0. In the following table, we've set Year 3 as the base year for our analysis.

	Year 1	Year 2	Year 3	Year 4	Year 5
Producer price index (Year 0)	1.09	1.15	1.21	1.25	1.33
Producer price index (Year 3)	0.90	0.95	1.00	1.03	1.10
Real value of $100 (base Year 3)	$111	$105	$100	$97	$91

Note that two steps were involved. First, the producer price index had to be adjusted for our chosen base, Year 3. That is, the index had to be set at 1.00 for Year 3 and then all index numbers were divided by the value of the index for the base year, which is 1.21. (However, the index could have been constructed on any other year because an index measures price changes year by year from whatever starting point is chosen.) The next step was to divide the adjusted index values on the second line into the nominal dollars of each year. We chose to use the amount of $100 for all years, but the process applies, of course, to any amount of nominal dollars in any one of the years. Using a single round figure permitted us to illustrate the shifts in value with a same dollar amount.

The example clearly shows that a dollar's purchasing power in Year 4 versus Year 3 declined by 3 percent. The implication from a business point of view is that a company must increase its nominal earnings power by 3 percent in order to keep up with inflation in the prices it must pay for goods and services. Anything less than that will leave the owners worse off.

This simple process allows us to convert nominal dollars into inflation-adjusted real dollars. Problems arise in choosing the proper index for a business situation, and also from the fact that the index embodies changes in economic value as well as in currency value, as we discussed earlier. Much thought has been expended on refining the process of inflation adjustment, but in the end, the judgment about its usefulness depends on the purpose of the analysis and the degree of accuracy desired.

Applications of Inflation Adjustment in Financial Analysis

Restatement of company data or projections in real dollar terms is at times useful to assess whether the company's performance has kept up with shifts in currency values. Such restatement may be used to value a company's assets and liabilities, or to show the real growth or decline in sales and earnings. As we observed, publicly traded companies are obligated to include an annual inflation-adjusted restatement of key data in their published shareholder reports.

Much effort can be spent on adjusting financial projections for inflation, particularly in the area of capital investment analysis. There are no truly satisfactory general rules for this process, however. When an analyst must project cash flows from a major capital investment, the easiest approach continues to be projection in nominal dollars, taking into account expected cost and price increases of the key variables involved, tailored specifically to the conditions of the business. The discount standard applied against the projection must also be based on nominal return expectations that, of course, embody the inflationary outlook.

To refine the analysis, many companies prepare projections in real dollars, attempting to forecast the true economic increases or decreases in costs and prices. Then an appropriate inflation index is applied to the figures to convert them into nominal dollars. The problem is, however, that the margin between revenues and costs may widen unduly, simply because the same inflation index is applied to the larger revenue numbers and to the smaller cost numbers. Often arbitrary adjustments have to be made to keep the margin spread manageable.

Another approach involves developing projections expressed in real dollars and discounting these with a return standard that has also been converted into real returns. The result will be internally consistent as far as the project is concerned. However, the result is not readily comparable with the current overall performance of the business—recorded and expressed in nominal dollar terms—unless the company has also found a way to convert and measure ongoing performance in real dollar terms. Some companies are beginning to experiment with such restated reports and measures, but the approach involves a massive effort, both in terms of data preparation and education of personnel generating and using the projections and performance data. It's instinctively easier to think about business in nominal dollars than real dollars, and progress in this area is being made only gradually. The complexities are such that the financial and planning staffs of companies wishing to use this approach face a lengthy conceptual and practical conversion problem.

Impact of Inflation

To restate quickly, the basic impact of inflation—and the much less common opposite situation, deflation—is a growing distortion of recorded values on a company's financial statements, and an ongoing partial distortion of operating results. Accounting methods discussed in Chapters 1 and 2 are designed to make the effect of the inflationary distortion at least consistent. In terms of cash flows, inflation distorts a company's tax payments if the taxes due are based on low historical cost apportionment, and it results in a cash drain if dividends are higher than they would be if real dollar earnings were considered, to name two examples. Inflation also affects financing conditions, particularly the repayment of principal on long-term debt obligations. As we observed before, however, the mediating influence of interest rates—which respond to inflation expectations—tends to prevent windfalls for the borrower looking to repay debt with "cheap" dollars. Normally, over the long run, distortions from inflation affect lenders and borrowers alike. Relative advantages gained by one over the other are only temporary.

Overall, the subject of inflation adjustments continues to evolve in financial analysis. It's unlikely that totally consistent methods that are generally applicable will be found.

APPENDIX V

Some Issues in Multinational Financial Analysis

In Chapter 3 we developed the principles of performance analysis and stressed the need for management to derive an economic return from the resources entrusted to them. The analysis involved such measures as profit margins, return on assets, and return on net worth, seen from different points of view. We also related the various measures within a system of ratios to show the different levers management can use to improve the profitability of the business and to create shareholder value. We'll briefly discuss some of the challenges generally encountered in measuring multibusiness companies, and then turn to the particular issues arising from operating with different national currencies.

General Performance Analysis Challenges

Performance measures work best when applied to a total business entity, where investment, operations, and financing are collectively controlled and managed by a management team. It's possible to derive both return on investment (ROI) and return on equity (ROE)—the latter allowing for the effect of financial leverage. Recall the expanded formula for return on equity:

$$\text{ROE} = \frac{\text{Net profit}}{\text{Sales}} \times \frac{\text{Sales}}{\text{Assets}} \times \frac{\text{Assets}}{\text{Assets} - \text{Liabilities}}$$

where the first element represents operations, the second element investment, and the third financial leverage. Also, as we discussed in Chapters 10 and 11, various cash flow analysis approaches can be applied to judge the performance and the value of the company.

Complications arise when the measures are applied to segments of a multiunit company, where individual units are responsible for investment and operations only, and financing remains a corporate headquarters function. In this case, the units are normally measured on a return on investment basis only, employing concepts such as return on total assets (ROA), return on net assets (RONA), or return on average assets employed (ROAE), modified to suit the needs of the particular company. The management of financial leverage doesn't enter in here. Recall the formula for return on assets:

$$\text{ROA} = \frac{\text{Net Profit}}{\text{Sales}} \times \frac{\text{Sales}}{\text{Assets}}$$

which, when applied to an operating unit, relates the unit's net profit (before or after taxes) to the unit's sales and its identifiable assets. Again, we can use cash flow

517

measures to judge the performance and the value of business units, but these require a variety of adjustments to make sure that all relevant cash flow elements have been considered, and that the appropriate return standards are applied.

Further complications arise when units within a large corporation supply goods and services to each other. The most difficult aspect is the issue of setting appropriate transfer prices for the value of the goods and services moving between units of the corporation. At times, readily available, clearly established market prices can be used to value these transfers. More often than not, however, transfer prices have to be set through negotiation or even by corporate decree. There are no entirely satisfactory approaches to resolving this often vexing issue, which not only can cause serious distortions in the results of individual units, but—even more significantly—may distort the decisions of unit managers and cause them to over- or underinvest, or to suboptimize their operations.

International Performance Analysis Challenges

The issue of measuring the performance of a business becomes particularly challenging when operations extend into the international arena, either when divisions are operating entirely within a foreign country, or when organizational entities perform transactions in several currencies. In the former situation, the division usually can be viewed as a rather independent entity—albeit operating with a foreign currency—whereas in the latter case, the flow of goods and services across borders introduces significant measurement problems. All of the measurement issues we mentioned earlier usually apply to foreign operations as well, but in addition there's the problem of measuring the impact of absolute and relative changes in the different currencies involved.

Foreign Subsidiaries Operating in a Single Country

The simplest case involves a wholly owned subsidiary, which for all practical purposes acts as part of the host country, and which keeps its books and financial statements in the local currency. The key measurements in which the U.S. parent company will be interested are current earnings performance and the valuation of the subsidiary.

Given that all transactions and cost accounting steps are carried out in the local currency, the calculation of earnings performance through various ratios will be internally consistent and unaffected by currency fluctuations and exchange rates. Whether the subsidiary operates in Euros, English pounds, or Brazilian cruzeiros, performance measures will indicate the effectiveness with which the subsidiary's assets are employed, and various ratios used to measure performance will give appropriate readings.

Because the U.S. parent company will also be interested in viewing the level of earnings as expressed in U.S. dollars, particularly for purposes of consolidating the earnings, exchange rates must be brought into play. We can represent the situation in the form of some simple formulas, revisiting the discussions of Chapters 3 and 5. If we simulate the subsidiary's earnings in dollars ($E\$$) by denoting unit price (P), variable costs (C), fixed costs (F), unit volume (V), and exchange rate (R), and denote all relevant components in terms of the foreign currency (f), the simple equation is

$$\text{Subsidiary } E_\$ = R\left[(P_f - C_f)\, V - F_f\right]$$

Clearly the exchange rate R affects all financial terms in the formulation, and the dollar earnings reported will be a function of the level of exchange between the dollar and the foreign currency involved. There's nothing the subsidiary management can do about the exchange rate, which may fluctuate wildly or may be very stable. The subsidiary's earnings as such aren't affected—only their expression in dollar terms will be altered. The U.S. parent, on the other hand, may be quite affected by rising or falling exchange rates that will change the subsidiary's dollar earnings. We observed some of these effects in 3M's financial statements in Chapter 3.

When we wish to develop the dollar return on investment (return on assets) of the subsidiary ROI$), the only additional item needed to complete the formula is the amount of the subsidiary's assets denoted in the foreign currency (A_f):

$$ROI_\$ = \frac{R\left[(P_f - C_f)\, V - F_f\right]}{R \times A_f} = \frac{(P_f - C_f)\, V - F_f}{A_f} = ROI_f$$

Note that the exchange rate R drops out of the equation and the return on investment in dollar terms is equivalent to the return in foreign currency terms. As we stated earlier, ratio analysis performed on an entity with consistent accounting in a single currency will provide meaningful results independent of exchange rate concerns. Only the distortions inherent in the accounting system itself, as discussed in Chapters 2 and 3, will affect the stated amount of the division's assets.

The implications of this discussion are rather straightforward. The management of a subsidiary operating as a unit completely within a given country can be judged by using all standard ratios expressed in the local currency. But the inclusion of the subsidiary's foreign currency earnings in consolidated U.S. financial statements will be affected by any movement in the dollar exchange rates, as will the recording of foreign assets in U.S. dollar terms. The U.S. parent's financial statements may have to be adjusted frequently to account for exchange rate differences alone.

Distortions arising from significant inflationary trends will affect a foreign subsidiary in much the same way as businesses experienced inflation in the United States during the 1970s. In essence, recorded asset values will tend to be understated over time. To the extent that inflationary conditions in the foreign country exceed U.S. levels, it may be desirable to revalue the foreign subsidiary's balance sheet elements for analysis purposes to make sure that ratios derived from the statement are internally consistent.

Valuation of the subsidiary in cash flow terms can be done by expressing the expected cash inflows in the foreign currency and discounting these to arrive at the present value, as we did in Chapter 10. Note that the issues of price, volume, and cost as well as ongoing value will remain consistent through the use of the foreign currency in which they occur. All of the issues surrounding the estimates of future conditions in markets, costs, economic developments, and so on will apply here as they would in the United States. The final result can then be translated into U.S. dollars at the prevailing exchange rate, if desired.

Subsidiaries Operating across Foreign Borders

A more common consequence of the continued expansion of international trade is the need for a corporate entity to do business in several countries and in their respective currencies. Now the issue of exchange rates begins to loom large, because both earnings calculations and performance measures will be affected by the mix of currencies on the company's books. Let's take the simplified example of a *cross-border subsidiary* that imports goods from the U.S. parent company and sells these goods within the foreign country in which it operates. Let's further assume that the U.S. parent requires payment for the goods in dollars, whereas the subsidiary quotes and sells the goods in the local currency. Moreover, all other costs of the subsidiary will be incurred in the local currency as well.

We can again write the equation for the dollar earnings of the subsidiary ($E\$$), taking into account the fact that its variable costs are incurred in dollars:

$$\text{Subsidiary } E_\$ = R \left[(P_f - \frac{C_\$}{R}) V - F_f \right]$$

This equation simply describes the subsidiary's condition in which prices and fixed costs have to be converted into dollars, while variable costs are already incurred in dollars.

The complications that can arise from this situation are apparent. No longer does the exchange rate simply apply to earnings as it did in the case of the single-country subsidiary. Now the exchange rate additionally affects a highly significant cost element in the subsidiary's cost structure. Any movement in the exchange rate during a period of operations will directly affect the subsidiary's cost of goods sold. For example, if the foreign currency weakens from four units per U.S. dollar to six, the subsidiary has suffered a 50 percent increase in its cost of goods sold because it must obtain dollars for payment to its U.S. parent that have become 50 percent more expensive. This could severely affect the subsidiary's competitive position in the local market unless it can readily pass on this price increase. An opposite effect will, of course, occur if the exchange rate moves in favor of the local currency, such as from four units per U.S. dollar to three.

The impact on the subsidiary's performance measures of exchange rate movement depends on a number of factors. If significant price changes in the subsidiary's cost of goods sold due to the U.S. dollar exchange rate don't affect its market position because it can adjust the price of the goods based on the change in cost—a highly unrealistic assumption—the performance ratios are likely to be unaffected. In reality, changes in the cost of goods sold will normally impact the subsidiary's ability to compete locally, and attempts to price according to cost will not only affect the volume of units sold, but also change operational costs because of these volume changes.

It's not possible to develop a simple formula approach here, because the total operating system of the subsidiary will be affected in largely unpredictable ways. For example, any attempted price changes are likely to be less than proportional to the change in the cost of goods sold, in order to minimize the competitive impact. Market reactions to these price changes will largely depend on the subsidiary's market position, the quality and price of competitive goods, the availability of competitive substitutes from sources not subject to similar exchange rate fluctuations, and so on. It will usually be best to model the major dimensions of the subsidiary's business system and to simulate a variety of assumptions about price, volume, and cost changes.

The basic calculation in Figure V–1 on the next page shows the type of analysis that will help gauge the effect on the subsidiary's earnings and ROA under several assumed conditions. Clearly, more specific knowledge about local market conditions would have to be applied to refine the range of estimates, and more of the underlying variables would have to be modeled to obtain a clearer picture of the impact of currency exchange rates.

This set of assumptions reflects conditions in two time periods, with exchange rates allowed to move significantly in the current period away from the conditions of the prior period. The foreign selling price was assumed to increase slightly in the current period under stable exchange rates (second column). The impact of this 10 percent price increase is a doubling of foreign earnings from f5,000 to f10,000, and a parallel doubling of the dollar earnings. Note that the ROI reflects this doubling as well.

As the dollar strengthens in the third column, the foreign purchase cost per unit jumps 50 percent, and the subsidiary tries to increase the price to recover the extra cost. This is likely to depress the volume sold—here it's assumed to drop by 25 percent. Higher-cost inventories will also increase the subsidiary's asset base by an assumed f6,000. While earnings in the foreign currency decline by 37.5 percent, the ROI is cut in half because of the impact of higher-cost inventories on the asset base. The dollar earnings, however, suffer an even greater decline due to the strengthening of the dollar exchange rate.

The fourth column reflects a weakening of the dollar, which makes U.S. goods cheaper to import. In fact, the cost to the subsidiary drops to 50 percent of the stronger dollar condition in the third column. We assume that the subsidiary will pass on much of this in the form of a lower price, which raises the number of units sold by 10 percent, to 1,100. Revenues are now the same as in the case of the stable exchange rate in the second column. Note, however, the impact of the reduction in costs on the foreign earnings, which soar to f17,000 and are reflected in the ROI of 63 percent—which in turn is boosted by the drop in assets due to

| FIGURE V–1 | | | | |

Impact on Subsidiary Earnings and ROA Using Several Assumed Exchange Rate Conditions

	Current Period			
Variable	Prior Period	Constant Exchange Rate	Dollar Strengthens	Dollar Weakens
Exchange rate (R)	$0.25	$0.25	$0.17	$0.33
(U.S. dollars/foreign currency)				
Selling price per unit (P_f)	f50.00	f55.00	f75.00	f50.00
Purchased cost per unit (C_s)	$10.00	$10.00	$10.00	$10.00
Purchased cost per unit (C_f)	f40.00	f40.00	f60.00	f30.00
Number of units sold (V)	1,000	1,000	750	1,100
Subsidiary assets (A_f)	f30,000	f30,000	f36,000	f27,000
Earnings, ROI in foreign currency:				
Revenues	f50,000	f55,000	f56,250	f55,000
Cost of goods sold	40,000	40,000	45,000	33,000
Fixed costs	5,000	5,000	5,000	5,000
Earnings	5,000	10,000	6,250	17,000
ROI	17%	33%	17%	63%
Earnings in U.S. dollars	$1,250	$2,500	$1,063	$5,610

lower-cost inventories. In addition, the weaker dollar exchange rate escalates the dollar earnings to more than twice the level of the second column, an increase of 124 percent!

It should be clear from this highly simplified example that we must thoroughly analyze the dynamics of the foreign markets and conditions in addition to assessing the mere reflection of currency exchange rates as changes occur. You're invited to trace through a variety of assumptions in this simple model to gain further insight into the dynamics at play.

More complexity is introduced when differing inflation rates in various countries are taken into account. As was experienced in the United States during the 1970s, inflationary conditions don't necessarily increase operating earnings proportionally, as the prices of inputs like materials, labor, and fuel don't necessarily move in concert. Thus, a detailed analysis of the impact of foreign operations requires much more insight than this brief exposure could provide.

We should briefly mention another aspect of foreign currency transactions here. Companies engaged in buying, selling, and operating in various foreign currencies will use, whenever possible, the concept of *hedging* to protect themselves from even temporary exposure to currency fluctuations. In simple terms, hedging involves the simultaneous purchase or sale of foreign currency contracts that offset the amounts of the commercial transaction undertaken. For example, if a U.S. company sells goods into a foreign market and expects to be paid in the foreign currency some 30 or 60 days hence, the company's treasurer may execute a simultaneous contract to sell an equivalent amount of foreign currency at that time, but based on today's exchange rate. Such a currency contract, called a *forward trade*, exemplifies a common transaction in the worldwide market for currencies. The purpose of currency hedging is in effect to lock in the prevailing exchange rate and to avoid the risk of fluctuations. Again, there are many more aspects of foreign currency management than we can cover in a book of this scope. Readers should turn to specialized materials on these subjects for in-depth coverage.

APPENDIX VI

Solutions to Self-Study
Exercises and Problems

This appendix contains solutions to selected end-of-chapter problems. Note that some of the exercises not shown here require use of the *Interactive Templates*, which are downloadable from the Web, and the available financial analysis software, *Financial Genome*, which is described in more detail in Appendix I.

Chapter 1

Both exercises at the end of this chapter are designed to explore and understand the business systems concept with the help of the Interactive Templates and Financial Genome. No specific solutions are intended here. You are urged to examine and follow the built-in help systems in both software applications to obtain the most benefits from this experience.

Chapter 2

1. *a*. ABC COMPANY

Beginning balance, retained earnings (12/31/02)		$167,300
Less:		
Net operating loss for 2003*	$14,100	
Common dividends paid	12,000	
Inventory-write-down	24,000	
Loss from sale of equipment	4,000	
Total effect on retained earnings		54,100
Ending balance, retained earnings (12/31/03)		$113,200

*Assume that depreciation and amortization were subtracted in the income statement, but not the loss on sale of equipment or the inventory write-down.

Cash Flow Items

Sources		Uses	
Depreciation	$21,000	Net operating loss	$14,100
Amortization of good will, patents	15,000	Dividends paid	12,000
		Investment in fixed assets	57,500
Total	$36,000	Total	$83,600

Depreciation (a noncash item) should be reflected as a source because it originally reduced operating profit/loss; loss conditions don't change its basic character. Similarly, amortization reduces assets and retained earnings equally; it does not affect cash and must also be added back. Loss from sale of equipment was offset by reduction in assets and does not affect cash as was the inventory write-down. A gain from a sale of equipment could be shown as a separate source, because it represents an increase in cash.

b. DEF COMPANY

The layout of the data is:

	Beginning Balance	Additions	Reductions	Ending Balance	Change
Gross property and fixed assets	$8,431,500*	$1,250,500*	$1,252,000†	$8,430,000*	$ (1,500)
Accumulated depreciation	3,513,000*	1,613,000*	1,252,000‡	3,874,000*	361,000
Net property and fixed assets	$4,918,500	$ (362,500)	-0-	$4,556,000	$(362,500)
					(Result)

The result is built up from:
˙Given information.
†Forced figures.
‡Assumption that fully depreciated assets were abandoned.

Observations   Any assumption about a gain or loss on sale and/or abandonment would be handled as in item *1a*. Any disposition of partially depreciated assets would cause greater "reductions" in assets than in accumulated depreciation, which in turn would raise the derived asset additions.

2.   CBA COMPANY
Changes in Balance Sheets 2002–2003
($ thousands)

Assets		Liabilities	
Cash	$(12.2)	Accounts payable	$11.8
Marketable securities	10.0	Notes payable	90.0
Accounts receivable	(8.8)	Accrued expenses	2.9
Inventories	60.7	Total current liabilities	$104.7
Total current assets	49.7		
Land	-0-	Mortgage payable	$ (15.2)
Plant and equipment (net)	19.6	Common stock	5.0
Total fixed assets	19.6	Retained earnings	(17.0)
Other assets	8.2	Total shareholders equity	$ (12.0)
Total assets	$ 77.5	Total liabilities and shareholders' equity	$ 77.5

Cash Flow Statement, 2003

Sources		Uses	
Depreciation	$ 32.2*	Loss from operations	$ 2.0*
Decrease in cash	12.2	Dividends paid	15.0†
Decrease in accounts receivable	8.8	Increase in securities	10.0
Increase in accounts payable	11.8	Increase in inventories	60.7
Increase in notes payable	90.0	Investment in plant	51.8†
Increase in accrued expenses	2.9	Increase in other assets	8.2
Increase in common stock	5.0	Decrease in mortgage	15.2
Total	$162.9	Total	$162.9

The results were built up from:

*Taken from 2003 income statement.

†Change in retained earnings matches the combination of loss from operations ($2,000) on the 2003 income statement and dividends paid ($15,000). No extraordinary items appear and no assumptions are necessary.

‡Since net plant and equipment increased by $19,600, and the only known element affecting the account is depreciation ($32,200), the amount of investment must have been the sum of these amounts ($51,800).

Observations   The biggest single use is a drastic rise in inventories, even though sales volume changed little. Are inventory controls failing? Dividends were wisely cut as profits plummeted. The key funds source was borrowing (short term) $90 which provided more than half the funds needs. Sizable capital investment (almost twice depreciation) points to optimistic future plans—any problems in sight? Is the company beginning to lean on suppliers? (Accounts payable are up somewhat.) Is equity capital called for?

4. ZYX Company

A variety of cash flow statements are possible here:
From peak to trough of season (two seasons).
From peak to peak, or trough to trough.
From April to April, or any other month.
Two-year span, July to July, to provide a long-term perspective.

Samples of these possible cash flow statements are:

	1/31/03 to 4/30/03	1/31/04 to 4/30/04	4/30/02 to 1/31/04	1/31/02 to 1/31/04	4/30/02 to 4/30/04	7/31/02 to 7/31/04
Sources of Cash						
Profit from operations	$ 10	$ 17	$ 67	$ 77	$ 84	$172
Depreciation	6	7	21	27	28	54
Decrease in cash	—	—	1	—	—	5
Decrease in receivables	191	237	—	—	—	11
Decrease in inventories	184	253	—	—	33	—
Decrease in other assets	1	—	—	—	—	—
Increase in payables	—	—	85	67	—	16
Increase in notes	—	—	342	48	—	45
Increase in common	—	—	25	25	25	25
Total sources	$392	$514	$541	$244	$170	$328
Uses of Cash						
Capital investments	$ 48	$ 50	—	$ 48	$ 50	$ 98
Increase in cash	17	13	—	16	12	—
Increase in receivables	—	—	$260	69	23	79
Increase in inventories	—	—	220	36	—	—
Increase in other assets	—	—	3	2	3	2
Decrease in payables	18	91	—	—	6	—
Decrease in notes	294	342	—	—	—	—
Decrease in mortgage	—	—	10	10	10	20
Dividends paid	15	18	48	63	66	129
Total uses	$392	$514	$541	$244	$170	$328

Observations   This strong seasonal pattern from January to April shows up vividly in the peak to trough and trough to peak comparisons, where receivables and inventories are matched with payables and sizable short-term notes. There's a lag effect in the buildup of inventories and receivables, as expected. Growth shows up in like to like comparisons, with no undue strains. This is a good example of the effect of thoughtful placement of cash flow analysis over alternative time periods.

Chapter 3

Note that exercises 1 and 2 are based on the use of Interactive Templates, downloadable from the Web, or the available financial analysis software, Financial Genome, which is described in more detail in Appendix I.

   3. *a.*

$$\frac{\text{Net profit}}{\text{Sales}} = 11.4\%; \frac{\text{Sales}}{\text{Assets}} = 1.34$$

$$\text{Assets} = \frac{\text{Sales}}{1.34} \text{ (i.e., Sales > Assets); Sales} = 1.34 \times \text{Assets}$$

Thus

$$\frac{\text{Net profit}}{\text{Assets}} = \frac{\text{Net profit}}{\dfrac{\text{Sales}}{1.34}} = 11.4\%(1.34) = 15.28\%$$

If we assume no debt in the capitalization, then shareholders' equity equals capitalization. Thus

$$\frac{\text{Net profit}}{\text{Capitalization}} = \frac{\text{Net profit}}{\text{Shareholders' equity}} = \frac{1}{0.67} \times \frac{\text{Net profit}}{\text{Assets}}$$

Return on shareholders' equity is

$$\frac{15.28}{0.67} = 22.8\%$$

A faster asset turnover means a smaller asset base and smaller capitalization relative to sales. Thus, return figures go up.

3. c.   Changes in current ratio and effect on working capital:

$$\text{Current ratio: 2.2 to 1} = \frac{\$573,100}{\$260,500}$$

(The $260,500 is derived from the relationship.)

Working capital: $573,100 − $260,500 = $312,600

(1) Payment of accounts payable:

Decrease in cash	$67,500
Decrease in payables	$67,500

Both current assets and current liabilities are reduced by the same amount; this improves the current ratio but leaves working capital unaffected:

$$\frac{\$573,100 - \$67,500}{\$260,500 - \$67,500} = \frac{\$505,600}{\$193,000} = 2.62 \text{ to } 1$$

This is a common action taken by small companies at year-end to improve their current ratio.

(2) Collection of note.

Increase in cash	$33,000
Decrease in notes receivable	$33,000

Both elements are within current assets; thus there's no net effect on either the current ratio or the working capital.

(3) Purchase on account:

Increase in inventory	$41,300
Increase in payables	$41,300

Both current assets and current liabilities are increased; thus the opposite effect of exercise (1), with working capital unaffected:

$$\frac{\$573,100 + \$41,300}{\$260,500 + \$41,300} = \frac{\$614,400}{\$301,800} = 2.04 \text{ to } 1$$

(4) Dividend payment:

Decrease in cash	$60,000
Decrease in accrued dividends	$42,000
Decrease in retained earnings	$18,000 (no effect)

The effect on the two elements is uneven; thus changes occur in both the current ratio and working capital:

$$\frac{\$573,100 - \$60,000}{\$260,500 - \$42,000} = \frac{\$513,100}{\$218,500} = 2.35 \text{ to } 1$$

The current ratio is slightly improved, while working capital drops by $18,000.

(5) Machine sale:

Increase in cash	$ 80,000
Decrease in fixed assets	$202,000 (no effect)
Decrease in accumulated depreciation	$112,000 (no effect)
Loss on sale of assets	$ 10,000 (no effect)

The only effect is an increase in current assets, which increases both the ratio and working capital:

$$\frac{\$573,100 + \$80,000}{\$260,500} = \frac{\$653,100}{\$260,500} = 2.51 \text{ to } 1$$

The current ratio rises to 2.51, while working capital improves by $80,000.

(6) Sale of merchandise:

Increase in receivables	$109,700*
Decrease in inventory	$ 73,500
Increase in operating profit	$ 36,200 (no effect)

*Derived from $\dfrac{\$73,500}{1.0 - 0.33} = \$109,700.$

There's a net increase in current assets, which improves the current ratio and working capital:

$$\frac{\$573,100 + \$109,700 - \$73,500}{\$260,500} = \frac{\$609,300}{\$260,500} = 2.34 \text{ to } 1$$

The current ratio rises to 2.34, while working capital improves by $36,200. (The potential increase in accrued income taxes has been ignored—it would worsen the current ratio and reduce working capital.)

(7) Write-offs:

Decrease in inventory	$20,000
Decrease in goodwill	$15,000 (no effect)
Decrease in retained earnings	$35,000 (no effect)

There's a reduction of current assets, which affects both the current ratio and working capital:

$$\frac{\$573,100 - \$20,000}{\$260,500} = \frac{\$553,100}{\$260,500} = 2.12 \text{ to } 1$$

The current ratio drops slightly to 2.12, while working capital is reduced by $20,000.

4. Three companies:

Calculating the various measures:

	A	B	C
ROE	15.0%	16.7%	25.0%
RONA	10.0%	8.3%	20.0%
ROS	12.0%	15.0%	10.0%
NOPAT	14	20	26
RONA before interest	11.7%	11.1%	20.8%

a. The best performance based on one year's operations is Company C, with all measures except return on sales superior, and at the same time having the lowest financial leverage. Company A and Company B are close; from an operational standpoint A is a little better, while B achieves a higher return on equity.

b. The difference is due to significant use debt (50 percent of capitalization). In a fluctuating environment Company A would likely do better. A series of data points and some insights into future expectations would be helpful.

c. RONA and operating return on net assets are differentiated by the interest paid on debt. A pure operational return puts A and B on about an equal footing.

d.   A new investment at 17 percent RONA will reduce overall RONA. But we know only about the first year, and not subsequent years, when depreciation charges will reduce the asset base, increasing the return given similar performance. However, investments cannot properly be judged on a one-year performance in accounting terms, but should be analyzed with discounted cash flow measures (Chapters 6 and 7).

e.   A combination of A and B will modify the results only slightly for the period shown. However, it is critical to know what future expectations will be for the two businesses, whether they reinforce each other, whether operational improvements can be expected, etc. Cash flow patterns would have to be established for this purpose (Chapters 10 and 11).

f.   A combination of A and C appears to benefit Company A and its owners, because all the measures are improved from their viewpoint, while Company C owners will see a reduced but still solid performance. The combination would make sense if Company A brought synergistic benefits to the combination, and also if the outlook for C was not as strong as the one year of performance indicates. The issue is a strategic one, not a question of ratio analysis alone (Chapters 10 and 11).

	A + B	A + C
Sales	$200	$350
Net assets	300	245
Shareholders equity	170	180
Long-term debt	130	65
Net profit after taxes	27	37
Aftertax interest	7	3
ROE	15.9%	20.6%
RONA	9.0%	15.1%
ROS	13.5%	10.6%
NOPAT	34	40
RONA before interest	11.3%	16.3%

5.   ABC Company

The various ratios are grouped by point of view:

a.   Management's view:

	2002	**2003**
Cost of goods sold	70.4%	70.6%
Gross margin	29.6%	29.4%
Profit margin	5.7%	5.4%
Profit before interest and taxes	10.7%	10.8%
Profit after taxes, before interest	5.8%	5.8%
Selling and administrative expenses	15.0%	14.4%
Employee profit sharing	4.1%	4.4%
Other income	0.2%	0.2%
Tax rate	46.0%	46.0%
Contribution	N.A.	N.A.
Gross asset turnover (Assets/Sales)	59.5%	64.6%
Net asset turnover (Assets/Sales)	39.4%	44.4%
Ending inventory turns (Cost of sales/Inventory)	5.2x	4.8x
Days' receivables	51.1 days	60.7 days
Days' payables (cost of sales)	34.0 days	37.0 days
Net profit to total assets	9.6%	6.3%
Net profit to capitalization	14.4%	12.1%
Net profit before interest and tax to total assets	18.0%	16.8%
Net profit before interest and tax to capitalization	27.2%	24.4%
Net profit after tax, before interest, to total assets	9.7%	9.0%
Net profit after tax, before interest, to capitalization	14.6%	13.2%

b.   Owner's view:

	2002	**2003**
Net profit to net worth (including deferred tax)	15.1%	16.3%
Net profit to common equity (w/o deferred tax)	15.2%	16.7%
Earnings per share	$3.69	$4.61
Cash flow per share	$6.48	$8.38
Dividends per share	$0.54	$0.59
Dividend coverage—earnings	6.8x	7.8x
Dividend coverage—cash flow	11.9x	14.2x

c.   Lender's view:

	2002	**2003**
Current ratio	2.1:1	2.2:1
Acid test (excluding advances)	1.3:1	1.4:1
Total debt to assets	35.7%	48.7%
Long-term debt to capitalization	3.0%	25.3%
Total debt to net worth	55.5%	95.0%
Long-term debt to net worth	3.1%	32.9%
Interest coverage (pretax)	70x	13x
Cash flow before taxes—interest coverage	98x	18x
Full interest coverage ($8.5 million)	—	11x

Observations   A slight worsening is shown in operating performance, at the same effective tax rate, which makes 2002 the better year. More investment has been committed both in working capital and fixed assets—collections are slowing, inventories are up, and profits on assets are down by every measure.

Leverage has improved the profit on net worth, however, and earnings per share are up sharply. No problems exist in covering dividends on interest, even if a full year's interest is assumed.

Comparisons should be made with companies in similar product lines, particularly on capital structure, return on net worth, and coverages. High-low analysis of good and bad years should highlight risk of earnings fluctuations. A two-year static picture isn't enough for good perspective.

Note that problems 6, 7, and 8 are open-ended analytical tasks using the available software program.

Chapter 4

   1. ***a.*** Change in credit policy:

        40 days' sales developed as follows:

$$\text{Daily sales: } \frac{\$9,137,000}{360} = \$25,381/\text{day}$$

        18 days' sales: 18 × \$25,381 = \$456,858
        40 days' sales: 40 × \$25,381 = \$1,015,240
        Increase in receivables: \$558,382

        60 days' sales:

        60 days' sales: 60 × \$25,381 = \$1,522,860
        Increase in receivables: \$1,066,002

Observations   Funds needs increase with 40 days is over \$500,000. Cash flow per year available from operations is only \$305,000. Likely the company must secure other funds. Need is doubled if policy is changed to 60 days.

       b. Inventory consignment:

          Average inventory: \$725,000.

$$\text{Current turnover: } \frac{\text{Cost of goods sold}}{\text{Average inventory}} = \frac{83\% \times \$9,137,000}{\$725,000}$$

$$= 10.5 \text{ times}$$

$$\text{Turnover slowdown: } \frac{\text{Cost of goods sold}}{7.0} = \frac{\$7,583,700}{7.0}$$

$$= \$1,083,400$$

Inventory increases by $1,083,400 less $725,000 = $358,400

$$\text{Turnover increase: } \frac{\text{Cost of goods sold}}{11.0} = \frac{\$7,583,700}{11.0} = \$689,400$$

Inventory decreases by $725,000 less $689,400 = $35,600

Observations   Funds needs change as indicated. The company likely will require increased production operations to achieve higher supply (about 5 percent), and also some increased purchases, which will provide some funds through higher payables. But the slowdown must be financed by other funds sources.

  e.   Sales growth:

  10 percent increase in sales ($913,700) requires:

Funds for receivables: 18 days of increased sales	$ 45,700
Funds for inventories: 10 percent increase	72,500
Funds from payables: 10 days of increased purchases	(14,800)
Total funds need	$103,400
Against additional profits of 10% (assume no efficiency of scale):	$ 13,100

Observations   Unless there are significant improvements in operations, the increase in sales requires funds of about $90,000. This makes dividends and capital expenditures suggested in item *(d)* barely possible from internal funds, and leaves no room for inefficiency.

3.

DEF COMPANY
Pro Forma Balance Sheet
December 31, 2005

Cash	$ 150,000	(desired level)
Receivables	348,300	(12 days on $10.45 mil.)
Inventories*	1,044,600	(as calculated below)
Total current assets	$1,542,900	
Land, buildings, etc.	$ 478,500	(plus $57,000)
Accumulated depreciation	248,700	(plus $31,400)
Net fixed assets	$ 229,800	
Other assets	21,700	(no change)
Total assets	$1,794,400	
Accounts payable	$ 648,300	(24 days' purchases)
Note payable—bank	468,900	(plug figure—up by $43,900)
Accrued expenses	63,400	(no change)
Total current liabilities	$1,180,600	
Term loan—properties	$ 110,000	(minus $10,000)
Capital stock	200,000	(no change)
Paid-in surplus	112,000	(no change)
Retained earnings	191,800	($184,400 + $19,900 − $12,500)
Total liabilities and shareholders' equity	$1,794,400	

*Beginning inventory	$ 912,700	
Purchases	9,725,000	
	$10,637,700	
Cost of goods sold	9,593,100	(91.8% of $10,450,000)
Ending inventory	$ 1,044,600	

Observations The main difference appears to be a rise in inventories that requires about $130,000, while receivables drop slightly. Apparently sales are leveling off or dropping. (If 12 days' sales are assumed outstanding in 2004, sales for the year must have been $10,836,000, while purchases keep going up.) Repayment of note and high dividend payout cause need for extra borrowing (plug figure) of about $44,000 even if cash is drawn down to $150,000.

4.

BCD COMPANY
Cash Budget for Six Months
October 1998 through March 2005
($ thousands)

	Oct.	Nov.	Dec.	Jan.	Feb.	Mar.	Total
Cash receipts:							
Collections from credit sales	$ 215	$ 245	$ 265	$ 385	$ 345	$ 505	$1,960
Cash sales	385	345	505	325	290	360	2,210
Total receipts	$ 600	$ 590	$ 770	$ 710	$ 635	$ 865	$4,170
Cash disbursements (see breakdown of purchases below):							
Cash purchases	$ 61	$ 54	$ 29	$ 32	$ 45	$ 48	$ 269
Credit purchases— 10 days (less 2%) (discount)	218	220	146	121	160	184	1,049
Credit purchases— 45 days	257	266	286	205	153	192	1,359
Salaries and wages	146	131	192	124	110	137	840
Operating expenses	108	97	141	91	81	101	619
Cash dividend	—	—	40	—	—	—	40
Income taxes	—	—	—	20	—	—	20
Mortgage payment	7	7	7	7	7	7	42
Total cash disbursements	$ 797	$ 775	$ 841	$ 600	$ 556	$ 669	$4,238
Net cash receipts (disbursements)	$(197)	$(185)	$ (71)	$ 110	$ 79	$ 196	$ (68)
Cumulative net cash flow	$(197)	$(382)	$(453)	$(343)	$(264)	$ (68)	
Analysis of cash requirements:							
Beginning cash balance	$ 95	$(102)	$(287)	$(358)	$(248)	$(169)	
Net cash receipts (disbursements)	(197)	(185)	(71)	110	79	196	
Ending cash balance	$(102)	$(287)	$(358)	$(248)	$(169)	$ 27	
Minimum cash balance	75	75	75	75	75	75	
Cash requirements	$ 177	$ 362	$ 433	$ 323	$ 244	$ 48	

Observations   In spite of sizable cash needs, which reach a peak of $433,000 in December, the pattern of cash movements winds up not far below the minimum cash balance six months hence. Seasonal short-term borrowing is indicated here to cover inventory buildup and lag in collection pattern.

5.   Pro forma statements developed from data given:

Initial cash	$250,000
Less: Equipment	175,000
	$ 75,000
Organization expenses	15,000
Cash remaining	$ 60,000

ZYX CORPORATION
Breakdown of Monthly Purchases

Terms	Aug.	Sep.	Oct.	Nov.	Dec.	Jan.	Feb.	Mar.
Cash	N.A.	$45	$61*	$54	$29	$32	$45	$48
2/10, n/30	N.A.	60/60/60*	81*/81*/82	71/71/72	38/39/39	42/43/43	60/60/60	64/64/64
n/45	145/145*	112*/113	153/152	134/133	72/73	80/80	112/113	120/120
Total	—	$450	$610	$535	$290	$320	$450	$480

*Due for payment in October. (September purchases are reconstructed from $60 amount purchased at 2/10, n/20, which must be one-third of 40 percent of total purchases.)

ZYX CORPORATION
Pro Forma Income Statement
Six Months Ended July 31, 2004
($ thousands)

Sales revenue		$2,400	(6 × $400,000)
Cost of goods sold:			
Labor	$ 360		(6 × $ 60,000)
Materials purchased	750		(6 × $125,000)
Rent	111		(6 × $ 18,500)
Overhead	456		(6 × $ 76,000)
Depreciation	36		(6 × $ 6,000)
Amortization	3		(6 × $ 500)
Total	$1,716		
Less: Prepaids	$ 12		
Inventories	205		
	$ 217	1,499	
Gross margin		$ 901	
Selling and administrative			
expenses		330	(6 × $55,000)
Profit before taxes		$ 571	
Taxes at 40%		228	
After-tax profit		$ 343	

ZYX CORPORATION
Pro Forma Balance Sheet
July 31, 2004
($ thousands)

Cash		$ 40	(minimum balance)
Accounts receivable		600	(45 days' sales)
Inventories		205	(given)
Total current assets		$ 845	
Equipment	$175		
Less: Depreciation	36	139	
Prepaid items		12	(given)
Patents		47	(net of amortization)
Organization expense		15	(given)
Total assets		$1,058	
Accounts payable		$ 125	(30 days' purchases)
Accrued expenses		15	(1 week's wages)
Accrued taxes		228	(from income statement)
Total current liabilities		$ 368	
Common stock ($1 par)		300	(given)
Retained earnings		343	(from income statement)
		$1,011	
Plug figure		47	(funds needs 7/31/04)
Total liabilities and shareholders' equity		$1,058	

Observations   The figures appear quite optimistic; no allowance is made for start-up problems. Profitability thus seems excessive. There are likely to be greater funds needs early in the period, as collections lag and production problems appear. Also, if taxes have to be prepaid, a major funds source will be affected. Moreover, growth will require additional funds:

10% increase in sales requires:	
10% increase in receivables, inventories	$80
Less: 10% increase in payables, accruals	34
	$46
10% increase in cash flow from operations	38
Need	$ 8

This need will increase drastically if any key assumptions are off the mark.

7.   XYZ Company (data contained in Interactive Templates, "Cash Budget Example: Projections and Key Drivers")

Observations   The key change is the transformation of receivables and inventories into cash, due to the change in policies. Note the dramatic drop in inventories b y 3/31/02, if the policies work as expected. No funds needs arise during the period, and the main collection impact is felt in October and December. If collections don't come in as expected $1,533 by 12/31/04 and $1,833 will be deferred and not available by 3/31/05.

Note that problems 8 and 9 are based on the use of the optional financial analysis software, Financial Genome, which is described in more detail in Appendix I.

Chapter 5

1. ABC Corporation

Break-even point calculation:

Price per unit	$5.50
Variable costs per unit	$3.25
Contribution	$2.25

Fixed costs: $360,000.
Units required to recover fixed costs with contribution:

$$\frac{\$360,000}{\$2.25} = 160,000 \text{ units}$$

a.   Operating leverage:

Profit Effect from Volume Increaes (20%)			***Profit Effect from Volume Decreases (20%)***		
Units	**Profit**	**Change**	**Units**	**Profit**	**Change**
160,000	-0-	—	160,000	-0-	—
192,000	$ 72,000	infinite	128,000	$ (72,000)	infinite
230,400	156,400	120.0%	102,400	(129,600)	80.0%
276,480	262,080	65.5%	81,920	(175,680)	39.8%
331,776	386,496	47.5%	65,536	(212,544)	21.0%

Note the declining rate of change as we move away from the break-even point.

b.   Changes in assumptions:

Price drop of 50 cents:
Change in contribution from $2.25 to $1.75:

$$\text{Break-even point: } \frac{\$360,000}{\$1.75} = 205,715 \text{ units}$$

Cost increase of 25 cents—variable:

Change in contribution from $2.25 to $2.00:

$$\text{Break-even point: } \frac{\$360,000}{\$2.00} = 180,000 \text{ units}$$

Cost increase of $40,000—fixed:

Change in fixed cost from $360,000 to $400,000:

$$\text{Break-even point: } \frac{\$400,000}{\$2.25} = 177,778$$

c.   Changing conditions by operating level:

Calculations must be made step by step to take account of changing conditions:

(1) Contribution from first 150,000 units:

Price	$5.50
Variable costs	3.25
	$2.25
Contribution	$2.25 x 150,000 = $337,500

(2) Contribution from next 25,000 units:

Price	$5.50
Vanabla costs	3.00
	$2.50
Contribution	$2.50 x 25,000 = $62,500

The break-even point will lie between 150,000 and 175,000 units, because the combined contribution of $400,000 exceeds fixed costs by $40,000. Thus the break-even point is based on fixed costs remaining after 150,000 units, i.e., $22,500 ($360,000 – $337,500).

$$\frac{\$22,500}{\$2.50} = 9,000 \text{ units added to } 150,000, \text{ or } 159,000 \text{ units}$$

The contribution from units after 175,000 units and after 190,000 does not come into play unless fixed costs were raised earlier.

ABC CORPORATION
Break-Even Chart

Original condition and price drop

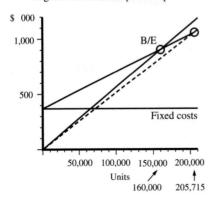

Original condition and variable cost increase

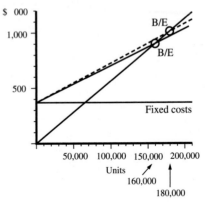

Original condition and fixed cost increase

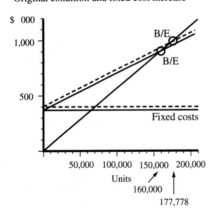

Original condition and step-wise changes

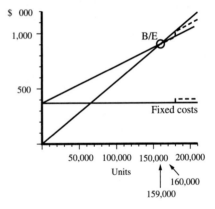

4. XYZ Company

The following data have been calculated from the information given:

	1998	1999	2000	2001	2002	2003
Profit margin	16.3%	15.9%	16.1%	15.3%	12.8%	13.6%
Asset turnover	1.12	1.23	1.27	1.26	1.31	1.29
Financial leverage	1.50	1.41	1.35	1.22	1.10	1.04
Earnings retention	63.1%	61.0%	65.4%	65.9%	59.5%	58.8%
Sustainable growth (from equation)	17.2%	16.8%	18.1%	15.5%	11.0%	10.7%
Actual growth in sales	10.3%	16.6%	22.6%	6.2%	5.6%	4.1%
Actual growth in shareholders' equity	11.6%	12.7%	23.3%	19.5%	12.5%	11.9%
Return on equity	27.3%	27.6%	27.7%	23.5%	18.5%	18.2%

The sustainable growth equation: $g = \dfrac{\text{Profit}}{\text{Sales}} \times \dfrac{\text{Sales}}{\text{Assets}} \times \dfrac{\text{Assets}}{\text{Equity}} \times \text{Retention }\%$

a.   Sustainable growth has dropped sharply in the later years due to the declining profit margin and higher payout. Still, actual growth in sales and equity has declined even more; the cash being generated has allowed a significant reduction in debt, with leverage going from 1.5 to 1.0.

b.   Future growth strategies depend mostly on the business outlook, not past performance. The company's stronger financial condition will allow for future borrowing, but the key is the profitability of future business.

c.   A higher dividend payout would be desirable if there is an outlook for modest growth in the business and solid profitability, and if future sources of business are not promising. Funds could also be applied to repurchases of shares if the outlook is modest.

d.   Future growth would be financed from a combination of debt, hopefully higher profit margins, and even new equity, all depending on the business outlook.

Note that problems 5, 6, and 8 are based on the use of the applicable Interactive Templates.

7. DEF Company five-year financial plan ($ thousands):

DEF Company	Year 1	Year 2	Year 3	Year 4	Year 5	Year 5 R
Capital structure:						
Debt as percent of capitalization	20.0%	20.0%	33.0%	33.0%	33.0%	43.0%
Debt to equity ratio	25.0%	25.0%	50.0%	50.0%	50.0%	75.0%
Debt	$ 300.0	$ 308.9	$ 638.6	$ 665.1	$ 706.7	$1,082.1
Equity	1,200.0	1,235.5	1,277.1	1,330.3	1,413.4	1,413.4
Net assets (capitalization)	1,500.0	1,544.3	1,915.7	1,995.4	2,120.1	2,495.5
Profitability (after taxes):						
Gross return on net assets*	8%	9%	10%	10%	10%	11%
Amount of profit	$ 120.0	$ 139.0	$ 191.6	$ 199.5	$ 212.0	$ 274.5
Interest rate	4.5%	4.5%	5.0%	5.0%	5.0%	4.5%
Amount of interest	13.5	13.9	31.9	33.3	35.3	48.7
Profit after interest	$ 106.5	$ 125.1	$ 159.6	$ 166.3	$ 176.7	$ 225.8
Disposition of profit:						
Dividend payout	67%	67%	67%	50%	50%	67%
Dividends paid	$ 71.0	$ 83.4	$ 106.5	$ 83.1	$ 88.3	$ 150.6
Reinvestment of profit	35.5	41.7	53.2	83.1	88.3	75.2
Financing (next year):						
New debt, old ratio	8.9	10.4	26.6	41.6	44.2	44.2
New debt, revised ratio	0.0	319.3	0.0	0.0	0.0	375.4
Funding potential	$ 44.3	$ 371.3	$ 79.7	$ 124.7	$ 132.5	$ 119.4
Cash flow implications:						
Amount of aftertax profit	106.5	125.1	159.6	166.3	176.7	225.8
Depreciation effect	75.0	78.0	80.0	90.0	92.0	92.0
Cash flow from operations	181.5	203.1	239.6	256.3	268.7	317.8
Dividends paid	71.0	83.4	106.5	83.1	88.3	150.6
Cash flow available for reinvestment	110.5	119.7	133.2	173.1	180.3	167.2
Additional debt	8.9	329.7	26.6	41.6	44.2	419.6
Total investment potential	$ 119.3	$ 449.3	$ 159.7	$ 214.7	$ 224.5	$ 586.8
Results:						
Net return on net assets	7.1%	8.1%	8.3%	8.3%	8.3%	9.0%
Return on equity	8.9%	10.1%	12.5%	12.5%	12.5%	16.0%
Growth in equity	3.0%	3.4%	4.2%	6.3%	6.3%	5.7%
Earnings per share (200,000 shares)	0.53	0.63	0.80	0.83	0.88	1.13
Dividends per share	0.36	0.42	0.53	0.42	0.44	0.75

*Profits before interest, after taxes related to net assets (capitalization).

Observations The results displayed are largely self-explanatory and show a rising level of performance as both operating and financial conditions are changed. The higher dividend payout in the revised Year 5 situation causes a drop in equity growth, even though operating conditions are more favorable. Note also that the depreciation effect adds to the basic funding potential, as we observed in Chapter 1, so that the total investment potential is always higher by the amount of depreciation. Part of this will clearly be needed for replacing worn-out and obsolescent facilities and equipment.

Chapter 6

1. Exercises:

   a. Present value of $1,500 to be paid in Year 7, discounted at 12 percent:

   $$\$1,500 \times 0.452 = \$678 \text{ (Table 6–1)}$$

   b. Future value of $678 in Year 7, compounded at 12 percent:

   $$\frac{\$678}{0.452} = \$1,500$$

   c. Future value of $1 250 in Year 11, compounded at 8 percent:

   $$\frac{\$1,250}{04.29} = \$2913.75 \text{ (Table 6–I) (also spreadsheet function } fxFV)$$

   d. Present value of $300 per year for 9 years, discounted at 18 percent:

   $$\$300 \times 4.303 = \$1,290.90 \text{ (Table 6–II) (also spreadsheet function } fxPV)$$

   e. Future value of $675 per year for 16 years, compounded at 5 percent (spreadsheet function $fxFV$): $15,969

   f. Annuity over five years, 6 percent discount, and principal of $50,000:

   $$\frac{\$50,000}{4.212} = \$11,870.84 \text{ (Table 6–II) (spreadsheet function } fxPMT: \\ \$11,869.82)$$

3. Trustee of major estate:
   Net investment: $100,000 in *a* and *b*.
   Yield:

   a. Yield factor: $\dfrac{\$100,000}{\$16,500} = 6.06$

   In Table 6–II on the eight-year line this corresponds to a yield of about 7 percent if a rough interpolation is made.

   Benefits: 8 × $16,500.

   Present value of benefits: 6.210 × $16,500 (Table 6–II) = $102,465.

   Net present value: + $2,465.

b. Yield factor: $\dfrac{\$100,000}{\$233,000} = 0.429$

In Table 6–I, on the 11-year line this corresponds exactly to a yield of 8 percent. Thus, the second proposition is preferable.

Net present value (6 percent):

Benefits: Lump sum in 11 years is $233.000.

Present value of benefits: .527 × $233.000 (Table 6–I) = $122,791

Net present value: + $22,791.

A spreadsheet analysis confirms the results, with slight rounding differences:

Direct IRR and NPV Calculation	Year 0	Year 1	Year 2	Year 3	Year 4	Year 5	Year 6	Year 7	Year 8
Annual cash payments	$-100,000	$16,500	$16,500	$16,500	$16,500	$16,500	$16,500	$16,500	$16,500
Result from function fx IRR	6.6%								
Net present value @ 6% from function fx NPV	2,462								

Direct IRR and NPV Calculation	Year 0	Year 1	Year 2	Year 3	Year 4	Year 5	Year 6	Year 7	Year 8	Year 9	Year 10	Year 11
Annual cash payments	$-100,000	0	0	0	0	0	0	0	0	0	0	$233,000
Result from function fx IRR	8.0%											
Net present value @ 6% from function fx NPV	22,741											

Observations   If a higher discount factor were used, the results would be reversed since proposition *(a)* provides continuous early benefits. The question of risk looms large here—11 years is a long time. Also, some argue that reinvestment of the cash flows makes *(a)* preferable—but the effect has been taken into account in the discount procedure. It's worthwhile to calculate a *compounding* of all cash flows to 11 years to prove this point. The question of changing earnings opportunities over time can be raised.

4. ABC Company

Net investment: 64% of $1,500,000 = $960,000
Past research and development: Not relevant here.
Profit improvement:

Year 1: 64% of $250,000	=	$ 160,000
Year 2: 64% of $450,000	=	288,000
Year 3: 64% of $750,000	=	480,000
Year 4: 64% of $500,000	=	320,000
Year 5: 64% of $300,000	=	192,000
Total	=	$1,440,000
Average yearly amount		$ 288,000

Measures calculated (000 omitted):

a. Payback (on average amount):

$\dfrac{\$960}{\$288} = 3.33$ years; almost four years on actual pattern

b.   Return on investment:

$$\frac{\$288}{\$960} = 30.0 \text{ percent: can't calculate on actual pattern}$$

c.   Average return:

$$\frac{\$288}{\$480} = 60.0 \text{ percent; can't calculate on actual pattern}$$

d.   Net present value (at 12 percent):

Based on average: 3.605 x $288 (Table 6–II)	+ $1,038,240
Outlay	−960,000
Net present value	$ 78,240

Based on actual pattern (factors from Table 6–I):

Present Value Analysis at 12 Percent

Actual Benefit Pattern	Totals	Year 0	Year 1	Year 2	Year 3	Year 4	Year 5	Average
Promotional outlay (outflow)	$−1,500,000	$−1,500,000	0	0	0	0	0	
Benefits (inflows)—actual pattern	2,250,000	0	$ 250,000	$ 450,000	$ 750,000	$ 500,000	$300,000	
Total outlays and benefits	750,000	−1,500,000	250,000	450,000	750,000	500,000	300,000	
Income tax adjustment	0.64	0.64	0.64	0.64	0.64	0.64	0.64	
Cash flows	480,000	−960,000	160,000	288,000	480,000	320,000	192,000	288,000
Present value factors @ 12%		1.000	0.893	0.797	0.712	0.636	0.567	
Present values of cash flows	1,026,560	−960,000	142,880	229,536	341,760	203,520	108,864	*
Cumulative present values		$−960,000	$−817,120	$−587,584	$−245,824	$−42,304	$ 66,560	
Net present value	66,560							
Profitability index	1.07							
Present value payback	Year 5							

*Benefits only

(Note that the actual pattern causes worsening of the result!)

e.   Profitability index:

$$\text{Based on average: } \frac{\$1,038,240}{960,000} = 1.08$$

$$\text{Based on pattern: } \frac{\$1,026,560}{960,000} = 1.07$$

f.   Internal rate of return:

Due to the closeness of the present value results, the IRR is approximately 15 percent in either case, higher on the average basis, and lower on the actual pattern. The spreadsheet calculations are shown below:

Direct Yield (IRR) Calculation	Year 0	Year 1	Year 2	Year 3	Year 4	Year 5
Actual cash flow pattern	$−960,000	$160,000	$288,000	$480,000	$320,000	$192,000
Result from function *fx* IRR	14.6%					

Direct Yield (IRR) Calculation	Year 0	Year 1	Year 2	Year 3	Year 4	Year 5
Average annual cash flows	$−960,000	$288,000	$288,000	$288,000	$288,000	$288,000
Result from function *fx* IRR	15.2%					

g. Present value payback:

Just over four years in both cases, with positive cumulative present values in Year 5.

h. Annualized net present value (factors from Table 6–II):

$$\text{Based on average: } \frac{\$78,240}{3,605} = \$21,703 \text{ each year}$$

$$\text{Based on pattern: } \frac{\$66,560}{3,605} = \$18,463 \text{ each year}$$

Actual pattern result calculated on a spreadsheet:

Direct Annualization Calculation

Net present value @ 12%	$66,560
Annualized net present value @ 12%; *fx*PMT	18,464 per year

Observations The project exceeds current return standard of 14 percent by but one-half percent, a slight margin. If the data had been available *before* the R&D expenditures were made, the combined expenditure pattern should not have been planned for. Because past outlays are *sunk* costs, however, this follow-on investment is acceptable if there is reasonable assurance that the benefit estimates are reasonable.

Chapter 7

1. XYZ Corporation

Past investment: $3.75 million (sunk)

Net investment data:

Original outlay	$6,300,000
Recovery in 12 years	1,260,000 (book value)
Working capital:	
Initial	1,500,000
Recovery in 12 years	1,250,000
Promotion expenditure	640,000 (aftertax) ($1.0 million x 0.64)
Life of proposition	12 years

Benefits:

	Years 1–3	Years 4–8	Years 9–12	Total
Profit improvement	$1,900	$2,200	$1,300	$21,900
Less: Depreciation	420	420	420	5,040
	$1,480	$1,780	$ 880	$16,860
Tax at 36% (rounded)	533	640	317	6,070
	$ 947	$1,140	$ 563	$10,790
Add back depreciation	420	420	420	5,040
Operating cash flow	$1,367	$1,560	$ 983	$15,830

Present value analysis at 12 percent:

Present Value Analysis at 12 Percent (thousands of dollars)

	Totals	Year 0	Year 1	Year 2	Year 3	Year 4	Year 5	Year 6	Year 7	Year 8	Year 9	Year 10	Year 11	Year 12
Investment outlay (outflow) and recovery	5,930	$-8,440	0	0	0	0	0	0	0	0	0	0	0	$2,510
Benefits (inflows)	15,833	0	$1,367	$1,367	$1,367	$1,560	$1,560	$1,560	$1,560	$1,560	$983	$983	$983	983
Present value factors @ 12%		1.000	0.893	0.797	0.712	0.636	0.567	0.507	0.452	0.404	0.361	0.322	0.287	0.257
Present value of investment	7,795	-8,440	0	0	0	0	0	0	0	0	0	0	0	645
Present values of operating cash flows	8,493	0	1,221	1,089	973	992	885	791	705	630	355	317	282	253
Cumulative present values		-8,440	-7,219	-6,130	-5,156	-4,164	-3,280	-2,489	-1,784	-1,154	-799	-482	-200	698
Net present value	698													
Profitability index—initial investment	1.08													
Profitability index—net investment	1.09													
Annualized net present value—*fx* PMT	113 per year													
Present value payback	11 + years													

Direct Yield (IRR) Calculation

		Year 0	Year 1	Year 2	Year 3	Year 4	Year 5	Year 6	Year 7	Year 8	Year 9	Year 10	Year 11	Year 12
Total cash flows		$-8,440	$1,367	$1,367	$1,367	$1,560	$1,560	$1,560	$1,560	$ 983	$983	$983	$3,493	
Result from function *fx* IRR		13.7%												

a. Net present value (PV) at 12 percent is about $698,000, indicating a somewhat better-than-standard result. In fact, the recovery of working capital and book values of equipment in Year 12 could be forgone and the project would still meet the standard.

b. Present value index at 12 percent:

Based on initial investment:

$$\frac{\$9,138}{\$8,440} = 1.08$$

Based on net investment:

$$\frac{\$8,493}{\$7,795} = 1.09$$

c.   Present value payback:

Just about 12 years because the recovery represents much of the positive net present value.

d.   Internal rate of return (IRR):

By trial and error a little under 14 percent. (See PV analysis above for exact result of 13.7 percent.)

e.   Annualized net present value:

$$\frac{\$698}{6.194} = \$112,700 \text{ per year (narrow margin for error)}$$

Observations   Project is close' to standard and not a real value creator; it shows problems of handling uneven cash flows. Can't recover past (sunk) R&D. Therefore similar future projects will be of doubtful value to the company. Not shown are potential new investments required during the project life, as well as changes in working capital, which would adversely affect the results.

3.   GSB Corporation

Initial investments:	$100,000 incremental equipment
	25,000 working capital
Follow-on investments:	$25,000 equipment in Year 3
	Incremental working capital
	(see schedules below)

Economic life: seven years

Net present value spreadsheet:

Present Value Analysis at 15 Percent	Totals	Year 0	Year 1	Year 2	Year 3	Year 4	Year 5	Year 6	Year 7
Investment outlays (outflows) and recovery	$-135,000	$-125,000	$-4,000	$-5,000	$-30,000	$-6,000	$-2,000	0	$37,000
Operating benefits after taxes									
(before depreciation)	240,000	0	15,000	25,000	40,000	65,000	45,000	$30,000	20,000
Depreciation tax shields @ 36% (7-yers ACRS)	41,390	0	5,144	8,816	7,583	6,701	4,789	4,339	4,019
Present value factors @ 15%		1.000	0.870	0.756	0.658	0.572	0.497	0.432	0.376
Present values of investments and recoveries	-142,514	-125,000	-3,480	-3,780	-19,740	-3,432	-994	0	13,912
Present values of operating cash flows	138,295	0	13,050	18,900	26,320	37,180	22,365	12,960	7,520
Present values of depreciation tax shields	25,728	0	4,476	6,665	4,989	3,833	2,380	1,874	1,511
Cumulative present values		0	$-110,954	$-89,169	$-77,600	$-40,019	$-16,268	$-1,434	$21,509
Net present value	21,509								
Annualized net present value—*fx* PMT	1,731 per year								
Profitability index—initial investment	1.17								
Profitability index—net investment	1.15								
Present value payback	Year 6+								

Internal rate of return:

Direct Yield (IRR) Calculation								
Total cash flows	$-125,000	$16,144	$28,816	$17,583	$65,701	$47,789	$34,339	$61,019	$146,390
Result from function *fx* IRR	19.5%								

Backup data:

Depreciation Patterns and Recoveries	Totals	Year 0	Year 1	Year 2	Year 3	Year 4	Year 5	Year 6	Year 7
Original equipment in Year 0 (ACRS 7 years)	$ 95,550	$100,000	$14,290	$24,490	$17,490	$12,490	$ 8,930	$ 8,930	$ 8,930
New investment in Year 3 (ACRS 7 years)	19,423	25,000	0	0	3,573	6,123	4,373	3,123	2,233
Total depreciation	114,973		14,290	24,490	21,063	18,613	13,303	12,053	11,163
Aftertax recovery of equipment									7,000
Partial recovery of working capital									30,000
Total recovery									37,000
Working capital investments (memo)	47,000	25,000	4,000	5,000	5,000	6,000	2,000	0	0

Net present value at $21,500 is quite positive, and the internal rate return is almost 20 percent.

Present value payback is achieved in the last year, but without having to rely on terminal value.

Given the 15 percent standard the project appears quite acceptable, assuming the risks of achieving the ambitious ramp-up of the cash flow pattern are not excessive. The annualized net PV shows that there is not much room for error in this regard.

The question about existing infrastructure can be resolved only in the context of the future strategy of the company. If several opportunities are competing, or likely to compete for this portion, it would be relevant to include it in each of the calculations; the idea is to maximize the use of this common resource by selecting the best opportunity. If there were no foreseeable expansion opportunities or plans, the issue would be sunk.

Observations   This example provides practice with different cash flow patterns, especially the accelerated depreciation impact as a tax shield. It also has a more realistic pattern of both investment and working capital needs and recoveries.

Chapter 8

2. KLN Company

   Weighted cost of capital calculation:

   Existing conditions:

Debt cost 11.0 (1 − 0.36)	7.04%
Preferred cost	12.0
Common equity cost (CAPM 5.5 + 1.2 [13.0 − 5.5])	14.5

   Incremental conditions:

Debt cost 8.0 (1 − 0.36)	5.12%
Preferred cost	9.00
Common equity (CAPM)	14.50

Assignment of weights:

Book value basis:

Debt	$250	35.8%
Preferred	50	7.1
Common equity	400	57.1
	$700	100.0%

Market value basis:

Debt (11.0/8.0 x 250)	$344	37.7%
Preferred (12.0/9.0 x 50)	67	7.4
Common equity $50/share	500	54.9
	$911	100.0%

Target basis:

Debt	42.0%
Preferred (12.0/9.0 x 50)	0.0
Common equity $50/share	58.0
	100.0%

Weighted cost (incremental):

	Book Value		Market Value		Target Basis	
Debt	35.8% × 5.12 =	1.83%	37.7% × 5.12 =	1.93%	42.0% × 5.12 =	2.15%
Preferred	7.1 × 9.00 =	0.64	7.4 × 9.00 =	0.67	0 × 9.00 =	0.0
Common equity	57.1 × 14.50 =	8.28	54.9 × 14.50 =	7.96	58.0 × 14.50 =	8.41
	100.0%	10.75%	100.0%	10.56%	100.0%	10.56%

Weighted cost (existing):

	Book Value		Market Value		Target Basis	
Debt	35.8% × 7.04 =	2.52%	37.7% × 7.04 =	2.65%	42.0% × 7.04 =	2.96%
Preferred	7.1 × 12.00 =	0.85	7.4 × 12.00 =	0.89	0 × 12.00 =	0.0
Common equity	57.1 × 14.50 =	8.28	54.9 × 14.50 =	7.96	58.0 × 14.50 =	8.41
	100.0%	11.65%	100.0%	11.50%	100.0%	11.37%

Observations The range of results is quite narrow in both circumstances. Even though significant changes occurred in the yields of the various securities, the changes in weights and the averaging process smoothed them out. There is roughly a 1 percent difference between the existing and incremental conditions. If we ignore the book value basis as not relevant, the market value and target results are even closer. If any use is made of the concept for future investments, the existing conditions aren't relevant either. Thus, the weighted cost is about 10.5 to 11 percent, perhaps a little higher. Note that great precision is unnecessary in the derivation of the cost of capital, a figure that is subject to shifting conditions and assumptions.

Note that problem 3 is based on the use of Financial Genome.

Chapter 9

1. *a.*

ABC CORPORATION
Per Share Analysis
($ thousands, except per share amounts)

	Old Level	New Level	
EBIT	$14,700	$17,400	(118%)
Interest (same)	1,100	1,100	
Profit before taxes	$13,600	$16,300	
Taxes at 34%	4,625	5,540	
Profit after taxes	$ 8,975	$10,760	
Number of common shares	300,000	350,000	
Earnings per share	$ 29.91	$ 30.74	
Sinking fund	$ 900	$ 900	
Sinking fund per share	$ 3.00	$ 2.57	
Uncommitted earnings per share	$ 26.91	$ 28.17	
Depreciation per share	$ 7.50	$ 6.43	
Cash flow per share	$ 37.41	$ 37.17	

Immediate dilution: $\dfrac{\$8,975,000}{350,000} - \$29.41 = ($3.77)$ dilution (12.8%).

Net dilution (strengthening): $30.74 − $29.41 = $1.33 strengthening (4.5%).

b. $5.0 million preferred stock (10%)
or $5.0 million debentures (9%), due in 15 years.

PER SHARE ANALYSIS
($ thousands, except per share amounts)

	Preferred		Debentures	
	Old Level	New Level	Old Level	New Level
EBIT	$14,700	$17,400	$14,700	$17,400
Interest—old	1,100	1,100	1,100	1,100
Interest—new	—	—	450	450
Profit before taxes	$13,600	$16,300	$13,150	$15,850
Taxes at 34%	4,625	5,540	4,475	5,390
Profit after taxes	$ 8,975	$10,760	$ 8,675	$10,460
Preferred dividends	500	500	—	—
Profits to common	$ 8,475	$10,260	$ 8,675	$10,460
Number of common shares	300,000	300,000	300,000	300,000
Earnings per share	$ 28.25	$ 34.20	$ 28.92	$ 34.86
Sinking fund	$ 900	$ 900	$ 900	$ 900
Sinking fund per share	$ 3.00	$ 3.00	$ 3.00	$ 3.00
Uncommitted earnings per share	$ 25.25	$ 31.20	$ 25.92	$ 31.86
Depreciation per share	$ 7.50	$ 7.50	$ 7.50	$ 7.50
Cash flow per share	$ 35.75	$ 41.70	$ 36.42	$ 42.36
Immediate dilution:				

Preferred: $28.25 − $29.91 = − $1.06; $\dfrac{\$1.66}{\$29.91}$ = 5.9%dilution

Debentures: $28.92 − $29.91 = − $0.99; $\dfrac{\$0.99}{\$29.91}$ = 3.4% dilution

Net dilution (strengthening):

Preferred: $34.20 − $29.91 = $4.29; 14.3% strengthening

Debentures: $34.86 − $29.91 = $4.95; 16.5% strengthening

c. Comparative cost of capital:

Common stock:

$5 million represents 50,000 shares, or $100 per share, far below the current average price of $130. EPS required to keep shareholders as well off as before: $29.91. Thus, the apparent "cost" of this issue is

$$\frac{\$29.91}{\$100.00} = 29.9\% \text{ after taxes, a very low P/E ratio, indeed.}$$

Based on the CAPM, the cost of common stock is

$$8.0 + 1.4\,(14.5 - 8.0) = 17.1\% \text{ after taxes}$$

This is obviously a risky company, from which the market is demanding a high risk premium. The other costs are:

- Preferred stock: 10% after taxes.
- Debentures: 5.9% after taxes.

Observations   Note the apparent attractiveness of the new investments, and the leverage effect of lower cost preferred or debt. (The example has been exaggerated with a low P/E to make the differences more apparent.)

3.

DEF COMPANY
EPS Calculations
($ thousands, except per share amounts)

	Common		*Preferred*		*Debentures*	
	Current*	**Low**	**Current***	**Low**	**Current***	**Low**
EBIT	$42,000	$22,000	$42,000	$22,000	$42,000	$22,000
Interest—old	1,200	1,200	1,200	1,200	1,200	1,200
Interest—new	—	—	—	—	$ 4,250	$ 4,250
Profit before taxes	$40,800	$20,800	$40,800	$20,800	$36,550	$16,550
Taxes at 46%	18,768	9,568	18,768	9,568	16,813	7,613
Profit after taxes	$22,032	$11,232	$22,032	$11,232	$19,787	$ 8,937
Preferred dividend—old	1,800	$ 1,800	1,800	1,800	1,800	1,800
Preferred dividend—new	—	—	4,750	4,750	—	—
Profit to common	$20,232	$ 9,432	$15,482	$ 4,682	$17,937	$ 7,137
Number of common shares (millions)	3.0	3.0	2.0	2.0	2.0	2.0
EPS	$ 6.74	$ 3.14	$ 7.94	$ 2.34	$ 8.97	$ 3.57
SFPS	$ 0.33	$ 0.33	$ 0.50	$ 0.50	$ 1.50	$ 1.50
UEPS	$ 6.41	$ 2.81	$ 7.24	$ 1.84	$ 7.47	$ 2.07
Dividend coverage (EPS)	3.37x	1.57x	3.87x	1.17x	4.49x	.79x

*Current EBIT plus incremental earnings on new capital.

Dilution Analysis

	Common	**Preferred**	**Debentures**
EBIT (old)	$34,000	$34,000	$34,000
Interest	1,200	1,200	5,450
Profit before taxes	$32,800	$32,800	$28,550
Taxes (46%)	15,088	15,088	13,133
Profit after taxes	$17,712	$17,712	$15,417
Preferred dividends	1,800	6,550	1,800
Profit to common	$15,912	$11,162	$13,617
Number of share (millions)	3.0	2.0	2.0
EPS (old – $7.96)	$ 5.30	$ 5.58	$ 6.81

Immediate dilution:

Common:	$7.96 − $5.30 = $2.66;	drop of 33.4%
Preferred:	$7.96 − $5.58 = $2.38;	drop of 29.9%
Debentures:	$7.96 − $6.81 = $1.15;	drop of 14.4%

Net dilution (strengthening):

Common:	$7.96 − $6.74 = $1.22;	drop of 15.3%
Preferred:	$7.96 − $7.74 = −$0.22;	drop of 2.8%
Debentures:	$7.96 − $8.97 = −$1.01;	drop of 12.7%

Cost of capital (after taxes):

Common: $7.96 per share for $50.00—apparent "cost" = 15.9%*
Preferred: 9.5 percent stated rate   = 9.5%
Debentures: 9.5 percent before tax $(1 − 0.46) \times 8.5\%$ = 4.6%

*Based on the CAPM, the cost of common is $7.5 + 1.2(14.0 − 7.5) = 15.2\%$.

Break-even points:

- Common versus preferred:

$$\frac{(E - 1,200)\,0.54 - 1,800}{3,000} = \frac{(E - 1,200)\,0.54 - 6,550}{2,000}$$
$$\text{(common)} \qquad\qquad \text{(preferred)}$$

$1,080E - 1,296,000 - 3,600,000 = 1,620E - 1,944,000 - 19,650,000$
$540E = 16,698,000;\ E = 30,922;\ \text{EBIT} = \$30,922,200$

- Common versus debentures:

$$\frac{(E - 1,200)\,0.54 - 1,800}{3,000} = \frac{(E - 5,450)\,0.54 - 1,800}{2,000}$$
$$\text{(common)} \qquad\qquad \text{(debentures)}$$

$1,080E - 1,296,000 - 3,600,000 = 1,620E - 8,829,000 - 5,400,000$
$540E = 9,333,000;\ E = 17,283;\ \text{EBIT} = \$17,283,300$

Dividend coverage:

Shown in the EPS calculations above.

Zero EPS:

- Common:

$$(E - 1,200)\,0.54 - 1,800 = 0$$
$$0.54E - 648 - 1,800 = 0$$
$$E = \$4,533,300\ \text{EBIT}$$

- Preferred:

$$(E - 1,200)\, 0.54 - 6,550 = 0$$
$$0.54E - 648 - 6,550 = 0$$
$$E = \$13,329,600 \text{ EBIT}$$

- Debentures

$$(E - 5,450)\, 0.54 - 1,800 = 0$$
$$0.54E - 2,943 - 1,800 = 0$$
$$E = \$8,783,300 \text{ EBIT}$$

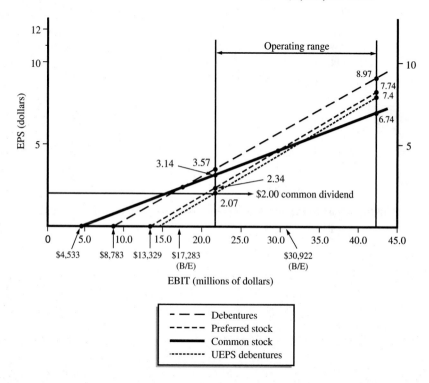

Observations   The example allows full treatment of the technical aspects of the three alternatives, and the display is useful in its exaggeration. Please review the key points beyond those represented by the figures, which are also necessary for choice. Otherwise the data are self-explanatory.

Note that problem 4 is based on the use of Financial Genome.

Chapter 10

1. Bond price examples:

   a. Price at 6%:

Principal due after 28 periods at 3%, plus premium of $75 (using calculator or spreadsheet) $1.075 x 0.437	$ 469.78
PV of 28 semiannual interest payments of $40, at 3% per period (factor from calculator) $40 x 18.764	750.56
Price to yield 6% per annum	$1,220.34

   Price at 10%

$1,075 x 0.255 (Table 6–I)	$ 274.12
$40 x 14.898 (Table 6–II)	595.92
Price to yield 10% per annum	$ 870.04

   b. Price at 9%:

$1,000 x 0.13 (interpolation, 4.5%)	$130.00
$42.50 x 18.7 (interpolation, 4.5%)	794.75
Price to yield 9% per annum	$924.75

If called:	
$1,100 x 0.33 (interpolatlon, 4.5%)	$363.00
$42.50 x 14.3 (interpolation, 4.5%)	607.75
Price to yield 9% per annum	$970.75

2. Bond yield examples:

   a. No interest accrued because the interest date coincides with the purchase date.

Market price 7/15/03	$1,241.25
Redemption price 7/15/17	1,100.00
	$2,341.25
Average investment (1/2)	$1,170.63

   Number of periods: 28

   Interest per period: $35.00

   Amortization of premium: $141.25÷28 = $5.04

   Averaqe periodic income $35.00 − $5.04 = $29.96, or $59.92 per year

   $$\text{Yield:} \frac{\$59.92}{\$1,170.63} = 5.12\%$$

   Exact yield from bond table: 4.65%

   b. Exact yield from bond table: 4.85%

3. Value of rights and subscription price:

a. Market value ex rights:

Subscription price (S) = \$65.00
Market price (M) = \$89.00
Number of rights (N) = 12

The following relationship holds where R = value of a right:

$$R = \frac{M - S}{N + 1}; \quad R = \frac{89 - 65}{13} = \$1.85$$

The market value ex rights will be approximately \$89.00 - 1.85 = \$87.15, reflecting the removal of the rights value.

b. Rights value for purchase of convertible preferred:

Value of preferred (V) = \$105.00
Subscription price (S) = \$82.00
Number of rights (N) = 6

The following relationship holds where R = value of a right:

$$R = \frac{V - S}{N^*} = \frac{105 - 82}{6} = \$3.83$$

*Number of common shares isn't affected.

if $N = 4$, $R = \$5.75$

c. Subscription price:

Market price (M) = \$123.00
Number of rights (N) = 11
Value of a right (R) = \$2.00

$$R = \frac{M - S}{N + 1}; \quad 2 = \frac{123 - S}{12}; \quad S = \$99.00$$

5. GHI Company

Based on current P/E ratio, the company is worth about $11 \times \$2.5$ million (\$27.5 million). The cash flow valuation using the general approach of Figure 10–5 appears as follows (the dividends are not relevant for this approach):

	Year 0	Year 1	Year 2	Year 3	Year 4	Year 5	Year 6
EBIT(1 − *t*)		$ 2.7	$ 2.9	$ 3.2	$ 3.6	$ 4.0	—
Add: write-offs and noncash items		1.0	1.3	1.5	1.6	1.8	—
Less: net new working capital		−0.4	−0.3	−0.5	−0.6	−0.4	—
Less: net new capital investments		−0.7	−2.1	−1.5	−1.5	−2.0	—
Add/less: significant nonoperating items		0.0	0.0	0.0	0.0	0.0	—
Free cash flow		2.6	1.8	2.7	3.1	3.4	3.6
Ongoing value @ 11 times earnings		—	—	—	—	44.0	
Present value factors @ 12%		0.893	0.797	0.712	0.636	0.567	
Present values @ cost of capital		2.3	1.4	1.9	2.0	26.9	
Cumulative present values		2.3	3.8	5.7	7.7	$	

Firm value	$ 34.5
Nonoperating assets (cash, marketable securities, etc.)	2.0
Total value	36.5
Value of outstanding long-term debt	12.2
Value of shareholders' equity	24.3

(a) Ongoing value with 6% growth assumed:
    $3.6/(0.12 − 0.6) = $60 million
    Present value of difference between $60.0 and $44.0:

$16.0 × 0.567	9.1
Revised firm value	43.6
Revised total value	45.6
Revised shareholders' equity value	33.4

(b) Ongoing value with no growth assumed:
    $3.6/0.12 = $30.0 million
    Present value of difference between $30.0 and $44.0:

$14 × 0.567	−7.9
Revised firm value	26.6
Revised total value	28.6
Revised shareholders' equity value	16.4

Observations   There is a wide range of results, caused by the ongoing value estimates, which must be interpreted against any assumptions that make sense in this case. Note that the book value of the capitalization of $23.5 million is lower than even the no-growth alternative of $28.6, and thus probably not meaningful. The 11 times earnings value at $44.0 million lies in between the extremes. Continued growth, of course, depends on the nature of the business and the competitive standing, and we would need to know quite a bit about the market, the company's capabilities, and the outlook for the product or service. Also, are there any comparable companies that could be checked out? Many more questions must be asked. This is just the start.

This problem allows the use of the Interactive Template for valuation, and you can test different assumptions directly. Note that problem 6 is based on the use of both the template and Financial Genome, while Problem 7 is based on the use of Financial Genome for an open-ended analysis of 3M Corporation.

Chapter 11

1. Potential merger:

	Company A	Company B
P/E ratio	12.0	20.0
Earnings per share	$8.00	$3.00
Dividends per share	$2.00	none
Aftertax earnings	$80.0 million	$3.0 million
Price range	$90 to $100	$45 to $70
Current price	$98.00	$54.00 ($65.00 offered)
Growth rate	6% per year	12% per year
Number of shares	10 million	1 million

a. Exchange ratio:

65 ÷ 98 = ⅔ share of A for 1 share of B = 667,000 shares

b. Impact on earnings:

$80.0 million plus $3.0 million = $83.0 million

10.0 million shares plus 667,000 = 10,667,000 shares

$83.0 ÷ 10,667,000 = $7.78 per share (22¢ dilution)

c. Impact on dividends: Each share of Company B now receives the equivalent of $1.33 per share in dividends versus none before.

d. Impact on earnings growth: Three years hence the situation is expected to be:

Company A @ 6 percent growth will earn $95.3 million ($9.53 EPS)

Company B @ 12 percent growth will earn $4.2 million ($4.20 EPS)

Total company earnings thus will grow to $99.5 million, and EPS will be $99.5 ÷ 10,667,000 = $9.53

Observations   This analysis clearly deals only with part of the valuation process in a merger situation. Thus the focus is on the accounting impact of the transaction. Without having a history and projection of cash flows and background data, one can only assume what the important issues might be.

The immediate dilution in earnings of 22 cents isn't likely to be overcome in the foreseeable future inasmuch as in three years the earnings per share of the combined company will be 20 cents lower than what Company A alone could have achieved, given the assumptions about their respective growth rates. On the other hand, synergy, if any, hasn't been considered, which could alter the outlook and improve the earnings picture. The difference in dividend policy is likely to affect the valuation from the standpoint of Company A's shareholders.

A cash flow projection (accompanied by an earnings projection) should be made for several years ahead in both cases, expressing the known strategies of the two companies and reflecting the past and future conditions of the industry. Also, synergistic elements should be identified and quantified. and tested in a range of assumptions. The value of Company B would then be determined by combining its individual performance outlook with identified synergies, and the combined cash flows and earnings analyzed. The exchange price could then be tested both on cash flow–based and market price-based information.

Note that problem 2 is based on the use of the Interactive Template on omparison of measures, whereas problem 3 is based on the use of Financial Genome for an open-ended analysis of 3M Corporation.

I N D E X